FOUNDATIONS OF BEHAVIORAL RESEARCH

Foundations of Behavioral Research

Educational and Psychological Inquiry

Fred N. Kerlinger

New York University

Holt, Rinehart and Winston, Inc.

New York, Chicago, San Francisco, Toronto, London

90123 9 98

Copyright © 1964 by Holt, Rinehart and Winston, Inc.
All Rights Reserved
Library of Congress Catalog Card Number 64-25229
03-044025-4
Printed in the United States of America

0123 22 9

To Betty, Paul, and Stephen

PREFACE

Some activities command more interest, devotion, and enthusiasm from man than others. So it seems to be with science and art. Why this is so is an interesting and significant psychological question to which there is no unequivocal answer. All that seems to be clear is that once men become immersed in scientific research or artistic expression they devote very large portions of their thoughts, energies, and emotions to these activities. It seems a far cry from science to art. But in one respect at least they are similar: men make passionate commitments to them.[1]

This is a book on scientific behavioral research. Above everything else, it aims to convey the exciting and absorbing quality of research in general, and educational and psychological research in particular. A large portion of the book is focused on abstract conceptual and technical matters, but behind the discussion is the conviction that research is a deeply absorbing and vitally interesting business.

It may seem strange in a book on research that I talk about interest, enthusiasm, and passionate commitment. Shouldn't we be objective? Shouldn't we develop a hardheaded attitude toward psychological, sociological, and educational phenomena? Yes, of course. But more important is somehow to catch the essential quality of the excitement of discovery that comes from research well done. Then the difficulties and frustrations of the research enterprise, while they never vanish, play a much less significant role. What I am trying to say is that strong subjective involvement is a powerful motivator for acquiring an objective approach to the study of phenomena. It is doubtful that any significant work is ever done without great personal involvement. It is doubtful that students can learn much about science, research design, and research methods without considerable personal involvement. Thus I would encourage students to discuss, argue, debate, and even fight about research. Take a stand. Be opinionated. Later try to soften the opinionation into intelligent conviction and controlled emotional commitment.

[1] The term "passionate commitment" is Polanyi's. M. Polanyi, *Personal Knowledge.* Chicago: University of Chicago Press, 1958.

The writing of this book has been strongly influenced by the book's major purpose: to help students understand the fundamental nature of the scientific approach to problem solution. Technical and methodological problems have been considered at length. One cannot understand any complex human activity, especially scientific research activity, without some technical and methodological competence. But technical competence is empty without an understanding of the basic intent and nature of scientific research: the controlled and objective study of the relations among phenomena. All else is subordinate to this. Thus the book, as its name indicates, strongly emphasizes the *fundamentals* or *foundations* of behavioral research.

To accomplish the major purpose indicated above, the book has four distinctive general features. First, it is a treatise on scientific research; it is limited to what is generally accepted as the scientific approach. It does not discuss historical research, legal research, library research, philosophical inquiry, and so on.[2] It emphasizes, in short, understanding scientific research problem solution.

Second, the student is led to grasp the intimate and often difficult relations between a research problem and the design and methodology of its solution. While methodological problems are treated at length, the book is not a "methods" book. Stress is always on the research problem, the design of research, and the relation between the two. The student is encouraged to think relationally, structurally, and architectonically.

Third, the content of much of the book is tied together with the notions of set, relation, and variance. These tools, together with those of probability theory, statistics, and measurement, are used to integrate the diverse content of research activity into a unified and coherent whole.

Fourth, a good bit of the book's discussion is slanted toward education and educational research problems, and very particularly toward the psychological aspects of educational research problems. It seemed to me that a foundational research book was needed in education. But there is little scientific research in education that is uniquely educational; for the most part it is behavioral research, research basically psychological and sociological in nature. In sum, while this is a book on the intellectual and technical foundations of scientific behavioral research in general, it concentrates heavily upon psychological and educational problems and examples.

The book's content is organized into eight parts. In Part One, the language and approach of science are studied. Its four chapters discuss the nature of science, scientific problems and hypotheses, the notions of variables, constructs, and definitions, and the important ideas of randomness and sampling. Part Two presents the conceptual and mathematical foundations. Much of the presentation of conceptual and technical mat-

[2] Historical and methodological research are briefly discussed in Appendix B.

ters, as indicated above, is based on the ideas of set, relation, and variance. These terms are defined using modern mathematical theory. Fortunately this theory is simple, though the reader may feel a bit strange at first. After becoming accustomed to the language and thinking, however, he will find that he possesses powerful instruments for understanding later subjects.

It is impossible to do competent research or to read and understand research reports without understanding the probabilistic and statistical thinking of social scientists. Part Three is thus devoted to the nature and purpose of statistics, statistical inference, and probabilistic thinking.

Parts One, Two, and Three provide an important part of the conceptual and mathematical foundations of behavioral education and psychological research. The remainder of the book uses these foundations to attack methodological problems of design, measurement, observation and data collection, and data analysis.

Part Four, "Designs of Research," is the structural heart of the book. Here the major designs of experimental and nonexperimental research are outlined and explained. Part Five, on types of research, follows naturally from Part Four: so-called ex post facto research and the distinctions among laboratory experiments, field experiments, field studies, and survey research are explored.

Part Six addresses itself mainly to theoretical measurement problems, while Part Seven addresses itself to practical and technical problems of gathering the data necessary for scientific problem solution. Standard methods of observation and data collection—interviews, objective tests and scales, direct observation of behavior, projective methods, and the use and analysis of available materials—are extensively discussed and illustrated in Part Seven. The newer methods of sociometry, Q methodology, and the semantic differential might have been subsumed under other methods. Because of their importance, distinctive nature, and frequent use by behavioral scientists, and because elementary yet detailed discussions of Q and the semantic differential seem not to exist, however, each has been assigned a separate chapter.

The book ends with a discussion of the analysis and interpretation of data. Actually, however, analysis and interpretation of data were necessarily discussed earlier in the book. When discussing statistics, for example, it is impossible not to discuss the interpretation of data. Part Eight formalizes the discussion and adds two subjects of large importance not often treated in an elementary way, the analysis of crossbreaks and factor analysis.

Some word on the book's level and audience is in order. The book is a behavioral scientific text intended for graduate students who have elementary backgrounds in psychology, statistics, and measurement. While many terms and ideas used in educational and psychological problems are defined, some familiarity with terms like intelligence, aptitude, socioeconomic status, learning, and the like is assumed. All technical terms are defined, though many students will probably need instructor help with some of them.

As usual, statistical terms and ideas may hinder the student's progress. While it is possible to study the book and master its contents without statistical background—an approach I have used successfully with many students who had not studied statistics—the student who has had an elementary statistics course will probably find the going easier. Suggestions are given in Part Three to help the student conquer certain statistical difficulties.

Foundations of Behavioral Research is perhaps best studied in a two-semester course. When used in one-semester courses, it should probably be selectively studied. Although individual instructors will of course make their own selection decisions, the following parts and chapters are recommended for one-semester courses: Parts One and Two and Chaps. 9, 10, 15-17, 21, 23-28, 34, and 35. (Chaps. 23, 24, and 25 can also be omitted.) For a two-semester course, all or most of the chapters may well be studied. Whatever selection is made, it should be borne in mind that later discussions often presuppose some understanding of earlier discussions.

To aid student study and understanding, and to help surmount some of the inherent difficulties of the subject, several devices have been used. One, many topics have been discussed at length. If a choice had to be made between repetition and possible lack of student understanding, material was repeated, though in different words with different examples. Two, many examples from actual research as well as many hypothetical examples have been used. The student who reads the book through will have been exposed to a large number and a wide variety of problems, hypotheses, designs, and data and to many actual research studies in the social sciences and education.

Three, an important feature of the book is the frequent use of simple numerical examples in which the numbers are only those between 0 and 9. The fundamental ideas of statistics, measurement, and design can be conveyed as well with small numbers as with large numbers, without the additional burden of tedious arithmetic computations. It is suggested that the reader work through each example at least once. Intelligent handling of data is indispensable to intelligent understanding of research design and methodology.

Four, most chapters have study suggestions that include suggested readings as well as problems designed to help integrate and consolidate the material presented in the chapters. Many of them arose from practical use with graduate students.

All books are cooperative enterprises. Though one person may undertake the actual writing, he is dependent on many others for ideas, criticism, and support. Among the many persons who contributed to this book, I am most indebted to those mentioned below.

Professor Theodore Newcomb not only read the whole manuscript and made many valuable and constructive suggestions for improvement; he also furnished the early prodding and encouragement needed to get the book going. Professor Dale Harris read drafts of early chapters and the final manuscript and made contributions whose worth cannot be weighed. Professor Jum Nunnally's trenchant and penetrating analysis of the first draft was invaluable.

Five other individuals—Professors Esin Kaya, Nathan Jaspen, and Jacob Cohen, Dr. Peter Norden, and Mrs. Frances Bennett—read and criticized one or more chapters. Professor Ernest Nagel helped me immeasurably with certain difficult logical scientific problems. His thinking enabled me to improve and clarify several sections of the book. I here express my admiration as well as my thanks.

It is doubtful that this book could have been written without the sabbatical year granted to me in 1961–62 by New York University. I am indeed grateful to the University for its generous sabbatical policy.

The price a family pays for an author's book is high. Its members put up with his obsession and his unpredictable writing ups and downs. I express my gratitude and indebtedness to my wife and sons by dedicating this book to them.

July 1964   *Fred N. Kerlinger*
Hartsdale, New York

CONTENTS

PART FOUR.   DESIGNS OF RESEARCH

PART FIVE.   TYPES OF RESEARCH

study. Characteristics and criteria of laboratory experiments, field experiments, and field studies. The field experiment. Field studies.

PART SIX. MEASUREMENT

PART SEVEN. METHODS OF OBSERVATION AND DATA COLLECTION

PART EIGHT. ANALYSIS AND INTERPRETATION

FOUNDATIONS OF BEHAVIORAL RESEARCH

PART ONE

THE LANGUAGE AND APPROACH OF SCIENCE

1   *SCIENCE AND THE SCIENTIFIC APPROACH*

To understand any complex human activity we must grasp the language and approach of the individuals who pursue the activity. So it is with understanding science and scientific research. One must know and understand, at least in part, scientific language and the scientific approach to problem-solving.

One of the most confusing things to the student of science is the special way the scientist uses ordinary words. To make matters worse, he invents new words. There are good reasons for this specialized use of language, which will become evident later. Suffice it to say now that we must understand and learn the language of psychological and educational scientists. When a psychological investigator tells us about his independent and dependent variables we must know what he means. When he tells us that he has randomized his experimental procedures, we must not only know what he means—we must understand why he does what he does.

Similarly, the scientist's approach to the solution of his problems must be clearly understood. It is not so much that this approach is different from the approach of the layman. It *is* different, of course, but it is not strange and esoteric. Quite the contrary. When understood, it will seem natural and almost inevitable that the scientist does what he does. Indeed, we will probably wonder why much more of human thinking and problem-solving is not consciously structured along such lines.

The purpose of Part I of this book, then, is to help the student learn and understand the language and approach of science and research. In the chapters of this section many of the basic constructs of the social and educational scientist will be studied. In some cases it will not be possible to give complete and satisfactory definitions because of lack of background at this early point in our development. In such cases we shall attempt to formulate and use reasonably accurate first approximations to later, more satisfactory definitions. Let us begin our study by considering how the scientist approaches his problems and how this approach differs from what might be called a common-sense approach.

SCIENCE AND COMMON SENSE

Whitehead has pointed out that in creative thought common sense is a bad master. "It's sole criterion for judgment is that the new ideas shall look like the old ones." [1] This is well said. Common sense may often be a bad master for the evaluation of knowledge. But how are science and common sense alike and how are they different? From one viewpoint, science and common sense are alike. This view would say that science is a systematic and controlled extension of common sense, since common sense, as Conant points out, is a series of concepts and conceptual schemes satisfactory for the practical uses of mankind.[2] But these concepts and conceptual schemes may be seriously misleading in modern science—and particularly in psychology and education. It was self-evident to many educators of the last century—it was only common sense—to use punishment as a basic tool of pedagogy. Now we have evidence that this older, common-sense view of motivation may be quite erroneous. Reward seems more effective than punishment in aiding learning.

Science and common sense differ sharply in five ways. These disagreements revolve around the words "systematic" and "controlled." First, the uses of conceptual schemes and theoretical structures are strikingly different. While the man in the street uses "theories" and concepts, he ordinarily does so in a loose fashion. He often blandly accepts fanciful explanations of natural and human phenomena. An illness, for instance, may be thought to be a punishment for sinfulness. An economic depression may be attributed to Jews. The scientist, on the other hand, systematically builds his theoretical structures, tests them for internal consistency, and subjects aspects of them to empirical test. Furthermore, he realizes that the concepts he is using are man-made terms that may or may not exhibit a close relation to reality.

Second, the scientist systematically and empirically tests his theories and hypotheses. The man in the street tests his "hypotheses," too, but he tests them in what might be called a selective fashion. He often "selects"

---

[1] A. Whitehead, *An Introduction to Mathematics.* New York: Holt, Rinehart and Winston, Inc., 1911, p. 157.

[2] J. Conant, *Science and Common Sense.* New Haven: Yale University Press, 1951, pp. 32, 33. A *concept* is a word that expresses an abstraction formed by generalization from particulars. "Aggression" is a concept, an abstraction that expresses a number of particular actions having the similar characteristic of hurting people or objects. A *conceptual scheme* is a set of concepts interrelated by hypothetical and theoretical propositions. (See *ibid.,* pp. 25, 47, 48.) A *construct* is a concept with the additional meaning of having been created or appropriated for special scientific purposes. "Mass," "energy," "hostility," "introversion," and "achievement" are constructs. They might more accurately be called "constructed types" or "constructed classes," classes or sets of objects or events bound together by the possession of common characteristics, characteristics defined by the scientist. The term "variable" will be defined in a later chapter. For now let it mean a symbol or name of a characteristic that takes on different numerical values.

evidence simply because it is consistent with his hypothesis. Take the stereotype: Negroes are musical. If a person believes this, he can easily "verify" his belief by noting that many Negroes are musicians. Exceptions to the stereotype, the unmusical or tone-deaf Negro, for example, are not perceived. The sophisticated social scientist, knowing this "selection tendency" to be a common psychological phenomenon, carefully guards his research against his own preconceptions and predilections and against selective support of his hypotheses. For one thing, he is not content with armchair exploration of a relation; he must test the relation in the laboratory or in the field. He is not content, for example, with the presumed relations between anxiety and school achievement, between methods of teaching and achievement, between intelligence and creativity, between pupil attitudes and learning. He insists upon systematic, controlled, and empirical testing of these relations.

A third difference lies in the notion of control. In scientific research, control means several things. For the present let it mean that the scientist tries systematically to rule out variables that are possible "causes" of the effects he is studying other than the variables that he has hypothesized to be the "causes." The layman seldom bothers to control his explanations of observed phenomena in a systematic manner. He ordinarily makes little effort to control extraneous sources of influence. He tends to accept those explanations that are in accord with his preconceptions and biases. If he believes that slum conditions produce delinquency, he will tend to disregard the incidence of delinquency in non-slum neighborhoods. The scientist, on the other hand, seeks out and "controls" delinquency incidence in different kinds of neighborhoods. The difference, of course, is profound.

Another difference between science and common sense is perhaps not so sharp. It was said earlier that the scientist is constantly preoccupied with relations among phenomena. So is the layman who invokes common sense for his explanations of phenomena. But the scientist cultivates relations almost for their own sake. More important, he consciously and systematically pursues relations. The layman does not do this. His preoccupation with relations is loose, unsystematic, uncontrolled. He often seizes, for example, on the fortuitous occurrence of two phenomena and immediately links them indissolubly as cause and effect.

Take the relation tested in a study by Hurlock.[3] In more recent terminology, this relation might be expressed: Positive reinforcement (reward) produces greater increments of learning than does negative reinforcement (punishment) or no reinforcement. The relation is between reinforcement (or reward and punishment) and learning. Educators and parents of the nineteenth century often assumed that negative reinforcement (punishment) was the more effective agent in learning. Educators

---

[3] E. Hurlock, "An Evaluation of Certain Incentives Used in Schoolwork," *Journal of Educational Psychology*, XVI (1925), 145–159.

and parents of the present often assume that positive reinforcement (reward) is the more effective agent. Both may say that their viewpoints are "only common sense." It is obvious, they may say, that if you reward (or punish) a child he will learn better. The scientist, on the other hand, while he may personally espouse one or the other or neither of these viewpoints, would probably insist on systematic and controlled testing of both (and other) relations, as Hurlock did.

A final difference between common sense and science lies in different explanations of observed phenomena. The scientist, when attempting to explain the relations among observed phenomena, carefully rules out what have been called "metaphysical explanations." A metaphysical explanation is simply a proposition that cannot be tested. To say, for example, that people are poor and starving because God wills it, that studying hard subjects improves the child's moral character, that delinquency is due to lack of moral fiber, that it is wrong to be authoritarian in the classroom, or that the evolving American public school is enhancing democracy is to talk metaphysically.

None of these propositions can be tested; thus they are metaphysical. As such, science is not concerned with them. This does not mean that a scientist would necessarily spurn such statements, rule them out of life, say they are not true, or claim they are meaningless. It simply means that *as a scientist* he is not concerned with them. In short, science is concerned with things that can be publicly observed and tested. If propositions or questions do not contain implications for such public observation and testing, they are not scientific questions.

FOUR METHODS OF KNOWING

Charles Peirce, the great American philosopher, said that there are four general ways of knowing or, as he put it, of fixing belief.[4] The first is the *method of tenacity*. Here men hold firmly to the truth, the truth that they know to be true because they hold firmly to it, because they have always known it to be true. Frequent repetition of such "truths" seems to enhance their validity. If one holds tenaciously to one's beliefs, even in the face of evidence that casts doubt on their validity, one seems to strengthen the beliefs. Recent psychological evidence has shown us that men will often cling to their beliefs in the face of clearly conflicting facts. And they will also infer "new" knowledge, new generalizations, from propositions that may be false.

A second method of knowing or fixing belief is the *method of au-*

[4] J. Buchler, ed., *Philosophical Writings of Peirce*. New York: Dover, 1955, chap. 2. In the ensuing discussion, I am taking some liberties with Peirce's original formulation in an attempt to clarify the ideas and to make them more germane to the present work. For a good discussion of the four methods, see M. Cohen and E. Nagel, *An Introduction to Logic and Scientific Method*. New York: Harcourt, 1934, pp. 193–196.

thority. This is the method of established belief. If the Bible says it, it is so. If a prominent professor says that modern education is soft and bad, it is so. If a noted physicist says there is a God, it is so. If an idea has the weight of tradition and public sanction behind it, it is so. As Peirce points out, this method is superior to the method of tenacity, because human progress, although slow, can be achieved using the method. Actually, life could not go on without the method of authority. We must take a large body of facts and information on the basis of authority. Thus, it should not be concluded that the method of authority is unsound; it is only unsound under certain circumstances.

The *a priori method* is the third way of knowing or fixing belief. (Cohen and Nagel call it the *method of intuition*.) It rests its case for superiority on the assumption that the propositions accepted by the "a priorist" are "agreeable to reason," are self-evident. Note that a priori propositions "agree with reason" and not necessarily with experience. The idea seems to be that men, by free communication and intercourse, can reach the truth because their natural inclinations tend toward truth. The difficulty with this rationalistic position lies in the expression "agree with reason." Whose reason? Suppose two good men, using rational processes, reach different conclusions, as they often do. Which one is right? Is it a matter of taste, as Peirce puts it? If something is self-evident to many men —for instance, that learning hard subjects trains the mind and builds moral character, that American education is inferior to Russian and European education, that women are poor drivers—does this mean it is so? According to the a priori method, it does—it just "stands to reason."

The fourth method is the *method of science*. Peirce says:

> To satisfy our doubts, . . . therefore, it is necessary that a method should be found by which our beliefs may be determined by nothing human, but by some external permanency—by something upon which our thinking has no effect. . . . The method must be such that the ultimate conclusion of every man shall be the same. Such is the method of science. Its fundamental hypothesis . . . is this: There are real things, whose characters are entirely independent of our opinions about them . . .[5]

The scientific approach[6] has one characteristic that no other method of attaining knowledge has: self-correction. There are built-in checks all along the way to scientific knowledge. These checks are so conceived and used that they control and verify the scientist's activities and conclusions to the end of attaining dependable knowledge outside himself. Even if a hypothesis seems to be supported in an experiment, the scientist will test

---

[5] Buchler, *op. cit.*, p. 18.

[6] It should be stated here that the position of this book is that there is no one scientific method as such. Rather, there are a number of methods that scientists can and do use, but it can probably be validly said that there is one scientific approach.

alternative hypotheses that, if also supported, may cast doubt on the first hypothesis. A scientist does not accept a statement as true, even though the evidence at first looks promising. He insists upon testing it. He also insists that any testing procedure be open to public inspection.

As Peirce says, the checks used in scientific research are anchored as much as possible in reality lying outside the scientist and his personal beliefs, perceptions, biases, values, attitudes, and emotions. Perhaps the best single word to express this is *objectivity*. But, as we shall see later, the scientific approach involves more than this. The point is that more dependable knowledge is attained through science because science ultimately appeals to evidence: propositions are subjected to empirical test. An objection might be raised to the effect that theory, which the scientist uses and exalts, is part of man himself. But, as Polanyi points out, "A theory is something other than myself" [7]; thus a theory helps the scientist to attain greater objectivity. In short, scientists systematically and consciously use the self-corrective aspect of the scientific approach.

SCIENCE AND ITS FUNCTIONS

What is science? This question is not easy to answer. Indeed, no definition of science will be directly attempted. We shall, instead, talk about notions and views of science and then try to explain the functions of science.

Science is a badly misunderstood word. There seem to be three popular stereotypes that impede popular understanding of scientific activity. One of these is the white coat-stethoscope-laboratory stereotype. The scientist seems to be perceived as a peculiar person who works only with facts in laboratories. He uses complicated equipment, does innumerable experiments, and piles up facts for the ultimate purpose of improving the lot of mankind. Thus, while he is somewhat of an unimaginative grubber after facts, he is redeemed by his noble motives. And you can believe him when, for example, he tells you that such-and-such a toothpaste is good for you or that you should not smoke cigarettes.

The second stereotype of the scientist is that he is a brilliant individual who thinks, spins complex theories, and generally spends his time in the ivory tower aloof from the world and its problems. The scientist in this stereotype is a rather impractical theorist, even though his thinking and theory occasionally lead to results of practical significance like atomic bombs.

The third stereotype equates science with engineering and technology. The building of bridges, the improvement of automobiles and missiles, the automation of industry, the invention of teaching machines, and the like are thought to be science. The scientist's job, in this conception,

[7] M. Polanyi, *Personal Knowledge*. Chicago: University of Chicago Press, 1958, p. 4.

is to work at the improvement of man's inventions and artifacts. The scientist himself is conceived to be a sort of highly skilled engineer working to make life smooth and efficient.

These stereotypical notions impede student understanding of science, the activities and thinking of the scientist, and scientific research in general. In short, they unfortunately make the student's task harder than it would otherwise be. Thus they should be cleared away to make room for more adequate notions.

In the scientific world itself there are two broad views of science: the static and the dynamic.[8] The *static view*, the view that seems to influence most laymen and students, is that science is an activity that contributes systematized information to the world. The scientist's job is to discover new facts and to add them to the already existing body of information. In short, science is even conceived to be a body of facts. Science, in this view, is also a way of explaining observed phenomena. The emphasis, then, is on the *present state of knowledge and adding to it,* on the extent of knowledge, and on the present set of laws, theories, hypotheses, and principles.

The *dynamic view,* on the other hand, regards science more as an *activity,* what scientists *do.* The present state of knowledge is important, of course. But it is important mainly because it is a base for further scientific operations, for further scientific theory and research. This has been called a *heuristic view.* The word "heuristic," meaning serving to discover or reveal, was used to describe arguments that were persuasive rather than logically compelling. The word now has the notion of self-discovery connected with it. A heuristic method of teaching, for instance, would be a method that emphasizes students' discovering things for themselves. The heuristic view in science emphasizes theory and interconnected conceptual schemata that are fruitful for further research. A heuristic emphasis is a discovery emphasis.

It is the heuristic aspect of science that distinguishes it in good part from engineering and technology. On the basis of a heuristic hunch, the scientist takes a risky leap. As Polanyi says, "It is the plunge by which we gain a foothold at another shore of reality. On such plunges the scientist has to stake bit by bit his entire professional life." [9] Heuristic may also be called problem-solving, but the emphasis is on imaginative and not routine problem-solving. The heuristic view in science stresses problem-solving rather than facts and bodies of information. Alleged established facts and bodies of information are important to the heuristic scientist because they help lead to further theory, further discovery, and further investigation.

Still avoiding a direct definition of science—but certainly implying one—we now look at the function of science. Here we find two distinct

[8] Conant, *op. cit.,* pp. 23–27.
[9] Polanyi, *op. cit.,* p. 123.

views. The practical man, the non-scientist generally, thinks of science as a discipline or activity aimed at improving things, at making progress. Some scientists, too, take this position. The function of science, in this view, is to make discoveries, to learn facts, to advance knowledge in order to improve things. Branches of science that are clearly and immediately of this character receive wide and strong support. Witness the strong support in the last forty to fifty years of medical research and military research. Recently, perhaps in good part because we have been threatened by alleged Soviet educational supremacy, educational research has been supported. This function of science, to improve man's lot, seems to be supported by most laymen and many scientists. The criterion of practicality is preeminent here. It can be argued (but we will not do so here) that educational research has been and is now dominated by this view.[10]

A very different view of the function of science is well expressed by Braithwaite: "The function of science . . . is to establish general laws covering the behaviors of the empirical events or objects with which the science in question is concerned, and thereby to enable us to connect together our knowledge of the separately known events, and to make reliable predictions of events as yet unknown." [11] The connection between this view of the function of science and the dynamic-heuristic view discussed earlier is obvious, except that an important element is added: the establishment of general laws—or theory, if you will. If we are to understand modern educational research and its strengths and weaknesses, we must explore the elements of Braithwaite's statement. We do so by considering the aims of science, scientific explanation, and the role and importance of theory.

THE AIMS OF SCIENCE, SCIENTIFIC EXPLANATION, AND THEORY

The basic aim of science is theory. Perhaps less cryptic, the basic aim of science is to find general explanations of natural events. Such general explanations are called theories. Instead of trying to explain each and every separate behavior of children, the scientific psychologist seeks general explanations that encompass and link together many different behaviors. Rather than try to explain children's methods of solving arithmetic problems, for example, the psychologist seeks general explanations of all kinds of problem-solving. He might call such a general explanation a theory of problem-solving.

This discussion of the basic aim of science as theory may seem strange

[10] See F. Kerlinger, "Practicality and Educational Research," *School Review*, LXVII (1959), 281–291.

[11] R. Braithwaite, *Scientific Explanation*. Cambridge: Cambridge University Press, 1955, p. 1.

to the student, especially the student of education, who has probably been inculcated with the notion that human activities have to pay off in practical ways. If we said that the aim of science is the betterment of mankind most readers would quickly read the words and accept them. But the basic aim of science is not the betterment of mankind. It is theory. Unfortunately, this sweeping and really complex statement is not too easy to understand. Still, we must try because it is important.

Other aims of science that have been stated are: explanation, understanding, prediction, and control. If we accept theory as the ultimate aim of science, however, explanation and understanding become simply sub-aims of the ultimate aim. This is because of the definition and nature of theory:

A theory is a set of interrelated constructs (concepts), definitions, and propositions that presents a systematic view of phenomena by specifying relations among variables, with the purpose of explaining and predicting the phenomena.

This definition says three things. One, a theory is a set of propositions consisting of defined and interrelated constructs. Two, a theory sets out the interrelations among a set of variables (constructs), and in so doing, presents a systematic view of the phenomena described by the variables. Finally, a theory explains phenomena. It does so by specifying what variables are related to what variables and how they are related, thus enabling the researcher to predict from certain variables to certain other variables.

One might, for example, have a theory of school failure. One's variables might be intelligence, verbal and numerical aptitudes, anxiety, social class membership, and motivation. The phenomenon to be explained, of course, is school failure—or, perhaps, more accurately, school achievement. School failure is explained by specified relations between each of the six variables and school failure, or by combinations of the six variables and school failure. The scientist, successfully using this set of constructs, then, "understands" school failure. He is able to "explain" and, to some extent at least, "predict" school failure.

It is obvious that explanation and prediction can be subsumed under theory. The very nature of a theory lies in its explanation of observed phenomena. Take reinforcement theory in psychology. A simple proposition flowing from this theory is: If a response is rewarded (reinforced) when it occurs, it will tend to be repeated. The psychological scientist who first formulated some such proposition did so as an explanation of the observed repetitious occurrences of responses. *Why* did they occur and reoccur with dependable regularity? Because they were rewarded. This is an explanation, although it may not be a satisfactory explanation to many people. Someone else may ask *why* reward increases the likelihood of a response's occurrence. A full-blown theory would have the explanation.

Today, however, there is no really satisfactory answer. All we can say is that, with a high degree of probability, the reinforcement of a response makes the response occur and reoccur. In other words, the propositions of a theory, the statements of relations, constitute the explanation, as far as that theory is concerned, of observed natural phenomena.

Now, about prediction and control. It can be said that scientists do not really have to be concerned with explanation and understanding. Only prediction and control are necessary. Proponents of this point of view would say that the adequacy of a theory is its predictive power. If by using the theory we are able to predict successfully, then the theory is confirmed and this is enough. We need not necessarily look for further underlying explanations. Since we can predict reliably, we can control because control is deducible from prediction.

The prediction view of science has validity. But as far as this book is concerned, prediction is considered to be an aspect of theory. By its very nature, a theory predicts. That is, when from the primitive propositions of a theory we deduce more complex ones, we are in essence "predicting." When we explain observed phenomena, we are always stating a relation between, say, the class A and the class B. Scientific explanation boils down to specifying the exact relations between one class of empirical events and another, under certain conditions. We say: If A, then B, A and B referring to classes of objects or events. But this *is* prediction, prediction from A to B. Thus a theoretical explanation implies prediction. And we come back to the idea that theory is the ultimate aim of science. All else flows from theory. This is perhaps what is meant by the expression "There is nothing more practical than a good theory."

It was not intended in the above discussion to discredit or denigrate research that is not specifically and consciously theory-oriented. Much valuable social scientific and educational research is preoccupied with the shorter range goal of finding specific relations; that is, merely to discover a relation is part of science. The ultimately most usable and satisfying relations, however, are those that are the most generalized, those that are tied to other relations in a theory.

The notion of generality is important here. Theories, because they are general, apply widely to many phenomena and to many people in many places. A specific relation, of course, is less widely applicable. If, for example, one finds that test anxiety is related to test performance, this finding, though interesting and important, is less widely applicable and less understood than if one first found the relation in a network of interrelated variables that are parts of a theory. Modest, limited, and specific research aims, then, are good. Theoretical research aims are better because, among other reasons, they are more widely applicable and more general.

SCIENTIFIC RESEARCH—A DEFINITION

Fortunately, it is much easier to define scientific research than it is to define science and theory. It would not be easy, however, to get scientists and researchers to agree on such a definition. Even so, we attempt one here:

Scientific research is systematic, controlled, empirical, and critical investigation of hypothetical propositions about the presumed relations among natural phenomena.

This definition requires little explanation since it is mostly a condensed and formalized statement of much that was said earlier or that will be said soon. Two points need emphasis, however. First, when we say that scientific research is systematic and controlled, we mean, in effect, that scientific investigation is so ordered that investigators can have critical confidence in research outcomes. As we shall see later, this means that the research situation is tightly disciplined. Among the many alternative explanations of a phenomenon, all but one are systematically ruled out. One can thus have greater confidence that a tested relation is as it is than if one had not controlled the situation, had not ruled out alternative possibilities.

Second, scientific investigation is empirical. If the scientist believes something is so, he must somehow or other put his belief to a test outside himself. Subjective belief, in other words, must be checked against objective reality. The scientist must always subject his notions to the court of empirical inquiry and test. That he is hypercritical of the results of his own and others' research results is a truism. Every scientist writing a research report has other scientists reading what he writes while he writes it. Though it is easy to err, to exaggerate, to overgeneralize when writing up one's own work, it is not easy to escape the feeling of scientific eyes constantly peering over one's shoulder. Considerable attention will of course be given in subsequent chapters to elaborating and clarifying this definition of scientific research.

THE SCIENTIFIC APPROACH

The scientific approach is a special systematized form of all reflective thinking and inquiry. Dewey, in his famous analysis of reflective thinking, *How We Think,* has given a general paradigm of problematical inquiry.[12] The present discussion of the scientific approach is based on Dewey's analysis. Dewey's treatment, however, is altered somewhat to suit the scientific framework in which we are working.

Problem-Obstacle-Idea The scientist will usually experience an obstacle to understanding, a vague unrest about observed and unobserved phenom-

12 J. Dewey, *How We Think.* Boston: Heath, 1933, pp. 106–118.

ena, a curiosity as to why something is as it is. His first and most important step is to get the idea out in the open, to express the problem in some reasonably manageable form. Rarely or never will the problem spring full-blown at this stage. He must struggle with it, try it out, live with it. Dewey says, "There is a troubled, perplexed, trying situation, where the difficulty is, as it were, spread throughout the entire situation, infecting it as a whole."[13] Sooner or later, explicitly or implicitly, he states the problem, even if his expression of it is inchoate and tentative. Here he intellectualizes, as Dewey puts it, "what at first is merely an *emotional* quality of the whole situation."[14] In some respects, this is the most difficult and most important part of the whole process. Without some sort of statement of the problem, the scientist can rarely go further and expect his work to be fruitful.

Hypothesis   After intellectualizing the problem, after turning back on experience for possible solutions, after observing relevant phenomena, the scientist may formulate a hypothesis. A hypothesis is a conjectural statement, a tentative proposition, about the relation between two or more observed (sometimes unobservable, especially in psychology and education) phenomena or variables. Our scientist will say, "If such-and-such occurs, then so-and-so results."

Reasoning-Deduction   This step or activity is one that is frequently overlooked or underemphasized. In some respects it is perhaps the most important part of Dewey's contribution to the analysis of reflective thinking. The scientist now deduces the consequences of the hypothesis he has formulated. Conant, in talking about the rise of modern science, says that the new element added in the seventeenth century was the use of deductive reasoning.[15] Here is where experience, knowledge, and perspicuity are important. Often the scientist, when deducing the consequences of a hypothesis he has formulated, will arrive at a problem quite different from the one he started with. On the other hand, he may find that his deductions lead him to believe that the problem cannot be solved with present technical tools. For example, before modern statistics was developed, certain educational research problems were insoluble. It was very difficult, if not impossible, to test two or three interdependent hypotheses at one time. It was next to impossible to test the interactive effect of variables. And we now have reason to believe that certain problems are insoluble unless they are tackled in a multivariate manner. An example of this is teaching methods and their relation to achievement and other variables. It is likely that teaching methods, *per se*, do not differ much if we only study their simple effects. Teaching methods probably work differ-

13 *Ibid.*, p. 108.
14 *Ibid.*, p. 109.
15 Conant, *op. cit.*, p. 46.

ently under different conditions, with different teachers, and with different pupils.

An example may help us to understand better this reasoning-deduction step. Suppose an investigator becomes intrigued with aggressive behavior. He wonders why people are often aggressive in situations where aggressiveness may not be too appropriate (Problem-Obstacle-Idea). He has noted that aggressive behavior seems to occur when people have experienced difficulties of one kind or another. (Note the vagueness of the problem here.) After thinking for some time, reading the literature for clues, and making further observations, he formulates a hypothesis: Frustration leads to aggression (Hypothesis). He defines "frustration" as prevention from reaching a goal and "aggression" as behavior characterized by physical or verbal attack on other persons or objects.

He may now reason somewhat as follows. If frustration leads to aggression, then we should find a great deal of aggression among children who are in schools that are very restrictive, schools that do not permit children much freedom and self-expression. Similarly, in very difficult social situations, assuming such situations are frustrating, we should expect more aggression than is "usual." Reasoning further, if we give experimental subjects interesting problems to solve and then prevent them from solving the problems, we should predict some kind of aggressive behavior.

Reasoning might, as indicated above, change the problem. We might realize that the initial problem was only a special case of a broader, more fundamental and important problem. We might, for example, have started with a narrower hypothesis: Restrictive school situations lead to negativism in children. Then we can generalize the problem to the form: Frustration leads to aggression. While this is a different form of thinking from that discussed earlier, it is important because of what might almost be called its heuristic quality. Reasoning can help lead to wider, more basic, and thus more significant problems, as well as provide operational (testable) implications of the original hypothesis.

Observation-Test-Experiment   It should be clear to the reader by now that the observation-test-experiment phase is only part of the scientific enterprise. If the problem has been well stated, the hypothesis or hypotheses adequately formulated, and the implications of the hypotheses carefully deduced, this step is almost automatic—assuming that the investigator is technically competent.

The essence of testing a hypothesis is to test the *relation* expressed by the hypothesis. We do not test the variables, as such; we test the relation between the variables. All observation, all testing, all experimentation is for one large purpose: putting the problem relation to empirical test. To test without knowing at least fairly well what and why one is testing is usually to blunder. Simply to have a vague and poorly stated problem (such as "What effect does the core curriculum have on students?") and then to test students for their achievement in, say, social studies is a very inadequate procedure that can lead only to ignorance and, worse, to misguided information. Similarly, to say one is going to study grouping practices (grouping children by intellectual level, reading level, and the like) of teachers without knowing, really, why one is doing it or without stating a relation between grouping practices and some other variable or variables is research nonsense.

Another point about testing hypotheses is that we do not test a hypothesis directly. As indicated in the previous step on reasoning, we test the deduced implications of the hypothesis. Our hypothesis might be, "Writing remarks on student papers will improve future papers," which was deduced, say, from a broader hypothesis, "Reinforcement of responses leads to an increment in response rate and strength." We are not testing "writing remarks on student papers" nor "the improvement of future papers." We are testing the relation between them.

Dewey emphasized that the temporal sequence of reflective thinking or inquiry is not fixed. We can repeat and re-emphasize what he says in our own framework. The steps of the scientific approach are not neatly fixed. The first step is not neatly completed before the second step begins. Further, we may test before adequately deducing the implications of the hypothesis. The hypothesis itself may seem to need elaboration or refinement as a result of deducing implications from it.[16]

Let us summarize the so-called scientific approach to inquiry. First there is doubt, a barrier, an indeterminate situation crying out, so to speak, to be made determinate. The scientist experiences vague doubts, emotional disturbance, inchoate ideas. He struggles to formulate the problem, even if inadequately. He studies the literature, scans his own experience and the experience of others. Often he simply has to wait for an inventive leap of the mind. Maybe it will occur; maybe not. With the problem formulated, with the basic question or questions properly asked, the rest is much easier. Then the hypothesis is constructed, after which its implications are deduced, mainly along experimental lines. In this process the original problem, and of course the original hypothesis, may be changed. It may be broadened or narrowed. It may even be abandoned. Lastly, but not finally, the relation expressed by the hypothesis is tested by observation and experimentation. On the basis of the research evidence, the hypothesis is accepted or rejected. This information is then

---

16 Hypotheses and their expression will often be found inadequate when implications are deduced from them. A frequent difficulty is when a hypothesis is so vague that one deduction is as good as another, that is, the hypothesis may not yield to precise test.

fed back to the original problem and it is kept or altered as dictated by the evidence. Dewey finally pointed out that one phase of the process may be expanded and be of great importance, another may be skimped, and there may be fewer or more steps involved. These things are not important. What is important is the over-all fundamental idea of scientific research as a controlled rational process of reflective inquiry, the interdependent nature of the parts of the process, and the paramount importance of the problem and its statement.

2 *PROBLEMS AND HYPOTHESES*

If research were limited simply to gathering so-called facts, scientific knowledge could not advance. Many people think that science is basically a fact-gathering activity. It is not. As Cohen says:

> There is . . . no genuine progress in scientific insight through the Baconian method of accumulating empirical facts without hypotheses or anticipation of nature. Without some guiding idea we do not know what facts to gather. Without something to prove, we cannot determine what is relevant and what is irrelevant.[1]

The scientifically uninformed person often has the idea that the scientist is a highly objective individual who gathers data without preconceived ideas. Poincaré long ago pointed out how wrong this idea is. He said:

> It is often said that experiments should be made without preconceived ideas. That is impossible. Not only would it make every experiment fruitless, but even if we wished to do so, it could not be done.[2]

PROBLEMS

It is not always possible for a researcher to formulate his problem simply, clearly, and completely. He may often have only a rather general, diffuse, even confused notion of the problem. This is in the nature of the complexity of scientific research. It may even take an investigator years of exploration, thought, and research before he can clearly say what questions he has been seeking answers to. Nevertheless, adequate statement of the research problem is one of the most important parts of research. That it may be difficult or impossible to state a research problem satisfactorily at this time should not allow us to lose sight of the ultimate desirability and necessity of doing so. Nor should the difficulty be used as a rationalization to avoid stating the problem.

1 M. Cohen, *A Preface to Logic.* New York: Meridian, 1956, p. 148.
2 H. Poincaré, *Science and Hypothesis.* New York: Dover, 1952, p. 143.

Bearing this difficulty in mind, a fundamental principle can be stated: If one wants to solve a problem, one must generally know what the problem is. It can be said that a large part of the solution of a problem lies in knowing what it is one is trying to do. Another part of the solution lies in knowing what a problem is and especially what a scientific problem is.

What is a good problem statement? Although research problems differ a great deal, and although there is no one "right" way to state a research problem, certain characteristics of problems and problem statements can be learned and used to good advantage. To start, let us take one or two examples of published research problems and study their characteristics. First, take the problem of the study by Hurlock mentioned in Chap. 1: What are the effects on pupil performance of different types of incentives? [3] Note that the problem is stated in question form. The simplest way is here the best way. Also note that the problem states a relation between variables, in this case between the variables incentives and pupil performance (achievement).

A *problem,* then, is an interrogative sentence or statement that asks: What relation exists between two or more variables? The answer to this question is what is being sought in the research. If the problem is a scientific one, it will almost always contain two or more variables. In the Hurlock example, the problem statement relates incentive to pupil performance. Another problem, by Page, is: Do teacher comments cause improvement in student performance? One variable is teacher comments (or reinforcement), and the other variable is student performance. The relational part of the question is expressed by the word "cause." Still another problem, by Harlow, is more complex: Under what conditions does learning how to learn transfer to new situations? One variable is "learning how to learn" (or set); the other variable is transfer (of learning).

Criteria of Problems and Problem Statements   There are three criteria of good problems and problem statements. One, the problem should express a relation between two or more variables. It asks, in effect, questions like: Is *A* related to *B?* How are *A* and *B* related to *C?* Is *A* related to *B* under conditions *C* and *D?* There are exceptions to this dictum, but they are rare. They occur mostly in taxonomic or methodological research. (See Appendix B.)

Two, the problem should be stated clearly and unambiguously in question form. Instead of saying, for instance, "The problem is . . . ," or "The purpose of this study is . . . ," ask a question. Questions have the virtue of posing problems directly. The purpose of a study is not necessarily the same as the problem of a study. The purpose of the Hurlock

[3] References for the problems and hypotheses in this chapter are given in the study suggestions at the end of the chapter. The original wording of the authors is not always used.

study, for instance, was to throw light on the use of incentives in school situations. The problem was the question about the relation between incentives and performance. Again, the simplest way is the best way: ask a question.

The third criterion is often difficult to satisfy. It demands that the problem and the problem statement should be such as to *imply* possibilities of empirical testing. A problem that does not contain implications for testing its stated relation or relations is not a scientific problem. This means not only that an actual relation is stated, but also that the variables of the relation can somehow be measured. Many interesting and important questions are not scientific questions simply because they are not amenable to testing. Certain philosophic and theological questions, while perhaps important to the individuals who consider them, cannot be tested empirically and are thus of no interest to the scientist as a scientist. The epistemological question, "How do we know?," is such a question. A medieval theological classic is "How many angels can dance on the head of a pin?" Education has many interesting but nonscientific questions, such as, "What effect is the changing ethos of American education having on American children?" "Does democratic education improve the learning of youngsters?" "Are group processes good for children?" These questions can be called metaphysical in the sense that they are, at least as stated, beyond empirical testing possibilities. The key difficulties are that some of them are not relations, and most of their constructs are very difficult or impossible to so define that they can be measured.

HYPOTHESES

A *hypothesis* is a conjectural statement of the relation between two or more variables. Hypotheses are always in declarative sentence form, and they relate, either generally or specifically, variables to variables. There are two criteria for "good" hypotheses and hypothesis statements. They are the same as two of those for problems and problem statements. One, hypotheses are statements about the relations between variables. Two, hypotheses carry clear implications for testing the stated relations. These criteria mean, then, that hypothesis statements contain two or more variables that are measurable or potentially measurable and that they specify how the variables are related. A statement that lacks either or both these characteristics is no hypothesis in the scientific sense of the word.[4]

---

[4] There are legitimate hypotheses that, at least on the surface, lack the relation criterion. For instance, in factor-analytic investigations, to be discussed later, we might have some such problem statement as: What are the factors underlying social attitudes? An hypothesis such as this might be used: There are two underlying factors behind social attitudes: (I) liberalism and (II) conservatism. In this book, however, only relational statements will be considered.

Let us take three hypotheses from the literature and apply the two criteria to them. First, consider a very simple hypothesis: Group study contributes to higher grade achievement. We have here a relation stated between one variable, group study, and another variable, grade achievement. Since measurement of the variables is readily conceivable, implications for testing the hypothesis, too, are readily conceivable. The criteria are satisfied. A second hypothesis is different because it states the relation in the so-called null form: Practice in a mental function has no effect on the future learning of that mental function. Note that the relation is stated directly and clearly: one variable, practice in a mental function, is related to another variable, future learning, by the words "has no effect on." On the criterion of potential testability, however, we meet with difficulty. We are faced with the problem of so defining "mental function" and "future learning" that they are measurable. If we can solve this problem satisfactorily, then we definitely have a hypothesis. Indeed, we have a famous one—but one that has usually not been stated as a hypothesis but as a fact by many educators of the past and the present.

The third hypothesis represents a very numerous and important class. Here the relation is indirect, concealed, as it were. It customarily comes in the form of a statement that Groups *A* and *B* will differ on some characteristic. For example, Middle-class children more often than lower-class children will avoid finger painting tasks. Note that this statement is one step removed from the actual hypothesis which might be stated: Finger painting behavior is in part a function of social class. If the latter statement were the hypothesis stated, then the first statement might be called a subhypothesis, or a specific prediction based on the original hypothesis.

Let us consider another hypothesis of this type but still one more step removed: Individuals having the same or similar occupational role will hold similar attitudes toward a cognitive object significantly related to the occupational role. ("Cognitive objects" are any concrete or abstract things perceived and "known" by individuals. Tables, houses, people, groups, the government, and education are examples of cognitive objects.) The relation in this case, of course, is between occupational role and attitudes (toward a cognitive object related to the role, for example, role of educator and attitudes toward education). In order to test this hypothesis, it would be necessary to have at least two groups, each representing a different occupational role, and then to compare the attitudes of the groups. For instance, we might take a group of teachers and compare their attitudes toward education to those of, say, a group of businessmen. Thus the hypothesis, as stated, is really a "difference" hypothesis. Still, it, too, could be reduced to the general relational form with which we started: Attitudes toward cognitive objects significantly related to occupational roles are in part a function of the behavior and expectations associated with the roles.

THE IMPORTANCE OF PROBLEMS AND HYPOTHESES

There is little doubt that hypotheses are important and indispensable tools of scientific research. There are three main reasons for this belief. One, they are, so to speak, the working instruments of theory. Hypotheses can be deduced from theory and from other hypotheses. If, for instance, we are working on a theory of aggression, we are presumably looking for causes and effects of aggressive behavior. We might have observed cases of aggressive behavior occurring after frustrating circumstances. The theory, then, might include the proposition: Frustration produces aggression. From this broad hypothesis we may deduce more specific hypotheses, such as: To prevent children from reaching goals they find desirable (frustration) will result in their fighting with each other (aggression); if children are deprived of parental love (frustration), they will react in part with aggressive behavior.

The second reason is that hypotheses can be tested and shown to be probably true or probably false. Isolated facts are not tested, as we said before; only relations are tested. Since hypotheses are relational propositions, this is probably the main reason they are used in scientific inquiry. They are, in essence, predictions of the form, "If A, then B," which we set up to test the relation between A and B. We let the facts have a chance to establish the probable truth or falsity of the hypothesis.

Three, hypotheses are powerful tools for the advancement of knowledge because they enable man to get outside himself. Though constructed by man, hypotheses exist, can be tested, and can be shown to be probably correct or incorrect apart from man's values and opinions. This is so important that we venture to say that there would be no science in any complete sense without hypotheses.

Just as important as hypotheses are the problems behind the hypotheses. As Dewey has well pointed out, research usually starts with a problem, with a problematic situation. Dewey says that there is first an indeterminate situation in which ideas are vague, doubts are raised, and the thinker is perplexed.[5] He further points out that the problem is not enunciated, indeed cannot be enunciated, until one has experienced such an indeterminate situation.

The indeterminacy, however, must ultimately be removed. Though it is true, as stated earlier, that a researcher may often have only a general and diffuse notion of his problem, sooner or later he has to have a fairly clear idea of what the problem is. Otherwise he can hardly get very far in solving it. Though this statement seems self-evident, one of the most difficult things to do, apparently, is to state one's research problem clearly and completely. In other words, you must know what you are

[5] J. Dewey, *Logic: The Theory of Inquiry.* New York: Holt, Rinehart and Winston, Inc., 1938, pp. 105–107.

trying to find out. And when you finally know this, the problem is a long way toward solution.

VIRTUES OF PROBLEMS AND HYPOTHESES

Problems and hypotheses, then, have powerful virtues in common. One, they direct investigation. The relations expressed in the hypotheses tell the investigator what to do, in effect. Two, problems and hypotheses, because they are ordinarily generalized relational statements, enable the researcher to deduce specific empirical manifestations implied by the problems and hypotheses. We say: "If Hypothesis 1 is true, then perhaps Hypothesis 2 is also true and 3 not true." Then we test Hypothesis 2 and 3. If Hypothesis 2 is true and Hypothesis 3 not true, as predicted, Hypothesis 1 is confirmed.

The third point is closely related to the second and refers to a difference between problems and hypotheses. Hypotheses, if properly stated, can be tested. While a particular hypothesis may be too broad to be directly tested, if it is a "good" hypothesis, then, as indicated under the second point, above, other testable hypotheses can be deduced from it. The point is that facts or variables are not tested as such. The relations stated by the hypotheses are tested. Another point is that a problem really cannot be scientifically solved if it is not reduced to hypothesis form because a problem is a question, usually of a broad nature, and is, in and of itself, not directly testable. One does not test the question: Does anxiety affect achievement? One tests one or more hypotheses implied by this question, for example: "Test anxiety reduces achievement test scores," or "Anxiety-provoking test situations will depress achievement test scores."

The fourth point is that problems and hypotheses advance scientific knowledge by helping the investigator to confirm or disconfirm theory. Suppose a psychological investigator gives a number of subjects three or four tests, among which is a test of anxiety and an arithmetic test. Routinely computing the intercorrelations between the three or four tests, he finds that the correlation between anxiety and arithmetic is negative. He concludes, therefore, that the greater the anxiety the lower the arithmetic score. But it is quite conceivable that the relation is fortuitous or even spurious. If, however, he had hypothesized the relation in advance on the basis of theory, the investigator could have greater confidence in the results. The investigator who does not hypothesize a relation in advance, in short, does not give the facts a chance to prove or disprove anything.[6]

---

[6] The words "prove" and "disprove" are not to be taken here in their usual literal sense. It should be remembered that a hypothesis is never really proved or disproved. To be more accurate we should probably say something like: The weight of evidence is on the side of the hypothesis, or the weight of the evidence casts doubt on the hypothesis. Braithwaite says: "Thus the empirical evidence of its instances never

This use of the hypothesis is similar to playing a game of chance. The rules of the game are set up in advance, and bets are made in advance. One cannot change the rules after an outcome, nor can one change one's bets after making them. That would not be "fair." One cannot throw the dice first and then bet. Similarly, if one gathers data first and then selects a datum and comes to a conclusion on the basis of the datum, one has violated the rules of the scientific game.

The reason is that the game is not "fair." And it is not fair because the investigator can easily capitalize on, say, two significant relations out of five tested. What happens to the other three? They are usually forgotten. But in a fair game every throw of the dice is counted in the sense that one either wins or does not win on the basis of the outcome of each throw. The main point, perhaps, is that the purpose of hypotheses is to direct inquiry. As Darwin pointed out long ago, all observations have to be for or against some view if they are to be of any use.

The last point to be made about hypotheses has already been made, but it needs formal statement, even repetition. Hypotheses incorporate the theory, or part of it, in testable or near-testable form. Earlier an example of reinforcement theory was given in which testable hypotheses were deduced from the general problem. The importance of recognizing this function of hypotheses may be shown by going through the back door and using a theory that is very difficult, or perhaps impossible, to test. Freud's theory of anxiety includes the construct of repression. Now, by repression Freud meant the forcing of unacceptable ideas deeply into the unconscious. In order to test the Freudian theory of anxiety it would be necessary to deduce relations suggested by the theory. These deductions would of course have to include the repression notion which includes the construct of the unconscious. Hypotheses can be formulated using these constructs, and, in order to test the theory, they would have to be so formulated. But testing them is another, more difficult matter because of the extreme difficulty of so defining terms like "repression" and "unconscious" that they can be measured. Up to the present, no one has succeeded in defining these two constructs without seriously departing from the original Freudian meaning and usage. Hypotheses, then, are important bridges between theory and empirical inquiry.

PROBLEMS, VALUES, AND DEFINITIONS

To clarify further the nature of problems and hypotheses, two or three common errors will now be discussed. First, scientific problems are

---

proves the hypothesis: in suitable cases we may say that it *establishes* the hypothesis, meaning by this that the evidence makes it reasonable to accept the hypothesis; but it never *proves* the hypothesis in the sense that the hypothesis is a logical consequence of the evidence." (R. Braithwaite, *Scientific Explanation*. Cambridge: Cambridge University Press, 1955, p. 14.)

not moral and ethical questions. What is the best way to teach fourth-grade children? Are punitive disciplinary measures bad? Is an authoritarian school system bad for the children's personal and social development? To ask these questions is to ask value and judgmental questions that science cannot answer. Many so-called hypotheses are not hypotheses at all. For instance, The small-group method of teaching is better than the lecture method. This is a value statement; it is an article of faith and not a hypothesis. If it were possible to state a relation between the variables, and if it were possible to define the variables so as to permit testing the relation, then we might have a hypothesis. But there is no way to test value questions scientifically.

A quick and relatively easy way to detect value questions and statements is to look for words like "should," "ought," "better than" (instead of "greater than"), and similar words that indicate cultural or personal judgments or preferences. Value statements, however, are tricky. While a "should" statement is obviously a value statement, certain other kinds of statements are not so obvious. Take the statement: Authoritarian methods of teaching lead to poor learning. Here there is a relation. But the statement fails as a scientific hypothesis because it uses two value expressions or words, "authoritarian methods of teaching" and "poor learning," neither of which can be defined for measurement purposes without deleting the words "authoritarian" and "poor." The word "poor" is obviously a value word: it expresses a value judgment. Again, science does not pass value judgments. Scientists may do so, but science never does. To attain scientific respectability, the expression "poor learning" would have to be deleted and some expression substituted like "decreased problem solving behavior," which implies measurement possibilities but no value judgment. The expression "authoritarian methods of teaching" is perhaps almost hopeless, at least at present, although its definition is conceivable if very difficult. The trouble is that the mere use of the word "authoritarian" expresses a value judgment, at least in this case. As used today, it says, in effect, that such methods are "bad." Another difficulty is that at present we do not know what "authoritarian methods of teaching" means. Most often it seems to mean the personal teaching biases of the person using this method.[7]

Other types of statements that are not hypotheses or are poor hypotheses are frequently formulated. One type, fortunately infrequent, is the definition. Consider, for instance, "The core curriculum is an enrichening experience." Another type, unfortunately frequent, is what might be called the vague generalization. Examples are: People react to special social resources; The existing curriculum thoroughly prepares

[7] An almost classic case in education of the use of the word "authoritarian" is the statement sometimes heard among educators: The lecture method is authoritarian. This seems to mean that the speaker does not like the lecture method and he is telling us that it is bad. Similarly, one of the most effective ways to criticize a teacher is to say that he is authoritarian or rigid.

students for successful teaching; Scholastic achievement is the major consideration in predicting the success of doctoral candidates; Listening ability can be increased in the third grade; Reading skills can be identified in the second grade; Arithmetic skills lend themselves to teaching.[8] Comment hardly seems necessary.

Another common defect of problem statements often occurs in doctoral theses: the listing of methodological points or "problems" as subproblems. These methodological points have two characteristics that make them easy to detect: (1) they are not substantive problems that spring from the basic problem; and (2) they clearly relate to techniques or methods of sampling, measuring, or analyzing. They are usually not in question form, but rather contain the words "test," "determine," "measure," and the like. "To determine the reliability of the instruments used in this research," "To test the significance of the differences between the means," and "To assign pupils at random to the experimental groups" are symptomatic of this mistaken notion of problems and subproblems.

GENERALITY AND SPECIFICITY OF PROBLEMS AND HYPOTHESES

One of the difficulties that the research worker usually encounters and that almost all students working on a thesis find bothersome is the generality and specificity of problems and hypotheses. If the problem is too general, it is usually too vague and cannot be tested. Thus, it is scientifically useless, though it may be interesting to read. Problems and hypotheses that are too general and too vague are common in the social sciences and education. For example, Creativity is a function of the self-actualization of the individual. Another is: Democratic education enhances social learning and citizenship. Still another is: Authoritarianism in the classroom inhibits the creative imagination of children. These are interesting problems. But, in their present form, they are worse than useless scientifically, because they cannot be tested and because they give one the spurious assurance that they are hypotheses that can "some day" be tested.

Terms like "creativity," "self-actualization," "democracy," "authoritarianism," and the like have, at the present time at least, no adequate empirical referents.[9] Now, it is quite true that we can define "creativity,"

---

8 All of these statements were prepared by doctoral students in the writer's classes in research design and methodology.

9 Although many studies of authoritarianism have been done with considerable success, it is doubtful that we know what authoritarianism in the classroom means. For instance, an action of a teacher that is authoritarian in one classroom might not be authoritarian in another classroom. The alleged democratic behavior exhibited by one teacher might even be called authoritarian if exhibited by another teacher. Such elasticity is not the stuff of science.

say, in a limited way by specifying one or two creativity tests. This may be a legitimate procedure. Still, in so doing, we run the risk of getting far away from the original term and its meaning. This is particularly true when we speak of artistic creativity. We are often willing to accept the risk in order to be able to investigate important problems, of course. Yet terms like "democracy" are almost hopeless to define, since the problem of measurement is very difficult. Even when we accomplish it we often find we have destroyed the original meaning of the term.

The other extreme is too great specificity. Every student has heard that it is necessary to narrow problems down to workable size. This is true. But, unfortunately, we can also narrow the problem out of existence. In general, the more specific the problem or hypothesis the clearer are its testing implications. But triviality may be the price we pay. While the researcher cannot handle problems that are too broad because they tend to be too vague for adequate research operations, in his zeal to cut the problems down to workable size or to find a workable problem, he may, as indicated above, cut the life out of it. He may make it trivial or inconsequential. A thesis, for instance, on the simple relation between speed of reading and size of type, while important and maybe even interesting, is too thin for doctoral study. Too great specificity is perhaps a worse danger than too great generality. At any rate, some kind of compromise must always be made between generality and specificity. The ability effectively to make such compromises is a function partly of experience and partly of much critical study of research problems.

CONCLUDING REMARKS—THE SPECIAL POWER OF HYPOTHESES

One will sometimes hear that hypotheses are unnecessary in research, that they unnecessarily restrict the investigative imagination, that the job of science and scientific investigation is to find out things and not to labor the obvious, that hypotheses are obsolete, and the like. Such statements are quite misleading. They misconstrue the purpose of hypotheses.

It can almost be said that the hypothesis is the most powerful tool man has invented to achieve dependable knowledge. Man observes a phenomenon. He speculates on possible causes. Naturally, his culture has a stock of answers to account for most phenomena, many correct, many incorrect, many a mixture of fact and superstition, many pure superstition and mythology. It is the scientist's business to doubt most explanations of the phenomena of his field. His doubts are systematic. He insists upon subjecting explanations of phenomena to controlled empirical test. In order to do this, he must so formulate explanations that they are amenable to controlled empirical test. He formulates the explanations in the form of theories and hypotheses. In fact, the explanations *are* hypotheses.

The scientist simply disciplines the business by writing systematic and testable hypotheses. If a causal explanation cannot be formulated in the form of a testable hypothesis, then it can be considered to be a metaphysical explanation and thus not amenable to scientific investigation. As such, it is dismissed by the scientist as being of no interest.

The power of hypotheses goes further than this, however. A hypothesis is a prediction. It says that if x occurs, y will also occur. That is, y is predicted from x. If, then, x is made to occur (vary), and it is observed that y also occurs (varies concomitantly), then the hypothesis is confirmed. This is more powerful evidence than simply observing, without prediction, the covarying of x and y. It is more powerful in the betting-game sense discussed earlier. The scientist makes a bet that x leads to y. If, in an experiment, x does lead to y, then he collects his money. He has won the bet. He cannot just enter the game at any point and pick a perhaps fortuitous common occurrence of x and y. Games are not played this way (at least in our culture). He must play according to the rules, and the rules in science are made to minimize error and man's fallibility. Hypotheses are part of the rules of the game.

Even when hypotheses are not confirmed, they have power. Even when y does not covary with x, knowledge is advanced. Negative findings are sometimes as important as positive ones, since they cut down the total universe of ignorance and sometimes point up fruitful further hypotheses and lines of investigation. *But the scientist cannot tell positive from negative evidence unless he uses hypotheses.* It is possible to conduct research without hypotheses, of course, particularly in exploratory investigations. But it is hard to conceive modern science in all its rigorous and disciplined fertility without the guiding power of hypotheses.

STUDY SUGGESTIONS

1. Collect a number of problems, say six to ten, from the research literature. Analyze the problems by using the criteria discussed in this chapter. Specify the variables. Rewrite the problems in different words, improving them if you can. Do not assume, because a research study is published, that its problem (or hypothesis) statement is irreproachable. On the contrary, assume that the author has not expressed his problem too well, and try to improve his statement.

   Do the same with completed theses in your institution's library.
2. Do the same as in Study Suggestion 1, with hypotheses.
3. Using the following constructs, write research problems and hypotheses: perception of self, level of aspiration, frustration, regression, academic achievement, intelligence, social class, sex, interests, reinforcement, teaching methods, reading readiness, introversion, incentives.

4. Six problems from published research studies are given below. Study them carefully and construct one or two hypotheses based on them.

    (a) Do teacher comments cause improvement in student performance? [10]

    (b) What are the effects on scholastic performance of different types of incentives? [11]

    (c) Does practice in a mental function improve future learning of the mental function? [12]

    (d) Does learning how to learn transfer to new situations? [13]

    (e) Do individuals with similar roles and role expectations hold similar values and attitudes toward a cognitive object significantly related to the role in question? [14]

    (f) What is the effect on his classmates of a misbehaving (deviant) student's response to teacher-exerted control? [15]

5. Six hypotheses are given below. Discuss the possibilities of testing them. Then read two or more of the original studies to see how the author(s) tested them.

    (a) The greater the cohesiveness of a group the greater its influence on its members.[16]

    (b) Prejudiced people identify minority-group members by their faces more readily than do unprejudiced people.[17]

    (c) Group study contributes to higher grade achievement.[18]

    (d) Practice in a mental function has no effect on the future learning of that mental function.[19]

[10] E. Page, "Teacher Comments and Student Performance: A Seventy-Four Classroom Experiment in School Motivation," *Journal of Educational Psychology*, XLIX (1958), 173–181. When citing problems and hypotheses from the literature, I have not always used the exact words of the author(s). In fact, the statements of some of the problems are this author's and not those of the cited authors. Some authors use only problem statements; some use only hypotheses; others use both.

[11] E. Hurlock, "An Evaluation of Certain Incentives Used in Schoolwork," *Journal of Educational Psychology*, XVI (1925), 145–159.

[12] A. Gates and G. Taylor, "An Experimental Study of the Nature of Improvement Resulting from Practice in a Mental Function," *Journal of Educational Psychology*, XVI (1925), 583–592.

[13] H. Harlow, "The Formation of Learning Sets," *Psychological Review*, LVI (1949), 51–65.

[14] F. Kerlinger, "The Attitude Structure of the Individual: A Q-Study of the Educational Attitudes of Professors and Laymen," *Genetic Psychology Monographs*, LIII (1956), 283–329.

[15] W. Gnagey, "Effects on Classmates of a Deviant Student's Power and Response to a Teacher-Exerted Control Technique," *Journal of Educational Psychology*, LI (1960), 1–8.

[16] S. Schachter, *et al.*, "An Experimental Study of Cohesiveness and Productivity," *Human Relations*, IV (1951), 229–238.

[17] G. Allport and B. Kramer, "Some Roots of Prejudice," *Journal of Psychology*, XXII (1946), 9–39.

[18] J. Blue, Jr., "The Effects of Group Study on Grade Achievement," *Journal of Educational Psychology*, XLIX (1958), 118–123.

[19] Gates and Taylor, *op. cit.*

(e) In failure situations, high test-anxious subjects assign blame for failure to themselves to a greater extent than do low test-anxious subjects.[20]

(f) The extent of role conflict is a function of the number and magnitude of incompatible expectations placed upon or held by the individual.[21]

[20] J. Doris, "Test Anxiety and Blame-Assignment in Grade School Children," *Journal of Abnormal and Social Psychology*, LVIII (1959), 181–190.

[21] J. Getzels and E. Guba, "Role, Role Conflict, and Effectiveness: An Empirical Study," *American Sociological Review*, XIX (1954), 164–175.

3 CONSTRUCTS, VARIABLES, AND DEFINITIONS

Scientists operate on two levels: the level of theory-hypothesis-construct and the level of observation. More accurately, they shuttle back and forth between these levels. A psychological scientist may say, "Frustration produces aggression." This statement is a hypothesis consisting of two concepts, "frustration" and "aggression," joined by a relation word, "produces." It is on the theory-hypothesis-construct level. Whenever the scientist utters relational statements and whenever he uses concepts, or constructs, as we shall call them, he is operating, so to speak, at this level.

The scientist must also operate at the level of observation. He must gather data that test his hypotheses. In order to do this, he must somehow get from the construct level to the observation level. He cannot simply make observations of "frustration" and "aggression." He must so define these constructs that observations are possible. The problem of this chapter is to examine and clarify the nature of scientific concepts or constructs and the way in which psychological and educational scientists get from the construct level to the observation level, how they shuttle from one to the other.

CONCEPTS AND CONSTRUCTS

The terms "concept" and "construct" have similar meanings. Yet there is an important distinction. A *concept* is a word that expresses an abstraction formed by generalization from particulars. "Weight" is a concept: it expresses numerous observations of things that are more or less "heavy" or "light." "Mass," "energy," and "force" are concepts used by physical scientists. They are of course much more abstract than concepts like "weight," "height," and "length."

A concept of more interest to readers of this book is "achievement." It is an abstraction formed from the observation of certain behaviors of children. These behaviors are associated with the mastery or "learning" of school tasks—reading words, doing arithmetic problems, drawing pictures, and so on. The various observed behaviors are put together and expressed in a word—"achievement." "Intelligence," "aggressiveness," "conformity," and "honesty" are all concepts used to express varieties of human behavior of interest to behavioral scientists.

A *construct* is a concept. It has the added meaning, however, of having been deliberately and consciously invented or adopted for a special scientific purpose. "Intelligence" is a concept, an abstraction from the observation of presumably intelligent and nonintelligent behaviors. But as a scientific construct, "intelligence" means both more and less than it may mean as a concept. It means that scientists consciously and systematically use it in two ways. One, it enters into theoretical schemes and is related in various ways to other constructs. We may say, for example, that *school achievement* is in part a function of *intelligence* and *motivation*. Two, "intelligence" is so defined and specified that it can be observed and measured. We can make observations of the intelligence of children by administering X intelligence test to them, or we can ask teachers to tell us the relative degrees of intelligence of their pupils.

VARIABLES

Scientists somewhat loosely call the constructs or properties they study "variables." Examples of important variables in psychology, sociology, and education are: social class, sex, income, level of aspiration, anxiety, religious affiliation, hostility, prejudice, authoritarianism, motivation, discipline, introversion, conformity, and, of course, intelligence and achievement. It can be said that a variable is a property that takes on different values. This says, to put it redundantly, that a variable is something that varies. While this manner of speaking gives us an intuitive notion of what variables are, we need a more general and yet more precise definition.

A *variable* is a symbol to which numerals or values are assigned. For instance, x is a variable: it is a *symbol* to which we assign numerical values. The variable x may take on any justifiable set of values, for example, scores on an intelligence test or an attitude scale. In the case of intelligence we assign to x a set of numerical values yielded by the procedure designated in a specified test of intelligence. This set of values, often called IQ's, ranges from low to high, from, say, 50 to 150.

A variable, x, however, may have only two values. If sex is the construct under study, then x can be assigned 1 and 0, 1 standing for one of the sexes and 0 standing for the other. It is still a variable. Other examples of two-valued variables are: alive-dead, citizen-noncitizen, middle class-working class, teacher-nonteacher, Republican-Democrat, and so on. Such variables are often called dichotomies or dichotomous variables.[1]

---

[1] The expression "qualitative variable" has sometimes been applied to dichotomies. Such usage reflects a somewhat distorted notion of what variables are. They are

Only a few of the variables ordinarily used in educational research are true dichotomies, that is, characterized simply by the presence or absence of a property. Most variables are theoretically capable of taking on continuous values. It is useful to remember, nevertheless, that it is often convenient or necessary to convert continuous variables to dichotomous or trichotomous variables. While it is not possible to convert a truly dichotomous variable like sex to a continuous variable, it is always possible to convert a continuous variable like intelligence or anxiety to a dichotomous variable. We shall meet several instances of such conversion later in the book.

CONSTITUTIVE AND OPERATIONAL DEFINITIONS OF CONSTRUCTS AND VARIABLES

The distinction made earlier between "concept" and "construct" leads naturally to another important distinction: that between kinds of definitions of constructs and variables. Words or constructs can be defined in two general ways. First, a word can be defined by using other words, which is what a dictionary usually does. "Intelligence" can be defined by saying it is "operating intellect," "mental acuity," or "the ability to think abstractly." Note that such definitions use other concepts or conceptual expresions in lieu of the expression being defined.

Second, we can define a word by telling what actions or behaviors the word expresses or implies. This type of definition of "intelligence" requires that we specify what behaviors of children are "intelligent" and what behaviors are "not intelligent." We might say that a child of seven who successfully reads a story we give him to read is "intelligent." If the child cannot read the story we might say he is "not intelligent." In other words, this kind of definition can be called a behavioral or observational definition. Both "other word" and "observational" definitions are used constantly in everyday living.

There is a looseness about this discussion that would disturb a scientist. Though he uses the types of definition just described, he does so in a more precise and articulated manner. We express this usage by defining and explaining Margenau's distinction between constitutive and operational definitions.[2]

A *constitutive definition* is a definition that defines a construct with

---

always quantifiable, or they are not variables. If x can take on only two values, 1 and 0, these are still values and the variable varies. If, however, we take two objects, a and b, grossly and genotypically different, then we have no adequate basis for quantification. Thus they might be called qualitatively different. Even in this case, we could quantify a and b simply by considering a to be of one class A and b not to be of the class A, or non-A, and assign 1's and 0's again.

[2] H. Margenau, *The Nature of Physical Reality.* New York: McGraw-Hill, 1950, chaps. 4, 5, and 12. The present discussion leans heavily on Margenau and on Torgerson's excellent presentation of the same distinction. W. Torgerson, *Theory and Methods of Scaling.* New York: Wiley, 1958, pp. 2–5.

other constructs. For instance, we can define "weight" by saying that it is the "heaviness" of objects. Or we can define "anxiety" as "subjectified fear." In both cases we have substituted one concept for another concept. Some of the constructs of a scientific theory may be defined constitutively. Torgerson, borrowing from Margenau, says that all constructs, in order to be scientifically useful, must possess constitutive meaning.[3] This means that they must be capable of being used in theories.

An *operational definition* is a definition that assigns meaning to a construct or a variable by specifying the activities or "operations" necessary to measure the construct or variable. Alternatively, an operational definition is a specification of the activities of the researcher in measuring a variable or in manipulating it. An operational definition is a sort of manual of instructions to the investigator. It says, in effect, "Do such-and-such in so-and-so a manner." In short, it defines or gives meaning to a variable by spelling out what the investigator must do to measure the variable.

A well-known, if extreme, example of an operational definition is: Intelligence (anxiety, achievement, and so forth) is scores on X intelligence test, or intelligence is what X intelligence test measures. Notice that this definition tells us what to do to measure intelligence. It says nothing about how well intelligence is measured by the specified instrument. (Presumably the adequacy of the test was ascertained prior to the investigator's use of it.) In this usage, an operational definition is an equation where we say, "Let intelligence equal the scores on X test of intelligence." We also seem to be saying, "The meaning of intelligence (in this research) is expressed by the scores on X intelligence test."

There are, in general, two kinds of operational definitions: (1) *measured* and (2) *experimental*. The definition given above is more closely tied to measured definitions than it is to experimental definitions. A *measured* operational definition is one that describes how a variable will be measured. For example, achievement may be defined by a standardized achievement test, by a teacher-made achievement test, or by grades. Hare defined the consensus of a group as follows: "The amount of consensus in the group is measured by having each individual rate the ten pieces of camping equipment before discussion, the group rate the equipment during the discussion, and the individual again rate them after discussion."[4] A study might include the variable *consideration*. It might be defined operationally by listing behaviors of children that are presumably considerate behaviors and then requiring teachers to rate the children on a five-point scale. Such behaviors might be when the children say to each other, "I'm sorry," or "Excuse me," when one child yields a toy to another

3 *Ibid.*, p. 5.

4 A. Hare, "A Study of Interaction and Consensus in Different Sized Groups," *American Sociological Review*, XVII (1952), 261–267.

child on request (but not on threat of aggression), or when one child helps another with a school task.

An *experimental* operational definition spells out the details (operations) of the investigator's manipulations of a variable. Reinforcement might be operationally defined by giving the details of how subjects are to be reinforced (rewarded) and not reinforced (not rewarded) for specified behaviors. In the Hurlock study discussed earlier, for example, some children were praised, some blamed, and some ignored. Dollard, *et al.,* define frustration as prevention from reaching a goal, or ". . . interference with the occurrence of an instigated goal response at its proper time in the behavior sequence . . ." [5] This definition contains clear implications for experimental manipulations. Barker, Dembo, and Lewin, apparently influenced by the definition of Dollard, *et al.,* operationally defined frustration by describing children put into a playroom with "a number of highly attractive, *but inaccessible,* toys." [6] (The toys were put behind a wire-net partition. The children could see the toys but could not touch them.) Other examples of both kinds of operational definitions will be given later.

Scientific investigators must sooner or later face the necessity of measuring the variables of the relations they are studying. Sometimes measurement is easy, sometimes difficult. To measure sex or social class is easy; to measure intelligence or anxiety is difficult. The importance of operational definitions cannot be overemphasized. They are indispensable ingredients of scientific research because they enable researchers to measure variables and because they are bridges between the theory-hypothesis-construct level and the level of observation. There can be no scientific research without observations, and observations are impossible without clear and specific instructions on what and how to observe. Operational definitions are such instructions.

Though indispensable, operational definitions yield only limited meanings of constructs. No operational definition can ever express all of a variable. No operational definition of intelligence can ever express the rich and diverse meaning of human intelligence. This means that the variables measured by scientists are always limited and specific in meaning. The "creativity" studied by psychologists is not the "creativity" referred to by artists, though there will of course be common factors.

Some scientists would say that such limited operational meanings are the only meanings that "mean" anything, that all other definitions are metaphysical nonsense. They might say that discussions of anxiety are metaphysical nonsense, unless adequate operational definitions of anxiety

[5] J. Dollard, *et al., Frustration and Aggression.* New Haven: Yale University Press, 1939, p. 7.

[6] R. Barker, T. Dembo, and K. Lewin, "Frustration and Regression." In R. Barker, J. Kounin, and H. Wright, *Child Behavior and Development.* New York: McGraw-Hill, 1943, p. 443.

are available and are used. This view is extreme, though it has healthy aspects. To insist that every term we use in scientific discourse be operationally defined would be too narrowing, too restrictive, and, as we shall see, scientifically unsound.[7]

Despite the dangers of extreme operationism, it can safely be said that operationism has been a healthy influence. It has been healthy, and still is healthy, because, as Skinner puts it, "The operational attitude, in spite of its shortcomings, is a good thing in any science but especially in psychology because of the presence there of a vast vocabulary of ancient and nonscientific origin." [8] When the terms used in education are considered, it is clear that education, too, has a vast vocabulary of ancient and nonscientific terms. Consider these: the whole child, horizontal and vertical enrichment, meeting the needs of the learner, core curriculum, administrative integration, progressivism, emotional adjustment, group atmosphere, and curricular enrichment.

To clarify constitutive and operational definitions—and theory, too —look at Fig. 3.1, which has been adapted after Margenau and Torger-

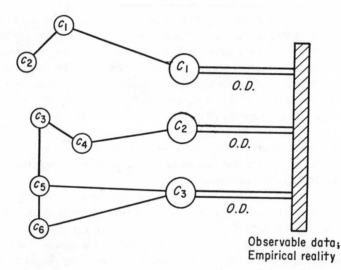

FIG. **3.1** CONSTRUCTS DEFINED OPERATIONALLY, THAT IS, CONNECTED TO OBSERVABLE DATA BY OPERATIONAL DEFINITIONS ($O.\,D.$'s): C_1, C_2, C_3. CONSTRUCTS DEFINED CONSTITUTIVELY: $c_1, c_2, \cdots, c_6$

[7] For a good discussion of this point, see F. Northrop, *The Logic of the Sciences and the Humanities.* New York: Macmillan, 1947, chaps. VI and VII. Northrop, in one place, for example, says, "The importance of operational definitions is that they make verification possible and enrich meaning. They do not, however, exhaust scientific meaning" (p. 130). Margenau makes the same point in his extended discussion of scientific constructs. (See Margenau, *op. cit.*, pp. 232ff.)

[8] B. Skinner, "The Operational Analysis of Psychological Terms." In H. Feigl and M. Brodbeck, eds., *Readings in the Philosophy of Science.* New York: Appleton, 1953, p. 586.

son. The diagram is supposed to illustrate a well-developed theory. The single lines represent theoretical connections or relations between constructs. These constructs, labeled with lower case letters, are defined constitutively. That is, c_4 is defined somehow by c_3, or vice versa. The double lines represent operational definitions. The C constructs, as can be seen, are directly linked to observable data and form indispensable links to empirical reality. But it is important to note that not all constructs in a scientific theory are defined operationally. Indeed, it would be a rather thin theory that has all its constructs operationally defined.

Let us build a "small theory" of underachievement to illustrate these notions. Suppose an investigator believes that underachievement is, in part, a function of pupils' self-concepts. He believes that pupils who perceive themselves "inadequately," who have negative self-percepts also tend to achieve less than their potential capacity and aptitude would indicate they should achieve. He further believes that "ego-needs" (which we will not define here) and motivation for achievement (call this n-ach, or need for achievement) are tied up with underachievement. Naturally, he is also aware of the relation between aptitude and intelligence and achievement in general. A diagram to illustrate this "theory" might look like that of Fig. 3.2.

The investigator has no *direct* measure of "self-concept," but he assumes that he can draw inferences about an individual's self-concept from

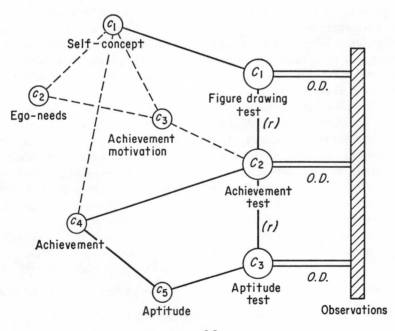

FIG. 3.2

a figure-drawing test. He operationally defines "self-concept," then, as certain responses to the figure-drawing test. This is probably the most common method of measuring psychological (and educational) constructs. The heavy single line between c_1 and C_1 indicates the relatively direct nature of the presumed relation between "self-concept" and the test. (The double line between C_1 and the level of observation indicates an operational definition, as it did in Fig. 3.1.) Similarly, the construct "achievement" (c_4) is operationally defined as the discrepancy between measured achievement (C_2) and measured aptitude (c_5). In this model the investigator has no direct measure of "achievement motivation," no operational definition of it. In another study, naturally, he may specifically hypothesize a relation between achievement and achievement motivation, in which case he would obviously try to define achievement motivation operationally.

The single solid lines between concepts, for example, between the construct "achievement" (c_4) and "achievement test" (C_2), indicates a relatively well-established relation between postulated achievement and what standard achievement tests measure. The single solid lines between C_1 and C_2 and between C_2 and C_3 indicate computed relations between the test scores of these measures. (The lines between C_1 and C_2 and between C_2 and C_3 are labeled r for "relation," or "coefficient of correlation.")

The broken single lines indicate postulated relations between constructs that are not relatively well-established, are more tenuous. A good example of this is the postulated relation between "self-concept" and "achievement motivation." One of the aims of science is to make these broken lines solid lines by bridging the operational definition-measurement gap. In this case, it is quite conceivable, even today, that both "self-concept" and "achievement motivation" can be operationally defined and fairly directly measured.

In essence, this is the way the psychological-educational scientist operates. He shuttles back and forth between the level of theory-constructs and the level of observation. He does this by operationally defining the variables of his theory that are amenable to such definition and then by testing the relations between the operationally defined and measured variables. From these computed relations he makes inferences as to the relations between the constructs. In the above example, he computes the relation between C_1 (Figure-drawing test) and C_2 (Achievement test) and, if the relation is established on this observational level, he infers that a relation exists between c_1 (Self-concept) and c_4 (Achievement).

TYPES OF VARIABLES

Independent and Dependent Variables   With definitional background behind us, we return to variables. Variables can be classified in several ways. In this book two kinds of variables are very important and will thus be emphasized: (1) independent and dependent variables and (2) active and assigned variables.

The most important and useful way to categorize variables is as independent and dependent. This categorization is common to science and to mathematics and should be used more in educational research because of its general applicability, its simplicity, and its special importance in designing research and communicating data. An *independent variable* is the *presumed* cause of the *dependent variable,* the *presumed* effect. The independent variable is the antecedent; the dependent variable is the consequent. Whenever we say "If *A,* then *B,*" whenever we have an implication, *A* implies *B,* we have an independent variable (*A*) and a dependent variable (*B*).

The terms "independent variable" and "dependent variable" come from mathematics. *X* is always the independent variable and *Y* the dependent variable. This is probably the best way to think of independent and dependent variables, because nothing is said about the touchy word "cause" and other related words and because such usage of symbols applies to most research situations. Indeed, it might even be said that scientific research is constantly pursuing the relations between *X*'s and *Y*'s, between independent and dependent variables.

In experiments the independent variable is the variable manipulated by the experimenter. When, for example, an educational investigator studies the effect of different teaching methods, he may manipulate method, the independent variable, by using different methods. In nonexperimental research, where there is no possibility of manipulation, the independent variable is the variable that has presumably been "manipulated" before he got it. He might, for instance, study the presumed effects on achievement of a ready-made teaching situation in which different methods have already been used. Methods, here, is also the independent variable. Or he might study the effect on school achievement of parental attitudes. Here parental attitudes is the independent variable.

The dependent variable, of course, is the variable predicted *to,* whereas the independent variable is predicted *from.* The dependent variable, *Y,* is the presumed effect, which varies concomitantly with changes or variation in the independent variable, *X.* It is the variable that is not manipulated. Rather, it is observed for variation as a presumed result of variation in the independent variable. In predicting from *X* to *Y,* we can take any value of *X* we wish, whereas the value of *Y* we predict to is of course "dependent on" the value of *X* we have selected. The dependent variable is ordinarily the condition we are trying to explain, especially in educational research. The most common dependent variable in education is achievement or "learning." In educational research we want to account for or explain achievement. In doing so we have a large number of possible *X*'s or independent variables to choose from.

When the relation between intelligence and school achievement is studied, intelligence is the independent variable and achievement the dependent variable. (Is it conceivable that it might be the other way around?) Other independent variables that can be studied in relation to the dependent variable, achievement, are social class, methods of teaching, personality types, types of motivation (reward and punishment), attitudes toward school, class atmosphere, and so on. When the presumed determinants of delinquency are studied, such determinants as slum conditions, broken homes, lack of parental love, and the like, are independent variables and, naturally, delinquency (more accurately, delinquent behavior) is the dependent variable. In the frustration-aggression hypothesis mentioned earlier, frustration is the independent variable and aggression the dependent variable. Sometimes a phenomenon is studied by itself, and either an independent or a dependent variable is implied. This is the case when teacher behaviors and characteristics are studied. The usual implied dependent variable is achievement or child behavior in general, though teacher behavior may be the dependent variable.

The relation between an independent variable and a dependent variable can perhaps be more clearly understood if we lay out two axes at right angles to each other, one axis representing the independent variable and the other axis the dependent variable. (When two axes are at right angles to each other, they are called *orthogonal* axes.) Following mathematical custom, X, the independent variable, is the horizontal axis and Y, the dependent variable, the vertical axis. (X is called the *abscissa* and Y the *ordinate*.) X values are laid out on the X axis and Y values on the Y axis. A very common and useful way to "see" and interpret a relation is to plot the pairs of XY values, using the X and Y axes as a frame of reference. Let us suppose, in a study of child development, that we have two sets of measures: the X measures chronological age, the Y measures reading age:[9]

X: Chronological Age (in Months)	Y: Reading Age (in Months)
72	48
84	62
96	69
108	71
120	100
132	112

These measures are plotted in Fig. 3.3.

[9] *Reading age* is a so-called growth age. Seriatim measurements of individuals' growths—in height, weight, intelligence, and so forth—are expressed as the average chronological age at which they appear in the standard population. The data reported above are from one of the author's studies: F. Kerlinger, "The Statistics of the Individual Child: The Use of Analysis of Variance with Child Development Data," *Child Development*, XXV (1954), 265–275. This article refers to the original sources of the growth data.

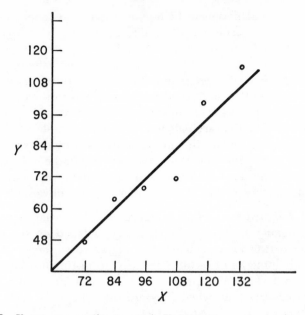

FIG. **3.3** *Y:* READING AGE (IN MONTHS); *X:* CHRONOLOGICAL AGE (IN MONTHS)

The relation between chronological age (*CA*) and reading age (*RA*) can now be "seen" and roughly approximated. Note that there is a pronounced tendency, as might be expected, for more advanced *CA* to be associated with higher *RA*, medium *CA* with medium *RA*, and less advanced *CA* with lower *RA*. In other words, the relation between the independent and dependent variables, in this case between *CA* and *RA*, can be seen from a graph such as this. A straight line has been drawn in to "show" the relation. It is a rough average of all the points of the plot. Note that if one has knowledge of independent variable measures and a relation such as that shown in Fig. 3.3 one can predict with considerable accuracy the dependent variable measures. Plots such as this can of course be used with any independent and dependent variable measures.

The student should be alert to the possibility of a variable being an independent variable in one study and a dependent variable in another. A good example of this is the variable "teacher satisfaction." It is possible to study the determinants of teacher satisfaction and equally possible to study the presumed results of teacher satisfaction. In the former case teacher satisfaction is the dependent variable; in the latter case it is the independent variable.

It is quite possible to consider school achievement as an independent variable, even though it is usually treated as a dependent variable. In studies of success in college, for instance, achievement in high school is often used as a predictor, or an independent variable. Here we have the interesting case of achievement being now the independent and now the dependent variable—achievement in different educational situations, naturally. In recent educational research, anxiety has been studied as an independent variable affecting the dependent variable achievement.[10] But anxiety can readily be conceived and used as a dependent variable, for example, if we wished to study the effectiveness of types of teaching or types of teacher supportive behavior, or types of tests, in reducing anxiety.[11] It is also possible—but too rarely done—to treat a variable as independent in one study and dependent in another study. We could even give a variable this dual role in the same study. In other words, the independent and dependent variable classification is really a classification of *uses* of variables rather than a distinction between different *kinds* of variables.

Active and Assigned Variables   A classification of variables that will be useful in our later study of research design is based on the distinction made earlier between experimental and measured variables. It is important when planning and executing research to distinguish between these two types of variables. Manipulated variables will be called *active* variables. Measured variables, when they are used in a way soon to be described, will be called *assigned* variables.

Any variable that is manipulated, then, is an active variable. Any variable that cannot be manipulated may be an assigned variable. When one uses different methods of teaching, rewarding the children of one group and punishing those of another, creating anxiety through worrisome instructions, one is *actively* manipulating the variables methods, reinforcement, and anxiety.

On the other hand, it is impossible, or at least very difficult, to manipulate many important variables. All variables that are characteristics of subjects—intelligence, aptitude, sex, socioeconomic status, race, education, level of aspiration, and anxiety, for example—can be assigned variables. Subjects come to our studies with these variables (characteristics) ready-made. They are, so to speak, already manipulated. Early environment, heredity, and other circumstances have made individuals what they are.[12]

[10] See S. Sarason, *et al.*, *Anxiety in Elementary School Children*. New York: Wiley, 1960.

[11] *Ibid.*, p. 280.

[12] Such variables are also called *organismic* variables. Any property of an individual, any characteristic or attribute, is an organismic variable. It is part of the organism, so to speak. In other words, organismic variables are those characteristics that individuals have in varying degrees when they come to the research situation. The term individual differences implies organismic variables.

Another related classification, used mainly by psychologists, is *stimulus* and *response* variables. A *stimulus variable* is any condition or manipulation by the experimenter of the environment that evokes a response in an organism. A *response variable* is any kind of behavior of the organism. The assumption is made that for any kind of behavior there is always a stimulus. Thus the organism's behavior is a response. This

The main reason for using the active-assigned terminology is this: in designing research, we often *assign* individuals to groups on the basis of their possession of different amounts of the characteristics these variables imply. For instance, we might, in a study of the effect of methods on achievement, break subjects down by sex (male-female), socioeconomic status (middle class-working class), or intelligence (high, medium, low), so that the possible joint effect on achievement of methods and one or more of these variables can be studied.

This active-assigned distinction is flexible and useful methodologically. For instance, we shall see later that some variables are by their very nature always assigned, but that other variables can be either active or assigned. This latter characteristic makes it possible for us to investigate the "same" relations in different ways. A good example is "anxiety." We can measure the anxiety of subjects and correlate these measures directly with other measures. Or we can take the same subjects, measure their anxiety, and break the whole group into, say, high anxiety and low anxiety subgroups. Here we obviously have an assigned variable. But we can manipulate anxiety, too. We can presumably induce different degrees of anxiety by telling the subjects of one experimental group that the task we are giving them is difficult, that we are measuring their intelligence, and that their futures depend on the scores they get, and by telling the subjects of another group to do their best but that they should relax, that the outcome is not too important, and that it will have no influence on their futures. Actually, however, we cannot assume that the two "anxieties" are the same. We may assume that both are "anxiety" in a broad sense, but they would certainly not be the same.

CONSTRUCTS, OBSERVABLES, AND INTERVENING VARIABLES

In much of the previous discussion of this chapter it has been implied, though not explicitly stated, that there is a sharp difference between constructs and observed or observable variables. In fact, we might say that constructs, as constructs, are nonobservables, and variables, when operationally defined, are observables. The distinction is important because if we are not always keenly aware of the level of discourse we are on when talking about variables, we can hardly be clear about what we are doing.

---

classification is reflected in the well-known equation: $R = f(O, S)$, which is read: "Responses are a function of the organism and stimuli," or "Response variables are a function of organismic variables and stimulus variables." For a systematic discussion of variables in relation to educational research, see R. Travers, *An Introduction to Educational Research*. New York: Macmillan, 1958, pp. 101ff. See, also, A. Edwards, "Experiments: Their Planning and Execution." In G. Lindzey, ed., *Handbook of Social Psychology*. Cambridge, Mass.: Addison-Wesley, 1954, vol. I, chap. 7.

Constructs have been called intervening variables.[13] *Intervening variables* are terms invented to account for internal and directly unobservable psychological processes that in turn account for behavior. Tolman, using William James' picturesque expression, says, ". . . the sole 'cashvalue' of mental processes lies . . . in this their character as a set of intermediate functional processes which interconnect between the initiating causes of behavior, on the one hand, and the final resulting behavior itself, on the other." [14] An intervening variable is an "in-the-head" variable. It cannot be seen, heard, or felt. It is inferred from behavior. "Hostility" is inferred from presumably hostile or aggressive acts. "Learning" is inferred from, among other things, increases in test scores. "Anxiety" is inferred from test scores, from skin responses, from heart beat, and so on.

The scientist, using such terms, is always aware that he is talking about invented constructs the "reality" of which he has inferred from behavior. If he wants to study the effects of different kinds of motivation, he must know that "motivation" is an intervening variable, a construct invented by man to account for presumably "motivated" behavior. He must know that its "reality" is only a postulated reality. He can only judge that a youngster is motivated or not motivated by observing the youngster's behavior. Still, in order to study motivation, he must measure it. But he cannot measure it directly because it is an in-the-head variable, an intervening variable, an unobservable entity. Other men have invented the construct to stand for "something" *presumed to be* inside the individual, "something" prompting him to behave in such-and-such manner. This means that he must always measure presumed indicants of motivation and not motivation itself. He must, in other words, always measure some kind of behavior, be it marks on paper, spoken words, or meaningful gestures, and then make inferences about presumed characteristics.

Examples of Constructs and Operational Definitions   A number of constructs and operational definitions have already been given. To illustrate and perhaps clarify the preceding discussion, especially that in which the distinction was made between experimental and measured variables and between constructs and operationally defined variables, several and varied examples of constructs and operational definitions are given below. If a definition is experimental, it is labeled (E). If it is measured, it is labeled (M).

The student should note that operational definitions differ in degree of specificity. Some are quite closely tied to observations. "Test" definitions like "Intelligence is defined as score on X intelligence test" are very specific. A definition like "Frustration is prevention from reaching a goal" is more general and requires further specification, such as that of

13 E. Tolman, *Behavior and Psychological Man.* Berkeley, Calif.: University of California Press, 1958, pp. 115–129.
14 *Ibid.,* p. 116.

the Barker, Kounin, and Wright definition, in order to be directly measurable.

SOCIAL CLASS   ". . . two or more orders of people who are believed to be, and are accordingly ranked by the members of a community, in socially superior and inferior positions." [15] (M) (To be operational this definition has to be specified by questions aimed at people's beliefs about other people's positions.)

This is a subjective definition of social class. Social class, or social status, is also defined more objectively by using such indices as occupation, income, and education, or by combinations of such indices. For example, "To get an index of SES (socioeconomic status), we combined a measure of occupational level with one of income." [16] (Then details of the definition follow.) (M)

ANXIETY (TEST ANXIETY)   "Our measure of test anxiety was a revised and shortened version of the Test Anxiety (TA) questionnaire which is described elsewhere." [17] (M) (The authors refer to a research study that describes the construction and development of the TA Scale. It is always good practice to refer to the original sources of tests and scales.)

ACHIEVEMENT (SCHOOL, ARITHMETIC, SPELLING)   Achievement is customarily defined operationally by citing a standardized test of achievement, for example, Iowa Every-Pupil Tests of Basic Skills, Elementary; Traxler Silent Reading Test, by grade-point averages (computed by assigning values, say, of 1 through 4 to letter grades and averaging the grades for each student), or by teacher estimates (via direct questions or grades assigned).

"Six alternate forms of a cancellation test were constructed in order to measure each pupil's work achievement under the various experimental conditions." [18] (M) (Then the authors describe, operationally, the tests and how the pupils were instructed to respond to them.)

"The Iowa Tests of Basic Skills . . . were used to assess achievement in vocabulary, reading, language, work study skills, and arithmetic." [19] (M)

SOCIAL ORGANIZATION (OF CLASSES)   ". . . has to do with the amount of social grouping and pupil autonomy in a class. A class scoring high was

[15] W. Warner and P. Lunt, *The Social Life of a Modern Community.* New Haven: Yale University Press, 1941, p. 82.

[16] R. Sears, E. Maccoby, and H. Levin, *Patterns of Child Rearing.* New York: Harper & Row, 1957, pp. 423–424.

[17] I. Sarnoff, *et al.*, "A Cross-Cultural Study of Anxiety among American and English School Children," *Journal of Educational Psychology*, XLIX (1958), 129–136.

[18] G. Thompson and C. Hunnicutt, "The Effects of Repeated Praise or Blame on the Work Achievement by 'Introverts' and 'Extroverts,'" *Journal of Educational Psychology*, XXXV (1944), 257–266.

[19] R. Gunderson and L. Feldt, "The Relationship of Differences between Verbal and Nonverbal Intelligence Scores to Achievement," *Journal of Educational Psychology*, LI (1960), 115–121.

one in which it was relatively common to find the class broken up into two or more groups working independently, and in which the teachers talked relatively little." [20] (M) (Note the relative looseness of this definition, a looseness introduced by such words as "relatively common" and "relatively little." But it is not too difficult to tighten up the definition.)

POPULARITY   Popularity is often defined operationally by the number of sociometric choices an individual receives from other individuals (in his class, play group, and so on). Individuals are asked: "With whom would you like to work?", "With whom would like to play?", and the like. Each individual is required to choose one, two, or more individuals from his group on the basis of such criterion questions.

"The sociometric popularity score (choices received) based on a criterion of enjoyment of participation, and the expansiveness (choices made), confidence (choices expected) . . ." [21] (M)

REINFORCEMENT   Reinforcement definitions come in a number of forms. Most of them involve, one way or another, the principle of reward. But note that both positive and negative reinforcement may be used.

". . . statements of *agreement* or *paraphrase*." [22] (E) Then the author gives specific experimental definitions of "reinforcement." For example, "In the second 10 minutes, every opinion statement S made was recorded by E and reinforced. For two groups, E agreed with every opinion statement by saying: 'Yes, you're right,' 'That's so,' or the like, or by nodding and smiling affirmation if he could not interrupt." [23] (E)

"In the first class of fifth-grade pupils the 'extroverts' were praised after each task, and the 'introverts' were blamed. In the second class of pupils this procedure was reversed and the 'extroverts' were blamed while the 'introverts' were praised." [24] (E)

"A single pellet of candy was released from a magazine and fed by chute to the tray. An impulse counter and a remote switch were wired in series with the release mechanism. Following the fall of each pellet, E opened the circuit to prevent 'jiggling' and thus ensure a discrete response for each reinforcement." [25] (E)

"Specified Comment students, regardless of teacher or student differences, all received comments designated in advance for each letter grade, as follows:

A. Excellent! Keep it up.

20 D. Medley and H. Mitzel, "Some Behavioral Correlates of Teacher Effectiveness," *Journal of Educational Psychology*, L (1959), 239–246.

21 E. Borgatta, "Analysis of Social Interaction: Actual, Role-Playing, and Projective," *Journal of Abnormal and Social Psychology*, LI (1955), 394–405.

22 W. Verplanck, "The Control of the Content of Conversation: Reinforcement of Statements of Opinion," *Journal of Abnormal and Social Psychology*, LI (1955), 668–676.

23 *Ibid.*

24 Thompson and Hunnicutt, *op. cit.*, p. 258.

25 P. Siegel and J. Foshee, "The Law of Primary Reinforcement in Children," *Journal of Experimental Psychology*, XLV (1953), 12–14.

B. Good work. Keep it up.

C. Perhaps try to do still better?

D. Let's bring this up.

F. Let's raise this grade!

Teachers were instructed to administer the comments 'rapidly and automatically, trying not even to notice who the students are.' " [26] (E) Two other experimental conditions, Free Comment and No Comment, were also operationally (experimentally) defined by the author.

ACQUISITION (OF LEARNING OR CONDITIONING) ". . . probability of occurrence, expressed as the number of trials on which a given subject produces a CR, or the percentage of subjects giving a CR on a given trial." [27] (E-M) (CR means conditioned response.)

EXTINCTION (OF LEARNING OR CONDITIONING) ". . . the decrease of response strength of nonreinforcement." [28] (E-M)

RESPONSE SET ". . . a general 'tendency to agree or disagree with questionnaire items, regardless of their content.' " [29] (M) The authors later operationalize this definition in different ways. One of these is: "An Overall Agreement Score (OAS) was computed for each S by taking the mean of their responses to the 360 items." [30]

COMMUNITY REPUTATION This is a variable of Newcomb's study of the attitudes of Bennington College girls. It was operationally defined by having knowledgeable students choose other students sociometrically. Twenty-eight criteria were used. For each of these the student judges nominated three individuals. Examples of the criteria are:

1. *Most absorbed* in social life, week–ends, etc.

2. *Most influenced* by faculty authority.

3. *Least likely* to engage actively in pursuits related to college interest.[31]

VALUES " 'Rank the ten goals in the order of *their importance to you.*' (1) financial success; (2) being liked; (3) success in family life; (4) being intellectually capable; (5) living by religious principles; (6) helping others; (7) being normal, well adjusted; (8) cooperating with others; (9) doing a thorough job; (10) occupational success." [32] (M)

". . . required S to categorize each of a group of value items in

26 E. Page, "Teacher Comments and Student Performance: A Seventy-Four Classroom Experiment in School Motivation," *Journal of Educational Psychology*, XLIX (1958), 173–181.

27 G. Kimble, *Hilgard and Marquis' Conditioning and Learning*, 2d. ed. New York: Appleton, 1961, p. 82.

28 *Ibid.*

29 A. Couch and K. Keniston, "Yeasayers and Naysayers: Agreeing Response Set as a Personality Variable," *Journal of Abnormal and Social Psychology*, LX (1960), 151–174.

30 *Ibid.*

31 T. Newcomb, *Personality and Social Change*. New York: Holt, Rinehart and Winston, Inc., 1943, pp. 66, 67, 184, 185.

32 T. Newcomb, *The Acquaintance Process*. New York: Holt, Rinehart and Winston, Inc., 1961, pp. 40 and 83.

terms of (a) *value importance,* that is, its importance to him as a 'source of satisfaction' and (b) *perceived instrumentality,* that is, his estimate as to whether, and to what extent, the value in question would tend to be achieved or blocked through the 'policy of allowing members of the Communist Party to address the public.' " [33] (M) (The author goes on to define and describe his method in detail.)

APPROVAL-DISAPPROVAL (OF PUPILS BY TEACHERS) ". . . time samples of classroom behavior were spread over an entire school year . . . interactions between teachers and pupils were classified into two categories: (a) praise contacts (teacher initiated interactions with a child in which she verbally expressed approval of some behavior which the child had displayed), and (b) blame contacts (teacher initiated interactions with a child in which she verbally expressed disapproval for some bit of behavior which the child had displayed)." [34] (M)

HONESTY "A child was considered 'dishonest' on the *Clapp-Young Arithmetic Test* in the correction of his paper if the inside of the test booklet showed: (a) that he had changed his answer by drawing a circle around his wrong response and had made an X for the correct response; (b) that he had erased the wrong response and marked the correct one; (c) that he marked the correct response when checking his paper but his work on the outside of the test booklet did not agree with his answer." [35] (M)

LEADERSHIP ". . . we shall deal with leader behavior defined as the behavior of the formally designated leader of a specified work-group. By definition, we shall designate all superintendents as leaders . . . we have chosen to measure two specific dimensions of leader behavior, 'Initiating Structure' and 'Consideration.' Initiating Structure refers to the leader's behavior in delineating the relationship between himself and the members of the work-group, and in endeavoring to establish well-defined patterns of organization, channels of communication, and methods of procedure. Consideration refers to behavior indicative of friendship, mutual trust, respect, and warmth in the relationship between the leader and the members of his staff." [36] (M) (Later, the author defines the two dimensions more precisely and operationally.)

COHESIVENESS ". . . attraction to a group." (M) (The authors then define and discuss "attraction to a group.")

"This total field of forces, which acts on members to remain in a

[33] M. Rosenberg, "Cognitive Structure and Attitudinal Affect," *Journal of Abnormal and Social Psychology,* LIII (1956), 367–372.

[34] W. Meyer and G. Thompson, "Sex Differences in the Distribution of Teacher Approval and Disapproval among Sixth-Grade Children," *Journal of Educational Psychology,* XLVII (1956), 385–396.

[35] Sister M. Gross, "The Effect of Certain Types of Motivation on the 'Honesty' of Children," *Journal of Educational Research,* XL (1946), 133–140.

[36] A. Halpin, *The Leadership Behavior of School Superintendents.* Chicago: Midwest Administration Center, University of Chicago, 1956, p. 4.

group, is called the cohesiveness of a group, and may be defined as the average for all members of the strength of resultant forces toward remaining in the group." [37]

Before leaving operational definitions and concepts, something that may puzzle the student should be discussed. In reading the literature, as often as not the student will not encounter operational definitions as such. Investigators may or may not *explicitly* define their terms operationally. A good research report, of course, should be so written that another investigator, if he chooses, can repeat the research. This implies that he will be able to measure the variables or manipulate the experimental conditions in the same way the original investigator did. To do this, naturally, he must know clearly and explicitly how to measure the variables or how to manipulate the experimental conditions. Therefore report writers must include operational definitions directly or indirectly. The commonest practice seems to be to mention the variables of the study early in the report and later to discuss the instruments used to measure the variables, or to discuss the experimental procedures used to manipulate the independent variables. Obviously the variables are thus operationally defined. An investigator will state a hypothesis, for example, that contains his variables: Underachievement is a function of inadequate self-concept. He will then probably discuss the hypothesis and in so doing say something about the concepts "underachievement" and "self-concept." But he may not define them operationally at this point. Later, in his section on method or procedure he will explain how he intends to measure underachievement and self-concept.

The benefits of operational thinking can be great. Although operationism can be carried to extremes, and although extreme operationism is dangerous because it tends to shut out the recognition of the importance of constructs and constitutive definitions in scientific theory and research and also tends to narrow research to perhaps trivial problems, there can be little doubt that it is a healthy scientific influence. As Underwood has said, in one of his fine chapters on operational definitions:

> . . . I would say that operational thinking makes better scientists. The operationist is forced to remove the fuzz from his empirical concepts . . .
> . . . operationism facilitates communication among scientists because the meaning of concepts so defined is not easily subject to misinterpretation.[38]

[37] D. Cartwright and A. Zander, *Group Dynamics*. New York: Harper & Row, 1953, pp. 76 and 102.
[38] B. Underwood, *Psychological Research*. New York: Appleton, 1957, p. 53.

STUDY SUGGESTIONS

1. The student can profit from study of some of the literature on constructs, variables, and operational definitions. Unfortunately, there are no very easy discussions. The five following references, however, are recommended:

> Kemeny, J., *A Philosopher Looks at Science*. Princeton, N.J.: Van Nostrand, 1959, Chap. 7.

> Margenau, H., *The Nature of Physical Reality*. New York: McMcGraw-Hill, 1950, Chaps. 4, 5, and 12.

> Northrop, F., *The Logic of the Sciences and the Humanities*. New York: Macmillan, 1947, Chaps. V, VI, and VII.

> Torgerson, W., *Theory and Methods in Scaling*. New York: Wiley, 1958, Chap. 1. Torgerson bases a large part of his discussion on Margenau, yet he goes beyond Margenau, particularly from the student's point of view and needs. This is an excellent chapter.

> Underwood, B., *Psychological Research*. New York: Appleton, 1957, Chaps. 3 and 7. Though Underwood takes a rather extreme operational position, these are excellent chapters.

2. Make up operational definitions for the following constructs. When possible, write two such definitions: an experimental one and a measured one.

permissiveness	underachievement
reinforcement	leadership
reading ability	class atmosphere
achievement	delinquency
interests	teacher control
needs	discipline
transfer of training	self-other attitudes
memory	conformity

Notice that some of these concepts or variables—for example, needs and transfer of training—are very difficult to define operationally. Why?

4 _SAMPLING AND RANDOMNESS_

Imagine the many situations in which we want to know something about people, about events, about things. To learn something about people, for instance, we take some few people whom we know—or do not know—and study them. After our "study," we come to certain conclusions about people, very often people in general. Some such method is behind much folk wisdom. Commonsensical observations about people, their motives, and their behaviors derive, for the most part, from observations and experiences with relatively few people. We make such statements as:

"Adolescents are delinquent"; "The world is deteriorating"; "People nowadays have no sense of moral values"; "Scientists are impractical"; "Politicians are corrupt"; and "Public school pupils are not learning the three R's."

The basis for making such statements is simple. People, mostly through their limited experiences, come to certain conclusions about other people and about their environment. In order to come to such conclusions, people must _sample_ their "experiences" of other people. Actually, they take relatively small samples of all possible experiences. The term "experiences" here has to be taken in a broad sense. It can mean direct experience with other people—for example, first-hand interaction with, say, Germans or Jews. Or it can mean indirect experience: hearing about Germans or Jews from friends, acquaintances, parents, and others. Whether experience is direct or indirect, however, does not concern us too much at this point. Let us assume that all such experience is direct. An individual believes that he "knows" something about Jews and says he "knows" they are clannish, because he has had direct experience with a number of Jews. He may even say, "Some of my best friends are Jews, and I know that . . ." The point is that his conclusions are based on a sample of Jews, or a sample of the behaviors of Jews, or both. He can never "know" all Jews; he must depend, in the last analysis, on samples. Indeed, most of the world's knowledge is based on samples, probably most often on inadequate samples.

SAMPLING AND RANDOM SAMPLING

Sampling is taking any portion of a population, or universe, as representative of that population or universe.[1] This definition does not say that the portion or sample taken—or drawn, as researchers say—*is* representative. It says, rather, taking a portion of a population and *considering* it to be representative. When a school administrator visits certain classrooms in his system "to get the feel of the system," he is sampling classes from all the classes in the system. He is probably assuming that if he visits, say, eight to ten classes out of forty "at random," as he may say, he will get a fair notion of the quality of teaching going on in the system. Or he may visit one teacher's class two or three times to sample her teaching. He is now sampling behaviors, in this case teaching behaviors, from the universe of all possible behaviors of the teacher. Such sampling is necessary and legitimate.

Random sampling is that method of drawing a portion (or sample) of a population or universe so that each member of the population or universe has an equal chance of being selected.[2] Let us define a universe to be studied as all fourth-grade children in X school system. Suppose there are 200 such children. We call them the population (or universe). We select, at random, one child from the population. His (or her) chance of being selected is $\frac{1}{200}$, if the sampling procedure is random. Likewise, a number of other children are similarly selected. Let us assume that after selecting a child we return him (or the symbol assigned to him) to the population. Then the chance of selecting any second child is also $\frac{1}{200}$. (If we had not returned him to the population, then the chance each of the remaining children has is, of course, $\frac{1}{199}$.)

A random sample can be said to be representative of the population from which it was drawn. We can really say a sample is representative only if it has been drawn randomly. Nonrandom samples may or may not be representative, but we cannot *say* they are representative. Although it will take us a while to understand fully why random samples can be said to be representative, we can anticipate later discussion now by noting that representativeness inheres in the definition of a random sample.

A sample drawn at random is an unbiased sample in the sense that no member of the population has any more chance of being selected than any other member. We have here a democracy of selection in which all members are equal before the bar of selection. A nonrandom sample, on

---

[1] The terms "population" and "universe" mean all the members of any well-defined class of people, events, or objects. For example, we might say that we will study such-and-such characteristics and the relations between them of the *fourth-grade children of X-school system.*

[2] This definition is not completely satisfactory from a mathematical point of view. A better definition is: a sample in which every possible combination of *n* elements of the population has the same probability of being selected.

the other hand, may be a biased sample. Nonrandom methods of selection may, and frequently do, yield samples in which some members of a population are over-represented or under-represented. Such over- and under-representation, of course, violates the definition of random samples. It is not so much that nonrandom samples may not be representative; in many cases they *may* be representative. It is that we cannot *say or assume* they are representative, whereas with random samples we can say or assume they are representative.

Here is a simple example. Suppose we have a population of 100 children. The children differ in intelligence. We want to know the mean IQ of the population, but for some reason we can only sample 30 of the 100 children. If we sample randomly, there are a large number of possible samples of 30 each. These samples have an equal and known probability of being selected. It can be shown that the means of most of these 30 samples will be relatively close to the mean of the population. A few will not be close. The probability of selecting a sample with a mean close to the population mean, then, is greater than the probability of selecting a sample with a mean not close to the population mean—if the sampling has been random.

If we do not draw our sample at random, however, some factor or factors unknown to us may predispose us to select a biased sample, in this case perhaps one of the samples with a mean not close to the population mean. The mean IQ of this sample will then be a biased estimate of the population mean. If the 100 children were known to us, we might unconsciously tend to select the more intelligent children. It should be emphasized that it is not so much that we would do so; it is that our method *allows* us to do so. Random methods of selection do not allow our own biases or any other systematic selection factors to operate.

It is possible that the reader is experiencing a vague and disquieting sense of dissatisfaction. He may ask: How can we be *sure* that random samples are representative? The answer is that we cannot be sure—ever. There is always the possibility of drawing samples that are not representative. In the above example of the population of 100 children, some of the samples would have means not close to the population mean. Later, we will learn ways of being more certain that our samples are representative. We will also learn that dead certainty can never be achieved. If he is to understand scientific research, the student must learn to live with this uncertainty. Fortunately, our lack of certainty and our lack of complete knowledge do not impair our research functioning.

RANDOMNESS

The notion of randomness is at the core of modern probabilistic methods in the natural and behavioral sciences. But it is difficult to define "random." The dictionary notion of haphazard, accidental, without aim or direction, does not help us much. In fact, scientists are quite systematic about randomness; they carefully select random samples and plan random procedures.

The position can be taken that nothing happens at random, that for any event there is a cause. The only reason, this position might say, that one uses the word random is that human beings do not know enough. To omniscience nothing is random. Suppose an omniscient being has an omniscient newspaper. It is a gigantic newspaper in which every event down to the last detail—for tomorrow, the next day, and the next day, and on and on into indefinite time—is carefully inscribed.[3] There is nothing unknown. And, of course, there is no randomness. Randomness is, as it were, ignorance, in this view.

Taking a cue from this argument, we define randomness in a backhand way. We say events are random if we cannot predict their outcomes. For instance, there is no known way to win a penny-tossing game. Whenever there is a system for playing a game that ensures our winning (or losing), then the event-outcomes of the game are random. More formally put, *randomness* means that there is no known law, capable of being expressed in language, that correctly describes or explains events and their outcomes.[4] In a word, when events are random we cannot predict them individually. Strange to say, however, we can predict them quite successfully in the aggregate. That is, we can predict the outcomes of large numbers of events. We cannot predict whether a coin tossed will be heads or tails. But, if we toss the coin 1000 times, we can predict, with considerable accuracy, the total number of heads and tails.

An Example of Random Sampling   To give the reader a feeling for randomness and random samples, we shall do an experiment using a table of random numbers. A table of random numbers contains numbers generated mechanically so that there is no discernible order or system in the numbers. It was said above that if events are random they cannot be predicted. But now we are going to predict the *general nature* of the outcomes of our experiment. We select, from a table of random digits, ten samples of ten digits each. Since the numbers are random, each sample should be representative of the universe of digits. The universe can be variously defined. We simply define it as the complete set of digits in the Rand Corporation table of random digits.[5] These digits are 0, 1, 2, 3, 4, 5,

3 See J. Kemeny, *A Philosopher Looks at Science.* Princeton, N. J.: Van Nostrand, 1959, p. 39.
4 *Ibid.*, pp. 68–75.
5 The source of random numbers used was: Rand Corporation, *A Million Random Digits With 100,000 Normal Deviates.* New York: Free Press, 1955. This is a large and carefully constructed table of random numbers. It is probably the best in existence. There are many other such tables, however, that are good enough for most practical purposes. Modern statistics texts have such tables. Useful tables of nonrepeating random

6, 7, 8, 9. We now draw samples from the table. If we compute the means of the ten samples, these means should be approximately equal—as a consequence of our representativeness of random samples idea. And the even numbers in each sample should approximately equal the odd numbers. The samples are given in Table 4.1.

TABLE 4.1   TEN SAMPLES OF RANDOM NUMBERS

1	2	3	4	5	6	7	8	9	10
9	0	8	0	4	6	0	7	7	8
7	2	7	4	9	4	7	8	7	7
6	2	8	1	9	3	6	0	3	9
7	9	9	1	6	4	9	4	7	7
3	3	1	1	4	1	0	3	9	4
8	9	2	1	3	9	6	7	7	3
4	8	3	0	9	2	7	2	3	2
1	4	3	0	0	2	6	9	7	5
3	1	8	8	4	5	2	1	0	3
2	1	4	8	9	2	9	3	0	1

Mean: 5.0 3.9 5.3 2.4 5.7 3.8 5.2 4.4 5.0 4.9 Total mean = 4.56

The means of the samples are given below each sample. Remember our question: How representative is each sample? Let us take the mean as an index of representativeness. A representative sample should have a mean of 4.5 or a mean near 4.5 since the mean of $U = \{0, 1, 2, 3, 4, 5, 6, 7, 8, 9\}$ is 4.5. (U means universe or population.) All 100 digits can be considered, too, to be a sample of the entire universe of the 1,000,000 digits in the complete table. Its mean is 4.56, which is, of course, very close to the population mean of 4.5. It can be seen that the means of the 10 samples vary around 4.5, the lowest being 2.4 and the highest 5.7. Only two of these means differs from 4.5 by more than 1. A statistical test—later we will learn the rationale of such tests—shows that the ten means do not differ from each other significantly. (The expression "do not differ from each other significantly" means that the differences are not greater than the differences that would occur by chance.) And by another statistical test nine of them are "good" estimates of the population mean of 4.5 and one (2.4) is not.

Changing the sampling problem, we can define the universe to consist of odd and even numbers. In the entire universe there should be an equal number of both. If our sample of 100 numbers is representative, then there should be approximately 50 odd and 50 even numbers. There are actually 54 odd and 46 even numbers. Is our sample representative,

numbers can be found in: A. Rosander, *Elementary Principles of Statistics*. Princeton, N. J.: Van Nostrand, 1951, pp. 681–683.

then? Yes, it is. A statistical test shows that the deviation of 4 for odd and 4 for even does not depart significantly from chance expectation.[6]

Similarly, if we sample human beings, and the numbers of men and women in the population being sampled is equal, then the numbers of men and women in our samples should be equal or nearly equal—if the sampling is random and our samples are large enough. If we measure the intelligence of our sample, and the mean intelligence quotient of the population is 100, then the mean of our sample should be close to 100.

THE PRINCIPLE OF RANDOMIZATION

Suppose an investigator wishes to test the hypothesis that counseling helps underachievers. He wants to set up two groups of underachievers, one to be counseled, one not to be counseled. Naturally, he wishes, also, to have the two groups equal in other independent variables that may have a possible effect on achievement. One way he can do this is to assign the children to both groups at random by, say, tossing a coin for each child in turn and assigning the child to one group if the toss is heads and to the other group if the toss is tails. (Note that if he had three experimental groups he could not use coin-tossing. He might use a die.) Or he could use a table of random numbers and assign the children as follows: if an odd number turns up, assign a child to one group, and if an even number turns up, assign the child to the other group. If he does this properly, he can then assume that the groups are approximately equal in all possible independent variables. The larger the groups, the safer the assumption. (Remember our recent random numbers experiment and the fact that the over-all mean derived from a sample of 100 was nearer to 4.5, the population mean, than any of the group means derived from samples of 10.) It might be said that the investigator has used the principle of randomization to equalize his groups.

An "ideal" experiment would be one in which *all* the factors or variables likely to affect the experimental outcome could be controlled. If we *knew* all these factors, in the first place, and *could control* them, in the second place, then we might have an ideal experiment. But the sad case is that we can never know all the pertinent variables nor can we control them even if we did know them. The principle of randomization, however, comes to our aid.

The *principle of randomization* may be stated thus: Since, in random procedures, every member of a population has an equal chance of being selected, members with certain distinguishing characteristics—male

---

[6] As indicated previously, the nature of such statistical tests, as well as the reasoning behind them, will be explained in detail in Part III. The student should not be too concerned if he does not completely grasp the statistical ideas expressed here. Indeed, one of the purposes of this chapter is to introduce some of the basic elements of such ideas.

and female, Republican and Democrat, extrovert and introvert, high and low intelligence, and so on and on—will, if selected, probably be counterbalanced in the long run by the selection of other members with the "opposite" quantity or quality of the characteristics. We might say that this is a practical principle that indicates what happens. We would not say that it is a law of nature. It is simply a statement of what usually happens when random procedures are used.

A Randomization Experiment   To show how, if not why, the principle of randomization works, we now set up a sampling and design experiment. The author recently made a study of the voting record of the Senate of the Eighty-Sixth Congress. The voting records of 100 senators on 12 important issues were reported in the *New York Times* on September 20, 1959. Omitting the two senators from Hawaii (they only voted on two of the issues), we have a population of 98 senators from which we can sample. In this population there are 64 Democrats and 34 Republicans, 65 northerners and 33 southerners. Each senator voted on each issue either Yea or Nay, except when he "paired for" or "paired against" an issue, or was absent. Thus we have a population of senators that can be broken down into subpopulations of Republicans and Democrats, northerners and southerners, "Yeaers" and "Nayers."

Let us pretend we are going to do an experiment using three groups, with 20 senators in each group. The nature of the experiment is not too relevant here, but let us say we want to test the efficacy of a film depicting the horrors of nuclear warfare in changing the attitudes of the senators toward nuclear test bans. We want the three groups of senators to be approximately equal in all possible characteristics. To accomplish this, we assign numbers from 1 through 98 to the senators in the *Times* table (omitting the senators from Hawaii), and then we select the 60 senators for the experiment in blocks of 20 using three separate pages of a large table of random numbers, the pages themselves being selected at random by entering the entire table anywhere and choosing three numbers at random.

We choose 20 two-digit numbers from the first page chosen, limiting our choices to numbers 1 through 98. Then we go to the second and third pages chosen and follow a similar procedure. The three groups of 20 numbers are given in Table 4.2, together with political party affiliation and regional origin (North-South) of each senator. In addition, for a purpose to be mentioned later, we enter the senatorial votes on Issues 1 and 5, assigning a 1 if a senator voted Yea and a 0 if he voted Nay.

How successful were we in equalizing the groups? In the total population of 98 senators, 64 are Democrats and 34 are Republicans, or 65 percent and 35 percent. In the total sample of 60, there are 41 Democrats and 19 Republicans, or 68 percent and 32 percent, a difference of only 3

TABLE 4.2   THREE GROUPS OF RANDOMLY SELECTED EIGHTY-SIXTH
CONGRESS SENATORS, THEIR POLITICAL PARTY AND REGION,
AND THEIR VOTES ON TWO ISSUES [a]

I	PP	R	1	5	II	PP	R	1	5	III	PP	R	1	5
34	D	S	0	1	60	D	S	0	0	4	D	N	0	0
35	R	S	0	1	42	D	S	1	0	38	D	N	0	0
50	D	S	0	0	66	D	N	0	0	75	D	N	1	0
15	R	N	0	1	98	D	N	0	0	37	D	N	1	1
86	D	S	0	1	41	D	S	0	0	30	D	S	0	0
29	D	S	0	1	51	D	S	0	0	31	D	N	1	0
79	D	N	1	0	9	R	N	0	1	65	D	S	0	1
16	D	N	1	0	1	R	N	1	1	13	D	N	0	0
21	D	N	1	0	46	R	N	0	1	7	D	N	0	0
17	R	N	1	1	40	D	N	0	0	67	D	N	1	0
76	D	N	0	0	53	R	N	1	1	2	R	N	0	1
87	R	N	0	1	32	D	S	0	1	85	R	N	1	1
8	R	N	1	1	93	R	N	1	1	78	R	N	0	1
92	D	S	0	1	89	D	S	0	1	12	D	S	0	0
57	R	N	1	1	90	D	S	1	0	84	R	N	0	1
52	D	S	0	1	64	D	N	1	0	20	D	N	0	0
26	D	N	1	1	63	R	N	0	1	44	D	S	0	0
11	D	S	0	1	43	R	N	0	1	23	R	N	0	1
36	D	S	0	0	80	D	S	0	0	73	D	N	0	0
96	D	S	0	0	3	D	N	0	0	72	R	N	0	1

[a] PP = Political Party; R = Region; D = Democrat; R = Republican (in body of table); 1 and 5 = Issues 1 and 5. See text for other explanations.

percent. There are 65 northerners and 33 southerners in the population, or 66 percent and 34 percent. In the sample of 60, there are 38 northerners and 22 southerners, or 63 percent and 37 percent, again a difference of 3 percent. We compute the frequencies for the three groups of 20 senators each. The data on political party and region are summarized in Table 4.3 It can be seen that the obtained frequencies in each sample on both variables are close to the expected frequencies.[7] In the total sample of 60, we would expect 39 Democrats and 39 northerners. Our sample gave us 41 Democrats and 38 northerners. All these differences are only chance fluctuations. We have evidently succeeded in equalizing the groups on political party and region. In addition, the total sample of 60 and the three samples of 20 each seem to be representative of the total population of 98—at least in these two variables.

[7] The expected frequencies are computed as follows: We take the proportions of Democrats, Republicans, northerners, and southerners in the total population of 98 and, using these proportions (or percentages) we compute the frequencies to be expected in the samples of 20. For example, 64 senators are Democrats, and 64/98 = .65. Thus 20 × .65 = 13, which is the number of Democrats to be expected in each of the samples of 20.

TABLE 4.3 OBTAINED AND EXPECTED FREQUENCIES OF POLITICAL PARTY
(DEMOCRAT) AND REGION (NORTH) IN SAMPLES OF 20 SENATORS [a]

| | Groups | | | | | | | |
| | I | | II | | III | | Total | |
	PP	R	PP	R	PP	R	PP	R
Obtained	14	10	13	12	14	16	41 (68%)	38 (63%)
Expected	13	13	13	13	13	13	39 (65%)	39 (66%)
Deviation	1	3	0	1	1	3	2	1

[a] Only the larger of the two totals of the Democrat-Republican split, the Democrat, is reported, and similarly, North is reported. PP = Political Party; R = Region. Expected frequencies have been rounded.

Now we check on the voting of the senators. To do this, we use Issues 1 and 5. We simply count the 1's (Yeas) in each column and compare the totals to the expected number of 1's computed by counting the Yeas on each issue, computing the proportion of Yeas on the issues in each sample of 20 and in the total sample of 60. For instance, in the total group of 98 senators there were 29 Yeas cast for Issue 1 and 50 Yeas cast for Issue 5, or proportions of $29/98 = .30$ and $50/98 = .51$. These same proportions should come up in each of the samples of 20. Multiplying 20 by .30 and by .51 gives us 6 and 10, respectively, as the numbers of Yeas expected on Issues 1 and 5. Similarly, multiplying 60 by .30 and by .51 yields expected frequencies of 18 and 31.

Table 4.4 reports the results of this simple analysis. All deviations obtained from expected frequencies are small (with one possible exception: Group I, Issue 5). They do not deviate very much from chance expectations. Thus we can say, again, that the samples are representative and that the principle of randomization has operated successfully.

TABLE 4.4 OBTAINED AND EXPECTED FREQUENCIES OF SENATORIAL YEA
AND NAY VOTES ON ISSUES 1 AND 5 [a]

| | Groups | | | | | | | |
| | I | | II | | III | | Total | |
	1	5	1	5	1	5	1	5
Obtained	7	13	6	9	5	8	18	30
Expected	6	10	6	10	6	10	18	31
Deviation	1	3	0	1	1	2	0	1

[a] If a senator voted Yea, this was counted as a frequency. The table is read, for example (first column): In the first sample of 20 senators (I), 7 voted Yea where 6 were expected to vote Yea, yielding a difference of 1.

RANDOM ASSIGNMENT

Instead of looking at this experiment as a sampling problem, we can look at it as an experimental *assignment* problem. We might have only 60 senators available to us for our experiment. In this case, let us say, we did not randomly sample the population of 98 senators but had the 60 handed to us, so to speak. This is analogous to many educational research situations where we must take groups as they are, for example, intact classes. Still, our experiment really showed us two things. One, our random sampling was successful. We can fairly safely assume that the random sample of 60 is representative of the total population of 98. Some evidence has been given above. And we can fairly safely assume that each of the samples of 20 is representative of the total population. Note, however, that had we not been able to randomly sample the population, that had we been "handed" the 60 senators to work with, we could make no assumption whatever about the representativeness of the sample and, of course, no assumption about the representativeness of each of the samples of 20—except as samples of the 60 senators.

Many educational research situations, as indicated above, are much like this. We must take as they are a class of seniors, two classes of sixth graders, a willing PTA. A general rule is: *When working with samples that have not been selected at random, generalization to the characteristics or relations between characteristics in the population is, strictly speaking, not possible.*

Stated positively the rule is: *When a sample of a population has been drawn at random, it is possible to make statements about the characteristics or the relations between characteristics in the population.*

An important corollary of this rule is that *such statements are never certain.* They are, rather, probabilistic statements, statements to which we always attach qualifications as to the probable certainty—if we can use a phrase that sounds like a contradiction—of the statements. If we make such statements with a random sample of 10,000, we can, for instance, be much more certain of their validity than we can with a random sample of 10, but in both cases the statements are probabilistic. To be sure, our estimates of the values of the population derived from the sample of 10,000 are much more certain—indeed, for all practical purposes, quite certain—than the estimates of the population values with a sample of only 10. In both cases, in other words, we *can* generalize to the population. It is simply that one generalization is much safer and much more certain than the other. In the case of the nonrandom sample, however, no matter what the size of the sample, we cannot generalize to the population.

Returning to the group of 60 senators that was handed to us and that was not a random sample of the 98 senators, we can still perform our experiment. We number the 60 senators from 1 through 60 and randomly *assign* the 60 senators to three groups of 20 each. Then we can assume that the three groups have been "equalized." This is called *random assignment*. It is a close relative of random sampling. Both operate on the principle of randomization. In fact, we can regard the random assignment as random sampling. In this case it would be random sampling of the *population* of 60 senators. That is, each of the groups of 20 senators *is* a random sample of the total group of 60 senators. (It is *not* a random sample of the 98 senators.) We sample randomly in order to have representative samples from which we can deduce the characteristics of the populations from which the samples were drawn. We randomly assign in order to have experimental groups that we can assume to be equal, within chance limits, in all possible characteristics.

SAMPLE SIZE

A rough and ready rule taught to beginning students of research is: Use as large samples as possible. Whenever a mean, a percentage, or anything else is computed from a sample, a population value is being estimated. A question that must be asked is: How much error is there likely to be in statistics calculated from samples of different sizes? The curve of Fig. 4.1 roughly expresses the relations between sample size and error, error meaning deviation from population values. The curve says that the smaller the sample the larger the error, and the larger the sample the smaller the error.

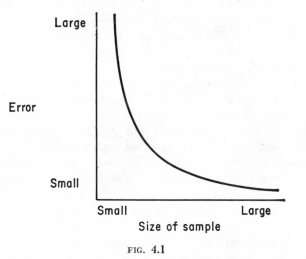

FIG. 4.1

Take the following rather extreme example of ten sets of two numbers each selected at random (using a table of random numbers) from a population of 293 IQ's given by Tate. These IQ's were themselves a sample from a much larger population of IQ's. We consider them to be a population from which we draw our small samples. Study Table 4.5. Note that the means of the samples diverge rather widely: The range is from 84.5 to 108.5, or 24.0 IQ points. The mean of all 20 scores is 93.55. Note that with very small samples like these we cannot depend too much on any one mean as an estimate of the population value, but that apparently we can depend much more on the total mean (calculated from 20 IQ's) as such an estimate. (The mean of the population of 293 IQ's is 95.0.)

TABLE 4.5   SAMPLES $(n = 2)$ OF IQ'S FROM A POPULATION OF 293 IQ'S
OF FOURTH-GRADE CHILDREN [a]

Samples									
117	85	84	92	83	82	83	96	93	101
75	84	107	103	87	96	100	121	103	79
Mean: 96.0	84.5	95.5	97.5	85.0	89.0	91.5	108.5	98.0	90.0
									Total mean = 93.55

[a] From M. Tate, *Statistics in Education*. New York: Macmillan, 1955, pp. 537–545.

Four more samples of 20 IQ's were drawn at random from the Tate data. The five means (including the mean of the sample of 20 IQ's in Table 4.5) were: 93.55; 90.20; 97.50; 94.80; and 90.50. The mean of all 100 IQ's was 93.31.

We are now in a position to answer some questions. First, large samples are more accurate, other things being equal, than small samples. The range of the means of samples of 20 was 90.20 to 97.50, or 7.30 IQ points, a relatively small range when the variability of the IQ's is considered (the range is from 54 to 125). The range of the means of the 10 samples of two IQ's each, on the other hand, was from 84.5 to 108.5, or 24.0 IQ points. Also attesting to the greater accuracy of larger samples are the means of our samples of 20. They were generally closer to the population mean of 95.0 than the means of the samples of two.

It should now be fairly clear why the research and sampling principle is: Use as large samples as possible. Large samples are not advocated because large numbers are good in and of themselves. They are advocated in order to give the principle of randomization, or simply randomness, a chance to "work," to speak somewhat anthropomorphically. For a rather dramatic example of what is meant, look back at the data of Table 4.2. Look at the political party of the first ten cases of Group III. They are all Democrats. Suppose, now, that we had chosen to work experimentally only with two groups of 10 each and one of our groups was the one with these 10 Democrats and the other had the remaining 10 cases of Group III in it. If our experiment had anything to do with political preference, the results might be very biased. With groups of 20, however, there is less danger.[8]

We do not know *why* the principle of randomization works. But random samples *do* give us dependable representative samples, and the assignment of subjects to groups at random *will* "equalize" the groups. To an omniscient being there is no randomness. By definition such a being would "know" the occurrence of any event with complete certainty.[9] As Poincaré points out, to gamble with such a being would be a losing venture. Indeed, it would not *be* gambling. When a coin is tossed ten times he would predict heads and tails with complete certainty and accuracy. When dice are thrown he would know infallibly what the outcomes will be. He would even be able to predict every number in a table of random numbers! And certainly he would have no need for research and science. What I seem to be saying is that randomness is a term for ignorance. If we, like the omniscient being, knew all the contributing causes of events, then there would be no randomness. The beauty of it is that man uses this "ignorance" and turns it to knowledge. How he does this should become more and more apparent as we go on with our study.

STUDY SUGGESTIONS

A variety of experiments with chance phenomena is recommended: games using coins, dice, cards, roulette wheels, and tables of random numbers. Such games, properly approached, can help one learn a great deal about fundamental notions of modern scientific research, statistics, probability, and, of course, randomness. Try the problems given in the suggestions below. Do not become discouraged by the seeming laboriousness of such exercises here and later on in the book. It is evidently necessary and, indeed, helpful occasionally to go through the routine involved in certain problems. After working the problems given, devise some of your own. If you can devise intelligent problems, you are probably well on your way to understanding.

1. From a table of random numbers draw 50 numbers, 0 through 9. List them in columns of 10 each.
    (a) Count the total number of odd numbers; count the total number of even numbers. What would you expect to get by chance? Compare the obtained totals with the expected totals.
    (b) Count the total number of numbers 0, 1, 2, 3, 4. Similarly count

---

8 This run of 10 Democrats is unusual. It has happened very seldom in all the random sampling the author has done. *But it can happen and does happen.*

9 For an eloquent discussion of this point, see Poincaré's essay on chance. H. Poincaré, *Science and Method*. New York: Dover, 1952, pp. 64–90.

5, 6, 7, 8, 9. How many of the first group should you get? The second group? Compare what you do get with these chance expectations. Are you far off?

(c) Count the odd and even numbers in each group of 10. Count the two groups of numbers 0, 1, 2, 3, 4 and 5, 6, 7, 8, 9 in each group of 10. Do the totals differ greatly from chance expectations?

(d) Add the columns of the five groups of 10 numbers each. Divide each sum by 10. (Simply move the decimal point one place to the left.) What would you expect to get as the mean of each group if only chance were "operating"? What did you get? Add the five sums and divide by 50. Is this mean close to the chance expectation? (*Hint:* To obtain the chance expectation, remember the population limits.)

2. Obtain a toy roulette wheel and "test" it for fairness. Spin the wheel and throw the ball 60 times. Write down the two kinds of results separately, that is, Red and Black and the numbers. Separate the 60 outcomes into three groups of 20 each. Compute, separately for the three groups and for the total number of spins:

(a) the numbers of Reds and the numbers of Blacks

(b) the means of the three groups

(c) the mean of the total group

Does the wheel seem to be biased or unbiased? Study the numbers to see if any one number seems to come up more than might be expected by chance. What does "biased" mean? (If you know statistics, compute a chi-square test of 2(*a*), and a simple analysis of variance of 2(*b*).)

PART TWO

SETS, RELATIONS, AND VARIANCE

5 *SETS*

Science works basically with group, class, or set concepts. When a scientist discusses individual events or objects, he does so always by considering such objects as members of sets of objects. For instance, we say "goose," but the word "goose" is meaningless without the concept of a gooselike group called "geese," or a flock of geese. We say "She's a beauty," but really mean she is a member of a class called "beauties." We talk about "brother," "sister," father," "mother," "husband," and "wife." Behind our talk, however, are the class notions of "siblings," "parents," and "family."

A *set* is a well-defined collection of objects or elements.[1] A set is well defined when it is possible to tell whether a given object does or does not belong to the set. Terms like aggregate, class, school, family, flock, and group indicate sets. There are two ways to define a set: (1) by listing all the members of the set, and (2) by giving a rule for determining whether objects do or do not belong to the set. Call (1) a "list" definition and (2) a "rule" definition. In research the rule definition is usually used, although there are cases where all members of a set are actually or imaginatively listed. For example, suppose we study the relation between voting behavior and political preference. Political preference can be defined as being a registered Republican or Democrat. We then have a large set of all people with political preferences with two smaller *subsets:* the subset of Republicans and the subset of Democrats. This is a rule definition of sets. Of course, we might list all registered Democrats and all registered Republicans to define our two subsets, but this is often difficult if not impossible. Besides, it is unnecessary; the rule is usually sufficient. Such a rule might be: A Republican is any person who is registered in the Republican party. Another such rule might be: A Republican is any person who says he is a Republican.

[1] J. Kemeny, J. Snell, and G. Thompson, *Introduction to Finite Mathematics.* Englewood Cliffs, N. J.: Prentice-Hall, 1956, p. 54.

SUBSETS

A *subset* of a set is a set that results from selecting sets from an original set. Each subset of a set is part of the original set. More succinctly and accurately, "A set *B* is a *subset* of a set *A* whenever all the elements of *B* are elements of *A*." [2] We designate sets by capital letters: *A, B, K, L, X, Y,* and so forth. If *B* is a subset of *A*, we write $B \subset A$, which means "*B* is a subset of *A*," "*B* is contained in *A*," or "All members of *B* are also members of *A*."

Whenever a population is sampled, the samples are subsets of the population. Suppose an investigator samples four eleventh-grade classes out of all the eleventh-grade classes in a large high school. The four classes form a subset of the population of all the eleventh-grade classes. Each of the four classes of the sample, too, can be considered a subset of the four classes—and also the total population of classes. All the children of the four classes can be broken down into two subsets of boys and girls. Whenever a researcher breaks down or partitions a population or a sample into two or more groups he is "creating" subsets using a "rule" or criterion to do so. Examples are numerous: religious preferences into Protestant, Catholic, Jew; intelligence into high and low; and so on. Even experimental conditions can be so viewed. The classic experimental-control group idea is a set-subset idea. Individuals are put into the experimental group; this is a subset of the whole sample. All other individuals used in the experiment (the control-group individuals) form a subset, too.

SET OPERATIONS

There are two basic set operations: *intersection* and *union*. An operation is simply "a doing-something to." In arithmetic we add, subtract, multiply, and divide. We "intersect" and "union" sets. We also "negate" them.

Intersection is the overlapping of two or more sets; it is the elements of two or more sets shared in common by the two or more sets. The symbol for intersection is ∩ (read "intersection" or "cap"). The intersection of the sets *A* and *B* is written $A \cap B$, and $A \cap B$ is itself a set. More precisely, it is the set that contains those elements of *A* and *B* that belong to *both A* and *B*. Intersection is also written $A \cdot B$, or simply AB.

Let $A = \{0, 1, 2, 3\}$; let $B = \{2, 3, 4, 5\}$. (Note that we use braces, "{ }," to symbolize sets. Then $A \cap B = \{2, 3\}$. This is shown in Fig. 5.1. $A \cap B$, or $\{2, 3\}$, is a new set composed of the members *common* to both sets. Note that $A \cap B$ might indicate the *relation* between the sets, the elements shared in common by *A* and *B*.

---

[2] R. Kershner and L. Wilcox, *The Anatomy of Mathematics.* New York: Ronald, 1950, p. 35.

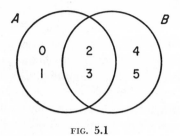

FIG. 5.1

Let A be a set of intelligence test scores on an administration of X test in January to 120 eighth graders. Let B be a set of intelligence test scores on a second administration in May of the same test to the same eighth graders. Some of the children will get the same scores or nearly the same scores both times. These scores can be indicated by $A \cap B$. To the extent the scores of A and B are the same or nearly the same, to this extent we may say that A and B are related. That is, $A \cap B$ can be conceived as a set name of a relation.

The *union* of two sets is written $A \cup B$. $A \cup B$ is a set that contains all the members of A and all the members of B. Mathematicians define $A \cup B$ as a set that contains those elements that belong either to A or to B or to both. In other words, we "add" the elements of A to those of B to form a new set $A \cup B$. Take the example of Fig. 5.1. A included 0, 1, 2, and 3; B included 2, 3, 4, and 5. $A \cup B = \{0, 1, 2, 3, 4, 5\}$. Note that the union of A and B in Fig. 5.1 is indicated by the whole area of the two circles. Note also that we do not count members of $A \cap B$, $\{2, 3\}$, twice.

Examples of union in research would be putting males and females together, $M \cup F$, or Republican and Democrats together, $R \cup D$. Perhaps more interesting, A might be all the children of the elementary schools and B all the children of the secondary schools of X school district. Then $A \cup B$ is the set of all the children in the district.

THE UNIVERSAL AND EMPTY SETS; SET NEGATION

The *universal set,* labeled U, is the set of all elements under discussion. It can be called the *universe of discourse or level of discourse.* (It is much like the terms *population* and *universe* discussed in Chapter 4.) This means that we limit our discussion to the fixed set of elements—all of them—from this fixed class, U. If we were to study determinants of achievement in the elementary school, for example, we might define U as all pupils in grades one through six. We could also define U, alternatively, as the scores on an achievement test of these same pupils. Subsets of U, perhaps to be studied separately, might be the scores of Grade 1 pupils, the scores of Grade 2 pupils, and so on.

U can be large or small. Returning to the example of Fig. 5.1, $A =$

$\{0, 1, 2, 3\}$ and $B = \{2, 3, 4, 5\}$. If $A \cup B = U$, then $U = \{0, 1, 2, 3, 4, 5\}$. Here U is quite small. Let $A = \{$Jane, Mary, Phyllis, Betty$\}$, and $B = \{$Tom, John, Paul$\}$. Then, if these individuals are all we are talking about, $U = \{$Jane, Mary, Phyllis, Betty, Tom, John, Paul$\}$. And, of course, $U = A \cup B$. This is another example of a small U. In research U's are more often large. If we random-sample the schools of a large county, then U is all the schools in the county, a rather large U. U might also be all the children or all the teachers in these schools, still larger U's.

In research it is important to know the U we are studying. Any ambiguity in the definition of U can lead to erroneous conclusions. Such ambiguities are common. If the characteristics of teachers are studied, it is imperative to define as precisely as possible what teachers we mean. Elementary and secondary teachers may differ considerably in some characteristics. In his study of teacher characteristics, for instance, Ryans separated elementary and secondary teachers. In effect, he defined two U's.[3] (It is possible, of course, to say that U was all elementary and secondary teachers and that U was broken down into two subsets.) Or the characteristics themselves might form a U, though it would be no mean job to define U in this case.

Like all sets, U is defined by a list or by a rule. In the case of teachers in the example just given, we would most likely use a rule definition. In the beginning of his study, Ryans limited the U of elementary teachers to those of Grades 3 and 4. He later defined U to include teachers from Grades 1 through 6.[4] With large U's rule definitions are ordinarily used because a list would be unwieldy and because it is often impossible to obtain or compile a list.

The *empty set* is the set with no members in it. We label it E. It can also be called the *null set*. Though it may seem peculiar to the student that we bother with sets with no members, the notion is quite useful, even indispensable. With it we can convey certain ideas economically and unambiguously. To indicate that there is no relation between two sets of data, for example, we can write the set equation $A \cap B = E$, which simply says that the intersection of the sets A and B is empty, meaning that no member of A is a member of B, and vice versa.

Let $A = \{1, 2, 3\}$; let $B = \{4, 5, 6\}$. Then $A \cap B = E$. Clearly there are no members common to A and B. The set of possibilities of the Democratic and Republican presidential candidates both winning the national election is empty. The set of cases of occurrences of rain without clouds is empty. The empty set, then, is another way of expressing the falsity of propositions. In this case we can say that the statement "Rain without

---

[3] D. Ryans, *Characteristics of Teachers.* Washington, D.C.: American Council on Education, 1960.
[4] *Ibid.,* p. 63.

clouds" is false. In set language this can be expressed $P \cap \sim Q = E$, where P = the set of all occurrences of rain, Q = the set of all occurrences of clouds, and $\sim Q$ = the set of all occurrences of no clouds.

The *negation* or *complement* of the set A is written $\sim A$. It means all members of U not in A. If we let A = all men, when U = all human beings, then $\sim A$ = all women (not-men). Simple dichotomization seems to be a fundamental basis of human thinking. In order to think, categorization is necessary: one must, at the most elementary level, separate objects into those belonging to a certain set and those not belonging to the set. We must distinguish men and not-men, me and not-me, early and not-early, good and not-good.

If $U = \{0, 1, 2, 3, 4\}$, and $A = \{0, 1\}$, then $\sim A = \{2, 3, 4\}$. A and $\sim A$ are of course subsets of U. An important property of sets and their negation is expressed in the set equation: $A \cup \sim A = U$. Note, too, that $A \cap \sim A = E$.

SET DIAGRAMS

We now pull together and illustrate the basic set ideas already presented by diagramming them. Sets can be depicted with various kinds of figures, but rectangles and circles are ordinarily used. They have been adapted from a system invented by John Venn. In this book rectangles, circles, and ovals will be used. Look at Fig. 5.2. U is represented by the rectangle. All members of the universe under discussion are in U. A set A has been drawn inside U. The members of the set A are a subset of U. All members of U not in A form another subset of U: $\sim A$. Note, again, that $A \cup \sim A = U$. Note, too, that $A \cap \sim A = E$, that is, there are no members common to both A and $\sim A$.

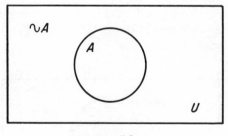

FIG. 5.2

Next, we depict, in Fig. 5.3, two sets, A and B, both subsets of U. From the diagram it can be seen that $A \cap B = E$. We adopt a convention: when we wish to indicate a set or a subset, we shade it either horizontally, vertically, or diagonally. The set $A \cup B$ has been shaded in Fig. 5.3.

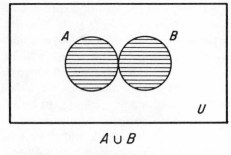

$$A \cup B$$

FIG. 5.3

Intersection, probably the most important set notion from the point of view of this book, is indicated by the shaded portion of Fig. 5.4. The situation can be expressed by the equation $A \cap B \neq E$; the intersection of the sets A and B is *not* empty.

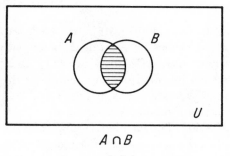

$$A \cap B$$

FIG. 5.4

When two sets, A and B are equal, they have the same set elements or members. The Venn diagram would show two congruent circles in U. In effect, only one circle would show. When $A = B$, then $A \cap B = A \cup B = A = B$.

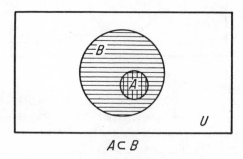

$$A \subset B$$

FIG. 5.5

We diagram $A \subset B$; A is a subset of B, in Fig. 5.5. B has been shaded horizontally, A vertically. Note that $A \cup B = B$ (whole shaded area) and $A \cap B = A$ (area shaded both horizontally and vertically). All members of A are also in B, or all a's are also b's, if we let $a =$ any member of A and $b =$ any member of B.

SET OPERATIONS WITH MORE THAN TWO SETS

Set operations are not limited to two subsets of U. Let A, B, and C be three subsets of U. Suppose the intersection of these three subsets of U is not empty, as shown in Fig. 5.6. The triply hatched area shows $A \cap B \cap C$. Note that there are four intersections, each hatched differently: $A \cap B, A \cap C, B \cap C$, and $A \cap B \cap C$.

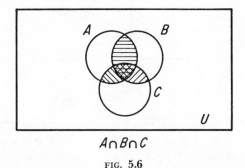

$A \cap B \cap C$

FIG. 5.6

Although four or more sets can be diagrammed, such diagrams become cumbersome and not easy to draw and inspect. There is no reason, however, why the intersection and union operations cannot be applied symbolically to four or more sets.

PARTITIONS AND CROSS PARTITIONS

It is obvious that U can be broken down into subsets that intersect. U can also be broken into subsets that do not exhaust all of U (unless we use set negation). On the other hand, U can be broken down into subsets that do not intersect and that exhaust all of U. When this is done the process is called *partitioning*.

Partitioning breaks a universal set down into subsets that are *disjoint* and *exhaustive* of the universal set. In set language, let U be a universe, and let A and B be subsets of U that are partitions. We label subsets of A: $A_1, A_2, \cdots, A_k$ and of B: $B_1, B_2, \cdots, B_k$. Now, $[A_1, A_2]$ and $[B_1 B_2]$,[5] for example, are partitions if:

---

[5] Partitions are usually set off by square brackets, [   ], while sets and subsets are set off by curled brackets or braces, {   }.

$$A_1 \cup A_2 = U \text{ and } A_1 \cap A_2 = E$$

$$B_1 \cup B_2 = U \text{ and } B_1 \cap B_2 = E$$

Diagrams make this clearer. The partitioning of U, represented by a rectangle, separately into the subsets A_1 and A_2 and into B_1 and B_2, is shown in Fig. 5.7. Note that both partitionings have been performed on the same U. We have met many examples of such partitions: middle class-working class, high income-low income, introvert-extrovert, Democrat-Republican, high achievement-low achievement, pass-fail, approve-disapprove, and so on. Some of these are true dichotomies; others are continuous variables.

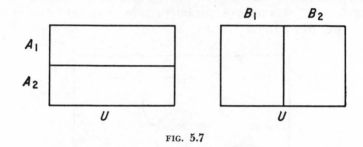

FIG. 5.7

It is possible to put the two partitions together into a *cross partition*. A *cross partition* is a new partitioning that arises from successively partitioning the same set U by forming all subsets of the form $A \cap B$. In other words, perform the A partitioning, then the B partitioning on the same U, or the same square. This is shown in Fig. 5.8. Each cell of the partitioning is an intersection of the subsets of A and B. We shall find in a later chapter that such cross-partitioning is very important in research design and in the analysis of data.

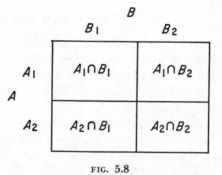

FIG. 5.8

Anticipating later developments, we give a research example of a cross partition. Such examples are called *crossbreaks*. Crossbreaks provide the most elementary way to show a relation between two variables. The example is from Miller and Swanson's study of child-rearing practices. One of the tables they report is a crossbreak in which the variables are social class (middle class and working class) and weaning (early and late). The data, converted to percentages by the writer, are given in Table 5.1.[6]

TABLE 5.1   CROSSBREAK TABLE: RELATION BETWEEN SOCIAL CLASS AND WEANING. MILLER AND SWANSON STUDY

		Weaning	
		Early (B_1)	Late (B_2)
Social	Middle Class (A_1)	60% (33)	40% (22)
Class	Working Class (A_2)	35% (17)	65% (31)

The frequencies reported by Miller and Swanson are given in the lower right corner of each cell. Evidently there is a relation between social class and weaning. Middle-class mothers show a tendency to wean their children earlier than lower-class mothers do.

The two conditions of disjointness and exhaustiveness are satisfied. The intersection of any two cells is empty, for example, $(A_1 \cap B_1) \cap (A_2 \cap B_2) = E$. And the cells exhaust all the cases: $(A_1 \cap B_1) \cup \cdots \cup (A_2 \cap B_2) = U$.

Partitioning extends beyond two subsets, of course. That is, instead of high and low income and high and low achievement, it is possible to have high-medium-low income and high-medium-low achievement. And one variable can be partitioned into five subsets. There is no theoretical limitation, either, on the number of variables.

Here is an example of a larger and more complex cross partition. We assign variable names to the set letters of a $2 \times 3 \times 2$ cross partition. It has been laid out in Fig. 5.9.

Let U be all fourth-grade children in X school system. Let U be partitioned and cross-partitioned according to three variables, A, B, and C, A being sex, B intelligence, and C motivation. Let U be partitioned first into A_1 and A_2, male and female. Let U be partitioned next into B_1, B_2, B_3, or high, medium, and low intelligence.[7] Finally, let U be partitioned into C_1 and C_2, high and low motivation (to do school work).

---

[6] D. Miller and G. Swanson, *Inner Conflict and Defense.* New York: Holt, Rinehart and Winston, Inc., 1960, p. 426.

[7] Naturally there has to be a clearcut system for setting up the categories. Such systems will be discussed when we study research design.

Next, we cross-partition or crossbreak A_1 and A_2 and B_1, B_2, and B_3 by forming subsets from the intersections of A and B, such as $A_1 \cap B_1$, $A_1 \cap B_2$, $\cdots$, $A_2 \cap B_3$. We do the same, theoretically, for A and C and B and C. Actually, we do not have to do all this. What we do do, after we have $A_1 \cap B_1$, $\cdots$, $A_2 \cap B_3$ is to cross-partition these intersection subsets with C_1 and C_2, arriving at the triple subsets, $A_1 \cap B_1 \cap C_1$, $A_1 \cap B_1 \cap C_2$, $\cdots$, $A_2 \cap B_3 \cap C_2$. (For simplicity we write these subsets in the diagram: $A_1 B_1 C_1$, $A_1 B_1 C_2$, and so forth.) This gives us $2 \times 3 \times 2 = 12$ cells, each of which represents the intersection of three sets.

	B_1		B_2		B_3	
	C_1	C_2	C_1	C_2	C_1	C_2
A_1	$A_1 B_1 C_1$	$A_1 B_1 C_2$	$A_1 B_2 C_1$	$A_1 B_2 C_2$	$A_1 B_3 C_1$	$A_1 B_3 C_2$
A_2	$A_2 B_1 C_1$	$A_2 B_1 C_2$	$A_2 B_2 C_1$	$A_2 B_2 C_2$	$A_2 B_3 C_1$	$A_2 B_3 C_2$

U

FIG. 5.9 $A_1 B_1 C_1$ STANDS FOR $A_1 \cap B_1 \cap C_1$

To classify any single individual, we learn whether "he" is a male or a female, whether he has high, medium, or low intelligence, and whether his motivation is high or low. We do this for each individual until all individuals or members of U are appropriately classified and assigned to their appropriate cells. Since our initial rules said that (1) the cells must be disjoint $[(A_1 \cap B_1 \cap C_2) \cap (A_2 \cap B_1 \cap C_3) = E$, for example], and (2) the union of all the cells must equal the universe $[(A_1 \cap B_1 \cap C_1) \cup (A_1 \cap B_1 \cap C_2) \cup \cdots \cup (A_2 \cap B_3 \cap C_2) = U]$, no individual can be in more than one cell and every individual must be assigned to a cell.

LEVELS OF DISCOURSE

When we talk about anything we talk about it, loosely put, in a context or frame of reference. The expressions context and frame of reference are closely related to U, the universe of discourse. The universe of discourse must be able to include any objects we talk about. If we go to another U, another level of discourse, the new level will not include all the objects. Indeed, it may not include any of the objects. If we are talking about people, for instance, we do not—or perhaps I should say "should not"—start talking about birds and their habits unless we somehow relate birds and their habits to people and make it clear that this is what we are doing. There are two levels of discourse or universes (U's) of

discourse here: people and birds. When discussing the democratic implications of segregation, we should not abruptly shift to religious problems
—unless, of course, we somehow relate the latter to the former. Otherwise
we lose our original universe of discourse, or we cannot assign the objects
of the level, religion, perhaps, to the old level, the education of Negro
children.

In research, similarly, we should not mix or shift our universes of
discourse. Set-thinking helps us avoid such mixing and shifting. As an
extreme example, suppose an investigator decided to study the toilet training, authoritarianism, musical aptitude, creativity, intelligence, reading
achievement, and general scholastic achievement of ninth-grade youngsters. While it is conceivable that some sort of relation or relations could
be teased out of this array of variables, it is more conceivable that it is an
intellectual mess. At any rate, remember sets. Ask yourself: "Do the objects I am now discussing or am about to discuss belong to the set or sets
of my present discussion?" If so, then you are one level of discourse. If
not, then another level of discourse, another set, or set of sets, is entering
the discussion. If this happens without your knowing it, the result is confusion. In short, ask: "What is my U and the subsets of my U?"

In addition, define your universal set precisely. "Precisely" means:
give a clear rule that tells you when an object is or is not a member of U.
Similarly, define subsets of U and the subsets of the subsets of U. If the
objects of U are people, then you cannot have a subset with objects that
are not people. (Though you might have the set A of people and set $\sim A$
of "not-people," this logically amounts to U being people. "Not-people"
is a class on the dimension of "people," by definition or convention.)

The set idea is fundamental in human thinking. This is because all
human thinking probably depends on putting things into categories and
labeling the categories, as indicated earlier. What we do is to group together classes of objects—things, people, events, phenomena in general—
and name these classes. Such names are then concepts, labels that we no
longer need to learn anew and that we can use for efficient thinking.

Applications of sets to the study of relations and functions (next
chapter), to crossbreaks, to probability problems and theory, and to measurement theory and problems are perhaps its most important research applications—at least in this book. But sets can be applied to other areas and
problems that are not usually considered mathematical. Piaget, for example, has used set algebra to help explain the thinking of children.[8] Hunt
has applied sets to his study of concept learning.[9] Restle has used set

    [8] J. Piaget, *Logic and Psychology*. New York: Basic Books, 1957. Also, B. Inhelder
and J. Piaget, *The Growth of Logical Thinking from Childhood to Adolescence*. New
York: Basic Books, 1958.
    [9] E. Hunt, *Concept Learning*. New York: Wiley, 1962.

theory to help conceptualize psychological problems of judgment and choice.[10] Coombs presents his theory of data largely in set terms.[11] It can fairly safely be predicted that social scientific and educational researchers will find set theory increasingly useful in the solution of theoretical and research problems.

STUDY SUGGESTIONS

1. There are several good references on sets for the beginning student. Here are four of them.

  Davis, R., ed., *Elementary Mathematics of Sets with Applications.* Committee on the Undergraduate Program, Mathematical Association of America, 1955. This book can be purchased inexpensively from the Secretary, Mathematical Association of America, University of Buffalo, Buffalo, N.Y.

  Insights into Modern Mathematics. Twenty-Third Yearbook. Washington, D.C.: The National Council of Teachers of Mathematics, 1957. See Chap. III. This is a good, solid presentation.

  Kemeny, J., J. Snell, and G. Thompson, *Introduction to Finite Mathematics.* Englewood Cliffs, N.J.: Prentice-Hall, 1956, Chap. II. One of finest sources, this book is an excellent source of modern mathematics for the student of the social sciences and education. In addition to sets, partitions are discussed at some length.

  Report of the Commission on Mathematics. *Appendices.* New York: College Entrance Examination Board, 1959, Chaps. 1, 2, and 9 (Appendices to *Program for College Preparatory Mathematics.*) This is an excellent book, in many ways the most suitable for the student of educational research. Careful study of the chapters mentioned is strongly recommended. (Can be obtained from College Entrance Examination Board, c/o Educational Testing Service, Princeton, N.J.)

2. Suppose an educational investigator has studied the relation between musical aptitude and abstract reasoning ability and has found no relation ($r = .00$). How would you indicate this (a) using a Venn diagram, (b) using a set equation?

  Suppose the same investigator had found a strong positive relation. How would you indicate this in the two ways suggested above?

3. Draw two overlapping circles, enclosed in a rectangle. Label the following parts: the universal set U, the subsets A and B, the intersection of A and B, and the union of A and B.

  (a) If you were working on a research problem involving fifth-grade

10 F. Restle, *Psychology of Judgment and Choice.* New York: Wiley, 1961.
11 C. Coombs, "A Theory of Data," *Psychological Review,* LXVII (1960), 143–159.

children, what part of the diagram would indicate the children from which you might draw samples?

(b) What might the sets A and B represent?

(c) What meaning might the intersection of A and B have?

(d) How would you have to change the diagram to represent the empty set? Under what conditions would such a diagram have research meaning?

4. Consider the following cross partition:

	Republican (B_1)	Democrat (B_2)
Male (A_1)		
Female (A_2)		

What is the meaning of the following sets, that is, what would we call any object in the sets?

(a) $(A_1 \cap B_1)$; $(A_2 \cap B_2)$.

(b) A_1; B_1.

(c) $(A_1 \cap B_1) \cup (A_1 \cap B_2) \cup (A_2 \cap B_1) \cup (A_2 \cap B_2)$.

(d) $(A_1 \cap B_1) \cup (A_2 \cap B_1)$.

5. Using the following sets, make a cross partition: intelligence test scores of third-grade children; socioeconomic backgrounds of the children; the children's sex.

6. Following the method outlined in the text, draw the cross partition of the following hypothesis: "Test performance in arithmetic is affected by anxiety and abstract reasoning aptitude." Outline the set reasoning involved. (*Note:* This is a difficult exercise. The student may want to postpone it until later in his development. *Hint:* Crossbreak all three variables.)

7. Under what conditions will the following set equation be true?

$$n(A \cup B) = n(A) + n(B)$$

(*Note:* $n(A)$ means the number of objects in the set A.)

6 *RELATIONS*

Relations are the essence of science. Cohen says, ". . . science is not a knowledge of mere particulars, but rather a knowledge of the way in which classes are related." [1] We know that large things are large only by comparing them to other smaller things. We thus establish the relations "greater than" and "less than." An educational scientist can "know" about achievement only as he studies achievement in relation to nonachievement and in relation to other variables. There is no "fact" of achievement in and of itself. Scientific "facts" are relations. The relations between intelligence and achievement, between group pressure and conformity, between aptitude and motivation, are, when established, "facts."

The relational nature of human knowledge is clearly seen even when seemingly obvious "facts" are analyzed. Is it a fact that a stone is hard? To speak of the truth or falsity of this statement we must first examine sets and subsets of different kinds of stones. Then, after operationally defining "hard," we compare the "hardness" of stones to other "hardnesses." The "simplest" facts turn out, on analysis, to be not so simple. Northrop, discussing concepts and facts, says, "The only way to get pure facts, independent of all concepts and theory, is merely to look at them and forthwith to remain perpetually dumb . . ." [2]

The dictionary tells us that a relation is a bond, a connection, a kinship. For most people this definition is good enough. But what do "bond," "connection," and "kinship" mean? Again, the dictionary says that a bond is a tie, a binding force, and that a connection is, among other things, a union, a relationship, an alliance. But a union, a tie, between what? And what do "union," "tie," and "binding force" mean? Such definitions, while intuitively helpful, are too ambiguous for scientific use.

---

[1] M. Cohen, *A Preface to Logic*. New York: Meridian, 1957, p. 170.

[2] F. Northrop, *The Logic of the Sciences and the Humanities*. New York: Macmillan, 1947, p. 317. See also, M. Cohen and E. Nagel, *An Introduction to Logic and Scientific Method*. New York: Harcourt, 1934, pp. 217–219.

RELATIONS AS SETS OF ORDERED PAIRS

Relations in science are always between classes or sets of objects. One cannot "know" the relation between social class and school achievement by studying one child. "Knowing" the relation is achieved only by abstracting the relation from sets of children, or more accurately, from sets of characteristics of children. Let us take examples of relations and intuitively develop a notion of what a relation is.

Let A be the set of all fathers and B the set of all sons. If we pair each father with his son (or sons), we have the relation "father-son." We might also call this relation "fatherhood," even though daughters have not been considered. Similarly we might pair parents (elements of A, each pair of parents being considered as an element) with their children. This would be the relation of "parenthood," or maybe "family."

Let A be the set of all husbands and B the set of all wives. The set of pairs then defines the relation "marriage." In other words, a new set is formed, a set of pairs with husbands always listed first and wives second and each husband paired only with his own wife.

Suppose the set A consists of the scores of a specified group of children on an intelligence test and the set B scores on an achievement test. If we pair each child's IQ with his achievement score, we define a relation between intelligence and achievement. Notice that we cannot so easily assign a name like "parenthood" or "marriage" to this relation. Suppose the sets of scores are as follows:

IQ	Achievement
136	55
125	57
118	42
110	48
100	42
97	35
90	32

Consider the two sets as one set of pairs. Then this set is a relation.

If we graph the two sets of scores on X and Y axes, as we did in Chap. 3 (Fig. 3.3), the relation becomes easier to "see." This has been done in Fig. 6.1. Each point is defined by two scores. For example, the point farthest to the right is defined by (136, 55), and the point farthest to the left is (90, 32). The set of pairs of scores, with IQ first and achievement score second in each pair, defines a relation. Graphs like Fig. 6.1 are convenient ways to express relations.

We are now prepared to define "relation" formally: *A relation is a set of ordered pairs.* Any relation *is* a set, a certain kind of set: a set of ordered pairs.

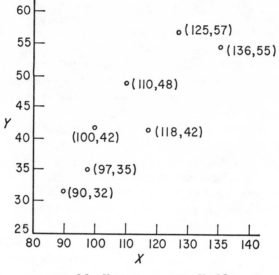

FIG. 6.1   *Y:* ACHIEVEMENT;   *X:* IQ

An *ordered pair* is two objects, or a set of two elements, in which there is a fixed order for the objects to appear. Actually, we speak of ordered pairs which means, as indicated earlier, that the members *of each pair* always appear in a certain order. If the members of the sets *A* and *B* are paired, then we must specify whether the members of *A* or the members of *B* come first in each pair. If we define the relation of marriage, for example, we specify the set of ordered pairs with, say, husbands always placed first in each pair. In other words, the pair (a, b) is not the same as the pair (b, a). (Ordered pairs are enclosed thus: (   ). A set of ordered pairs is indicated in this manner: $\{(a, k), (b, l), (c, m)\}$.)

We have fortunately left the previous ambiguity of the dictionary definition behind. The definition of relations as sets of ordered pairs, though it may seem a bit strange and even curious to the student, is unambiguous and general. Moreover, the scientist, like the mathematician, can work with it.

DETERMINING RELATIONS IN RESEARCH

Though we have avoided ambiguity with our definition of relations, we have not cleared up the definitional and especially the practical problem of "determining" relations. There is another way to define a relation that may help us. Let *A* and *B* be sets. If we pair each individual member of *A* with every member of *B*, we obtain *all the possible pairs* between the two sets. This is called the Cartesian product of the two sets and is labeled $A \times B$. A relation is then defined as a subset of $A \times B$, that is, *any* subset of ordered pairs drawn from $A \times B$ is a relation.[3]

To illustrate this idea very simply, let the set $A = \{a_1, a_2, a_3\}$ and the set $B = \{b_1, b_2, b_3\}$.[4] Then the Cartesian product, $A \times B$, can be diagrammed as in Fig. 6.2. That is, we generate nine ordered pairs: (a_1, b_1), (a_1, b_2), $\cdots$, (a_3, b_3). With large sets, of course, there would be many pairs, in fact mn pairs, where m and n are the numbers of elements in A and B, respectively.

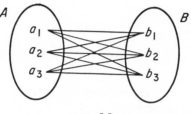

FIG. 6.2

This is not very interesting—at least in the present context. What do we do to determine or "discover" a relation? We determine empirically which elements of A "go with" which elements of B according to some criterion. Obviously there are many subsets of pairs of $A \times B$, most of which do not "make sense" or which do not interest us. Kershner and Wilcox say that a relation is "a method for distinguishing some ordered pairs from others; it is a scheme for singling out certain pairs from all of them." [5] According to this way of viewing relations, the relation of "marriage" is a method or procedure for distinguishing married couples from all possible pairings of men and women. In this way we can even think of religion as a relation. Let $A = \{a_1, a_2, \cdots, a_n\}$ be the set of all people in the United States, and let $B = \{$Catholic, Protestant, Jew, and so forth$\}$ be the set of religions. If we order pairs, in this case each person with his religion, then we have the "relation" of religion, or perhaps more accurately, "religious affiliation."

Lest the student be too disturbed by the perhaps jarring sensation of defining a relation as a subset of $A \times B$, we may hastily add, again, that many of the possible subsets of ordered pairs of $A \times B$, naturally, will make no sense. Then, too, some of them may make very good sense. Perhaps the main point to be made is that our definition of relation is unambiguous and completely general. No matter what sets of ordered

[3] See R. Kershner and L. Wilcox, *The Anatomy of Mathematics*. New York: Ronald, 1950, chap. 5, for an excellent discussion of relations.

[4] The subscript integers merely label and distinguish individual members of sets. They do not imply order. Note, too, that there do not have to be equal numbers of members in the two sets.

[5] Kershner and Wilcox, *op. cit.*, p. 46.

pairs we pick, it *is* a relation. It is up to *us* to decide whether or not the sets we pick make scientific sense according to the dictates of the problems to which we are seeking answers and the hypotheses we are testing. But we should not automatically rule out relations just because they seem at the moment not to make sense.

The student may wonder why so much trouble has been taken to define relations. First, the ordered pair definition, as already indicated, is unambiguous. Second, it applies to research situations generally and thus is a useful intellectual tool that helps us to unify varied kinds of relations in varied kinds of research situations. Third, it tells us, in effect, what we must do to study relations empirically: we must somehow study ordered pairs and find ways to distinguish meaningful ordered pairs from those that are not meaningful to a particular research problem.

RULES OF CORRESPONDENCE AND MAPPING

Any objects—people, coffee beans, numbers, railroad cars, gambling outcomes, points in space, symbols, and so on and on—can be members of sets and can be related in the ordered-pair sense. It is said that the members of one set are *mapped* on to the members of another set by means of a rule of correspondence. A *rule of correspondence* is a prescription or a formula that tells us how to map the objects of one set on to the objects of another set. It tells us, in brief, how the correspondences between set members are achieved.

To illustrate the mapping and correspondence notions, study Fig. 6.3, which shows a simplified ordinary map on the left and the names of map objects on the right. We have here literally a mapping, a mapping of actual geographical objects on to the names of the objects (or vice versa). This is of course a relation, a set of ordered pairs, each geographical object being paired with its name.

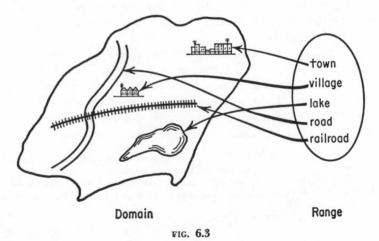

Domain   Range

FIG. 6.3

In a relation the two sets whose objects are being related are named the *domain* and the *range,* or *D* and *R*. *D* is always the set of first elements, and *R* the set of second elements. Suppose we have a group of boys and girls and want to study the relation between sex and some other variable. We assign 1 to male and 0 to female. An illustration of the mapping is given in Fig. 6.4, where to each member of the domain is appropriately assigned a member of the range. $D = \{$Jane, Arthur, Michael, Alberta, Ruth$\}$, and $R = \{0, 1\}$. The rule of correspondence says: If the object of *D* is female assign a 0, if male assign a 1.

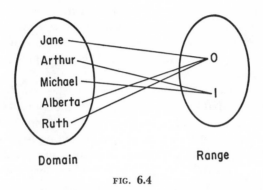

FIG. **6.4**

In other words, objects, especially numbers, are assigned to other objects—persons, places, numbers, and so on—according to rules. The process is highly varied in its applications but simple in its conception. This is why sets are stressed in this book: they are generally applicable and simple in conception. Instead of thinking of all the different ways of expressing relations separately, we realize that they are all sets of ordered pairs and that the objects of one set are simply mapped on to the objects of another set. All the varied ways of expressing relations—as mappings, correspondences, equations, sets of points, tables, or statistical indices—can be reduced to sets of ordered pairs.

FUNCTIONS

A *function* is a rule, a rule of correspondence. It is a rule, often designated by the letters f, g, F, and so on, that assigns to each member of a domain *some one* member of a range. All functions are relations, sets of ordered pairs. Figure 6.4 depicts a function: to each member of the domain $\{$Jane, Arthur, Michael, Alberta, Ruth$\}$ one and only one member of the range $\{0, 1\}$ is assigned.

Functions are written in various ways. One frequent way is $y = f(x)$. Here x stands for the objects of the domain; $f(x)$ denotes the objects assigned to the x's of the domain. That is, $f(x)$ stands for the objects of the range. These objects are called the *values* of f at x; $y = f(x)$ is ordinarily read, "y is a function of x." Unfortunately, this tends to be confused with common sense usages of the word function: school achievement is a function of intelligence. This usage seems to mean that one thing depends on or is caused by another. This is not the meaning intended here; $y = f(x)$ is better read "y equals the object (a set member) that corresponds to x."

Another way to write functions, one that is close to the purposes of this chapter, is exemplified in this equation: $f = \{(x, y); x$ is a number and $y = x + 2\}$. Translated into words, this says: "The function, f, or the rule of correspondence, is equal to the set of ordered pairs (x, y) such that x is a number and each corresponding y, also a number, is equal to $x + 2$." In brief, given a value of x, say 4, we add 2 to it to obtain y, in this case 6. The rule is f which, spelled out, is the expression on the right side of the equation.

It was said above that all functions are relations. It should be understood, however, that not all relations are functions. A function can have assigned to any member of its domain only one member of its range. If we pair sons and fathers, with sons always coming first, we would have a function—and, of course, a relation. Each son can have assigned to him only one father. This is shown in Fig. 6.5 where five sons are "related" to three fathers. Note that each object of the domain has only one object of the range associated with it. Naturally each son can have only one father.

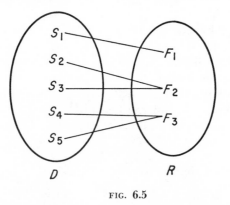

FIG. 6.5

Figure 6.6 turns the situation around. Fathers come first and sons second. Notice that F_2 and F_3 have two lines connecting them to objects of R. Thus Fig. 6.6 illustrates a relation but not a function.

It is important for the student of research at least to know what a function is. Functions, functional expressions, and functional laws occur frequently in research literature. More important, one of the principal goals of science is to discover and state functional laws, laws of the kind,

"If p, then q," which can be stated $q = f(p)$. In addition to discovering relations, the scientist would like to state precise mathematical functional laws which he can use for prediction from independent variables to dependent variables. For example, learning theorists have long used functional equations. The famous so-called "learning curves" and the equations that underly them are functions—and, of course, relations. The relation in this case is between time or practice, the independent variables (or domains), and correct or incorrect responses, the dependent variables (the ranges). The student, reading the learning theory literature, is in difficulty if he knows nothing about relations and functions.

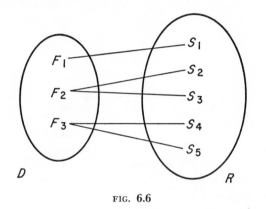

FIG. 6.6

More and more, in fact, social scientists are using sets, relations, and functions in their work. This usage reflects the growth of the social sciences. Though the actual mathematical statements look complex and abstruse to the uninitiated, they are fortunately based on the relatively simple and unambiguous ideas outlined in these chapters. More to the scientific point, they are powerful tools for conceptualizing the foundations of scientific thinking and research and for aiding the discovering and testing of relations.

SOME WAYS TO SHOW RELATIONS

It was said earlier that relations can be expressed in various ways. In the previous discussion, some of these ways were illustrated. One way was simply to list and pair the members of sets. Figures 6.2, 6.3, 6.4, 6.5, and 6.6 illustrate the method. Another way to illustrate a relation is with graphs. Figure 6.1 is an example. Still another way is with equations.

Tables are often convenient ways to show relations. The situation indicated in Fig. 6.4 might be expressed in a table. Here is one table that shows the ordered pairs clearly:

x	Jane	Arthur	Michael	Alberta	Ruth
y	0	1	1	0	0

Here is a simple example from actual research. Newcomb, in studying the acquaintance process, reports a table that epitomizes the relation
between need for affiliation and attitude change.[6] The substantive details
need not concern us here since we are interested only in tables as convenient devices to show relations. Part of Newcomb's table is given in
Table 6.1.

TABLE **6.1**   RELATION BETWEEN NEED FOR AFFILIATION AND ATTITUDE
CHANGE, NEWCOMB STUDY [a]

	Change of Attitude	No Change of Attitude
High Need for Affiliation	6	0
Low Need for Affiliation	2	6

[a] The numbers are the numbers of individuals who exhibited the joint characteristics indicated by the variables on the top and side of the table. For example, 2
individuals with low need for affiliation showed change of attitude.

The table is of course a cross partition or crossbreak. Actually, it
condenses a set of 14 ordered pairs, the first members being individuals
and the second members 1's and 0's. The mapping, or functional rule, is
contained in the intersection of the subsets (the four cells) and their joint
names. For example, the lower left cell is $A_2 \cap B_1$, using the convention
adopted in Chap. 5, A_2 is Low Need for Affiliation, and B_1 is Change of
Attitude. The two individuals who satisfy both these conditions (part of
the rule) are mapped from their domain (containing 14 individuals) on
to $A_2 \cap B_1$, which is part of the range of the four intersections (cells). The
other 12 individuals would be similarly mapped. We have here a relation
that is also a function. In a later chapter we shall examine similar crossbreaks, as well as other kinds of tables that express relations and functions.

It is instructive to examine statistical measures of relation together
with graphs. Suppose we have two sets, X and Y, consisting of scores of
the same individuals on two tests. The scores are:

X	Y
1	1
2	1
2	2
3	3

[6] T. Newcomb, *The Acquaintance Process.* New York: Holt, Rinehart and Winston, Inc., 1961, p. 140.

The two sets form a set of ordered pairs. This set is of course a relation. (Is it a function?) It can also be written, letting R stand for relation $R = \{(1, 1), (2, 1), (2, 2), (3, 3)\}$.

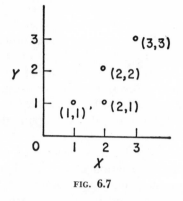

FIG. 6.7

Though we can often get a rough idea of the direction and degree of a relation by inspection of lists of ordered pairs, such a method is imprecise. Graphs, such as those of Figures 6.1 and 6.7, tell us more. It can more easily be "seen" that X values "go along" with Y values: higher values of Y accompany higher values of X, and lower values of Y accompany lower values of X. In this case the relation, or correlation, as it is commonly called, is positive. If we had the equation: $R = \{(1, 3), (2, 1), (2, 2), (3, 1)\}$, the relation would be negative. (The student should plot these values. Note that this relation is not a function because the X value of 2 has two different Y values paired with it. This is easily seen in the graph. A function can never have more than one Y value with each X value.)

If the equation were $R = \{(1, 2), (2, 1), (2, 2), (3, 2)\}$, the relation would be null or zero. This is plotted in Fig. 6.8. It can be seen that Y

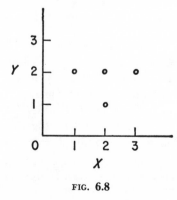

FIG. 6.8

values do not "go along" with X values in any systematic way. This does not mean that there is "no" relation. There is always a relation—by definition—since there is a set of ordered pairs. It is commonly said, however, that there is "no" relation. It is more accurate to say that the relation is null or zero.

Social scientists commonly calculate indices of relation, usually called coefficients of correlation, between sets of ordered pairs in order to obtain more precise estimates of the direction and degree of relations. If one such index, the product-moment coefficient of correlation, or r, is calculated for the ordered pairs of Table 6.7, $r = .85$ is obtained. For the pairs of $R = \{(1, 3), (2, 1), (2, 2), (3, 1)\}$, the relation we said was negative, $r = -.85$. For the pairs of Fig. 6.8, the set of pairs that showed a null or zero relation, $r = 0$.[7]

Product-moment and related coefficients of correlation, then, are based on the concomitant variation of the members of sets of ordered pairs. If they *covary*, vary together—high values with high values, medium values with medium values, and low values with low values, or high values with low values, and so on—it is said that there is a positive or negative relation as the case may be. If they do not covary, it is said there is "no" relation. The most useful such indices range from $+1.00$ through 0 to -1.00, $+1.00$ indicating a perfect positive relation, -1.00 a perfect negative relation, and 0 no discernible relation, or zero relation. Some indices range only from 0 to $+1.00$. Other indices may take on other values.

TABLE 6.2   THREE SETS OF ORDERED PAIRS SHOWING DIFFERENT DIRECTIONS
AND DEGREES OF CORRELATION

(I) $r = 1.00$		(II) $r = -1.00$		(III) $r = 0$	
X	Y	X	Y	X	Y
1	1	1	5	1	2
2	2	2	4	2	5
3	3	3	3	3	3
4	4	4	2	4	1
5	5	5	1	5	4

Most coefficients of relation tell us how similar the rank orders of two sets of measures are. Table 6.2 presents three examples to illustrate this going together of rank orders. The coefficients of correlation are given with each of the sets of ordered pairs. I and II are fairly obvious: the rank orders of the X and Y scores of I go together perfectly. So do the X and Y scores of II, but in the opposite direction. In III, no relation be-

---

[7] Methods of calculating these r's and other coefficients of correlation are discussed in statistics texts. These texts also discuss at greater length than is possible in this book the interpretation of correlation coefficients.

tween the rank orders can be discerned. In I and II, one can predict perfectly from X to Y, but in III one cannot predict values of Y from knowledge of X. Coefficients of correlation are rarely 1.00 or 0. They ordinarily take on intermediate values.

STUDY SUGGESTIONS

1. The following selected references contain excellent discussions of sets, relations, and functions. Students should try to study the pertinent sections of at least two of these books.

   Kershner, R., and L. Wilcox, *The Anatomy of Mathematics*. New York: Ronald, 1950, pp. 41–60. The most abstract and in some ways the most satisfactory of all the references. Its rigorous treatment of sets, relations, and functions is especially good. The text is difficult, however, and is recommended for more advanced students.

   Luchins, A., and E. Luchins, "Variables and Functions," *Psychological Review*, LXI (1954), 315–322. An older, but still useful, notion of functions and relations is discussed.

   Report on the Commission on Mathematics. *Appendices*. New York: College Entrance Examination Board, 1959. This is an excellent reference, with clear, simple exposition. Chapter 2 is highly recommended; Chap. 9 is good. The beginning student should use this and the following reference.

   The Growth of Mathematical Ideas, Grades K–12. Twenty-Fourth Yearbook. Washington, D.C.: The National Council of Teachers of Mathematics, 1959, Chap. 3. This book is very strongly recommended for its excellent presentation, clear exposition, and good examples.

   Little seems to have been written on the applications of sets, relations, and functions to social scientific and educational research. One important work has been written for psychologists: Bush, R., R. Abelson, and R. Hyman, *Mathematics for Psychologists: Examples and Problems*. New York: Social Science Research Council, 1956. Part II is on sets, relations, and functions. This reference is rather difficult, although the range of difficulty is wide. The exposition is also limited. It is, however, interesting and valuable, particularly for psychologists, and can be obtained from the Social Science Research Council.

2. Five examples of relations and/or functions are given below. Assume that the first-named set is the domain and the second the range. Why are all of these relations? Which are functions?

   (a) Book pages and page numbers
   (b) Chapter numbers and pages of a book

(c) Population table headings or categories and population figures in a census report

(d) A class of third-grade children and their arithmetic scores on a standardized test

(e) $y = 2x$

(f) $y > 5 - x$. (*Hint:* Substitute values for x and y and plot some points.)

3. An educational investigator has studied the relation between anxiety and school achievement. Express the relation in set language.

4. The aptitude and achievement scores of 10 children are as follows:

Child	Aptitude	Achievement
1	9	10
2	9	9
3	7	9
4	6	7
5	6	7
6	5	7
7	4	5
8	3	4
9	2	3
10	2	3

(a) What is the direction and approximate magnitude of the relation?

(b) Graph the aptitude and achievement scores. Make aptitude scores X, and achievement scores Y. Judge the direction and magnitude of the relation again.

7 VARIANCE

To study scientific problems and to answer scientific questions, differences among phenomena must be studied. Without differences, without variation, there is no way to determine the relations among variables. Therefore it is necessary to explore the variance notion analytically and in some depth. To do so adequately, it is also necessary to skim some of the cream off the milk of statistics.

Studying sets of numbers as they are is unwieldy. It is usually necessary to reduce the sets in two ways: (1) by computing averages or measures of central tendency, and (2) by computing measures of variability. The measure of central tendency used in this book is the *mean*. The measure of variability most used is the *variance*. Both kinds of measures epitomize sets of scores, but in different ways. They are both "summaries" of whole sets of scores, "summaries" that express two important facets of the sets of scores: their central or average tendency and their variability. Solving research problems without these measures is next to impossible. We start our study of variance, then, with some simple computation.

COMPUTATION OF MEANS AND VARIANCES

Take the set of numbers $X = \{1, 2, 3, 4, 5\}$. The mean is defined:

$$M = \frac{\Sigma X}{n} \tag{7.1}$$

n = the number of cases in the set of scores; Σ means "the sum of" or "add them up." X stands for any one of the scores, that is, each score is an X. The formula, then, says, "Add the scores and divide by the number of cases in the set." Thus:

$$M = \frac{1 + 2 + 3 + 4 + 5}{5} = \frac{15}{5} = 3$$

The mean of the set X is 3.

Computing the variance, while not as simple as computing the mean, is still simple. The formula is:[1]

$$V = \frac{\Sigma x^2}{n} \qquad (7.2)$$

V means variance; n and Σ are the same as in Eq. 7.1. Σx^2 is called the *sum of squares;* it needs some explanation. The scores are listed in a column:

X	x	x^2
1	−2	4
2	−1	1
3	0	0
4	1	1
5	2	4

ΣX: 15

M: 3

Σx^2:   10

In this computation x is a deviation from the mean. It is defined:

$$x = X - M \qquad (7.3)$$

Thus, to obtain x, simply subtract from X the mean of all the scores. For example, when $X = 1$, $x = 1 - 3 = -2$; when $X = 4$, $x = 4 - 3 = 1$; and so on. This has been done above. Equation 7.2, however, says to square each x. This has also been done above. (Remember, that the square of a negative number is always positive.) In other words, Σx^2 tells us to subtract the mean from each score to get x, square each x to get x^2, and then add up the x^2's. Finally, the average of the x^2's is taken by dividing Σx^2 by n, the number of cases. Σx^2, the *sum of squares,* is a very important statistic which we will use often.

The variance, in the present case, is

$$V = \frac{(-2)^2 + (-1)^2 + (0)^2 + (1)^2 + (2)^2}{5} = \frac{4 + 1 + 0 + 1 + 4}{5} = \frac{10}{5} = 2$$

The variance is also called the *mean square* (when it is calculated in a slightly different way which we take up in a future chapter). It is called this because, obviously, it is the mean of the x^2's. Clearly it is not difficult to compute the mean and the variance.[2]

---

[1] "V" will be used for "variance" in this book. Other symbols commonly used are σ^2 and s^2. It is not necessary to go into their usage here. In this text, N is used for the number of cases in U, whereas n is used for the number of cases in a subset or sample of U. Appropriate subscripts will be added and explained as necessary. For example, if we wish to indicate the number of elements in the set A, a subset of U, we can write n_A or n_a. Similarly we attach subscripts to x, V, and so on. When double subscripts are used, such as r_{xy}, the meaning will usually be obvious.

[2] The method of computing the variance used in this chapter differs from the

The question is: Why compute the mean and the variance? The rationale for computing the mean is easily disposed of. In research, means of different experimental groups are compared to study relations. We may be testing the relation between teaching methods and achievement, for instance. We may have used three methods of teaching and may be interested in the question of which method has the greatest effect on achievement. In such cases means are customarily compared. For instance, of three groups, treated by Methods A_1, A_2, and A_3, which has the greatest mean on, say, a standardized achievement test?

The rationale for computing and using the variance in research is more difficult to explain. In the usual case of ordinary scores the variance is a measure of the dispersion of the set of scores. It tells us how much the scores are spread out. If a group of pupils is very heterogeneous in reading achievement, then the variance of their reading scores will be large compared to the variance of a group that is homogeneous in reading achievement. The variance, then, is a measure of the spread of the scores; it is a description of the extent to which the scores differ from each other.[3] The remainder of this chapter and later parts of the book will explore other aspects of the use of the variance statistic.

KINDS OF VARIANCE

Variances come in a number of forms. When you read the research and technical literature, you will frequently come across the term sometimes with a qualifying adjective, sometimes not. To understand the literature, it is necessary to have a good idea of the characteristics and purposes of these different variances. And to design and do research, one must have a rather thorough understanding of the variance concept as well as considerable mastery of statistical variance notions and manipulations.

A goodly part of statistics consists in comparing variances. In order to get answers to research questions, in order to test research hypotheses, different kinds of variance are compared. Take a simple example. A teacher has two classes that he knows are approximately equal in arith-

---

methods ordinarily used. In fact, the method given above is impracticable in most situations. Our purpose is not to learn statistics, as such. Rather, we are pursuing basic ideas. Methods of computation, examples, and demonstrations have been constructed to aid this pursuit of basic ideas. The student should therefore *not* learn the computational methods of this chapter.

[3] For descriptive purposes, the square root of the variance is ordinarily used. It is called the *standard deviation*. Because of certain mathematical properties, however, the variance is more useful in research. It is suggested that the student supplement his study with study of appropriate sections of an elementary statistics text, since it will not be possible in this book to discuss all the facets of meaning and interpretation of means, variances, and standard deviations. Two good elementary texts for this purpose are: A. Edwards, *Statistical Analysis,* rev. ed. New York: Holt, Rinehart and Winston, Inc., 1958; S. Diamond, *Information and Error.* New York: Basic Books, 1959.

metic ability, that is, the means of the classes are approximately equal. The teacher thinks, however, that the classes differ considerably in variability. He can easily check his belief by computing the variances of both classes and then dividing the smaller variance into the larger variance. If the result of this operation is large—"large" means considerably greater than 1—then his belief is substantiated. If the ratio is small, then his belief is not substantiated. From this simple beginning the comparison of variances gets very elaborate indeed, as we will see.

Population and Sample Variances   The *population variance* is the variance of U, a universe or population of measures. If all the measures of a defined universal set, U, are known, then the variance is known. More likely, however, all the measures of U are not available. In such cases the variance is estimated by computing the variance of one or more samples of U. A good deal of statistical energy goes into this important problem. A question may arise: How variable is the intelligence of the citizens of the United States? This is a U or population question. If there were a complete list of all the millions of people in the United States—and there were also a complete list of intelligence test scores of these people— the variance could be easily if wearily computed. No such list exists. So samples—hopefully representative samples—of Americans are tested and means and variances computed. The samples are used to estimate the mean and variance of the whole population.

Sampling variance is the variance of statistics computed from samples. If four random samples are drawn from a population and the means of the samples are computed, the means will differ. If the sampling is truly random and the samples are large enough, the computed means of the four samples should not vary too much. That is, the *variance of the means* should be relatively small.[4]

Systematic Variance   Perhaps the most general way to classify variances is as *systematic variance* and *error variance*. *Systematic variance* is the variation in measures due to some known or unknown influences that

---

[4] Unfortunately, in much actual research only one sample is usually available— and this one sample is frequently rather small. We can, however, estimate the sampling variance of the means very simply by using what is called the *standard variance of the mean(s)*. (The term "standard error of the mean" is usually used. The standard error of the mean is simply the square root of the standard variance of the mean.) The formula is

$$V_M = \frac{V_s}{n_s}$$

where V_M is the standard variance of the mean, V_s the variance of the sample, and n_s the size of the sample.

Notice an important conclusion that can be reached from this equation. If the size of the sample is increased, V_M is decreased. In other words, to be quite sure that the sample is close to the population mean, make n very large. Conversely, the smaller the sample, the riskier the estimate.

"cause" the scores to lean in one direction more than another. Any natural or man-made influences that "cause" events to happen in a certain predictable way are systematic influences. The achievement test scores of the children in a wealthy suburban school will tend to be *systematically* higher than the achievement test scores of the children in a city slum area school. Expert teaching may systematically influence the achievement of children—as compared to the achievement of children taught inexpertly.

"Fair" dice will turn up all the numbers 1 through 6 about equally often. Loaded dice, on the other hand, lean in one direction systematically: certain numbers will turn up more often than other numbers. Similarly, marked cards and crooked roulette wheels show systematic variance.

There are many, many causes of systematic variance. The scientist seeks to separate those in which he is interested from those in which he is not interested. And he must also separate from his systematic variances, as we shall see, variance that is random. Indeed, research may narrowly and technically be defined as controlled study of variances.

Between-Groups (Experimental) Variance The type of systematic variance most important in research is between-groups or experimental variance. *Between-groups* or *experimental variance,* as the name indicates, is the variance that reflects systematic differences between groups of measures. The variance discussed previously as score variance reflects the differences between individuals in a group. We can say, for instance, that, on the basis of present evidence and current tests, the variance in intelligence of a random sample of eleven-year-old children is about 225 IQ points.[5] This figure is a statistic that tells us how much the individuals differ from each other. Experimental variance, on the other hand, is the variance due to the differences between *groups* of individuals. It is often called "between-groups" variance. If the achievement of northern and southern children in comparable schools is measured, there would be differences between the northern and southern groups. Groups as well as individuals differ or vary, and it is perfectly possible and appropriate to compute the variance between these groups.

Between-groups variance and experimental variance are fundamentally the same. Both arise from differences between groups. Between-groups variance is a term that covers all cases of systematic differences between groups, experimental and nonexperimental. Experimental variance is usually associated with the variance engendered by active manipulation of independent variables by experimenters. In this book the term "between groups" will most often be used. It will be clear from the con-

[5] This is computed simply by squaring the known standard deviation reported in a test manual. The standard deviation of the California Test of Mental Maturity for eleven-year-old children is about 15, and $15^2 = 225$.

text of future discussions whether experimental manipulation is or is not involved.[6]

Here is a simple example of between-groups—in this case experimental—variance. Suppose an investigator tests the relative efficacies of three different methods of teaching a physical education skill. After teaching three groups of children, each group being taught by a different method, he computes the means of the groups. Suppose that they are 30, 23, and 19. The mean of the three means is 24, and we calculate the variance *between the means* or *between the groups:*

		x	x^2
	30	6	36
	23	-1	1
	19	-5	25
$\Sigma X:$	72		
$M:$	24		
$\Sigma x^2:$			62

$$V_b = \frac{62}{3} = 20.67$$

In other words, the three means are treated as three scores, and their variance is calculated as before. This variance between groups (V_b) is an index of the variability of the three group means, or the variability of the three groups taken as wholes. Later we will see how V_b is used.

In the methods experiment just described, presumably the methods tend to "bias" the achievement scores one way or another. This is, of course, the experimenter's purpose: he wants Method A, say, to increase all the achievement scores of an experimental group. He may believe that Method B will have no effect on achievement, and that Method C will have a depressing effect. If he is correct, the scores under Method A should all tend to go up, whereas under Method C they should all tend to go down. Thus the scores of the groups, as wholes—and, of course, their means—differ systematically. Methods is an *active* variable, a variable deliberately manipulated by the experimenter with the conscious intent to "bias" the scores differentially. Thus any experimenter-manipulated variables are intimately associated with systematic variance. When Hurlock differentially reinforced her experimental groups of children by praising one group, reproving another, ignoring another, and doing nothing to still another, she was deliberately attempting to build systematic variance into her outcome measures.[7]

6 Even nonexperimental variance can be called experimental variance. For example, suppose in a methods experiment we split a group in two on the basis of intelligence. The between-groups intelligence variance can be called experimental variance.

7 E. Hurlock, "An Evaluation of Certain Incentives Used in Schoolwork," *Journal of Educational Psychology,* XVI (1925), 145–149.

The basic idea behind the famous "classical design" of scientific research, in which experimental and control groups are used, is that, through careful control and manipulation, the experimental group's outcome measures (also called "criterion measures") are made to vary systematically, to all go up or down together, while the control group's measures are ordinarily held at the same level. The variance, of course, is between the two groups, that is, the two groups are made to differ. For example, in an interesting little experiment on arithmetic readiness in the kindergarten child, Koenker manipulated experimental groups by giving them an enriched-numbers and arithmetic-concepts program.[8] He held his control groups constant or at the same level by not giving them a readiness program, by letting them have the regular kindergarten program "without enrichment." Statistically speaking, he was trying to increase the between-groups variance. (He succeeded.)

This is clear and easy to see in experiments. In research that is not experimental, in research where already existing differences between groups are studied, it is not always so clear and easy to see that one is studying between-groups variance. But the idea is the same. The principle may be stated in a somewhat different way: The greater the differences between groups, the more an independent variable or variables can be presumed to have operated. If there is no or little difference between groups, on the other hand, then the presumption must be that an independent variable or variables have not operated, that their effects are too weak to be noticed, or that their influences have canceled each other out. If, for example, the achievement scores of two or three classes are the same or nearly the same, then one or more of these presumptions can be made. We judge the effects of independent variables that have been manipulated or that have worked in the past, then, by between-groups variance. It makes no difference whether the independent variables have or have not been manipulated. The principle is the same.

To illustrate the principle, we can go back to the example of anxiety and school achievement discussed earlier. It is possible to manipulate anxiety by having two experimental groups and inducing anxiety in one and not in the other. This can be done by giving each group the same test with different instructions. We tell the members of one group that their grades depend wholly on the test. We tell the members of the other group that the test does not matter particularly, that its outcome will not affect grades. On the other hand, the relation between anxiety and achievement may also be studied by comparing groups of individuals on whom it can be assumed that different environmental and psychological circumstances have acted to produce anxiety. (Of course, the experimentally induced anxiety and the already existing anxiety—the stimulus variable and the organismic variable—are not assumed to be the same.) A study to test the hypothesis that different environmental and psychological circumstances act to produce different levels of anxiety has been done by Sarnoff, *et al.*[9] The investigators predicted that, as a result of the English 11-plus examinations, English school children would exhibit greater test anxiety than would American school children. In the language of this chapter, the investigators hypothesized a between-groups variance larger than could be expected by chance because of the differences between English and American environmental, educational, and psychological conditions. (The hypothesis was supported.)

Error Variance   It is probably safe to say that the most ubiquitous kind of variance in research is error variance. *Error variance* is the fluctuation or varying of measures due to chance. Error variance is random variance. It is the variation in measures due to the usually small and self-compensating fluctuations of measures—now here, now there; now up, now down. The sampling variance discussed earlier in the chapter, for example, is random or error variance.

Reasoning along the lines of the discussion of randomness of Part I, it can be said that error variance is the variance in measures due to ignorance. Imagine the great dictionary described in Chap. 4 in which everything in the world—every occurrence, every event, every little thing, every great thing—is given in complete detail. To understand any event that has occurred, that is now occurring, or that will occur, all one needs to do is look it up in the dictionary. With this dictionary there are obviously no random or chance occurrences. Everything is accounted for. In brief, there is no error variance; all is systematic variance.

Unfortunately—or more likely, fortunately—we do not have such a dictionary. Many, many events and occurrences cannot be explained. Much variance eludes identification and control. This is error variance—at least as long as identification and control elude us.

While seemingly strange and even a bit bizarre, this mode of reasoning is useful, provided we remember that some of the error variance of today may not be the error variance of tomorrow. Suppose that we do an experiment on teaching methods in which we assign pupils to three groups at random. After we finish the experiment, we study the differences between the three groups to see if the methods have had an effect. We know that the scores will always show minor fluctuations, now plus a point or two or three, now minus a point or two or three, which we can probably never control. Something or other makes these scores fluctuate in this fashion. According to the view under discussion, they do not just fluctuate for no reason, there is probably no "absolute randomness." As-

---

[9] I. Sarnoff, *et. al.*, "A Cross-Cultural Study of Anxiety among American and English School Children," *Journal of Educational Psychology*, XLIX (1958), 129–136. Also reported in S. Sarason, *et. al.*, *Anxiety in Elementary School Children*. New York: Wiley, 1960, pp. 151–157.

suming determinism, there must be some cause or causes for the fluctuations. True, we can learn some of them and possibly control them. When we do this, however, we have systematic variance.

We find out, for instance, that sex "causes" the scores to fluctuate, since boys and girls are mixed in the experimental groups. (We are, of course, talking figuratively here. Obviously sex does not make scores fluctuate.) So we do the experiment and control sex by using, say, only boys. The scores still fluctuate, though to a somewhat lesser extent. We remove another presumed cause of the perturbations: intelligence. The scores still fluctuate, though to a still lesser extent. We go on removing such sources of variance. We are controlling systematic variance. We are also gradually identifying and controlling more and more unknown variance.

Now note that before we controlled or removed these systematic variances, before we "knew" about them, we would have to label all such variance error variance—partly through ignorance, partly through inability to do anything about such variance. We could go on and on doing this and still there would be variance left over. Finally we give in; we "know" no more; we have done all we can. There will still be variance. A practical definition of error variance, then, would be: *Error variance* is the variance left over in a set of measures after all known sources of systematic variance have been removed from the measures. This is so important it deserves a numerical example.

An Example of Systematic and Error Variance   Suppose a teacher is interested in knowing whether writing critical comments on student essays, in addition to assigning grades, is more effective in improving subsequent student writing than merely assigning grades.[10] Call "critical comments" and "no critical comments" the variable A, divided into A_1 and A_2. The teacher assigns ten students at random to two groups and assigns treatments A_1 and A_2 at random. She gives a written assignment and follows the procedure indicated. A week later she gives a similar assignment and grades the papers. The scores are as follows:

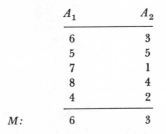

	A_1	A_2
	6	3
	5	5
	7	1
	8	4
	4	2
M:	6	3

10 This little example is a miniature experiment modeled after Page's much larger experiment: E. Page, "Teacher Comments and Student Performance: A Seventy-Four Classroom Experiment in School Motivation," *Journal of Educational Psychology,* XLIX (1958), 173–181.

A_1 is the critical comments-plus-grades group, A_2 the grades-only group. The means are different; they vary. Thus there is between-groups variance. Computing it just as we did with an earlier example, we get:

	x	x^2
6	1.5	2.25
3	−1.5	2.25
$M:$ 4.5		
$\Sigma x^2:$		4.50

$$V_b = \frac{4.50}{2} = 2.25$$

In other words, we calculate the between-groups variance just as we earlier calculated the variance of the five scores 1, 2, 3, 4, and 5. We simply treat the two means as though they were individual scores, and go ahead with an ordinary variance calculation. The between-groups variance, V_b, is, then, 2.25. An appropriate statistical test would show that the difference between the means of the two groups is what is called a "statistically significant" difference. (The meaning of this will be taken up in another chapter.)[11]

If we put the 10 scores in a column and calculate the variance, we obtain:

X	x	x^2
6	1.5	2.25
5	.5	.25
7	2.5	6.25
8	3.5	12.25
4	− .5	.25
3	−1.5	2.25
5	.5	.25
1	−3.5	12.25
4	− .5	.25
2	−2.5	6.25
$M:$ 4.5		
$\Sigma x^2:$		42.50

$$V_t = \frac{42.50}{10} = 4.25$$

[11] The method of computation used here is *not* what would be used to test statistical significance. It is used here purely as a pedagogical device. Note, too, that the small numbers of cases in the examples given and the small size of the numbers are used only for simplicity of demonstration. Actual research data, of course, are usually more complex, and many more cases are needed.

This is the total variance, V_t. $V_t = 4.25$ contains all sources of variation in the scores. We already know that one of these is the between-groups variance, $V_b = 2.25$. Let us compute still another variance. We do this by computing the variance of A_1 alone and the variance of A_2 alone and then averaging the two:

A_1	x	x^2	A_2	x	x^2
6	0	0	3	0	0
5	−1	1	5	2	4
7	1	1	1	2	4
8	2	4	4	1	1
4	−2	4	2	−1	1

ΣX:	30		15		
M:	6		3		
Σx^2:		10			10

$$V_{A_1} = \frac{10}{5} = 2 \qquad\qquad V_{A_2} = \frac{10}{5} = 2$$

The variance of A_1 is 2, and the variance of A_2 is 2. The average of these two is 2. Since each of these variances was computed *separately* and then *averaged*, we call the average variance computed from them the "within-groups variance." We label this variance V_w, meaning within variance, or within-groups variance. Thus $V_w = 2$. It is important to note here that this variance is unaffected by the difference between the two means.[12]

Now write an equation: $V_t = V_b + V_w$. This equation says that the total variance is made up of the variance between the groups and the variance within the groups. Is it? Substitute the numerical values: $4.25 = 2.25 + 2.00$. Our methods works—it shows us, too, that these variances are additive.

The variance ideas under discussion can perhaps be clarified with a diagram. In Fig. 7.1, a circle broken up into two parts has been drawn. Let the area of the total circle represent the total variance of the 10 scores, or V_t. The larger shaded portion represents the between-groups variance, or V_b. The smaller unshaded portion represents the error variance, or V_w or V_e. From the diagram one can see that $V_t = V_b + V_e$. (Note the similarity to set thinking and the operation of union.)

A measure of all sources of variance is represented by V_t and a measure of the between-groups variance (or a measure of the effect of the experimental treatment) by V_b. Evidently, the adding of critical comments to the papers of the A_1 group "caused" the scores on subsequent A_1 individuals' papers to rise. But what is V_w, the within-groups vari-

[12] This is easily shown by subtracting a constant of 3 from the scores of A_1. This makes the mean of A_1 equal to 3. Then, if the variance of A_1 is computed, it will be the same as before: 2. Obviously the within-groups variance will be the same: 2.

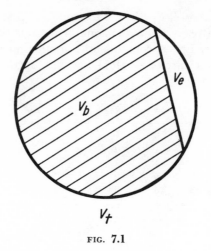

V_t

FIG. **7.1**

ance? Since, of the total variance, we have accounted for a known source of variance, via the between-groups variance, we assume that the variance remaining is due to chance or random factors. We call it error variance. But, you may say, surely there must be other sources of variance? How about individual differences in intelligence, sex, and so on? Since the teacher assigned the students to the experimental groups at random, we assume that these sources of variance are equally, or approximately equally, distributed between A_1 and A_2. And because of the random assignment we cannot isolate and identify any other sources of variance. So we call the variance remaining error variance, knowing full well that there are probably other sources of variance but assuming, and hoping our assumption is correct, that they have been equally distributed between the two groups.

A Subtractive Demonstration: Removing Between-Groups Variance from Total Variance   Let us demonstrate all this another way by removing from the original set of scores the between-groups variance, using a simple subtractive procedure. First, we let each of the means of A_1 and A_2 be equal to the total mean. The total mean is 4.5. (See above where the mean of all 10 scores was computed.) Second, we adjust each individual score of A_1 and A_2 by subtracting or adding, as the case may be, an appropriate constant. Since the mean of A_1 is 6, $6 - 4.5 = 1.5$ is the constant to be *subtracted* from each A_1 score. The mean of A_2 is 3. Therefore we add $4.5 - 3 = 1.5$ to each of the A_2 scores.

Study the "corrected" scores. Compare them with the original scores. Note that they vary less than they did before. Naturally. We removed the between-groups variance, a sizeable portion of the total variance. The variance that remains is that portion of the total variance due, presum-

Correction:	− 1.5	+ 1.5
	A_1	A_2
	$6 - 1.5 = 4.5$	$3 + 1.5 = 4.5$
	$5 - 1.5 = 3.5$	$5 + 1.5 = 6.5$
	$7 - 1.5 = 5.5$	$1 + 1.5 = 2.5$
	$8 - 1.5 = 6.5$	$4 + 1.5 = 5.5$
	$4 - 1.5 = 2.5$	$2 + 1.5 = 3.5$
ΣX:	22.5	22.5
M:	4.5	4.5

ably, to chance. We compute the variance of the "corrected" scores of A_1, A_2, and the total, and note these surprising results:

A_1	x	x^2	A_2	x	x^2
4.5	0	0	4.5	0	0
3.5	−1	1	6.5	2	4
5.5	1	1	2.5	−2	4
6.5	2	4	5.5	1	1
2.5	−2	4	3.5	−1	1
ΣX: 22.5			22.5		
M: 4.5			4.5		
Σx^2:		10			10

$$V_{A_1} = \frac{10}{5} = 2 \qquad\qquad V_{A_2} = \frac{10}{5} = 2$$

The within-groups variance is the same as before. It is unaffected by the correction operation. Obviously the between-groups variance is now zero. What about the total variance, V_t? Computing it, we obtain $\Sigma x_t^2 = 20$, and $V_t = 20/10 = 2$. Thus the within-groups variance is now equal to the total variance. The reader should study this example carefully until he has firmly grasped what has happened and *why*.

Although the previous example is perhaps sufficient to make the essential points, it may solidify the student's understanding of these basic variance ideas if we extend the example by putting in and pulling out another source of variance. The reader may recall that we knew that the within-groups variance contained variation due to individual differences. Now assume that, instead of randomly assigning all the students to the two groups, the teacher had matched the students on intelligence—and intelligence was related to the criterion measure. That is, she put into the two groups members of pairs with IQ's approximately equal. The outcome of the experiment might be:

	A_1	A_2
	6	3
	5	1
	7	4
	4	2
	8	5
M:	6	3

Note carefully that the *only* difference between this setup and the previous one is that the matching has caused the scores to covary: the A_1 and A_2 measures have nearly the same rank order now. In fact, the coefficient of correlation between the two sets of scores is .90. We have here another source of variance: that due to individual differences in intelligence which is reflected in the rank order of the pairs of criterion measures. (The precise relation between the rank order and matching ideas and their effects on variance will be taken up in another chapter. The student should take it on faith for the present that matching produces systematic variance.)

This variance can be computed and pulled out as before, except that there is an additional operation. First equalize the A_1 and A_2 means and "correct" the scores as before. This yields:

Correction:	-1.5	$+1.5$
	A_1	A_2
	4.5	4.5
	3.5	2.5
	5.5	5.5
	2.5	3.5
	6.5	6.5
M:	4.5	4.5

Second, by equalizing the rows (making each *row* mean equal to 4.5 and "correcting" the row scores accordingly) we find the following data:

Correction:	A_1	A_2	Original Means	Corrected Means
0	$4.5 + 0 \ = 4.5$	$4.5 + 0 \ = 4.5$	4.5	4.5
$+1.5$	$3.5 + 1.5 = 5.0$	$2.5 + 1.5 = 4.0$	3.0	4.5
-1.0	$5.5 - 1.0 = 4.5$	$5.5 - 1.0 = 4.5$	5.5	4.5
$+1.5$	$2.5 + 1.5 = 4.0$	$3.5 + 1.5 = 5.0$	3.0	4.5
-2.0	$6.5 - 2.0 = 4.5$	$6.5 - 2.0 = 4.5$	6.5	4.5
M:	4.5	4.5		$M_t = 4.5$

The doubly corrected measures now show very little variance. The computed variance of the ten doubly corrected scores is .10, very small indeed. There is no between-groups (columns) or between-individuals (rows) variance left in the measures, of course. After double correction, all of the total variance is error variance. (As we will see later, when the variances of both columns and rows are extracted like this—although with a quicker and more efficient method—there is no within-groups variance.)

This has been a long operation. A brief recapitulation of the main points may be useful. Any set of measures has a total variance. If the measures from which this variance is computed have been derived from the responses of human beings, then there will always be at least two sources of variance. One will be due to systematic sources of variation like individual differences of the subjects whose characteristics or accomplishments have been measured and differences between the groups or subgroups involved in research. The other will be due to chance or random error, fluctuations of measures that cannot be accounted for. Sources of systematic variance tend to make scores lean in one direction or another. This is reflected in differences in means, of course. If sex is a systematic source of variance in a study of school achievement, for instance, then the sex variable will tend to act in such a manner that the achievement scores of girls will tend to be higher than those of boys. Sources of random error, on the other hand, tend to make measures fluctuate now this way now that way. Random errors, in other words, are self-compensating; they tend to balance each other out.

In any experiment or study, the independent variable (or variables) is a source of systematic variance—at least it should be. The researcher "wants" the experimental groups to differ systematically. He usually seeks to maximize such variance while controlling or minimizing other sources of variance, both systematic and error. The experimental example given above illustrates the additional idea that these variances are additive, and that because of this additive property, it is possible to analyze a set of scores into systematic and error variance.

COMPONENTS OF VARIANCE

The discussion so far may have convinced the student that any total variance has what will be called "components of variance." The case just considered, however, included one experimental component, A_1 and A_2, one component due to individual differences, and a third component due to random error. We will now study the case of two components of systematic experimental variance. To do this, we will synthesize the experimental measures, creating them from *known* variance components. We will go backwards, in other words. Because we shall start from "known" sources of variance, from "known" scores, there will be no error in the synthesized scores.

We have a variable X which has three values. Let $X = \{0, 1, 2\}$. We also have another variable Y, which has three values. Let $Y = \{0, 2, 4\}$. X and Y, then, are *known* sources of variance. We assume an ideal experimental situation where there are two independent variables acting *in concert* to produce effects on a dependent variable, Z. That is, each score of X operates with each score of Y to produce a dependent-variable score Z. For example, the X score, 0, has no influence. The X score, 1, operates with Y as follows: $\{(1 + 0), (1 + 2), (1 + 4)\}$. Similarly, the X score, 2, operates with Y: $\{(2 + 0), (2 + 2), (2 + 4)\}$. All this is easier to see if we generate Z in clear view, as in the following matrix:

			Y					Z	
		0	2	4			0	2	4
	0	$0+0$	$0+2$	$0+4$		0	0	2	4
X	1	$1+0$	$1+2$	$1+4$	$=$	1	1	3	5
	2	$2+0$	$2+2$	$2+4$		2	2	4	6

The set of scores in the 3×3 matrix (a matrix is any rectangular set or array of numbers) is the set of Z scores. The purpose of this example will be lost unless the reader remembers that in practice we do *not* know the X and Y scores; we only know the Z scores. We are assuming that we know X and Y. In actual experimental situations we manipulate or set up X and Y. But we only hope they are effective. They may not be. In other words, the sets $X = \{0, 1, 2\}$ and $Y = \{0, 2, 4\}$ can never be known like this. The best we can do is to estimate their influences by estimating the amount of variance in Z due to X and to Y.

The sets X and Y have the following variances:

	X	x	x^2		Y	y	y^2
	0	-1	1		0	-2	4
	1	0	0		2	0	0
	2	1	1		4	2	4
$\Sigma X:$	3				6		
$M:$	1				2		
$\Sigma x^2:$			2				8

$$V_x = \frac{2}{3} = .67 \qquad\qquad V_y = \frac{8}{3} = 2.67$$

The set Z has variance as follows:

Z	z	z^2
0	−3	9
2	−1	1
4	1	1
1	−2	4
3	0	0
5	2	4
2	−1	1
4	1	1
6	3	9

ΣX: 27

M: 3

Σx^2: 30

$$V_z = \frac{30}{9} = 3.33$$

Now .67 + 2.67 = 3.34, or $V_z = V_x + V_y$, within errors of rounding.

This example illustrates that, under certain conditions, variances operate additively to produce the experimental measures we analyze. While the example is "pure" and therefore unrealistic, it is not at all unreasonable. It is possible to think of X and Y as independent variables. They might be intelligence and motivation. And Z might be school achievement, a dependent variable. That real scores do not behave in exactly this way does not alter the idea. They behave in approximately this way. We plan research to make this principle as true as possible, and we analyze data as though it were true. And it works!

COVARIANCE

Covariance is really nothing new. Recall, in an earlier discussion of sets and correlation, that we talked about the relation between two or more variables being analogous to the intersection of sets. Let X be $\{0, 1, 2, 3\}$, a set of intelligence measures of four children. Let Y be $\{1, 2, 3, 4\}$, a set of achievement measures of the same children, but not in the same order. Let R be a set of ordered pairs of the elements of X and Y, the rule of pairing being: each individual's intelligence and achievement measures are paired, with the intelligence measure placed first. Assume that this yields $R = \{(0, 2), (1, 1), (2, 3), (3, 4)\}$. By our previous definition of relation, this set of ordered pairs is a relation, in this case the relation between X and Y. The results of the computation of the variance of X and the variance of Y are:

X	x	x^2	Y	y	y^2
0	-1.5	2.25	2	$-.5$	.25
1	$-.5$	.25	1	-1.5	2.25
2	.5	.25	3	.5	.25
3	1.5	2.25	4	1.5	2.25

ΣX:	6		10		
M:	1.5		2.5		
Σx^2:		5.00			5.00

$$V_x = \frac{5}{4} = 1.25 \qquad\qquad V_y = \frac{5}{4} = 1.25$$

We now set ourselves a problem. (Note carefully in what follows that we are going to work with deviations from the mean, x's and y's, and not with the original raw scores.) We have computed the variances of X and Y above by using the x's and y's, that is, the deviations from the respective means of X and Y. If we can compute the variance of any set of scores, is it not possible to compute the relationship *between* any two sets of scores in a similar way? Is it conceivable that we can compute the variance of the two sets simultaneously? And if we do so, will this be a measure of the variance of the two sets together? Will this variance also be a measure of the relationship between the two sets?

What we want to do is to use some statistical operation analogous to the set operation of intersection, $X \cap Y$. To compute the variance of X or of Y, we squared the deviations from the mean, the x's or the y's, and then added and averaged them. A natural answer to our problem is to perform an analogous operation on the x's and y's *together*. To compute the variance of X, we did this first: $(x_1 \cdot x_1), \cdots, (x_4 \cdot x_4) = x_1^2$, $\cdots, x_4^2$. Why, then, not follow this through with *both* x's and y's, multiplying the ordered pairs like this: $(x_1 \cdot y_1), \cdots, (x_4 \cdot y_4)$? Then, instead of writing Σx^2 or Σy^2, we write Σxy, as follows:

x	$\cdot$	y	$=$	xy
-1.5	$\cdot$	$-.5$	$=$	.75
$-.5$	$\cdot$	-1.5	$=$	.75
.5	$\cdot$	.5	$=$	.25
1.5	$\cdot$	1.5	$=$	2.25

$$\Sigma xy = 4.00$$

$$V_{xy} = CoV_{xy} = \frac{4}{4} = 1.00$$

If we compute the variance of these products—symbolized as V_{xy} or CoV_{xy}—we obtain 1.00, as indicated above. This 1.00, then, can be taken as an index of the relation between the two sets. But it is an unsatisfactory index because its size fluctuates with the ranges and scales of different X's and Y's. That is, it might be 1.00 in this case and 8.75 in another case, making comparisons from case to case difficult and unwieldy.

Before going further, let us give names to Σxy and V_{xy}. Σxy is called the *cross product,* or the sum of the cross products. V_{xy} is called the *co-variance.* We will write it CoV with suitable subscripts. Returning to the problem, we need a measure that is comparable from problem to problem. Such a measure—an excellent one, too—is obtained simply by writing a fraction or ratio: the covariance, CoV_{xy}, divided by an average of the variances of X and Y. The average usually taken is the square root of the product of V_x and V_y. The whole formula for our index of relationship, then, is

$$R = \frac{CoV_{xy}}{\sqrt{V_x \cdot V_y}}$$

This is one form of the well-known, product-moment coefficient of correlation. Computing it for our little problem, we obtain

$$R = \frac{1.00}{\sqrt{(1.25)\,(1.25)}} = \frac{1.00}{1.25} = .80$$

This index, usually written r, can range from $+1.00$ through 0 to -1.00, as we learned in Chap. 6.

So we have another important source of variation in sets of scores, provided the set elements, the X's and Y's, have been ordered into pairs after conversion into deviation scores. The variation is aptly called *co-variance* and is a measure of the relation between the sets of scores.

It can be seen that the definition of relation as a set of ordered pairs leads to several ways to define the relation of the above example:

$$R = \{(x, y); \ x \text{ and } y \text{ are numbers, } x \text{ always coming first}\}$$

$$xRy = \text{the same as above}$$
$$\text{or "}x \text{ is related to } y\text{"}$$

$$R = \{(0, 2), (1, 1), (2, 3), (3, 4)\}$$

$$R = \{(-1.5, -.5), (-.5, -1.5), (.5, .5), (1.5, 1.5)\}$$

$$R_{xy} = \frac{CoV_{xy}}{\sqrt{V_x \cdot V_y}} = \frac{1.00}{1.25} = .80$$

COMMON FACTOR VARIANCE

The previous discussion of covariance and correlation leads naturally to another expression used a great deal in statistics and research: *common factor variance.* Common factor variance is the variance shared by two or more variables. The term *factor* is a construct used to indicate a common entity or influence present in different variables. In brief, a factor is a source of variance common to two or more variables. Common factor variance will be symbolized: V_{co}. If only two variables, A and B, are under study, and if certain operations are performed, then the common factor variance is covariance. The operations alluded to involve too much statistics so we will tackle the problem another way. If a coefficient of correlation has been computed, then the common factor variance is the coefficient of correlation squared. Squaring the coefficient computed in the previous section, for example, yields $.80^2 = .64$. This number now has a direct meaning. It means that 64 percent of the variance of B is shared in common with A, or vice versa.[13]

Assume that $r = 1.00$. (We change R to r, the usual symbol for the coefficient of correlation.) Then $r^2 = 1.00$, and all the variance of the sets A and B is common factor variance. The same is true if $r = -1.00$, since $(-1.)^2 = 1$. Now assume that $r = .00$. Then, obviously, there is no variance common to the two variables. If we let $V(A)$ equal the variance of the set A, and $V(B)$ equal the variance of the set B, then $V(A \cap B)$ equals the variance common to the two sets or variables. In this case $V(A \cap B) = 0$, or $A \cap B = E$, the empty set.

Venn diagrams to illustrate $r = .00$ and $r = 1.00$ would show the extreme possibilities of set intersection. With $r = .00$, the two sets do not intersect; there would be no overlapping or common area. No variance is shared by A and B. With $r = 1.00$ (or $r = -1.00$), the two sets intersect completely, that is, there is complete overlapping or common area— virtual identity. The variances of A and B are one and the same.

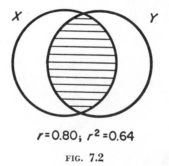

$r = 0.80; \; r^2 = 0.64$

FIG. 7.2

Now take the case above where $r_{xy} = .80$ and $r_{xy}^2 = .64$, or 64 percent. We attempt to show the percentage of variance shared in common

[13] The squared coefficient of correlation is called the *coefficient of determination*. If the two correlated variables are A and B, it indicates the percentage of variance in B associated with or "determined by" the variance in A. For a discussion of the coefficient of determination, see J. Guilford, *Fundamental Statistics in Psychology and Education*, 3d ed. New York: McGraw-Hill, 1956, pp. 378, 379.

by the two variables (Fig. 7.2).[14] If $r = .90$, then $r^2 = .81$, or 81 percent (Fig. 7.3). On the other hand, take a contrasting case of little shared variance, $r = .30$ and $r^2 = .09$, or 9 percent (Fig. 7.4).

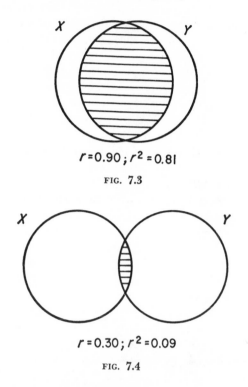

$r = 0.90 ; r^2 = 0.81$

FIG. 7.3

$r = 0.30 ; r^2 = 0.09$

FIG. 7.4

This reasoning can be applied to more than two variables. Assume that we have three variables A, B, and C. Let these variables be represented by the sets A, B, and C. Further, $r_{ab} = .70$, $r_{ac} = .60$, and $r_{bc} = .60$. Then $r_{ab}^2 = .49$, $r_{ac}^2 = .36$, and $r_{bc}^2 = .36$. This is approximately depicted in Fig. 7.5.

Consider the sets A and B and $A \cap B$, just as we did before. Note that about half the areas of the A and B circles are shared ($r_{ab}^2 = .49$). Now consider A and C and $A \cap C$ separately. Here the shared area is 36 percent. Sets B, C, and $B \cap C$ are interpreted in the same manner. If we had only the sets (variables) A and B, then the common factor variance would be $A \cap B$, and similarly for A and C considered apart from B, and B and C considered apart from A. But now we have an area of the three

[14] It should be noted that Venn circles usually do not represent actual areas: they are diagrammatic representations of abstractions and are usually not to be literally perceived and interpreted. In what ensues, however, the circles are used to represent areas (roughly). This is a special case, where we consider each variable represented by a Venn circle to be equal to 1.

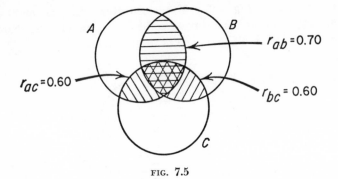

FIG. 7.5

circles common to all three variables (triply hatched area of Fig. 7.5). This represents the common factor variance, or, in set terms: $V(A \cap B \cap C)$. In other words, $V(A \cap B \cap C)$, or V_{co}, represents whatever the three variables or measures share in common. In later chapters of the book these ideas will serve us well.

PART THREE

PROBABILITY AND STATISTICAL INFERENCE

8 *PROBABILITY*

Probability is an obvious and simple subject. It is a baffling and complex subject. It is a subject we know a great deal about, and a subject we know nothing about. Kindergartners can study probability, and philosophers do. It is dull; it is interesting. Such contradictions are the stuff of probability.

Take the expression "laws of chance." The expression itself is contradictory. Chance or randomness, by definition, is the absence of law. If events can be explained lawfully, they are not random. Then why say "laws of chance"? The answer, too, is contradictory—seemingly. It is possible to gain knowledge from ignorance if we view randomness as ignorance. This is because random events, *in the aggregate,* occur in lawful ways with monotonous regularity. From the disorder of randomness the scientist welds the order of scientific prediction and control.

It is not easy to explain these disconcerting statements. Indeed, philosophers disagree on the answers. Fortunately there is no disagreement on the empirical probabilistic events—or at least very little. Almost all scientists and philosophers will agree that if two dice are thrown a number of times, there will probably be more sevens than twos or twelves. They will also agree that certain events like finding a hundred-dollar bill or winning a sweepstakes are extremely unlikely.

DEFINITION OF PROBABILITY

What is probability? We ask this question and immediately strike a perplexing problem. Philosophers cannot seem to agree on the answer.[1] This seems to be because there are two broad definitions, among others, which seem irreconcilable: the a priori and the a posteriori. The *a priori definition* we owe to a controversial, interesting, and very human genius,

[1] For discussions of the disagreement, see J. Kemeny, *A Philosopher Looks at Science.* Princeton, N. J.: Van Nostrand, 1959, chap. 4; H. Margenau, *The Nature of Physical Reality.* New York: McGraw-Hill, 1950, chap. 13.

Simon Laplace.[2] The probability of an event is the number of favorable cases divided by the total number of (equally possible) cases, or $p = f/f + u$, where p is probability, f the number of favorable cases, and u the number of unfavorable cases. This is an a priori definition because the method of calculating probability implied by the definition is a priori in the sense that probability is given, that we can determine the probabilities of events before empirical investigation. This definition is the basis of mathematical theoretical probability. The a priori nature of Laplace's definition is revealed to some extent by Laplace's saying that the theory of probability is nothing more than common sense reduced to calculation. Yet Laplace's great work on probability is considered an extremely difficult work. (Laplace was famous for using that exasperating expression of mathematicians and statisticians, "It is easy to see that . . .")

The a posteriori, or frequency, definition is empirical in nature. It says that probability is the ratio of the number of times an event occurs in an actual series of tests to the total number of trials. With this definition, one approaches probability empirically by performing a series of tests, counting the number of times a certain kind of event happens, and then computing the ratio. The result of the computation is the probability of the certain kind of event.

A brief and simple example will make the distinction clear. The a priori probability of throwing a 6 with a die is $\frac{1}{6}$, since there are 6 sides to the die, and any side is equally likely to turn up as any other. (Note that the latter part of this statement uses the important assumption of equiprobability—which is not always justified.) That is, out of six possible outcomes, there is one only that is "favorable." Thus $p = 1/6$. Similarly, if one throws two dice, the a priori probability of a 12 is $\frac{1}{36}$ since there are 36 possibilities $(6 + 6, 6 + 5, \cdots, 6 + 1, \cdots, 5 + 5, 5 + 4, \cdots, 1 + 1)$ and among these possibilities only one $(6 + 6)$ yields a 12.

The same samples with an a posteriori or frequency definition, on the other hand, would lead to throwing a die a large number of times and counting the number of 6's to obtain the probability that a 6 will turn up on any one throw. If we throw a die 60 times, the a priori definition tells us that a 6 should appear 10 times, or close to 10 times. (Actually, this is not accurate. There should be many throws. How many is many? An infinite number!) At this point, I took a die and threw it 60 times, shaking it thoroughly before each throw. Six turned up 8 times. The fre-

2 For a good brief discussion of Laplace and his work, see J. Newman, *The World of Mathematics*, vol. 2. New York: Simon and Schuster, 1956, pp. 1316–1324. For Laplace's own definition of probability, see *ibid.*, pp. 1325–1333. Discussions of the two kinds of definitions are given in Kemeny, *op. cit.*, chap. 4, and Margenau, *op. cit.*, chap. 13.

quency interpretation of probability would say, then, that the probability that 6 will turn up is $\frac{8}{60}$. This is called a *relative frequency*. With a small number of throws, obviously, this is not a very good definition of probability.

Practically speaking and for our purposes, the distinction between the a priori and a posteriori definitions is not too vital. Following Margenau, we put the two together by saying that the a priori approach supplies a constitutive definition of probability, whereas the a posteriori approach supplies an operational definition of probability.[3] We need to use both approaches; we need to supplement one with the other.

SAMPLE SPACE, SAMPLE POINTS, AND EVENTS

To compute the probability of any outcome, first determine the total number of possible outcomes. With a die the outcomes are 1, 2, 3, 4, 5, 6. Call this the set U. U is called the *sample space,* or universe of possible outcomes. The sample space includes all possible outcomes of an "experiment" that are of interest to the experimenter. The primary elements of U are called *elements* or *sample points*. Then let us write $U = \{1, 2, 3, 4, 5, 6\}$, and bring this chapter in line with the set reasoning and method of Part II. Letting x_i = any sample point or element in U, we write $U = \{x_1, x_2, \cdots, x_n\}$. Examples of different U's are: (1) all possible outcomes of tossing two dice (see below), (2) all kindergarten children in such-and-such a school system, and (3) all arithmetic achievement test scores of seventh- and eighth-grade children of X school in an experiment involving only these grades in the school.

Sometimes the determination of the sample space is easy; sometimes it is difficult. The problem is directly analogous to the definition of sets of Chap. 5: sets can be defined by listing all the members of the set, and by giving a rule for the inclusion of elements in a set. In probability theory, both kinds of definition are used. What is U in tossing two coins? This is, of course, the same as asking: What are the sample points of U? We list all the possibilities: $U = \{(H, H), (H, T), (T, H), (T, T)\}$. This is a list definition of U. A rule definition—although we would not use it —might be: $U = \{x; x$ is all combinations of H and $T\}$. In this case U is the Cartesian product. Let $A_1 = \{H_1, T_1\}$, the first coin; let $A_2 = \{H_2, T_2\}$, the second coin. Recalling that a Cartesian product of two sets is the set of *all* ordered pairs whose first entry is an element of one set and whose second entry is an element of another set, we can diagram the generation of the Cartesian product of this case, $A_1 \times A_2$, as in Fig. 8.1. Notice that there are four lines connecting A_1 and A_2. Thus there are four possibilities: $\{(H_1, H_2), (H_1, T_2), (T_1, H_2) (T_1, T_2)\}$. This thinking

---

[3] Margenau, *op. cit.*, p. 264.

and procedure can be used in defining many sample spaces or U's, although the actual procedure can be tedious.

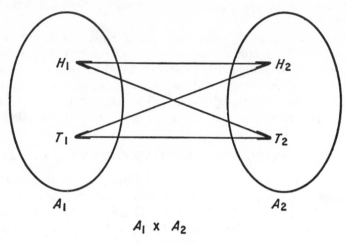

$$A_1 \times A_2$$

FIG. 8.1

With two dice, what is U? Think of the Cartesian product of two sets and you will probably have little trouble. Let A_1 be the outcomes or points of the first die: $\{1, 2, 3, 4, 5, 6\}$. Let A_2 be the outcomes or points of the second die. Then $U = A_1 \times A_2 = \{(1, 1), (1, 2), \cdots, (5, 6), (6, 6)\}$. We can diagram this as we diagramed the coin example, but counting the lines would be more difficult. There are too many of them. We can know the number of possible outcomes simply by $6 \times 6 = 36$, or in a formula: mn, where m is the number of possible outcomes of the first set, and n is the number of possible outcomes of the second set.

It is often possible to solve difficult probability problems by using trees. Trees define sample spaces, logical possibilities, with clarity and precision. A *tree* is a diagram that gives all possible alternatives or outcomes for combinations of sets by providing paths and set points. This definition is a bit unwieldy. Illustration is better. Take the coin example (we turn the tree on its side). Its tree is shown in Fig. 8.2.

To determine the number of possible alternatives, just count the number of alternatives or points at the "top" of the tree. In this case, there are four alternatives. To name the alternatives, read off, for each end point, the points that led to it, for example, the first alternative is (H_1, H_2). Obviously, three, four, or more coins can be used. The only trouble is that the procedure is tedious because of the large number of alternatives. The tree for three coins is illustrated in Fig. 8.3. There are eight possible alternatives, outcomes, or sample points: $U = \{(H_1, H_2, H_3), (H_1, H_2, T_3), \cdots, (T_1, T_2, T_3)\}$. (The elements of this set are called ordered triples.)

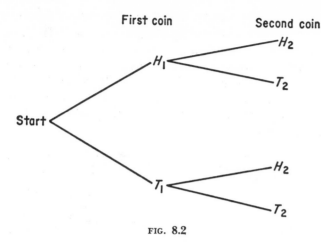

FIG. 8.2

Sample points of a sample space may seem to be a bit confusing to the reader, because two kinds of points have been discussed without differentiation. Another term and its use may help clear up this possible confusion. An *event* is a subset of U. Any element of a set is also a subset of the set. Recall that with set $A = \{a_1, a_2\}$, for example, both $\{a_1\}$ and $\{a_2\}$ are subsets of A, as well as $\{a_1, a_2\}$, and $\{\quad\}$, the empty set. Identically, all the outcomes of Figs. 8.2 and 8.3, for example, (H_1, T_2), (T_1, H_2), and (T_1, H_2, T_3), are subsets of their respective U's, Therefore they are events, too—by definition. But in the usual usage, events are more encompassing than points. All points are events (subsets), but not all events are points. Or, a point or outcome is a special kind of event, the simplest kind. Any time we state a proposition, we describe an event. We ask, for instance, "If two coins are thrown, what is the probability of getting two heads?" The "two heads" is an event. It so happens, in this case, that it is also a sample point. But suppose we asked, "What is the probability of getting at least one head?" "At least one head" is an event, but not a sample point, because it includes, in this case three sample points: (H_1, H_2), (H_1, T_2), and (T_1, H_2). (See Fig. 8.2.)

DETERMINING PROBABILITIES WITH COINS

Suppose we toss a new coin 100 times. We write $p(\text{H}) = 1/2$ and $p(\text{T}) = 1/2$, meaning the probability of heads is $\frac{1}{2}$, and similarly for tails. We assume, then, equiprobability. The sample space can only be imagined here. It has 100 sample points: $HHH \cdots H$, $HHH \cdots T$, $\cdots$. There are 100 possible outcomes, some of which duplicate others: three of them might each have 45 heads and 55 tails but in different ways. To make this clear, we write the sample space with all its sample points for three tosses of a coin (or one toss of three coins): $U = \{(H, H, H),$

(H, H, T), (H, T, H), (H, T, T), (T, H, H), (T, H, T), (T, T, H), (T, T, T)}. Note that if we pay no attention to the order of heads and tails, we obtain one case of 3 heads, one case of 3 tails, three cases of 2 heads and 1 tail, and three cases of 2 tails and 1 head. The probability of each of the eight outcomes is obviously $\frac{1}{8}$. Thus the probability of 3 heads is $\frac{1}{8}$, and the probability of 3 tails is $\frac{1}{8}$. The probability of 2 heads and 1 tail, on the other hand, is $\frac{3}{8}$, and similarly for the probability of 2 tails and 1 head.

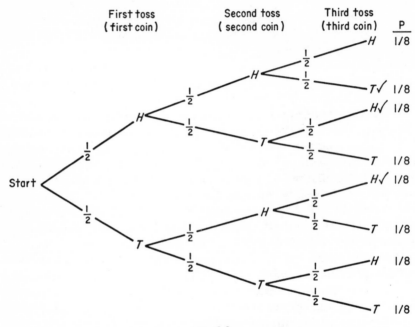

FIG. **8.3**

The probabilities of all the points in the sample space must add up to 1.00. It also follows that *probabilities are always positive.* If we write a probability tree for the three-toss experiment, it looks like Fig. 8.3. Each complete path of the tree (from the start to the third toss) is a sample point. All the paths comprise the sample space. The single path sections are labeled with the probabilities, in this case all of them are labeled with "$\frac{1}{8}$." This leads naturally to the statement of a basic principle: If the outcomes at the different points in the tree, that is, at the first, second, and third tosses, are independent of each other (that is, if one outcome does not influence another in any way), then the probability of any sample point (HHH perhaps) is the product of the probabilities of the separate outcomes. For example, the probability of 3 heads is $1/2 \times 1/2 \times 1/2 = 1/8$.

Another principle is: *To obtain the probability of any event, add the probabilities of the sample points that comprise that event.* For example, what is the probability of tossing 2 heads and 1 tail? We look at the paths in the tree that have 2 heads and 1 tail. We find that there are 3 of them. (They are checked in Fig. 8.3). Thus, $1/8 + 1/8 + 1/8 = 3/8$. In set language, we find the subsets (events) of U and note their probabilities. The subset of U of the type "2 heads and 1 tail" are, from the tree or the previous definition of U, $\{(H, H, T), (H, T, H), (T, H, H)\}$. Call this the set A_1. Then $p(A_1) = 3/8$.

This procedure can be followed with the experiment of 100 tosses, but it is much too laborious. Instead, to get the theoretical expectations, we merely multiply the number of tosses by the probability of any one of them, $100 \times 1/2 = 50$, to get the *expected* number of heads (or tails). This can be done because all the probabilities are the same. A big and important question is: In actual experiments in which we throw 100 coins, will we get *exactly* 50 heads? No, not often: about 8 times in 100 such experiments. This can be written: $p = 8/100$ or .08. (Probabilities can be written in fractional or decimal forms, more usually in decimal form.)

AN EXPERIMENT WITH DICE

I threw two new dice 72 times under carefully controlled conditions. If I add the number of spots on the two dice on all 72 throws, I will obtain a set of sums from 2 to 12. Some of these outcomes (sums) will turn up more frequently than others simply because there are more ways for them to do so. For example, there is only one way for 2 or for 12 to turn up: $1 + 1$ and $6 + 6$, but there are three ways for a 4 to turn up: $1 + 3$, $3 + 1$, and $2 + 2$. If this be so, then the probabilities for getting different sums must be different. The game of craps is based on these differences in frequency expectations.

To solve the a priori probability problem, we must first define the sample space: $U = \{(1, 1), (1, 2), (1, 3), \cdots, (6, 4), (6, 5), (6, 6)\}$. That is, we pair each number of the first die with each number of the second die in turn (the Cartesian product again). This can easily be seen if we set up this procedure in a matrix (see Table 8.1). Suppose we want to know the probability of the event—a very important event, too—"a 7 turns up." Simply count the number of 7's in the table. There are six of them nicely arrayed along the center diagonal. There are 36 sample points in U, obtained by some method of enumerating them, as above, or simply by using the formula mn, which says: Multiply the number of possibilities of the first thing by the number of possibilities of the second thing. This method can be defined: When there are m ways of doing something, A, and n ways of doing something else, B, then, if the n ways of doing B are independent of the m ways of doing A, there are $m \cdot n$ ways of doing both A and B.[4]

---

[4] This principle can be extended to more than two things. If, for example, there are three things, A, B, and C, then the formula is mnr.

TABLE 8.1   MATRIX OF POSSIBLE OUTCOMES WITH TWO DICE

		Second Die					
		1	2	3	4	5	6
	1	2	3	4	5	6	7
	2	3	4	5	6	7	8
First	3	4	5	6	7	8	9
Die	4	5	6	7	8	9	10
	5	6	7	8	9	10	11
	6	7	8	9	10	11	12

Applied to the dice problem, $mn = 6 \times 6 = 36$. Assuming equipossibility again, the probability of any *single* outcome is $\frac{1}{36}$. The probability of a 12, for instance, is $\frac{1}{36}$. The probability of a 4, however, is different. Since 4 occurs three times in the table above, we must add the probabilities for each of these elements of the sample space: $1/36 + 1/36 + 1/36 = 3/36$. Thus $p(4) = 3/36 = 1/12$. As we have seen, the probability of a 7 is $p(7) = 6/36 = 1/6$. The probability of an 8 is $p(8) = 5/36$. Note, too, that we can compute the probabilities of combinations of events. Gamblers often bet on such combinations. For example, what is the probability of a 4 *or* a 10? In set language, this is a *union* question: $p(4 \cup 10)$. Count the number of 4's and 10's in the table. There are three 4's and three 10's. Thus $p(4 \cup 10) = 6/36$.

Counting, in Table 8.1, the probabilities of each kind of outcome, we lay out a table of expected frequencies (f_e) for 36 throws. Then simply double these frequencies to get the expected (a priori) frequencies for 72 throws. We juxtapose against these expected frequencies the frequencies obtained when two dice were actually thrown 72 times. The absolute differences between expected and obtained frequencies are then apparent. The results are laid out in Table 8.2.

TABLE 8.2   EXPECTED AND OBTAINED FREQUENCIES OF SUMS
OF TWO DICE THROWN 72 TIMES

Sum of Dice	2	3	4	5	6	7	8	9	10	11	12
$f_e(36)$	1	2	3	4	5	6	5	4	3	2	1
$f_e(72)$	2	4	6	8	10	12	10	8	6	4	2
$f_o(72)$	4	2	6	6	10	15	7	11	6	4	1
Difference	2	2	0	2	0	3	3	3	0	0	1

The discrepancies are not great. In fact, by actual statistical test, they do not differ significantly from chance expectations. The a priori method seems to have virtue.

A COMPOUND EXPERIMENT

Suppose we do another somewhat more interesting experiment: toss a coin *and* throw one die simultaneously and record the outcomes after reasoning out the a priori probabilities. The probabilities can be read from the tree given in Fig. 8.4. There are twelve sample points.

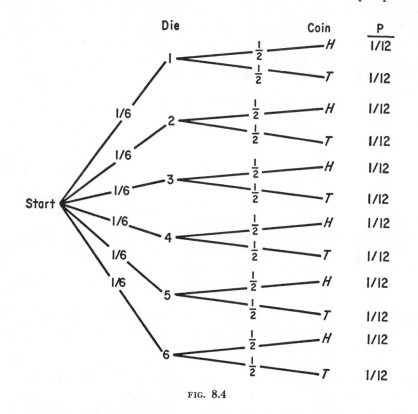

FIG. 8.4

Thus any particular combination of a die face and a coin face is $\frac{1}{12}$. The same probabilities can of course be computed using the *mn* principle: $1/6 \times 1/2 = 1/12$. What is the probability of getting an even-numbered die face *and* heads? Just count the number of paths; 2-*H*, 4-*H*, 6-*H*. There are three. Therefore $1/12 + 1/12 + 1/12 = 3/12 = 1/4$. What is the probability of getting an even number die face and heads *or* tails? Count the paths leading to all even numbers *and* both heads and tails: 2-*H*, 2-*T*, 4-*H*, 4-*T*, 6-*H*, 6-*T*. There are six. Thus $6/12 = 1/2$. But, of course, we could have obtained this in an easier fashion. Let $H =$ the set of heads and $T =$ the set of tails. Then the union of these two sets, $H \cup T$, includes all possibilities. Thus the probability is 1.00. So our only consideration is the die and its numbers, and obviously the probability of an even number is $\frac{1}{2}$.

Another way to look at this problem leads to more fruitful applications later in our study of analysis. Consider an experiment in which a die and a coin are thrown many times. Let U be all the outcomes as given above. Let P, a subset of U, be the coin outcomes. Let, Q, another subset of U, be the die outcomes. Let P_1 and P_2 be subsets of P, P_1 being the heads outcomes and P_2 the tails outcomes. Let Q_1, Q_2, $\cdots$, Q_6 be subsets of Q, the die outcomes 1, 2, $\cdots$, 6. In the experimental situation any particular outcome can be assigned to some intersection of P and Q. For example, if tails and a 3 are thrown, this outcome is assigned to the set of outcomes, $P_2 \cap Q_3$. All this is seen in Table 8.3.

TABLE 8.3   SET OUTCOMES OF TOSSING A COIN (P) AND THROWING A DIE (Q)

			Q			
	Q_1	Q_2	Q_3	Q_4	Q_5	Q_6
P_1	$P_1 \cap Q_1$	$P_1 \cap Q_2$	$P_1 \cap Q_3$	$P_1 \cap Q_4$	$P_1 \cap Q_5$	$P_1 \cap Q_6$
P						
P_2	$P_2 \cap Q_1$	$P_2 \cap Q_2$	$P_2 \cap Q_3$	$P_2 \cap Q_4$	$P_2 \cap Q_5$	$P_2 \cap Q_6$

Each of the cells is equivalent to one of the paths of the tree of Fig. 8.4. Therefore in my experiment the probability of any particular combined outcome is $\frac{1}{12}$. We can write $p(P_1 \cap Q_2) = 1/12$, meaning "The probability of the outcome, heads and 2, is $\frac{1}{12}$." We can also write such relations as $p(P_1 \cup P_2) = 1.00$, $p[(P_1 \cap Q_3) \cup (P_2 \cap Q_4)] = 2/12 = 1/6$, and so on. If we toss the coin and throw the die 72 times (a convenient multiple of 12), the expected (a priori) frequency in each cell is $72 \cdot 1/12 = 6$. The actual results of the 72 tosses are given in Table 8.4.

The degree of departure from the chance expectation of 6 in each cell can be measured by the differences between the obtained and the expected frequencies. Only one cell, H-3, departs seriously from the chance expectation. (By actual statistical test, the departures are not significant.) Note that we can also easily see the frequencies of the heads and tails, and the 1, 2, $\cdots$, 6 frequencies and their departures from chance expectations. They are all relatively small and insignificant.

To this point the assumption of equiprobability has been accepted. The probability of each outcome (sample point) is assumed to be equal to the probability of any other outcome (sample point). Are we justified in using this assumption? In many research situations we are. In general, when we have no reason to believe otherwise we use the equiprobability

TABLE 8.4   OBTAINED FREQUENCIES FROM 72 TOSSES AND THROWS OF A COIN AND A DIE ^{a}

	1	2	3	4	5	6	Totals	
H	5	4	11	7	9	6	42	(6)
	−1	−2	5	1	3	0		
T	5	6	4	9	4	2	30	(−6)
	−1	0	−2	3	−2	−4		
Total	10	10	15	16	13	8	72	
	(−2)	(−2)	(3)	(4)	(1)	(−4)		

^{a} The numbers directly under the main column headings are the obtained frequencies. The numbers to the lower right of the obtained frequencies are the discrepancies from theoretical expectation. The numbers in parentheses on the right and at the bottom of the table are the discrepancies of the marginal totals from expectation.

assumption. Of course, in experiments we can frequently assure ourselves to a large extent of the validity of the assumption by careful control. Yet there are many situations in which the assumption of equiprobability is not justified. Notice how absurd it would be to reason like this: The probability of one's dying tomorrow is one-half. Why? Because one will either die tomorrow or not die tomorrow. Since there are two possibilities, they each have probability of occurrence of one-half. Any insurance company that operated this way would go out of business. Suppose that a political scientist were studying, among other things, the relation between political preferences and religious preferences. If he assumed that the probabilities that a Catholic would be a Democrat or a Republican were equal, he would err seriously. Obviously, researchers have to know something about the phenomena they are studying. Some attempt must be made, before using probability theory, to check the assumptions being used. In the social sciences and education, as we will see, this is not always easy.

SOME FORMAL THEORY

We have the *sample space* U, with subsets A, B, · · · · . The elements of U—and *of* A, B, · · —are a_i, b_i, · · · , that is, a_1, b_2, · · · , a_n and b_1, b_2, · · · , b_n, and so forth. A, B, and so forth, are *events*. Actually, although we have often talked about the probability of a single occurrence, we really mean the probability of a type of occurrence. When we talk about the probability of any single event of U, for instance, we can only do so because any particular member of U is conceived as representative of all of U. And similarly for the probabilities of subsets A, B, · · · K of U. The probability of U is 1; the probability of E, the empty set, is 0. Or $p(U) = 1.00$; $p(E) = 0$. To determine the probability of any subset of U, a *measure* of the set must be assigned. In order to assign such a measure, we must assign a *weight* to each element of U and thus to each element of the subsets of U. A weight is defined:[5]

A *weight* is a positive number assigned to each element, x, in U, and written $w(x)$, such that the sum of all these weights, $\Sigma w(x)$, is equal to 1.

This is a function notion; w is called a *weight function*. It is a rule that assigns weights to elements of a set, U, in such a way that the sum of the weights is equal to 1, that is, $w_1 + w_2 + w_3 + \cdots + w_n = 1.00$, and $w_i = 1/n$. The weights are equal, assuming equiprobability; each weight is a fraction with 1 in the numerator and the number of cases, n, is the denominator. In the previous experiment of the tosses and throws of a coin and a die, the weights assigned to each element of U, U being all the outcomes, are all $\frac{1}{12}$. The sum of all the weight functions, $w(x)$, is $1/12 + 1/12 + \cdots + 1/12 = 1$. In probability theory, the sum of the elements of the sample space must always equal 1.

To get from weights to the measure of a set is easy. We define the measure of a set thus: The *measure* of a set is the sum of the weights of the elements of the set:[6]

$$\sum_{x \text{ in } U} w(x), \text{ or } \sum_{x \text{ in } A} w(x)$$

We write $m(A)$, meaning "The measure of the set A." This simply means the sum of the weights of the elements in the set A.

By way of example, suppose that we randomly sample children from the 400 children of the fourth grade of a school system. Then U is all 400 children. Each child is a sample point of U. Each child is an x in U. The probability of selecting any one child at random is $\frac{1}{400}$. Let $A =$ the boys in U, and $B =$ the girls in U. There are 100 boys and 300 girls. Each boy is assigned the weight $\frac{1}{400}$, and each girl is assigned the weight $\frac{1}{400}$. Suppose we wish to sample, all together, 100 children. Our expectation is, then, 25 boys and 75 girls in the sample. The measure of the set A, $m(A)$, is the sum of the weights of all the elements in A. Since there are 100 boys in U, we sum the 100 weights: $1/400 + 1/400 + \cdots + 1/400 = 100/400 = 1/4$, or

$$m(A) = \sum_{x \text{ in } A} w(x) = \frac{1}{4}$$

[5] The approach used here follows to some extent that found in J. Kemeny, J. Snell, and G. Thompson, *Introduction to Finite Mathematics.* Englewood Cliffs, N. J.: Prentice-Hall, 1956, chap. IV, and J. Kemeny, H. Mirkil, J. Snell, and G. Thompson, *Finite Mathematical Structures.* Englewood Cliffs, N. J.: Prentice-Hall, 1959, chap. 3.
[6] Note that the sum of the weights in a subset A of U does not have to equal 1. In fact, it is usually less than 1, as we shall see.

Similarly,

$$m(B) = \sum_{x \text{ in } B} w(x) = \frac{3}{4}$$

For the set B, the girls, we sum 300 weights, each of them being $\frac{1}{400}$. In short, the sums of the weights are the probabilities. That is, the measure of a set is the probability of a member of the set's being chosen. Thus we can say that the probability that a member of the sample of 400 children will be a boy is $\frac{1}{4}$, and the probability that the selected member will be a girl is $\frac{3}{4}$. To determine the expected frequencies, simply multiply the sample size by these probabilities: $1/4 \times 100 = 25$ and $3/4 \times 100 = 75$.

Probability has three fundamental properties:

1. The measure of any set, as defined above, is greater than or equal to 0 and less than or equal to 1. In brief, probabilities (measures of sets) are either 0, 1, or in between.

2. The measure of a set, $m(A)$, equals 0 if and only if there are no members in A, that is, A is empty.

3. Let A and B be sets. If A and B are disjoint, that is, $A \cap B = E$, then:

$$m(A \cup B) = m(A) + m(B)$$

This equation simply says that when no members of A and B are shared in common, then the probability of either A or B or both is equal to the combined probabilities of A and B.

There is no need to give an example to illustrate (1). We have had several earlier. To illustrate (2), assume, in the boys-girls example, that we asked the probability of drawing a teacher in the sample. But U did not include teachers. Let C be the set of fourth-grade teachers. In this case, the set C is empty, and $m(C) = 0$. Use the same boys-girls example to illustrate (3). Let A be the set of boys, B the set of girls. Then $m(A \cup B) = m(A) + m(B)$. But $m(A \cup B) = 1.00$, because they were the only subsets of U. And we learned that $m(A) = 1/4$ and $m(B) = 3/4$. It is obvious that the equation holds.

COMPOUND EVENTS AND THEIR PROBABILITIES

The coin-dice example studied above was an example of a compound event. The other examples were simple events. It is now necessary to examine compound events and their probabilities and conditional events and their probabilities. First, we examine certain counting problems and the ways in which counting is related to set theory and probability theory. It will be found that if the basic theory is understood, the application of probability theory to research problems is considerably facilitated. In addition, the interpretation of data becomes less subject to error.

Assume that a group of sixth-grade children has been studied, that there are 100 children altogether in the group, 60 boys and 40 girls. A useful function is the *numerical function,* which assigns to any set the number of members in the set. The number of members in A is $n(A)$. In this case $n(U) = 100$, $n(A) = 60$, and $n(B) = 40$, where A is the set of boys and B the set of girls, both subsets of U, the 100 sixth-grade children. If there is no overlap between two sets, $A \cap B = E$, then the following equation holds:

$$n(A \cup B) = n(A) + n(B) \tag{8.1}$$

Recall that earlier the frequency definition of probability was given as:

$$p = \frac{f}{f + u} \tag{8.2}$$

where f is the number of favorable cases, and u the number of unfavorable cases. The numerator is $n(F)$ and the denominator $n(U)$, the total number of possible cases. Similarly, we can divide through the terms of Eq. 8.1 by $n(U)$:

$$\frac{n(A \cup B)}{n(U)} = \frac{n(A)}{n(U)} + \frac{n(B)}{n(U)} \tag{8.3}$$

This reduces to probabilities, analogously to Eq. 8.2:

$$p(A \cup B) = p(A) + p(B) \tag{8.4}$$

Using the example of the 100 children, and substituting values in Eq. 8.3, we get

$$\frac{100}{100} = \frac{60}{100} + \frac{40}{100}$$

which yields for Eq. 8.4:

$$1.00 = .60 + .40$$

In many cases, two (or more) sets in which we are interested are not disjoint. Rather, they overlap. When this is so, then $A \cap B \neq E$, and it is not true that $n(A \cup B) = n(A) + n(B)$. Look at Fig. 8.5.

Here A and B are subsets of U; sample points are indicated by dots. The number of sample points in A is 8; the number in B is 6. There are two sample points in $A \cap B$. Thus the equation above does not hold. If we try to compute all the points in $A \cup B$ with Eq. 8.1, we would get $8 + 6 = 14$ points. But there are only 12 points. The equation has to be altered to a more general equation that fits all cases:

$$n(A \cup B) = n(A) + n(B) - n(A \cap B) \tag{8.5}$$

It should be clear that the error when Eq. 8.1 is used results from counting the two points of $A \cap B$ twice. Therefore we subtract $n(A \cap B)$ once, which corrects the equation. It now fits any possibility. If, for example, $n(A \cap B) = E$, the empty set, Eq. 8.5 is reduced to (8.1). Equation 8.1

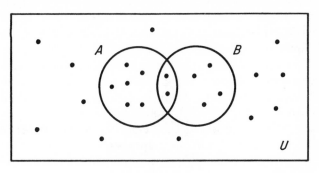

FIG. 8.5

is a special case of (8.5). Computing the number of sample points in $A \cup B$ of Fig. 8.5, then, we get: $n(A \cup B) = 8 + 6 - 2 = 12$. If we divide Eq. 8.5 through by $n(U)$, as in (8.3):

$$p(A \cup B) = p(A) + p(B) - p(A \cap B) \qquad (8.6)$$

Substituting our number of dots or sample points, we find that

$$\frac{12}{24} = \frac{8}{24} + \frac{6}{24} - \frac{2}{24}$$

$$.50 = .33 + .25 - .08$$

In a random sample of U, then, the probabilities of an element's being a member of A, B, $A \cap B$, and $A \cup B$, respectively, are .33, .25, .08, and .50.

INDEPENDENCE, MUTUAL EXCLUSION, AND EXHAUSTIVENESS

Think of the following questions, variants of which must be asked by any researcher. Does the occurrence of this event, A, preclude the possibility of the occurrence of this other event, B? Does the occurrence of event A have an influence on the occurrence of event B? Are the events A, B, and C related? When A has occurred, does this influence the outcomes of B—and, perhaps, C? Do the events A, B, C, and D exhaust the possibilities? Or are there, perhaps, other possibilities E, F, and so on? Suppose, for instance, that a researcher is studying board of education decisions and their relation to, say, political preference, religious preference, education, and others. In order to relate these variables to board decisions, he has to have some method of classifying the decisions. One of the first questions he must ask is, "Have I exhausted all possibilities in my classification system?" He should also ask, "If a board makes one kind of decision, does this preclude the possibility of making another kind of decision?" "If the board members vote Yes on this issue, does this make it logically impossible for them to vote Yes on the next issue?" Perhaps the most important question the researcher can ask, however, is, "If a board makes a particular decision, does this decision influence its action on any other decision?"

We have been talking about exhaustiveness, mutual exclusiveness, and independence. The first two of these were discussed in an earlier chapter, though not in detail. We now define them in a more detailed manner. Then we will use them in probability examples.

Let A and B be subsets of U. We ask the questions: Are there any other subsets of U (other than the empty set)? Do A and B exhaust the sample space? Are all the sample points of the sample space U included in A or in B? A simple example is: Let $A = \{$H, T$\}$; let $B = \{$1, 2, 3, 4, 5, 6$\}$. This is our coin-die problem. If we toss a coin and throw a die together, what are the possibilities? Unless *all* the possibilities are exhausted, we cannot solve the probability problem. There are 12 possibilities, as we saw before. The sets A and B exhaust the sample space. (This is of course obvious, since A and B generated the sample space.) Now take a more realistic example. Suppose a researcher is studying religious preferences. He sets up the following system to categorize individuals: $\{$Protestants, Catholics, Jews$\}$. What he has done, implicitly, is to set up $U =$ all people (with or without religious preferences) and subsets of U, $A =$ Protestants, $B =$ Catholics, $C =$ Jews. The set question is: Does $A \cup B \cup C = U$? Has he exhausted all religious preferences? How about Buddhists? How about atheists? And so on.

To define *exhaustiveness*, let $U =$ a sample space, and let A, B, and C be subsets (events) of U. This principle is like saying that we have to know what we are talking about. (Recall the levels of discourse idea discussed in Part I.) It is also the same as saying, in probability language: $p(A \cup B \cup C) = 1.00$.

Mutual exclusiveness is easier to understand. Succinctly, two events, A and B, are *mutually exclusive* when they are disjoint, or when $A \cap B = E$. That is, when the intersection of two (or more) sets is the empty set —or when two sets have no elements in common—the sets are said to be mutually exclusive. This is the same as saying, again in probability language, $p(A \cap B) = 0$. It is more convenient for the researcher when events are mutually exclusive, because he can then add the probabilities of events. We state a principle in set and probability terms: If the events (sets) A, B, and C are *mutually exclusive*, then $p(A \cup B \cup C) = p(A) + p(B) + p(C)$. This is the special case of the more general principle we discussed in the previous section. (See Eq. 8.1, 8.4, 8.5, and 8.6 and the accompanying discussion, above.)

One of the chief purposes of research design is to set up conditions of independence of events so that conditions of dependence of events can be adequately studied. Easy and clear examples of independent events are coin-tossing and dice-throwing. If we toss a coin 10 times, one toss has no influence whatever on any other toss. The tosses are independent. If we throw a die or two dice several times, one throw has no effect on any other throw. The throws are independent. Similarly, when we simultaneously tossed a coin and threw a die, the *events* of tossing a coin, A, and throwing a die, B, were independent. The outcome of any coin toss could have no influence on the outcome of any die throw. In other words, $A \cap B = E$, and $p(A \cap B) = 0$. Unfortunately, this neat model does not always apply in research situations, as we shall see.

Suppose 30 students in a college class are taking an examination. They are working under the usual conditions of no communication, no looking at each other's papers, and so forth. The responses of any student can be considered independent of the responses of any other student. Can the responses to the items within the test be considered independent? Suppose that the answer to one item later in the test is embedded in an item earlier in the test. The probability of getting the later item correct by chance, say, is $\frac{1}{4}$. But the fact that the answer was given earlier can change this probability. With some students it might even become 1.00. What is important for the researcher to know is that independence is often difficult to achieve and that lack of independence when research operations assume independence can seriously affect the interpretation of data.

Suppose we rank order examination papers and then assign grades on the basis of the ranks. This is a perfectly legitimate and useful procedure. In fact it is better than the system in which the instructor reads a paper and then assigns a grade on the basis of his judgment of the absolute quality of the answers to the questions. But it must be realized that the grades given by the rank-order method are not independent (if they ever could be). Let us take five such papers. After reading them one is ranked as the first (the best), the second next, and so on through the five papers. We assign the number "1" to the first, "2" to the second, "3" to the third, "4" to the fourth, and "5" to the fifth. After using up 1, we have only 2, 3, 4, and 5 left. After using up 2, only 3, 4, and 5 remain. When we assign 4, obviously we must assign 5 to the remaining examination. In short, the assignment of 5 was influenced by the assignment of 4—and also 1, 2, and 3. The assignment events are not independent. One may ask, "Does this matter?" Suppose we take the ranks, treat them as scores, and make inferences about mean differences between groups, say between two classes. The statistical test used to do this is probably based on the coin-dice paradigm with its pristine independence. But we have not followed this model—one of its most important assumptions, independence, has been ignored.

When research results lack independence, statistical tests applied to them lack a certain validity. A χ^2 test, for example, assumes that the events—responses of individuals to an interview question, say—recorded in the cells of a crossbreak table, are independent of each other. If the recorded events are not independent of each other, then the basis of the statistical test and the inferences drawn from it are corrupted.

TABLE 8.5   EXAMPLE OF DATA EXHIBITING POSSIBLE LACK OF
INDEPENDENCE, HEBB DATA [a]

	Males ($n = 8$)	Females ($n = 22$)
Quasi-Aggression, then Aggression	37	0
Friendly Behavior, then Aggression	0	15

[a] Table entries are numbers of acts of male and female chimpanzees of the kinds indicated by the margin labels on the left.

It will be instructive to illustrate this discussion of independence with two interesting examples, one from actual research, one hypothetical. In a fascinating account of research on the aggressive behavior of apes, Hebb and Thompson present the data of Table 8.5.[7] The problem was the relation between sex and aggression. Samples of the behavior of 30 adult chimpanzees were taken in an effort to study individual differences in ape temperament. Without going into details, it can be said that one analysis of the observations showed that males and females displayed friendly behavior about equally often, but that males were more aggressive. Hebb and Thompson's data on this observation seem to say: "Watch out for males!" But, the authors point out, this is quite out of line with the experience of the apes' caretakers. Nineteen out of 20 cuts and scratches were inflicted by females! Then Hebb and Thompson pursued the interesting, if disconcerting, idea of tabulating incidence of aggressive acts in two ways: (1) when such were preceded by quasi-aggression, that is, by warning of attack, and (2) when aggressive acts were preceded by friendly behavior. The resulting incidences of behavior are given in Table 8.5. The table seems to indicate: "Watch out for females when they are friendly!"

[7] D. Hebb and W. Thompson, "The Social Significance of Animal Studies." In G. Lindzey, ed., *Handbook of Social Psychology*, vol. I. Cambridge, Mass.: Addison-Wesley, 1954, pp. 532–562. The table is on p. 546.

The data in the table cannot be validly analyzed statistically, since the numbers in the table indicate the frequency of kinds of acts. But all 37 acts by males may have been committed by only one or two of them. If one ape had committed all 37 acts, then it should be clear that the acts were not independent of each other. The ape might simply have had a bad temper. And bad tempers notoriously create lack of independence in animal and human acts.

The concluding example is hypothetical. Take the example of the board of education decision given earlier. Suppose the researcher decided to sample 100 board of education decisions. He has a variety of ways to do this. He can sample many decisions from a few boards, or he can sample many decisions from many boards. Or he might do both. If he wants to be assured of the independence of the decisions, then he should sample many decisions from many boards of education. Theoretically, he should take only one decision from each board. Then he is assured of independence—at least as much as such assurance is possible. True, his sample of education boards might include two in adjoining districts, one of which watches the other's decisions before making its own. But this is not too likely. As soon as he takes more than one decision from the same board, however, he must entertain the notion that decisions of the kind A may influence decisions of the kind B. Decision A may influence decision B, for example, not because the board members consider A and B separately and independently but because they may wish to appear consistent. Both decisions may involve expenditures for instructional equipment, and since the board adopted a liberal policy on A it must adopt a liberal policy on B.

It is now time for a mathematical definition of independence. Actually, it has already been implied. Remember the case of tossing a coin. Look back at Fig. 8.3. The probability of heads on the first toss is $\frac{1}{2}$. The probability of heads on the second toss is $\frac{1}{2}$. The probability of heads on the third toss, too, is $\frac{1}{2}$. And the probability of three heads in three tosses is $1/2 \times 1/2 \times 1/2 = 1/8$. Each of the tosses is clearly independent. Getting heads or tails on one toss has no effect whatever on getting heads or tails on any subsequent toss.

The common-sense notion of the so-called "law of averages" is utterly erroneous, but it nicely illustrates a lack of understanding of independence. It says something to the effect that if there is a large number of occurrences of an event, then the chances of that event's occurring on the next trial is smaller. Suppose a coin is being tossed. Heads has come up five times in a row. The common-sense notion of the "law of averages" would lead one to believe that there is a greater chance of getting tails on the next toss. Not so. The probability is still $\frac{1}{2}$. Each toss is an independent event. This suggests a principle or definition: If A and B are two independent events, then:

$$p(A \cap B) = p(A) \cdot p(B) \qquad (8.7)$$

If we translate into the above example, and let A be the event "heads on the first toss" and B the event "heads on the second toss," the probability that the events A and B will both occur is the probability of the first toss times the probability of the second toss. Using two dice, and letting A be the event "8 on the first toss" and B the event "8 on the second toss" (or any similar pair of events), we find that the probability of two 8's in a row is the probability of A times the probability of B. In this case, since there are five ways 8 can turn up with two dice (see Table 8.1)—(2, 6), (6, 2), (3, 5), (5, 3), (4, 4)—$p(A) = 5/36$, $p(B) = 5/36$, and $p(A \cap B) = 5/36 \cdot 5/36 = 25/1296$, or about .02.

Take an example more directly pertinent to research. Suppose an investigator is studying a relation, and he calculates the probability that the result obtained—for example, the difference between two means—was due to chance. This probability is $5/100$, or .05. This means that there are approximately five chances in 100 that his result is due to chance. That is, if he repeated the experimental conditions 100 times *without* the experimental manipulation, approximately five of those times he could obtain a mean difference as large as the one he obtained *with* the experimental manipulation. Feeling shaky about the result—after all, there *are* five chances in 100 that the result could be due to chance—he carefully repeats the whole experiment. He obtains substantially the same result (luck!). Having controlled everything carefully to be sure the two experiments are independent, he now computes the probability that the two results are due to chance. This probability is approximately .02. Thus we see both one of the values of independence in experimentation and the importance of replication of results.[8]

Note, finally, that the formula for independence works two ways. One, it tells us, if events are independent and we know the probabilities of the separate events, the probability of both events occurring *by chance.* If it is found that dice repeatedly show 12's, say, then there is probably something wrong with the dice. If a gambler notes that another gambler seems always to win, he will of course get suspicious. The chances of continually winning a fair game or a relatively fair game are small. It could

---

[8] The method of computing these combined probabilities was discovered by Fisher and is described in F. Mosteller and R. Bush, "Selected Quantitative Techniques." In G. Lindzey, ed., *Handbook of Social Psychology,* vol. I. Cambridge, Mass.: Addison-Wesley, 1954, pp. 328–331. The astute student may wonder why the set principle applied to probability, $p(A \cap B) = p(A) \cdot p(B)$, is not applicable. That is, why not compute $.05 \times .05 = .0025$? Mosteller and Bush explain this point. Since it is a rather difficult and moot point, we do not consider it in this book. All the reader need do is to remember that the probability of getting, say, a large difference between means in the same direction on repeated experiments is considerably smaller than getting such a difference once. Thus one can be surer of one's data and conclusions, other things being equal.

happen, of course, but it is unlikely to happen. In research, it is unlikely that one would get two or three significant results by chance. *Something beyond chance must probably be operating*—hopefully the hypothesized independent variable.

Two, the formula can be turned around, so to speak. It can tell the researcher what he must do to allow himself the advantage of the multiplicative probabilities. He must, if it is at all possible, plan his research so that events are independent. That this is easier said than done will become quite evident before this book is finished.

CONDITIONAL PROBABILITY

In all research and perhaps especially in social scientific and educational research, events are often not independent. Look at independence in another way. When two variables are related they are not independent. Our previous discussion of sets makes it clear; if $A \cap B = E$, then there is no relation (more accurately, a zero relation), or A and B are independent; if $A \cap B \neq E$, then there is a relation, or A and B are not independent. When events are not independent, when they are related, scientists can sharpen their probabilistic inferences. The meaning of this statement can be explicated to some extent by studying conditional probability. In addition, its study may give the student more insight into both probability and scientific problems of sampling and prediction.

When events are not independent, the probability approach must be altered. Here is a simple example. What is the probability that, of any married couple picked at random, both mates are Republicans? First, assuming equiprobability and that everything else is equal, the sample space U (all the possibilities) is $\{RR, RD, DR, DD\}$, where the husband comes first in each possibility or sample point. Thus the probability that both husband and wife are Republicans is $p(RR) = 1/4$. But suppose we know that one of them is a Republican. What is the probability of both's being Republicans now? U is reduced to $\{RR, RD, DR\}$. The knowledge that one is a Republican deletes the possibility DD, thus reducing the sample space. Therefore, $p(RR) = 1/3$. Suppose we have the further information that the wife is a Republican. Now, what is the probability that both mates are Republicans? Now $U = \{RR, DR\}$. Thus $p(RR) = 1/2$. The new probabilities are, in this case, "conditional" on prior knowledge or facts.

Formal Definition of Conditional Probability Let A and B be events in the sample space U, as usual. The conditional probability is denoted: $P(A|B)$, which is read, "The probability that the event A (an occurrence of the type A) will occur, given that B has occurred." Of course, we can write $p(B|A)$, too. The formula for the conditional probability involving two events is:[9]

$$p(A|B) = \frac{p(A \cap B)}{p(B)} \tag{8.8}$$

The formula simply takes an earlier formula definition of probability and alters it for the conditional probability occasion. Remember that in probability problems the denominator has to be the sample space. The formula above changes the denominator of the ratio and thus *changes the sample space. The sample space has, through knowledge, been cut down from U to B.* To demonstrate this point take two examples, one of independence or simple probability and one of dependence or conditional probability.

TABLE **8.6**   PROBABILITY MATRIX SHOWING JOINT PROBABILITIES
OF TWO INDEPENDENT EVENTS

		Second Toss		
		H_2	T_2	
	H_1	¼	¼	½
First Toss	T_1	¼	¼	½
		½	½	

Toss a coin twice. The events are independent. What is the probability of getting heads on the second toss if heads appeared on the first toss? We already know: ½. Let us compute this relation using Eq. 8.8. First we write a probability matrix (see Table 8.6). For the probabilities of heads (H) and tails (T) on the first toss, read the marginal entries on the right side of the matrix. Similarly for the probabilities of the second toss: they are on the bottom of the matrix. Thus $p(H_1) = 1/2$, $p(H_2) = 1/2$, and $p(H_2 \cap H_1) = 1/4$. Therefore,

$$p(H_2|H_1) = \frac{p(H_2 \cap H_1)}{p(H_1)} = \frac{¼}{½} = \frac{1}{2}$$

The result agrees with our previous simpler reasoning. If we make the problem a bit more complex, however, maybe the formula will be of more use. Suppose, somehow, that the probability of getting heads on the second toss were increased to .60 instead of .50—the events are still inde-

---

[9] The theory extends to more than two events, but will not be discussed in this book. The reasoning is the same.

pendent. Does this change the situation? The new situation is set up in Table 8.7. (The .30 in the cell $H_1 \cap H_2$ is computed by the probabilities

TABLE **8.7** MATRIX OF JOINT PROBABILITIES OF TWO INDEPENDENT EVENTS, UNEQUAL PROBABILITIES OF EVENTS

		Second Toss		
		H_2	T_2	
First Toss	H_1	.30	.20	.50
	T_1	.30	.20	.50
		.60	.40	1.00

on the margins: $.50 \times .60 = .30$. This is permissible since we know that the events are independent. If they are not independent, conditional probability problems cannot be solved without knowledge of at least one of the values.) The formula gives us:

$$p(H_2|H_1) = \frac{p(H_2 \cap H_1)}{p(H_1)} = \frac{.30}{.50} = .60$$

But this .60 is the same as the simple probability of H_2. When events are independent, we always get the same results. That is, in this case:

$$p(H_2|H_1) = p(H_2)$$

and in the general case:

$$p(A|B) = p(A) \tag{8.9}$$

We have here another definition or condition of independence. If Eq. 8.9 holds, the events are independent.

An Academic Example There are many much more interesting examples of conditional probability than coins and other such chance devices. Take the interesting, if baffling and frustrating, problem in the graduate school of predicting the success of doctoral students. Can the coin-dice models be used in such a complex situation? Yes—under certain conditions. Unfortunately, these conditions are difficult to arrange. There is some limited success, however. Provided that we have certain empirical information, the model can be quite useful. Assume that the administrators of a graduate school of education are interested in predicting the success of their doctoral students. They are distressed by the poor performance of many of their graduates and want to set up a selection system. The school continues to admit all doctoral applicants as in the past, but for three years all incoming students take the Miller Analogies Test (MAT), a test that has been found to be fairly successful in prediction in other fields. An arbitrary cutoff point of a raw score of 65 is selected.

The school administration finds that 30 percent of all the candidates of the three-year period score 65 or above. The proportions of men and women candidates is .60 and .40. The school administration is interested in the relation between sex and score on the MAT. The empirical proportions are given in Table 8.8. Note that the obtained proportions differ only slightly from the proportions that would be obtained if sex and MAT score were independent. For example, assuming independence, the proportion for the $\geq$ 65-Male cell would be .30 $\times$ .60 = .18. This follows from the equation: $P(A \cap B) = p(A) \cdot p(B)$.

TABLE **8.8**   HYPOTHETICAL PROBABILITIES, GRADUATE-SCHOOL PROBLEM

		Sex		
		Male	Female	
MAT	$\geq$ 65	.20	.10	.30
	$<$ 65	.40	.30	.70
		.60	.40	1.00

The question is now asked: What is the probability, given a candidate is male, that he will get an MAT score equal to or greater than 65? We compute:

$$p(\geq 65|M) = \frac{p(\geq 65 \cap M)}{p(M)} = \frac{.20}{.60} = .33$$

A similar calculation for females yields:

$$p(\geq 65|F) = \frac{p(\geq 65 \cap F)}{p(F)} = \frac{.10}{.40} = .25$$

Evidently men have a somewhat higher probability than women of getting an MAT score 65 or higher.

The school needs to know more than this. So, after following up all the students of the three-year period, each one was categorized as a success (*s*) or a failure (*f*). The criterion was simple: Did he or she get the degree? If so, this was defined as success. It was found that 40 percent of the total number succeeded. To determine the relation between MAT score and success or failure, the administration, again using a cutoff point of 65, determined the proportions shown in Table 8.9.

TABLE **8.9** HYPOTHETICAL JOINT PROBABILITIES, SUCCESS OF PREDICTION:
GRADUATE-SCHOOL PROBLEM

	Success (s)	Failure (f)	
$\geqq 65$	.20	.10	.30
< 65	.20	.50	.70
	.40	.60	1.00

The MAT divides the successful group in half (.20 and .20), but sharply differentiates in the failure group (.10 and .50). Now, the questions are asked: What is the probability of getting the doctor's degree if a candidate gets an MAT score of 65 or higher? What is the probability of a candidate's getting the degree if he gets an MAT score lower than 65? The computations are

$$p(S|\geqq 65) = \frac{p(S \cap \geqq 65)}{p(\geqq 65)} = \frac{.20}{.30} = .67$$

$$p(S|< 65) = \frac{p(S \cap <65)}{p(<65)} = \frac{.20}{.70} = .29$$

Clearly, it would seem that the MAT is a good predictor of success in the program.

Note carefully what happens in all these cases. When we can write $p(A|B)$ instead of simply $p(A)$, in effect we cut down the sample space from U to B. Take the example just given. The probability of success without any other knowledge is a probability problem on the whole sample space U. This probability is .40. But given knowledge of MAT score, the sample space is cut down from U to a subset of U, $\geqq 65$. The actual number of occurrences of the success event, of course, does not change; the same number of persons succeed. But the probability fraction gets a new denominator. Put differently, the probability estimate is refined by knowledge of "pertinent" subsets of U. In this case, $\geqq 65$ and < 65 are "pertinent" subsets of U. By "pertinent" subsets we mean that the variable implied is related to the criterion variable, success and failure.

Maybe the following mode of looking at the problem will help. An area interpretation of the graduate-student problem is diagramed in Fig. 8.6. The idea of a *measure of a set* is used here. Recall that a measure of a set or subset is the sum of the weights of the set or subset. The weights are assigned to the elements of the set or subset. Figure 8.6 is a square with ten equal parts on each side. Each part is equal to $\frac{1}{10}$ or .10. The area of the whole square is the sample space U, and the measure of U, $m(U)$, equals 1.00. This simply means that all the weights assigned to all the elements of the square add up to 1.00. The measures of the subsets have been inserted: $m(F) = .60$, $m(< 65) = .70$, $m(S \cap \geq 65) = .20$. The measures of these subsets can be calculated by multiplying the lengths of their sides. For example, the area of the upper left (doubly hatched) box is $.5 \times .4 = .20$. Recall that the probability of any set (or subset) is the measure of the set (or subset). So the probability of any of the boxes in Fig. 8.6 is as indicated. We can find the probability of any two boxes by adding the measures of sets; for example, the probability of success is .20 $+ .20 = .40$.

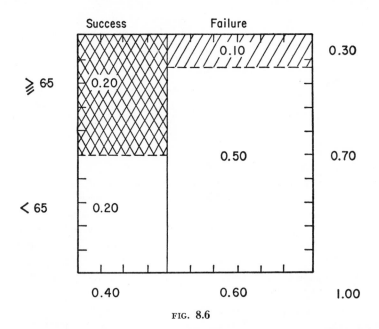

FIG. 8.6

These measures (or probabilities) are defined on the whole area, or $U = 1.00$. The probability of success is equal to $.40/1.00$. We have knowledge of the students' performances on the MAT. The areas indicating the probabilities associated with ≥ 65 and < 65 are marked off by horizontal dashed lines. The simple probability of ≥ 65 is equal to $.20 + .10 = .30$, or $.30/1.00$. The whole shaded area on the top indicates this probability. The areas of the "success" and "failure" measures are indicated by the heavy lines separating them on the square.

Our conditional probability problem is: What is the probability of success, given knowledge of MAT scores, or given ≥ 65 (it could also be < 65, of course)? We have a new small sample space, indicated by the whole shaded area at the top of the square. In effect U has been cut down to this smaller space because we know the "truth" of the smaller space. Instead of letting this smaller space be equal to .30, we now let it be equal to 1.00. (You might say it becomes a new U.) Consequently the measures of the boxes that constitute the new sample space must be recomputed. For instance, instead of computing the probability of $p(\geqq 65 \cap S) = .20$ because it is $\frac{2}{10}$ of the area of the whole square, we must compute, since we now know that the elements in the set $\geqq 65$ do have MAT scores greater than or equal to 65, the probability on the basis of the area of $\geqq 65$ (the whole shaded area at the top of the square). Having done this, we get $.20/.30 = .67$, which is exactly what we got when we used Eq. 8.8.

What happens is that the additional knowledge makes U no longer relevant as the sample space. *All probability statements are relative to a sample space.* It is a question of adequately defining the sample space. In the earlier problem of husbands and wives, we asked the question: What is the probability of both mates being Republican? The sample space was $U = \{RR, RD, DR, DD\}$. But when we add the knowledge that one of them is certainly a Republican and ask the same question, in effect we make the original U irrelevant to the problem. A new sample space, call it U', is required. Consequently the probability that both are Republicans is different when we have more knowledge.

We can compute other probabilities similarly. Suppose we wanted to know the probability of failure, given an MAT score less than 65. Look at Fig. 8.6. The probability we want is the box on the lower right, labeled .50. Since we know that the score is < 65, we use this knowledge to set up a new sample space. The two lower boxes whose area equals $.20 + .50 = .70$ represent this sample space. Thus we compute the new probability: $.50/.70 = .71$. The probability of failure to get the degree if one has an MAT score less than 65 is .71.

STUDY SUGGESTIONS

1. The student who chooses to pursue probability further is lucky. There are a number of very good, even excellent, references. Here are four particularly good ones.

   Davis, R., ed. *Elementary Mathematics of Sets with Applications.* Committee on the Undergraduate Program, Mathematical Association of America, 1955. Chapter V is an excellent chapter on probability. *Highly recommended.*

   Introductory Probability and Statistical Inference, An Experimental Course. New York: Commission on Mathematics, College Entrance Examination Board, 1959. If the student were to own one reference and one reference only, this would probably be it. The book is a relatively complete elementary presentation of probability that contains all most students of research need. *A Teachers' Notes and Answer Guide,* which has solutions to the problems of *Introductory Probability,* is also available. Write to: College Entrance Examination Board, c/o Educational Testing Service, Box 592, Princeton, New Jersey. *Very highly recommended.*

Kemeny, J., J. Snell, and G. Thompson. *Introduction to Finite Mathematics.* Englewood Cliffs, N. J.: Prentice-Hall, 1956, Chap. IV. A square area of interpretation of probability can be found on pp. 133–135. *Highly recommended.*

The Growth of Mathematical Ideas, Grades K-12. Twenty-Fourth Yearbook. Washington, D. C.: The National Council of Teachers of Mathematics, 1959, Chap. 6. This chapter, by David Page, is unique. Oriented toward the teaching of probability by elementary and secondary teachers, it has many examples and activities that can be used to enhance the understanding of probabilistic ideas.

2. Suppose that you are sampling ninth-grade youngsters for some research purposes. There are 250 ninth graders in the school system, 130 boys and 120 girls.

   (a) What is the probability of selecting any youngster?

   (b) What is the probability of selecting a girl? A boy?

   (c) What is the probability of selecting either a boy or a girl? How would you write this problem in set symbols? (*Hint:* Is it equivalent to set intersection or union?)

   (d) Suppose you drew a sample of 100 boys and girls. You got 90 boys and 10 girls. What conclusions might you reach?

   (*Answers:* (a) $\frac{1}{250}$; (b) $\frac{120}{250}$, $\frac{130}{250}$; (c) 1.)

3. Toss a coin and throw a die once. What is the probability of getting heads on the coin *and* a six on the die? Draw a tree to show all the possibilities. Label the branches of the tree with the appropriate weights or probabilities. Now answer some questions. What is the probability of getting:

   (a) tails and either a 1, a 3, or a 6?

   (b) heads and either a 2 or a 4?

   (c) heads or tails and a 5?

   (d) heads or tails and a 5 or a 6?

   (*Answers:* (a) $\frac{1}{4}$; (b) $\frac{1}{6}$; (c) $\frac{1}{6}$; (d) $\frac{1}{3}$.)

4. Toss a coin and roll a die 72 times. Write the results side-by-side on a ruled sheet as they occur. Check the obtained frequencies against the theoretical expected frequencies. Now check your answer to each of the questions in Question 3. Do the obtained results come close to the expected results? (For example, suppose you computed a cer-

tain probability for 3(a), above. Now count the number of times tails is paired with a 1, a 3, or a 6. Does the obtained fraction equal the expected fraction?)

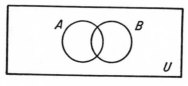

FIG. E, 8.1

5. Note Fig. E, 8.1. There are 20 elements in U, of which 4 are in A, 6 in B, and 2 in $A \cap B$. If you randomly select one element, what is the probability
   (a) that it will be in A?
   (b) that it will be in B?
   (c) that it will be in $A \cap B$?
   (d) that it will be either in A or B? (*Hint:* Remember the equation: $p(A \cup B) = p(A) + p(B) - p(A \cap B)$.)
   (e) that it will be neither in A nor in B.
   (f) that it will be in B but not in A.
6. Consider Fig. E, 8.2. There are 20 elements in U, 4 in B, and 8 in A.

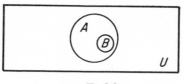

FIG. E, 8.2

If an element of U is selected at random, what are the probabilities that the element will be in
   (a) A?   (d) $A \cup B$?
   (b) B?   (e) U?
   (c) $A \cap B$?
(*Answers:* (a) $\frac{2}{5}$; (b) $\frac{1}{5}$; (c) $\frac{1}{5}$; (d) $\frac{2}{5}$; (e) 1.)
7. Using the diagram of Question 6 (Fig. E, 8.2) answer the following questions:
   (a) Given A (knowing that a sampled element came from A), what is the probability of B?
   (b) Given B, what is the probability of A?
(*Answers:* (a) $\frac{1}{2}$; (b) 1.)

8. Using the diagram of Question 5 (Fig. E, 8.1), answer the following questions:

    (a) Given B, what is the probability of A?

    (b) Given A, what is the probability of B?

(*Answers:* (a) $\frac{1}{3}$; (b) $\frac{1}{2}$.)

9 STATISTICS: PURPOSE, APPROACH, AND METHOD

THE BASIC APPROACH

The basic principle behind the use of statistical tests can be summed up in one sentence: *Compare obtained results with chance expectations.* Whenever a research study is done and statistical results are obtained, the results must be checked against the statistical results expected on the basis of chance. A large part of the theoretical activity of mathematical statisticians is devoted to the problems of determining what these chance expectations are. In Chap. 8 we met several examples of checking empirical results of coin-tossing and dice-throwing against theoretical expectations. For example, if a die is thrown a large number of times, the expected proportion of occurrences of a 4, say, is one sixth of the total number of throws. If two dice are thrown a large number of times, the theoretical expectation of an 11's turning up is $2/36$.

The dice were thrown 72 times in an experiment described in Chap. 8. The theoretically expected number of times a 7 should turn up is $1/6 \cdot 72 = 12$. But Table 8.1 showed that 7 turned up 15 times in 72 throws, rather than 12 times. We must now ask an important question: Does this obtained result differ from the theoretically expected result *significantly?* Or we might put it: Does this obtained result differ from chance expectation enough to warrant a belief that something other than chance is at work?

Recall that when a coin was tossed 100 times, 48 heads and 52 tails turned up. The theoretical expectation was 50 heads and 50 tails. Is the difference of two *significant?* Is the difference of two small enough to warrant our saying that the result was due to chance fluctuations? Is it large enough to lead us to believe that it is a *significant* departure from chance expectation? Such questions are the essence of the statistical approach. The statistician is a skeptic. He does not believe in the "reality" of empirical results until he has applied statistical tests to them. He assumes that all results are chance results until shown to be otherwise.

He is what might be called an inveterate probabilist. The core of his approach to empirical data is to set up chance expectation as his hypothesis and to try to fit the empirical data to the chance model. If the empirical data "fit" the chance model, then it is said that they are "not significant." If they do not fit the chance model, if they depart "sufficiently" from the chance model, it is said that they are "significant."

This chapter and the ensuing chapters of Part III are devoted to an attempt to elucidate the statistical approach to research problems. In so doing, several actual statistical procedures and techniques will be used and explained. In this chapter, statistical methods associated with frequencies are emphasized and the interpretation of the normal probability curve is introduced. In the next chapter, a detailed discussion of an important statistical notion, the standard error, is combined with a discussion of testing statistical hypotheses. Certain fundamental ideas are repeated in the two chapters on the assumption that such repetition in different contexts may aid student comprehension. The remaining chapters of Part III will take up the analysis of variance and the ideas behind this important statistical technique and way of thinking, correlation, and so-called nonparametric statistics.

DEFINITION AND PURPOSES OF STATISTICS

Statistics is the theory, discipline, and method of studying quantitative data gathered from samples of observations in order to study and compare sources of variance of phenomena, to help make decisions to accept or reject hypothesized relations between the phenomena so studied, and to aid in making reliable inferences from observations.

Four purposes of statistics are suggested, if not specifically stated in this definition. The first is the commonest and most traditional purpose of statistics: to reduce large quantities of data to manageable and understandable form. It is impossible to digest 100 scores, for instance, but if a mean and a standard deviation are computed the scores can be readily managed and interpreted by a trained person. The definition of "statistic" stems from this traditional usage and purpose of statistics. A *statistic* is a measure computed from a sample. A statistic contrasts with a *parameter*, which is a population value. If, in U, a population or universe, we compute the mean, this would be a parameter. Now take a subset (sample) A of U. The mean of A is a statistic. For our purposes, parameters are of theoretical interest only. They cannot usually be computed or known. They are *estimated* with statistics. Thus we deal almost exclusively with sample or subset statistics. These samples or subsets are usually conceived to be representative of U. Statistics are, then, epitomes or summaries of the samples—and often, presumably, of the populations—from which they are computed. Means, medians, variances, standard deviations, percentiles, percentages, and so on, computed from samples, are statistics.

A second purpose of statistics is to aid in the study of populations and samples. This use of statistics is so well-known that it will not be discussed. Besides, we studied something of populations and samples in earlier chapters.

A third purpose of statistics is to aid in decision-making. If a manufacturer needs to know which of three manufacturing methods yields the most reliable product with the least cost, he can use statistics to help him gain this knowledge. This use of statistics is comparatively recent. Some of the basic ideas of statistical decision theory, without the technical ramifications, will be used in this book. In fact, this purpose is subsumed under the inference purpose to be discussed below. Bross says that a decision-maker consists of (1) a set of actions; (2) a set of outcomes associated with the actions; (3) a set of probabilities associated with the outcomes of the actions; and (4) the desirability of the outcomes.[1] Although we shall not follow the pragmatic method of decision theory, as such, we will be influenced by it.

Although most decision situations are more complex, we use an example that is quite familiar by now. A decision-maker dice gambler would first lay out the outcomes for dice throws. These are, of course, 2 through 12. He notes the differing frequencies of the numbers. For example, 2 and 12 will probably occur much less often than 7 or 6. He computes the probabilities for the various outcomes. Finally, on the basis of how much money he can expect to make, he devises a betting system. He decides, for instance, that, since 7 has a probability of $\frac{1}{6}$, he will require that his opponent give him, say, odds of 5 to 1 instead of even money on the first throw. (We here take liberties with craps.) To make this whole thing a bit more dramatic, suppose that two players operate with different decision-makers.[2] One player, A, proposes the following game: A will win if 2, 3, or 4 turns up; his opponent, B, will win if 5, 6, or 7 turns up (outcomes 8 through 12 are to be disregarded). It is obvious that A's decision-maker is faulty. It is based on the assumption that 2, 3, 4, 5, 6, and 7 are equiprobable. B should have a good time with this game.

The fourth and last purpose of statistics, to aid in making reliable inferences from observational data, is closely allied to, indeed, is part of, the purpose of helping to make decisions among hypotheses. An *inference* is a proposition or generalization derived by reasoning from other propositions, or from evidence. Generally speaking, an inference is a conclusion arrived at through reasoning. In statistics, a number of inferences may be drawn from tests of statistical hypotheses. We "conclude" that Meth-

---

[1] I. Bross, *Design for Decision*. New York: Macmillan, 1953, p. 28. Bross' wording has been changed a bit.

[2] This example is suggested by Bross: *ibid.*, p. 51.

ods A and B really differ. We conclude from evidence, say $r = .67$, that two variables are really related.

Statistical inferences have two characteristics. One, the inferences are usually made *from samples to populations*. When we say that the variables *A* and *B* are related because the statistical evidence is $r = .67$, we are inferring that because $r = .67$ in *this* sample it is $r = .67$, or near .67, in the population from which the sample was drawn. The second kind of inference is used when investigators are not interested in the populations or only interested secondarily in the populations. An educational investigator is studying the presumed effect of the relationships between board of education members and chief educational administrators, on the one hand, and teacher morale, on the other hand. His hypothesis is that, when relationships between boards and chief administrators are strained, teacher morale is lower than otherwise. He is interested only in testing this hypothesis in Y County. He makes the study and obtains statistical results that support the hypothesis, for example, morale is lower in System A than in Systems B and C. He *infers*, from the statistical evidence of a difference between Systems A, on the one hand, and Systems B and C, on the other hand, that his hypothetical proposition is correct—in Y County. And it is possible for his interest to be strictly limited to Y County.

To summarize much of the above discussion, the purposes of statistics can be reduced to one major purpose: *to aid in inference-making*. This is one of the basic purposes of research design, methodology, and statistics. Scientists want to draw inferences from data. Statistics, via its power to reduce data to manageable forms (statistics) and its power to study and analyze variances, enables scientists to attach probability estimates to the inferences they draw from data. Statistics says, in effect, "The inference you have drawn is correct at such-and-such a level of significance. You may act as though your hypothesis were true, remembering that there is such-and-such a probability that it is untrue." It should be reasonably clear why some contemporary statisticians call statistics the discipline of decision-making under uncertainty.

It should also be reasonably clear that, whether you know it or not, you are always making inferences, attaching probabilities to various outcomes or hypotheses, and making decisions on the basis of statistical reasoning. Statistics, using probability theory and mathematics, simply makes the process more exact. Put somewhat differently than before, statistics helps us to know how much we can depend on our inferences and to control our research, so that our inferences can be depended upon.

STATISTICAL SIGNIFICANCE AND THE χ^2 TEST

What does it mean to say that an obtained result is "statistically significant," that it departs "significantly" from chance expectation? Suppose that we were to do an actual experiment 100 times just as we tossed a coin 100 times. Each experiment is like a coin toss or a throw of the dice. The outcome of each experiment can be considered a sample point. The sample space, properly conceived, is an infinite number of such experiments or sample points. For convenience, we conceive of the 100 replications of the experiment as the sample space U. This is nothing new. It is what we did with the coins and the dice. The difference is that with the coins and the dice *all* the outcomes were presumably due to chance, whereas with the actual experiments we hoped that the experimental outcomes were not due to chance. Yet we must entertain the notion that all or some of them are due to chance.

Take a simple example. A university administration is considering the wisdom of changing the marking system, but it wants to know faculty attitudes toward the proposed change, since it has found from experience that if most of the faculty does not approve a change the new system can run into serious trouble. By means of a suitable procedure 100 faculty members, selected at random, are asked their attitudes toward the proposed change. Sixty faculty members approve the change, and 40 disapprove. The administration now has to ask: Is this a "significant" majority? The administration reasons this way. If the faculty members were completely indifferent, their responses would be like chance: now this way, now that way. The expected frequency on an indifference hypothesis would of course be 50/50, the result to be expected by chance.

TABLE **9.1**   CALCULATION OF χ^2: FACULTY APPROVAL AND DISAPPROVAL OF PROPOSED CHANGE IN MARKING SYSTEM

	Approve	Disapprove
f_o	60	40
f_e	50	50
$f_o - f_e$	10	-10
$(f_o - f_e)^2$	100	100
$\dfrac{(f_o - f_e)^2}{f_e}$	$\dfrac{100}{50} = 2$	$\dfrac{100}{50} = 2$

To answer the question whether 60/40 differs significantly from indifference or chance a statistical test known as χ^2 (*chi* square) is performed. A table is set up to obtain the necessary terms for the computation of χ^2. The term f_o means "frequency obtained" and f_e means "frequency expected." Remember that the function of statistical tests is to compare obtained results with those to be expected on the basis of chance. Here, then, we compare f_o with f_e. On the indifference or chance assumption (and the equiprobable assumption discussed earlier), we write 50 and 50. But 60 and 40 were obtained. The difference is 10. Could a difference as large as 10 have happened by chance? Another way to put the question is: If we performed the same experiment 100 times and only chance were operating, that is, the faculty members answered the questions indifferently or, in effect, randomly, how many times in the 100 could we expect to get a deviation as large as 60/40? If we tossed a coin 100 times, we know that sometimes we would get 60 heads and 40 tails and 40 heads and 60 tails. How many times would such a large discrepancy, if it *is* a large discrepancy, happen by chance? The x^2 test is one convenient way to get an answer.

We now compute x^2:

$$x^2 = \Sigma \left[\frac{(f_o - f_e)^2}{f_e} \right] \tag{9.1}$$

which simply says: "Subtract each expected frequency, f_e, from the comparable obtained frequency, f_o, square this difference, divide the difference squared by the expected frequency, f_e, and then add up these quotients." This was done in Table 9.1. To make sure the reader knows what is happening, we write it out:

$$x^2 = \frac{(60 - 50)^2}{50} + \frac{(40 - 50)^2}{50} = \frac{100}{50} + \frac{100}{50} = 4$$

But what does $x^2 = 4$ mean? x^2 is a measure of the departure of obtained frequencies from the frequencies expected by chance. Provided we have some way of knowing what the chance expectations are, and provided the observations are independent, we can always compute x^2. The larger x^2 is the greater the obtained frequencies deviate from the expected chance frequencies. Chi-square ranges from 0, which indicates no departure of obtained from expected frequencies, through a large number of increasing values.

In addition to the formula, above, it is necessary to know the so-called *degrees of freedom* of the problem and to have a x^2 table. Chi-square tables are found in almost any statistics book, together with instructions on how to use them. So are explanations of degrees of freedom. We may say here that "degrees of freedom" means the latitude of variance a statistical problem has. In the problem above, there is one degree of freedom because the total number of cases is fixed, 100, and as soon as one of the frequencies is given the other is immediately determined. That is, there are no degrees of freedom when two numbers must sum to 100 and one of them, say 40, is given. Once 40, or 45, or any other number is given, there are no more places to go. The remaining number has no freedom to vary.[3]

---

[3] Similarly, if one computes a mean of 100 scores, one uses up one degree of freedom, by imposing one restriction on the data. Probably the best explanation of degrees of freedom is Walker's. See H. Walker, "Degrees of Freedom," *Journal of Educational*

To understand more about what is going on here, suppose we compute all the χ^2's for all possibilities: 40/60, 41/59, 42/58, $\cdots$, 50/50, $\cdots$, 60/40. Doing so we get the following set of values:

TABLE 9.2 FREQUENCIES AND CORRESPONDING χ^2's [a]

Frequencies	χ^2
40/60	4.00
41/59	3.24
42/58	2.56
43/57	1.96
44/56	1.44
45/55	1.00
46/54	.64
47/53	.36
48/52	.16
49/51	.04
50/50	0

[a] *The values of* χ^2 *for* 51/49, . . . , 60/40 *are, of course, the same as those in the table but in reverse order.*

(In reading the table, it is helpful to conceive of the first frequency of each pair as "Heads," or "Agrees with," or "Male," or any other variable.) Only two of these χ^2's, the values of 4.00 associated with 40/60 and 60/40, are statistically significant. They are statistically significant—some of these values must be taken on faith until we learn about χ^2 and the table —because by checking the χ^2 table on one degree of freedom we find an entry of 3.841 at what is called the .05 level of significance. All the other χ^2's in Table 9.2 are less than 3.841. Take the χ^2 for 42/58, which is 2.56. If we consult the table, 2.56 falls between the values of χ^2 with probabilities of .10 and .25, or 2.706 and 1.323, respectively. This is actually a probability of about .14. In most cases, we do not need to bother finding out where it falls. All we need to do is to note that it does not make the .05 grade of 3.841. If it does not, we say that it is not statistically significant—*at the .05 level.* The reader may now ask: "What is the .05 level?" and "Why the .05 level?" "Why not .10 or even .15?" To answer these questions, we must digress a little.

LEVELS OF STATISTICAL SIGNIFICANCE

The .05 level means that an obtained result that is significant at the .05 level could occur *by chance* only 5 times in 100 trials. With our responses to the administrations's question of 60 Agrees and 40 Disagrees, we can say that a discrepancy as large as this *could happen by chance* only about 5 times in 100 trials. It *could* happen more often or less often, but it probably will happen about 5 times in 100.

A level of statistical significance is to some extent chosen arbitrarily.[4] But it is certainly not completely arbitrary. Another level of significance frequently used is the .01 level. The .05 and .01 levels correspond fairly well to two and three standard deviations from the mean of a normal probability distribution. (A normal probability distribution is the symmetric bell-shaped curve which the student has probably often seen. We shall take it up later.)

Think back to the coin-tossing experiment, when a penny was tossed 100 times. Heads turned up 52 times and tails 48 times. Consult Table 9.2. $x^2 = .16$, a result clearly not significant. But suppose the coin had been tossed not one set of 100 tosses but 100 sets of 100 tosses, which would be tantamount to 100 experiments. From these 100 experiments we would get a variety of results: 58/42, 46/54, 51/49, and so on. About 95 or 96 of these experiments would yield heads within the bounds of 40 and 60. That is, only 4 or 5 of the experiments would yield less than 40 or greater than 60 heads. Similarly, if we perform an experiment and find a difference between two means which, after an appropriate statistical test, is at the .05 level of significance, then we have reason to believe that the obtained mean difference is not merely a chance difference. It *could* be a chance difference, however. If the experiment were done 100 times and there really were no difference between the means, 5 of these 100 replications might show differences as large as the actual obtained differences.

While this discussion may help to clarify the meaning of statistical significance, it does not yet answer all the questions asked before. The .05 level was originally chosen—and has persisted with researchers—because it is considered a reasonably good gamble. It is neither too high nor too low for most social scientific research. Many researchers prefer the .01 level of significance. This is quite a high level of certainty. Indeed, it is "practical certainty." Some researchers say that the .10 level might sometimes be used. Others say that 10 chances in 100 are too many, so that they are not willing to risk a decision with such odds. Others say that the .01 level, or 1 chance in 100, is too stringent, that "really" significant results may be discarded in this manner.

Should a certain level of significance be chosen and adhered to? This is a difficult question. The .05 and .01 levels have been widely advocated. There is a newer trend of thinking that advocates reporting the significance levels of all results. That is, if a result is significant at the .12

4 The .05 level was apparently first chosen by Fisher. See R. Fisher, *Statistical Methods for Research Workers*, 11th ed. New York: Hafner, 1950, pp. 80ff.

level, say, it should be reported accordingly. Some practitioners object to this practice. They say that one should make a bet and stick to it. Another school of thought advocates working with what are called "confidence intervals." [5] The latter approach is probably the best one, and the student is urged to learn it—after he has mastered statistical fundamentals. In this book, however, the statistical "levels" approach will be used because it is simpler. For the student who does not plan to do any research, the matter is not serious. But it is emphasized that those who will engage in research should study other procedures, such as statistical estimation methods, confidence intervals, and exact probability methods.

STATEMENT OF THE STATISTICAL PROBLEM

In solving statistical and probabilistic problems, it is very necessary to state the problem correctly and explicitly. Note that the reason people are usually surprised when they are told that the probability of obtaining 50 heads in 100 coin tosses is only about .08 is because they have not grasped the problem behind the proposition. Likewise, with the 60/40 problem, if we ask what the problem is of getting 60/40 we will have handicapped ourselves. Asking it in this way really means the *exact* probability of getting *just* 60/40. It excludes other possibilities.

The sheer abundance of words needed in any verbal explanations of statistical problems is confusing. In this case, we are not asking the question: What is $p(60 \text{ Agrees})$? We are asking: What is $p(60 \cup 59 \cup 58 \cup \cdots \cup 40)$? Our previous additive set principle, expanded to include k events, is

$$p(A \cup B \cup \cdots \cup K) = p(A) + p(B) + \cdots + p(K) \qquad (9.2)$$

(Since the events are presumably independent we do not need the final intersection term.) Translating this into the actual problem, we write

[5] Most investigators simply say that the results are not significant if they do not make the .05 or .01 grade. For a penetrating discussion of this obviously difficult issue, which cannot be adequately discussed here, see W. Rozeboom, "The Fallacy of the Null-Hypothesis Significance Test," *Psychological Bulletin,* LVII (1960), 416–428. Rozeboom advocates the use of confidence intervals and the reporting of precise probability values of experimental outcomes. See also J. Nunnally, "The Place of Statistics in Psychology," *Educational and Psychological Measurement,* XX (1960), 641–650; H. Walker and J. Lev, *Statistical Inference.* New York: Holt, Rinehart and Winston, Inc., 1953, pp. 52ff. The basic idea is that, instead of categorically rejecting hypotheses if the .05 grade is not made, we say the probability is .95 that the unknown value falls between .30 and .50. Now, if the obtained empirical proportion is, say, .60, then this is evidence for the correctness of the investigator's substantive hypothesis, or in null hypothesis language, the null hypothesis is rejected. A well-balanced discussion of these and other statistical problems can be found in C. Harris, "Statistical Methods," in C. Harris, ed., *Encyclopedia of Educational Research,* 3d ed. New York: Macmillan, 1960, pp. 1397–1410. A discussion of the difference between the terms "significance" and "confidence" can be found in R. Chandler, "The Statistical Concepts of Confidence and Significance," *Psychological Bulletin,* LIV (1957), 429, 430.

$$p(60 \cup 59 \cup \cdots \cup 40) = p(60) + p(59) + \cdots + p(40)$$

The set rationale behind this is that the sample space has 100 sample points, each sample point being an ordered pair of Agree and Disagree, with Agree coming first:

$$U = \{(0, 100), (1, 99), (2, 98, \cdots, (50, 50), \cdots, (98, 2), (99, 1), (100, 0)\}$$

The 100 sample points do *not* have equal probability. This is easily seen when we realize that (0, 100), (1, 99), and (100, 0), for example, each occur very rarely, but that such pairs as (49, 51) and (50, 50) occur much more often. Now, $p(U) = 1.00$, and the sum of the probabilities of all the sample points must equal 1.00. As we have seen, the sample points in the middle of U occur more frequently than do those at the ends of U. Therefore most of $p(U) = 1.00$ will be used up in the middle of U. Without doing the calculations, we can say, as before, that $p(60, 59, \cdots, 40)$ is approximately equal to .96.

Most statistical questions are asked, then, from the middles of U's. In this 60/40 case, we do not particularly care whether it is 60/40, 62/38, 40/60, 41/59, or what not. We want to know how far from random theoretical expectations are our results. And the theoretical expectation, in this case, is in the middle of U: 50/50. To ask whether 60/40 is statistically significant is to ask the question: *How often can we expect a deviation as great as* 60/40 *to occur by chance?* Another, perhaps clearer, way to ask the question is: *Does this result fall into the region covered by chance expectation?* Earlier it was seen that this region extended from (59, 41) to (41, 59). Beyond these sample points chance expectation ends, so to speak.[6]

BINOMIAL STATISTICS

When things are counted, the number system used is simple and useful. Whenever objects are counted, they are counted on the basis of some criterion, some variable or attribute, in research language. Many examples have already been given: heads, tails, numbers on dice, sex, aggressive acts, political preference, and so on. If a person or a thing possesses the attribute, the person or thing is "counted in," we say. When something is "counted in" because it possesses the attribute in question, it is assigned a 1. If it does not possess the attribute, it is assigned a 0. This is a binomial system.

Earlier, the mean was defined as $M = \Sigma X / n$. The variance is $V =$

---

[6] Note that the choice of 50/50 as the theoretical expectation is not sacred. With lack of any knowledge, we use the equiprobable assumption. But if we had knowledge that the "true" frequencies were, say, 65/35, then we would have to calculate with 65/35 instead of with 50/50. The principle is always the same, however: statistically compare obtained results with expected results whatever form the expected results take.

$\Sigma x^2/n$, where $x = X - M$ (each x is a deviation from the mean). The standard deviation is $SD = \sqrt{V}$. Of course, these formulas work with any scores. Here we use them only with 1's and 0's. And it is useful to alter the formula for the mean. The formula $\Sigma X/n$ is not general enough. It assumes that all scores are equiprobable. A more general formula, which can be used when equiprobability is not assumed, is

$$M = \Sigma[X \cdot w(X)] \qquad (9.3)$$

where $w(X)$ is the weight assigned to an X. $w(X)$ simply means the probability each X has of occurring. The formula says: Multiply each X, each score, by its weight (probability), and then add them all up. Notice that if all X's are equally probable, this formula is the same as $\Sigma X/n$.

The mean of the set $\{1, 2, 3, 4, 5\}$ is

$$M = \frac{1 + 2 + 3 + 4 + 5}{5} = \frac{15}{5} = 3$$

By formula (Eq. 9.3), it is of course the same, but its computation looks different:

$$M = 1 \cdot \frac{1}{5} + 2 \cdot \frac{1}{5} + 3 \cdot \frac{1}{5} + 4 \cdot \frac{1}{5} + 5 \cdot \frac{1}{5} = 3$$

Why the hair-splitting? Let a coin be tossed. $U = \{H, T\}$. The *mean number of heads* is, by Eq. 9.3,

$$M = 1 \cdot \frac{1}{2} + 0 \cdot \frac{1}{2} = \frac{1}{2}$$

Let two coins be tossed. $U = \{HH, HT, TH, TT\}$. The mean number of heads, or the *expectation* of heads, is

$$M = 2 \cdot \frac{1}{4} + 1 \cdot \frac{1}{4} + 1 \cdot \frac{1}{4} + 0 \cdot \frac{1}{4} = \frac{4}{4} = 1$$

This means that if two coins were tossed many times, the average number of heads per toss would be 1. If we sample one person from 30 men and 70 women, the mean of men is: $M = 3/10 \cdot 1 + 7/10 \cdot 0 = .3$. The mean for women is: $M = 3/10 \cdot 0 + 7/10 \cdot 1 = .7$. These are the means for one outcome. (This is a little like saying "an average of 2.5 children per family.")

What has been said in these examples is that the mean of any single experiment (a single coin toss, a sample of one person) is the probability of the occurrence of one of two possible outcomes (head, a man) which, if the outcome occurs, is assigned a 1 and, if it does not occur, is assigned a 0. This is tantamount to saying: $p(1) = p$ and $p(0) = 1 - p$. In the one-toss experiment, let 1 be assigned if heads turns up and 0 if tails turns up. Then $p(1) = 1/2$ and $p(0) = 1 - 1/2 = 1/2$. In tossing a coin twice, let

1 be assigned to each head that occurs and 0 to each tail. We are interested in the outcome "heads." $U = \{HH, HT, TH, TT\}$. The mean is

$$M = \frac{1}{4} \cdot 2 + \frac{1}{4} \cdot 1 + \frac{1}{4} \cdot 1 + \frac{1}{4} \cdot 0 = 1$$

Can we arrive at the same result in an easier manner? Yes. Just add the means for each outcome. The mean of the outcome of one coin toss is $\frac{1}{2}$. For two coin tosses it is simply $1/2 + 1/2 = 1$. To assign probabilities with one coin toss, we weight 1 (heads) with its probability and 0 (tails) with its probability. This gives $M = p \cdot 1 + (1 - p) \cdot 0 = p$. Take the men-women sampling problem, Let $p =$ the probability of a man's being sampled on a single outcome and $1 - p = q =$ the probability of a woman's being sampled on a single outcome. Then $p = 3/10$ and $q = 7/10$. We are interested in the mean of a man being sampled. Since $M = p \cdot 1 + q \cdot 0 = p$, $M = 3/10 \cdot 1 + 7/10 \cdot 0 = 3/10 = p$. The mean is $\frac{3}{10}$ and the probability is $\frac{3}{10}$. Evidently $M = p$, or the mean is equal to the probability.

How about a series of outcomes? We write S_n for the sum of n outcomes. One example, the tossing of two coins, was given above. Let us take the men-women sampling problem. The mean of a man's occurring is $\frac{3}{10}$ and of a woman's occurring $\frac{7}{10}$. We sample 10 persons. What is the mean number of men? Put differently, what is the expectation of men? If we sum the 10 means of the individual outcomes, we get the answer:

$$M(S_{10}) = M_1 + M_2 + \cdots + M_{10} \tag{9.4}$$

$$= \frac{3}{10} + \frac{3}{10} + \cdots + \frac{3}{10} = \frac{30}{10} = 3$$

In a sample of 10, we would expect to get the answer: 3 men. The same result could have been obtained by $3/10 \cdot 10 = 3$. But $3/10 \cdot 10$ is pn, or

$$M(S_n) = pn \tag{9.5}$$

In n trials the mean number of occurrences of the outcome associated with p is pn.

THE VARIANCE

Recall that in Chap. 7 the variance was defined as $V = \Sigma x^2/n$. Of course, it will be the same in this chapter, with a change in symbols (for the same reason given with the formula for the mean):

$$V = \Sigma[w(X)(X - M)^2] \tag{9.6}$$

To make clear what a variance—and a standard deviation—is in probability theory, we work two examples. Recall that, binomially, only two outcomes are possible: 1 and 0. Therefore X is equal to 1 or 0. We set up a table to help us compute the variance of the heads outcome of a coin throw:

Outcome	X	$w(X) = p$	$(X - M)^2$
H	1	$\frac{1}{2}$	$(1 - \frac{1}{2})^2 = \frac{1}{4}$
T	0	$\frac{1}{2}$	$(0 - \frac{1}{2})^2 = \frac{1}{4}$

The variance is, then,

$$V = \frac{1}{2}(1 - \frac{1}{2})^2 + \frac{1}{2}(0 - \frac{1}{2})^2 = \frac{1}{2} \cdot \frac{1}{4} + \frac{1}{2} \cdot \frac{1}{4} = \frac{1}{8} + \frac{1}{8} = \frac{2}{8} = \frac{1}{4}$$

The mean is ½ and the variance is ¼. The standard deviation is simply the square root of the variance, or $\sqrt{1/4} = 1/2$.

The variance of an individual outcome, however, does not have too much meaning. We really want the variance of the sum of a number of outcomes. If the outcomes are independent, the variance of the sum of the outcomes is the sum of the variances of the outcomes:

$$V(S_n) = V_1 + V_2 + \cdots + V_n \tag{9.7}$$

Or, analogously to Eqs. 9.4 and 9.5, if all the outcomes have the same mean:

$$V(S_n) = nV_i \qquad (i = 1, 2, \cdots n) \tag{9.8}$$

For 10 coin tosses, the variance of heads, then, is $V(H_{10}) = 10 \cdot 1/4 = 10/4 = 2.5$.

Earlier we showed that $M(S_n) = np$. We now want a formula for the variance. That is, instead of Eq. 9.7 we want a direct, simple formula. With a little algebraic manipulation we can arrive at such a formula:

$$V = p(1 - p) = pq \tag{9.9}$$

This is the variance of one outcome. The variance of the number of times that an outcome occurs is, analogously to Eqs. 9.4, 9.5, and 9.8, the sum of the individual outcome variances, or

$$V(S_n) = npq \tag{9.10}$$

The standard deviation is

$$SD(S_n) = \sqrt{npq} \tag{9.11}$$

Equations 9.5, 9.10, and 9.11 are important and useful. They can be applied in many statistical situations. Take two or three applications of the formula: first, the Agree-Disagree problem. Since a sample of 100 was taken, $n = 100$. On the assumption of equiprobability, $p = 1/2$ and

$q = 1/2$. Therefore, $M(S_{100}) = np = 100 \cdot 1/2 = 50$, $V(S_{100}) = npq$ $= 100 \cdot 1/2 \cdot 1/2 = 25$, and $SD(S_{100}) = \sqrt{25} = 5$. It was found that there were 60 Agrees. So, this is a deviation of two standard deviations from the mean of 50, $60 - 50 = 10$, and $10/5 = 2$. Second, take the coin-tossing experiment of the chapter on probability. In one experiment, 52 heads turned up in 100 tosses. The computations are exactly the same as those just given. Since there were 52 heads, the deviation from the mean, or expected frequency, is $52 - 50 = 2$. In standard deviation terms or units, this is $2/5 = .4$ standard deviation units from the mean. We now get back to one of the original questions we asked: Are these differences "statistically significant"? We found, via χ^2 and the exact probability method, that the result of 60 Agrees was statistically significant and that the result of 52 heads was not statistically significant. Can we do the same thing with the present formula? Yes, we can. Further, the beauty of the present method is that it is applicable to all kinds of numbers, not just to binomial numbers. Before demonstrating this, however, we must study, if only briefly, the so-called "law of large numbers" and the properties of the standard deviation and the normal probability curve.

THE LAW OF LARGE NUMBERS

The law of large numbers took Jacob Bernoulli twenty years to work out. In essence it is so simple that one wonders why he took so long to develop it.[7] Roughly, the law says that as you increase the size of samples, you also decrease the probability that the observed value of an event, A, will deviate from the "true" value of A by no more than a fixed amount, k. Provided the members of the samples are drawn independently, the larger the sample the closer the "true" value of the population is approached. The law is also a gateway to the testing of statistical hypotheses, as we shall see.

Toss a coin 1, 10, 50, 100, 400, and 1000 times. Let heads be the outcome in which we are interested. We compute means, variances, standard deviations, and two new measures. The first of these new measures is the proportion of favorable outcomes, heads in this case, in the total sample. We call this measure H_n and define it as $H_n = S_n/n$. (Recall that S_n is the total number of times the favorable outcome occurs in n trials.) Then, the fraction of the time that the favorable outcome occurs is H_n. The mean of H_n is p, or $M(H_n) = p$. (This follows from Eq. 9.5, where $M(S_n)$ $= pn$, and since $H_n = S_n/n$, $M(H_n) = M(S_n)/n = np/n = p$.) In short,

[7] A brief statement of the law by Bernoulli himself can be found in J. Newman, *The World of Mathematics*, vol. 3. New York: Simon and Schuster, 1956, pp. 1452–1455. For more exact statements than are possible in this text, see *ibid.*, pp. 1448, 1449. A rigorous mathematical treatment is given in J. Kemeny, *et. al.*, *Finite Mathematical Structures*. Englewood Cliffs, N. J.: Prentice-Hall, 1959, pp. 165–178.

$M(H_n)$ equals the expected probability. The second measure is the variance of H_n. It is defined: $V(H_n) = pq/n$. The variance, $V(H_n)$, is a measure of the variability of the mean, $M(H_n)$. Later more will be said about the square root of $V(H_n)$, called the *standard error of the mean*. The results of the calculation are given in Table 9.3.

TABLE **9.3**   MEANS, VARIANCES, STANDARD DEVIATIONS, AND EXPECTED
PROBABILITIES OF THE OUTCOME HEADS WITH DIFFERENT SIZE SAMPLES [a]

n	$M(S_n) = np$	$V(S_n) = npq$	$SD(S_n)$	$M(H_n) = p$	$V(H_n) = pq/n$
1	$\frac{1}{2}$	.25	.50	$\frac{1}{2}$	$\frac{1}{4}$
10	5	2.50	1.58	$\frac{1}{2}$	$\frac{1}{40}$
50	25	12.50	3.54	$\frac{1}{2}$	$\frac{1}{200}$
100	50	25.00	5.00	$\frac{1}{2}$	$\frac{1}{400}$
400	200	100.00	10.00	$\frac{1}{2}$	$\frac{1}{1600}$
1000	500	250.00	15.81	$\frac{1}{2}$	$\frac{1}{4000}$

[a] See text for explanation of the symbols in this table.

Notice that, although the means, variances, and standard deviations of the sums increase with the sizes of the samples, the $M(H_n)$'s or p's remain the same. That is, the average number of heads, or $M(H_n)$, is always $\frac{1}{2}$. But the variance of the average number of heads, $V(H_n)$, gets smaller and smaller as the sizes of the samples increase. Again, $V(H_n)$ is a measure of the variability of the averages. As Table 9.3 clearly indicates, the average number of outcomes should come closer and closer to the "true" value, in this case $\frac{1}{2}$. (The student should ponder this example carefully before going further.)

THE NORMAL PROBABILITY CURVE AND THE STANDARD DEVIATION

The normal probability curve is the lovely bell-shaped curve encountered so often in statistics and psychology textbooks. Its importance stems from the fact that chance events in large numbers tend to distribute themselves in the form of the curve. The so-called "theory of errors" uses the curve. Many natural phenomena, physical and psychological, distribute themselves in normal form. Height, intelligence, and achievement are three familiar examples. The means of samples distribute themselves normally.[8] It is hard to conceive of modern statistics without this curve.

---

[8] The reader should avoid the untested belief that all or even most phenomena are normally distributed. Whenever possible, data should be checked by appropriate methods, especially by plotting or graphing. Data are often subtle. Take height, for example. In the whole population, height is very probably normally distributed. But suppose we are studying men of high talent. Is height normally distributed? (Some people may think short people are more talented; others that tall people are more

Every statistics text has a table called the "table of the normal deviate," or "table of the normal curve."

The most important statistical reason for using the normal curve is to be able easily to interpret the probabilities of the statistics one computes. If the data are, as is said, "normal" or approximately normal, one has a clear interpretation for what one does.

There are two types of graphs ordinarily used in research in the social sciences and education. In one of these, as we have seen, the values of a dependent variable are plotted against the values of an independent variable. The second major type of graph has a different purpose: to show the distribution of a single variable. On the horizontal axis, values are laid out similarly to the first type of graph. But, on the vertical axis, *frequencies* or frequency intervals or probabilities are laid out.

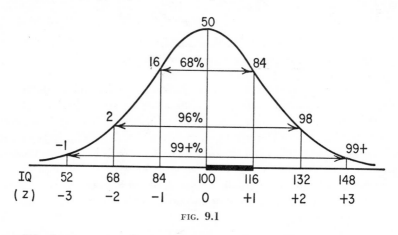

FIG. 9.1

We draw a normal curve, and lay out two sets of values on the horizontal axis. In one set of values, we use IQ's with a mean of 100 and a standard deviation of 16. Say we have a sample of 400 and the data (the IQ's) are in normal form. (It is said that the data are "normally distributed.") The curve looks like that of Fig. 9.1. Imagine a *Y* (vertical) axis with frequencies (or propositions) marked off on the axis. The major characteristics of normal curves are unimodality (one curve), symmetry (one side the same as the other), and certain mathematical properties. It is the mathematical properties that interest us, because they allow us to make statistical inferences of considerable power.

---

talented.) Havelock Ellis, in his study of British genius, lists 270 men of high talent according to their heights: 103 tall, 57 medium, and 100 short. Although we can well question the sampling and the source data, the example is instructive. (See H. Ellis, *A Study of British Genius.* Boston: Houghton Mifflin, 1926, pp. 278–281.) Margenau gives a powerful *rational* argument for normality: H. Margenau, *The Nature of Physical Reality.* New York: McGraw-Hill, 1950, pp. 114, 115. For an enlightening discussion of the normality concept, see M. Tate, *Statistics in Education.* New York: Macmillan, 1955, pp. 203–209.

A standard deviation can be conceived as a length along the base line of the curve from the mean or middle of the base line out to the right, or left to the point where the curve inflects. It can also be visualized as a point on the base line a certain distance from the mean. One standard deviation from the mean of this particular distribution is $100 + 16 = 116$. The distance from 100 to 116 has been indicated by a heavy line in Fig. 9.1. Similarly, one standard deviation below the mean is $100 - 16 = 84$. Two standard deviations are represented by $100 + (2)(16) = 132$ and $100 - (2)(16) = 68$. If one can be reasonably confident that one's data are normally distributed, then one can draw a curve like the one above, mark the mean, and lay out the standard deviations. This has also been done in Fig. 9.1. The base line of Fig. 9.1 has also been labeled in *standard deviation units* (labeled z in the figure.) That is, instead of raw scores (IQ's) of 100, 116, and 68, for instance, standard deviation scores can be used. They are 0, $+1$, -2, and so on; points between these marked points can be indicated. For example, one half of a standard deviation above the mean, in raw scores, is $100 + (1/2)(16) = 108$. In standard deviation scores, it is $0 + .5 = .5$. These standard deviation scores are called *standard* scores or z scores. z scores range, in practical usage, from about -3 through 0 to about $+3$.[9]

If z scores are used, and the total area under the curve is set equal to 1.00, the curve is said to be in *standard form*. This immediately suggests probability. Portions of the area of the curve are conceived as probabilities and interpreted as such. If the total area under the whole curve is equal to 1.00, then if a vertical line is drawn upward from the base line at the mean $(z = 0)$ to the top of the bell, then the areas to the left and to the right of the vertical line are each equal to $\frac{1}{2}$ or 50 percent. But vertical lines might be drawn elsewhere on the base line, at one standard deviation above the mean $(z = 1)$ or two standard deviations below the mean $(z = -2)$. To interpret such points in area terms—and in probability terms—we must know the area properties of the curve.

The *approximate* percentages of the areas one, two, and three standard deviations above and below the mean have been indicated in Fig. 9.1. For our purposes, it is not necessary to use the exact percentages. The area between $z = -1$ and $z = +1$ is approximately 68 percent. The area between $z = -2$ and $z = +2$ is approximately 96 percent. (The exact figure is .9544. We use .96 because it makes interpretation easier.) The area between $z = -3$ and $z = +3$ is 99+ percent. Similarly all other possible baseline distances and their associated areas can be translated into

[9] To transform any raw score to a z score, use the formula $z = x/s$, where $x = X - M$ and s is the sample standard deviation. The x's are called deviation scores, as we saw in an earlier chapter. Now we can divide the standard deviation into any x to convert the X (raw score) to a z score. As an example, take $X = 120$. Then $z = 120 - 100/16 = 20/16 = 1.25$. That is, a raw score of 120 is equivalent to a z score of 1.25. Or, it is one and a quarter standard deviations above the mean.

percentages of the whole curve. An important point to remember is that, since the area of the whole curve is equal to 1.00, or 100 percent, and thus is equivalent to U in probability theory, the percentages of area can be interpreted as probabilities. In fact, the normal probability table entries are given in percentages of areas corresponding to z scores.

INTERPRETATION OF DATA USING THE NORMAL PROBABILITY CURVE—FREQUENCY DATA

We now inquire about the probabilities of events. To do this, we first go back to the rather silly, but simple and useful, task of tossing coins. Strictly speaking, the frequencies of heads and tails are discontinuous events, whereas the normal probability curve is continuous. But this need not worry us, since the approximations are close. It is possible to specify with great accuracy and considerable ease the probabilities that chance events will occur. Instead of computing exact probabilities as we did before, we can estimate probabilities from knowledge of the properties of the normal curve.

Suppose we again, somewhat wearily, perhaps, toss 100 coins. We found that the mean number of times heads will probably turn up is $M(S_{100}) = np = 100 \cdot 1/2 = 50$, and the standard deviation was $SD(S_{100}) = \sqrt{V(S_{100})} = \sqrt{npq} = \sqrt{100 \cdot 1/2 \cdot 1/2} = \sqrt{25} = 5$. Using the percentages of the curve (probabilities), we can make probability statements. We can say, for example, that in 100 tosses the probability that heads will turn up between one standard deviation below the mean ($z = -1$) and one standard deviation above the mean ($z = +1$) is approximately .68. Roughly, then, there are two out of three chances that the number of heads will be between 45 and 55 (50 ± 5). There *is* one chance in three, approximately, that the number of heads will be less than 45 or greater than 55. That is, $q = 1 - p = 1 - .68 = .32$, approximately.

Take two standard deviations above and below the mean. These points would be $50 - (2)(5) = 40$ and $50 + (2)(5) = 60$. Since we know that about 95 or 96 percent of the cases will probably fall into this band, that is, between $z = -2$ and $z = +2$, or between 40 and 60, we can say that the probability that the number of heads will be no less than 40 or no greater than 60 is about .95 or .96. That is, there are only about 4 or 5 chances in 100 that less than 40, or more than 60, heads will occur. It *could* happen. But it is quite unlikely to happen. (Recall that earlier it was said that by the exact probability method of computation the probability was about .96.)

If we want or need to be practically certain (as in certain kinds of medical or engineering research), then we can go out to three standard deviations, $z = -3$ and $z = +3$, or perhaps somewhat less than three standard deviations. (The .01 level is about two and a half standard deviations.) Three standard deviations means the numbers of heads between 35 and 65. Since three standard deviations above and below the mean in Fig. 9.1 take up more than 99 percent of the area of the curve, we can say that we are practically certain that the number of heads in 100 tosses of a fair coin will not be less than 35 nor more than 65. The probability is greater than .99. If you tossed a coin 100 times and got, say, 68 heads, you might conclude that there was probably something wrong with the coin. Of course, 68 heads could occur, but it is very, very unlikely that they would.

The earlier Agree-Disagree problem is treated exactly the same as the coin problem above. The result of 60 Agrees and 40 Disagrees is unlikely to happen. There are only about 4 chances in 100 that 60 Agrees and 40 Disagrees could happen by chance. We knew this before from the χ^2 test and from the exact probability test. Now we have a third way that is generally applicable to all kinds of data—provided the data are distributed normally or approximately so.

INTERPRETATION OF DATA USING THE NORMAL PROBABILITY CURVE—CONTINUOUS DATA

Suppose we have the social studies test scores of a sample of 100 fifth-grade children. The mean of the scores is 70; the standard deviation is 10. From previous knowledge we know that the distribution of test scores on this test is approximately normal. Obviously we can interpret the data using the normal curve. Our interest is in the reliability of the mean. How much can we depend on this mean? With future samples of similar fifth-grade children, will we get the same mean? If the mean is undependable, that is, if it fluctuates widely from sample to sample, obviously any interpretation of the test scores of individual children is in jeopardy. A score of 75 might be average this time, but if the mean is unreliable this 75 might become, on a future testing, a superior score. In other words, we must have a dependable or reliable mean.

Imagine giving this same test to the same group of children again and again and again. Go further. Imagine giving the test under exactly the same conditions 100,000 times, or even an infinite number of times. Assume that all other things are equal: the children learn nothing new in all these repetitions; they do not get fatigued; environmental conditions remain the same; and so on.

If we compute a mean and a standard deviation for each of the many times, we obtain a gigantic distribution of means (and standard deviations). What will this distribution be like? First, it will form a beautiful bell-shaped normal curve. Means always do. They have the property of falling nicely into the normal distribution, even when the original distributions from which they are computed are not normal. This is because

we assumed "other things equal" and thus have no source of mean fluctuations other than chance. The means will fluctuate, but the fluctuations
will all be chance fluctuations. Most of these fluctuations will cluster
around what we will call the "true" mean, the "true" value of the gigantic population of means. A few will be extreme values. If we repeated the
100 coin-tosses experiment many many times, we would find that heads
would cluster around what we know is the "true" value: 50. Some would
be a little higher, some a little lower, a few considerably higher, a few
considerably lower. In brief, the heads and the means will obey the same
"law." Since we assumed that nothing else is operating, we must come to
the conclusion that these fluctuations are due to chance. And chance
errors, given enough of them, distribute themselves into a normal distribution. This is the theory. It is called the *theory of errors.*

Continuing our story of the mean, if we had the data from the very
many administrations of the social studies test to the same group, we
could compute a mean and a standard deviation. The mean so computed
would be very close to the "true" mean. If we had an infinite number of
means from an infinite number of test administrations and computed the
mean of the means, we would then obtain the "true" mean. Similarly for
the standard deviation of the means. Naturally, we cannot do this, for we
do not have an infinite or even a very large number of test administrations. There is fortunately a simple way to solve the problem. It consists
in accepting the mean computed from the sample as the "true" mean and
then estimating how accurate this acceptance (or assumption) is. To do
this, a statistic known as the *standard error of the mean* is computed. It
is defined:

$$SE_M = \frac{\sigma_{pop}}{\sqrt{n}} \tag{9.12}$$

where the standard error of the mean is SE_M; the standard deviation of
the population (σ is read "sigma"), σ_{pop}, and the number of cases in the
sample, n.

There is a little snag here. We do not know, nor can we know, the
standard deviation of the population. Recall that we also did not know
the mean of the population, but that we estimated it with the mean of the
sample. Similarly, we estimate the standard deviation of the population
with the standard deviation of the sample. Thus the formula to use is

$$SE_M = \frac{SD}{\sqrt{n}} \tag{9.13}$$

The social studies test mean can now be studied for its reliability.
We compute:

$$SE_M = \frac{10}{\sqrt{100}} = \frac{10}{10} = 1$$

Again imagine a large population of means of this test. If they are computed and put into a distribution and the curve of the distribution plotted, the curve would look something like the curve of Figure 9.2. Keep firmly in mind: this is an imaginary distribution of means of samples. It is *not* a distribution of scores. It is easy to see that the means of this distribution are not very variable. If we double the standard error of the mean we get 2. Subtract and add this to the mean of 70: 68 to 72. The probability is approximately .95 that the population ("true") mean lies within the interval 68 to 72, that is, approximately 5 percent of the time the means of random samples of this size would lie outside this interval.

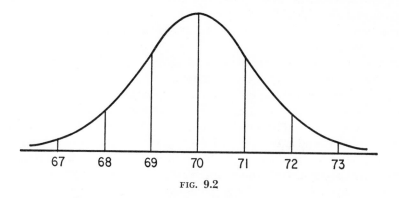

FIG. 9.2

If we do the same computation for the intelligence test data of Fig. 9.1, we obtain

$$SE_M = \frac{16}{\sqrt{400}} = \frac{16}{20} = .80$$

Three standard errors above and below the mean of 100 give the range 97.60 to 102.40, or we can say that the "true" mean very probably (less than 1 percent chance of being wrong) lies within the interval 98 to 102. Means *are* reliable—with fair size samples.[10]

The standard error of the mean, then, is a standard deviation. It is

[10] Even with relatively small samples, the mean is quite stable. (See the IQ data in chap. 4.) Five samples of 20 IQ's each were drawn from a population of IQ's with a mean of 95. The means of the five samples were computed. Standard errors of the mean were computed for the first two samples, and interpretations were made. Then comparisons were made to the "true" value of 95. The mean of the first sample was 93.55 with a standard deviation of 12.22. $SE_M = 2.73$. The .05 level range of means was: 88.09 to 99.01. Obviously 95 falls within this range. The mean of the second sample was more deviant: 90.20. The standard deviation was 9.44. $SE_M = 2.11$. The .05 level range was 85.98 to 94.42. Our 95 does not fall in this range. The .01 level range is: 83.87 to 96.53. Now 95 is encompassed. This is not bad at all for samples of only 20. For samples of 50 or 100 it would be even better. The mean of the five means was 93.31; the standard deviation of these means was 2.73. Compare this to the standard errors computed from the two samples: 2.73 and 2.11.

a standard deviation of an infinite number of means. Only chance error makes the means fluctuate. Thus the standard error of the mean—or the standard deviation of the means, if you like—is a measure of chance or error in its effect on one measure of central tendency.

A caution is in order. All of the theory discussed is based on the assumptions of random sampling and independence of observations. If these assumptions are violated, the reasoning, while not entirely invalidated, practically speaking, is open to question. Estimates of error may be biased to a greater or lesser extent. The trouble is we cannot tell how much a standard error is biased. Guilford gives some interesting examples of the biases encountered when the assumptions are violated.[11] With large numbers of Air Force pilots, he found that estimates of standard errors were sometimes considerably off. No one can give hard and fast rules. The best maxim probably is: Use random sampling and keep observations independent, if at all possible.

If random sampling cannot be used, and if there is doubt about the independence of observations, compute the statistics and interpret them. But be circumspect about interpretations and conclusions; they may be in error. Because of such possibilities of error, it has been said that statistics are misleading, and even useless. Like any other method—consulting authority, using intuition, and the like—statistics *can* be misleading. But even when statistical measures are biased, they are usually less biased than authoritative and intuitive judgments. It is not that numbers lie. The numbers do not know what they are doing. It is that the human beings using the numbers may be informed or misinformed, biased or unbiased, knowledgeable or ignorant, intelligent or stupid. Treat numbers and statistics neither with too great respect nor too great contempt. Compute statistics and act as though they were "true," but always maintain a certain reserve toward them, a willingness to disbelieve them if the evidence indicates such disbelief.

11 J. Guilford, *Fundamental Statistics in Psychology and Education,* 3d ed. New York: McGraw-Hill, 1956, pp. 169–173.

10   STATISTICS: THE STANDARD ERROR AND TESTING HYPOTHESES

The standard error, as a measure of chance fluctuations of experimental measurements, is the measure against which the outcomes of experimental manipulations are checked. Is there a difference between the means of two experimental groups? If so, is the difference a "real" difference or merely a consequence of the many relatively small differences that could have arisen by chance? To answer this question, the standard error of the differences between means is computed and the obtained difference is compared to this standard error. If it is sufficiently greater than the standard error, it is said to be a "significant" difference. Similar reasoning can be applied to any statistic. Thus, there are many standard errors: of correlation coefficients, of differences between means, of means, of medians, of proportions, and so on. The purpose of this chapter is to examine the general notion of the standard error and to see how hypotheses are tested using the standard error.

EXAMPLES: DIFFERENCES BETWEEN MEANS

A number of years ago, Ojemann and Wilkinson, using an experimental group and a control group of 33 Ss each, performed an interesting and educationally provocative experiment.[1] Personality and environmental data (obtained by suitable means) on an experimental group of children were made available to their teachers. The teachers of the children in the control group did not get this information. One of the dependent variables was school achievement measured by grade points. (Presumably the authors meant grade-point averages, which are the averages of achievement scores converted to grade levels via suitable tables.) The means of the experimental and control groups in grade points, at the end of the experimental period of a school year, were 3.21 and 2.97, respectively, a

[1] R. Ojemann and F. Wilkinson, "The Effect on Pupil Growth of an Increase in Teachers' Understanding of Pupil Behavior," *Journal of Experimental Education,* VIII (1939), 143–147.

mean difference of .24. The authors asked this question: Is the mean difference of .24 large enough to warrant the conclusion that the experimental condition had a "real" effect? Or the question may be stated: Can the difference of .24 just as well be considered a manifestation of chance? That is, differences like this will occur by chance if no experimental manipulations were used. Will such chance differences be as large as .24? The authors found this not to be the case. The .24 was "statistically significant" at a high level of significance. They could thus come to the conclusion that their experimental manipulations were effective, an interesting result indeed.[2]

Gross, Mason, and McEachern, in an important study of board of education members and superintendents, report one intriguing if perhaps obvious result.[3] They administered a questionnaire on division of labor to a sampling of board members and superintendents. The hypothesis they tested was that incumbents of subordinate (superintendent) and superordinate (board of education) positions will assign more responsibility to their own position than incumbents of the other position will assign to it. The means of the two groups on the instrument, which indicates the relative amount of responsibility, were 1.41 and 2.54 for board members and superintendents, respectively. (The higher the mean the greater the responsibility assigned to the superintendent role.) The direction of the difference was as predicted. Is the size of the difference, 1.13, sufficient to warrant the authors' claim that their hypothesis is supported? A test of the statistical significance of this difference showed that it was highly significant.

The point of these two examples in the present context is that both these mean differences were tested for statistical significance with a standard error. The standard error in this case was the standard error of the differences between two means. In both cases the differences were found to be significant. Now let us look at an example in which the difference between means was not significant.

Gates and Taylor, in a well-known early study of transfer of training, set up two matched groups of 16 pupils each.[4] The experimental

2 An important note on the absolute and relative size of statistics is in order here. The student may wonder about a difference of .24, and ask about the psychological and practical significance of a difference of this magnitude. This is a relative matter. Remember the scale on which an experimenter is working. The difference of .24 is about 8 percent of the average mean of about 3.00, an appreciable increase. Sometimes, however, a difference of .24 is trivial, whether or not it is statistically significant. Once again, the researcher should use experienced and informed judgment. We shall have to return to this point later.

3 N. Gross, W. Mason, and A. McEachern, *Explorations in Role Analysis*. New York: Wiley, 1958, pp. 123–126.

4 A. Gates and G. Taylor, "An Experimental Study of the Nature of Improvement Resulting from Practice in a Mental Function," *Journal of Educational Psychology*, XVI (1925), 583–592.

group was given practice in digit memory; the control group was not given such practice. The mean gain of the experimental group right after the practice period was 2.00; the mean gain of the control group was .67, a mean difference of 1.33. Four to five months later, the children of both groups were tested again. The mean score of the experimental group was 4.71; the mean score of the control group was surprising— 4.77. The mean gains over the initial tests were .35 and .36. Statistical tests are hardly necessary with data like these.

EXAMPLES: CORRELATION COEFFICIENTS

Correlation coefficients are reported in large quantities in every issue of every psychology and education research journal. Since correlation coefficients are measures of the relations between variables, questions as to the significance of the coefficients—and the "reality" of the relations —must be asked. Although this is probably not too serious a problem since perhaps most of the coefficients of correlation reported in educational research are reasonably high, it can be a serious problem if the investigator is not aware of the facts. For example, in order to be statistically significant, a coefficient of correlation computed between 30 pairs of measures, has to be approximately .36 to be significant at the .05 level and approximately .46 at the .01 level. With about 100 pairs of measures the problem is less acute (the law of large numbers again). To carry the .05 day, an r of about .20 is sufficient; to carry the .01 day, an r of about .25 does it. If r's are less than these levels, they are considered to be not significant.

If one takes a table of random numbers and draws, say, 30 pairs of numbers and correlates them, theoretically the computed r should be near zero. Clearly there should be a zero relation between the two sets of random numbers, but every once in a while such a set of pairs can yield a reasonably high r *by chance.*[5] At any rate, coefficients of correlation, as well as means and differences have to be weighed in the balance by stacking them up against their standard errors. Fortunately, this is easy to do since tables of r's for different levels of significance and for different size samples are given in most statistics texts. Thus, with r's it is not necessary to compute and use the standard error of an r. The reasoning behind the tables has to be understood, however.

In presenting data on the validity of their Test Anxiety Scale (TASC), Sarason, *et al.,* present a number of coefficients of correlation

[5] I drew 30 pairs of numbers from a table of random numbers. The coefficient of correlation was −.19, clearly not significant. With more patience and time, one could draw 100 such samples and correlate them. At least one or more would probably be greater than about .40, either plus or minus.

between the TASC and mean school achievement of children and between teacher ratings (TR) of test anxiety and mean achievement.[6] Most of the r's between the TASC and achievement were low. In Greenwich, Conn., only one r out of eight was significant. It was $-.234$ ($n = 120$). In Milford, Conn., however, all the r's were significant. The samples were considerably larger. Curiously, the r's between TR and achievement were considerably higher but with a larger range: $-.127$ to $-.533$. All were significant. Here is a case of a type that occurs frequently in the literature where r's are low and borderline. It has been said that it is inappropriate to bother with r's of .10, .20, and .30. With r's of about .10 or less, this point is well taken. But with r's of about .30, the point is not well-taken. If an r of .30 is statistically significant, it may help the investigator later to find an important relationship—if he can clear up, say, his measurement problems. That is, he might, by dropping a statistically significant r of .30, be losing a valuable lead for theory and subsequent research. The point is that r's, like other statistics, must be tested for statistical significance.

A few more examples may help to drive this point home. Sears, Maccoby, and Levin, in their large study of child-rearing practices, report a large number of relations, some of them in coefficient of correlation form.[7] Most of these r's are quite small, sometimes so small that one wonders whether they are "psychologically significant." But it must be known that Sears and his colleagues were measuring very complex variables and their measures were relatively crude (but not inept—quite the contrary). They report, for instance, the correlation between an accepting tolerant attitude toward the child's dependent behavior and being warm toward the child: .37.[8] This r is not high, true. But since it is based presumably on an N of 379, it is statistically significant. Also, it reflects, very probably, an important relation. Other significant, but low, relations reported are between tolerant attitude toward dependent behavior and gentleness in toilet training (.30); low physical punishment (.30); high in esteem for self (.39); and high in esteem for husband (.32). Such relations, though low, are the makings of important research findings and theory building. The role of the standard error is obvious here. If the correlations were not significant, we could come to no definite conclusions. Here, however, sets of relations go together, and, from a scientific point of view, lend credence to the purposes of the whole investigation.

In an important book recently published, Rokeach reports a number of important relations, among which the following are interesting because they were computed from samples with very low numbers in each

[6] S. Sarason, *et al.*, *Anxiety in Elementary School Children.* New York: Wiley, 1960, p. 129.

[7] R. Sears, E. Maccoby, and H. Levin, *Patterns of Child Rearing.* New York: Harper & Row, 1957.

[8] *Ibid.*, p. 166.

sample.[9] The correlation between Dogmatism and Opinionation (interpreting these terms with their usual meanings will not be too misleading for the present purpose) is .66. Since $n = 13$, this is significant at the .05 level but not quite significant at the .01 level. The correlation between Authoritarianism and Ethnocentrism is .46. But since $n = 10$, this r is *not* significant at the .05 level. These examples illustrate two points. One, tests of the significance of r's are essential to adequate interpretation of computed relations. Two, working with samples that are too small can be dangerous. Small samples yield relatively large standard errors.

HYPOTHESIS TESTING: SUBSTANTIVE AND NULL HYPOTHESES

The main research purpose of inferential statistics is to test research hypotheses by testing statistical hypotheses. Another way to put it is that inferential statistics helps the researcher make decisions between alternative hypotheses.

Broadly speaking, the scientist uses two types of hypothesis, substantive and statistical. A *substantive hypothesis* is the usual type of hypothesis discussed in Chap. 2 in which a conjectural statement of the relation between two or more variables is expressed, for example, "The greater the cohesiveness of a group the greater its influence on its members" [10] is a substantive hypothesis. An investigator's theory dictates that this variable is related to that variable. The statement of this relation is a substantive hypothesis.

A substantive hypothesis itself, strictly speaking, is not testable. It has first to be translated into operational and experimental terms. One very useful way to test substantive hypotheses is through statistical hypotheses. A *statistical hypothesis* is a conjectural statement, in statistical terms, of statistical relations deduced from the relations of the substantive hypothesis. This rather clumsy statement needs translation. A statistical hypothesis expresses an aspect of the original substantive hypothesis in quantitative and statistical terms. $M_A > M_B$, Mean A is greater than Mean B; $r > +.20$, the coefficient of correlation is greater than $+.20$; $M_A > M_B > M_C$, at the .01 level; the interaction F ratio is significant at the .05 level; and so on. A statistical hypothesis is a prediction of how the statistics used in analyzing the quantitative data of a research problem will turn out.

Statistical hypotheses must be tested against something, however. It is not possible simply to test a statistical hypothesis as it stands. That is, we do not actually and directly test the statistical proposition $M_A > M_B$

[9] M. Rokeach, *The Open and Closed Mind.* New York: Basic Books, 1960, p. 131.
[10] S. Schachter, *et al.,* "An Experimental Study of Cohesiveness and Productivity," *Human Relations,* IV (1951), 229–238.

in and of itself. We test it against an alternative proposition. Naturally, there can be several alternatives to $M_A > M_B$. The alternative usually selected is the null hypothesis, which was invented by Sir Ronald Fisher. The *null hypothesis* is a statistical proposition which states, essentially, that there is no relation between the variables (of the problem). The null hypothesis says, "You're wrong, there is no relation; disprove me if you can." It says this in statistical terms such as $M_A = M_B$, or $M_A - M_B = 0$; $r_{xy} = 0$; F is not significant; t is not significant; and so on.[11]

Fisher says, "Every experiment may be said to exist only in order to give the facts a chance of disproving the null hypothesis." [12] Aptly said. What does it mean? Suppose you entertain a hypothesis to the effect that teaching Method A is superior to teaching Method B. If you satisfactorily solve the problems of defining what you mean by "superior," of setting up an experiment, and the like, you now must specify a statistical hypothesis. In this case, you might say $M_A > M_B$ (the mean of Method A is, or will be, greater than the mean of Method B on such-and-such a criterion measure). Assume that after the experiment the two means are 68 and 61, respectively. It would seem that your substantive hypothesis is upheld since $68 > 61$, or M_A is greater than M_B. As we have already learned, however, this is not enough since this difference may be one of the many possible similar differences due to chance and its fluctuations.

In effect, we set up what can be called the chance hypothesis: $M_A = M_B$, or $M_A - M_B = 0$, or $M_B - M_A = 0$. These are all null hypotheses. What we do, then, is write hypotheses. First we write the statistical hypothesis which reflects the operational-experimental meaning of the substantive hypothesis. Then we write the null hypothesis against which we test the first type of hypothesis. Here are the two kinds of hypothesis suitably labeled:

$$H_1: M_A > M_B$$
$$H_o: M_A = M_B$$

H_1 simply means "Hypothesis 1." There is often more than one such hypothesis. They are labeled H_1, H_2, H_3, and so on. H_o means "null hypothesis." Note that the null hypothesis could in this case have been written:

$$H_o: M_A - M_B = 0$$

11 Many graduate students use the null form of hypothesis in writing their theses. Instead of saying that Method A is more conducive to learning arithmetic than Method B, to take a simple example, they may say that there is no difference between Methods A and B. In the author's opinion, this is poor practice because it begs the scientific question. Assume that an investigator believes $M_A > M_B$, but hypothesizes $M_A = M_B$. Then, either $M_A > M_B$ or $M_B < M_A$, which is a very wide range. The power of the substantive hypothesis, that the investigator can make a more or less specific *nonchance* prediction, is thus lost.

12 R. Fisher, *The Design of Experiments*, 6th ed. New York: Hafner, 1951, p. 16.

This form shows where the null hypothesis got its name; the difference between M_A and M_B is zero. But it is a little unwieldy in this form, especially when there are three or more means or other statistics being tested. $M_A = M_B$ is general, and of course means the same as $M_A - M_B = 0$ and $M_B - M_A = 0$. Notice that we can write quite easily $M_A = M_B = M_C = \cdots = M_N$.

The null hypothesis is a succinct way to express the testing of obtained data against chance expectation. The null hypothesis is the chance expectation. The standard error is a means of testing the null hypothesis. Indeed, it expresses the null hypothesis since it is a measure of expected chance fluctuations around a mean of zero. We can express these ideas in variance terms. How much does the obtained result vary? Does it vary significantly? Vary from what? Vary significantly from chance. The null hypothesis and the statistical tests that use it give us the answers to these questions.

THE GENERAL NATURE OF A STANDARD ERROR

If this were the best of all possible research worlds, there would be no random error. And if there were no random error, there would be no need for statistical tests of significance. The word "significance" would be meaningless, in fact. Any difference at all would be a "real" difference. But such is never the case, alas. There are *always* chance errors (and biased errors, too), and in educational and psychological research they often contribute substantially to the total variance. Standard errors are measures of this error, and are used, as has repeatedly been said, as a sort of yardstick against which experimental or "variable" variance is checked.

The *standard error* is the standard deviation of the sampling distribution of any given measure—the mean or the correlation coefficient, for instance. In most cases, population or universe values (parameters) cannot be known; they must be estimated, as we said earlier, from sample measures, usually from single samples.

Suppose we draw a random sample of 100 children from eighth-grade classes in such-and-such a school system. It would be difficult or impossible, say, to measure the whole universe of eighth-grade children for reasons we need not go into here. We compute the mean and the standard deviation from a test we give the children and find these statistics to be $M = 110$; $SD = 10$. An important question we must ask ourselves is "How accurate is this mean?" Or, if we were to draw a large number of random samples of 100 eighth-grade pupils from this same population, would the means of these samples be 110 or near 110? And, if they are near 110, how near? What we do, in effect, is to set up a *hypothetical distribution of sample means*, all computed from samples of 100 pupils each drawn from the parent population of eighth-grade pupils. If we could compute the means of this population *of means,* or if we knew what it was, everything would be simple. But we do not know this value, and we are not able to know it since the possibilities of drawing different samples are so numerous. The best we can do is to *estimate it with our sample value, or sample mean.* We simply say, in this case, let the sample mean equal the mean of the population mean—and hope we are right. Then we must test our equation. This we do with the standard error.

A similar argument applies to the standard deviation of the whole population (of the original scores). We do not know and probably can never know it. But we can estimate it. And we estimate it with the standard deviation computed from our sample. Again, we say, in effect, let the standard deviation of the sample equal the standard deviation of the population. We know they are probably not the same value, but we also know, if the sampling has been random, that they are probably close.

In Chap. 9 the sample standard deviation was used as a substitute for the standard deviation of the population in the formula for the *standard error of the mean:*

$$SE_M = \frac{SD}{\sqrt{n}} \tag{10.1}$$

This is also called the *sampling error.* Just as the standard deviation is a measure of the dispersion of the original scores, the standard error of the mean is a measure of the dispersion of the distribution of sample means. It is *not* the standard deviation of the population of individual scores if, for example, we could test every member of the population and compute the mean and standard deviation of this population.

Suppose we draw five samples of 100 scores from a population of scores. Let the scores be intelligence test scores and the population be all children in American suburban communities. These five samples are represented in Fig. 10.1:

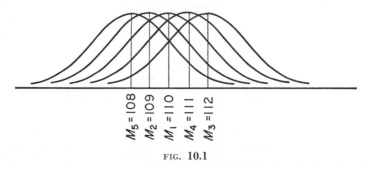

$M_5 = 108$ $M_2 = 109$ $M_1 = 110$ $M_4 = 111$ $M_3 = 112$

FIG. 10.1

Note that the distributions overlap, and that their means are quite close. (Remember that the means of samples are very stable, more stable, in fact, than the raw scores from which they are derived.) The means are: M_1 = 110; M_2 = 109; M_3 = 112; M_4 = 111; M_5 = 108. Now compute the *standard deviation of this sample of means.* The mean of the means is 110. The standard deviation is

$$SD = \sqrt{\frac{\Sigma x^2}{n}} = \sqrt{\frac{10}{5}} = \sqrt{2} = 1.414$$

This 1.414 is *akin to* the standard error of the mean. (It is of course not the standard error of the mean because it has been computed from only five means.) If, as usual, only one sample had been drawn with a mean of 110 and a standard deviation of 10, we could have estimated this, as follows:

$$SE_M = \frac{SD}{\sqrt{n}} = \frac{10}{\sqrt{100}} = 1$$

This value of 1 is the standard error of the distribution of means, or the estimate of the standard deviation of the population of means. For obvious reasons there is a discrepancy. But the idea should be clear.

Suppose we have two randomly selected groups of 100 eighth-grade pupils each. We show a movie on intergroup relations to one group, for example, and none to the other group. Next, we give both groups an attitude measure. The mean score of Group A (saw the movie) is 110 and the mean score of Group B (did not see the movie) is 100. Our problem is: Is the difference of 10 units a "real" difference, a statistically significant difference? Or is it a difference that could have arisen by chance—more than 5 times in 100, say, or some other amount—when no difference actually exists?

If we similarly draw double samples of 100 and compute the differences between the means of these samples, and go through the same experimental procedure, would we consistently get this difference of 10? Again, we use the standard error to evaluate our differences, but this time we have a *sampling distribution of differences between means.* It is as if we took each $M_i - M_j$ and considered it as an X. Then the several differences between the means of the samples are considered as the X's of a new distribution. At any rate, the standard deviation of this sampling distribution of differences is *akin to* the standard error. (See the previous discussion of the use of several means.) But this procedure is only for illustration; actually we do not do this. Here, again, we estimate the standard error from our first two groups, A and B, by using the formula:

$$SE_{M_A - M_B} = \sqrt{SE_{M_A}{}^2 + SE_{M_B}{}^2} \tag{10.2}$$

where $SE_{M_A}{}^2$ and $SE_{M_B}{}^2$ are the standard errors squared, respectively, of Groups A and B, as previously stated.[13]

Suppose we did the experiment with five double groups, that is, ten groups, two at a time. The five differences between the means were 10, 11, 12, 8, 9. The mean of these differences is 10; the standard deviation is 1.414. This 1.414 is again *akin to* the standard error of the sampling distribution of the differences between the means, in the same sense as the standard error of the mean in the previous discussion. Now, if we compute the standard error of the mean for each group (by making up standard deviations for the two groups, $SD_A = 8$ and $SD_B = 9$), we would obtain

$$SE_{M_A} = \frac{SD_A}{\sqrt{n_A}} = \frac{8}{\sqrt{100}} = .8 \qquad SE_{M_B} = \frac{SD_B}{\sqrt{n_B}} = \frac{9}{\sqrt{100}} = .9$$

By Eq. 10.2 we compute the standard error of the differences between the means:

$$SE_{M_A - M_B} = \sqrt{SE_{M_A}{}^2 + SE_{M_B}{}^2} = \sqrt{(.8)^2 + (.9)^2} = \sqrt{.64 + .81}$$

$$= \sqrt{1.45} = 1.20$$

What do we do with the 1.20 now that we have it? If the scores of the two groups had been chosen from a table of random numbers and there were no experimental conditions, we would expect no difference between the means. But we have learned that there are always differences that are relatively small, which are due to chance factors. These differences are random. *The standard error of the differences between the means is an estimate of the dispersion of these differences.* But it is a measure of these differences that is an estimate for the whole population of such differences. For instance, the standard error of the differences between the means is 1.20. This means that, by chance alone, around the difference of 10 between M_A and M_B there would be random fluctuations —now 10, now 10.2, now 9.8, and so on. Only rarely would the differences exceed, say, 13 or 7 (about three times the *SE*). Another way of putting it is to say that the standard error of 1.20 indicates the limits (if we multiply the 1.20 by the appropriate factor) beyond which sample differences between the means probably will not go.

What has all this to do with our experiment? It is precisely here that we evaluate our experimental results. The standard error of 1.20 estimates random fluctuations. Now our difference was 10, that is, $M_A - M_B = 10$. Could this have arisen by chance, as a result of random fluctuations as just described? It should by now be halfway clear that this cannot be, except under very unusual circumstances. We evaluate this differences of 10 by comparing it with our estimate of random or chance

13 Other formulas are applicable under other circumstances, for example, if we start off with matched pairs of subjects.

fluctuations. *Is it one of them?* We make the comparison by means of the *t* ratio, or *t* test (formerly called the critical ratio):[14]

$$t = \frac{M_A - M_B}{SE_{M_A - M_B}} = \frac{110 - 100}{1.20} = \frac{10}{1.20} = 8.33$$

This means that our measured difference between M_A and M_B would be 8.33 standard deviations away from an hypothesized mean of zero (zero difference, no difference between the two means).

We would not have any difference, theoretically, if our subjects were well randomized and there had been no experimental manipulation. We would have, in effect, two distributions of random numbers from which we could expect only chance fluctuations. But here we have, comparatively, a huge difference of 10, compared to an insignificant 1.20 (our estimate of random deviations). Decidedly, something is happening here besides chance. And this something is just what we are looking for. It is, presumably, the effect of the movie, or the effect of the experimental condition, other conditions having been sufficiently controlled, of course.

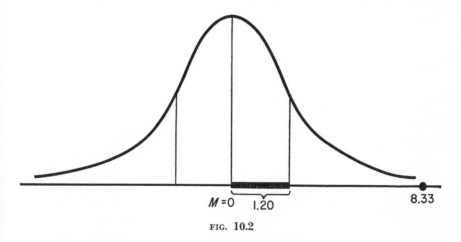

M = 0   1.20   8.33

FIG. 10.2

Look at Fig. 10.2. It represents *a population of differences between means* with a mean of zero and a standard deviation of 1.20. (The mean is set at zero, because we assume that the mean of all the mean differences is zero.) Where would the difference of 10 be placed on the base line of the diagram? In order to answer this question, the 10 must first be converted into standard deviation (or standard error) units. (Recall standard scores from the last chapter.) This is done by dividing by the standard deviation

[14] The term "critical ratio" (*CR*) is a fraction in which a statistic is divided by its standard error. With samples larger than 30, the *t* ratio and the *CR* are almost the same. The *CR*'s can be referred to any table of the normal deviate. The *t* ratios must be referred to a *t* table, especially with *n*'s less than 30. We use the *t* ratio in this text because it is more general (includes the *CR*) and because it is a more accurate test.

(standard error), which is $1.20:10/1.20 = 8.33$. But this is what we got when we computed the t ratio. It is, then, simply the difference between M_A and M_B, 10, expressed in standard deviation (standard error) units. Now we can put it on the base line of the diagram. Look far to the right for the little dot. Clearly the difference of 10 is a deviate. It is so far out, in fact, that it probably does not belong to the population in question. In short, the difference between M_A and M_B is statistically significant, so significant that it amounts to what Bernoulli called "moral certainty." Such a large difference, or deviation from chance expectation, can hardly be attributed to chance. The odds are actually greater than a billion to one. It *could* happen. But it is hardly likely to happen.[15]

A RESEARCH EXAMPLE

Sims and Patrick, in studying the attitudes of northern and southern students toward Negroes, report certain statistics that it will be instructive and interesting to analyze.[16] They used three groups of students: 156 from southern homes, 115 from northern homes going to a southern university, and 97 students from northern homes going to a northern university. The present analysis is limited to the 156 southern students and the 97 northern students. A scale constructed to measure the attitude of the students toward the Negro was administered. The means, standard deviation, and n's of the northern and southern students were:

$$M_N = 6.7 \qquad M_S = 5.0$$
$$SD_N = 1.0 \qquad SD_S = 1.0$$
$$n = 97 \qquad n = 156$$

(As a matter of interest, the mean of the 115 north-in-south students was 5.9, perhaps interesting evidence of the influence of environment.)

We ask the question: Do these means differ significantly from each other? Sims and Patrick used an older statistical technique to test the significance of the difference. We use the t test, for which the computations are

[15] An important question is: How large a difference, or in the language of statistics, how far away from the hypothetical mean of zero must a deviation be to be significant? This question cannot be answered definitively in this book. The .05 level is 1.96 standard deviations from the mean, and the .01 level is 2.58 standard deviations from the mean. But there are complications, especially with small samples. The student must, as usual, study a good statistics text. A simple rule is: 2 standard deviations (SE's) are significant (about the .05 level); 2.5 standard deviations are very significant (about the .01 level); and 3 standard deviations are highly significant (a little less than the .001 level).

[16] V. Sims and J. Patrick, "Attitude toward the Negro of Northern and Southern College Students," *Journal of Social Psychology,* VII (1936), 192–204.

$$SE_{M_N} = \frac{SD_N}{\sqrt{n_N}} = \frac{1}{\sqrt{97}} = \frac{1}{9.85} = .102$$

$$SE_{M_S} = \frac{SD_S}{\sqrt{n_S}} = \frac{1}{\sqrt{156}} = \frac{1}{12.49} = .080$$

$$SE_{M_N - M_S} = \sqrt{(.102)^2 + (.080)^2} = \sqrt{.0104 + .0064} = \sqrt{.0168} = .13$$

$$t = \frac{6.7 - 5.0}{.13} = \frac{1.70}{.13} = 13.1 \ (.001)$$

Actually, the difference is much more significant than .001, since, in the distribution of differences, this particular difference falls about 13 standard deviations (standard errors) from the mean of zero difference. There seems to be little doubt that the northern students of this sample scored significantly higher on the attitude scale than did the southern students.

These students were not random samples of northern and southern students. (It would be difficult to obtain such random samples, though perhaps not impossible.) So the results cannot be generalized to other northern and southern students. You may ask: Of what use are the results, then? This question is a difficult and embarrassing one for the behavioral scientist. Can we come to no conclusions at all? Some researchers would tell us to limit our generalizations strictly to the present group of students. Others would not be so strict. The position taken here is that, if we have no other evidence than the present sample, we should limit conclusions to this sample. Random samples are difficult and often impossible to obtain. Because of this obstacle, should one discontinue research? By no means.

Suppose Sims and Patrick, or some other investigators, had measured the attitudes of northern and southern students in other institutions at different times and had gotten very similar results. These results would be better. The samples are still not random, however, but with reasonable care and circumspection, we can strengthen our conclusions. It is less likely that a mean difference as large as this one, if found in two or three other similar investigations, is a function of characteristics other than attitudes toward the Negro. The objection to a nonrandom sample is that measures computed from it—in this case, mean attitude scores and standard deviations—are not representative of a larger population. The behavioral scientist usually wants to go beyond his present samples; he wants, if possible, to talk about the behavior and characteristics of all men —not just the behavior and characteristics of, say, college students. If, however, the investigator extends his investigation to different kinds of samples—to businessmen, housewives, and graduate students, perhaps— and gets similar results despite the nonrandomness of the samples, his conclusions are strengthened.

Such is the standard error and its use. The standard error of other statistics is used in the same way. A very important, useful, and neat tool. It is a basic instrument in contemporary research. Indeed, it would be hard to imagine modern research methodology, and impossible to imagine modern statistics, without the standard error. As a key to statistical inference its importance cannot be overestimated. Much of statistical inference boils down to a family of fractions epitomized by the fraction,

$$\frac{\text{Statistic}}{\text{Standard error of the statistic}}$$

STATISTICAL INFERENCE

To *infer* is to derive a conclusion from premises or from evidence. To *infer statistically* is to derive probabilistic conclusions from probabilistic premises. We conclude probabilistically, that is, at a specified level of significance.[17] We infer, probabilistically, if an experimental result deviates from chance expectation, if the null hypothesis is not "true," that a "real" influence is at work. If, in the teaching methods experiment, $M_A > M_B$ and $M_A \neq M_B$, or H_1 is "true" and H_o is not "true," we infer that Method A is "superior" to Method B, "superior" being accepted in the sense defined in the experiment.

Another form of inference, discussed at length in the chapter on sampling, is that from a sample to a population. Since, for instance, 55 percent of a random sample of 2000 people in the United States say they will vote for a certain presidential candidate, it is inferred that the whole population of the United States will so vote. This is rather a big inference. One of the gravest dangers of research—or perhaps I should say, of any human reasoning—is the inferential leap from sample data to a population fact. In education, inferential leaps of no mean size are constantly being made. Witness the recommendations for teaching elementary school youngsters foreign languages on the basis of little research. Aided by large inferential leaps, teaching machines by the thousands are being made and sold. But scientists, too, make inferential leaps, often very large ones—with one important difference. The scientist is (or should be) aware that he is making such leaps and that they are always risky.

It can be said, in sum, that statistics enables the scientist to test substantive hypotheses indirectly by enabling him to test statistical hypotheses directly (if it is at all possible to test anything directly). In this process, he uses the null hypothesis, which he considers to be a hypothesis

---

[17] Sometimes the words "significance" and "confidence" are used interchangeably. The two words do not mean the same thing. In this book, however, the difference is not elaborated. For a discussion of the difference, see Q. McNemar, *Psychological Statistics*, 2d ed. New York: Wiley, 1955, pp. 98, 99.

written by chance. He tests the "truth" of substantive hypotheses by subjecting null hypotheses to statistical tests on the basis of probabilistic reasoning. He then makes appropriate inferences. Indeed, the objective of all statistical tests is to test the justifiability of inferences.

STUDY SUGGESTIONS

1. Good references on statistics are plentiful. Those given below are only a small sample. The student should select one or two of them to supplement his study. The references marked with an asterisk are especially recommended to the beginning student. In reading a statistics book, you should not be too discouraged if you do not completely understand everything you read the first and second times. Some of the references below will contain passages that may be a stumbling block at first. Most of these difficulties tend to disappear as you acquire an understanding of the language and methods of the statistician.

   Bross, I., *Design for Decision*. New York: Macmillan, 1953. This is an excellent and readable book with a strong emphasis on decision-making.

   * Diamond, S., *Information and Error*. New York: Basic Books, 1959, Chaps. 5, 6, and 7. Witty and original, this different kind of statistics book has excellent presentation. It is well worth one or two months of study. *Highly recommended.*

   * Edwards, A., *Statistical Analysis.*, rev. ed. New York: Holt, Rinehart, and Winston, Inc., 1958. Chaps. 5, 7, 8, 9, 10, and 11. One of the best books for the beginning student, this text is clear, readable, and sound. *Highly recommended.* (Start with this book, and supplement it with the Diamond book.)

   Hebb, D., *A Textbook of Psychology*. Philadelphia: Saunders, 1958, Chap. 11. This is a chapter stressing statistical thinking, written by a distinguished psychological investigator.

   Lindquist, E., *Statistical Analysis in Educational Research*. Boston: Houghton Mifflin, 1940, Chaps. 2 and 3. The author of this text has specifically slanted it toward educational research. *Very good.*

   Tate, M., *Statistics in Education*. New York: Macmillan, 1955. Chaps. 5, 7, and 8. This is an excellent text specifically designed for educational problems and research. Good discussions of the reliability and validity of statistical evidence (Chap. 7) and statistical inference (Chap. 8). Some of Chap. 8 is a bit difficult, but well worth the effort of studying it. *Highly recommended.*

2. An educational investigator drew a random sample of 64 ninth-grade students in a junior high school and asked them if they favored

monthly conferences with their homeroom teacher. Of the 64 students, 40 said Yes.

(a) Is this a "real" majority opinion? Is it a statistically significant response?

(b) Test the response for significance. Use χ^2, and assume equiprobability (that is, if the students answered Yes and No at random, what responses would you expect to get?) A χ^2 as great as, or greater than, 3.84 is significant at the .05 level, 6.64 at the .01 level.

(c) Test the response using binomial statistics and the normal probability curve. (Use the formulas and reasoning of the last chapter.)

(*Answers:* (b) $\chi^2 = 4$ (.05); (c) $M = 32$; $SD = 4$; 40 is 2 standard deviations above the mean, significant at about .05.)

3. The proportions of middle- and working-class children in an entire school system are .70 and .30, respectively. In one school of 400 children there are 300 middle-class and 100 working-class children. Can it be said that this school's proportions of middle- and working-class children differ significantly from those of the entire school system? (*Answer:* No. $\chi^2 = 2.66$. See .05 and .01 levels in Question 2.)

4. There are 120 teachers in X School System: 36 have done some graduate work, 72 have bachelor degrees but no graduate work, and 12 have no degrees. In one junior high school of 40 teachers, 10 have done some graduate work, 20 have bachelor degrees but no graduate work, and 10 have no degrees. Do the proportions in the junior high school differ significantly from those in the whole school system? What contributes most to this result? (*Hint:* Compute χ^2 exactly as with two cells. Just add the three quantities computed from each of the discrepancies. To be significant at .05, χ^2 has to be 5.99 or greater. To be significant at .01, it has to be 9.21 or greater.)

(*Answer:* $\chi^2 = 10$ (.01). The disproportionately large number of teachers with no degrees contributes most to the result.)

5. Investigators interested in the possible effect of a new motion picture on attitudes toward minority-group members were also interested in whether discussion after the picture would enhance the effect of the picture. (Prior to this, results with other similar pictures had been disappointing, which was thought to be due to the fact that no discussion had followed the pictures.) The investigators randomly selected students and randomly assigned them to two groups. One group, the experimental group, selected at random from the two groups, was shown the picture, after which a twenty-minute discussion period followed. The other group, the control group, was only shown the film. Both groups were tested with a scale designed to measure attitudes toward minority group members. The means of

the two groups on the attitude scale, after the experimental session, were experimental group, 18; control group, 14. The standard error of the difference between the means was .80. Was the film plus discussion significantly more effective than the film alone?

(*Answer:* Yes. $18 - 14/.80 = 4/.80 = 5$ standard deviations from the mean.)

6. On a new test constructed by a professor, the mean was 62, the standard deviation 8, and the standard error of the mean 1.30. On the basis of this evidence, what can the professor say about the reliability of the mean of this test?

7. An investigator in the field of prejudice experimented with various methods of answering the prejudiced person's remarks about minority group members. He randomly assigned 32 subjects to two groups, 16 in each group. With the first group he used Method A; with the second group he used Method B. The means of the two groups on an attitude test, administered after the methods were used, were A: 27; B: 25. Each group had a standard deviation of 4. Do the two group means differ significantly?

(*Answer:* No. $27 - 25/1.4 = 2/1.4 = 1.3$.)

8. In a study of the manifest anxiety of retarded children, Malpass, Mark, and Palermo report the means and standard deviations on the Children's Manifest Anxiety Scale (CMAS) of two groups: institutionalized retardates (IR) and educable mentally handicapped (EMH) children.[18] The EMH children lived in their own homes; the IR children lived at a special school for a year. The statistics are as follows:

	IR	EMH
n:	53	41
M:	25.98	21.49
SD:	7.31	7.24

Compute the *t* ratio, using these statistics. What conclusion might be reached about these children?

(*Answer:* $t = 2.97$, significant at .01.)

9. In Stouffer's fine study of tolerance and civil liberties, two independent samples totaling approximately 5900 were drawn.[19] It is customary in survey research to check the accuracy of the sampling by comparing proportions of sociological variables—rural-urban, sex,

[18] L. Malpass, S. Mark, and D. Palermo, "Responses of Retarded Children to the Children's Manifest Anxiety Scale," *Journal of Educational Psychology*, LI (1960), 305–308.

[19] S. Stouffer, *Communism, Conformity, and Civil Liberties.* Garden City, N. Y.: Doubleday, 1955.

education, and so on—with the proportions reported in the national census. One such comparison, drawn from many made by Stouffer, is urban-rural. The percentage figures are: Survey: 64 percent; Census: 66 percent.[20] Does the survey figure differ significantly from the census figure? $(n = 4900.)$ *Hint:* What proportion are you testing? Against what expectation?

(*Answer:* The difference is significant. $t = 3$, approximately.)

[20] *Ibid.,* p. 238.

11 *ANALYSIS OF VARIANCE: FOUNDATIONS*

The analysis of variance is not just a statistical method. It is an approach and a way of thinking. From one point of view at least, modern statistical methods culminate in analysis of variance and factor analysis. Both methods are general. Both have aims of scientific data analysis hardly conceived of fifty years ago. Both attain their results in fundamentally the same way although the outcomes are different: the total variance of any statistical situation is broken down into component sources of variance.

In this chapter and in Chaps. 12 and 13 we explore the analysis of variance. The emphasis in these chapters is on the few fundamental and general notions that underlie the method. To accomplish the pedagogical purpose, simple examples are used. It makes little difference, however, if 5 scores or 500 scores are used, or if 2 or 20 variables are used. The fundamental ideas, the common conceptions, remain the same. The examples of this chapter exemplify what is called *simple* or *one-way analysis of variance*. The next two chapters consider so-called factorial analysis of variance and the analysis of variance of correlated groups. By then the student should have a good basis for the study of research design.[1]

VARIANCE BREAKDOWN: A SIMPLE EXAMPLE

In Chap. 7, two sets of scores were analyzed in a variance fashion. It was shown that the *total variance* of all the scores could be broken down into a *between-groups variance* and a *within-groups variance*. It is now necessary to pick up the thread of Chap. 7. We do so by using, in altered form, the simple two-group example given there, and by correcting the incorrect method of calculation. Then we extend analysis of variance ideas considerably.

Suppose an educational investigator is interested in the relative efficacies of two methods of teaching, A_1 and A_2. Selecting ten students

[1] At this point the student should review Chap. 7. The basic ideas presented in that chapter will be applied in this one.

as a sample, he divides them into two groups at random and assigns the experimental treatments to the two groups at random. After a suitable length of time, he measures the learning of the children of both groups on some measure of achievement. The results, together with certain computations, are given in Table 11.1.

TABLE 11.1   TWO SETS OF HYPOTHETICAL EXPERIMENTAL DATA WITH
SUMS, MEANS, AND SUMS OF SQUARES

	A_1	x	x^2	A_2	x	x^2
	4	0	0	3	0	0
	5	1	1	1	−2	4
	3	−1	1	5	2	4
	2	−2	4	2	−1	1
	6	2	4	4	1	1
ΣX:	20			15		$\Sigma X_t = 35$
M:	4			3		$M_t = 3.5$
Σx^2:			10		10	

Our job, with the data given, is to locate and compute the different variances that make up the total variance. The total variance and the other variances are computed as before, with an important computational difference. Instead of using N or n in the denominator of variance fractions, we use so-called degrees of freedom. Degrees of freedom are ordinarily defined as one case less than N or n, that is, $N - 1$ and $n - 1$. In the case of groups, instead of k (the number of groups), we use $k - 1$. While this method has a great advantage from a statistical point of view, from a mathematical-conceptual point of view it makes our job a bit more difficult. First, we do the computations, and then return to the difficulty.

To compute the total variance, we use the formula:

$$V_t = \frac{\Sigma x^2}{N - 1} \tag{11.1}$$

where $\Sigma x^2 =$ the sum of squares, as before, $x = X - M$, or deviation from the mean of any score, and $N =$ number of cases in the total sample. To compute V_t, simply take all the scores, regardless of their grouping, and compute the necessary terms of Eq. 11.1, as follows: see Table 11.2. Since $N - 1 = 10 - 1 = 9$, $V_t = 22.50/9 = 2.5$. Thus, if we arrange the data of Table 11.1 without regard to the two groups, $V_t = 2.5$.

It will be recalled that there is variance between the groups and that this variance was due, presumably, to the experimental manipulations. That is, the experimenter did something to one group and something different to the other group. These different treatments should

TABLE 11.2 COMPUTATION OF V_t OF DATA OF TABLE 11.1

	X	x	x^2
	4	.5	.25
	5	1.5	2.25
	3	− .5	.25
	2	− 1.5	2.25
	6	2.5	6.25
	3	− .5	.25
	1	− 2.5	6.25
	5	1.5	2.25
	2	− 1.5	2.25
	4	.5	.25
ΣX:	35		
M:	3.5		
Σx^2:			22.50

make the groups and their means different. Thus the groups are different, they vary. They have *between-groups variance*. Take the two means, treat them like any other scores (X's), and compute their variance (see Table 11.3).

TABLE 11.3 COMPUTATION OF V_b OF DATA OF TABLE 11.1

	X	x	x^2
	4	.5	.25
	3	.5	.25
ΣX:	7		
M:	3.5		
Σx^2:			.50

$$V_b = \frac{\Sigma x_b^2}{k-1} = \frac{.50}{2-1} = .50$$

There is a remaining source of variance left over: the ubiquitous random error. We saw in Chap. 7 that this could be obtained by computing the variance *within* each group separately and then averaging these separate variances. We do this using the figures given earlier. Each group had $\Sigma x^2 = 10$. Dividing each of these variances by its degrees of freedom, we get

$$\frac{\Sigma x_{A_1}^2}{n_{A_1} - 1} = \frac{10}{4} = 2.5$$

and

$$\frac{\Sigma x_{A_2}^2}{n_{A_2} - 1} = \frac{10}{4} = 2.5$$

The averaging yields, of course, 2.5. Therefore the *within-groups variance*, V_w, is 2.5.

Three variances have been computed: V_t, V_b, and V_w. They are, respectively, 2.5, .50, and 2.5. The theoretical equation given in Chap. 7 says that the total variance is made up of separate sources of variance: the between-groups and the within-groups variances. Logically, they should add up to the total variance. The theoretical equation is

$$V_t = V_b + V_w \tag{11.2}$$

Since 2.5 is not equal to .50 and 2.5, something must be wrong. The trouble is easily located. Degrees of freedom were used in the denominators of the variance formula instead of N, n, and k. Had N, n, and k been used, the relation of Eq. 11.2 would have held (see Chap. 7).

The student may ask: Why not follow the N, n, and k procedure? And if you cannot follow it, why bother with all this rigmarole? The answer is that the computation of the variances with N, n, and k is mathematically correct but statistically "incorrect." Another important aspect of the analysis of variance is the estimation of population values. It can be shown that using degrees of freedom in the denominators of the variance formula yields unbiased estimates of the population values, a matter of great statistical concern. The reason we bother going through the present procedure is to show the reader clearly the mathematical basis of the reasoning. One should remember, though, that variances, as used in the analysis of variance, are not necessarily additive.

Sums of squares, on the other hand, are always additive. (They are computed from the scores and not *divided* by anything.) The sum of squares, of course, is also a measure of variability. Except at the final stage of analysis variance, sum of squares are computed, studied, and analyzed. To convince ourselves of the additive property of sums of squares, note that the between-groups and the within-groups sums of squares add to the total sum of squares. If we multiply the between-groups sum of squares by n, the number of cases in each group:

$$\Sigma x_t^2 = n \Sigma x_b^2 + \Sigma x_w^2$$

or numerically, $22.50 = (5)(.50) + 20$. (Why Σx_b^2 is multiplied by 5 will be taken up later.)

ANOTHER METHOD OF ANALYSIS

Using the data of Table 11.1, we calculate several statistics for the A_1 and A_2 data separately: the variances, standard deviations, standard errors of the means, and standard variances of the means.[2] These calcu-

---

[2] The methods of analysis used in the first part of this chapter are not actually used in computing the analysis of variance. They are too cumbersome. They are used

lations are shown in Table 11.4. (Note that V is now calculated with $n - 1$ instead of n.) Computing the between-groups variance, we obtain

$$V_b = \frac{\Sigma x^2}{k - 1} = \frac{.50}{2 - 1} = .50$$

TABLE 11.4   VARIOUS STATISTICS COMPUTED FROM TABLE 11.1 DATA

	A_1	A_2
V:	$\dfrac{\Sigma x^2}{n - 1} = \dfrac{10}{4} = 2.5$	$\dfrac{10}{4} = 2.5$
SD:	$\sqrt{2.5} = 1.58$	$\sqrt{2.5} = 1.58$
SE_M:	$\dfrac{SD}{\sqrt{n}} = \dfrac{1.58}{\sqrt{5}} = .705$	$\dfrac{1.58}{\sqrt{5}} = .705$
SV_M:	$\dfrac{V}{n} = \dfrac{2.5}{5} = .50$	$\dfrac{2.5}{5} = .50$

Now we consider the central statistical idea behind the analysis of variance. The question the investigator has to ask himself is: Do the means differ significantly? It is obvious that 4 does not equal 3, but the question has to be asked statistically. We know that if sets of random numbers are drawn, the means of the sets will not be equal. They should, however, not be too different, that is, they should differ only within the bounds of chance fluctuations. Thus the question becames: Does 4 differ from 3 *significantly?* Again the null hypothesis is set up: $H_o:M_{A_1} - M_{A_2} = 0$, or $M_{A_1} = M_{A_2}$. The substantive hypothesis was: $H_1:M_{A_1} > M_{A_2}$. Which hypothesis does the evidence support? In other words, it is not simply a question of 4's being absolutely greater than 3. It is, rather, a question of whether 4 differs from 3 beyond the differences to be expected on the basis of chance.

This question can be quickly answered using the method of the last chapter. First, compute the standard error of the differences between the means:

$$SE_{M_{A_1} - M_{A_2}} = \sqrt{SE_{M_{A_1}}{}^2 + SE_{M_{A_2}}{}^2} = \sqrt{(.705)^2 + (.705)^2}$$
$$= \sqrt{.994} = .997 = 1.00 \text{ (rounded)}$$

Now compute the t ratio:

$$t = \frac{M_{A_1} - M_{A_2}}{SE_{M_{A_1} - M_{A_2}}} = \frac{4 - 3}{1.00} = \frac{1}{1} = 1$$

Since the difference being evaluated is no greater than the measure of error, it is obvious that the difference is not significant. The numerator

---

here purely for pedagogical reasons. Unfortunately, the usual computing method tends to obscure the important relations and operations underlying the analysis of variance.

and the denominator of the t ratio are equal. The difference, $4 - 3 = 1$, is clearly one of the differences that could have occurred with random numbers. Remember that a "real" difference would be reflected in the t ratio by a considerably larger numerator than denominator.

In the analysis of variance, the approach is conceptually similar, although the method differs. The method is general: differences of more than two groups can be tested for statistical significance, whereas the t test applies only to two groups. (With only two groups, as we shall see shortly, the results of the two methods are really identical.) The method of analysis of variance uses variances entirely, instead of using actual differences and standard errors, even though the actual difference-standard error reasoning is behind the method. Two variances are always pitted against each other. One variance, that presumably due to the experimental (independent) variable or variables is pitted against another variance, that presumably due to error or randomness. This is a case, again, of information versus error, as Diamond would put it,[3] or, as information theorists say, information versus noise. To get a grip on this idea, go back to the problem.

We found that the between-groups variance was .50. Now we must find a variance that is a reflection of error. This is the within-groups variance. After all, since we compute the within-groups variance, essentially, by computing the variance of each group separately and then averaging the two (or more) variances, this estimate of error is unaffected by the differences between the means. Thus, *if nothing else is causing the scores to vary,* it is reasonable to consider the within-groups variance as a measure of chance fluctuations. If this is so, then we can *stack up the variance due to the experimental effect, the between-groups variance, against this measure of chance error, the within-groups variance.* The only question is: How is the within-groups variance computed?

Remember that the variance of a population of means can be estimated with the standard variance of the mean (the standard error squared). One way to compute the within-groups variance is to compute the standard variance of each of the groups and then average them for all of the groups. This should yield an estimate of error that can be used to evaluate the variance of the means of the groups. The reasoning here is basic. To evaluate the differences between the means, it is necessary to refer to a theoretical population of means that would be gotten from the random sampling of groups of scores like the groups of scores we have. In the present case, we have two means from samples with five scores in each group. (It is well to remember that we might have three, four, or more means from three, four, or more groups. The reasoning is the same.) If the sampling has been random and nothing else has operated—that is, there have been no experimental manipulations and no other systematic

---

[3] S. Diamond, *Information and Error.* New York: Basic Books, 1959.

influences have been at work—then it is possible to estimate the variance of the means of the population of means with the standard variance of the means ($SE_M{}^2$, or simply SV_M). Each group provides such an estimate. These estimates will vary to some extent among themselves. We can pool them by averaging to form an over-all estimate of the variance of the population means.

Recall that the standard error of the mean formula was: $SE_M = SD/\sqrt{n}$. Simply square this expression to get the standard variance of the mean: $SE_M{}^2 = (SD)^2/n = SV_M = V/n$. The variances of each of the groups was 2.5. Computing the standard variances, we obtain for each group: $SV_M = V/n = 2.50/5 = .50$. Averaging them obviously yields .50. Note carefully that each standard variance was computed from each group *separately and then averaged*. Therefore this average standard variance is uninfluenced by differences between the means, as noted a bit earlier. The average standard variance, then, is a *within-groups variance*. It is an estimate of random errors, or the random sampling fluctuations *of means*.

But if random numbers had been used, the same reasoning applies to the between-groups variance, the variance computed from the actual means. We computed a variance from the means of 4 and 3. It was found to be .50. If the numbers were random, estimating the variance of the population of means should be possible by calculating the variance of the obtained means.

Note carefully, however, that if any extraneous influence has been at work, if anything like experimental effects have operated, then no longer will the variance calculated from the obtained means be a good estimate of the population variance of means. If an experimental influence—or some influence other than chance—has been operative, the effect may be to increase the variance of the obtained means. In a sense, this is the purpose of experimental manipulation: to increase the variance between means, to make the means different from each other. This is the crux of the analysis of variance matter. *If* an experimental manipulation has been influential, then it should show up in differences between means above and beyond the differences that would arise by chance alone. And the between-groups variance should show the influence by becoming greater than could be expected by chance. Clearly we can use V_b, then, as a measure of experimental influence. Equally clearly, as we showed above, we can use V_w as a measure of chance variation. Therefore, we have almost reached the end of a rather long but profitable journey: we can evaluate the between-groups variance, V_b, with the within-groups variance, V_w. Or information, experimental information, can be weighed against error or chance.

It would conceivably be possible to evaluate V_b by subtracting V_w from it. In the analysis of variance, however, V_b is divided by V_w. The ratio so formed is called the F ratio. (The F ratio was named by Snedecor in honor of Ronald Fisher, the inventor of the analysis of variance. It was Snedecor who worked out the F tables used to evaluate F ratios.) One calculates the F ratio from observed data and checks the result against an F table. (The F table with directions for its use can be found in any recent statistics text.) If the obtained F ratio is as great or greater than the appropriate tabled entry, the differences that V_b reflects are statistically significant. In such a case the null hypothesis of no differences between the means is rejected at the chosen level of significance. In the present case:

$$F = \frac{V_b}{V_w} = \frac{.50}{.50} = 1$$

One obviously does not need the F table to see that the F ratio is not significant. Evidently the two means of 4 and 3 do not differ from each other significantly. In other words, of the many possible random samples of pairs of groups of five cases each, this particular case could easily be one of them. Or it is possible to say that 4 and 3 could readily belong to the same population of means. Had the difference been considerably greater, great enough to tip the F ratio balance scale, then the conclusion would be quite different, as we shall see.[4]

AN EXAMPLE OF A STATISTICALLY SIGNIFICANT DIFFERENCE

Suppose that the investigator had obtained quite different results. Say the means had been 6 and 3, rather than 4 and 3. We now take the above example and *add a constant of 2 to each A_1 score.* This operation of course merely restores the scores used in Chap. 7. It was said earlier that adding a constant to a set of scores (or subtracting a constant) changes the mean by the constant *but has no effect whatsoever on the variance.* The figures are given in Table 11.5.

It is very important to note carefully that the Σx^2 amounts are the same as they were before, 10. Note, too, that the variances, V, are the same, 2.5. So are the standard variances, each being .50. As far as these statistics are concerned, then, there is no difference whatsoever between this example and the previous example. But now we calculate the between-groups variance (Table 11.6). V_b is nine times greater than it was before: 4.50 versus .50. But V_w *is exactly the same as it was before.* This is the important point. To repeat: adding a constant to one set of scores— which is tantamount to an experimental manipulation, since one of the

---

[4] Note that the t test and analysis of variance yielded the same result. With only two groups, or one degree of freedom $(k-1)$, $F = t^2$, or $t = \sqrt{F}$. This equality shows that it does not matter, in the case of two groups, whether t or F is computed. (But the analysis of variance is a bit easier to compute than t, in most cases.) With three or more groups, however, the equality breaks down; F must always be computed. Thus F is the general test of which t is a special case.

TABLE 11.5 HYPOTHETICAL EXPERIMENTAL DATA FOR TWO GROUPS:
TABLE 11.1 DATA ALTERED

	A_1	x	x^2	A_2	x	x^2
	$4+2=6$	0	0	3	0	0
	$5+2=7$	1	1	1	-2	4
	$3+2=5$	-1	1	5	2	4
	$2+2=4$	-2	4	2	-1	1
	$6+2=8$	2	4	4	1	1
ΣX:	30			15		
M:	6			3		
Σx^2:			10			10
V:	$\frac{10}{4}=2.5$			$\frac{10}{4}=2.5$		
SV:	$\frac{V}{n}=\frac{2.5}{5}=.50$			$\frac{2.5}{5}=.50$		

purposes of an experiment of this kind is to augment or diminish one set of measures (the experimental group measures) while the other set does not change (the control group measures)—has no effect on the within-groups variance while the between-groups variance changes drastically. Another way to put this is to say that *the estimates of V_b and V_w are independent of each other.* (If they are not, by the way, the F test is vitiated.)

TABLE 11.6 COMPUTATION OF BETWEEN-GROUPS VARIANCE OF TABLE 11.7 DATA

	X	x	x^2
	6	1.5	2.25
	3	-1.5	2.25
ΣX:	9		
M:	4.5		
Σx^2:			4.50

$$V_b = \frac{\Sigma x_b^2}{k-1} = \frac{4.50}{2-1}$$
$$= 4.50$$

The F ratio is $F = V_b/V_w = 4.50/.50 = 9$. Evidently information is much greater than error. Does this mean that the difference $6-3=3$ is a statistically significant difference? If we check an F table, we find that, in this case, an F ratio of 7.71 or greater is significant at the .05 level. (The details of how to read an F table are omitted here. They are not essential to the argument.) To be significant at the .01 level, the F ratio in this case would have to be 21.20 or greater. Our F ratio is 9. It is greater than 7.71 but less than 21.20. It seems that the difference of 3 is a statistically significant difference at the .05 level. Therefore, $6 \neq 3$, and the null hypothesis is rejected.

COMPUTATION OF ONE-WAY ANALYSIS OF VARIANCE

Simple one-way analysis of variance is easier to compute than the above procedure and discussion have indicated. To show the method, the example just considered will be used. By now the reader should be able to follow the procedure without difficulty. Note that deviation scores (x's) are not used at all. One can and does calculate entirely with raw scores. There will be certain differences in the variances computed. In the preceding examples, standard variances were used in order to show the underlying rationale of the analysis of variance. In the following method, however, although the same method is used, certain steps are omitted because it is possible to arrive at the ultimate goal, the F ratio and the conclusions thereto, in a much easier way.

TABLE 11.7   CALCULATION OF ANALYSIS OF VARIANCE: FICTITIOUS DATA

X_{A_1}	$X_{A_1}{}^2$	X_{A_2}	$X_{A_2}{}^2$	
6	36	3	9	$N = 10$
7	49	1	1	$n = 5$
5	25	5	25	$k = 2$
4	16	2	4	
8	64	4	16	
ΣX: 30		15		$\Sigma X_t = 45$
$(\Sigma X)^2$: 900		225		$(\Sigma X_t)^2 = 2025$
M: 6		3		$M_t = 4.5$
ΣX^2:	190		55	$\Sigma X_t{}^2 = 245$

$$C = \frac{(\Sigma X_t)^2}{N} = \frac{(45)^2}{10} = \frac{2025}{10} = 202.50$$

$$\text{Total } (\Sigma x_t{}^2) = \Sigma X_t{}^2 - C = 245 - 202.50 = 42.50$$

$$\text{Between } (\Sigma x_b{}^2) = \left[\frac{(\Sigma X_{A_1})^2}{n_{A_1}} + \frac{(\Sigma X_{A_2})^2}{n_{A_2}} \right] - C$$

$$= \left[\frac{(30)^2}{5} + \frac{(15)^2}{5} \right] - 202.50 = (180 + 45) - 202.50 = 22.50$$

Source	df	s.s.	m.s.	F
Between Groups	$k - 1 = 1$	22.50	22.50	9. (.05)
Within Groups	$N - k = 8$	20.00	2.50	
Total	$N - 1 = 9$	42.50		

The calculations of Table 11.7 speak for themselves and can easily be followed right from the table. First, in the body of the table, note that the raw scores, the X's, are each squared.[5] Then they are added to yield the ΣX^2's at the bottom of the table (190 and 55). The purpose of doing this is to obtain $\Sigma X_t^2 = 245$ (190 + 55), at the right and bottom. Read ΣX_t^2: "The total sum of all the squared X's." The ΣX's and M's are calculated as usual (even though we do not really need the M's, except for interpretation later). Next, each group sum is squared and written $(\Sigma X)^2$. They are $(30)^2 = 900$ and $(15)^2 = 225$. (Be careful here. A frequent mistake is to confuse ΣX^2 and $(\Sigma X)^2$.) At the bottom right of the table proper, ΣX_t, $(\Sigma X_t)^2$, M_t, and ΣX_t^2 are entered. They are simply the total statistics and are calculated in the same way as the individual group statistics.

Next, the calculations of the sums of squares (Σx^2). In the analysis of variance, mostly sums of squares are calculated and used. The variances are reserved for the final analysis of variance table (at the bottom of Table 11.7). What we are after in this procedure are the total, the between and the within *sums of squares*, or Σx_t^2, Σx_b^2, and Σx_w^2. First, the calculation of C, the correction term. Since we are using raw scores, and since we are aiming at sums of squares, which are the *sums of the deviations* squared, we must reduce the raw scores to deviation scores. To accomplish this, we subtract C from every calculation. This accomplishes the reduction: it changes, in effect, X's to x's. The actual calculation of C is obvious. Here it is 202.50.

The total sum of squares, Σx_t^2, is now calculated. The result is obvious and yields 42.50. The between, or between-groups, or between-means, sum of squares is not as obvious. The sum of each group's scores is squared and then divided by the number of scores in the group. These averages are then added. From this sum C is subtracted. The result is the between-groups sum of squares, or Σx_b^2. And this is all there is to the simple one-way analysis of variance. The within-sum of squares, Σx_w^2, is calculated by subtraction. The following equation is important and should be remembered:

$$\Sigma x_t^2 = \Sigma x_b^2 + \Sigma x_w^2 \qquad (11.3)$$

Recall Eq. 11.2: $V_t = V_b + V_w$. Equation 11.3 is the same equation in the sum of squares form. Equation 11.2 cannot be used since, as was pointed out earlier, it is a theoretical formulation that only works exactly under the conditions specified. Equation 11.3 always works precisely, that is, sums of squares in the analysis of variance are always additive. So, with a little algebraic manipulation we see that $\Sigma x_w^2 = \Sigma x_t^2 - \Sigma x_b^2$. To obtain the within-sum of squares, in other words, simply subtract the between

---

[5] The calculations of Table 11.7 are not difficult to do by hand. With most realistic problems, however, a desk calculator is needed. Therefore the prospective research student should sooner or later learn to use a desk calculator.

from the total sum of squares. In the table, $42.50 - 22.50 = 20$. (It is of course possible to calculate the within-sum of squares directly.)

After completing the above calculation, the degrees of freedom (df) are entered into the final table. Although formulas have been entered, they are not necessary to the operation. For the total degrees of freedom, simply take 1 case less than the total number of subjects used. If, for example, there were three experimental groups with 30 Ss in each group, the total degrees of freedom are $N - 1 = 90 - 1 = 89$. The between-groups degrees of freedom are one less than the number of experimental groups. With three experimental groups, $k - 1 = 3 - 1 = 2$. With the example of Table 11.7, $k - 1 = 2 - 1 = 1$. The within-groups degrees of freedom, like the within-groups sum of squares, are obtained by subtraction. In this case, $9 - 1 = 8$. Next, divide the degrees of freedom into the sums of squares ($s.s./df$) to obtain the between and within variances, labeled "$m.s.$" in the table. In the analysis of variance, the variances are called "mean squares." Finally, compute the F ratio by dividing the within or error variance or mean square into the between variance or mean square: $F = V_b/V_w = m.s._b/m.s._w = 22.50/2.50 = 9$. This final F ratio, also called the variance ratio, is checked against appropriate entries in an F table to determine its significance, as discussed previously.

TWO RESEARCH EXAMPLES

To illustrate the research use of one-way analysis of variance, data from two different kinds of research studies are given below. The first set of data is from an early experimental study by Hurlock, described earlier in this book.[6] The data were not analyzed in this manner by Hurlock, the analysis of variance not being available at the time of the study. Hurlock divided 106 fourth- and sixth-grade pupils into four groups, E_1, E_2, E_3, and C. Five forms of an addition test, A, B, C, D, and E, were used. Form A was administered to all the Ss on the first day. For the next four days the experimental groups, E_1, E_2, and E_3, were given a different form of the test. The control group, C, was separated from the other groups and given different forms of the test on four separate days. The Ss of Group C were told to work as usual. But each day before the tests were given, the E_1 group was brought to the front of the room and *praised* for its good work. Then the E_2 group was brought forward and *reproved* for its poor work. The members of the E_3 group were *ignored*. On the fifth day of the

---

[6] E. Hurlock, "An Evaluation of Certain Incentives Used in Schoolwork," *Journal of Educational Psychology*, XVI (1925), 145–159. The first three lines of figures in Table 11.8 are reported by Hurlock. All the other figures were calculated by the author from these figures. The analysis of variance was done by recreating necessary figures from Hurlock's reported figures. A simple way to conduct one-way analysis of variance from reported means, standard deviations, and n's is given in Diamond, *op. cit.*, pp. 129, 130.

experiment, Form E was administered to all groups. Scores were the number of correct answers on this form of the test. Summary data are given in Table 11.8, together with the table of the final analysis of variance.

TABLE 11.8 SUMMARY DATA AND ANALYSIS OF VARIANCE
OF DATA FROM HURLOCK STUDY

	E_1 Praised	E_2 Reproved	E_3 Ignored	E_4 Control
n:	27	27	26	26
M:	20.22	14.19	12.38	11.35
SD:	7.68	6.78	6.06	4.21

Source	df	$s.s.$	$m.s.$	F
Between Groups	3	1260.06	420.02	10.08 (.001)
Within Groups	102	4249.29	41.66	
Total	105	5509.35		

Since $F = 10.08$, which is significant at the .001 level, the null hypothesis of no differences between the means has to be rejected. Evidently the experimental manipulations were effective. There is not much difference between the Ignored and Control groups, a very interesting finding. The Praised group has the largest mean, with the Reproved group mean in between the Praised group and the other two groups. The student can complete the interpretation of the data.[7]

The second research study is different in type from Hurlock's in that it is not experimental. There was no manipulation of the independent variable, no random sampling, and no random assignment of subjects. In a factor analytic study of attitudes toward education, 598 Ss—136 undergraduate education students, 157 graduate education students, and 305 persons outside the university—were administered a scale constructed to measure attitudes toward education.[8] This scale presumably measured

---

[7] After an analysis of variance of this kind, some investigators test pairs of means with t tests. Unless specific differences between pairs have been predicted beforehand, this procedure is incorrect for reasons that cannot be discussed here. There are tests that can be used to test the differences between *any* pairs of means after an analysis of variance, two of which are Tukey's and Scheffé's. A good description of Tukey's method can be found in T. Ryan, "Multiple Comparisons in Psychological Research," *Psychological Bulletin*, LVI (1959), 26–47, but especially 45, 46. This is an authoritative article on the subject of such comparisons. The Scheffé test, which the writer prefers, is a very conservative test. If used with discretion, however, it is a general test that can be conveniently applied to all comparisons of means after an analysis of variance.

[8] F. Kerlinger and E. Kaya, "The Predictive Validity of Scales Constructed to Measure Attitudes toward Education," *Educational and Psychological Measurement*, XIX (1959), 305–317.

two basic attitude factors: Progressivism and Traditionalism. In a part of the study analyses of variance were performed. The summary data and analysis of variance of the Traditionalism attitude scores of the three groups are given in Table 11.9.

TABLE 11.9   SUMMARY DATA AND ANALYSIS OF VARIANCE OF DATA FROM STUDY ON ATTITUDES TOWARD EDUCATION

	Graduate Students	Undergraduates	Persons Outside
n:	157	136	305
M:	3.84	4.43	5.19
SD:	.93	.84	.86

Source	df	$s.s.$	$m.s.$	F
Between Groups	2	197.20	98.60	128.05 (.001)
Within Groups	595	457.85	.77	
Total	597	655.05		

The F ratio of 128.05 is highly significant. The investigator's prediction was that people outside the university would have the highest mean and graduate students of education the lowest mean. The null hypothesis is clearly rejected, and the substantive prediction upheld. The three means are significantly different, and the differences are in the predicted direction.

STRENGTH OF RELATIONS: CORRELATION AND THE ANALYSIS OF VARIANCE

Tests of statistical significance like t and F unfortunately do not reveal to the research scientist the magnitude or strength of the relations he is studying. A t test of the difference between two means, if significant, simply tells the investigator that there *is* a relation. That there is a relation between two variables is inferred from the significant difference between the means. An F test, similarly, if significant, simply says that a relation exists. The relational fact is inferred from the significant differences between two, three, or more means. A statistical test like F says in a relatively indirect way that there is or is not a relation between the independent variable (or variables) and the dependent variable.

In contrast to tests of statistical significance like t and F, coefficients of correlation are relatively direct measures of relationship. They have an easily "seen" and direct intuitive message since the joining of two sets of scores more obviously seems like a relation, plus the fact that this follows our earlier definition of a relation as a set of ordered pairs. If, for example, $r = .90$, it is easy to see that the rank orders of the measures of two variables are very similar. But t and F ratios are one or two steps removed from the actual relation. An important research technical question, then, is how t and F, on the one hand, and measures like r, on the other hand, are related.

We first compute a simple measure of relation between an independent variable and a dependent variable. In an analysis of variance, the variable on the margins of the data table—methods of incentive as in the Hurlock example, and group membership, as in the Kerlinger and Kaya example—is the independent variable. The measures in the body of the table reflect the dependent variable: arithmetic achievement in the Hurlock example and attitudes toward education in the Kerlinger and Kaya example. The analysis of variance works with the relation between these two kinds of variables. If the independent variable has had an effect on the dependent variable, then the "equality" of the means of the experimental groups that would be expected if the numbers being analyzed were simply random numbers is upset. The effect of a really influential independent variable is to make means unequal. We might say, then, that any relation that exists between the independent and dependent variables is reflected in the inequality of the means. The more unequal the means, the wider apart they are, the higher the relation, other things being equal.

If no relation exists between the independent variable and the dependent variable, then it is as though we had sets of random numbers, and consequently, random means. The differences between the means would only be chance fluctuations. An F test would show them not to be significantly different. If a relation does exist, if there is a tie or bond between the independent and dependent variables, the imposition of *different* aspects of the independent variable, like different methods of instruction, should make the measures of the dependent variable vary accordingly. Method A_1 might make achievement scores go up, whereas Method A_2 might make them go down. Note that we have the same phenomenon of concomitant variation that we did with the correlation coefficient. Take two extreme cases: a very strong relationship and zero relationship. We lay out a hypothetically very strong relation between methods and achievement in Table 11.10.

Note that the dependent variable scores vary directly with the independent variable methods: Method A_1 has high scores, Method A_2 medium scores, and Method A_3 has low scores. The relation is also shown by comparing methods and the means of the dependent variable.

Compare the example of Table 11.10 with chance expectation. If there were no relation between methods and achievement, then the achievement means would not covary with methods. That is, the means would be nearly equal. In order to show this, I wrote the 12 achievement scores of Table 11.10 on separate slips of paper, mixed them up thor-

TABLE 11.10   HYPOTHETICALLY STRONG RELATION BETWEEN METHODS
OF INSTRUCTION AND ACHIEVEMENT

Independent Variable (Methods of Instruction)	Dependent Variable (Achievement)	Means
Method A_1	10 9 9 8	9
Method A_2	7 7 7 7	7
Method A_3	5 4 4 3	4

oughly in a hat, threw them all on the floor, and picked them up 4 at a time, assigning the first four to A_1, the second four to A_2, and the third four to A_3. The results are shown in Table 11.11.

TABLE 11.11   HYPOTHETICALLY ZERO RELATION BETWEEN METHODS
OF INSTRUCTION AND ACHIEVEMENT

Independent Variable (Methods of Instruction)	Dependent Variable (Achievement)	Means
Method A_1	4 8 10 7	7.25
Method A_2	3 5 4 9	5.25
Method A_3	7 7 7 9	7.50

Now it is difficult, or impossible, to "see" a relation. The means differ, but not much. Certainly the relation between methods and achievement scores (and means) is not nearly as clear as it was before. Still, we have to be sure. Analyses of variance of both sets of data were performed.

The F ratio of the data of Table 11.10 (strong relation) was 57.59, highly significant, whereas the F ratio of the data of Table 11.11 (low or zero relation) was 1.29, not significant. The statistical tests confirm our visual impressions. We now know that there is a relation between methods and achievement in Table 11.10 but not in Table 11.11.

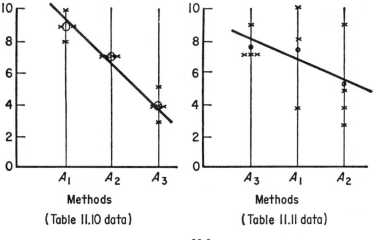

FIG. 11.1

The problem, however, is to show the relation between significance tests like the F test and the correlation method. This can be done in several ways. We illustrate with two such ways, one graphical and one statistical. In Fig. 11.1 the data of Tables 11.10 and 11.11 have been plotted much as continuous X and Y measures in the usual correlation problem are plotted, with the independent variable—Methods—on the horizontal axis, and the dependent variable—Achievement—on the vertical axis, as usual. To indicate the relation, lines have been drawn as near to the means as possible. A diagonal line making a 45-degree angle with the horizontal axis would indicate a strong relation. A horizontal line across the graph would indicate no relation. Note that the plotted scores of the data of Table 11.10 clearly indicate a strong relation: the height of the plotted scores (crosses) and the means (circles) varies with the method. The plot of the data of Table 11.11, even with a rearrangement of the methods for purposes of comparison, shows a weak relation or no relation.

Let us now look at the problem statistically. It is possible to compute correlation coefficients with data of this kind. If one has done an analysis of variance, a simple (but not entirely satisfactory) coefficient is yielded by the following formula:

$$E = \sqrt{\frac{\Sigma x_b^2}{\Sigma x_t^2}}$$

(11.4)

Of course, Σx_b^2 and Σx_t^2 are the between-groups sum of squares and the total sum of squares, respectively. One simply takes these sums of squares from the analysis of variance table to compute the coefficient. The symbol E is the letter associated with the Greek symbol η (Greek eta) that is usually used with this coefficient. E, usually called the *correlation ratio*, is a general coefficient or index of relation which is often used with data that are not linear. (*Linear*, roughly speaking, means that, if two variables are plotted one against another, the plot tends to follow a straight line.) Its values vary from 0 to 1.00. We are interested here only in its use with analysis of variance and in its power to tell us the *degree* of relation between independent and dependent variables.

Recall that the means of the data of Table 11.1 were 3 and 4. They were not significantly different. Therefore there is no relation between the independent variable (Methods) and the dependent variable (Achievement). If an analysis of variance of the data of Table 11.1 is done, using the method outlined in Table 11.7, $\Sigma x_b^2 = 2.50$ and $\Sigma x_t^2 = 22.50$. Computing $E = \sqrt{2.50/22.50} = \sqrt{.111} = .33$ yields the correlation between methods and achievement. Since we know that the data are not significant ($F = 1$), E is not significant. In other words, $E = .33$ is here tantamount to a zero relation. Had there been no difference at all between the means, then, of course, $E = 0$. If $\Sigma x_b^2 = \Sigma x_t^2$, then $E = 1.00$. This could only happen if all the scores of one group were the same, and all the scores of the other group were the same as, and yet different from, those of the first group, which is a highly unlikely phenomenon. For example, if the A_1 scores were 4, 4, 4, 4, 4, and the A_2 scores were 3, 3, 3, 3, 3, then $\Sigma x_b^2 = \Sigma x_t^2 = 2.5$, and $E = \sqrt{2.5/2.5} = \sqrt{1} = 1$. It is obvious that there is no within-groups variance—again, an extremely unlikely phenomenon.

Take the data of Table 11.7. The means are 6 and 3. They are significantly different since $F = 9$. Compute E:

$$E = \sqrt{\frac{\Sigma x_b^2}{\Sigma x_t^2}} = \sqrt{\frac{22.50}{42.50}} = \sqrt{5.29} = .727 = .73$$

Note the substantial increase in E. And since F is significant, $E = .73$ is significant. There is a substantial relation between methods and achievement.

Much more interesting are the E's of the data of the two research studies reported earlier (see Tables 11.8 and 11.9). The E of the Hurlock study is $E = \sqrt{1260.06/5509.35} = \sqrt{.229} = .48$. The E of the educational attitudes study is $E = \sqrt{197.20/665.05} = \sqrt{.301} = .549 = .55$. Both E's are of course significant. They are also substantial, if not very high. In the Hurlock study, other things being equal, incentive is substantially related to arithmetic achievement, as defined. The relation of the educational attitudes study is more subtle. Calling graduate students-undergraduates-persons outside "occupational role" (as the authors did), there is a substantial relation between occupational role and attitudes toward education.

By now the student has sufficient background to interpret E in variance terms. In Chap. 7, this was done for r, where it was explained that r^2 indicated the variance shared by two variables. This variance was called *common factor variance*. E can be given a similar interpretation. If E is squared, E^2 indicates, in essence, the variance shared by the independent and dependent variables. Perhaps more to the point, E indicates the proportion of the variance of the dependent variable, say Achievement, taking one of the examples above, determined by the variance of the independent variable, Methods, or Incentives. For example, in the Hurlock example, $E^2 = (.48)^2 = .23$, which indicates that 23 percent of the variance of the arithmetic addition scores is accounted for by the different modes of incentive used by Hurlock.

Other measures of association or correlation that can be used with the analysis of variance are readily available. Fortunately, they are based on the same basic idea: the relations between different variances. One of these is the *intraclass coefficient of correlation, R*. Like the correlation ratio E, R is a general measure of association readily used with the analysis of variance.[9]

Although it would take us too far afield to discuss R in detail, it is worthwhile to indicate one of the R formulas to show how it is calculated with one-way analysis of variance. The formula is

$$R = \frac{V_b - V_w}{V_b + (n - 1)V_w} \tag{11.5}$$

All the symbols are familiar: they are the between-groups variance (V_b), or between-groups mean square, the within-groups variance (V_w), and the number of cases in each group (n). Now, compute R for the Hurlock example, using the statistics of Table 11.10:[10]

$$R = \frac{420.06 - 41.66}{420.06 + (26.50 - 1)(41.66)} = \frac{378.46}{1482.35} = .255 = .26$$

Compare this value of .26 to the value of E^2, .23. R is comparable to E^2 rather than to E. Both R and E^2 indicate the proportion of variance in a dependent variable due to the presumed influence of an independent variable.

[9] An important reference is E. Haggard, *Intraclass Correlation and the Analysis of Variance*. New York: Holt, Rinehart and Winston, Inc., 1958. Other than Haggard's book, there is very little discussion of intraclass correlation in the literature. And it is an important idea, as Haggard competently shows in his book. Fisher, of course, discussed R many years earlier. In fact, in his *Statistical Methods*, one chapter is entitled "Intraclass Correlation and the Analysis of Variance." See R. Fisher, *Statistical Methods for Research Workers*, 11th ed. New York: Hafner, 1950, chap. VII.

[10] In the computation n is slightly altered, because the n's were unequal. (See Haggard, *op. cit.*, p. 14.) Ordinarily this is no problm, since n's are usually equal.

Calculating R for the data of the educational attitudes study, we obtain $R = .41$. For the very strong relation of the example of Table 11.10 and the example of the very weak relation of Table 11.11, we get .93 and .07, respectively. These R's more adequately reflect the actual relations of the data because R is an unbiased estimate of the degree of the relation, whereas E^2 is not.

The purpose of this exposition of E and R, however, is not to discuss the relative merits of these and other indices. It is, rather, to point up the similarity of the principle and structure of the analysis of variance and correlational methods. R, like E, depends on the relative magnitudes of the different variances. The larger the variance due to the independent variable, indicated by $\Sigma x_b{}^2$ *or* V_b, relative to the total variance or to the variance due to error, the larger the correlation. Under certain conditions, R can be defined as the proportion of between-groups variance to the total variance, or V_b/V_t.[11] It is thus seen that the conceptualization of E and that of R are very similar.

The total variance, of course, is the variance of the dependent variable, Y. What E and R tell us is the proportion of the variance of Y attributable to the variable (influence) of X (the independent variable). The means of achievement, in the Hurlock example, varied significantly. This variance can be attributed to X, the experimental manipulation. The total variance is the total variance of Y, arithmetic achievement. (Remember that in an experimental situation—or we might also call it an analysis of variance situation—it is the variances of the Y scores that are analyzed.)

COMPONENTS OF VARIANCE

The analysis of variance is usually used to test statistical hypotheses about the significance of the differences between means. But it has another important use, which needs emphasis. This is the problem of estimating *component variances*. Each statistical problem has a total amount of variance. As in probability theory, we let this amount of variance equal 100 percent. Then each variance source contributes so much percent of the variance. It is certainly important and useful to know what proportion of the variance of a dependent variable an experimental independent variable contributes. It is often also important to know what proportion of the total variance the error variance is. (This notion is used in measurement theory, for example.)

It is possible to derive expressions for the average values of the variances of large numbers of samples from a large population. It can be shown that V_w, the within-groups variance, is an unbiased or best estimate of the variance of this population. Thus, if we let σ^2 be the

[11] See *ibid.*, pp. 12 and 54.

symbol for the population variance, then V_w is an unbiased estimate of σ^2. The between-groups variance V_b is defined as $V_b = n \Sigma x_b{}^2/k - 1$, where $\Sigma x_b{}^2$ is the sum of squares calculated from the means (as previously shown), and k is the number of groups.[12] This between-groups variance is also an estimate of the variance of the population. If the samples have been random samples from the same population, then these two estimates, V_w and V_b, should be pretty nearly the same.

Now let us assume that V_w and V_b are not equal, that V_b is significantly greater than V_w. In this case, we must reason that there is something in V_b over and above chance. Thus we must conclude that V_b *includes both error variance and some systematic variance.* That is, V_b includes V_w, plus some other variance. If we had a way to estimate these components of variance of V_b, we would have valuable information as to the relative contributions of systematic and error variance, or the contribution of the independent variable and the contribution of error to the total variance. Luckily, this is easily determined. Subtract the within-groups variance from the between-groups variance and divide the remainder by the number of cases in each group, n. This gives the component of variance due to the independent variable. Now add to this the component due to error. Dividing each of these components by the sum of the two, we obtain the relative contributions (percentages) of each to the total variance. Two or three examples will clarify the procedure.

TABLE 11.12 COMPUTATION OF COMPONENTS OF VARIANCE
FOR DATA OF TABLE 11.7

n	*m.s.*	Components of Variance	Percent
5	22.50	$\dfrac{20}{5} = 4.00$	62
	−2.50	2.50	38
	20.00	6.50	

Take the fictitious data of Table 11.7, where the means of 6 and 3 were found to be significantly different. The computations of the components of variance are laid out in Table 11.12. The independent variable, the experimental manipulation, contributes 62 percent of the total variance. Contrast this to the data of Table 11.1, the problem in which the difference between the means of 4 and 3 was not significant. The between-groups and within-groups variances were both 2.50. Therefore 2.5

[12] The reasoning behind this equation is as follows. The definition of an unbiased estimate of the variance of the population of means is $V_M = \Sigma x^2/n - 1$. But from our reasoning on the standard error and the standard variance, we know that $V_M = SV_M = V/n$. Substituting in the first equation, we get $V/n = \Sigma x^2/k - 1$, and thus $V = n\Sigma x^2/k - 1$.

$- 2.5 = 0$, and the between-groups component of variance is 0, contributing nothing to the total variance. (If this sounds confusing, remember that it is a theoretical estimation of population variances. Actually, in the obtained data, some variance was contributed by the difference between the means, but did not exceed chance expectation.)

TABLE 11.13   CALCULATION OF COMPONENTS OF VARIANCE
OF HURLOCK EXAMPLE

n	$m.s.$	Components of Variance	Percent
26.50	420.02	$\dfrac{378.36}{26.50} = 14.28$	26
	-41.66	41.66	74
	378.36	55.94	

Actual research examples are more interesting. The Hurlock example (Table 11.8) components of variance are calculated in Table 11.13. The independent variable, the incentives, contributed approximately 26 percent of the total variance. A similar calculation of the components of variance of the educational attitudes example of Table 11.9 shows that the independent variable, the occupational role, contributed approximately 41 percent of the total variance.

Insight into the nature of R, the intraclass coefficient of correlation, is achieved when we compare the R's for these three examples with the percentages of the between-groups components of variance. In each case they are the same. In fact, the procedure outlined for computing components of variance is algebraically identical to the formula previously given for R. Therefore R tells us not only about the relative homogeneity and heterogeneity of the scores in the groups and the group means, and thus about the relation between the independent and dependent varibles; it also tells us the approximate proportion of the total variance of the dependent variable accounted for by the variance of the independent variable. Probably most important, however, for the purposes of this book and its central theme, R is an excellent illustration of the logical identity of different research approaches and different statistical approaches.

We have come a long, perhaps hard, way on the analysis of variance road. One may wonder why so much space has been devoted to the analysis of variance. There are several reasons for this emphasis. One, the analysis of variance has wide practical applicability. It is hard to conceive of contemporary educational, psychological, and sociological research without the analysis of variance. Analysis of variance takes many forms that are applicable in psychology, sociology, economics, agriculture, biology, education, and other fields. It frees us from the Procrustean task of working with one independent variable at a time and gives us a powerful lever for solving measurement problems. It increases the possibilities of making our experiments exact and precise. The analysis of variance also permits us to test several hypotheses at one time, as well as to test hypotheses that cannot be tested in any other way, at least with precision. Thus its generality of application is great.

More germane to the purposes of this book, the analysis of variance gives us an insight into modern research approaches and methods. No other method of statistical analysis gives quite so much. It does this by focusing sharply and constantly on variance thinking. As we know by now, variance thinking is basic to research design and data analysis.

STUDY SUGGESTIONS

1. There are a number of good references on analysis of variance, varying in difficulty and clarity of explanation (for the beginning student). Seven are listed below. Those marked with an asterisk should be particularly valuable for the reader who has not had much training in statistics. For the reader who is just beginning the study of the analysis of variance, the Edwards' references are suggested; they offer a good clarification of computational procedures. Start with *Statistical Analysis* or *Statistical Methods* and then proceed to *Experimental Design*. Supplement these books by reading Diamond. The McNemar and Lindquist chapters are more difficult. The Lindquist reference is for the student who already has a fairly good statistical background.

  * Diamond, S., *Information and Error*. New York: Basic Books, 1959. Chaps. 3, 4, and 8. This book has a refreshing approach. It also stresses an understanding of principles.

  Edwards, A., *Experimental Design in Psychological Research*. Chap. 10. New York: Rinehart, 1950. A new edition of this valuable book has been published (1960), but the old edition is probably better for the beginning student.

  * Edwards, A., *Statistical Analysis*, rev. ed. New York: Holt, Rinehart and Winston, Inc., 1958, Chap. 12. This is a good book for the beginner. Since the author does not go very deeply into principles in this book, however, supplementary reading is recommended.

  Edwards, A., *Statistical Methods of the Behavioral Sciences*, Chap. 16. New York: Holt, Rinehart, and Winston, Inc. 1954. If the reader has grasped the analysis of variance discussion in the present text fairly well, this chapter is a good supplement for clarifying his understanding. Although more advanced than *Statistical Analysis*, the discussion is clear.

Hays, W., *Statistics for Psychologists.* New York: Holt, Rinehart and Winston Inc., 1963. This book is more advanced than the above references, but is perhaps the finest book in the field. It is based on set theory and written with actual research constantly in mind. *Very highly recommended.*

Lindquist, E., *Design and Analysis of Experiments.* Boston: Houghton Mifflin, 1953, Chap. 3. The most difficult of these references, this text is excellent in several ways. Since Lindquist concentrates on educational experimentation, the book is particularly valuable for students of education—but only for those students with fairly good statistical backgrounds.

McNemar, Q., *Psychological Statistics,* 2d ed. New York: Wiley, 1955, Chap. 15. This text is an excellent one for the serious student to consult and study after the unfamiliarity of statistics has worn off.

Moroney, M., *Facts from Figures,* rev. ed. Baltimore: Penguin, 1953, Chap. 19. Since an interesting and instructive method of partitioning sums of squares is used in this book, it is well worth studying.

2. An educational investigator has conducted an experiment to test the relative efficacies of three methods of instructions: A_1, Lecture; A_2, Large-Group Discussion; and A_3, Small-Group Discussion. From a universe of sophomores, 30 were selected at random and randomly assigned to three groups. The three methods were randomly assigned to the three groups. The students were tested for their achievement at the end of four months of the experiment. The scores for the three groups are given below.

Test the null hypothesis, using simple one-way analysis of variance and the .01 level of significance. Compute E and R. Interpret the results. Draw a graph of the data similar to those in the text.

Methods

4 A_1 (Lecture)	5 A_2 (Large Group Discussion)	3 A_3 (Small Group Discussion)
7	6	5
9	3	1
6	8	4
9	3	4
6	2	5
5	5	7
7	6	3
7	7	5
10	5	3

(Answers: F = 7.16 (.01); E = .59; R = .16.)
3. From a table of random numbers, draw three samples of 10 each of numbers 0 through 9.
   (a) Do an analysis of variance of the three sets of numbers. Compute *E* and *R*. Draw a graph of the results.
   (b) Add a constant of 2 to each of the scores of the third group. Use the analysis of variance method and compute *E* and *R* again. What changes take place in the statistics? (Examine the sums of squares especially, taking careful note of the within-groups variance of both examples.) Draw a graph of the data, and compare it with that drawn in (a).
   (c) Compute the components of variance and then interpret them.
4. Take the scores given of the highest and lowest groups in Question 2 (Groups A_1 and A_3).
   (a) Using the analysis of variance, compute the square root of $F, \sqrt{F}$.
   (b) Now do a *t* test as described in the last chapter. Compare *t* with the result of (a) above.
   (c) If you had done an analysis of variance of the original three groups, would it be legitimate to use the analysis described above and then draw conclusions about the difference between the two methods? (Consult your instructor, if necessary—this point is difficult.)
   (d) Compute *E* and *R*. Compare them to *E* and *R* of Question 2, above. Discuss.
   (Answers: (a) $F = 14.47$; $\sqrt{F} = 3.80$; (b) $t = 3.80$; (d) $E = .67$; $R = .57$.)*
5. In an interesting study with important implications for the problem of transfer of training, Wickens conditioned *S*s to tones.[13] He used four groups: Group I was conditioned to the same tone; Group II was conditioned to a tone one octave from the original tone; Group III was conditioned to a tone three octaves from the original tone; Group IV was a control: it received no conditioning. (The unconditioned stimulus was shock.) The following *n*'s, means, and standard deviations are reported by Wickens for Groups I, II, and III. Prepare an analysis of variance and interpret the results. Compute *R*. Interpret.

   Group I: $M = 5.87$; $SD = 3.66$; $n = 15$
   Group II: $M = 3.69$; $SD = 3.45$; $n = 16$
   Group III: $M = 4.19$; $SD = 4.33$; $n = 16$
   (Hint: What terms do you need to compute an *F* ratio? In the statis-

---

[13] D. Wickens, "Studies of Response Generalization in Conditioning. I. Stimulus Generalization during Response Generalization," *Journal of Experimental Psychology,* XXXIII (1943), 221–227.

tics given above, how could you get an estimate of the within-groups variance quite directly? What terms do you need to compute the between-groups variance? Are they given in the table?)

(*Answers:* $F = 1.36$ (*n.s.*); $R = .02$.)

6. Aronson and Mills tested the interesting and perhaps humanly perverse hypothesis that individuals who undergo an unpleasant initiation to become members of a group have more liking for the group than do members who do not undergo such an initiation.[14] Three groups of 21 young women each were subjected to three experimental conditions: (1) *severe condition,* in which the Ss were asked to read obscene words and vivid descriptions of sexual activity in order to become members of a group; (2) *mild condition,* in which Ss read words related to sex but not obscene; and (3) *control condition,* in which Ss were not required to do anything to become members of the group. After a rather elaborate procedure, the Ss were asked to rate the discussion and the group members of the group to which they then ostensibly belonged. The means and standard deviations of the total ratings are *severe:* $M = 195.3, SD = 31.9$; *mild:* $M = 171.1, SD = 34.0$; *control:* $M = 166.7, SD = 21.6$. Each n was 21.

(a) Do an analysis of variance of these data. Interpret the data. Was the hypothesis supported?

(b) Compute R. Is the relation strong? Would you expect the relation to be strong in an experiment of this kind?

(*Answers:* (a) $F = 5.39$ (.01); (b) $R = .17$.)

14 E. Aronson and J. Mills, "The Effect of Severity of Initiation on Liking for a Group," *Journal of Abnormal and Social Psychology,* LIX (1959), 177–181.

12 ANALYSIS OF VARIANCE: FACTORIAL ANALYSIS

In factorial analysis of variance two or more independent variables vary independently or interact with each other to produce variation in a dependent variable. *Factorial analysis of variance is the statistical method that analyzes the independent and interactive effects of two or more independent variables on a dependent variable.*

One of the most significant and revolutionary developments in modern research design and statistics is the planning and analysis of the simultaneous operation and interaction of two or more variables. Scientists have long known that variables do not act independently. Rather, they often act in concert. The virtue of one method of teaching contrasted with another method of teaching depends on the teachers using the methods. The educational effect of a certain kind of teacher depends, to a large extent, on the kind of pupil being taught. An anxious teacher may be quite effective with anxious pupils but less effective with non-anxious pupils. Different methods of teaching in colleges and universities may depend on the intelligence and personality of both professors and students.

The traditional conduct of experimental research has been to study the effect of one independent variable on one dependent variable.[1] Educational scientists knew that the study of the effects of different pedagogical methods and techniques on educational outcomes was in part a function of other variables, such as the intelligence of the students, the personality of the teachers, the social background of both the teachers and the students, and the general atmosphere of the class and the school. In the past most researchers (this is also true of many researchers today) believed that the most effective research method was to vary one independent variable while controlling, as best one could, other independent variables that might contribute to the variance of the dependent variable.

It is by no means implied that scientists did not arrive at important

[1] See R. Fischer, *The Design of Experiments*, 6th ed. New York: Hafner, 1951, pp. 91, 92.

and valid generalizations before the advent of modern research design and statistics. They did. Factorial analysis of variance and other multivariate notions, as well as the research designs they imply, however, make it possible to expand greatly our conceptions and our methods of research and analysis.

RESEARCH EXAMPLES

Educators have long believed that both praise and blame, reward and punishment, have different effects on learning. In previous centuries, great emphasis was put upon the efficacy of punishing pupils for poor work. Good work was only to be expected, because it was only right and proper that children should do good work. If the children did poor work, they were considered to be bad, and their teachers were admonished to correct this defect, even by ruthless and cruel methods if necessary.

In the twentieth century educational thought has changed radically. Influenced by more enlightened thinking, by increased knowledge of the growth of the child, and by more valid knowledge of the learning process in general, we now believe that learning is encouraged more by reward than by punishment. But is it possible that reward and punishment have varying effects on different kinds of children in different kinds of educational institutions with different kinds of teachers?

Thompson and Hunnicutt attempted to answer part of this question in an experimental manner.[2] Five groups of fifth-grade children were used—four experimental and one control. The children were divided into the four experimental groups as follows. On the basis of an extroversion-introversion test, the children were split into two groups, those above the median and those below the median (a common method of dividing experimental groups), called "extroverts" and "introverts." Six alternate forms of a cancellation test were given in six test periods of 30 seconds each. Two of the four classes were designated as "praise" groups and two as "blame" groups. The fifth group, the control group, was neither praised nor blamed. (In subsequent discussion, this control group will be omitted from consideration, since it is not pertinent to our purpose.) In effect, then, the authors had two independent variables, Praise-Blame and Extroversion-Introversion, and one dependent variable, Achievement (via cancellation score gains).

The results showed that both praise and blame increased cancellation scores. More important, it was found that extroverts who were blamed and introverts who were praised achieved higher scores. Apparently an interaction existed between the two independent variables.

2 G. Thompson and C. Hunnicutt, "The Effect of Praise and Blame on the Work Achievement of 'Introverts' and 'Extroverts,'" *Journal of Educational Psychology*, XXXV (1944), 257–266.

We shall concentrate here on the basic design and omit other details. What Thompson and Hunnicutt did, in effect, was to assign the total number of students to four groups by dichotomizing the entire group on extroversion-introversion, and by administering the experimental treatments of praise-blame to half of each of these two groups. The design looks like this (Fig. 12.1):

Incentive

Praise   Blame

Extrovert   CANCELLATION

Type   TEST

Introvert   SCORES

FIG. **12.1**

Although Thompson and Hunnicutt did not clearly conceptualize or analyze the study in this way, it is a good example of a factorial design.

Note that three statistical hypotheses can be tested: the significance of the differences between Praise-Blame, between Extrovert-Introvert, and the significance of the interaction or mutual interplay of these two variables. An important characteristic of factorial analysis of variance is that several hypotheses can be tested simultaneously. Thompson and Hunnicutt were naturally interested in the effects of praise and blame, but they were *more* interested in whether praise and blame worked differently with different kinds of children, in this case with extroverts and introverts. In other words, they wanted to know whether or not Praise-Blame *interacted* with Extroversion-Introversion. They asked these questions of the data, the theoretical and practical implications of which are important: Does praise work better with introverts than with extroverts? Does blame work better with extroverts? (The answer to both questions was Yes.)

In a British study reported by Quenouille, the question was asked: Are parental encouragement and child initiative related to intelligence? [3] To obtain an answer to this question, 48 eleven-year-old children were tested on the three variables. The study is unusual in several ways: (1) it is not an experimental study; no independent variables were manipulated; (2) intelligence is the dependent variable rather than, as usual, an independent variable; and (3) the results included a significant interaction between the two independent variables. The design of the study is shown in Fig. 12.2.

[3] M. Quenouille, *Introductory Statistics*. London: Pergamon, 1950, p. 73. Quenouille unfortunately does not give references for the studies he cites.

Parental Encouragement

High P.E.   Low P.E.

	High I	INTELLIGENCE
Initiative		TEST
	Low I	SCORES

FIG. 12.2

The results are particularly interesting, since all of the effects were statistically significant. From the evidence presented, it would seem that initiative is related to intelligence. Parental encouragement, too, is related to intelligence. The most provocative finding, however, is the significant interaction effect which in this case means that, with children of high initiative, parental encouragement is quite effective, whereas with children of low initiative it has less effect.

In both of these studies, then, the conclusions go beyond the simple differences between effects or groups. In both studies it was possible to qualify the conclusions in important ways because the authors studied the simultaneous working of the two independent variables. They were consequently able to talk about the *differential effect* of their variables. They could say, for example, that Treatment A_1 is effective when coupled with Level B_1, but not effective when alone or when coupled with Level B_2, and that, perhaps, A_2 is effective only when coupled with B_1. The balance of this chapter will be devoted to clarifying these statements, as well as explaining the logic and machinery of factorial analysis of variance.

A SIMPLE FICTITIOUS EXAMPLE

As usual we take a very simple, if unrealistic, example which highlights the basic problems and characteristics of factorial analysis of variance. Assume that an educational investigator is interested in the relative efficacy of two methods of teaching, A_1 and A_2. Call this variable Methods. He believes that methods of teaching, in and of themselves, do not differ very much. They differ only when used with certain kinds of students, by certain kinds of teachers, in certain kinds of educational situations, and with certain kinds of motives. Studying all of these variables at one time is too large an order for him, though not necessarily impossible. So he decides to study Methods and Motivations, which gives him two independent variables and one dependent variable. Call the dependent variable Achievement. (Some type of achievement measure will be used, perhaps scores on a standardized test.)

The investigator conducts an experiment with eight sixth-grade children. (Obviously he would work with many more than eight children.) He randomly assigns the eight children to four groups, two per group. He also randomly assigns Methods A_1 and A_2 and Motivations B_1 and B_2 to the four groups. Refer back to the earlier discussion on partitions of sets. Recall that we can partition and cross-partition sets of objects. The objects can be assigned to a partition or subpartition on the basis of the possession of certain characteristics. But they can also be assigned at random—and then presumably be "given" certain characteristics by the experimenter. In either case the partitioning logic is the same. The experimenter will end up with four subpartitions: A_1B_1, A_1B_2, A_2B_1, and A_2B_2. The experimental paradigm is shown in Fig. 12.3.

	Methods	
	A_1	A_2
B_1	A_1B_1	A_2B_1
Motivations		
B_2	A_1B_2	A_2B_2

FIG. 12.3

Each cell in the design is the intersection of two subsets. For instance, Method A_1 combined with Motivation B_2 is conceptually $A_1 \cap B_2$. Method A_2 combined with Motivation B_2 is the intersection $A_2 \cap B_2$. In this design, we write simply A_1B_2 and A_2B_2 for simplicity. Now two children have been assigned at random to each of these four cells. This means that each child will get a combination of two experimental manipulations, but each pair of children will get a different combination.

Call A_1 "recitation," and A_2 "no recitation." Call B_1 "praise," and B_2 "blame." The children in cell A_1B_1, then, will be taught with recitation and will be praised for their work. The children in cell A_1B_2 will be taught with recitation but will be "blamed" for their work. And similarly for the other two cells. If the experimental procedures have been adequately handled, it is possible to conceive of the variables as being independent, that is, two separate experiments are actually being run with the same subjects. One experiment manipulates Methods; the other, Types of Motivations. The design of the experiment, in other words, makes it possible for the investigator to test *independently* the effects on a dependent variable, in this case, achievement, of (1) Methods and (2) Types of Motivation. To show this and other important facets of factorial designs, let us jump to the hypothetical data of the experiment. These "data" are reported in Table 12.1, together with the necessary computations for a factorial analysis of variance.

TABLE 12.1 DATA OF HYPOTHETICAL FACTORIAL EXPERIMENT
WITH ANALYSIS OF VARIANCE CALCULATIONS

Types of Motivation	Methods A_1	A_2	
B_1	8 6	4 2	
ΣX	14	6	$\Sigma X_{B_1} = 20$
$(\Sigma X)^2$	196	36	$(\Sigma X_{B_1})^2 = 400$
M	⑦	③	$M_{B_1} =$ ⑤
B_2	8 6	4 2	
ΣX	14	6	$\Sigma X_{B_2} = 20$
$(\Sigma X)^2$	196	36	$(\Sigma X_{B_2})^2 = 400$
M	⑦	③	$M_{B_2} =$ ⑤
ΣX_A	28	12	$\Sigma X_t = 40$
$(\Sigma X_A)^2$	784	144	$(\Sigma X_t)^2 = 1600$
M_A	⑦	③	$M_t =$ ⑤ $\Sigma X_t^2 = 240$

First, we calculate the sums of squares that we would for a simple one-way analysis of variance. There is of course a *total sum of squares,* calculated from all the scores, using $C,$ the correction term:

$$C = \frac{(40)^2}{8} = \frac{1600}{8} = 200$$

$$\text{Total} = 240 - 200 = 40$$

Since there are four groups, there is a sum of squares associated with the means of the four groups. Simply conceive of the four groups placed side by side as in simple analysis of variance, and calculate the sum of squares as in the last chapter. Now, however, we call this the *"between all groups" sum of squares* to distinguish it from sums of squares to be computed later.

$$\text{Between all groups} \atop (A_1, A_2, B_1, B_2) = \left(\frac{196}{2} + \frac{36}{2} + \frac{196}{2} + \frac{36}{2} \right) - 200 = 32$$

This sum of squares is a measure of the variability of all four group means. Therefore, if we subtract this quantity from the total sum of squares, we should obtain the sum of squares due to error, the random fluctuations of the scores within the cells (groups). This is familiar: it is the *within-groups sum of squares:*

$$\text{Within groups} = 40 - 32 = 8$$

Since the experiment is concerned with Methods and Types of Motivation, we need not bother with the final analysis of variance table. Instead, we go on to compute the sum of squares of experimental concern.

To compute the *sum of squares for methods,* proceed exactly as with the simple analysis of variance: treat the scores (X's) and sums of scores (ΣX's) of the columns (Methods) as though these two groups were not subdivided:

	A_1	A_2
	8	4
	6	2
	8	4
	6	2
ΣX:	28	12

The computation is:

$$\text{Between methods} \atop (A_1, A_2) = \left(\frac{(28)^2}{4} + \frac{(12)^2}{4} \right) - 200 = \left(\frac{784}{4} + \frac{144}{4} \right) - 200 = 32$$

Similarly, treat Types of Motivation (B_1 and B_2) as though there were no Methods (A_1 and A_2):

	B_1	B_2
	8	8
	6	6
	4	4
	2	2
ΣX:	20	20

The computation of the between-types sum of squares is really not necessary. Since the sums (and the means) are the same, the between types sum of squares is zero:

$$\text{Between types} \atop (B_1, B_2) = \left(\frac{(20)^2}{4} + \frac{(20)^2}{4} \right) - 200 = 0$$

There is another possible source of variance, the variance due presumably to the *interaction* of the two independent variables. The between-all-groups sum of squares comprises the variability due to the means of the four groups: 7, 3, 7, 3. This sum of squares was 32. If this were not a contrived example, part of this sum of squares would be due to Methods, part to Types of Motivation, and a remaining part left over, *which is due to the joint action, or interaction, of* Methods and Types. In many cases it would be relatively small, no greater than chance expectation. In other cases, it would be large enough to be statistically significant; it would exceed chance expectation. In the present problem it is clearly zero since the between-methods sum of squares was 32, and this is equal to the between-all-groups sum of squares. To complete the computational cycle we calculate:[4]

Interaction: methods × types = between all groups − (between methods + between types) = 32 − (32 + 0) = *0*

We are now in a position to set up the final analysis of variance table. We postpone this, however, until we perform a minor operation on these scores.

We use exactly the same scores, but rearrange them slightly: we reverse the scores of A_1B_2 and A_2B_2. Since all the individual scores (X's) are exactly the same, the total sum of squares must also be exactly the same. Further, the sums and sums of squares of B_1 and B_2 (Types) must also be exactly the same. Table 12.2 shows just what was done and its effect on the means of the four groups.

TABLE 12.2   DATA OF HYPOTHETICAL FACTORIAL EXPERIMENT OF TABLE 12.1 WITH B_2 FIGURES REARRANGED

Types of Motivation	*Methods* A_1	A_2	
B_1	8 6	4 2	
ΣX M	14 ⑦	6 ③	$\Sigma X_{B_1} = 20$ $M_{B_1} = ⑤$
B_2	4 2	8 6	
ΣX M	6 ③	14 ⑦	$\Sigma X_{B_2} = 20$ $M_{B_2} = ⑤$
ΣX M	20 ⑤	20 ⑤	$\Sigma X_t = 40$ $M_t = ⑤$ $\Sigma X_t^2 = 240$

Study the figures of Tables 12.1 and 12.2 and note the differences. To emphasize the differences, the means have been circled in both tables. To make the differences still clearer, the means of both tables have been

---

[4] In a more complex factorial analysis of variance it is not possible to compute the interactions so easily. Since the purpose of these chapters is not basically computational, we do not take up the computation of more complex forms of analysis of variance. See A. Edwards, *Experimental Design in Psychological Research.* New York: Holt, Rinehart and Winston, Inc., 1950, chaps. 12 and 13.

laid out in Table 12.3. The little table on the left shows two variabilities: between all four means and between A_1 and A_2 means. In the little table on the right, there is only one variability, that between the four means. In both little tables, the variability of the four means is the same since they both have the same four means: 7, 3, 7, 3. Obviously, there is no variability of the B means in both tables. There are two differences between the tables, then: the A means and the arrangement of the four means inside the squares. If we analyze the sum of squares of the four means, the between-all-groups sums of squares, we find that B_1 and B_2 contribute nothing to it in both tables, since there is no variability with 5, 5, the means of B_1 and B_2. In the table on the right, the A_1 and A_2 means of 5 and 5 contribute no variability. In the table on the left, however, the A_1-A_2 means differ considerably, 7 and 3, and thus they contribute variance.

TABLE 12.3 MEANS OF THE DATA OF TABLES 12.1 AND 12.2

	Table 12.1 Means				Table 12.2 Means		
	A_1	A_2			A_1	A_2	
B_1	7	3	5	B_1	7	3	5
B_2	7	3	5	B_2	3	7	5
	7	3			5	5	

Assuming for the moment that the means of 7 and 3 differ significantly, we can say that Methods of the data of Table 12.1 had an effect irrespective of Types of Motivation. That is, $M_{A_1} \neq M_{A_2}$, or $M_{A_1} > M_{A_2}$. As far as this experiment is concerned, Methods differ significantly *no matter what the type of motivation*. And, obviously, Types of Motivation had no effect, since $M_{B_1} = M_{B_2}$. In Table 12.2, on the other hand, the situation is quite different. Neither Methods nor Types of Motivation had an effect *by themselves*. Yet there *is* variance. The problem is: What is the source of the variance? It is in the *interaction of the two variables,* the interaction of Methods and Types of Motivation.

If we had performed an experiment and obtained data like those of Table 12.2, then we could come to the likely conclusion that there was an interaction between the two variables in their effect on the dependent variable. In this case, we would interpret the results as follows. Methods A_1 and A_2, operating in and of themselves, do not differ in their effect. Types of Motivation B_1 and B_2, in and of themselves, do not differ in their effect. When Methods and Types of Motivation are allowed to "work together," when they are permitted to interact, they are significantly effective. Specifically, Method A_1 is superior to Method A_2 when combined with Type of Motivation B_1. When combined with Type of Motivation B_2, it is inferior to A_2. This interaction effect is indicated on the right-hand side of Table 12.3 by the crisscrossed arrows. Qualitatively interpreting the original methods, we find that "recitation" seems to be superior to "no recitation" under the condition of "praise," but that it is inferior to "no recitation" under conditions of "blame" (reproof).

It is instructive to note, before going further, that interaction can be studied and computed by a subtractive procedure. In a 2 × 2 design, this procedure is simple. Subtract one mean from another in each row, and then compute the variance of these differences. Take the fictitious means of Table 12.3. If we subtract the Table 12.1 means, we get $7 - 3 = 4$; $7 - 3 = 4$. Clearly the mean square is zero. Thus, the interaction is zero. Follow the same procedure for the Table 12.2 means (right-hand side of the table): $7 - 3 = 4$; $3 - 7 = -4$. If we now treat these two differences as we did means in the last chapter and compute the sum of squares and the mean square, we will arrive at the interaction sum of squares and the mean square, 32 in each case. The reasoning behind this procedure is simple. If there were no interaction, we would expect the differences between row means to be approximately equal to each other and to the difference between the means at the bottom of the table, the Methods means, in this case. Note that this is so for the Table 12.1 means: the bottom row difference is 4, and so are the differences of each of the rows. The row differences of Table 12.2, however, deviate from the difference between the bottom row (Methods) means. They are 4 and −4, whereas the bottom-row difference is $5 - 5 = 0$.

From this discussion and a little reflection, it can be seen that a significant interaction can be caused by one deviant row. For example, the means of the above example might be:

7	3	5
5	5	5
6	4	

Subtract the rows. $7 - 3 = 4$; $5 - 5 = 0$; and $6 - 4 = 2$. There is obviously some variance in these remainders.[5]

It will be profitable to write the final analysis of variance tables in which the different variances and F ratios are calculated. Table 12.4 gives the final analysis of variance tables for both examples.[6]

[5] For a more complete discussion, see E. Lindquist, *Design and Analysis of Experiments in Psychology and Education*. Boston: Houghton Mifflin, 1953, pp. 119, 125. Lindquist also discusses more complex examples.

[6] The between-all-groups sums of squares have not been included in the table. They are only useful for computing the within-groups sums of squares. The degrees of freedom for the main effects (Methods and Types) and for between all groups and

TABLE 12.4   FINAL ANALYSIS OF VARIANCE TABLES: DATA
OF TABLES 12.1 AND 12.2

| Source | df | Data of Table 12.1 | | | Data of Table 12.2 | | |
		s.s.	m.s.	F	s.s.	m.s.	F
Between Methods (A_1, A_2)	1	32	32	16 (.05)	0	0	....
Between Types (B_1, B_2)	1	0	0	....	0	0	....
Interaction: A × B	1	0	0	....	32	32	16 (.05)
Within Groups	4	8	2		8	2	
Total	7	40			40		

The sum of squares and mean square and the resulting F ratio of 16 on the left-hand side of the table indicate what we already know from the preceding discussion: Methods are significantly different (at the .05 level), and Types of Motivation and interaction are not significant. The parallel figures of the right-hand side of the table indicate that only the interaction is significant.

THE MEANING OF INTERACTION

In the last chapter, it was said that if sampling was random the means of the k groups would be approximately equal. If, for example, there were four groups and the general mean, M_t, was 4.5, then it would be expected that each of the means would be approximately 4.5. Similarly, in factorial analysis of variance, if random samples of numbers are drawn for each of the cells, then the means of the cells should be approximately equal. If the general mean, M_t, were 10, then the best expectation for any cell means in the factorial design would be 10. These means, of course, would very rarely be exactly 10. Indeed, some of them might be considerably far from 10. The fundamental statistical question is: Do they differ from 10 significantly? The means of combinations of means, too, should hover around 10. For example, in a design like that of the previous example the A_1 and A_2 means should be approximately 10, and the B_1 and B_2 means should be approximately 10. In addition, the means of each of the cells, A_1B_1, A_1B_2, A_2B_1, and A_2B_2, should hover around 10.

within groups are calculated in the same way as in the simple analysis of variance. This should become apparent upon studying the table. The interaction degrees of freedom is the product of the degrees of freedom of the main effects, that is, $1 \times 1 = 1$. If Methods had had four groups and Types three groups, the interaction degrees of freedom would have been $3 \times 2 = 6$.

Using a table of random numbers, I drew 60 digits, 0 through 9, to fill the six cells of a factorial design. The resulting design has two levels or independent variables, A and B. A is subdivided into A_1, A_2, and A_3, B into B_1 and B_2. This is called a 3×2 factorial design. (The examples of Tables 12.1 and 12.2 are 2×2 designs.)

Conceive of A as Types of Appeal. In a social psychological experiment designed to test hypotheses of the best ways to appeal to prejudiced people to change their attitudes, the question is asked: What kinds of appeal work best to change prejudiced attitudes? [7] Assume that three types of appeal, "Religious," "Fair-Play," "Democratic," have been tried with unclear results. The investigator suspects that the situation is more complex, that Types of Appeal interact with the Manner of Appeal in which appeals are made. So he sets up a 3×2 factorial design, in which the second level or variable, B, is divided into B_1 and B_2, impassioned and calm manner of appeal. That is, the religious appeal is given in an impassioned manner to some subjects and in a calm manner to others, and similarly for the other two types of appeal. We will not explore this research problem further, but simply use it to color the abstract and perhaps skeleton quality of our discussion. Imagine the experiment to have been done with the results given in Table 12.5, which gives the design paradigm and the means of each cell, as well as the means of the two variables, A and B, and the general mean, M_t. These means were computed from the 60 random numbers drawn in lots of 10 each and inserted in the cells.

TABLE 12.5   TWO-WAY FACTORIAL DESIGN: MEANS OF GROUPS
OF RANDOM NUMBERS 0 THROUGH 9

	Types of Appeal			
Manner of Appeal	A_1 Religious	A_2 Fair-Play	A_3 Democratic	
B_1 Impassioned	4.1	5.0	3.9	4.33
B_2 Calm	5.6	3.9	4.2	4.57
	4.85	4.45	4.05	$M_t = 4.45$

We hardly need a test of statistical significance to know that these means do not differ significantly. Their total range is 3.9 to 5.6. The mean expectation, of course, is the mean of the numbers 0 through 9,

[7] The idea for this fictitious experiment was taken from an actual experiment: A. Citron, I. Chein, and J. Harding, "Anti-Minority Remarks: A Problem for Action Research," *Journal of Abnormal and Social Psychology*, XLV (1950), 99–126.

or 4.5. The closeness of the means to $M_t = 4.45$ or to 4.5 is remarkable, even for random sampling. At any rate, if these were the results of an actual experiment, the experimenter would probably be most chagrined. Types of Appeal, Manner of Appeal, and the interaction between them are all insignificant. He might just as well have drawn random numbers.

Remark how many different outcome possibilities other than chance there would be if one or both variables had been effective. The three means of Appeal, M_{A_1}, M_{A_2}, and M_{A_3}, might have been significantly different, with the means of Manner, M_{B1}, and M_{B2}, not significantly different. Or the Manner means might be significantly different, with the Appeal means not significantly different; or both sets of means could be different; or both could turn out not to be different, with their interaction significant. The possibilities of *kinds* of differences and interactions are considerable, too, although it would take too many words and numbers to illustrate even a small number of them. If the student will juggle the numbers a bit, he can get considerable insight into both statistics and design possibilities. For instance, increase the A_1 mean by 2, $4.85 + 2 = 6.85$, and increase the two cell means of A_1, A_1B_1 and A_1B_2, by 2, also; then $4.1 + 2 = 6.1$ and $5.6 + 2 = 7.6$. At the same time, decrease the A_3 means by 1 and its two cell means by 1: $4.05 - 1 = 3.05$; $3.9 - 1 = 2.9$; and $4.2 - 1 = 3.2$. Naturally, recompute M_t and the B_1 and B_2 means. What conclusions might then be drawn? Now try altering one of the B means, making appropriate adjustments throughout the table. Such alterations can be very informative.

Since our present preoccupation is with interaction, let us alter the means to cause a significant interaction. We increase the A_1B_1 mean by 2, decrease the A_1B_2 mean by 2, increase the A_3B_2 mean by 1, and decrease the A_3B_1 mean by 1. We let the A_2 means stand as they are, and alter the main effect means accordingly. The changes are shown in Table 12.6.

TABLE 12.6   MEANS OF TABLE 12.8 ALTERED SYSTEMATICALLY
BY ADDING AND SUBTRACTING CONSTANTS

Manner of Appeal	Types of Appeal			
	A_1	A_2	A_3	
B_1	(4.1 + 2) 6.1	5.0	(3.9 − 1) 2.9	4.67
B_2	(5.6 − 2) 3.6	3.9	(4.2 + 1) 5.2	4.23
	4.85	4.45	4.05	4.45

Table 12.6 should be studied carefully. Compare it to Table 12.5. Interaction has been produced by the arbitrary alterations. The cell means have been unbalanced, so to speak, while the marginal means $(A_1, A_2, A_3, B_1, B_2)$ are almost undisturbed. The total mean remains unchanged at 4.45. The three A means are the same. (Why?) The two B means are changed very little. A factorial analysis of variance of the appropriately altered random numbers—which, of course, are no longer random—yields the final analysis of variance table given in Table 12.7.

TABLE 12.7   FINAL ANALYSIS OF VARIANCE TABLE OF ALTERED
RANDOM NUMBER DATA

Source	df	m.s.	s.s.	F
Between All Groups	5	70.15		
Within Groups	54	476.70	8.83	
Between Appeals (A_1, A_2, A_3)	2	6.40	3.20	$< 1.$ (n.s.)
Between Manners (B_1, B_2)	1	2.82	2.82	$< 1.$ (n.s.)
Interaction: $A \times M$	2	60.93	30.47	3.45 (.05)
Within Groups	54	476.70	8.83	
Total	59	546.85		

Neither of the main effects (Appeal and Manner) is significant. That is, the means of A_1, A_2, and A_3 do not differ significantly from chance. Neither do the means of B_1 and B_2. The only significant F ratio is that of interaction, which is significant at the .05 level.[8] Evidently the alteration of the scores has had an effect. If we were interpreting the results, as given in Tables 12.6 and 12.7, we would say that, in and of themselves, neither types of appeal to the bigot nor the manner of appeal differ. But a religious appeal delivered in an impassioned manner and a democratic appeal in a calm manner seem to be most effective. Perhaps a bit more clearly, the democratic appeal in an impassioned manner is relatively ineffectual, as is the religious appeal in a calm manner. (It is not possible to say much about the fair play appeal.)

[8] The random numbers that generated Table 12.5 were also subjected to an analysis of variance. The F ratios were not significant.

FACTORIAL ANALYSIS OF VARIANCE
WITH THREE OR MORE VARIABLES

Factorial analysis of variance can work with more than two independent variables. Three, four, and more variables are possible and do appear in the literature. Designs with more than four variables, however, are uncommon and not too fruitful. It is not so much because the statistics become complex and unwieldy. Rather, it is a matter of practicality. It is very difficult just to get enough subjects to fill the cells of complex designs. And it is even more difficult to manipulate four, five, or six independent variables at one time. For instance, take an experiment with four independent variables. The smallest arrangement possible is $2 \times 2 \times 2 \times 2$, which yields 16 cells into each of which some minimum number of subjects must be put. If 10 Ss are placed in each cell, it will be necessary to handle the total of 160 Ss in four different ways. Yet one should not be dogmatic about the number of variables. Perhaps in the next ten years factorial designs with more than four variables will become common with the increased support of behavioral research and the use of high speed computers.

The simplest form of a three-variable factorial analysis of variance is a $2 \times 2 \times 2$ design. Consider the immediately preceding sample. Suppose the investigator decided to use, in a new experiment, a third independent variable. He drops the fair play appeal and keeps the religious and democratic appeals. He has noticed that there seems to be a greater effect on the prejudiced person if he personalizes the appeal. So he adds another variable, C, which he calls Personalization. This variable he defines as the degree of appeal to the person as an individual rather than as a member of any group. In the design this variable has two *modes* which he calls "Personalized" and "Objectified," C_1 and C_2. The design now looks like that in Fig. 12.4.

Appeals

		A_1 (Religious)		A_2 (Democratic)	
	Mode	C_1 Personalized	C_2 Objectified	C_1 Personalized	C_2 Objectified
Manner	B_1 (Impassioned)	$A_1B_1C_1$	$A_1B_1C_2$	$A_2B_1C_1$	$A_2B_1C_2$
	B_2 (Calm)	$A_1B_2C_1$	$A_1B_2C_2$	$A_2B_2C_1$	$A_2B_2C_2$

FIG 12.4

The researcher can now test seven hypotheses: the differences between A_1 and A_2 (Appeal), between B_1 and B_2 (Manner), and between C_1 and C_2 (Mode). These are called the *main effects*. Four interactions can also be tested: $A \times B$, $A \times C$, $B \times C$, and $A \times B \times C$. A final analysis of variance table would look like Table 12.8.

TABLE 12.8   FINAL ANALYSIS OF VARIANCE TABLE FOR THE
2 × 2 × 2 DESIGN OF FIG. 12.4

Source	df	s.s.	m.s.	F
Between Appeals (A_1, A_2)	1			
Between Manners (B_1, B_2)	1			
Between Modes (C_1, C_2)	1			
Interaction: $A \times B$	1			
Interaction: $A \times C$	1			
Interaction: $B \times C$	1			
Interaction: $A \times B \times C$	1			
Within Groups	$N - 7$			
Total	$N - 1$			

It is evident that a great deal of information can be obtained from this one experiment. Contrast it with the one variable experiment in which only *one* hypothesis can be tested. The difference is not only great—it indicates a fundamentally different way of conceptualizing research problems.

Multiple Interactions among Variables   In most research studies using factorial designs, the main effects are probably of most interest. Interactions, particularly triple and quadruple interactions, seem most often not to be significant. Even so, this information is important. To know, say, that a variable, *A,* is effective in and of itself is important information, and it cannot be known unless the interaction is specifically tested.

Interactions are called first order, second order, third order, and so on. A two-variable interaction, $A \times B$, is a first-order interaction; a three-variable interaction, $A \times B \times C$, is a second-order interaction. Significant first-order interactions seem to be fairly common, and students of research, especially students of behavioral research, should be familiar with them and be able to handle them. In the opinion of some educational thinkers, the study of interactions in educational research is becoming increasingly important and should become a central preoccupation of educational research workers.

By now the reader no doubt realizes that in principle the breakdowns of the independent variables are not restricted to just two or three subpartitions. It is quite possible to have 2×4, 2×5, 4×6, $2 \times 3 \times 3$, $2 \times 5 \times 4$, $4 \times 2 \times 3 \times 5$. . . . The main obstacle, as mentioned above, is practicability. As always, the problem under investigation and the judgment of the researcher are the criteria that determine what a design and its concomitant analysis shall be. A point to be emphasized is that the student should be flexible and should know what *can* be done. Another point is that research by no means needs to be limited to one variable at a time. It may even be said that it is wrong to so limit it, as Fisher has so strongly indicated.

GOALS OF FACTORIAL ANALYSIS OF VARIANCE

Factorial analysis of variance, as we have seen, accomplishes several purposes. First, factorial design and factorial analysis of variance enable the researcher to manipulate and control two or more variables simultaneously. Not only is it possible to study the effects of teaching methods on achievement. We can study the effects of teaching methods and also the effects of, say, types of reinforcement of responses. In addition, we can control variables like sex, intelligence, and social class. These research possibilities should be fairly evident by now.

A second possible accomplishment of the factorial approach has been touched upon above: variables that are not manipulated can be controlled. Instead of the ubiquitous procedure of matching for intelligence or aptitude, for instance, we can build these variables—and many other such variables—into our designs in a factorial fashion. We may be interested only in the differential effects of certain methods. Certain variables that are known or suspected to influence achievement, like intelligence, sex, and social class, may at the time be merely unnecessary complications. They must be controlled; this we know. Instead of matching pairs of subjects—a procedure that may be inadequate—we can build them into our designs. Not only can we thus control these variables, but we can obtain additional information of possibly great value and significance. One easy way to control the sex variable, for instance, is to confine the experiment to one of the sexes only or to match on sex. But why not introduce sex as a variable in a factorial design?

The third possible accomplishment is the most important: the study of the interactive effects of independent variables on dependent variables. This was discussed earlier.

A fourth and final accomplishment is that factorial analysis of variance is more precise than simple one-way analysis of variance. Here we see one of the virtues of combining research design and statistical considerations. It can be said that, other things being equal, factorial designs are "better" than one-way designs. This value judgment has been implicit in most of the preceding discussion. The multivariate, control, and inter-action reasons support the judgment. The precision argument adds even more weight to it.

FACTORIAL ANALYSIS OF VARIANCE AND PRECISION

In a simple one-way analysis of variance, there are two *identifiable* sources of variance: that presumed to be due to the experimental effects and that presumably due to error or chance variation. We now look at the latter more closely. When subjects have been assigned to the experimental groups at random, the only possible estimate of chance variation is the within-groups variance. But—and this is important—it is clear that the within-groups variance contains not only variance due to error; it also contains variance due to individual differences among the subjects. Two simple examples are intelligence and sex. There are, of course, many others. If both girls and boys are used in an experiment, randomization can be used in order to balance the individual differences that are con-comitant to sex. Then the number of girls and boys in each experimental group will be approximately equal. We can also arbitrarily assign girls and boys in equal numbers to the groups. This method, however, does not accomplish the over-all purpose of randomization, which is to equal-ize the groups on *all* possible variables. It *does* equalize the groups as far as the sex variable is concerned, but we can have no assurance that other variables are equally distributed among the groups. Similarly for intelli-gence. Randomization, if successful, will equalize the groups such that the intelligence test means and standard deviations of the groups will be ap-proximately equal. Here, again, it is possible arbitrarily to assign young-sters to the groups in a way to make the groups approximately equal, but then there is no assurance that other possible variables are similarly controlled, since randomization has been interfered with.

Now, let us assume that randomization has been successful. Then theoretically there will be no differences between the groups in intelli-gence and all other variables. *But there will still be individual differ-ences in intelligence—and other variables—within each group.* With two groups, for instance, Group 1 might have IQ's ranging from, say, 88 to 145, and Group 2 might have IQ's ranging from 90 to 142. This range of IQ's, in and of itself, shows, just as the presence of boys and girls within the groups shows, that there are individual differences in intelligence *within* the groups. If this be so, then how can we say that the within-groups variance can be an estimate of error, of chance variation?

The answer is that it is the best we can do under the design circum-stances. If the design is of the simple one-way kind, there is no other meas-ure of error obtainable. So we compute the within-groups variance and treat it as though it were a "true" measure of error variance. It should be clear that the within-groups variance will be larger than the "true" error variance, since it contains variance due to individual differences as well as error variance. Therefore, an F ratio may not be significant when in fact there is "really" a difference between the groups. Obviously if the F ratio is significant, there is not so much to worry about, since the between-groups variance is sufficiently large to overcome the spuriously high estimate of error variance.

To summarize what has been said, let us rewrite an earlier theoretical equation. The earlier equation was

$$V_t = V_b + V_w \qquad (12.1)$$

Since the within-groups variance contains more variance than error variance, the variance due to individual differences, in fact, we can write

$$V_w = V_i + V_e \qquad (12.2)$$

where $V_i =$ variance due to individual differences and $V_e =$ "true" error variance. If this be so, then we can substitute the right-hand side of Eq. 12.2 for the V_w in Eq. 12.1:

$$V_t = V_b + V_i + V_e \qquad (12.3)$$

In other words, Eq. 12.3 is a shorthand way to say what we have been saying above.

The practical research significance of Eq. 12.3 is considerable. If we can find a way to control or measure V_i, to separate it from V_w, then it follows that a more accurate measure of the "true" error variance is possible. Put differently, our ignorance of the variable situation is decreased because we identify and isolate more systematic variance. A portion of the variance that was attributed to error is identified. Consequently the within-groups variance is reduced.

Many of the principles and much of the practice of research design is occupied with this problem, which is essentially a problem of control— the control of variance. When it was said earlier that factorial analysis of variance was more precise than simple one-way analysis of variance, we meant that, by setting up levels of an independent variable, say intelligence, we could decrease the estimate of error, the within-groups variance, and thus get closer to the "true" error variance. Instead of writing Eq. 12.3, let us now write a more specific equation, substituting for V_i, the variance of individual differences, V_{int}, the variance for intelligence —and reintroducing V_w:

$$V_t = V_b + V_{\text{int}} + V_w \qquad (12.4)$$

Compare this equation to Eq. 12.1. More of the total variance, other than the between-groups variance, has been identified and labeled. This variance, V_{int}, has in effect been taken out of the V_w of Eq. 12.1.

SOME RESEARCH EXAMPLES

A large number of interesting uses of factorial analyses of variance have been reported in recent years in the psychological and educational literature, but especially in the psychological literature. Four of them have been selected to illustrate the usefulness and strength of the method. Two analyses of the use of two variables were outlined early in the chapter. The following studies are a mixture of types.

Attitudes toward the Negro Young, Benson, and Holtzman, in a non-experimental but important study of student attitudes toward the Negro in a southern university, used a 2 × 2 factorial analysis to study the possible interaction of two variables, Sex and Year.[9] This study is also distinctive because the sampling procedure was random. Two surveys of student attitudes, measured with a 26-item attitude scale (imbedded in a larger scale), were made in 1955 and 1958. No appreciable change from 1955 to 1958 was found in the student body as a whole, but a factorial analysis of variance using the variables Year of Survey, Sex, and Fraternity (or Sorority) Membership yielded interesting results. The authors state that they were specifically looking for significant interactions, despite the over-all lack of a significant difference between the 1955 and 1958 means. They found fraternity affiliation to be related to attitudes; the *F* ratio between fraternity membership and no fraternity membership was significant at the .05 level. Unaffiliated students were more tolerant of the Negro. The only other significant *F* ratio (.05 level) was that for the interaction between Sex and Year. The data (means) reported are given in Table 12.9.

TABLE 12.9 MEANS OF CROSS-CLASSIFICATION OF SEX AND YEAR; YOUNG, BROWN, AND HOLTZMAN STUDY

	Year of Survey	
	1955	1958
Men	44.8	47.9
Women	45.1	42.3

This is a good example of interaction. Study of the table shows that both male and female students changed from 1955 to 1958, but that they changed in opposite directions. In 1958 the men were *less* tolerant than they had been in 1955, whereas the women were *more* tolerant in 1958 than they had been in 1955.

[9] R. Young, W. Benson, and W. Holtzman, "Changes in Attitudes toward the Negro in a Southern University," *Journal of Abnormal and Social Psychology*, LX (1960), 131–133.

Comments on Test Papers In a study already mentioned, Page analyzed his data in several ways.[10] One of these analyses, a factorial analysis of variance, should be of interest to educators. Recall that Page used three types of reinforcements on tests: No Comment, Free Comment, and Specified Comment. Objective tests were returned to students with (1) No Comment at all on them; (2) Free Comment, that is, the teachers made any comments they thought desirable; (3) Specified Comment(s), which were short remarks provided by Page to be used by the teachers. The criterion measures were scores on the next test given. Page found significant differences between the three treatments. But he also explored the interaction between the types of comment and the pupils' letter grades (A, B, and so forth). The interaction was significant and surprising. He found that the F (failing) pupils' performance mostly caused the interaction. Contrary to the expectation of common sense, the failing students profited most from the free comments on the tests. The mean score (rank) of the free comment students was considerably higher than that of any of the other mean scores. Had Page not used factorial analysis and the idea behind this method, he would not have unearthed this rather startling fact.

Relation between Aggressiveness and Anti-Semitism Berkowitz, studying the relation between anti-Semitism and the displacement of aggression, asked whether prejudiced persons were more likely to respond to frustration with displaced aggression than less prejudiced individuals.[11] He selected 48 female *S*s and separated them into 8 groups in a $2 \times 2 \times 2$ factorial design. He formed two groups of *S*s on the basis of high and low Anti-Semitism. Each of these two groups was then split into two further groups based on high and low Aggressive Drive. (This variable was a control variable, which will not be explained here.) The third variable was an experimental manipulation, Hostility Arousal. In one experimental group hostility was aroused by the experimenter's using sarcasm, deprecating performances, and questioning the student's ability to do well in college. The non-hostility *S*s were treated in a neutral manner. Each *S* was paired with a confederate of the experimenter with whom the *S* was to work to solve a problem. *S*s were asked whether they liked their partners by means of two questions that could be scored 0 ("definitely yes") to 23 ("definitely no"). This was the dependent variable. It was predicted that the more anti-Semitic *S*s would exhibit more displaced aggression, induced by the hostility arousal, than the less anti-Semitic *S*s. This should be manifested in less liking for the work partners by the highly anti-Semitic *S*s. We have here, then, an interaction hypothesis.

[10] E. Page, "Teacher Comments and Student Performance: A Seventy-Four Classroom Experiment in School Motivation," *Journal of Educational Psychology,* XLIX (1958), 173–181.

[11] L. Berkowitz, "Anti-Semitism and the Displacement of Aggression," *Journal of Abnormal and Social Psychology,* LIX (1959), 182–187.

The outcome was interesting and psychologically significant. None of the main effects, Anti-Semitism, Aggressive Drive, or Hostility Arousal, in and of themselves, were significant in the liking-for-partner measure. That is, each pair of groups had approximately equal mean scores on the measure. But one of the interactions, Anti-Semitism by Hostility Arousal, was significant. The mean scores of the crossbreak of these variables is given in Table 12.10. (This table is constructed from part of Berkowitz's larger table.) It seems clear that when hostility is aroused, high anti-Semites respond with more displaced aggression than do low anti-Semites.

TABLE 12.10   MEAN LIKING-FOR-PARTNER SCORES AS RELATED TO HOSTILITY AND ANTI-SEMITISM, BERKOWITZ STUDY [a]

	Hostility Arousal	No Hostility Arousal
High Anti-Semitism	18.4	14.2
Low Anti-Semitism	12.2	16.3

[a] The higher the score the less the liking for partner.

Lecture vs. No Lecture   The last study to be summarized is a contribution to an old educational problem: Do college students learn as much from a textbook alone as they do from lectures plus a text? Marr, *et al.,* used factorial analysis of variance to test the major hypothesis and to control two independent variables.[12] To test the hypothesis implied by the question stated above, Marr, *et al.,* had four sections of a psychology class, the control group, taught in the conventional manner with formal lectures at class sessions. Four other sections, the experimental group, received no lectures. Instead, they were given the class reading assignments and met once a week at which time the instructor merely answered their questions about the reading assignments without any discussion. This was the main variable, Treatments.

To test another variable, Achievement, each class was divided into three groups on the basis of grade-point averages, six students being selected at random from each level. A third independent variable was Instructors. Four instructors taught two sections, one experimental and one control. One of the dependent variables was Course Achievement, as measured by the final course examination. The design is shown in Fig. 12.5.

12 J. Marr, *et. al.,* "The Contribution of the Lecture to College Teaching," *Journal of Educational Psychology,* LI (1960), 277–284.

Methods

		Lecture			No Lecture	
Levels	High	Medium	Low	High	Medium	Low
1						
2			FINAL			
3			EXAMINATION			
4			SCORES			

Instructors (label at left, spanning rows)

FIG. **12.5**

The results are easy to report. Only the variable Levels (as measured by grade-point averages) was significant. These differences, of course, were built into the design, and were to be expected. No other main effect or interaction effect was significant.

This study is unique in three ways. One, it tested an important educational hypothesis—which happens also to be a substantive null hypothesis—that methods make little or no difference in achievement. Two, it is a neat example of building control of possibly important independent variables right into the design. Achievement levels, if not controlled, can contaminate the results. That is, significant results of an experiment can perhaps be due not to the experimental treatments but to the differences in achievement, aptitude, or intelligence levels of the subjects. Here, Levels is explicitly built into the framework of the design and the analysis. A similar argument is valid for the differences between teachers. Again, this possible source of contamination is built into the design, tested, and thus controlled. A third point is that possible interactions of these contaminating variables with the experimental variable of major interest (Lecture vs. No Lecture) is also provided for.

A FURTHER WORD ON INTERACTION

Although the various combinations of data (and means) that can generate significant interactions cannot be discussed in this book, a further word on the manifestations of interaction is necessary. The interactions discussed previously have been what may be called symmetrical interactions. In the situations described, an independent variable has usually operated in one way at one level and in the opposite way at another level. Let us lay out several sets of means, showing some of the main possibilities. There are of course many possibilities of which the six in Table 12.11 can indicate the factorial possibilities with two independent variables. The first three setups show the three possibilities of the significant main effects. They are so obvious that they need not be discussed. (There is, naturally, another possibility: neither A nor B is significant.)

TABLE 12.11   VARIOUS SETS OF MEANS SHOWING DIFFERENT KINDS OF INTERACTION

	A_1	A_2	
B_1	30	20	25
B_2	30	20	25
	30	20	

(a) A significant; B not significant; Interaction not significant

	A_1	A_2	
B_1	30	30	30
B_2	20	20	20
	25	25	

(b) A not significant; B significant; Interaction not significant

	A_1	A_2	
B_1	30	20	25
B_2	40	30	35
	35	25	

(c) A significant; B significant; Interaction not significant

	A_1	A_2	
B_1	30	20	25
B_2	20	30	25
	25	25	

(d) Interaction significant (symmetrical)

	A_1	A_2	
B_1	30	20	25
B_2	20	20	20
	25	20	

(e) Interaction significant (not symmetrical)

	A_1	A_2	
B_1	20	20	20
B_2	30	20	25
	25	20	

(f) Interaction significant (not symmetrical)

When there is a significant interaction, on the other hand, the situation is not so obvious. The setups (d), (e), and (f) show three common possibilities. In (d), what might be called a "classical" pattern is shown. The means crisscross, as indicated by the arrows in Table 12.11. Here the interpretation is symmetrical: opposite at the two levels of B. It can be said, for example, that A is effective in one direction at B_1, but is effective in the other direction at B_2. Or, $A_1 > A_2$ at B_1, but $A_1 < A_2$ at B_2. In this chapter, the simple fictitious example of Table 12.2 was of this kind. (See also Table 12.3.) The fictitious example of Table 12.6, where interaction was deliberately induced by adding and subtracting constants, is another symmetric case. An example from actual research was given in Table 12.9. An almost classic example occurs in the Berkowitz study, reported in Table 12.10.

The setups in (e) and (f), however, are different. Here one independent variable is effective at one level only of the other independent variable. In (e), $A_1 > A_2$ at B_1, but $A_1 = A_2$ at B_2. In (f), $A_1 = A_2$ at B_1, but $A_1 > A_2$ at B_2. The interpretation changes accordingly. In the case of (e), we would say that A is effective at B_1 level, but makes no difference at B_2 level. The case of (f) would take a similar interpretation.

A simple way to study the interaction with a 2×2 setup (it is more complex with more complex models) is to subtract one entry from another in each row, as we did earlier. If this be done for (a), we get, for rows B_1 and B_2, 10 and 10. For (b), we get 0 and 0, and for (c), 10 and 10 again. When these two differences are equal, as in these cases, there is no interaction. But now try it with (d), (e), and (f). We get 10 and -10 for (d), 10 and 0 for (e), and 0 and 10 for (f). When these differences are significantly unequal, interaction is present. The student can interpret these differences as an exercise.

It is also possible—and often very profitable—to graph interactions. Set up one independent variable by placing the experimental groups (A_1, A_2, and so on) at equal intervals on the horizontal axis and appropriate values of the dependent variable on the vertical axis. Then plot, against the horizontal axis group positions ($A_1\ A_2$, and so on), the mean values in the table at the levels of the other independent variable (B_1, B_2, and so on). This method can quite easily be used with 2×3, 3×3, and other such designs. The plots of (a), (c), (d), and (e) are given in Fig. 12.6.

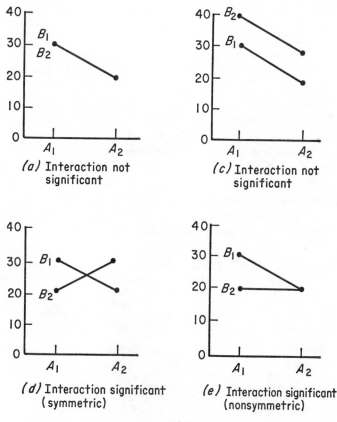

FIG. 12.6

We can discuss these graphs with brief remarks since both graphs and graphing relations have been discussed before.[13] In effect, we ask first if there is a relation between the main effects (independent variables) and the measures of the dependent variables. Each of these relations is plotted as in the preceding chapter, except that the relation between one independent variable and the dependent variable is plotted at both levels of the other independent variables; for instance, A is plotted against the dependent variable (vertical axis) at B_1 and B_2. The slope of the lines roughly indicates the extent of the relation. In each case, we have chosen to plot the relations using A_1 and A_2 on the horizontal axis. If the plotted line is horizontal, obviously there is no relation. There is no relation between A and the dependent variable at level B_2 in (e) of Fig. 12.6, but there is a relation at level B_1. In (a), there is a relation between A and the dependent variable at both levels, B_1 and B_2. The same is true of (c). The nearer the line comes to being diagonal, the higher the relation. If the two lines make approximately the same angle in the same direction (that is, they are parallel), as in (a) and (c), the relation is approximately the same magnitude at each level. To the extent that the lines make different angles with the horizontal axis (are not parallel), to this extent there is interaction present.

If the graphs of Fig. 12.6 were plotted from actual research data, we could interpret them as follows. Call the measure of the dependent variable (on the vertical axis) Y. In (a), A is related to Y *regardless of B*. It makes no difference what B is; A_1 and A_2 differ significantly. The interpretation of (c) is similar: A is related to Y at both levels of B. There is no interaction in either (a) or (c). In (d) and (e), however, the case is very different. The graph of (d) shows interaction. A is related to Y, but the kind of relation depends on B. Under the B_1 condition, A_1 is greater than A_2. But under the B_2 condition A_2 is greater than A_1. The graph of (e) says that A is related to Y at level B_1 but not at level B_2, or A_1 is greater than A_2 at B_1 but at B_2 they are equal. (Note that it is possible to plot B on the horizontal axis. The interpretations would differ accordingly.)

---

[13] The student can find extended discussions of interaction in: A. Edwards, *Experimental Design in Psychological Research*, rev. ed. New York: Holt, Rinehart and Winston, Inc., 1960, pp. 184–197. More thorough discussion—but without graphs—can be found in Lindquist, *op. cit.*, pp. 20–23, 118–120, 123–127. The method of graphing, strictly speaking, is questionable because the A variable laid out along the horizontal axis may not be an ordered variable. The method serves, however, to accomplish the pedagogical purpose of helping the student to understand interaction better. The two references cited also discuss proper error terms to use in the factorial analysis of variance. See, also, Q. McNemar, *Psychological Statistics*, 2d ed. New York: Wiley, 1955, pp. 303–311. One does not always use the within-groups variance as the error term in the complex factorial analysis of variance. In certain cases, interactions are used. The subject is too advanced and technical, however, for discussion in this book. If the reader wants to use complex designs, he is advised to get special help.

A NOTE OF CAUTION

As Lindquist has pointed out, interaction is not always a result of the "true" interaction of experimental treatments.[14] There are, rather, three possible causes of a significant interaction. One is "true" interaction, the variance contributed by the interaction that "really" exists between two variables in their mutual effect on a third variable. Another is error. A significant interaction *can* happen by chance, just as the means of experimental groups can differ significantly by chance, if a contradiction in terms is permitted. A third possible cause of interaction is some extraneous, unwanted, uncontrolled effect operating at one level of an experiment but not at another. Such a cause of interaction is particularly to be watched for in nonexperimental uses of the analysis of variance, that is, in the analysis of variance of data gathered after independent variables have already operated. Suppose, for example, that the levels in an experiment on methods was schools. Extraneous factors in such a case can cause a significant interaction. Assume that the principal of one school, although he had consented to having the experiment run in his school, was negative in his attitude toward the research. This attitude could easily be conveyed to teachers and pupils, thus contaminating the experimental treatment, methods. In short, significant interactions must be handled with the same care as any other research results. They are interesting, even dramatic, as we have seen. Thus they can perhaps cause us momentarily to lose our customary caution.

STUDY SUGGESTIONS

1. A research worker has done an experiment in which he tested two methods of instruction, A_1 and A_2. Dividing the group in two at the median of an intelligence test, he treated intelligence as an independent variable (B_1 and B_2). The dependent variable was achievement as measured by scores on an objective examination. The results are summarized as follows (the tabled entries are means):

		Methods		
		A_1	A_2	
Intelligence	B_1	78	70	74
	B_2	72	60	66
		75	65	($M_t = 70$)

The A effect was significant at the .01 level. So was the B effect. The interaction was not significant.

[14] Lindquist, *op. cit.*, p. 124.

    (a) Interpret the results specifically and discuss the differences between the means and the relations they presumably reflect.

    (b) Draw a graph of the results, and interpret the graph.

2. Use Problem 1 again, but now assume that the tabled entries are a bit different:

	A_1	A_2	
B_1	70	78	74
B_2	72	60	66
	71	69	$(M_t = 70)$

The only change is that the A_1B_1 and A_2B_1 means have been interchanged. (Of course, the marginal means at the bottom of the table, too, are changed.) A factorial analysis of variance shows that this time the A means are not significantly different, and the B means, as before, are significantly different. The interaction is also significant.

    (a) Interpret the results. Compare the interpretation to that of Problem 1.

    (b) Draw a graph, and then interpret it. Compare this graph to the one drawn in Problem 1.

    (c) Do you suppose data like these might occur in actual research? *Why?*

    (d) What value does the factorial analysis of variance have in research situations like this? Could you reach the same conclusions by two separate experiments? For example, the investigator has conducted an experiment by randomly assigning Ss of varying intelligence to two groups. What might have been the results and why?

3. We are interested in testing the relative efficacies of different methods of teaching foreign languages (or any other subject). We believe that foreign language aptitude is a possibly influential variable. How might an experiment be set up to test the efficacies of the methods? Now add a third variable, sex, and lay out the paradigms of both researches. Discuss the logic of each design from the point of view of statistics. What statistical tests of significance would you use? What part do they play in interpreting the results?

4. Wallach and Gahm, studying the relation between Graphic Expansiveness and Constriction, Anxiety, and Extroversion-Introversion, measured the doodling of female subjects (a measure of Expansiveness) and analyzed it in a factorial analysis of variance with the results (the means):[15]

---

15 M. Wallach and R. Gahm, "Personality Functions of Graphic Constriction and Expansiveness," *Journal of Personality*, XXVIII (1960), 73–88.

	High Social Extroversion	High Social Introversion
High Anxiety	8.67	11.33
Low Anxiety	14.20	6.73

The final analysis of variance table in the Wallach-Gahm study was:

Source	df	m.s.	F	p
Extroversion-Introversion	1	86.40	3.36	.08
Anxiety	1	3.26	.13	n.s.
Interaction: $E \times A$	1	385.07	14.99	.001
Within	56	25.68		

(*Note:* This final analysis of variance table is a little different from those in the earlier text of this chapter. The sums of squares and the total are not reported; they are often omitted in published reports to save space.)

Interpret the results.

13 *ANALYSIS OF VARIANCE: CORRELATED GROUPS OR SUBJECTS*

DEFINITION OF THE PROBLEM

The problem of this chapter is to understand the principles and mechanics of research designs and statistical analyses in which correlation between groups or subjects is present. What does correlation between groups mean? It is not easy to answer this question with a simple statement.

In simple one-way analysis of variance and in factorial analysis of variance, the independence of groups and subjects was a sine qua non of the designs, that is, in these two approaches the subjects are assigned to groups at random. If the correlation between the experimental groups were computed somehow, the result should be zero. A relation was earlier defined as a set of ordered pairs. In one-way analysis of variance, when subjects are assigned to groups at random, there is clearly no systematic way to pair subjects (or their measures). If there were a way to do this, then the assumption of independence would be untenable.

The definition of random assignment precludes the possibility of ordering pairs of subjects. In ordering pairs, as we learned earlier, there must be either a list of the pairs or a rule to tell us how to pair a member of the domain with a member of the range. In other words, of all the possible pairings of the sets A and B, there must be a systematic method for pairing certain a's with certain b's. But by the definition of randomness, this is not possible.

If a way could be found to pair elements of the sets of the experimental groups, and if this pairing led to a systematic covarying of the elements of the set of pairs, then the set and statistical situation would change radically. There would then be a systematic relation (correlation) between the sets, which would introduce an identifiable variance into the total variance picture. This situation is analogous to that of the preceding chapter on the factorial analysis of variance, where we saw that introducing levels of a second independent variable enabled us to extract from the total variance the variance due to this second variable, thus decreasing the error term. To make this abstract discussion concrete, we return to an example used earlier.

A Fictitious Example A principal of a school and the members of his staff decided to introduce a program of education in intergroup relations as an addition to the school's curriculum. One of the problems that arose was in the use of motion pictures. Films were shown in the initial phases of the program, but the results were not too encouraging. The staff hypothesized that the failure of the films to have impact might have resulted from their not making any particular effort to bring out the possible applications of the film to intergroup relations. They decided to test the hypothesis that seeing the films and then discussing them would improve the viewers' attitudes toward minority group members more than would just seeing the films.

For a preliminary study the staff randomly selected a group of students from the total student body and attempted to pair the students on intelligence and socioeconomic background until ten pairs were obtained, each pair being approximately equal in intelligence and socioeconomic background. The reasoning behind the experiment was that intelligence and socioeconomic background are related to attitudes toward minority groups. Each member of each pair was randomly assigned to either an experimental or a control group, and then both groups were shown a new film on intergroup relations. The A_1 (experimental) group had a discussion session after the picture was shown; the A_2 (control) group had no such discussion after the film. Both groups were tested with a scale designed to measure attitudes toward minority groups. The attitude scores and the necessary calculations for an analysis of variance procedure to be described are given in Table 13.1.

TABLE 13.1 ATTITUDE SCORES AND CALCULATIONS FOR ANALYSIS OF VARIANCE—FICTITIOUS EXAMPLE

Pairs	Groups A_1 (Experimental)		A_2 (Control)		Σ	Σ^2
1	8	64	6	36	14	196
2	9	81	8	64	17	289
3	5	25	3	9	8	64
4	4	16	2	4	6	36
5	2	4	1	1	3	9
6	10	100	7	49	17	289
7	3	9	1	1	4	16
8	12	144	7	49	19	361
9	6	36	6	36	12	144
10	11	121	9	81	20	400
ΣX:	70		50		$\Sigma X_t = 120$	
$(\Sigma X)^2$:	4900		2500		$(\Sigma X_t)^2 = 14{,}400$	
M:	7		5		$\Sigma X_t^2 = 930$	
					$\Sigma(\Sigma)^2 = 1804$	

First we do a one-way analysis of variance as though the investigators had not matched the subjects. We disregard the matching procedure and analyze the scores as though all the Ss had been randomly assigned to the two groups without regard to intelligence and socioeconomic background. The necessary calculations are

$$C = \frac{14{,}400}{20} = 720$$

$$\text{Total} = 930 - 720 = 210$$

$$\underset{(A_1, A_2)}{\text{Between columns}} = \left(\frac{4900}{10} + \frac{2500}{10} \right) - 720 = 20$$

The final analysis of variance table of this analysis is given in Table 13.2. According to this analysis, then, the two group means of 7 and 5 do not differ significantly. The interpretation of these data would lead the experimenters to believe that the film plus discussion had no effect. This conclusion would be erroneous. The difference in this case is really significant at the .01 level. Let us assume that this statement is true; if it *is* true, then there must be something wrong with the analysis of the data.

TABLE 13.2   FINAL ANALYSIS OF VARIANCE TABLE. ONE-WAY ANALYSIS
OF FICTITIOUS DATA

Source	df	s.s.	m.s.	F
Between Groups (A_1, A_2)	1	20.	20.	1.89 (n.s.)
Within Groups	18	190.	10.56	
Total	19	210.		

An Explanatory Digression   When subjects are matched on variables *significantly related to the dependent variable one is studying,* correlation is introduced into the statistical picture. In Chap. 12 we saw that it was often possible to identify and control more of the total variance of an experimental situation by setting up levels of one or more variables presumably related to the dependent variable. The setting up of two or three levels of intelligence, for example, makes it possible to identify and measure the variance in the total scores due to intelligence. Now, simply shift gears a bit. The matching of the present experiment has actually set up ten levels, one for each pair. The members of the first pair had IQ's of 130 and 132, the members of the second pair 124 and 125, and so on to the tenth pair, the members of which had IQ's of 89 and 92. Each pair (level) has a different mean. If this is the case, the matching has "introduced" variance between pairs, or *between-rows variance.*

Consider another hypothetical example to dramatize what happens when there is correlation between sets of scores. An investigator has matched three groups of subjects on intelligence. In setting up the analysis, intelligence was perfectly correlated with the dependent variable, achievement of some kind. The first trio of subjects had IQ's of 141, 142, and 140; the second trio 130, 126, and 128; and so on through the fifth trio of 82, 85, and 82. If we check the rank orders in columns of the three sets of scores, they are exactly the same: 141, 130, $\cdots$, 82; 142, 126, $\cdots$, 85; 140, 128, $\cdots$, 82. Since we assume that $r = 1.00$ between intelligence and achievement, then the rank orders of the achievement scores must be the same in the three groups. The assumed achievement test scores are given on the left-hand side of Table 13.3. The rank orders of these scores, from high to low, are given in parentheses beside each achievement score. Note that the rank orders are the same in the three groups.

TABLE 13.3   CORRELATED AND UNCORRELATED SCORES, FICTITIOUS EXAMPLE

I. Correlated Groups				II. Uncorrelated Groups			
A_1	A_2	A_3	M	A_1	A_2	A_3	M
73 (1)	74 (1)	72 (1)	73	63 (2)	74 (1)	46 (5)	61.00
63 (2)	65 (2)	61 (2)	63	45 (5)	55 (3)	61 (2)	53.67
57 (3)	55 (3)	59 (3)	57	50 (4)	50 (4)	59 (3)	53.00
50 (4)	50 (4)	53 (4)	51	57 (3)	65 (2)	53 (4)	58.33
45 (5)	44 (5)	46 (5)	45	73 (1)	44 (5)	72 (1)	63.00

$$M_t = 57.80 \qquad\qquad\qquad M_t = 57.80$$

Now suppose that the correlation between intelligence and achievement were approximately zero. In such a case, no prediction could be made of the rank orders of the achievement scores, or, to put it another way, the achievement scores would not be matched. To simulate such a condition of zero correlation, I broke up the rank orders of the scores on the left-hand side of Table 13.3 with the help of a table of random numbers. After drawing three sets of numbers 1 through 5 I rearranged the scores in columns according to the random numbers. (Before doing this, all the column rank orders were 1, 2, 3, 4, 5. The first set of random numbers was 2, 5, 4, 3, 1.) The second number of column A_1 was put first. I next took the fifth number of A_1 and put it second. This process was continued until the former first number became the fifth number. The same procedure was used with the other two groups of numbers, with, of course, different sets of random numbers. The final results are given on the right-hand side of Table 13.3. The means of the rows are also given. The ranks of the column scores are also included in the table (in parentheses).

First, study the ranks of the two sets of scores. In the left-hand portion of the table, labeled I, are the correlated scores. Since the ranks are the same in each column, the average correlation between columns is 1.00. The numbers of the set labeled II, which are essentially random, present quite a different picture. The 15 numbers of both sets are exactly the same. So are the numbers in each column (and their means). Only the row numbers—and, of course, the row means—are different. Look at the rank orders of II. No systematic relations can be found between them. The average correlation should be approximately zero, since the numbers were randomly shuffled. Actually it is .11.

Now study the variability of the row means. Note that the variability of the means of I is considerably greater than that of II. If the numbers are random, the expectation for the mean of any row is the general mean. The means of the rows of II hover rather closely around the general mean of 57.80. The range is $63 - 53 = 10$. But the means of the rows of I do not hover closely around 57.80; their variability is much greater, as indicated by a range of $73 - 45 = 28$. Computing the variances of these two sets of means (called *between-rows variance*), we obtain 351.60 for I and 58.27 for II. The variance of I is six times greater than the variance of II. This large difference is a direct effect of the correlation that is present in the scores of I but not in II. It may be said that the correlation is an indirect index and the variance a direct index of individual differences. The reader should pause here and go over this example, especially the examples of Table 13.3, until the effect of correlation on variance is clear to him.

What is the effect on the estimate of the error variance of correlated scores? Clearly the variance due to the correlation is *systematic* variance, which must be removed from the total variance if a more accurate estimate of error variance is desired. Otherwise, as shown in the last chapter, the error variance estimate will include the variance due to individual differences and the result will thus be too large. In the example, we know that the shuffling procedure has concealed the systematic variance due to the correlation or individual differences. By rearranging the scores the possibility of identifying this variance is removed. This variance is still in the scores of II, but it cannot be extracted. To show this, we compute the variance of the error terms of I and II; that of I was 3.13; that of II, 149.79. By removing from the total variance the variance due to the correlation, it is possible to reduce the error term greatly, with the result that the variance of I is 48 times smaller than the variance of II. If there is systematic variance in the sets of measures, then, and it is possible to isolate and identify this variance, it is clearly worthwhile to do so.

Actual research data will probably not be as dramatic as the above example. Correlations are almost never 1. But they are often greater than .50 or .60. *The higher the correlation, the larger the systematic variance that can be extracted from the total variance and the more the error term can be reduced.* This principle becomes very important not only in designing research, but also in measurement theory and practice. Sometimes it is possible to build correlation into the scores and then extract the variance due to the resulting correlated scores. For example, we can obtain a "pure" measure of individual differences by using the same subjects on different trials. Obviously a subject's own scores will be more alike than they will be like the scores of others.

Re-examination of Table 13.1 Data We return to the fictitious research data on the effects of films on attitudes towards minority groups (see Table 13.1). Earlier we computed a between-columns sum of squares and variance exactly as in one-way analysis of variance. We found that the difference between the means was not significant when this method was used. From the above discussion, we can surmise that if there is correlation between the two sets of scores, then the variance due to the correlation should be removed from the total variance and, of course, from the estimate of the error variance. If the correlation is substantial, this procedure should make quite a difference: the error term should get considerably smaller. The correlation between the sets of scores of A_1 and A_2 of Table 13.1 is .93. Since this is a high degree of correlation, the error term when properly computed should be much lower than it was before.

The additional operation required is simple. Just add the scores in each row of Table 13.1 and compute the *between-rows* sum of squares and the variance. Square the sum of each row and divide the result by the number of scores in the row; for example, in the first row: $8 + 6 = 14$; $(14)^2/2 = 196/2 = 98$. Repeat this procedure for each row, add the quotients, and then subtract the correction term C. This yields the *between-rows* sum of squares. (Since the number of scores in each row is always 2, it is easier, especially with a desk calculator, to add all the squared sums and then divide by 2.)

$$\begin{array}{c} \text{Between rows} \\ (1, 2, \cdots, 10) \end{array} = \left[\frac{(14)^2 + (17)^2 + \cdots + (20)^2}{2} \right] - 720$$
$$= 902 - 720 = 182$$

This between-rows sum of squares is a measure of the variability due to individual differences, as indicated earlier.

We have extracted from the total sum of squares the between columns and the between-rows sums of squares. Now, set up a familiar equation:

$$\Sigma x_t^2 = \Sigma x_b^2 + \Sigma x_w^2 \tag{13.1}$$

This is the equation used in one-way analysis of variance. The analysis of Table 13.2 is an example. We must alter this equation to suit the present circumstances. The former between-groups sum of squares, Σx_b^2, is re-labeled Σx_c^2, which means the sum of squares of the columns. The sum of squares of the rows, Σx_r^2, is added, and Σx_w^2 must be re-labeled since we now no longer have a within-groups variance. (Why?) We label it Σx_{res}^2, meaning the sum of squares of the *residuals*. As the name indicates, the *residual* sum of squares means the sum of squares left over after the sums of squares of columns and rows have been extracted from the total sum of squares. The equation then becomes

$$\Sigma x_t^2 = \Sigma x_c^2 + \Sigma x_r^2 + \Sigma x_{res}^2 \tag{13.2}$$

Briefly, the total variance has been broken down into two identifiable or systematic variances and one error variance. And this error variance is a more accurate estimate of error or chance variation of the scores than that of Table 13.2.

TABLE 13.4   FINAL COMPLETE ANALYSIS OF VARIANCE TABLE:
DATA OF TABLE 13.1

Source	df	s.s.	m.s.	F
Between Columns (A_1, A_2)	1	20.	20.00	22.47 (.001)
Between Rows (1, 2, · · · , 10)	9	182.	20.22	22.72 (.001)
Residual: $C \times R$	9	8.	.89	
Total	19	210.		

Rather than substitute in the equation, we set up the correct final analysis of variance table (Table 13.4). The *F* ratio of the columns is now $20.00/.89 = 22.47$, which is significant at the .001 level. In Table 13.1 the *F* ratio was not significant. This is quite a difference. Since the between-columns variance is exactly the same, the difference is due to the greatly decreased error term, now .89 when it was 10.56 before. By computing and extracting the rows sum of squares and the variance, it has been possible to reduce the error term to about $\frac{1}{12}$ of its former magnitude. In this situation, obviously, the former error variance of 10.56 was greatly over-inflated. Returning to the original problem, it is now possible to say that adding discussion after the motion picture seems to have had a significant effect on attitudes towards minority groups.

Before leaving this example, two points need to be clarified. The first involves the error term and the contrast between the within-groups variance and the residual variance. As to the disappearance of the within-groups variance, remember that this variance—and any other type of error variance—*is only an estimate of the error variance*. In the one-way situation, it is the only such estimate possible. We know that the within-groups variance contains other sources of systematic variance, such as the variance due to individual differences. When it is possible to extract any of these other variances, we do so. In the case of the Table 13.1 data, it was possible. And when the variances of the columns and the rows are computed, it is no longer possible to compute a within-groups variance since, by computing the between-rows variance, we have in effect extracted much of the variance that would normally be a part of the within-groups variance.

The second point to be cleared up has to do with the t test. Students ask: "Why not use the t test?" The answer is simple: "Do so if you wish." If the t test is used, the outcome will be identical provided that the transformation noted earlier is made: $t = \sqrt{F}$, or $F = t^2$. The t ratio of the data of Table 13.4 is simply: $\sqrt{22.47} = 4.74$. Another answer to the query is that the analysis of variance works with any number of groups, whereas the t test does not. The t test can be used only with two groups. An additional point is that the analysis of variance yields more information. The analysis of variance of Table 13.4 tells us that the difference between the attitude scores of the experimental and control groups is significantly different. We would obtain the same results with the t test, of course. Table 13.4 also informs us, simply and clearly, that the matching was effective. Had the between-rows F ratio not been significant, we would know that the matching had not been successful, which is important information indeed. (Why is this true?) Finally, the analysis of variance is a bit easier to compute than the t test, and once understood, the computational procedure is very easily remembered, whereas the equations used for estimating the standard error of the differences between the means seem to confuse the beginning student.[1] Although either method may be used, the analysis of variance method is recommended for the above reasons.

EXTRACTING VARIANCES BY SUBTRACTION

To make quite sure that the reader understands the points being made, previous examples are repeated here. In Table 13.5, two sets of numbers, labeled I and II, are given. The numbers in these sets are exactly the same; only their arrangements differ. In I, there is no correlation between the two columns of numbers; the coefficient of correlation is

---

[1] It is possible to integrate set reasoning with the formulas for the standard error of the differences between means. The reader may wish to think about this. The clue is gotten from an important theorem of set theory, which we used in Chap. 8:

$$m(A \cup B) = m(A) + m(B) - m(A \cap B)$$

If the sets A and B do not intersect, then $A \cap B = E$, and $m(A \cap B) = 0$, and

$$m(A \cup B) = m(A) + m(B)$$

Now check the formulas for the standard error of differences in any statistics text.

exactly zero. This is analogous to the assignment of subjects to the two groups at random. One-way analysis of variance is applicable. In II, on the other hand, the A_2 numbers have been rearranged so that there is correlation between the A_1 and A_2 numbers. (Check the rank orders.) In fact, $r = .90$. One-way analysis of variance is not applicable here. If it is used with the numbers of II, the result would be exactly the same as it would be with the numbers of I, but then we would be disregarding the variance introduced by the correlation.

TABLE 13.5   ANALYSES OF VARIANCE OF RANDOMIZED AND CORRELATED
FICTITIOUS DATA

	I $r = .00$				II $r = .90$		
A_1	A_2	Σ	Σ^2	A_1	A_2	Σ	Σ^2
1	5	6	36	1	2	3	9
2	2	4	16	2	4	6	36
3	4	7	49	3	3	6	36
4	6	10	100	4	5	9	81
5	3	8	64	5	6	11	121
ΣX: 15	20	$\Sigma X_t = 35$		15	20	$\Sigma X_t = 35$	
$(\Sigma X)^2$: 225	400	$(\Sigma X_t)^2 = 1225$				$(\Sigma X_t)^2 = 1225$	
M: 3	4	$\Sigma X_t{}^2 = 145$				$\Sigma X_t{}^2 = 145$	
		$\Sigma(\Sigma)^2 = 265$				$\Sigma(\Sigma)^2 = 283$	

$$C = \frac{1225}{10} = 122.50 \qquad\qquad C = \frac{1225}{10} = 122.50$$

$$\text{Total} = 145 - 122.50 = 22.50 \qquad\qquad \text{Total} = 145 - 122.50 = 22.50$$

$$\text{Between } C = \frac{225 + 400}{5} - 122.50 \qquad\qquad \text{Between } C = \frac{225 + 400}{5} - 122.50$$

$$= 2.50 \qquad\qquad\qquad = 2.50$$

$$\text{Between } R = \frac{6^2 + 4^2 + \cdots + 8^2}{2} \qquad\qquad \text{Between } R = \frac{3^2 + 6^2 + \cdots + 9^2}{2}$$

$$- 122.50 = 132.50 - 122.50 = 10 \qquad\qquad - 122.50 = 141.50 - 122.50 = 19$$

The calculations in Table 13.5 yield all the sums of squares except the residual sums of squares, which are obtained by subtraction. Since the calculations are so straightforward, we proceed directly to the final analysis of variance tables which are given in Table 13.6. The sums of squares for totals, columns, and rows are entered as indicated, with the appropriate degrees of freedom. The between-rows degrees of freedom are the number of rows minus one ($5 - 1 = 4$). The residual degrees of free-dom, like the interaction degrees of freedom in factorial analysis of variance, are obtained by multiplying the between-columns and between-rows degrees of freedom: $1 \times 4 = 4$. Or simply subtract the between-columns and between-rows degrees of freedom from the total degrees of freedom: $9 - 1 - 4 = 4$. The residual sums of squares, similarly, are obtained by subtracting the between-columns and between-rows sums of squares from the total sums of squares. For I, $22.5 - 2.5 - 10.0 = 10$; for II, $22.5 - 2.5 - 19.0 = 1$.

TABLE 13.6 FINAL ANALYSIS OF VARIANCE TABLES

Source	df	I (r = .00)			II (r = .90)		
		s.s.	m.s.	F	s.s.	m.s.	F
Between C	1	2.5	2.5	1. (*n.s.*)	2.5	2.50	10. (.05)
Between R	4	10.0	2.5		19.0	4.75	
Residual $C \times R$	4	10.0	2.5		1.0	.25	
Total	9	22.5			22.5		

These analyses need little elaboration. Note particularly that where there is correlation, the between-columns F ratio is significant, but where the correlation is zero it is not significant. Note particularly the error terms. For I ($r = .00$), it is 2.5. For II ($r = .90$), it is .25, which is *ten* times smaller.

Removal of Systematic Sources of Variance We now use the subtractive procedure of Chap. 7 to remove the two systematic sources of variance in the two sets of scores. First, remove the between-columns variance by correcting each mean so that it equals the general mean of 3.5. Then correct each score in each column similarly (as done for I and II in Table 13.7).

TABLE 13.7 REMOVAL OF BETWEEN-COLUMNS VARIANCE BY EQUALIZING COLUMN MEANS AND SCORES

	I (r = .00)			II (r = .90)		
Correction	.5	—.5		.5	—.5	
	A_1	A_2	M	A_1	A_2	M
	1.5	4.5	3.0	1.5	1.5	1.5
	2.5	1.5	2.0	2.5	3.5	3.0
	3.5	3.5	3.5	3.5	2.5	3.0
	4.5	5.5	5.0	4.5	4.5	4.5
	5.5	2.5	4.0	5.5	5.5	5.5
M:	3.5	3.5	$M_t = 3.5$	3.5	3.5	$M_t = 3.5$

If we now compute the total sums of squares of I and II, in both cases we obtain 20. Compare this result to the former figure of 22.5. The correction procedure has reduced the total sums of squares by 2.5. These are of course the sums of squares between columns. Note, again, that the correction procedure has had no effect whatever on the variance within each of the four groups of scores. Nor has it had any effect on the means of the rows.

Now remove the rows variance by letting each row mean equal 3.5, the general mean, and by correcting the row scores accordingly. This has been done in Table 13.8, which should be carefully studied. Note that the variability of both sets of scores has been reduced, but that the variability of the correlated set (II) has been sharply reduced. In fact, the scores of II have a range of only $4 - 3 = 1$, whereas the range of the I scores is $5 - 2 = 3$. The matching of the scores in II and its concomitant correlation enables us, via the corrective procedure, to reduce the error term sharply by "correcting out" the variance due to the correlation. The only variance now in the twice-corrected scores is the residual variance. "Residual variance" is an apt term. It is the variance left over after the two systematic variances have been removed. If we compute the *total* sums of squares of I and II, we find them to be 10 and 1, respectively. If we compute the sums of squares *within* the groups as with one-way analysis of variance, we find them also to be 10 and 1. Evidently there is no more systematic variance left in the scores—only error variation remains. The most important point to note is that the residual sum of squares of the uncorrelated scores is ten times greater than the residual sum of squares of the correlated scores. Exactly the same operation was performed on both sets of scores. With the uncorrelated scores it is not possible to extract as much variance as with the correlated scores.

TABLE 13.8   REMOVAL OF BETWEEN-ROWS VARIANCE BY EQUALIZING ROW MEANS AND SCORES

	I $(r = .00)$				II $(r = .90)$		
Correction	A_1	A_2	M	*Correction*	A_1	A_2	M
$+ \ .5$	2.0	5.0	3.5	$+ 2.0$	3.5	3.5	3.5
$+ 1.5$	4.0	3.0	3.5	$+ \ .5$	3.0	4.0	3.5
0	3.5	3.5	3.5	$+ \ .5$	4.0	3.0	3.5
$- 1.5$	3.0	4.0	3.5	$- 1.0$	3.5	3.5	3.5
$- \ .5$	5.0	2.0	3.5	$- 2.0$	3.5	3.5	3.5
M:	3.5	3.5	(3.5)		3.5	3.5	(3.5)

APPLICATIONS TO EDUCATIONAL SETTINGS

The type of analysis discussed in this chapter can be applied to a variety of research situations. The matching of subjects, perhaps the commonest application, can also be used to match any objects. For instance, when a subject is matched with himself by using two or more measurements of him, the analysis applies. We have already mentioned the obvious fact that a subject's performances are more alike than they are like other people's performances. In this way, correlation is introduced.

An important educational use of two-way analysis of variance is with so-called schools designs. Suppose a research study is done in five or more different schools. It is well-known that schools differ systematically on educationally important variables like intelligence, socio-economic level, general atmosphere, and administrative procedure. If classes are selected at random from five or more different schools for a research study, it is as though they had been matched; the classes will tend to be more alike within schools than they are between different schools. As we shall see later, two-way analysis of variance allows us to extract the variance due to the differences among the schools on whichever dependent variable we are studying. Return to Table 13.1 and substitute schools for subjects. If two scores per school, say the means of classes, are used, the design and statistical analysis are identical to those used in this chapter.[2]

Two-way analysis of variance is useful in the solution of certain measurement problems, particularly in psychology and education. Individual differences are a constant source of variance that needs to be identified and isolated. A good example is its use in the study of raters and ratings. It is possible to separate the variance of raters from the variance of the objects being rated. Two-way analysis can also be very useful in the study of the reliability of measuring instruments. The variance of items can be separated from the variance of the persons responding to the items.

Research Examples   EFFECT OF TRAINING ON MENTAL FUNCTIONS   In a justly well-known study of the presumed effect of training on mental functions, Gates and Taylor matched two groups of 16 four and five-year-old children *on twelve variables:* sex, age, mental age, scholastic maturity, and various kinds of memory.[3] Matching on so many variables at one time would be considered inefficient today. Although the details of the experiment do not concern us here, the authors found that a period of training

---

[2] It should of course be noted that more elaborate and better analyses are possible. See E. Lindquist, *Statistical Analysis in Educational Research.* Boston: Houghton Mifflin, 1940, pp. 104–114, *et passim.*

[3] A. Gates and G. Taylor, "An Experimental Study of the Nature of Improvement Resulting from Practice in a Mental Function," *Journal of Educational Psychology,* XVI (1925), 583–592.

on digit memory had no transfer effect on other kinds of memory: the experimental group trained in digit memory showed no appreciable gain over the control group that had not been so trained. Their results were quite clear-cut; had they been less so, the use of analysis of variance could have been helpful. Even a small gain in transferred memory might be theoretically and practically important. In such a case a precise test of significance might be invaluable. Since one wonders, too, how effective the matching on twelve variables was, the analysis of variance might give some indication of this effectiveness.

USING HUMAN SUBJECTS AS THEIR OWN CONTROLS   It is common to use subjects as their own controls. Haslerud and Meyers, in another study of transfer of training, had Ss solve problems (1) with specific directions or rules for problem solution (G problems), and (2) with no directions for solution (D problems).[4] (The problem was coding.) The experimental Ss were all trained in both ways. They were tested on a later test which included G and D problems, with the result that they did better on the G (rule-given) problems than on the D (rule-derived) problems. But on a second test a week later, the results were reversed: the scores on those problems that had been rule-derived (D) by the Ss *increased,* whereas the scores on the problems that had been rule-given (G) *decreased.* The experimenters here used each S as his own control, so to speak, since the scores used were $D_2 - D_1$ and $G_2 - G_1$ difference scores.

TABLE 13.9   MEAN RATINGS ON 10 TRAITS, STECKLE STUDY

Trait	1940	1941	M
Self-Control	10.9	13.4	12.15
Enthusiasm	11.1	12.3	11.70
Good Judgment	10.6	12.6	11.60
Magnetism	11.7	13.4	12.50
Considerateness	8.9	11.7	10.30
Adaptability	11.7	13.3	12.50
Breadth of Interest	11.7	12.6	12.15
Honesty	13.8	14.3	14.05
Refinement	11.3	13.7	12.50
Leadership	11.9	13.1	12.50
M:	11.36	13.04	

INSTRUCTOR EVALUATION   Can a teacher improve his teaching by considering his students' evaluation and criticism, of himself and his teaching? Steckle asked this question of himself and tried to answer it empirically.[5] He had his students rate him in 1940 on a scale constructed

4 G. Haslerud and S. Meyers, "The Transfer Value of Given and Individually Derived Principles," *Journal of Educational Psychology,* XLIX (1958), 293–298.

5 L. Steckle, "The Utility of the Instructor's Rating Scale," *Journal of Educational Psychology,* XXXII (1941), 631–635.

for evaluating instructor performance. In 1941 he again had his students rate him on the same scale. The mean ratings on each of the items of the scale for both the 1940 and 1941 ratings are given in Table 13.9. The question was: Did the instructor improve himself? Inspection of the table seems to indicate that the instructor improved: all ten measures increased. That this result is statistically significant is evident when it is realized that increases in scores in one direction on all ten measures are highly unlikely to occur by chance. That is, chance results would fluctuate, now this way now that way. These results are consistently a one-way street. Despite this fact, a two-way analysis of variance was run on the data. The *F* ratio for columns (years) was 50.39, significant at the .001 level. The *F* ratio for rows (traits) was 6.39, significant at the .01 level. Clearly the 1941 mean of 13.04 is significantly greater than the 1940 mean of 11.36, and the students seemed to discriminate significantly between the traits.

STUDY SUGGESTIONS

1. Do two-way analyses of variance of the two sets of fictitious data of Table 13.5. Use the text as an aid. Interpret the results. Now do two-way analyses of variance of the two sets of Table 13.7; do the same for Table 13.8. Lay out the final analysis of variance tables and compare. Think through carefully how the adjustive corrections have affected the original data.

2. Do a one-way analysis of variance of the data of Table 13.9; follow this with a two-way analysis of variance. Compare the results. Interpret the two-way analysis.

3. Draw 30 digits, 0 through 9, from a table of random numbers. Divide them arbitrarily into three groups of 10 digits each.
    (a) Do a two-way analysis of variance. Assume that the numbers in each row are data from one individual.
    (b) Now add constants to the three numbers of each row as follows: 20 to the first two rows, 15 to the second two rows, 10 to the third two rows, 5 to the fourth two rows, and 0 to the last two rows. Do a two-way analysis of variance of these "data."
    (c) In effect, what have you done by "biasing" the row numbers in this fashion?
    (d) Compare the sum of squares and the mean squares of (a) and (b). Why are the *total* sums of squares and mean squares different? Why are the *between-columns* and the *residual* sums of squares and mean squares the same? Why are the *between-rows* sums of squares and mean squares different?
    (e) Create a research problem out of all this and interpret the "results." Is the example realistic?

4. In a study of the effect of group psychotherapy on the reading of retarded readers, Fisher matched two groups of six delinquent boys

on age, IQ, and reading ability.[6] Both groups received remedial reading instruction, but one group was "arbitrarily chosen" to participate in group therapy once a week for six months. Part of the data reported by Fisher, the gains in months on a reading test of the boys in both groups, are given below.

Matched Pairs	Therapy	Nontherapy
A	16.0	9.0
B	8.5	9.0
C	18.5	16.5
D	6.0	13.5
E	7.5	2.0
F	12.5	— .5
M:	11.5	8.25

In discussing the group that received therapy, Fisher said, "This group showed a 39.4 percent greater improvement in reading than did the control group. It is therefore concluded that . . . the pyschotherapeutic relationship was an important factor in the correction of reading disabilities." [7]

(a) Do a two-way analysis of variance of the above data, and interpret the results.

(b) Make your own critical estimate of Fisher's conclusion.

(c) Did Fisher's matching have any effect?

(*Answers:* (a) Both F ratios of the columns (therapy and nontherapy) and the row (pairs) are not significant: 1.29 and 1.75, respectively.)

[6] B. Fisher, "Group Therapy with Retarded Readers," *Journal of Educational Psychology*, XLIV (1953), 354–360.

[7] *Ibid.,* pp. 358, 359.

14 *NONPARAMETRIC STATISTICS*

The student of education and the behavioral sciences should be aware that so-called parametric statistics are sometimes not appropriate to some educational, psychological, and sociological data. He must, therefore, be aware of the existence of a new and important branch of statistics known as nonparametric statistics. This chapter has two main purposes: (1) to introduce the reader to nonparametric statistics, if only briefly, and (2) to attempt, again, to show the basic similarity of all tests of statistical significance, parametric and nonparametric.

PARAMETRIC AND NONPARAMETRIC STATISTICS

A *parameter,* as we learned in an earlier chapter, is a population value. If all the scores of a defined population are available and a mean is computed, this mean is a parameter. Similarly, the variance and the standard deviation of a population, or any other population measure, is a parameter. It may not even be possible to compute population measures. They are still referred to as parameters. A *statistic,* on the other hand, is a measure computed from a sample. In Chap. 4 we drew random samples from a population of intelligence test scores and computed statistics from the samples, our purpose being to estimate the parameter known as the mean.

Whenever statistical tests, parametric or nonparametric, are used, certain assumptions are made. Nonparametric statistical tests are hemmed in by fewer and less stringent assumptions than parametric tests. They are particularly free of assumptions about the characteristics or the form of the distributions of the populations of research samples. Thus they are also called distribution-free tests. As Siegel puts it, "A nonparametric statistical test is a test whose model does not specify conditions about the parameters of the population from which the sample was drawn." [1]

[1] S. Siegel, *Nonparametric Statistics for the Behavioral Sciences.* New York: McGraw-Hill, 1956, p. 31.

Assumption of Normality   The most famous but apparently not the most important assumption behind the use of many parametric statistics is the *assumption of normality*. It is assumed in using the t and F tests (and thus the analysis of variance), for example, that the samples with which we work have been drawn from populations that are normally distributed. It is said that, if the populations from which samples are drawn are not normal, then statistical tests that depend on the normality assumption are vitiated. As a result, the conclusions drawn from sampled observations and their statistics will be in question. When in doubt about the normality of a population, or when one knows that the population is not normal, one should use a nonparametric test that does not make the normality assumption. Some teachers urge students of education and psychology to use *only* nonparametric tests on the questionable ground that most educational and psychological populations are not normal. The issue is not this simple.

Homogeneity of Variance   The next most important assumption is known as the *homogeneity of variance* assumption. It is assumed, in analysis of variance, that the variances within the groups are statistically the same. That is, variances are assumed to be homogeneous from group to group, within the bounds of random variation. If this is not true, the F test is vitiated. There is good reason for this statement. We saw earlier that the within-groups variance was an average of the variances within the two, three, or more groups of measures. If the variances differ widely, then such averaging is questionable. The effect of widely differing variances is to inflate the within-groups variance. Consequently an F test may be not significant when in reality there are significant differences between the means. The homogeneity of variance assumption can easily be taken out of the assumption class. Readily available tests can be used.[2]

These two assumptions have both been examined rather thoroughly by empirical methods. Artificial populations have been set up, samples drawn from them, and t and F tests performed. The evidence to date is that the importance of normality and homogeneity is overrated,[3] a view

[2] The most widely used test is Bartlett's. See A. Edwards, *Experimental Design in Psychological Research*, rev. ed. New York: Holt, Rinehart and Winston, Inc., 1960, pp. 125–128. A much easier test to use is given in E. Pearson and H. Hartley, eds., *Biometrika Tables for Statisticians*, Vol. I. Cambridge: Cambridge University Press, 1954, pp. 60, 61, 179. The student should note that the use of the Bartlett test, which is "nonrobust," has been likened to going to sea in a rowboat to see if an ocean liner would be safe.

[3] Two important large scale studies were done by Norton and by Boneau. Lindquist gives an admirable summary of the Norton study: E. Lindquist, *Design and Analysis of Experiments*. Boston: Houghton Mifflin, 1953, pp. 78–86. Boneau discusses the whole problem of assumptions and reports his own definitive study in a brilliant article: C. Boneau, "The Effects of Violations of Assumptions Underlying the t Test," *Psychological Bulletin*, LVII (1960), 49–64. Another useful article by Boneau is C. Boneau, "A Note on Measurement Scales and Statistical Tests," *American Psychologist*,

that is shared by the author. Unless there is good evidence to believe that populations are rather seriously non-normal and that variances are heterogeneous, it is usually unwise to use a nonparametric statistical test in place of a parametric one. The reason for this is that parametric tests are almost always more powerful than nonparametric tests. (The power of a statistical test is the probability that the null hypothesis will be rejected when it is actually false.) Relative simplicity and number of calculations are hardly good scientific arguments for using statistical tests. Current fashion may be one argument, but it lacks scientific cogency.

To return to the evidence on normality and homogeneity, Lindquist says, ". . . the F distribution is amazingly insensitive to the form of the distribution of criterion measures in the parent population . . ."[4] Lindquist also says, on the basis of Norton's data, that unless variances are so heterogeneous as to be readily apparent, that is, relatively large differences exist, the effect on the F test will probably be negligible. Boneau confirms this. He says that in a large number of research situations the probability statements resulting from the use of t and F tests, even when these two assumptions are violated, will be highly accurate.[5] In brief, in most cases in education and psychology, it is probably safer—and usually more effective—to use parametric tests rather than nonparametric tests. Anderson, in an excellent and definitive article on the whole subject, says, "It was concluded that parametric procedures are the standard tools of psychological statistics, although nonparametric procedures are useful minor techniques."[6]

Continuity and Equal Intervals of Measures A third assumption is that the measures to be analyzed are continuous measures with equal intervals. As we shall see in a later chapter, this assumption is behind the arithmetic operations of adding, subtracting, multiplying, and dividing. Parametric tests like the F and t tests of course depend on this assumption, but many nonparametric tests do not. A rank-order method, for example, may take no account of the continuity and equal intervals of measures.

Despite the conclusions of Lindquist, Boneau, Anderson, and others, it is well to bear these assumptions in mind. It is not wise to use statistical procedures—or, for that matter, any kind of research procedures—without due respect for the assumptions behind the procedures. If they are too seriously violated, the conclusions drawn from research data may be in

---

XVI (1961), 260, 261. An excellent but more general article is N. Anderson, "Scales and Statistics: Parametric and Nonparametric," *Psychological Bulletin,* LVIII (1961), 305–316.

[4] Lindquist, *op. cit.,* p. 81.

[5] Boneau, "The Effects of Violations of Assumptions Underlying the t Test," *op. cit.,* p. 62. There is one case that is particularly difficult to resolve, however: when variances are heterogeneous and the sample sizes of experimental groups differ.

[6] Anderson, *op. cit.,* p. 315.

error. To the reader who has been alarmed by some statistics books the best advice probably is: Use parametric statistics, as well as the analysis of variance, routinely, but keep a sharp eye on data for gross departures from normality, homogeneity of variance, and equality of intervals. Be aware of measurement problems and their relation to statistical tests, and be familiar with the basic nonparametric statistics so that they can be used when necessary. Also bear in mind that nonparametric tests are often quick and easy to use and are excellent for preliminary, if not always definitive, tests.

THE BINOMIAL TEST, χ^2, THE RANK-ORDER COEFFICIENT OF CORRELATION, AND THE COEFFICIENT OF CONCORDANCE

The two significance tests of this section have already been described in this book. We simply review them here and note that they can be considered nonparametric or distribution-free tests. They are nonparametric in the sense that such tests and the probability statements associated with them do not depend on the shape of the population distributions of observations from which sample observations are drawn.

The binomial test is associated with two-class problems about which we have spoken so much: male-female, graduate-nongraduate, smoker-nonsmoker, Republican-Democratic, and so on. The exact test is most useful with small samples. It uses an equation that cannot be explained here, since the explanation would require considerable space.[7] With large samples, the binomial distribution approaches the normal distribution, so that approximations discussed earlier can be used. The test is used when we ask questions such as: What is the probability that the observed values (frequencies, proportions) could have occurred by chance? Research questions analogous to the coin and die examples of Chap. 8 are such questions.

The χ^2 test, too, was discussed earlier. It need only be noted that we do not need to know anything about the distribution of the population observations to use the χ^2 test, but that it is not too useful when samples are very small. In the latter case, there is a better test: the Kolmogorov-Smirnov test, which has the important virtue not only of being capable of use with very small samples, but also of treating individual observations separately.[8]

The rank-order coefficient of correlation, ρ, is quick and useful, especially in classroom situations. It is, of course, not a test of statistical significance, although the significance of ρ is easily determined. In order

---

[7] See Siegel, *op. cit.*, pp. 36–42.
[8] *Ibid.*, pp. 47–52. The Kolmogorov-Smirnov test should be better known by educational and psychological investigators.

to use ρ, all that is necessary is to be able to produce ranks from the research data or to gather the data in the form of ranks. Further, ρ should not be indiscriminately used in place of r because it is so easy to compute (except in certain practical situations as when it is used by teachers in simple classroom experiments or in teacher-made tests), or because one is worried about the assumption of normality behind r. It is not necessary to assume normality to compute r. It *is* necessary to assume normality if one wishes to make statistical inferences from sample r's to population values. But if one only wants to know the relation between two variables, one needs no such assumption.[9]

The last statistic in this section is mentioned because it is closely related to ρ. This is the *coefficient of concordance, W,* which was developed by Kendall.[10] When data are in rank form and there are more than two sets of such data, W is applicable. It tells the over-all degree of association between the ranks. Discussion of the computation and rationale of W is postponed until later, when we consider it in an analysis-of-variance context.

THE SIGN TEST

A simple, but efficient, test for small samples is the *sign test*. It is used with matched pairs. All one does is to list the observations for all the pairs and to record with + or − the direction of the differences between the paired values. Assume that we have an experimental and control group, and scores on some measure. The hypothetical scores for 10 such pairs are given in Table 14.1, with the signs of the differences between the pairs.

TABLE 14.1 HYPOTHETICAL OBSERVATIONS OF 10 PAIRS OF MATCHED SUBJECTS AND SIGNS OF DIFFERENCES

Experimental	Control	Sign $(E - C)$
8	6	+
9	8	+
5	3	+
2	4	−
2	1	+
7	10	−
3	1	+
10	7	+
6	5	+
7	4	+

[9] See Q. McNemar, *Psychological Statistics,* 2d ed. New York: Wiley, 1955, pp. 136, 137.

[10] M. Kendall, *Rank Correlation Methods.* London: Griffin, 1948, chap. 6.

Obviously we can compute the significance of the difference between the means with a *t* test or a two-way analysis of variance. If, however, there is serious question as to the appropriateness of a parametric test because of violation of assumptions, a nonparametric test can be used. Suppose the above is such a case. The significance of the difference between the two groups can be tested by using binomial statistics. An exact test is appropriate here, but it would take too much space and mathematics to illustrate. Therefore, an approximation to the binomial test is used. There is no point to using this test with smaller samples, however, since convenient tables have been constructed to make the test.[11] We use it here simply to show the logic of the method.

The mean, variance, and standard deviation of a binomial distribution is given by the following formulas:

$$M = np \tag{14.1}$$

$$V = npq \tag{14.2}$$

$$SD = \sqrt{V} = \sqrt{npq} \tag{14.3}$$

where n is the number of pairs, $p = 1/2$, and $q = 1/2$. These formulas were discussed earlier. In the present case of 10 pairs,

$$M = 10 \cdot \frac{1}{2} = 5$$

$$V = 10 \cdot \frac{1}{2} \cdot \frac{1}{2} = 2.5$$

$$SD = \sqrt{2.5} = 1.58$$

On the basis of the null hypothesis, we would expect to obtain approximately equal number of pluses and minuses. Does the present number of 8 pluses and 2 minuses differ significantly from 5, the chance expectation? Forming a critical ratio with the equation used earlier, we get

$$z = \frac{x - M}{SD} \tag{14.4}$$

where $x =$ the number of like signs, in this case 8. Substituting, we obtain

$$z = \frac{8 - 5}{1.58} = 1.90$$

This is a little less than 2 *SD*'s above the mean. It is not quite significant at the .05 level. Actually, a better approximation is obtained with a corrected formula.[12]

---

[11] See Siegel, *op. cit.*, pp. 68–75 and 250 (Table D). A rather convenient table is given by Mosteller and Bush. See F. Mosteller and R. Bush, "Selected Quantitative Techniques," in G. Lindzey, ed., *Handbook of Social Psychology*, Vol. I. Cambridge, Mass.: Addison-Wesley, 1954, p. 313.

[12] *Ibid.*, p. 312.

$$z = \frac{(x - M) - .5}{SD} = \frac{8 - 5 - .5}{1.58} = \frac{2.5}{1.58} = 1.58$$

This is not significant. It seems clear that the reasoning behind this non-parametric test is basically the same as that used for parametric tests.[13]

NONPARAMETRIC ANALYSIS OF VARIANCE AND MEASURES OF ASSOCIATION

The nonparametric analysis of variance methods studied here, like so many other nonparametric methods, depend on ranking.[14] We study two basic forms: one-way analysis and two-way analysis.

One-Way Analysis of Variance: The Kruskal-Wallis Test An investigator interested in the differences in conservatism of three boards of education is unable to administer a measure of conservatism to the board members. He therefore has an expert judge rank order all the members of the three boards on the basis of private discussions with them. The three boards have six, six, and five members, respectively. The ranks of the board members are given in Table 14.2.

TABLE 14.2 RANKS OF 17 MEMBERS OF THREE BOARDS OF EDUCATION ON JUDGED CONSERVATISM

	Boards	
I	II	III
12	11	4
14	16	3
10	5	8
17	7	1
15	6	9
13	2	
ΣRanks: 81	47	25

If there were no differences in conservatism between the three boards, then the ranks should be randomly distributed in the three columns. If they are randomly distributed in the three columns, then the sums of the ranks (or their means) in the three columns should be approximately equal.[15] (It is assumed, in this reasoning, that the numbers

[13] The noncorrelated (independent groups) analogue of the sign test is the Mann-Whitney U test, one of the most powerful of nonparametric tests. A useful alternative to the t test, it is not discussed in this chapter because the explanation is too lengthy. See Siegel, *op. cit.*, pp. 116–127.

[14] Other forms of nonparametric analysis of variance are now being developed. There seems to be lack of agreement, however, as to their virtues.

[15] Kendall has ingeniously shown how it is appropriate to add ranks. See Kendall, *op. cit.*, p. 1.

of ranks in each column are the same.) On the other hand, if there are differences in conservatism between the three groups, then the ranks in one column should generally be higher than the ranks in another column —with a consequent higher sum of ranks.

Kruskal and Wallis give a simple formula for assessing the significance of these differences.[16] The formula is

$$H = \frac{12}{N(N+1)} \Sigma \frac{R^2}{n} - 3(N+1) \tag{14.5}$$

where N is the total number of ranks, n the number of ranks in one group, and R the sum of the ranks in any one column. Applying Eq. 14.5 to the ranks of Table 14.3, we first compute $\Sigma(R^2/n)$:

$$\Sigma \frac{R^2}{n} = \frac{(81)^2}{6} + \frac{(47)^2}{6} + \frac{(25)^2}{5} = 1093.50 + 368.17 + 125. = 1586.67$$

Substituting in Eq. 14.5, we find that

$$H = \frac{12}{17(17+1)} \cdot 1586.67 - 54 = 62.22 - 54 = 8.22$$

H is approximately distributed as χ^2. The degrees of freedom are $k - 1$, where k is the number of columns or groups, or $3 - 1 = 2$. Checking the χ^2 table, we find this to be significant at the .02 level. Thus the ranks are not random.

Two-Way Analysis of Variance: The Friedman Test In situations in which subjects are matched or the same subjects are observed more than once, a form of rank order analysis of variance, first devised by Friedman, can be used.[17] An ordinary two-way analysis of variance of the ranks can also be used. In addition, it is possible to compute a measure of association, W, of the rankings. Many cases arise in psychological, sociological, and educational research where the measurement procedure is such that it is doubtful whether parametric analyses are legitimate. Of course, doubtful measures can also be transformed into less doubtful ones.[18] But

[16] W. Kruskal and W. Wallis, "Use of Ranks in One-Criterion Variance Analysis," *Journal of the American Statistical Association*, XLVII (1952), 583–621. The test is also described in statistics texts, including Siegel, *op. cit.*, pp. 184–193, and Mosteller and Bush, *op. cit.*, pp. 320, 321.

[17] M. Friedman, "The Use of Ranks to Avoid the Assumption of Normality Implicit in the Analysis of Variance," *Journal of the American Statistical Association*, XXXII (1937), 675–701. The Friedman test is also described in the references mentioned earlier.

[18] The problem of transformation of scores exceeds the bounds of this book. The student can find discussion of transformations in Edwards, *op. cit.*, pp. 128–131. Perhaps the most complete discussion—but a difficult one—is in M. Bartlett, "The Use of Transformations." *Biometrics*, III (1947), 39–52. The essence of the idea of transformations is that measures that are not respectable, due to lack of normality and other reasons, are transformed to respectability via a linear function of the sort $y = f(x)$, where y is a transformed score, x the original score, and f is some operation ("the square root of") on x.

in many cases it is easily possible to rank order the scores and perform the analysis on the ranks.

Many research situations, too, are such that the only form of measurement possible is rank order, or ordinal, measurement. In such cases, one can use the analysis of variance of ranks. Certain other research situations require that we know the degree of association among several sets of ranks. Again, one can use the analysis of variance of ranks and compute Kendall's W, the coefficient of concordance. One can also easily compute the intraclass coefficient of correlation for ranks. We proceed to these matters using the same set of simple numbers to illustrate the different techniques. The research examples to go with the numbers, however, will be varied.

RESEARCH EXAMPLES An educational researcher, concerned with the relation between role and perception of teaching competence, asked groups of professors to rate each other on an instructor evaluation rating instrument. He also asked administrators and students to rate the same professors. Since the numbers of professors ("peers"), administrators, and students differed, he lumped the ratings of the members of each rating group together by averaging. In effect the hypothesis stated that the three groups of raters would differ significantly in their ratings. The researcher also wanted to know whether there were significant differences among the professors. The data of one part of the study are given in Table 14.3. The numbers in parentheses to the right of each number are the ranks of the numbers in the columns, from low to high. The numbers in parentheses to the left of each number are the ranks of the numbers in the rows, from low to high.

TABLE 14.3 HYPOTHETICAL DATA (MEANS) OF RATINGS, WITH RANKS, OF PROFESSORS BY PEERS, ADMINISTRATORS, AND STUDENTS [a]

Professors	Peers			Administrators			Students			ΣR
A	(3)	28	(3)	(1)	19	(1)	(2)	22	(1)	5
B	(1)	22	(1)	(2)	23	(2)	(3)	36	(3)	6
C	(2)	26	(2)	(1)	24	(3)	(3)	29	(2)	7
D	(2)	44	(6)	(1)	34	(4)	(3)	48	(6)	16
E	(1)	35	(4)	(2)	39	(6)	(3)	40	(4)	14
F	(2)	40	(5)	(1)	38	(5)	(3)	45	(5)	15
ΣR:	11			8			17			

[a] The numbers in the table are composite ratings. The numbers in parentheses to the right and left of the composite ratings are ranks. Those to the right are the ranks in columns; those to the left are the ranks in rows.

There are a number of ways these data can be analyzed. First, of course, ordinary two-way analysis of variance can be used. If the numbers being analyzed seem to conform reasonably well with the assumptions discussed earlier, this would be the best analysis. In the analysis of variance, the F ratio for columns (between raters) is 4.71, significant at the .05 level, and the F ratio for rows is 12.73, significant at the .01 level. From this analysis, the hypothesis of the investigator is supported. This is indicated by the significant differences between the means of the three groups. The professors, too, differ significantly.

Now assume that the investigator is disturbed by the type of data he has and decides to use nonparametric analysis of variance. Clearly he should not use the Kruskal-Wallis method; he decides to use the Friedman method, rank ordering the data *by rows*. In so doing he tests the differences between the columns, because by using ranks by rows he is minimizing the between-rows differences. Obviously if two or more raters are given the same ranking system, say 1, 2, 3, 4, 5, it is apparent that the sums and means of the ranks of the different raters will always be the same. In this analysis, then, he concentrates on the differences between the raters and ignores the differences between the professors (as rated). In what follows, then, we concentrate on the ranks in the parentheses to the *left* of each composite rating. Also concentrate on the sums of the ranks in the *columns* at the bottom of the table and ignore the sums in the last column of the table.

The formula given by Friedman is

$$\chi_r^2 = \frac{12}{kn(n+1)} \Sigma R^2 - 3k(n+1) \tag{14.6}$$

where $\chi_r^2 = \chi^2$, ranks; k is the number of rankings; n the number of objects being ranked; R the sum of the ranks in each column; and ΣR^2 is the sum of these squared sums. First compute ΣR^2:

$$\Sigma R^2 = (11)^2 + (8)^2 + (17)^2 = 474$$

Now determine k and n. The number of rankings is k, or the number of times that the rank-order system, whatever it is, is used. Here $k = 6$. The number of objects being ranked, n, or the number of ranks, is 3. (Actually, the raters are not being ranked: 3 is the number of ranks in the rank-order system being used.) Now compute χ_r^2:

$$\chi_r^2 = \frac{12}{(6)(3)(4)} \cdot 474 - (3)(6)(4) = 79 - 72 = 7$$

This value is checked against a χ^2 table, at $df = k - 1 = 6 - 1 = 5$. The value happens not to be significant.[19]

The investigator was also interested in the significance of the differences between the professors as rated. Clearly if these differences are not significant, there may be something wrong with the raters and/or

___

[19] With n and k relatively small, the significance level is in doubt. For details, see Siegel, *op. cit.*, pp. 166–169.

the rating system. Note that the reasoning is the same here—with minor modifications—as it was with one-way analysis of variance of ranks. If the rating composites in Table 14.3 were random, then the totals of the ranks (ΣR's) would be roughly the same. What is being tested, in effect, is whether they *are* random. Returning to the example, the investigator then assigns ranks to the rating composites in *columns* (in parentheses to the *right* of each rating composite). These are the ranks that the rater-groups assigned to the six professors. The professor who is rated high should get the higher ranks, which can be determined by adding his ranks across the rows. The data for all six professors appear in Table 14.3. (See ΣR column on the right-hand side of the table.) This time $k = 3$ and $n = 6$. We compute x_r^2 using Eq. 14.6 again:

$$x_r^2 = \frac{12}{(3)(6)(7)} \cdot 787 - (3)(3)(7) = 11.95$$

Checking this value in a χ^2 table, at $df = k - 1 = 3 - 1 = 2$, we find it to be significant at the .01 level. The instructors, as rated, seem to be different.

It is interesting to compare these results with the ordinary analysis of variance results. In the latter, the three groups were found to be significantly different at the .05 level, but according to x_r^2, they are not significantly different. This discrepancy may be due to the fact that the usual analysis of variance uses more information than the ranking method. Or it may be due to the rough χ^2 approximation with small k and n. (They are still not too discrepant, however.) In the case of the significance of the differences between the professors, both analyses showed significance. In general, the methods should agree fairly well.[20]

The Coefficient of Concordance, W Perhaps a more direct test of the investigator's hypothesis is provided by using a measure of the association of the ranks. Such a measure, called the *coefficient of concordance, W*, has been worked out by Kendall.[21] We are now interested in the degree of agreement or association in the ranks of the columns of Table 14.3. Each rater-group has virtually assigned a rank to each professor. If there were no association whatever between two of the rater groups, and a rank-order coefficient of correlation were computed between the ranks, it should be near zero. On the other hand, if there is agreement, the coefficient should be significantly different from zero.

---

[20] Using another method of analysis of variance based on ranges rather than variances, the results of the Friedman test are confirmed. This method, called the *studentized range test*, is very useful. For the details see Pearson and Hartley, *op. cit.*, pp. 51–54 and 176–179. Ranges are good measures of variation for small samples but not for large samples. The principle of the studentized range test is similar to that of the F test in that a "within-groups range" is used to evaluate the range of the means of the groups. Another useful method, that of Link and Wallace, is described in detail in Mosteller and Bush, *op. cit.*, pp. 304–307. Both methods have the advantage that they can be used with one-way and two-way analyses.

[21] Kendall, *op. cit.*, chap. 6.

The coefficient of concordance, W, expresses the average agreement, on a scale from .00 to 1.00, between the ranks. There are two ways to define W. The Kendall method, which is quite simple, will be presented first. According to this method W can be expressed as the ratio between the *between-groups* (or ranks) sum of squares and the *total* sum of squares of a complete analysis of variance of the ranks. This ratio, then, is the correlation ratio squared, E^2, of ranked data, another manifestation of the close relationships existing in statistics.

Where there are k rankings of n individual objects, Kendall's coefficient of concordance is defined by

$$W = \frac{12\,S}{k^2(n^3 - n)} \tag{14.7}$$

S is the sum of the deviations squared of the totals of the n ranks from their mean. S is a between-groups sum of squares for ranks. It is like Σx_b^2. (In fact, if we divide S by k, S/k, we obtain the between sum of squares we would obtain in a complete analysis of variance of the ranks.)

Consider the data of Table 14.3. We are interested in the six ranks of the three-column measures and their over-all relation. These are given in parentheses to the *right* of the original composite ratings. Add them across the rows. The sums of the six rows are 5, 6, 7, 16, 14, and 15. Then S can be computed in two ways. In the first method, square each total, add them up, and subtract the total of all the ranks squared divided by n. In a formula, $S = \Sigma X^2 - (\Sigma X_t)^2/n$, where ΣX is the sum of the ranks in any row (or column), $\Sigma X_t =$ the sum of all the ranks. Using this formula, we find that

$$S = [(5^2 + 6^2 + \cdots + 15^2)] - (63)^2/6 = 787 - 661.5 = 125.5$$

Kendall uses another method that gives the same results: subtract each individual sum of ranks from the mean of the sums, square the resulting figures, and then add them. The mean of the six totals is $63/6 = 10.5$. Therefore,

$$S = (5 - 10.5)^2 + (6 - 10.5)^2 + \cdots + (15 - 10.5)^2$$
$$= (-5.5)^2 + (-4.5)^2 + \cdots + (4.5)^2 = 125.5$$

Since $k = 3$ and $n = 6$,

$$W = \frac{12 \times 125.50}{3^2(6^3 - 6)} = \frac{1506}{9(216 - 6)} = \frac{1506}{1890} = .797 = .80$$

The relation between the three sets of ranks is quite substantial.

To evaluate the significance of W, the following formula for the F ratio can be used:

$$F = \frac{(k - 1)W}{1 - W} \tag{14.8}$$

By substitution we find that

$$F = \frac{(3-1)(.797)}{1-.797} = \frac{1.594}{.203} = 7.85$$

The significance of the F ratio (which is significant at the .01 level) will not be discussed here. The reader can check such methods in the Kendall or Siegel books. We now note that we could have used Friedman's x_r^2 to obtain the F ratio, as follows:

$$F = \frac{(k-1)\,x_r^2}{k(n-1) - x_r^2} \tag{14.9}$$

Previously we found that $x_r^2 = 11.95$. Thus,

$$F = \frac{(3-1)(11.95)}{3(6-) - 11.95} = \frac{23.90}{3.05} = 7.84$$

Now, let us do a two-way analysis of variance of the ranks, treating the ranks as though they were scores. The table of ranks and the calculations are given in Table 14.4 for the assistance of the reader.

TABLE 14.4 RANKS OF HYPOTHETICAL DATA OF TABLE 14.3
WITH CALCULATIONS FOR ANALYSIS OF VARIANCE

Professors	Peers	Administrators	Students	Σ	Σ^2
A	3	1	1	5	25
B	1	2	3	6	36
C	2	3	2	7	49
D	6	4	6	16	256
E	4	6	4	14	196
F	5	5	5	15	225
ΣX	22	22	22		

$\Sigma X_t = 63$
$(\Sigma X_t)^2 = 3969$
$\Sigma X_t^2 = 273$
$\Sigma(\Sigma)^2 = 787$

$$C = \frac{3969}{18} = 220.50$$

$$\text{Total} = 273 - 220.50 = 52.50$$

$$\text{Between raters} = 0$$

$$\text{Between professors} = \frac{787}{3} - 220.50 = 41.83$$

Source	df	s.s.	m.s.	F
Between raters	2	0	0	
Between professors	5	41.83	8.366	7.84 (.01)
Residual: $R \times P$	10	10.67	1.067	
Total	17	52.50		

Note that the F ratio computed by Eqs. 14.8 and 14.9 and by the analysis of variance are the same (within errors of rounding). Now, we perform one more calculation, E^2:

$$E^2 = \frac{\Sigma x_b{}^2}{\Sigma x_t{}^2} = \frac{41.83}{52.50} = .797 = .80$$

This is the same as W. (Note that if we multiply the between-sum of squares by k, we obtain S: $41.83 \times 3 = 125.5$.) Since the above methods produce results similar to those of earlier analyses of the relations among variances, further discussion is unnecessary. (The possibilities have still not been exhausted, though. For example, R, the intraclass coefficient of correlation can be calculated with ranks.) The reader may find it profitable, however, to go through the calculations of these various methods carefully.

STUDY SUGGESTIONS

1. A teacher interested in studying the effect of workbooks, decides to conduct a small experiment with her class. She randomly divides the class into 3 groups of 7 pupils each, calling these groups A_1, A_2, and A_3. A_1 was taught without any workbooks at all, A_2 was taught with the occasional use of workbooks at the teacher's direction, and A_3 was taught with heavy dependence on workbooks. At the end of four months, the teacher tested the children in the subject matter. The scores she obtained were in percentage form, and she knew that it might be questionable to use parametric analysis of variance.[22] So she used the Kruskal-Wallis method. The data are as follows:

A_1	A_2	A_3
.55	.82	.09
.32	.24	.35
.74	.91	.25
.09	.36	.36
.48	.86	.20
.61	.80	.07
.12	.65	.36

Convert the percentages into ranks (from 1 through 21) and compute H. Interpret. (To be significant, H must be 5.99 or greater for the .05 level, and 9.21 at the .01 level. This is at $k - 1 = 2$ degrees of freedom, the χ^2 table.)

[22] When scores are in percentage form, they can easily be transformed to scores amenable to parametric analysis. The appropriate transformation is called the *arc-sine transformation,* a table for which can be found in R. Fisher and F. Yates, *Statistical Tables for Biological, Agricultural, and Medical Research,* 5th ed. New York: Hafner, 1957, Table X, p. 70.

Note: Two cases of tied percentages and consequently tied ranks occur in these data. When ties occur, simply take the median (or mean) of the ties. For example, there are three .36's in Table 14.5, occurring at the tenth, eleventh, and twelfth ranks. The median (or mean) is 11. All three .36's, then, will be assigned the rank of 11. The next higher rank must then be 13, since 10, 11, and 12 have been "used up." Similarly there are two .09's, which occur at the second and third ranks. The median of 2 and 3 is 2.5. Both .09's are assigned 2.5 and the next higher rank, of course, is 4. (*Answer:* H = 7.79 (.05).)

2. Koenker, in his study of arithmetic readiness, reports, among other data, difference scores.[23] These scores are the differences between the final *gain* scores of the matched pairs of his experimental and control groups on an arithmetic test. Among the 27 *D* (difference) scores, 24 are positive and 3 are negative, that is, 24 of the experimental group *S*s made greater gains than their control-group partners did, and 3 of them did not gain as much as their control-group partners.

   (a) Use the sign test and Eqs. 14.1, 14.3, and 14.4 to test the significance of this result. Interpret.

   (b) Koenker reports a *t* ratio of 5.23, significant at the .01 level—actually significant at the .001 level. How does the result of the sign test compare with Koenker's result?

   (*Answer:* z = 4.04.)

3. An educational sociologist, studying the relation between racial membership and over-all school achievement, used the usual analysis of variance procedure to test the significance of the differences between his racial groups. He obtained $F = 7.34$, which is significant at the .01 level. A statistician, criticizing his work, used a nonparametric test on the data and obtained $H = 8.50$, which is also significant at the .01 level.

   (a) Is there any difference in the interpretation of these two results?

   (b) From a purely statistical point of view, *is* there any difference?

4. The relation between the discussion behavior of members of boards of education and their decisions was studied by a social psychological researcher. In this research, a particularly complex facet of discussion behavior, say antagonistic behavior, was to be measured. He wondered if this behavior could be reliably measured. The researcher trained three observers and had them rank order the antagonistic behavior of the members of one board of education during a two-hour session. The ranks of the three observers are shown in the table on p. 272 (high ranks show high antagonism):

   (a) What is the degree of agreement or concordance between the three observers? (Use *W*.)

[23] R. Koenker, "Arithmetic Readiness at the Kindergarten Level," *Journal of Educational Research*, XLII (1948), 218–223.

| | Observers | | |
Board Members	0_1	0_2	0_3
1	3	2	2
2	2	4	1
3	6	6	7
4	1	1	3
5	7	7	6
6	4	3	5
7	5	5	4

(b) Is W statistically significant? (If $F \geqq 5.32$, W is significant at the .01 level. If $F \geqq 9.58$, W is significant at the .001 level.)

(c) Can the social psychologist say that he is reliably measuring "antagonism" or "antagonistic behavior"?

(d) Use another method to compute the W of (a).

(*Answers:* (a) $W = .86$; (b) $F = 11.99$ (.001); (c) Yes.)

5. Use the numerical example of Problem 4 and compute a two-way analysis of variance, using Friedman's method.

(a) What is χ_r^2? Is it statistically significant? (At $df = 2$, if $\chi_r^2 \geqq 9.21$, it is significant at the .01 level; if $\chi_r^2 \geqq 13.82$, it is significant at the .001 level.)

(b) Do the board of education members differ in antagonistic behavior? Could you have known this from the results of Problem 4?

(c) Compare these results with those of Problem 4.

(d) Compute F, using Eq. 14.9. Compare this F to that computed in Problem 4.

(*Answers:* (a) $\chi_r^2 = 15.43$ (.001); (b) Yes; (d) $F = 11.9$.)

PART FOUR

DESIGNS OF RESEARCH

15 RESEARCH DESIGN: MEANING, PURPOSE, AND PRINCIPLES

Research design is the plan, structure, and strategy of investigation conceived so as to obtain answers to research questions and to control variance. The *plan* is the overall scheme or program of the research. It includes an outline of everything the investigator will do from writing the hypotheses and their operational implications to the final analysis of data. The *structure* of the research is more specific. It is the outline, the scheme, the paradigm of the operation of the variables.[1] When we draw diagrams that outline the variables and their relation and juxtaposition we build structural schemes for accomplishing operational research purposes. *Strategy,* as used here, is also more specific than plan. It includes the methods to be used to gather and analyze the data. In other words, strategy implies *how* the research objectives will be reached and *how* the problems encountered in the research will be tackled.

PURPOSES OF RESEARCH DESIGN

Research design has two basic purposes: (1) *to provide answers to research questions* and (2) *to control variance.* Naturally, research design does not *do* these things; only the investigator does. Design helps the investigator obtain answers to the questions of research and also helps him to control the experimental, extraneous, and error variances of the particular research problem under study. Since all research activity can be said to have the purpose of providing answers to research questions, it is possible to omit this purpose from the discussion and to say that research design has one grand purpose: to control variance. Such a delimitation of the purpose of design, however, is dangerous. Without strong stress on the research questions and on the use of design to help provide

[1] A "paradigm" is a model, or an example. The word "model" is a synonym for a paradigm, but "paradigm" evades the value connotation of "model." Diagrams, graphs, and verbal outlines are paradigms. The word will be used here, however, in the sense of a structure and a guiding model, particularly in connection with research design.

answers to these questions, the study of design can degenerate into an interesting, but sterile, technical exercise.

Research designs are invented to enable the researcher to answer research questions as validly, objectively, accurately, and economically as possible. Any research plan is deliberately and specifically conceived and executed to bring empirical evidence to bear on the research problem. Research problems are stated in the form of hypotheses. At some point in the research they are stated so that they can be empirically tested. There is a wide range of possibilities of testing; theoretically, at least, as many designs of research exist as there are possibilities. Designs are carefully worked out to yield dependable and valid answers to the research questions epitomized by the hypotheses. We can make one observation and infer that the hypothesized relation exists on the basis of this one observation, but it is obvious that we cannot accept the inference so made. On the other hand, it is also possible to make hundreds of observations and to infer that the hypothesized relation exists on the basis of these many observations. In this case we might or might not accept the inference as a valid one. The result depends on how the observations and the inference were made. Adequately planned and executed design helps greatly in permitting us to rely on both our observations and our inferences.

How does design accomplish this? Research design sets up the framework for "adequate" tests of the relations among variables. Design tells us, in a sense, what observations to make, how to make them, and how to analyze the quantitative representations of the observations. Strictly speaking, design does not "tell" us precisely what to do, but rather "suggests" the directions of observation-making and analysis. An adequate design "suggests," for example, how many observations should be made, and which variables are active and which are assigned. We can then act to manipulate the active variables and to dichotomize or trichotomize or otherwise categorize the assigned variables. A design tells us what type of statistical analysis to use. Finally, an adequate design outlines possible conclusions to be drawn from the statistical analysis.

An Example We wish to test the hypothesis that the efficacy of two methods of teaching spelling depends upon the intelligence of the children being taught. Method A_1 is a holistic approach; Method A_2 is a syllabic-memory approach. We believe that A_1 works better with more intelligent children and that A_2 works better with less intelligent children. The measures of the dependent variable might be supplied by a standardized or a teacher-made spelling test. This is a good example of another point to be emphasized later: research problems suggest research designs. Since the above hypothesis is one of interaction, a factorial design would seem to be appropriate. A is *methods*; B is *intelligence*. A is subpartitioned into A_1 and A_2, and B into as many levels as desired, say B_1 and B_2, high intelligence and low intelligence. Now we have a familiar 2×2 factorial paradigm. (See Fig. 15.1.)

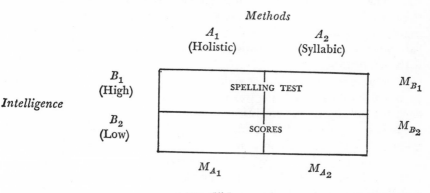

FIG. 15.1

The paradigm of Fig. 15.1 suggests a number of things. First and most obviously, a fairly large number of subjects are needed. Specifically, $4n$ subjects are necessary (n = number of Ss in each cell). If we decide that n should be 10, then we must have 40 Ss for the experiment. Note the "wisdom" of the design here. If we were only testing the methods and ignoring intelligence, only $2n$ Ss would be needed.

Second, the design indicates that the subjects can and should be randomly assigned to A_1 and A_2, but not to B_1 and B_2. Third, according to the design the observations made on the children, the spelling test measures, must be made independently. The score of one child must not be affected by the score of another child. This is simply a statistical requirement of factorial design. The mere act of reducing a design to an outline like that of Fig. 15.1, by prescribing statistical tests of significance, at the same time also prescribes the measures and operations necessary for obtaining the measures that are appropriate to the statistical analysis. An F test depends upon the assumption of the independence of the measures; therefore such variables as hints from the teacher during the testing and the possibility of one child's being able to see another child's paper must be prevented—not on moral grounds but as a prerequisite of sound design and sound statistics.

Fourth, the design of Fig. 15.1 indicates the use of analysis of variance and F tests. If the research is well-designed before the data are gathered, most statistical problems can be solved. In addition, certain troublesome problems can be avoided before they arise or can even be prevented from arising at all. With an inadequate design, however, problems of appropriate statistical tests may be very troublesome. One reason for the strong emphasis in this book on treating design and statistical problems concomitantly is to point out ways to avoid those problems. If design and statistical analysis are planned simultaneously, the analytical work is usually straightforward and uncluttered.

The last function of design discussed here is this: it outlines clearly the possible conclusions the investigator can reach, by specifically outlining or suggesting the statistical tests that can be made. A simple one-variable randomized design with two subpartitions, for example, methods with two methods A_1 and A_2, permits only a statistical test of the difference between the two statistics yielded by the data. These statistics might be two means, two medians, two ranges, two variances, two percentages, and so forth. Only one statistical test is ordinarily possible. If subjects are matched, on the other hand, two statistical tests are possible, one of them being the really important one, as we learned in Part III.

With the design of Fig. 15.1 three statistical tests are possible: (1) between A_1 and A_2; (2) between B_1 and B_2; and (3) the interaction of A and B. In most investigations, all the statistical tests are not of equal importance. The important ones, naturally, are those directly related to the research problems and hypotheses. In the present case, Test 3 is the important one, since the hypothesis is that the efficacy of the methods depends upon the intelligence of the children with whom the methods are used. Symbolically, this can be written:

$$H_3:\ A_1 > A_2|B_1$$
$$A_2 > A_1|B_2$$

This says that Method A_1 (holistic) is more effective than A_2 (syllabic) with level B_1 (high intelligence) children, and Method A_2 is more effective than A_1 with level B_2 (low intelligence) children. The "|" in the symbolism indicates "under the condition," so that the first line is read "A_1 is greater than A_2, under the condition B_1." In addition to testing H_3 (Hypothesis 3), it is possible to test A_1 against A_2 and B_1 against B_2. The first of these is important; the second is not, except to tell us whether the assignment of intelligence has been effective.

It should be evident that research design is not static. A knowledge of design can help us to plan and do better research and can also suggest the testing of hypotheses. Probably more important, we may be led to realize that the design of a study is not in itself adequate to the demands we are making of it. What is meant by this somewhat peculiar statement?

Assume that we formulate the interaction hypothesis as outlined above without knowing anything about factorial design. We set up a design consisting, actually, of two experiments. In one of these experiments we test A_1 against A_2 under condition B_1. In the second experiment we test A_1 against A_2 under condition B_2. The paradigm would look like that in Fig. 15.2.

| B_1 Condition | | B_2 Condition | |
| Methods | | Methods | |
A_1	A_2	A_1	A_2
M_{A_1}	M_{A_2}	M_{A_1}	M_{A_2}

FIG. 15.2

The important point to note is that no *adequate* test of the hypothesis is possible with this design. A_1 can be tested against A_2 under both B_1 and B_2 conditions, to be sure. But it is not possible to know, clearly and unambiguously, whether there is a significant interaction between A and B. Even if $M_{A_1} > M_{A_2}|B_1$, as hypothesized, the design does not offer a clear confirmation of the fact of interaction, since we cannot obtain any information about the difference between B_1 and B_2. This information is necessary to test the interaction hypothesis. If the statistical conditions were as indicated in the expression above, then there is good *presumptive* evidence that the interaction hypothesis is true. But presumptive evidence is not good enough, especially when we know that it is possible to obtain better evidence.

In Fig. 15.2, suppose the means of the cells were, from left to right: 40, 30; 30, 30. This result would seem to support the interaction hypothesis, since there is a significant difference between A_1 and A_2 at level B_1, but not at level B_2. But we could not know this to be certainly so, even though the difference between A_1 and A_2 is statistically significant. Figure 15.3 shows how this would look if a factorial design had been used.

	A_1	A_2	
B_1	40	30	35
B_2	30	30	30
	35	30	

FIG. 15.3

(The figures in the cells and on the margins are means.) Assuming that the main effects, A_1 and A_2; B_1 and B_2, were significant, it is still possible that the interaction is not significant. Unless the interaction hypothesis is specifically tested, the evidence for interaction is merely presumptive, because the authentic ring of a planned statistical interaction test that a factorial design would provide is lacking. It should be clear that a knowl-edge of design could have improved this experiment greatly.

RESEARCH DESIGN AS VARIANCE CONTROL

The main technical function of research design is *to control vari-ance.* A research design is, in a manner of speaking, a set of instructions to the investigator to gather and analyze his data in certain ways. It is there-fore a control mechanism. The statistical principle behind this mechan-ism, as stated earlier is: *Maximize systematic variance, control extraneous systematic variance, and minimize error variance.* In other words, we must *control variance.* The word "control" actually implies the rest of the state-ment.

According to this principle, by constructing an efficient research de-sign the investigator attempts (1) to maximize the variance of the variable or variables of his substantive research hypothesis, (2) to control the vari-ance of extraneous or "unwanted" variables that may have an effect on his experimental outcomes, but in which he is not interested, and (3) to minimize the error or random variance, including so-called errors of meas-urement. Let us look at an example.

An Example   An educational investigator decides to test the hypothesis that the teaching of reading is facilitated more by an opportunistic method than by a systematic method.[2] The *systematic method,* call it A_1, uses a course of study that is definitely outlined and organized and ori-ented basically to the subject matter. The *opportunistic method,* call it A_2, explores the inclinations and interest of children. The teacher waits for opportunities to introduce reading skills, on the supposition that this study will be better motivated by the children's interests. The investiga-tor knows very well that other possible independent variables influence reading outcomes: intelligence, sex, social class background, previous ex-perience with verbal materials, and so on. As in many such studies, he can attempt to match experimental subjects with control subjects on these variables, but he has reason to believe that the methods may work differ-ently with different kinds of children. They may work one way with chil-dren of different intelligent levels and another way with children of vary-ing home backgrounds. Children from relatively strict homes may respond better to one method than to the other method, and the same is true for children from relatively permissive homes.

What kind of design shall the investigator set up? To answer this

[2] The idea for this example was taken from A. Gates, M. Batchelder, and J. Betz-ner, "A Modern Systematic versus an Opportunistic Method of Teaching," *Teachers College Record,* XXVII (1926), 679–700. The design notions used in the example are not those of the original authors, who used a matching method.

question, it is important to assemble and label the variables and to know clearly what questions the investigator wants to answer. The variables are:

Methods	*Type of Home*
systematic, A_1,	*restrictive, B_1,*
opportunistic, A_2	*permissive, B_2*

He might also include *intelligence* as an independent variable, but he decides not to do so. Instead, he decides that random assignment will take care of intelligence and other possible influential independent variables. His dependent variable measure is provided by a standardized reading test to be administered after four months of the experiment.

The investigator's problem seems to call for a factorial design. (The investigator might use a mixture of factorial and matching designs, also.) There are two reasons for this choice. One, there are two independent variables. Two, the investigator has quite clearly an interaction hypothesis in mind, though he may not have stated it in so many words, since he has the belief that the methods will work differently with different kinds of children. We set up the design structure in Fig. 15.4.

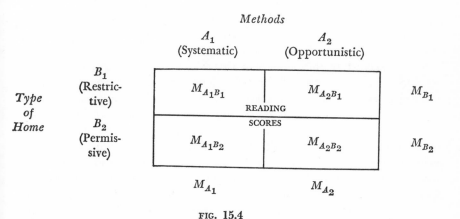

FIG. 15.4

Note that all the marginal and cell means have been appropriately labeled. Note, too, that there is one *active variable,* Methods, and one *assigned* variable, Type of Home.[3] The experimenter obviously cannot use randomization with the assigned variable. All he can do is to categorize his subjects as coming from restrictive and permissive homes and assign them accordingly to B_1 and B_2. He can, however, and *does* randomly assign the

[3] It will be remembered from chap. 3 that an *active variable* is a manipulated variable, and an *assigned variable* is one engendered by subjects having been assigned to different cells of a design on the basis of their possession of certain characteristics, like intelligence, sex, social class, and so on.

children to A_1 and A_2, the methods groups. This he does in two stages: (1) he randomly assigns the B_1, restrictive home, children to A_1 and A_2, and (2) he assigns the B_2, permissive home, children to A_1 and A_2. By so randomizing the subjects the investigator can assume that before the experiment begins, the children in A_1 are approximately equal to the children in A_2 in all possible characteristics. Now he is ready to perform the experiment.

Rather than continue the experiment, however, we now study its variance aspects. Our present concern is with the different roles of variance in research design and the variance principle. Before going further, we name the variance principle for easy reference—the "maxmincon" principle. The origin of this name is obvious: *max*imize the systematic variance under study; *con*trol extraneous systematic variance; and *min*imize error variance—with two of the syllables reversed for euphony.

Before tackling the application of the maxmincon principle in the present example, an important point should be discussed. Whenever we talk about variance, we must be sure to know *what* variance we are talking about. We speak of the variance of the methods, of intelligence, of sex, of type of home, and so on. This sounds as though we were talking about the independent variable variance. This is true and not true. We always mean *the variance of the dependent variable, the variance of the dependent variable measures,* after the experiment has been done.[4] Our way of saying "independent variable variance" stems from the fact that, by manipulation and control of independent variables, we *influence,* presumably, the variance of the dependent variable. Somewhat inaccurately put, we "make" the measures of the dependent variable behave or vary as a presumed result of our manipulation and control of the independent variables. In an experiment, it is always the dependent variable measures that are analyzed. Then, from the analysis we *infer* that the variances present in the total variance of the dependent variable measures are due to the manipulation and control of the independent variables and to error. In fact, this is part of the basis of the analysis of variance. In the analysis of variance, it is the analysis of the variance of the dependent variable that is presumably influenced by the manipulated and controlled variance, the individual differences variance, and the error variance. Now, back to our principle.

MAXIMIZATION OF EXPERIMENTAL VARIANCE

The experimenter's most obvious, but not necessarily most important, concern is to maximize what we will call the *experimental variance.*

---

[4] This is not true in so-called correlational studies where, when we say "the variance of the independent variable," we mean just that. When correlating two variables, we study the variances of the independent and dependent variables "directly."

This term is introduced to facilitate subsequent discussions and, in general, simply refers to the variance presumably introduced into the dependent variable by the independent variable or variables being manipulated or controlled. It is the variance of the independent variable or variables of the substantive hypothesis. In this particular case, the experimental variance is the variance in the dependent variable presumably due to Methods, A_1 and A_2, and Types of Home, B_1 and B_2. Although experimental variance can be taken to mean only the variance due to a manipulated or *active* variable, like Methods, we shall also consider *assigned* variables, like intelligence, sex, and, in this case, Type of Home, experimental variables. One of the main tasks of an experimenter is to maximize this variance. He must "pull" the methods apart as much as possible to make A_1 and A_2 (and A_3, A_4, and so on, if they are in the design) as unlike as possible. Very briefly, if his experiment is to succeed, he has to make his experimental variables really vary.

If the independent variable does not vary substantially, there is little chance of separating its effect from the total variance of the dependent variable, so much of which is often due to chance. It is necessary to give the variance of a relation a chance to show itself, to separate itself, so to speak, from the total variance, which is a composite of variances due to perhaps numerous other sources, especially chance. Remembering this subprinciple of the maxmincon principle, we can write a research precept: *Design, plan, and conduct research so that the experimental conditions are as different as possible.*[5]

In the present research example, this subprinciple means that the investigator must take pains to make A_1 and A_2, the systematic and opportunistic methods, as different as possible. Next, he must so categorize his types of homes into restrictive and permissive, B_1 and B_2, that they are as different as possible on the restrictive-permissive dimension. This latter problem is essentially one of measurement. In an experiment, the investigator is like a puppeteer making the independent variable puppets do what he wants. He holds the strings of the A_1 and A_2 puppets in his right hand and the strings of the B_1 and B_2 puppets in his left hand. (We assume there is no influence of one hand on the other, that is, the hands must be independent.) He makes the A_1 and A_2 puppets dance apart, and he makes the B_1 and B_2 puppets dance apart. He then watches his audience (the dependent variable) to see and measure the effect of his manipulations. If he is successful in making A_1 and A_2 dance apart, and if there is a relation between A and the dependent variable, the audience reaction—

---

[5] There are, of course, exceptions to this subprinciple, but they are probably rare. An investigator might want to study the effects of small gradations of, say, motivational incentives on the learning of some subject matter. Here he would not make his experimental conditions as different as possible. Still, he would have to make them vary somewhat or there would be no discernible resulting variance in the dependent variable.

if separating A_1 and A_2 is funny, for instance—then he should get a reaction from the audience, laughter. He may even observe that he only gets laughter when A_1 and A_2 dance apart and, at the same time, B_1 or B_2 dance apart (interaction again).

CONTROL OF EXTRANEOUS VARIABLES

The control of extraneous variables means that the influences of independent variables extraneous to the purposes of the study are minimized, nullified, or isolated. In other words, the variance of such variables is in effect reduced to zero or near zero, or, what amounts to fundamentally the same thing, it is separated from the variance of other independent variables.

There are three ways to control extraneous variables. The first is the easiest, if it is possible: to eliminate the variable as a variable. If we are worried about intelligence as a possible contributing factor in studies of achievement, its effect on the dependent variable can be virtually eliminated by using subjects of only one intelligence level, say IQ's within the range of 90 to 110. If we are studying achievement, and racial membership is a possible contributing factor to the variance of achievement, it can be eliminated by using only members of one race. The subprinciple here is: *To eliminate the effect of a possible influential independent variable on a dependent variable, one can choose subjects so that they are as homogeneous as possible on that independent variable.*

This method of controlling unwanted or extraneous variance is very effective. If we select only one sex for an experiment, then we can be sure that sex cannot be a contributing independent variable. But then we lose the power of generalization; for instance we can say nothing about the relation under study with girls if we use only boys in the experiment. If the range of intelligence is restricted, then we can discuss only this restricted range. Is it possible that the relation, if discovered, is nonexistent or quite different with children of high intelligence or children of low intelligence? We simply do not know; we can only surmise or guess.

The second way to control extraneous variance is through randomization. This is the best way, in the sense that you can have your cake and eat some of it, too. Theoretically, randomization is the only method of controlling *all* possible extraneous variables. Another way to phrase it is: if randomization has been thoroughly accomplished, then the experimental groups can be considered statistically equal in all possible ways. This does not mean, of course, that the groups *are* equal in all the possible variables. We already know that by chance the groups can be unequal, but the probability of their being equal is much greater, with proper randomization, than the probability of their not being equal. For this reason control of the extraneous variance by randomization is the best possible method of control. All other methods leave many possibilities of inequality. If we match for intelligence, we may successfully achieve statistical equality in intelligence (at least in those aspects of intelligence measured), but we may suffer from inequality in other significantly influential independent variables like aptitude, motivation, and social class. A subprinciple that springs from this equalizing power of randomization, then, is: *Whenever it is possible to do so, randomly assign subjects to experimental groups and conditions, and randomly assign conditions and other factors to experimental groups.*

The third means of controlling an extraneous variable is to build it right into the design as an independent variable. For example, assume that sex was to be controlled in the experiment discussed earlier and it was considered inexpedient or unwise to eliminate it, and it was not possible to assign subjects to groups at random. One could add a third independent variable, sex, to the design. Unless one were interested in the actual difference between the sexes on the dependent variable or wanted to study the interaction between one or two of the other variables and sex, however, it is unlikely that this form of control would be resorted to. One might want information of the kind just mentioned and also want to control sex, too. In such a case, adding it to the design as a variable might be desirable. The point is that building a variable right into an experimental design "controls" the variable, since it then becomes possible to extract from the total variance of the dependent variable the variance due to the variable. (In the above case, this would be the "between-sexes" variance.) Variables of this kind are too seldom built into designs.

These considerations lead to another subprinciple: *An extraneous variable can be controlled by building it into the research design as an assigned variable, thus achieving control and yielding additional research information about the effect of the variable on the dependent variable and about its possible interaction with other independent variables.*

The fourth method, the most frequently used, but not necessarily the best, way to control extraneous variance is to match subjects (see Part III for detailed discussion). The control principle behind matching is the same as that for any other kind of control, the control of variance. Matching is similar—in fact, it might be called a corollary—to the principle of controlling the variance of an extraneous variable by building it into the design. The basic principle is to split a variable into two or more parts, say into high and low intelligence in a factorial design, and then randomize within each level as described above. Matching is a special case of this principle. Instead of splitting the subjects into two, three, or four parts, however, they are split into $N/2$ parts, N being the number of subjects used; thus the control of variance is identified and built into the design. Matching is theoretically a more powerful method of achieving this aim, because it uses most of the variance due to the variable.

In using the matching method several problems may be encountered. To begin with, the variable on which the subjects are matched
must be fairly substantially related to the dependent variable or the
matching is a waste of time. Even worse, it can be misleading. In addition,
matching has severe limitations. If we try to match on, say, more than two
variables, or even more than one, we lose subjects. It is difficult to find
matched subjects on more than two variables. For instance, if one decides
to match intelligence, sex, and social class, one may be fairly successful in
matching the first two variables but not in finding pairs that are fairly
equal on all three variables. Add a fourth variable and the problem becomes very difficult, often impossible to solve.

Let us not throw the baby out with the bath, however. When there
is a substantial correlation between the matching variable or variables
and the dependent variable ($>$ .50 or .60), then matching reduces the error term and thus increases the precision of an experiment, a very desirable outcome. If the same subjects are used with different experimental
treatments, we have the most powerful control of variance there is. How
match better on all possible variables than by matching a subject with
himself? Other negative considerations usually rule out this possibility,
unfortunately.

A subprinciple suggested by this discussion is: *When a matching
variable is substantially correlated with the dependent variable, matching
as a form of variance control is profitable and desirable. Before using
matching, however, carefully weigh its advantages and disadvantages in
the particular research situation. Complete randomization or the analysis
of covariance may be better methods of variance control.*

Still another form of control, statistical control, was discussed at
length in Part III, but one or two further remarks are in order here. Statistical methods are, so to speak, forms of control in the sense that they
isolate and quantify variances. But statistical control is inseparable from
other forms of design control. If matching is used, an appropriate statistical test must be used, or the matching effect, and thus the control, will be
lost.

More germane to the notion of control being discussed in this chapter, and especially useful in educational research, is the statistical method
known as the analysis of covariance. This method matches *for* us—under certain conditions and with certain limitations.[6] Other values of this
method will be discussed later.

[6] A good discussion of analysis of covariance can be found in A. Edwards, *Experimental Design in Psychological Research.* New York: Holt, Rinehart, and Winston, Inc.,
1950, chap. 17.

MINIMIZATION OF ERROR VARIANCE

Error variance is the variability of measures generated by random fluctuations whose basic characteristic is that they are self-compensating, varying now this way, now that way, now positive, now negative, now up, now down. Random errors tend to balance each other so that their mean is zero, but systematic variance is in essence predictable. Error variance is unpredictable.

There are a number of determinants of error variance, for instance, factors associated with individual differences among subjects. Ordinarily we call this variance due to individual differences "systematic variance." But when such variance cannot be, or is not identified and controlled, we have to lump it with the error variance. Because many determinants interact and tend to cancel each other out (or at least we assume that they do), the error variance has this random characteristic.

Another source of error variance is that associated with what are called errors of measurement: variation of responses from trial to trial, guessing, momentary inattention, slight temporary fatigue and lapses of memory, transient emotional states of subjects, and so on.

Minimizing error variance has two principal aspects: (1) the reduction of errors of measurement through controlled conditions, and (2) an increase in the reliability of measures. The more uncontrolled the conditions of an experiment, the more the many determinants of error variance can operate. This is one of the main reasons for carefully setting up controlled experimental situations and conditions. In studies under field conditions, of course, such control is difficult; still, constant efforts must be made to lessen the effects of the many determinants of error variance. This can be effected, in part, by specific and clear instructions to subjects and by excluding from the experimental situation problems that are extraneous to the research purpose.

To increase the reliability of measures is to reduce the error variance. Pending fuller discussion later in the book, reliability can be taken to be the *accuracy* of a set of scores. To the extent that scores do not fluctuate randomly, to this extent they are reliable and contribute to good research procedure. Imagine a completely unreliable measurement instrument, one that could not allow us to predict the future performance of individuals at all, one that would give one rank ordering of a sample of subjects and a completely different rank ordering on another administration. With such an instrument, it would not be possible to identify and extract systematic variances, since the scores yielded by the instrument would be like the numbers in a table of random numbers. This would be the extreme case. Now imagine differing amounts of reliability and unreliability in the measures of the dependent variable. The more reliable the measures, the better we can identify and extract systematic variances and the smaller the error variance in relation to the total variance.

Another reason for reducing error variance as much as possible is to give systematic variances a chance to show their significance—if they *are* significant. We cannot do this if the error variance, and thus the error term, is too large. If a relation exists, we seek to discover it. One way of discovering this relation or of letting it appear, is by finding significant differences between the means. But if the error variance is relatively large due to uncontrolled errors of measurement (and thus unreliable), the systematic variances—called earlier "between" variances—will not have a chance to be significant. Thus the relation, although it exists, will probably not be, or perhaps cannot be, discovered.

The problem of error variance can be put into a neat mathematical nutshell: remember the equation,

$$V_t = V_b + V_e \qquad (15.1)$$

where V_t is the total variance in a set of measures; V_b is the between-groups variance, the variance presumably due to the influence of the experimental variables; and V_e is the error variance (in analysis of variance, the within-groups variance and the residual variance). Obviously, the larger V_e is, the smaller V_b must be, with a given amount of V_t.

Better yet, consider the following equations:

$$t = \frac{\text{statistic}}{\text{standard error of the statistic}} \qquad (15.2)$$

and

$$F = \frac{V_b}{V_e} \qquad (15.3)$$

Both equations say the same thing: in order for the numerators of the fractions on the right to be accurately evaluated for significant departures from chance expectations, the denominators should be accurate measures of "true" chance or random error.

A familiar example should make this clear. Recall that in the discussions of factorial analysis of variance and the analysis of variance of correlated groups we talked about variance due to individual differences being present in experimental measures. We said that, while adequate randomization would effectively equalize experimental groups, there would be variance in the scores due to individual differences, for instance, differences due to intelligence, aptitude, and so forth. Now, in some situations, these individual differences can be quite large. If they are, then the error variance and, consequently, the denominators of Eqs. 15.2 and 15.3 will be "too large" relative to the numerators; that is, the individual differences will have been randomly scattered among, say, two, three, or four experimental groups. Still, they are sources of variance and, as such, will inflate the within-groups or residual variance or the standard variance (standard error squared), the denominators of the above equations.

16 GENERAL DESIGNS OF RESEARCH: "POOR" DESIGNS

All man's disciplined creations have form. Architecture, poetry, music, painting, mathematics, scientific research—all have form. Man puts great stress on the content of his creations, often not realizing that without strong structure, no matter how rich and how significant the content, the creations may be weak and sterile.

So it is with scientific research. The scientist needs viable and plastic form with which to express his scientific aims. Without content—without good theory, good hypotheses, good problems—the design of research is empty. But without form, without structure adequately conceived and created for the research purpose, little of value can be accomplished. Indeed, it is no exaggeration to say that many of the failures of behavioral research have been failures of disciplined and imaginative form.

EXPERIMENTAL AND EX POST FACTO APPROACHES

Discussion of design must be prefaced by an important distinction: that between the experimental and so-called ex post facto approaches to research. Indeed, this distinction is so important that a separate chapter will be devoted to it later. The literal meaning of ex post facto is "from what is done afterward." It means something done or occurring *after* an event with a retroactive effect on the event. It is used in contradistinction to "experimental" in this text, and has been assigned a specific and, hopefully, unambiguous meaning.

An experiment is taken to mean a scientific investigation in which an investigator manipulates and controls one or more independent variables and observes the dependent variable or variables for variation concomitant to the manipulation of the independent variables. An *experimental design,* then, is one in which the investigator has *direct* control over at least one independent variable and *manipulates* at least one independent variable. Hurlock manipulated incentives to produce different amounts of retention. Page manipulated reinforcement by having his experimental group teachers write different comments on student tests. Koenker manipulated methods by giving one group of kindergartners readiness experience and not giving it to another group.

In a *true* experiment, the investigator has the power to assign subjects to experimental groups. Ideally, he should have the power to *select* his subjects, at random if possible, but unfortunately, this ideal situation is frequently denied him. If the experimenter does not have the *power* either to assign subjects to experimental groups or to assign experimental treatments to the groups, then his study may be an experiment, but not a *true* experiment. Note the word "power." The experimenter may not so assign subjects or treatments, but it is essential that he have the power to do so.

In ex post facto research one cannot manipulate or assign subjects or treatments, because in this kind of research the independent variable or variables have already occurred. The investigator starts with observation of the dependent variable and retrospectively studies independent variables for their possible effects on the dependent variable. When Getzels and Jackson compared the characteristics of highly intelligent "noncreative" children and less intelligent "creative" children, their "creative" and "noncreative" and highly intelligent and less intelligent groups had already been formed for them.[1] These independent variables had already "occurred," so to speak. Getzels and Jackson could not manipulate creativity or intelligence, nor could they assign, randomly or otherwise, subjects to groups or treatments to subjects (unless, of course, they had chosen another independent variable to manipulate, say methods of teaching). While experimental and ex post facto research differ sharply, then, on these and other counts, they share structural and design features, which we will attempt to point out in this and the following chapters on design.

It should be clear, then, that the ideal of science is the controlled experiment. Except, perhaps, in taxonomic research, research with the purpose of discovering, classifying, and measuring natural phenomena and the factors behind such phenomena, the controlled experiment is the desired model of science. It may be difficult for many students to accept this rather categorical statement since its logic is not readily apparent. Earlier it was said that the main goal of science was to discover relations among phenomena. Why, then, assign a priority to the controlled experiment? Do not other methods of discovering relations exist? Yes, of course they do. The main reason for the preeminence of the controlled experiment, however, is that the researcher can have more confidence that the relations he discovers *are* the relations he thinks they are, since he discovers

[1] J. Getzels and P. Jackson, "Occupational Choice and Cognitive Functioning: Career Aspirations of Highly Intelligent and of Highly Creative Adolescents," *Journal of Abnormal and Social Psychology*, LXI (1960), 119–123.

them under the most carefully *controlled* conditions of inquiry known to man. The unique virtue of experimental inquiry, then, is control.

In short, a perfectly conducted, an ideal if nonexistent, experimental research, which yields information that A is related to B, is more trustworthy than a perfectly conducted, an ideal if also nonexistent, ex post facto research. Why this is so should become more apparent as we advance in our study of research design.

FAULTY DESIGNS

There are three or four inadequate designs of research that have been used, and unfortunately are still used, in behavioral research. It is doubtful that the investigators who use these designs are aware of their inadequacies. These inadequacies are basically structural weaknesses that lead to no control or poor control of independent variables. The faulty designs to be discussed furnish us with examples that, although poor, are instructive. Dangers cannot be avoided if they are not recognized.

Definitions   Before beginning the main discussion, some explanation of the symbolism to be used in these chapters is necessary. We shall assign X to be the experimental manipulation of the independent variable or variables. Then X_1, X_2, X_3, etc., mean that X is partitioned into independent variables X_1, X_2, X_3, and so on. The symbol (X) indicates that the independent variable is *not manipulated*—is not under the direct control of the investigator, but is *measured* or *imagined*. The dependent variable is Y, or perhaps more accurately, the measure of the dependent variable; Y_b the dependent variable *before* the manipulation of X, and Y_a the dependent variable *after* the manipulation of X. With $\sim X$, we borrow the negation sign of set theory; $\sim X$ means that the experimental variable, the independent variable X, is *not* manipulated. (Note: (X) is a nonmanipulable variable and $\sim X$ is a manipulable variable that is *not* manipulated.) The symbol $\boxed{R}$ will be used for the random assignment of subjects to experimental groups and the random assignment of experimental treatments to experimental groups.

An experimental group, or *the* experimental group, is the group that is manipulated or given the independent variable treatment. In testing the frustration-aggression hypothesis, the experimental group is the group whose subjects are systematically frustrated. By contrast, a *control group* is one that is given "no" treatment, is not manipulated.

In modern multivariate research, it is necessary to expand these notions. They are not changed basically; they are only expanded. It is quite possible to have more than one experimental group, as we have seen. Different degrees of manipulation of the independent variable are not only possible; they are often also desirable or even imperative. Furthermore, it is possible to have more than one control group, a statement that at first seems like nonsense. How can one have different degrees of "no" experimental treatment?—because the notion of *control* is generalized. When there are more than two groups, and when any two of them are treated differently, one or more groups serve as "controls" on the others. Recall that control is always control of variance. With two or more groups treated differently, variance is engendered by the experimental manipulation. So the traditional notion of X and $\sim X$, treatment and no treatment, is generalized to $X_1, X_2, \cdots, X_k$, different forms or degrees of treatment.

If X is circled, (X), this means that the investigator "imagines" the manipulation of X, or he assumes that X occurred and that it is *the* X of his hypothesis. It may also mean that X is measured and not manipulated. Actually, we are saying the same thing here in different ways. The context of the discussion should make the distinction clear. Suppose an educational sociologist is studying delinquency and the frustration-aggression hypothesis. He observes delinquency, Y, and imagines that his delinquent subjects were frustrated in their earlier years, or (X). All ex post facto designs will have (X). Generally, then, (X) means an independent variable not under the control of the investigator.

One more point—each design in this chapter will ordinarily have an a and a b form. The a form will be the experimental form, or that in which X is manipulated. The b form will be the ex post facto form, that in which X is not under the control of the investigator, or (X). Obviously, $(\sim X)$ is also possible.

DESIGN **16.1**   ONE GROUP

(a)	X	Y	(Experimental)
(b)	(X)	Y	(Ex Post Facto)

This design has also been called the "One-Shot Case Study," an apropos expression.[2] Case studies fall under this rubric, but so do certain types of research. Design 16.1 (a) is an "experimental" type. For example, a school faculty decides to institute a new curriculum, and also decides to "study" or "evaluate" the effects of the new curriculum, represented by X, a manipulated independent variable. After one year, Y,

---

2 D. Campbell, "Factors Relevant to the Validity of Experiments in Social Settings," *Psychological Bulletin*, LIV (1957), 297–312. This is an excellent article. The author has been influenced by Campbell's thinking and the thinking of Solomon, Stouffer, and Underwood, but has altered their formulations to fit the design discussion of this book. See S. Stouffer, "Some Observations on Study Design," *American Journal of Sociology*, LV (1950), 355–361; R. Solomon, "An Extension of Control Group Design," *Psychological Bulletin*, XLVI (1949), 137–150; B. Underwood, *Psychological Research*. New York: Appleton, 1957, chaps. 4 and 5; and D. Campbell and J. Stanley, "Experimental and Quasi-Experimental Designs for Research on Teaching," in N. Gage, ed., *Handbook of Research on Teaching*. Skokie, Ill.: Rand McNally, 1963, chap. 5.

student achievement, and perhaps student attitudes—but more likely, faculty opinion—are studied. Student achievement is found to be "the same" or "better," say. The value of the new curriculum is established.[3] Another example is that of the school principal who wishes to write his doctoral thesis on the effects of reforms he has produced in a school over a five-year period.

Design 16.1 (b) is the ex post facto form of the one-group design. Here the dependent variable Y, the outcome, is studied or examined, and the independent variable X is assumed or imagined. A case in point would be to study delinquency by taking a group of juvenile delinquents and looking into the past for causative factors that might have led to their anti-social behavior. Another example is to study student failure or underachievement (Y) by seeking out possible X's in the students' backgrounds.

Scientifically speaking, Design 16.1 is worthless; worse, it can be badly misleading. As Campbell points out, the minimum of useful scientific information requires at least one formal comparison.[4] The new curriculum example requires, *at the very least,* comparison of a group that experienced the curriculum with a group that did not experience it. The design is worthless scientifically because Y, the presumed effect, might have occurred as it did without X, the presumed cause. The presumed effect of the new curriculum, say such-and-such achievement, might well have been about the same under any kind of curriculum. The point is not that the new curriculum did or did not have an effect, but that, in the absence of any formal, controlled comparison of the performance of the members of the "experimental" group with the performance of the members of some other group not experiencing the new curriculum, nothing can be said about the effect of the new curriculum. Unfortunately, much *has* been said about the presumed results of such "experiments," and faith has even been placed in these utterances.

An important distinction must be emphasized. We are not saying that the method is *universally* worthless and misleading, but that it is *scientifically* worthless and misleading. In studying life we depend on such "experimental" evidence. We act, we say, on the basis of our experience, and this is the only way we *can* act. We hope that we use our experience rationally and critically. Thus, the paradigm of thinking in practical affairs, which is implied by Design 16.1, is not being criticized, although it might well be. It is only when such a paradigm is labeled as scientific, or believed to be scientific, that difficulties arise. Even in high intellectual pursuits, this paradigm must be used. Freud's brilliant observations and

---

[3] The implication here is not that *evaluation,* in the sense of informed and careful discussion and appraisal, is undesirable. It is often not feasible to use controlled experiments in such situations. To call such appraisal "research," or to set up an experiment of the one-group kind, however, is misleading.

[4] Campbell, *op. cit.,* p. 298.

analyses of neurotic behavior seem to fall into this category. The only quarrel we have is not with Freud but rather with the assertions that his conclusions were "scientifically established."

Design 16.2 is only a small improvement on Design 16.1. The essential characteristic of this mode of research is that a group is compared with itself. Theoretically, there is no better control since all possible independ-

DESIGN 16.2 ONE GROUP, BEFORE-AFTER (PRETEST-POSTTEST)

(a) Y_b X Y_a (Experimental)

(b) Y_b (X) Y_a (Ex Post Facto)

ent variables associated with the subjects' characteristics have been controlled. The procedure dictated by such a design is as follows. A group is measured on the dependent variable, Y, before any experimental manipulation. This is usually called a *pretest*. Two important dependent variables that are used quite frequently are school achievement and attitudes. Let us assume that the attitudes of a group of subjects toward education are to be measured. An experimental manipulation designed to change these attitudes is accomplished. An experimenter might expose the group to expert opinion on educational issues. After the interposition of this X, the attitudes of the subjects are again measured. The difference scores, or $Y_a - Y_b$, are examined for any change in opinion on the part of the subjects.

At face value, this would seem to be a good way to accomplish the experimental purpose. After all, if the difference scores are statistically significant, does this not indicate a change in attitudes? The situation, however, is not so simple—there are a number of other factors that may have contributed to the change in scores. Campbell gives an excellent, detailed discussion of these factors,[5] only a brief discussion of which can be given here.

First is the possible effect of the measurement procedure: measuring subjects changes them. Could it be that the post-X measures were influenced not by the manipulation of X but by increased sensitization due to the pretest? In some research situations, this factor may make no difference; in others, it may make a considerable difference. Controversial attitudes, for example, seem to be especially susceptible to such sensitization. Campbell calls the measures of such variables *reactive measures*, because they cause the subject to react. Achievement measures, though probably less reactive, are still reactive. Measures involving memory are quite reactive. If you take a test now, you are more likely to remember later things

5 *Ibid.*, pp. 298–300. The first point discussed, the possible interaction effect of the pretest, seems first to have been pointed out by Solomon in his excellent article, cited above, pp. 140 and 141. Campbell has elaborated Solomon's original point: Campbell, *op. cit.*, pp. 298, 299.

that were included in the test. In short, observed changes may be due to reactive measures.

Two other important sources of extraneous variance are *history* and *maturation.* Between the Y_b and Y_a testings, many things can occur other than X. In other words, extraneous independent variables can operate in the interval. The longer the period of time, the greater the chance of extraneous variables affecting the subjects and thus the Y_a measures. This is what Campbell calls *history.* These variables or events are *specific* to the particular experimental situation. *Maturation,* on the other hand, covers events that are not specific to any particular situation. They are, rather, *general.* They are connected with change or growth in the organism studied. The mental age of a child increases with time. This increase could easily affect achievement measures. Children learn during any given time interval, and the learning might affect the dependent variable measure. In fact, this is one of the exasperating features of educational research. Children refuse to stand still while studies are progressing. Again, the longer the time interval, the greater the possibility that such extraneous variables, such unwanted possible sources of systematic variance, will influence the dependent variable measures. Other difficulties, too, are involved.[6]

Design 16.2 is inadequate, not so much because these extraneous variables can operate (they operate whenever there is a time interval between pretest and posttest), but *because we do not know whether or not they have operated, whether or not they have affected the dependent variable measures.* The design affords no opportunity to know or to test such possible influences.

The peculiar title of Design 16.3 stems in part from its very nature. It is similar to Design 16.2 in that it is a before-after design. Instead of using the before and after (or pretest-posttest) measures of one group, the

DESIGN **16.3**   SIMULATED BEFORE-AFTER FORM

$$\frac{\qquad\qquad X \qquad\qquad\qquad\qquad Y_a \qquad}{Y_b}$$

measures of another group which are chosen to be as similar as possible to the experimental group and thus a control group of a sort, are used as pretest measures. (The line between the two levels, above, indicates separate groups.) This design is subject to even more weaknesses than Design 16.2. It satisfies the condition of having a control group, and is thus a gesture toward the comparison that is necessary to scientific investigation. Unfortunately, the controls are weak, a result of our inability to know

---

[6] The so-called *regression effect* is important. A clear discussion can be found in A. Anastasi, *Individual Differences,* 3rd ed. New York: Macmillan, 1958, pp. 203–205. Regression is particularly important in research when groups from different populations are compared.

that the two groups were equivalent before X, the experimental manipulation.

Design 16.4 is a common one. In Design (a) the experimental group is administered treatment X; the "control" group, taken to be, or assumed to be, similar to the experimental group, is not given X. The Y measures

DESIGN **16.4** TWO-GROUPS, NO-CONTROL

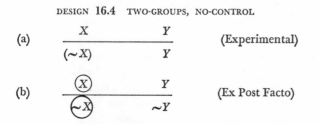

are compared to ascertain the effect of X. Groups or subjects are taken "as they are," or they may be matched. The ex post facto version of the same design is labeled (b). An effect, Y, is observed to occur in one group (top line) but not in another group, or to occur in the other group to a lesser extent (indicated by the $\sim Y$ in the bottom line). The first group is found to have experienced X, the second group not to have experienced X.

This design has a basic weakness. The two groups are assumed to be equal in all independent variables other than X (except, perhaps, in Design 16.4 (a), for the variables on which subjects may have been matched). It is sometimes possible to check the equality of the groups roughly by comparing them on different pertinent variables, for example, age, sex, income, intelligence, ability, and so on. This should be done if it is at all possible, but, as Stouffer says, ". . . there is all too often a wide-open gate through which other uncontrolled variables can march." [7] Because there is no randomization used, that is, the subjects are not assigned to the groups at random, it is not possible to assume that the groups are equal. Design 16.4 (b) is weaker than (a) because X is manipulated in Design 16.4 (a) but not in (b). Both versions of the design, however, suffer seriously from lack of control of independent variables due to lack of randomization. Yet Design 16.4 (a) has two advantages over (b); the treatments may be assigned to the two groups at random, and the assumption that Y varies concomitantly with X is stronger since the investigator performs the manipulation of X and observes Y for concomitant variation. In Design 16.4 (b), he works backwards in time, that is, from Y to X, thus losing one important source of control, manipulation.

[7] Stouffer, *op. cit.*, p. 522.

CHARACTERISTICS LACKING IN "POOR"
RESEARCH DESIGNS

It might be well to pause before considering "good" or adequate research designs in order to discuss the basic characteristics that are missing in poor research designs. The desiderata of good design may be called "criteria"; with these criteria in mind, the student should be in a better position to understand why "good" designs are "good."

The main criterion or desideratum of a research design can be expressed in a question: *Does the design answer the research questions?* or *Does the design adequately test the hypotheses?* Perhaps the most serious weakness of designs often proposed by students is that they are not capable of adequately answering the research questions, or they can only answer the research questions inadequately. A common example of this lack of congruence between the research questions and hypothesis, on the one hand, and the research design, on the other, is matching subjects for reasons irrelevant to the research and then using an experimental group-control group type of design. Students often assume, because they match pupils on intelligence and sex, for instance, that their experimental groups are equal. They have heard that one should match subjects for "control" and that one should have an experimental group and a control group. Frequently, however, the matching variables may be irrelevant to the research purposes. That is, if there is no relation between, say, sex and the dependent variable, then matching on sex is irrelevant.

Another example of this weakness is the case where three or four experimental groups are needed—for example, three experimental groups and one control group, or four groups with different amounts of X, the experimental treatment—and the investigator uses only two because he has heard that an experimental group and a control group are necessary and desirable.

The example discussed earlier in this book (Chap. 15) of testing an interaction hypothesis by performing, in effect, two separate experiments is another example. The hypothesis to be tested was that the efficacy of two methods of teaching spelling depends upon the intelligence of the children being taught. This is an interaction hypothesis and most probably calls for a factorial type design. To set up a two-experiment design, one test for children of high intelligence and one for children of low intelligence, is poor practice because such a design, as shown earlier, cannot decisively test the stated hypothesis. Similarly, to match subjects on intelligence and then set up a two-group design would escape the research question entirely. These considerations lead to a general precept: *Design research to answer the research questions.*

The second criterion is *control.* The question must be asked: Does this design adequately control independent variables? Since this criterion has already been discussed at considerable length in earlier chapters, no more need be said here. One aspect of control, however—the most important aspect—needs to be repeated in a research design framework. This aspect of control can be succinctly expressed in another principle:

Randomize whenever possible: select subjects at random; assign subjects to groups at random; assign experimental treatments to groups at random.

While it may not be possible to *select* subjects at random, it may be possible to *assign* them to groups at random. This "equalizes" the groups in the statistical sense discussed in Part III. If such random assignment of subjects to groups is not possible, then every effort should be made to assign experimental treatments to experimental groups at random. And, in educational experiments, if experimental treatments are administered at different times with different teachers, times and teachers should be assigned at random.

To the extent that randomization is ignored or is not possible, to this extent research designs are weak. The whole structure of probabilistic-statistical reasoning depends upon randomization. So, again, whenever possible, *randomize*. Since the reasoning behind randomization and its power have been discussed at great length elsewhere in this book, we move on to the third criterion.

The third criterion is the general one discussed in previous chapters: *control*. A rather complex and difficult-to-execute precept is: *Control the independent variables so that extraneous and unwanted sources of systematic variance have minimal opportunity to operate.* According to this precept a relation between two or more variables is to be sought. In an effort to state pRq, p is related to q, with confidence, we manipulate p and observe that q covaries with the manipulation of p. But how confident can we be that pRq is really true? Our confidence is directly related to the completeness and adequacy of the controls. If we use a design similar to Designs 16.1 through 16.4, we cannot have too much confidence in pRq, since our control of the extraneous independent variable variance is weak or nonexistent. Because such control is not always possible in much educational, psychological, and sociological research, should we then give up research entirely? By no means. Nevertheless, we must be aware of the weaknesses of intrinsically poor design. Frequently it is possible to construct and use a better design than is at first thought possible.

The negative approach of this chapter was taken in the belief that an exposure to poor but commonly used and *accepted* procedures, together with a discussion of their major weaknesses, would provide a good starting point for the study of research design. This method is especially justified because the student has already been exposed to good designs and design principles in previous chapters, though they may not have been so labeled. Other inadequate designs are possible, but all such designs are inadequate on design-structural principles alone. This point should be emphasized because in the next chapter we shall find that a perfectly good design structure can be poorly used. Thus it is necessary to learn and understand the two sources of research weakness: intrinsically poor designs and intrinsically good designs poorly used.

17 GENERAL DESIGNS OF RESEARCH: "GOOD" DESIGNS

Design is data discipline. The implicit purpose of all research design is to impose controlled restrictions on observations of natural phenomena. The research design tells the investigator, in effect: Do this and this; don't do that or that; be careful with this; ignore that; and so on. It is the blueprint of the research architect and research engineer. If the design is poorly conceived structurally, the ultimate product will be faulty. If it is at least well conceived structurally, the ultimate product has a greater chance of being worthy of serious scientific attention. The problem of this chapter is to continue the discussion of the last chapter, but on a positive note of good, well-conceived design.

We should recognize that almost no research design can satisfy all criteria, yet we should strive to satisfy as many as possible. In addition to the criteria discussed in the last chapter, there are two general ones (discussed at length by Campbell)[1] that must be borne in mind: *internal validity* and *external validity*.

Internal validity asks the question: Did X, the experimental manipulation, really make a significant difference? The three criteria of the last chapter are actually aspects of internal validity. Indeed, anything affecting the *controls* of a design becomes a problem of internal validity. If a design is such that one can have little or no confidence in the relations, as shown by significant differences between experimental groups, say, this is a problem of internal validity. Henceforth, when the term internal validity is used, it will be a general way of denoting the three criteria.

A difficult criterion to satisfy, *external validity* means *representativeness* or *generalizability*. When an experiment has been completed and a

[1] D. Campbell, "Factors Relevant to the Validity of Experiments in Social Settings," *Psychological Bulletin,* LIV (1957), 297–312. For a more complete discussion of external and internal validities, see D. Campbell and J. Stanley, "Experimental Designs and Quasi-Experimental Designs for Research on Teaching," in N. Gage, ed., *Handbook of Research on Teaching.* Skokie, Ill.: Rand McNally, 1963, chap. 5. I am indebted to Professors Campbell and Stanley for making this chapter available before publication, and to them and Professor Gage for permission to use their material.

relation found, to what populations can it be generalized? Can we say that *A* is related to *B* for *all* school children? All eighth-grade children? All eighth-grade children in this school system or the eighth-grade children of this school only? Or must the findings be limited to the eighth-grade children with whom we worked? This is a very important scientific question that should always be asked—*and answered.*

Not only must sample generalizability be questioned. It is necessary to ask questions about the ecological and variable representativeness of studies. If the social setting in which the experiment was conducted were changed, would the relation of *A* and *B* still hold? Would *A* be related to *B* if the study were replicated in a lower class school? In a western school? In a southern school? These are questions of *ecological representativeness.*

Variable representativeness is a more subtle matter. A question not often asked, but that should be asked, is: Are the variables of this research representative? When an investigator works with psychological and sociological variables, he assumes that his variables are "constant." If he finds a difference in achievement between boys and girls, he assumes that sex as a variable is "constant."

In the case of variables like achievement, aggression, aptitude, and anxiety, can the investigator assume that the "aggression" of his suburban subjects is the same "aggression" to be found in city slums? Is the variable the same in a European suburb? The representativeness of "anxiety" is more difficult to ascertain. When we talk of "anxiety," what kind of anxiety do we mean? Are all kinds of anxiety the same? If anxiety is manipulated in one situation by verbal instructions and in another situation by electric shock, are the two induced anxieties the same? If anxiety is manipulated by, say, experimental instruction, is this the same anxiety as that measured by an anxiety scale? [2] Variable representativeness, then, is another aspect of the larger problem of external validity, and thus of generalizability.

Unless special precautions are taken and special efforts made, the results of research are frequently not representative, and hence not generalizable. Campbell and Stanley say that internal validity is the sine qua non of research design, but that the ideal design should be strong in both internal validity and external validity, even though they are frequently contradictory.[3] This point is well taken. In these chapters, the main emphasis will be on internal validity, with a vigilant eye on external validity.

---

2 This is the problem of the equivalence of definitions. See A. Baldwin, "The Study of Child Behavior and Development." In P. Mussen, ed., *Handbook of Research Methods in Child Development.* New York: Wiley, 1960, pp. 12, 13.

3 Campbell and Stanley, *op. cit.*

ADEQUATE DESIGNS

Unlike the designs of the last chapter, those of this section will have no ex post facto counterparts because the ex post facto approach precludes the possibility of randomization. This problem will be discussed in detail in a later chapter (Chap. 20).

Design 17.1 and its variants with more than two groups are the "best" designs available for most experimental purposes in education. Its structural similarity to Design 16.4 is apparent. The $\boxed{R}$ placed before

DESIGN 17.1   EXPERIMENTAL GROUP-CONTROL GROUP: RANDOMIZED SUBJECTS

$$\boxed{R} \quad \frac{X \qquad Y}{(\sim X) \qquad Y} \quad \begin{array}{l} \text{(Experimental)} \\ \text{(Control)} \end{array}$$

the paradigm indicates that subjects have been *randomly assigned* to the experimental group (top line) and the control group (bottom line). This randomization removes the objections mentioned in Chap. 16. Theoretically, *all* possible independent variables are controlled. Practically, of course, this may not be so. If enough subjects are included in the experiment to give the principle of randomization a chance to "operate," then we have powerful control indeed. In other words, the claims of internal validity are rather well satisfied.

External validity is another matter. Too often subjects cannot be *selected* from a defined population at random. We must be satisfied with, or at least reconciled to, the nonrandom selection of subjects. Thus, while Design 17.1 gives us good answers to internal validity questions, unless subjects (and, theoretically, situations) have been selected at random, we cannot generalize beyond the samples at our disposal. This problem is not as difficult to resolve as it seems, however. By replicating experiments, with and without variants, it is possible to increase generalizability considerably. If, for instance, an experiment is repeated at different times and in different places with the hypothesized relations holding up in each experiment, then we can have much more confidence in the scientific validity of the relations.

If extended to more than two groups, and if it is capable of answering the specific research questions asked, Design 17.1 is the ideal design of educational and social scientific research. To summarize the advantages of this design: (1) it has the best built-in theoretical control system of any other design, with one or two possible exceptions in special cases; (2) it is flexible, being theoretically capable of extension to any number of groups with any number of variables; (3) if extended to the multivariate case, it can test several hypotheses at one time; and (4) it is statistically and probabilistically elegant.

We do not mean to say that Design 17.1 is the be-all and end-all of research design—it is not universal or perfect. Obviously, it cannot, as it stands, test experiments of change as well as do pretest-posttest designs, and if extended to the multivariate case, practical considerations may limit its applicability in behavioral research situations. From most points of research view, however, it is very effective for two reasons:

1. The control group gives the comparability required by science. Comparisons are essential in *all* scientific investigation. The classical experimental group-control group design using equated experimental and control groups provides such comparisons in an efficient manner, which makes it an intellectual achievement of the first order.

2. The second reason for the virtue of Design 17.1 is randomization. In order to make the experimental group-control group idea valid, it is necessary for the experimenter to have some assurance that his groups are approximately (statistically) equal on *any* variables possibly related to the dependent variable or variables. Matching cannot accomplish this, as we learned earlier, nor can intuitive or experienced judgments. Experimenters seem to be reluctant to accept the outline of this design, and its logical offshoots such as three, four, or five-group, one-way designs and 2×2, 2×4, and $3 \times 2 \times 4$ factorial designs. They find it difficult to believe that a table of random numbers can be so effective.

Before discussing mechanics, let us say a word about the extension of Design 17.1. The "classical design" involves an experimental group and a control group—that is, two groups, usually matched. But there is no reason, especially if we drop the matching requirement, why we cannot have two, three, or more experimental groups and one, two, or more control groups (see Chap. 18 for examples).

THE NOTION OF THE CONTROL GROUP

Evidently the word "control" and the expression "control group" did not appear in the scientific literature before the late nineteenth century.[4] The notion of controlled experimentation, however, is much older: Boring says that Pascal used it as early as 1648. Solomon searched the psychological literature and could not find a single case of the use of a control group before 1901.[5] He says that control-group design apparently had to await statistical developments and the development of statistical sophistication among psychologists.

Perhaps the first use of control groups in psychology occurred in

---

[4] E. Boring, "The Nature and History of Experimental Control," *American Journal of Psychology,* LXVII (1954), 573–589.

[5] R. Solomon, "An Extension of Control Group Design," *Psychological Bulletin,* XLVI (1949), 137–150.

1901.[6] One of the two men who did this research, E. L. Thorndike, extended the basic and revolutionary ideas of this first research series to education.[7] Thorndike's controls, in this gigantic study of 8564 pupils in many schools in a number of cities were independent educational groups. Among other comparisons, he contrasted the gains in intelligence test scores presumably engendered by the study of English, history, geometry, and *Latin* with the gains in intelligence test scores presumably engendered by the study of English, history, geometry, and *shopwork*. He tried, in effect, to compare the influence of Latin and shopwork. He also made other comparisons of a similar nature. Despite the weaknesses of design and control, Thorndike's experiments and those he stimulated others to perform were remarkable for their insight. Thorndike even berated colleges for not admitting students of stenography and typing who had not studied Latin, because he claimed to have shown that the influence of various subjects on intelligence was similar. It is interesting to note that he thought huge numbers of subjects were necessary—he called for 18,000 more cases. He was also quite aware, in 1924, of the need for random samples.[8]

It seems clear, then, that the expression "control group" was not used before this century. Furthermore the importance of control seems not to have been clearly and generally understood or applied in psychological, sociological, and educational research much before 1920.[9] Indeed, to judge from studies published in the 1950s, the importance of experimental control does not seem to be completely understood yet in education, even though psychology, which has had a great influence on educational research, long ago mended most of its control fences.

Today, a half century after its inception in educational research, the notion of the control group still needs generalization. Assume that in an educational experiment we have four experimental groups as follows. A_1 is the reinforcement of every response, A_2 the reinforcement at regular time intervals, A_3 the reinforcement at random intervals, and A_4 no reinforcement. Technically, there are three experimental groups and one control group, in the traditional sense of the control group. However, A_4 might be another "experimental treatment"; it might be some kind of minimal reinforcement. Then, in the traditional sense, there would be *no* control group. The traditional sense of the term "control group" lacks generality. If the notion of control is generalized, the difficulty dis-

[6] E. Thorndike and R. Woodworth, "The Influence of Improvement in One Mental Function upon the Efficiency of Other Functions," *Psychological Review*, VIII (1901), 247–261, 384–395, 553–564.

[7] E. Thorndike, "Mental Discipline in High School Subjects," *Journal of Educational Psychology*, XV (1924), 1–22, 83–98.

[8] See *Ibid.*, pp. 93, 97, and 85, for the three points mentioned.

[9] Solomon says that the Peterson and Thurstone study of attitudes in 1933 was the first serious attempt to use control groups in the evaluation of the effects of educational procedures. Solomon, *op. cit.*, p. 175.

appears. Whenever there is more than one experimental group and any two groups are given different treatments, control is present in the sense of comparison previously mentioned. As long as there is an attempt to make two groups systematically different on a dependent variable, a comparison is possible. Thus the traditional notion that an experimental group should receive the treatment not given to a control group is a special case of the more general rule that comparison groups are necessary for the internal validity of any scientific research.

If we assume this reasoning to be correct, we can set up designs such as the following:

$$\boxed{R} \quad \begin{array}{cc} X_1 & Y \\ \hline X_2 & Y \\ \hline X_3 & Y \end{array}$$

or

$$\boxed{R} \quad \begin{array}{cc} X_{1a} & Y \\ \hline X_{1b} & Y \\ \hline X_{2a} & Y \\ \hline X_{2b} & Y \end{array}$$

These designs will be more easily recognizable if they are set up in a different notation in the form used in Part III, as in Fig. 17.1.

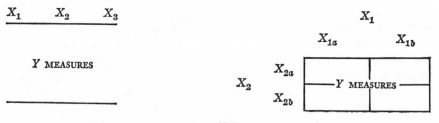

FIG. 17.1

The left-hand design is a simple one-way analysis of variance design and the second one on the right a 2×2 factorial design. In the right-hand design, X_{1a} might be experimental and X_{1b} control, with X_{2a} and X_{2b} either a manipulated or active variable or a dichotomous assigned variable.

The structure of Design 17.2 is the same as that of Design 17.1. The only difference is that, instead of all subjects being randomly assigned to groups, they are matched on one or more characteristics. For the design to take its place as an "adequate" design, however, randomization must enter the picture, as noted by the small r attached to the M (for "matched"). It is not enough that matched subjects are used; the members of each pair must be assigned to the two groups at random. Ideally, too, whether a group is to be an experimental or a control group is also decided at random. In either case, each decision can be made by flipping a coin or by using a table of random numbers, letting odd numbers mean one group and even numbers the other group. If there are more than two groups, naturally a random number system must be used.

DESIGN **17.2** EXPERIMENTAL GROUP-CONTROL GROUP: MATCHED SUBJECTS

$\boxed{M_r}$	X	Y	(Experimental)
	$(\sim X)$	Y	(Control)

As in Design 17.1, it is possible, though not often easy, to use more than two groups. (The difficulty of matching more than two groups was discussed earlier.) There are times, however, when a matching design is an inherent element of the research situation. When the same subjects are used for two or more experimental treatments, or when subjects are given more than one trial, matching is inherent in the situation. In educational research, when schools or classes are in effect variables—when, say, two or more schools or classes are used and the experimental treatments are administered, as they should be, in each school or class—then Design 17.2 is the basis of the design logic. Study the paradigm of a schools design in Fig. 17.2. It is seen that variance due to the differences between schools, and such variance can be substantial, can be readily controlled in this design.

Schools	X_{e_1} Experimental 1	X_{e_2} Experimental 2	X_c Control
1			
2			
3		Y MEASURES	
4			
5			

FIG. **17.2**

MATCHING—PRO AND CON

Matching is not limited to the matching of subjects. If we think of matching in variance terms, we can readily apprehend this point. When certain subsets of the total set of sampled units are more alike than other subsets, the variance due to the differences between the subsets is probably present. The extreme case is when the same subjects are used on more than one trial, because a subject is naturally more like himself than he is like other persons. The three experimental groups of Fig. 17.2 could be the same subjects on different trials, which introduces systematic variance, individual differences variance. When pretests and posttests are used, matching is of course present, too. Schools are known to differ in important characteristics: classes differ, school districts differ, neighborhoods differ, teachers differ. These differences can be used in the study and the variances arising from their use can be isolated by building their sources into the design. In fact, failure to build such variables into designs of educational and behavioral research can lead to the confounding of the experimental variables.[10]

The benefits to be derived from matching are sometimes considerable. It is imperative to use a matching design of some sort when objects in the environment are naturally matched. To have matched objects in a research experiment and not to take advantage of the variance due to the matching is a statistical and design blunder.

We now consider Design 17.3. This design has many advantages and is used frequently. Its structure is similar to that of Design 16.2, but with two important differences: Design 16.2 lacks a control group and ran-

DESIGN **17.3** BEFORE AND AFTER CONTROL-GROUP DESIGN (PRETEST—POSTTEST)

(a)	$\boxed{R}$	Y_b	X	Y_a	(Experimental)
		Y_b	$(\sim X)$	Y_a	(Control)
(b)	$\boxed{M_r}$	Y_b	X	Y_a	(Experimental)
		Y_b	$(\sim X)$	Y_a	(Control)

domization. Design 17.3 is similar to Designs 17.1 and 17.2 except that the "before" or pretest feature has been added. This design can also be called the "classical design" of research. For studies of change, or so-called

---

[10] The term "confounding," often used in treatises of statistical and research design, means the "mixing" of the variance of one or more independent variables, usually extraneous to the research purpose, with the independent variable or variables of the research problem. As a result it cannot be clearly said that the relation found is between the independent variables and the dependent variable of the research, or between the extraneous independent variables and the dependent variable, or both. Underwood points out that there is only one basic principle of research design: ". . . design the experiment so that the effects of the independent variables can be evaluated unambiguously." [B. Underwood, *Psychological Research*. New York: Appleton, 1957, p. 86.] When this cannot be done—it is a difficult procedure—more likely than not the independent variables have been confounded. The term evidently came from statistics where "confounding" is sometimes deliberately practiced.

change experiments, it is the classical design. As in the cases of Designs 17.1 and 17.2, it can be expanded to more than two groups.

In Design 17.3 (a), subjects are assigned to the experimental group (top line) and the control group (bottom line) at random and are pre-tested on a measure of Y, the dependent variable. The investigator can then check the equality of the two groups on Y. The experimental manipulation X is performed, after which the groups are measured on Y. The difference between the two groups is tested statistically. An interesting characteristic of this design is the nature of the scores analyzed. Usually, the difference scores, $Y_a - Y_b = D$, are analyzed, a simple and efficient procedure. In Design 16.2, the departure of the D scores from zero is tested. Since there is a control group in Design 17.3, the significance of the difference between the D scores of the experimental and control groups can be tested with a t or an F test (see Fig. 17.3).

X_e: Experimental			X_c: Control		
Before	After	Difference	Before	After	Difference
.	.	.	.	.	.
.	.	.	.	.	.
Y_b	Y_a	$Y_a - Y_b = D$	Y_b	Y_a	$Y_a - Y_b = D$
.	.	.	.	.	.
.	.	.	.	.	.

FIG. 17.3

There are two analytical possibilities. The simplest method has already been mentioned: analyze the D scores with a t test or an F test. This is merely a statistical test of the significance of the differences between the D means of the experimental and the control groups. Secondly, before and after measures can also be analyzed. Because there are before and after measures on the same subjects, correlation is introduced.

Design 17.3 (b) adds matching and, consequently, correlation to the design. Since the previous remarks on matching and on Design 17.3 (a) are applicable here, and since there is a better alternative, Design 17.3 (b) will not be discussed separately.

It would easily be possible to devote one or two whole chapters to a discussion of Design 17.3. For rather elaborate details, the student is referred to the Campbell and the Campbell and Stanley references.[11] Only the main strengths and weaknesses of the design will be discussed here.

---

[11] An informative comparison of before-after and after-only designs discussing strengths, weaknesses, measurement problems, and statistical tests can be found in C. Hovland, A. Lumsdaine, and F. Sheffield, *Experiments on Mass Communication*. Princeton: Princeton University Press, 1949, Appendix C, pp. 308–328.

Probably most important, Design 17.3 overcomes the great weakness of Design 16.2, namely, it supples a comparison control group against which the difference, $Y_a - Y_b$, can be checked. With only one group, we can never know whether history, maturation (or both), or the experimental manipulation X produced the change in Y. When a control group is added, the situation becomes radically altered. After all, if the groups are equated, the effects of history and maturation, if present, should be present in both groups. If the mental ages of the children of the experimental group increase, so should the mental ages of the children of the control group. Then, if there is still a difference between the Y measures of the two groups, it should not be due to history or maturation. That is, if something happens to affect the experimental subjects between the pretest and the posttest, this something should also affect the subjects of the control group. Similarly, the effect of testing—Campbell's *reactive* measures—should be controlled. For if the testing affects the members of the experimental group it should similarly affect the members of the control group. (There is, however, a concealed weakness here, which will be discussed later.) This is the main strength of the well-planned and well-executed before-after, experimental-control group design.

On the other hand, before-after designs have a troublesome aspect, which decreases the external validity of the experiment, although the internal validity is not affected. This source of difficulty is the pretest. A pretest can have a *sensitizing effect* on subjects. For example, the subjects may possibly be alerted to certain events in their environment that they might not ordinarily notice. If the pretest is an attitude scale, it can sensitize subjects to the issues or problems mentioned in the scale. Then, when the X treatment is administered to the experimental group, the subjects of this group may be responding not so much to the attempted influence, the communication, or whatever method is used to change attitudes, as to a combination of their increased sensitivity to the issues *and* the experimental manipulation.

Since such interaction effects are not immediately obvious, and since they contain a threat to the external validity of experiments, it is worthwhile to consider them a bit further. One would think that, since both the experimental and the control groups are pretested, the effect of pretesting, if any, would ensure the validity of the experiment. Let us assume that no pretesting was done, that is, that Design 17.2 was used. Other things equal, a difference between the experimental and the control groups after experimental manipulation of X can be assumed to be due to X. There is no reason to suppose that one group is more sensitive or more alert than the other, since they both face the testing situation *after* X. But when a pretest is used, the results differ. While the pretest sensitizes both groups, it can make the experimental subjects respond to X, wholly or partially, because of the sensitivity. What we have, then, is a lack of generalizability: it may be possible to generalize to pretested groups but not to unpretested ones. Clearly such a situation is disturbing to the researcher, since who wants to generalize to pretested groups?

If this weakness is important, why do we say that this is a good design? While the possible interaction effect described above may be serious in some research, it is doubtful that it is very serious in educational research, provided that adequate precautions are taken. Testing is an accepted and normal part of most school and college situations, and as such, should have no great sensitizing effect. Still, there may be times when it does. The rule Campbell and Stanley give is a good one: when highly unusual testing procedures are to be used, it is best to use designs that do not involve pretests, such as Design 17.4.

DESIGN **17.4**   SIMULATED BEFORE-AFTER FORM—RANDOMIZED

$$\boxed{R} \quad \frac{\qquad\qquad X \qquad\qquad Y_a}{Y_b}$$

The value of this design is doubtful, even though it is included among the adequate designs. The scientific demand for a comparison is satisfied: there is a comparison group (lower line). A major weakness of Design 16.3 (a pallid version of Design 17.4) is, of course, remedied by the randomization. Recall that with Design 16.3 we were unable to know beforehand that the experimental and control groups were equivalent. Design 17.4 calls for subjects to be assigned to the two groups at random. Thus, it can be assumed that they are statistically equal. Such a design might be used when one is worried about the reactive effect of pretesting, or when, due to the exigencies of practical situations, one has no other choice. Such an educational situation occurs when one has the opportunity to try a method or some educational innovation only once. To test the method's efficacy, one provides a base line for judging the effect of X on Y by pretesting a group similar to the experimental group. Then Y_a is tested against Y_b.

This design is a borderline design. Its validity breaks down if the two groups are not both randomly selected from the same population or if the subjects are not assigned to the two groups at random. Even then, it has the weaknesses mentioned in connection with other similar designs, namely, other possible variables may be influential in the interval between Y_b and Y_a. In other words, Design 17.4 is superior to Design 16.3, but it should not be used if a better design is available.

Among possible better designs are Designs 17.5 and 17.6, first proposed by Solomon.[12] In most respects they are the strongest designs, since

---

[12] Solomon, *op. cit.*, pp. 137–150. Although this design can have a matching form, it is not discussed here, nor is Solomon's symbolism used.

DESIGN **17.5**   THREE-GROUP FORM—EXPERIMENTAL AND CONTROL

	Y_b	X	Y_a	(Experimental)
$\boxed{R}$	Y_b	$(\sim X)$	Y_a	(Control 1)
		X	Y_a	(Control 2)

to the assets of Design 17.3 they provide a way to avoid possible inter-active effects due to the pretest. In Design 17.5, this is achieved by the second control group (third line). (It seems a bit strange to have a control group with an X, but the group of the third line is really a control group.) With the Y_a measures of this group available, it is possible to check the interaction effect. Suppose the mean of the experimental group is significantly greater than the mean of the first control group (second line). We may doubt whether this difference was really due to X. It might have been produced by increased sensitization of the subjects after the pretest and the interaction of their sensitization and X. We now look at the mean of Y_a of the second control group (third line). It, too, should be significantly greater than the mean of the first control group. If it is, we can assume that the pretest has not unduly sensitized the subjects, or that X is sufficiently strong to override any sensitization-X interaction effect.

DESIGN **17.6**   FOUR-GROUP FORM—EXPERIMENTAL AND CONTROL

	Y_b	X	Y_a	(Experimental)
$\boxed{R}$	Y_b	$(\sim X)$	Y_a	(Control 1)
		X	Y_a	(Control 2)
		$(\sim X)$	Y_a	(Control 3)

An extension of Design 17.5 with one more control group yields a design with potent controls. Actually, if we change the designation of Control 2 to Experimental 2, we have a combination of Designs 17.3 and 17.1, our two best designs, where the former design forms the first two lines and the latter the second two lines. The virtues of both are combined in one design. Campbell says that this design has become the new ideal for social scientists.[13] While this is a strong statement, probably a bit too strong, it indicates the high esteem in which this design is held.

Among the reasons why Design 17.6 is a strong design is that (1) the demand for comparison is well satisfied with the first two lines *and* the second two lines, (2) the randomization assures statistical equivalence of the groups, and (3) history and maturation are controlled with the first two lines of the design. The possible interaction effect due to possible

[13] Campbell, *op. cit.*, p. 303.

pretest subject sensitization is controlled by the first three lines. By adding the fourth line possible temporary contemporaneous effects that may have occurred between Y_b and Y_a can be controlled. The clearest way to look at this design is as a combination of Designs 17.3 and 17.1. If we combine these designs, we see that we have the power of each test separately and the power of replication because, in effect, there are two experiments. If Y_a of Experimental is significantly greater than Control 1, and Control 2 is significantly greater than Control 3, together with a consistency of results between the two experiments, this is strong evidence, indeed, of the validity of our research hypothesis.

What is wrong with this paragon of designs? It certainly looks fine on paper. There seem to be only two sources of weakness. One is practicability—it is harder to run two simultaneous experiments than one and the researcher encounters the difficulty of locating more subjects of the same kind.

The other difficulty is statistical. Note that there is a lack of balance of groups. There are four actual groups, but not four complete sets of measures. Using the first two lines, that is, with Design 17.3, one can subtract Y_b from Y_a and work with difference scores. With the second two lines, one can test the Y_a's against each other with a t test or F test, but the problem is how to obtain one over-all statistical approach? One solution is to test the Y_a's of Controls 2 and 3 against the average of the two Y_b's (the first two lines), as well as to test the significance of the difference of the Y_a's of the first two lines. In addition, Solomon originally suggested a 2×2 factorial analysis of variance, using the four Y_a sets of measures.[14] Solomon's suggestion is outlined in Fig. 17.4.

	X	~X
Pretested	Y_a, Experimental	Y_a, Control 1
Not Pretested	Y_a, Control 2	Y_a, Control 3

FIG. 17.4

A careful study will reveal that this design is a fine example of research thinking, a nice blending of design and analysis. With this analysis we can study the main effects, X and $\sim X$, and Pretested and Not Pretested. What is more interesting, we can test the interaction of pretesting and X and get a clear answer to the previous problem.

While this and other complex designs have decided strengths, it is doubtful that they can be used routinely. In fact, they should probably be saved for very important experiments in which, perhaps, hypotheses

[14] Solomon, *op. cit.*, p. 146; Campbell, *op. cit.*, p. 303.

already tested with simpler designs are again tested with greater rigor and control. Indeed, it is recommended that designs like those of Designs 17.5 and 17.6 and certain variants of Design 17.6 to be discussed later, be reserved for definitive tests of research hypotheses after a certain amount of preliminary experimentation has been done.

VARIANTS OF BASIC DESIGNS

Designs 17.1 through 17.6 are the *basic* "true" experimental designs. Some variants of these designs have already been indicated. Additional experimental and control groups can be added as needed, but the basic core ideas remain the same. It is always wise to consider the possibility of adding experimental and control groups. Within reason, the addition of such groups provides more evidence of the validity of the study hypotheses as we saw clearly with Design 17.6. We saw that this design was a combination of two other basic designs, combining the strengths of both and adding replication power, as well as further controls. Such advantages lead to the principle that, whenever we consider a research design, we should always consider the possibility of adding more experimental groups as *replications* or *variants* of experimental and control groups.

Important variants of the basic design are *time designs*. The form of Design 17.6 might be altered to include a span of time:

Y_b	X	Y_a
Y_b	$(\sim X)$	Y_a
	X	Y_a
	$(\sim X)$	Y_a

The Y_a's of the third and fourth lines are observations of the dependent variable at any specified later date. Such an alteration, of course, changes the purpose of the design and would cause some of the virtues of Design 17.6 to be lost. We might, if we had the time, the patience, and the resources, retain all the former benefits and still extend in time by adding two more groups to Design 17.6 itself.

Compromise Designs   It is possible, indeed necessary, to use designs that are compromises with true experimentation. Recall that true experimentation requires at least two groups, one receiving an experimental treatment and one not receiving the treatment or receiving it in different form. The true experiment requires the manipulation of at least one independent variable, the random assignment of subjects to groups, and the random assignment of treatments to groups. When one or more of these prerequisites is not present for one reason or another, we have a *compromise design*. Although there are of course many possibilities of compromise design, only one will be discussed at length below.

COMPROMISE EXPERIMENTAL GROUP-CONTROL GROUP DESIGN Perhaps the most commonly used design is the experimental group-control group pattern in which one has no clear assurance that the experimental and control groups are equivalent. The structure of this design has already been considered in Design 17.3. The compromise form is as follows:

DESIGN 17.7 COMPROMISE EXPERIMENTAL GROUP-CONTROL GROUP

Y_b	X	Y_a	(Experimental)
Y_b	$(\sim X)$	Y_a	(Control)

The difference between Designs 17.3 and 17.7 is sharp. In Design 17.7, there is no randomized assignment of subjects to groups, as in 17.3 (a), nor is there matching of subjects and then random assignment, as in 17.3 (b). Design 17.7, therefore, is subject to the weaknesses due to the possible lack of equivalence between the groups in variables other than X. Researchers commonly take pains to establish equivalence by other means, and to the extent they are successful in doing so, to this extent the design is valid. This is done in ways discussed below.

The fact must be faced that very frequently in research it is extremely difficult or impossible to equate groups by random selection or random assignment, or by matching. Should one then give up doing the research? By no means. Every effort should be made, first, to select and to assign at random. If both of these are not possible, perhaps matching and random assignment can be accomplished. If they are not, an effort should be made at least to use samples from the same population or to use samples as alike as possible. The experimental treatments should be assigned at random. Then the similarity of the groups should be checked using any information available—sex, age, social class, and so on. The equivalence of the groups should be checked using the means and standard deviations of the pretests: t tests and F tests will do. The distributions should also be checked. Although one cannot have the assurance that randomization gives, if these items all check one can go ahead with the study knowing at least that there is no evidence against the equivalence assumption.

These precautions increase the possibilities of attaining internal validity. Since the groups are "equal" on the dependent variable, one can assume, if the differences (D scores) between the pretest and the posttest of the experimental group are significantly greater than the differences of the control group, that the discrepancy is explained not by history and maturation, for example, but by the experimental manipulation, X. There are still difficulties, all of which are subordinate to one main difficulty, called *selection*. (These other difficulties will not be discussed here. For detailed discussion, see the Campbell and Stanley chapter previously cited. Another valuable reference is Underwood's book, *Psychological Research*.[15])

Selection is one of the difficult and troublesome problems of research. Since its aspects will be discussed in detail in Chap. 20 on ex post facto research, only a brief description will be given here. The most important reason for the insistence on random selection, and especially random assignment, is to avoid the difficulties of selection. When subjects are selected into groups on bases extraneous to the research purposes, we call this "selection," or more accurately, "self-selection." To take an example, let us assume that volunteers are used in the experimental group and other subjects are used as controls. If the volunteers differ in a characteristic related to *Y*, the dependent variable, the ultimate difference between the experimental and control groups may be due to this characteristic rather than to *X*. Volunteers, for instance, may be more intelligent (or less intelligent) than nonvolunteers. If we were doing an experiment with some kind of learning as the dependent variable, obviously the volunteers might perform better on *Y* because of superior intelligence, despite the initial likeness of the two groups on the pretest. (Note that, if we had used only volunteers and had assigned them to experimental and control groups at random, the selection difficulty would disappear. External validity or representativeness, however, is decreased.)

Another more frequent example in educational research is to take some school classes for the experimental group and others for the control group. If a fairly large number of classes are selected and assigned at random to experimental and control groups, there is no great problem. But if they are not assigned at random, certain ones may select themselves into the experimental groups, and these classes may have characteristics that predispose them to have higher mean *Y* scores than the other classes. For example, their teachers may be more alert, more intelligent, more aggressive. These characteristics interact with the selection to produce, irrespective of *X*, the manipulation, higher experimental group than control group *Y* scores. In other words, something that influences the selection process, as do the volunteer subjects, also influences the dependent variable measures. This happens even though the pretest may show the groups to be the same on the dependent variable. The *X* manipulation is "effective," but it is not effective in and of itself. It is effective because of selection, or *self-selection*.

Time Designs   A common research problem, especially in studies of the development and growth of children, involves the study of individuals and groups using time as a variable. Such studies are longitudinal studies

---

[15] Underwood, *op. cit.*, chaps. 4 and 5.

of subjects, often children, at different points in time. One such design among many might be:

DESIGN 17.8   A LONGITUDINAL TIME DESIGN

$$Y_1 \qquad Y_2 \qquad X \qquad Y_3 \qquad Y_4$$

Note the similarity to Design 16.2 where a group is compared to itself. The use of Design 17.8 allows us to avoid one of the difficulties of Design 16.2. Its use makes it possible to separate reactive measurement effects from the effect of X. It also enables us to see, if the measurements have a reactive effect, whether X has an effect over and above that effect. The reactive effect should show itself at Y_2; this can be contrasted with Y_3. If there is an increase at Y_3 over and above the increase at Y_2, it can be attributed to X. A similar argument applies for maturation and history.

One difficulty with longitudinal or time studies, especially with children, is the growth or learning that occurs over a period of time. Children do not stop growing and learning for research convenience. The longer the time period, the more of a problem this becomes. In other words, time itself is a variable in a sense. With a design like Design 16.2, $Y_b \quad X \quad Y_a$, these time variables can confound X, the experimental independent variable. If there is a significant difference between Y_a and Y_b, one cannot tell whether X or a time variable caused the change. But with Design 17.8, one has other measures of Y and thus a base line against which to compare the change in Y presumably due to X.

Campbell and Stanley believe that history is the most serious problem in this design. The idea here is that it was not X that produced a change in Y but some other event or combination of events occurring during the experimental period. History *is* a problem, but if other X's are operative, they should show up between, say Y_1 and Y_2, as well as between Y_2 and Y_3. If there are constantly recurring extraneous events or variables other than the experimental X, naturally history will decrease the internal validity of any time study. Researchers must be particularly alert to such other possibilities to prevent their occurrence, and should either take them into account in the interpretation of results or demonstrate that the experimental manipulation X is greater than any such extraneous influences.

Take an educational example to illustrate time research and possible extraneous influences. Suppose a board of education, concerned about the morale of its teaching staff, institutes a new policy calculated to improve morale. The administrative staff has two measures of staff morale gathered at three-month intervals, Y_1 and Y_2. The new policy, X, is instituted. The staff's morale is measured again on two subsequent occasions, Y_3 and Y_4. Assume that the results, when graphed (time data should probably always be graphed), are as shown in Fig. 17.5. It can be seen that X

seems to have had an effect over and above the effect of time. While morale seems to have been increasing before X, a relatively sharp rise occurred after X. Then the previous rate of rise continued. The only trouble is: Did something else occur between Y_2 and Y_3 to cause the rise in morale? It is probably unlikely, but one must examine the situation carefully. Maybe the superintendent took some other action at the same time the board of education changed the policy in question.

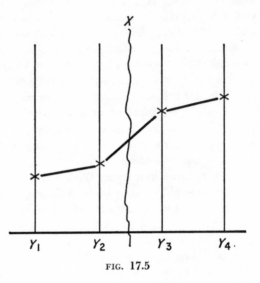

FIG. 17.5

It is easy to transfer the above example to studies of child growth and learning data. The Y's might be measurements of reading proficiency; X might be a new method of teaching reading. Results like those of Fig. 17.5 would look encouraging to the teacher. Here we have to be even more cautious. If a learning study is being done, one or more control groups are essential for reasons already considered and also because of the Hawthorne effect.[16] Almost any change, any extra attention, any experimental manipulation, or even the absence of manipulation but the knowledge that a study is being done, is enough to cause subjects to change. In short, if we pay attention to people, they respond. In the example, above, perhaps any method, as long as it was different from the usual classroom routine, would cause reading scores to rise—thus the need for a control group to which another placebo method could be given. (It is difficult to conceive of a control group in the board of education-staff morale situation.)

[16] This effect is named after the Hawthorne plant of the Western Electric Corporation where it was first noted. A good, brief, and readily available account of some of this research may be found in G. Homans, "Group Factors in Worker Productivity," in E. Maccoby, T. Newcomb, and E. Hartley, eds., *Readings in Social Psychology*, 3rd ed. New York: Holt, Rinehart and Winston, Inc., 1958, pp. 583–595.

The statistical analysis of time measures is a special and troublesome problem: the usual tests of significance applied to time measures can yield spurious results. One reason is that such data tend to be highly variable, and it is easy to interpret changes not due to X as due to X. That is, in time data, individual and mean scores tend to move around a good bit. It is easy to fall into the trap of seeing one of these shifts as "significant," especially if it accords with our hypothesis. If we can legitimately assume that influences other than X, both random and systematic, are uniform over the whole series of Y's, the statistical problem can be solved.[17] But such an assumption may be, and probably often is, unwarranted.

The researcher who does time studies should make a special study of the statistical problems and should consult a statistician. For the classroom teacher and educational administrator, this statistical complexity is unfortunate in that it may discourage needed practical studies. Since longitudinal single-group designs are particularly well-suited to individual class research, it is recommended that in longitudinal studies of methods or studies of children in educational situations analysis be confined to drawing graphs of results and interpreting them qualitatively. Crucial tests, especially those for published studies, however, must be buttressed with statistical tests.

Naturally, there are possible variations of Design 17.8. One important variation is to add one or more control groups; another is to add more time observations. Still another is to add more X's, more experimental interventions.

EXPERIMENTAL AND NONEXPERIMENTAL RESEARCH

Two strong tendencies seem to exist among researchers: one toward experimental research and one toward nonexperimental research. We have the individual who says that most educational and psychological research should be experimental and then the individual who says experiments in education and psychology are absurd. Perhaps half the research in psychology and education, and most of the research in sociology and anthropology, are nonexperimental. Some psychological, sociological, and educational researchers might even say that the most important and interesting research problems do not lend themselves to an experimental approach.

Ideally, we should, whenever possible, approach research problems and test research hypotheses both experimentally and nonexperimentally. Whenever an independent variable can be manipulated, an experimental approach can and should be used.

[17] For a statistical discussion, see A. Edwards, *Experimental Design in Psychological Research*, rev. ed. New York: Holt, Rinehart and Winston, Inc., 1960, pp. 148–152 and chap. 14.

Many important variables, however, cannot be studied experimentally, because they are not manipulable—at least not in our society. Think of intelligence, aptitudes, child training, religious values, conscience, honesty, characteristics of teachers, juvenile delinquency, home environment, and many others. Some of these variables can conceivably be manipulated, but by their very nature most of them cannot be. Many other variables are inherently manipulable: reinforcement, drill, teaching methods, disciplinary methods, school and class environments, and certain teacher behaviors. There are other variables that are both measurable and manipulable. Anxiety and frustration are good examples. In short, the very multiplicity and complexity of variables tell us that it is misleading to insist upon a preponderance of experimental or nonexperimental research in education, psychology, and sociology.

STUDY SUGGESTIONS

1. Suppose that you are an educational psychologist and plan to test the hypothesis that feeding-back psychological information to teachers effectively enhances the children's learning, by increasing the teacher's understanding of the children. Outline an *ideal* research design to test this hypothesis, assuming that you have complete command of the situation and plenty of money and help. (*These are important conditions*, which are included to free the reader from the practical limitations that so often compromise good research designs out of existence.) Set up alternative designs, as follows:
   (a) A design with complete randomization.
   (b) A matching design, with randomization.
   Now compromise the ideal. Set up alternative designs, as follows:
   (c) A matching design, without randomization.
   (d) A compromise design.
   How do these four designs compare in their control powers? Which design, do you think, best tests the hypothesis? In the findings of which design can you put the greatest faith? Why?
2. A college faculty group is to study a core curriculum program instituted during the previous year. All incoming freshmen are to be required to take this program. Discuss the problems and difficulties the researchers face. How much faith can be put in their findings?
3. The faculty of a university school of education decides to begin a core curriculum for all undergraduates and to study its effectiveness. A faculty research group is asked to study the program for two years. The research group, wishing to have a group with which to compare the core curriculum group, requests that the regular program be continued for two years and that students be allowed to volunteer

for the core program or the regular program. In this way, the group feels it will have an experimental and a control group.

Discuss the group's proposal critically. Would you have faith in its findings at the end of the two years? Give reasons for reacting positively or negatively to the proposal. What research design would you like to set up?

4. Imagine that you are a graduate school professor and that you are asked to judge the worth of a proposed doctoral thesis. The doctoral student is a school superintendent who is instituting a new type of administration into his school system. He plans to study the effects of the new administration for a three-year period and then write his Doctor of Education thesis. To keep the study objective he will not study any other school situation.

Discuss the candidate's proposal, keeping this question in mind: If the study is completed, should he be awarded the degree? Is such a study suitable for doctoral work?

5. In a study of the relation between the attitudes of children toward school and counseling in the junior high school, an investigator took 30 eighth-grade children who, because of disciplinary problems, had been referred for counseling during the previous year, and matched each child with another eighth-grade child, not referred for counseling, on sex and intelligence. He compared the attitudes of the two groups toward school at the beginning and at the end of the year and found a significant difference at the beginning of the year but no significant difference at the end. He concluded that counseling had a salutary effect on children's attitudes toward school.

Criticize this research: Is it good? Is it bad? How good? How bad? Bear the following in mind: sampling, group comparability, and control.

6. The first sentence of this chapter is: "Design is data discipline." What does this sentence mean? Justify it.

18 RESEARCH DESIGN AND APPLICATIONS: RANDOMIZED GROUPS

It is difficult to tell anyone how to do research. About all one can do is to try to make sure that the beginner has a grasp of the possibilities. The selection among the possibilities then becomes *his* problem. In tackling a research problem, the investigator should let his mind roam, speculate about possibilities, even guess. Once the possible alternatives are known, the intuitive stage of thinking can enrich the research conception by leading more effectively to the analytical stage of organizing and structuring the problem. The investigator is then ready to plan his approach to the problem and to decide what research and analytical methods he will use to execute his ideas. Good research design is not pure analysis. Intuitive thinking, too, is essential because it helps the investigator to arrive at solutions that are not routine. Perhaps most important, it should be remembered that intuitive thinking and analytical thinking depend upon knowledge, understanding, and experience.

The main purposes of this chapter and the next are to enrich previous design and statistical discussions with actual research examples and to suggest basic possibilities for structuring research, so that the student can ultimately solve research problems.

SIMPLE RANDOMIZED SUBJECTS DESIGN

In Chaps. 11 and 12 the statistics of simple one-way and factorial analyses of variance were discussed and illustrated. The design behind the earlier discussion is here called *randomized subjects design*. The general design paradigm is Design 17.1:[1]

$$\boxed{R} \quad \frac{X \qquad Y}{(\sim X) \qquad Y}$$

[1] Henceforth, when the term "general design" is used, we refer to the type of paradigm given above and discussed in chaps. 16 and 17. "Analysis of variance design" will refer to the type of paradigm used in the earlier statistical chapters, in this chapter, and in chap. 19.

Research Examples   Examples of Design 17.1 in educational research, strange to say, are not numerous. Three examples are given here, in two of which we do not know whether or not randomization was used. Unfortunately, many investigators do not report *how* subjects were assigned to groups, but the studies have been included to point up the need to use randomization whenever possible.

HURLOCK INCENTIVES STUDY   An excellent example of a randomized subjects design is the Hurlock experiment (see Chap. 11). Three experimental groups and one control group were used: Praised, Reproved, Ignored, and Control. Pupils were assigned to the four groups at random (12 pupils to each group). The independent variable was Incentive and the dependent variable Achievement, the latter measured by the number of correct answers on an addition test. Assigning X and Y symbols to the independent and dependent variables, the design paradigm is:

$$X_1 \qquad X_2 \qquad X_3 \qquad X_4$$

Y Measures

The design is simple, clearcut, and effective—simple one-way analysis of variance.

WICKENS' STIMULUS AND RESPONSE GENERALIZATION STUDY   An interesting, ingenious, and important study with significant implications for education is Wickens' study of stimulus and response generalization using conditioning.[2] This study is noteworthy on two related counts: (1) evidently no randomization was used, and (2) randomization was probably deemed unnecessary. The second point needs elaboration. With any type of human response, especially physiological response, that is universal to *homo sapiens* and that *does not exhibit a wide range of individual differences,* it is sometimes fairly safe not to randomize. If all people are pretty much alike in a characteristic under study, it obviously makes no difference whether or not randomization is used. In this respect, any single individual is representative of the whole human race. The possession of blood, a heart beat, and lungs are examples. Of course, the type of blood and the rate of the heart beat and lung action, when used as variables, radically change the picture. At any rate, in Wickens' study, it was probably assumed that all subjects are conditionable. Still, it would have been better to assign subjects to groups at random, because we know that there are individual differences in conditioning or conditionability. It is conceivable that such differences might affect the experimental outcomes.

Returning to Wickens' experiment, the responses of subjects to

[2] D. Wickens, "Studies of Response Generalization in Conditioning. I. Stimulus Generalization during Response Generalization," *Journal of Experimental Psychology,* XXXIII (1943), 221–227.

shock were conditioned to a tone. After being conditioned, the subjects' hands were turned over and their conditioned responses to the first tone and to other tones were tested. Three experimental groups and one control group were used. Groups I, II, and III, the experimental groups, were conditioned and then tested differently. Although the details do not concern us, in general, the Ss were conditioned to one tone and either tested with that tone or with tones one or two octaves above or below the original conditioned tone. The results, in mean number of responses (flexion in a new hand position), indicated that stimulus generalization and response generalization had occurred. The means for the four groups were: I, 5.87; II, 3.69; III, 4.19; and control, .16.

Wickens did a one-way analysis of variance of the data of Groups I, II, and III to show that they did not differ in mean response. The F ratio was not significant. This demonstrated stimulus generalization (since the Ss responded similarly to the original tone *and* to the tones one and two octaves away from the original tone). He then tested each of the experimental groups against the control group. Each comparison was significant, which demonstrated response generalization (because the control group was shocked but not conditioned, and the responses were given with the hand turned over).

BIRCH AND RABINOWITZ TRANSFER OF TRAINING STUDY   Birch and Rabinowitz in essence asked the questions: What is the relation between past experience and productive thinking? Does past experience, under some circumstances, have a negative effect on productive thinking? [3] This study has a simple design of two experimental groups and one control group. It lacks randomization, partly for good reason. It still belongs in the Design 17.1 classification, because subjects could at least have been assigned at random to the two experimental groups. (The authors do not say how subjects were assigned to the groups, except in the case of the control group.) Such assignment is particularly important in this case since the dependent variable is problem-solving, a variable strongly influenced by a number of individual characteristics. The study is so original and potentially significant for education, however, that its weaknesses can perhaps be overlooked.

The two experimental groups were called R and S. All experimental subjects were given experience completing electrical circuits, R subjects with a *relay* and S subjects with a *switch*. Ss had little or no prior experience with electrical wiring. Control subjects, C, engineering students who had considerable experience with electrical wiring, were given no training. All Ss were given a problem-solving task in which each S was required to tie together the ends of two cords suspended from the ceiling. The two

[3] H. Birch and H. Rabinowitz, "The Negative Effect of Previous Experience on Productive Thinking," *Journal of Experimental Psychology*, XLI (1951), 121–125.

cords were so placed that the problem could only be solved if the end of one cord were weighted and swung like a pendulum. In the present experiment, the only objects that could have been used for weighting were the relay and the switch.

Birch and Rabinowitz's notion was that, because the subjects had had prior experience with the relay and the switch *as* a relay and *as* a switch, they would exhibit "functional fixedness." This is an inability to solve a problem using the switch or the relay *as tools,* because their use had become "fixed" in another functional context. The results supported this hypothesis. The control Ss used the relay and the switch indiscriminately: half used one and half used the other. But the experimental Ss seemed to be "functionally fixed." All the relay Ss used the switch, and most of the switch Ss used the relay. When asked why they chose the implement they did, they gave "good" reasons for doing so. The authors concluded that learning broad, general, nonspecific notions about things gives the experience necessary for productive thinking, and that experiences and perceptions of a limited kind lead to "functional fixedness."

FACTORIAL DESIGNS

The basic general design is still Design 17.1, although the variation of the basic experimental group-control group pattern is drastically altered by the addition of other experimental conditions or independent variables. Following a definition of factorial analysis of variance given earlier, it can be said that *factorial design is the structure of research where two or more independent variables are juxtaposed in order to study their independent and interactive effects on a dependent variable.*

The reader may find it difficult to fit the older and simpler experimental group-control group paradigm into the factorial framework. There are a number of possibilities. Recall that an *active* variable is a manipulated variable and an *assigned* variable is one using subjects who are apportioned or assigned to cells of the design on the basis of differential possession of characteristics. We have the independent variables A and B and the dependent variable Y.[4] The simplest factorial design, the 2×2, has three possibilities: both A and B active; A active, B assigned (or vice versa); and both A and B assigned. The last possibility, both independent variables assigned, is the ex post facto case. Returning to the experimental group-control group notion, A can be divided into A_1 and A_2, experimental and control, as usual, with the additional independent variable B par-

---

[4] Instead of using X for the independent variables, we now return to the earlier practice of using the early letters of the alphabet. To be consistent with the other paradigms of Part IV, Y will be used to indicate the dependent variable. (In statistics texts, X's are used in the cells of statistical design paradigms.)

titioned into B_1 and B_2. B can be either active or assigned. Since this structure is very familiar to us by now, we need only discuss one or two procedural details.

The ideal subject assignment procedure is to assign subjects to the four cells at random. If both A and B are active variables, this is possible and easy. Simply give the subjects numbers arbitrarily from 1 through N, N being the total number of subjects. Then, using a table of random numbers, write down numbers 1 through N as they turn up in the table. Place the numbers into four groups as they turn up and then assign the four groups of subjects to the four cells. To be safe, assign the groups of subjects to the experimental treatments (the four cells) at random, too. Label the groups 1, 2, 3, and 4. Then draw these numbers from a table of random numbers. Assume that the table yielded the numbers in this order: 3, 4, 1, 2. Assign Group 3 subjects to the upper left cell, Group 4 subjects to the upper right cell, and so on.

Often B will be an assigned variable, like sex, intelligence, achievement, anxiety, self-perception, race, and so on. The subject assignment must be altered. First, since B is an assigned variable, there is no possibility of assigning subjects to B_1 and B_2 at random. If B were the variable sex, the best we can do is to assign males first at random to the cells A_1B_1 and A_2B_1, and then females to the cells A_1B_2 and A_2B_2. With the ex post facto case where both variables are assigned, random assignment is, of course, not possible.

Factorial Designs with More than Two Variables   We can often improve the design and sharpen up the information obtained from a piece of research by adding groups. Instead of A_1 and A_2, and B_1 and B_2, the experiment might profit from A_1, A_2, A_3, and A_4, and B_1, B_2, and B_3. There are limitations to the use of this procedure, of course: more subjects and a mode of measurement sufficiently reliable to warrant partitioning are needed. Moreover, some variables are natural dichotomies. In other words, while partitioning and its rules are good guides to proper procedures, the research benefits to be derived and the cost of these benefits must be calculated.

Practical and statistical problems increase and sometimes become quite difficult as variables are added. Suppose we have a $3 \times 2 \times 2$ design that has $3 \times 2 \times 2 = 12$ cells, each of which has to have at least two subjects, and preferably many more. (It is possible, but not very sensible, to have one subject per cell if one can have more than one. There are, of course, designs that have only one subject per cell.) If we decide that 10 subjects per cell are necessary, $12 \times 10 = 120$ subjects will have to be obtained and assigned at random. The problem is more acute with one more variable and the practical manipulation of the research situation is also more difficult. But the successful handling of such an experiment allows us to test a number of hypotheses and yields a great deal of information.

Four-variable factorial designs are not too uncommon in the psychological literature, but they seem to be rare in educational research. The possibilities of combinations of three, four, and five-variable designs give a wide variety of possible designs: $2 \times 5 \times 3$, $4 \times 4 \times 2$, $3 \times 2 \times 4 \times 2$, $4 \times 3 \times 2 \times 2$, and so on.

Research Examples of Factorial Designs Several good examples of two- and three-dimensional factorial designs were described in Chap. 12. (The restudy of these examples is recommended, because the reasoning behind the essential design can now be more easily grasped.) Four more factorial studies of unusual interest are summarized below. The first, second, and fourth are essentially Design 17.1 studies, despite the fact that one is a 3×2, another a 2×2, and the third a $2 \times 2 \times 3 \times 3$. The third is a Design 17.6 study in which a factorial analysis of variance was worked into the analysis, as suggested in Chap. 17.

DI VESTA AND BOSSART STUDY OF LABELING AND ATTITUDES[5] The first example is one of the many psychological studies that have important implications for education. It is distinguished, too, by a very large number of subjects and a 3×2 factorial design. Di Vesta and Bossart tested the hypothesis that attitudes expressed toward situations are influenced by the labels attached to the situations. (Note the interesting educational implications. Studies like this should be done with children in a wide variety of school and class situations.) Three types of "sets" were presented randomly to 1087 entering freshmen of a large university. (A *set* is a temporary predisposition to behave or react in a certain way.) The sets were engendered by differing instructions about a housing communication. One set advocated *ethical* considerations; another advocated the *betterment of society;* still another stressed the *management of one's financial affairs.* In other words, *S*s were instructed to consider the communication ethically, societally, and financially; the subjects' attitudes toward the issues were then measured. The responses of men and women students were kept separate.

This is a 3×2 factorial design with one active variable, Sets, and one assigned variable, Sex. In order to use factorial analysis of variance, the experimenters randomly eliminated 283 *S*s so that there were 134 *S*s in each cell. (This is one solution to the frequently difficult problem of disproportionate numbers in cells.) The design and the results are given in Table 18.1. The analysis of variance results showed that the Sex means were significantly different, indicating that females responded more negatively than males to the somewhat unethical situation. The *F* ratio for Sets (the differences between the three Sets means) was also significant, thus

5 F. DiVesta and P. Bossart, "The Effect of Sets Induced by Labeling on the Modification of Attitudes," *Journal of Personality*, XXVI (1958), 379–387.

supporting the original hypothesis. The interaction was not significant. Evidently the evaluations people put on situations and problem solutions depend upon the points of view from which the evaluations are made.

TABLE 18.1   DESIGN AND DATA OF DI VESTA AND BOSSART STUDY [a]

| | *Set* | | | |
	Ethical	Social	Economic	*M*
Male	3.31	2.91	3.01	3.08
Female	3.89	3.69	3.48	3.69
M:	3.60	3.30	3.25	

[a] Table entries are means. Marginal means added by the author: the larger the mean, the more negative the attitude.

This study is clean-cut. The randomization gave good assurance of equality. The control of sex by adding it as a variable was a good move. The experimental situation was simple, economical, and effective. The main drawback—a very common one, but with not too serious an effect on the results—is the population: college students. Would the general population react similarly? This question can naturally not be answered using these data. Thus the study lacks external validity despite its good internal validity.

AMIDON-FLANDERS STUDY OF TEACHER INFLUENCE[6]   The problem of the relation between teacher presentation and student learning is an old and important one. Amidon and Flanders used a basic 2×2 factorial design to investigate the problem among eighth-grade students with a tendency toward dependence. Dependent students were used for the study because it was believed that they might be overly concerned with authority figures and group pressures. Students were selected at random from an eighth-grade population from which the top 25 percent in dependent-proneness were used for the experiment (140 students). Unfortunately, the authors do not say whether or not *S*s were assigned to treatments at random.

Influence

Direct   Indirect

Goals

Clear

ACHIEVEMENT

MEASURES

Unclear

FIG. 18.1

6 E. Amidon and N. Flanders, "The Effects of Direct and Indirect Teacher Influence on Dependent-Prone Students Learning Geometry," *Journal of Educational Psychology*, LII (1961), 286–291. Only the barest skeleton of this study is given. The analysis was much more complex than is indicated here.

The independent variables were Influence and Goals. Influence had two experimental aspects or treatments: *direct* and *indirect;* Goals had two aspects: *clear* and *unclear.* The design, then, looks like that of Fig. 18.1. There was a significant difference between direct and indirect influences. The students who experienced indirect influence achieved more than the students who experienced direct influence. (*Direct influence* consisted of a lecture, questions, and explanations. *Indirect influence* consisted of discussion and explanations.) Somewhat strangely, there was no difference between the achievement of students under the different goal conditions. Nor was the interaction significant.

LANA STUDY OF PRETEST INTERACTION EFFECTS[7]   This is a methodological study using the Solomon design discussed in Chap. 17 as Design 17.6. It may be recalled that this design is a four-group design, with one experimental group and three control groups, the experimental group and one control group being administered pretests. Lana put Solomon's and Campbell's notions to empirical test. Do pretests have a sensitizing effect on attitudes? Recall one of the major purposes of the Solomon design: to control for possible pretest effects on Y, the dependent variable. Recall also that Solomon suggested, among other statistical analyses, a 2×2 factorial analysis of the four sets of posttest measures to separate the pretest-posttest variance from the variance of the other independent variables. Lana adopted these ideas and put them to good use.

Group I, the experimental group, and Group II, the first control group, were administered an attitudinal pretest. Groups III and IV were not given the pretest. One experimental variable, then, was Pretest-No Pretest. Another experimental variable was Communication-No Communication. Unlike most such attitudinal studies, this latter variable was less important than the pretest variable. The design and part of Lana's data are given in Table 18.2.[8] The difference between the communication and no communication means was significant at the .05 level. The pretest–no-pretest means difference was not significant, but most important, the interaction was not significant. The pretest apparently had no sensitizing effect.

TABLE 18.2   DESIGN AND DATA OF LANA STUDY OF PRETEST
INTERACTION EFFECT

	Pretest	No-Pretest
Communication	42.96	42.90
No communication	40.28	40.77

[7] R. Lana, "Pretest-Treatment Interaction Effects in Longitudinal Studies," *Psychological Bulletin*, LVI (1959), 293–300.

[8] Lana actually used five groups. His design and analysis were more elaborate than indicated above. Still, the basic design is shown. Additional tests were control tests.

To understand this clever study and its findings, we must know clearly what Lana was trying to do: he was testing an interaction hypothesis, that the pretest and the treatment would interact. Listening to Campbell's warning about the danger of pretesting, we might expect that pretested groups, because they were pretested, would be sensitized to receive the communication whereas unpretested groups would not be sensitized. This sensitization, if present, would be demonstrated by a difference between the means of the pretested communication-no communication groups with no such difference present between the means of the unpretested communication-no communication groups. That is, in Table 18.2, the means of the two cells on the top of the table would differ significantly, but the means of the bottom cells would not differ significantly.

HOYT STUDY OF TEACHER KNOWLEDGE AND PUPIL ACHIEVEMENT[9]   This study was planned to answer an important theoretical and practical educational question: What are the effects on the achievement and attitudes of pupils if the teachers are given knowledge of the characteristics of their pupils? An earlier study by Ojemann and Wilkinson had purported to show that such knowledge feedback enhances pupil achievement and personality.[10] Hoyt's study explored several related aspects of the basic question and used recent design and statistical developments to enhance the internal validity of the investigation. He used three factorial designs: $2 \times 2 \times 3 \times 3$; $2 \times 3 \times 3 \times 3$; and 3×3. The first design was used three times for each of three school subjects, and the second and third were used twice, once in each of two school systems.

			Treatments			
	N		T		TO	
Sex	M	F	M	F	M	F
School A { High IQ / Medium IQ / Low IQ						
School B { High IQ / Medium IQ / Low IQ			DEPENDENT VARIABLE MEASURES			

FIG. 18.2

[9] K. Hoyt, "A Study of the Effects of Teacher Knowledge of Pupil Characteristics on Pupil Achievement and Attitudes towards Classwork," *Journal of Educational Psychology*, XLVI (1955), 302–310.

[10] R. Ojemann and F. Wilkinson, "The Effect on Pupil Growth of an Increase in Teachers' Understanding of Pupil Behavior," *Journal of Experimental Education*, VIII (1939), 143–147.

We sketch the design for the first of these designs. The independent variables were Treatments, Ability Level, Sex, and Schools. The three treatments were: no information (*N*), test scores (*T*), and test scores plus other information (*TO*). These are self-explanatory. They were assigned at random to experimental groups. Ability Levels were high, medium, and low IQ. The remaining two variables, Sex and Schools, are obvious. Eighth-grade students were assigned at random *within sex and scholastic aptitude populations*.[11] The design is shown in Fig. 18.2. Since this design is complex, it will be well to examine what a final analysis of variance table of such a design would look like and to know the hypotheses that can be tested. Before doing so, however, it should be noted that the achievement results were mostly indeterminate (or negative). With one interaction exception, the *F* ratios were not significant. A notable positive result was that pupil attitudes toward teachers seemed to improve when there were increases in teacher knowledge, an interesting and important finding.

TABLE 18.3 SOURCES OF VARIANCE AND DEGREES OF FREEDOM FOR A $3 \times 3 \times 2 \times 2$ FACTORIAL DESIGN WITH VARIABLES TREATMENTS, ABILITY, SEX, AND SCHOOL. (TOTAL AND WITHIN DEGREES OF FREEDOM ARE OMITTED)

Source	df
Main Effects:	
*Between Treatments	2
Between Ability Levels	2
Between Sexes	1
Between Schools	1
First-Order Interactions:	
*Interaction: Treatments × Ability	4
*Interaction: Treatments × Sex	2
*Interaction: Treatments × School	2
Interaction: Ability × Sex	2
Interaction: Ability × School	2
Interaction: Sex × School	1
Second-Order Interactions:	
*Interaction: Treatments × Ability × Sex	4
*Interaction: Treatment × Ability × School	4
Interaction: Ability × Sex × School	2
Third-Order Interaction:	
Interaction: Treatment × Ability × Sex × School	4
Within	
Total	

[11] Though not often done, this is very desirable. The procedure is to select and assign within each sex separately and within each ability level separately.

The sources of variance and degrees of freedom of the analysis of variance table are given in Table 18.3. One experiment yields 14 tests! Naturally, a number of these tests are not important and can be ignored. The tests of greatest importance (marked with asterisks in the table) are those involving the treatment variable. The most important test is between Treatments, the first of the main effects. Next in importance, perhaps equally important, are the interactions involving Treatments. Take the interaction Treatments × Sex. If this were significant, it would mean that the amount of information a teacher possesses about students has an influence on student achievement, but boys are influenced differently than girls. Boys with teachers who possess information about their pupils may do better than boys whose teachers do not have such information, whereas it may be the opposite with girls, or it may make no difference one way or the other.[12]

Second-order or triple interactions are harder to interpret. It is probably true that they are rarely significant. If they *are* significant, however, they require special study; one of the best ways to study them is by graphic representation (discussed in an earlier chapter). Crossbreak tables of means are also helpful. The student will find guidance in Edwards' book.[13]

EVALUATION OF RANDOMIZED SUBJECTS DESIGNS

Randomized subjects designs are all variants or extensions of Design 17.1, the basic experimental group-control group design in which subjects are assigned to the experimental and control groups at random. As such they have the strengths of the basic design, the most important of which is the randomization feature and the consequent ability to assume the pre-experimental approximate equality of the experimental groups in all possible independent variables. History and maturation are controlled because very little time elapses between the manipulation of X and the observation and measurement of Y. There is no possible contamination due to pretesting.

Two other strengths of these designs, springing from the many variations possible, are flexibility and applicability. They can be used to help solve many educational research problems, since they seem to be peculiarly well-suited to the types of design problems that arise from educa-

12 The student will find it very helpful to lay out and study the tables for these interactions. For example, the one under discussion would be:

$$N \qquad T \qquad TO$$

Female

Male

Fill in the means and interpret the results for the various combinations.

13 A. Edwards, *Experimental Design in Psychological Research*, rev. ed. New York: Holt, Rinehart and Winston, Inc., 1960, pp. 186–188, 206, 207.

tional problems and hypotheses. The one-way designs, for example, can incorporate any number of methods, and the testing of methods is a major educational need. The variables that constantly need control in educational research—sex, intelligence, aptitude, social class, schools, and many others—can be incorporated into factorial designs and thus be controlled. With factorial designs, too, it is easily possible to have mixtures of active and assigned variables, another important educational research need.

There are weaknesses in these designs, too. One criticism has been that randomized subjects designs do not permit tests of the equality of groups as do before-after designs. Actually, this is not a valid criticism for two reasons: (1) with enough subjects and careful randomization, it can be assumed that the groups are equal, as we have seen, and (2) it *is* possible to check the groups for equality on variables other than Y, the dependent variable. Attributes like sex and social class are easily checked. Data on such variables as intelligence, aptitude, and achievement usually exist in readily available school records. It is an easy matter to count the numbers of boys and girls in the experimental groups, or to run an analysis of variance on, say, intelligence.

Another difficulty is statistical. One should have equal numbers of cases in the cells of factorial designs. (It is possible to work with unequal n's, but it is both clumsy and a threat to interpretation. Small discrepancies are easily cured by dropping out cases at random.) This imposes a limitation on the use of such designs, because it is often not possible to have equal numbers in each cell. One-way randomized designs are not so delicate: unequal numbers are not a difficult problem.[14]

Compared to matched groups designs, randomized subjects designs are usually less precise, that is, the error term is ordinarily larger, other things equal. It is doubtful, however, whether this is a matter for great concern. In some cases it certainly is, for example, where a very sensitive test of a hypothesis is needed. In much behavioral research, though, it is probably desirable to consider as nonsignificant any effect that is insufficiently powerful to make itself felt over and above the random noise of a randomized subjects design.

All in all, then, these are powerful, flexible, useful, and widely applicable designs for educational research. In the opinion of the writer, they are the best all-round designs, perhaps the first to be considered when planning the design of a research study.

[14] The advanced student will find a discussion of unequal n's and the problem of disproportionality in G. Snedecor, *Statistical Methods,* 4th ed. Ames, Iowa: Iowa State College Press, 1946, pp. 284ff.

1. In studying research design, it is useful to do analyses of variance—as many as possible: simple one-way analyses and two-variable factorial analyses. Try even a three-variable analysis. By means of this statistical work you can get a better understanding of the designs. You might well attach variable names to your "data," rather than work with numbers alone. Some useful suggestions for projects with random numbers follow.

   (a) Draw three groups of random numbers, 0 through 9. Name the independent and dependent variables. Express a hypothesis and translate it into design-statistical language. Do a one-way analysis of variance. Interpret.

   (b) Repeat 1 (a) with five groups of numbers.

   (c) Now increase the numbers of one of your groups by 2, and decrease those of another group by 2. Repeat the statistical analysis.

   (d) Draw four groups of random numbers, 10 in each group. Set them up, at random, in a 2 × 2 factorial design. Do a factorial analysis of variance.

   (e) Bias the numbers of the two right-hand cells by adding 3 to each number. Repeat the analysis. Compare with the results of 1 (d).

   (f) Bias the numbers of the data of 1 (d), as follows: add 2 to each of the numbers in the upper left and lower right cells. Repeat the analysis. Interpret.

2. Look up Study Suggestion 2, Chap. 11. Three groups are used. What general design does this example fall under? Why? Is there a "control group"?

3. Look up Study Suggestions 1 and 2, Chap. 12. Work through both examples again. (Are they easier for you now?) Pay particular attention to 2 (d).

4. Suppose that you are the principal of an elementary school. Some of the fourth and fifth-grade teachers want to dispense with workbooks. The superintendent does not like the idea, but he is willing for you to test the notion that workbooks do not make much difference. (One of the teachers even suggests that workbooks may have bad effects on both teachers and pupils.) Set up two research plans and designs to test the efficacy of the workbooks: a one-way design and a factorial design. Consider the variables achievement, intelligence, and sex. You might also consider the possibility of teacher attitude toward workbooks as an independent variable.

5. Here is a difficult research design problem. Imagine that you are the chairman of a committee appointed to evaluate the effects of a core curriculum soon to be established in your school of education undergradu-

ate division. The proponents of the program say that the core program is superior to the conventional program on all counts: achievement, student attitude, and so on. Draw up a research plan and design to test the efficacy of the new program. What are the limitations of the design? What would be the limitations of *any* design in a problem of this kind?

6. Suppose an investigation using methods and sex as the independent variables and achievement as the dependent variable has been done with the results shown in Table 18.4. The numbers in the cells are fictitious means. The F ratios of Methods and Sex are not significant. The interaction F ratio is significant at the .01 level. Interpret these results statistically and substantively. To do the latter, name the three methods.

TABLE 18.4 HYPOTHETICAL DATA (MEANS) OF A FICTITIOUS
FACTORIAL EXPERIMENT

Methods

	A_1	A_2	A_3	
Male	45	45	36	42
Female	35	39	40	38
	40	42	38	

7. A provocative series of researches on writing essays, using rather elaborate factorial designs, has been launched by Julian Stanley and his colleagues at the University of Wisconsin.[15] A number of questions are being asked: about sex differences, reader differences, essay differences, and differences due to different lengths of exposure to English composition writing. Stanley, in one study, plans to use three treatments: much English composition, some English composition, little English composition. This is the active variable. Then he plans to have cross-partitioning on Sex of Reader, Sex of Student, Essays, and certain other characteristics. His design may look something like that of Fig. 18.3.

This design is a new and striking conception. Here is a combination of experimental-educational and psychometric-methodological research. Such a fresh and original approach to old and difficult educational problems is only possible because design conceptions have grown so richly and rapidly in the last 20 years. Study the design and the ideas

---

[15] Personal communications to the writer of January 20 and 30, 1962. Dr. Stanley has requested that the tentative nature of the Wisconsin plans be emphasized and that he be credited only with the initial suggestion for the studies. For the sake of simplicity Dr. Stanley's original tentative design has been altered as shown in Fig. 18.3.

behind it. What questions can be answered by the data gathered from the implementation of this design? Specify three or four of the hypotheses that can be tested. Are possible interactions important?

		Treatments					
		Little Composition		Some Composition		Much Composition	
		Reader Male	Reader Female	Reader Male	Reader Female	Reader Male	Reader Female
Student Male	Essay 1						
	Essay 2			DEPENDENT VARIABLE MEASURES			
Student Female	Essay 1						
	Essay 2						

FIG. **18.3**

19 RESEARCH DESIGN AND APPLICATIONS: CORRELATED GROUPS

One basic principle is behind all correlated-groups[1] designs: there is systematic variance in the dependent variable measures due to the correlation between the groups in some variable related to the dependent variable. This correlation and its concomitant variance can be introduced into the measures—and the design—in three ways: (1) use the same units, for example, subjects, in each of the experimental groups, (2) match units on one or more independent variables that are related to the dependent variable, and (3) use more than one group of units, like classes or schools, in the design. Despite the seeming differences among these three ways of introducing correlation into the dependent variable measures, they are basically the same (see Chap. 13). Now, without repeating the discussion of Chap. 13, we examine the design implications of this basic principle and discuss the three ways of implementing the principle.

THE GENERAL PARADIGM

With the exception of correlated factorial designs, all analysis of variance paradigms of correlated groups designs can be easily outlined. The general paradigm is given in Fig. 19.1. To emphasize the sources of variance, means of columns and rows have been indicated. The individual dependent variable measures (Y's) have also been inserted.[2] It can be

---

[1] The word "group" should be taken to mean set of scores. Then there is no confusion when a repeated trials experiment is classified as a multigroup design.

[2] It is useful to know the system of subscripts to symbols used in mathematics and statistics. A rectangular table of numbers is called a *matrix*. The entries of a matrix are letters and/or numbers. When letters are used, it is common to identify any particular matrix entry with two (sometimes more) subscripts. The first of these indicates the number of the *row*, the second the number of the *column*. Y_{32}, for instance, indicates the Y measure in the third row and the second column. Y_{57} indicates the Y measure of the fifth row and the seventh column. It is also customary to generalize this system by adding letter subscripts. In this book, i symbolizes *any row number* and j *any column number. Any* number of the matrix is represented by Y_{ij}; *any* number of the third row, Y_{3j}; and *any* number of the second column, Y_{i2}.

seen that there are two sources of systematic variance: (1) that due to columns, or treatments, and (2) that due to rows—individual or unit differences. Analysis of variance must be the two-way variety.

Units	X_1	X_2	X_3	.	.	.	X_k	
			Treatments					
1	Y_{11}	Y_{12}	Y_{13}	.	.	.	Y_{1k}	M_1
2	Y_{21}	Y_{22}	Y_{23}	.	.	.	Y_{2k}	M_2
3	Y_{31}	Y_{32}	Y_{33}	.	.	.	Y_{3k}	M_3
.	.	.	.	.	.	.	.	.
.	.	.	.	.	.	.	.	.
.	.	.	.	.	.	.	.	.
n	Y_{n1}	Y_{n2}	Y_{n3}				Y_{nk}	M_n
	M_{X_1}	M_{X_2}	M_{X_3}	.	.	.	M_{X_k}	(M_t)

FIG. 19.1

The student who has studied the correlation-variance argument of Chap. 13, where the statistics and some of the problems of correlated-groups designs were presented, will have no difficulty with the variance reasoning of Fig. 19.1. The intent of the design is to maximize the between-groups variance, identify the between-pairs variance, and minimize the error (residual) variance. The *maxmincon* principle applies here as elsewhere. The only difference, really, between designs of correlated groups and randomized subjects is the rows variance introduced by the correlation.

Units   The units used do not alter the variance principles in the slightest. It is necessary to understand this point clearly. The usual conception of the correlated-groups design seems to be fixed rather rigidly in the matching of subjects. The word "units" was deliberately used in Fig. 19.1 to overcome this conception and to substitute a generalized conception. In principle it does not matter what is substituted for "units." "Subjects," "pairs," "classes," "schools," "school districts," "cities," and "counties" are all appropriate substitutions for "units." The important consideration is whether the units, whatever they are, differ from each other. If they do, *variance between units* is introduced. In this sense, talking about correlated groups or subjects is the same as talking about variance between groups or subjects. The notion of individual differences is extended to *unit differences.*

The real value of correlated-groups designs would seem to be that not only do they enable the investigator to isolate and estimate the variance due to correlation, they also guide him to design research to capitalize on the differences that frequently exist between units. If a research study involves different classes in the same school, these classes are a possible source of variance. Thus it may be wise to use "classes" as units in the design. The well-known differences between schools are very important sources of variance in educational research. They may be handled factorially, or they may be handled in the manner of the designs in this chapter. Indeed, if one looks carefully at a factorial design with two independent variables, one of them *schools,* and at a correlated groups design with units *schools,* one finds, in essence, the same design. Study Fig. 19.2. On the left is a factorial design and on the right a correlated-groups design. But they look the same! They are the same, in variance principle. (The only differences might be numbers of scores in the cells and statistical treatment.)

	Treatments			Treatments	
	A_1	A_2	Schools	A_1	A_2
B_1			1		
Schools B_2			2		
B_3			3		
Factorial Design			Correlated-Groups Design		

FIG. 19.2

One-group Repeated Trials Design   In the one-group repeated trials design, as the name indicates, one group is given different treatments at different times or is measured at different times. In a learning experiment, the same group of subjects may be given several tasks of differing complexity, or the experimental manipulation may be to present learning principles in different orders, say from simple to complex, from complex to simple, from whole to part, from part to whole. Many longitudinal studies fall into this category. Studies of the physical and mental growth of children using this design have been successful, despite its inherent weaknesses. This success is probably due to the resistance of growth processes to other than massive external influences.

It was said earlier that the best possible matching of subjects is to match a subject with himself, so to speak. The difficulties in using this solution of the control problem have also been mentioned. One of these difficulties resembles pretest sensitization, which may produce an interaction between the pretest and the experimentally manipulated variable. Another is simply that subjects mature and learn over time. A subject who has experienced one or two trials of an experimental manipulation and is facing a third trial is a different person than the one who faced trials one and two (especially trial one). Experimental situations differ a great deal, of course. In some situations, repeated trials might not unduly affect the performances of subjects on later trials; in other situations, they might. The problem of how individuals learn or become unduly sensitized during an experiment is a difficult one to solve. In short, *history, maturation,* and *sensitization* are possible weaknesses of repeated trials.

Despite the basic time difficulties, there may be occasions when a one-group repeated trials design would be useful. Certainly in ex post facto analyses of "time" data this is the implicit design. If we have a series of growth measurements of children, for instance, the different times at which the measurements were made correspond to treatments. The paradigm of the design is the same as that of Fig. 19.1. Simply substitute "subjects" for "units" and label $X_1, X_2, \cdots$ "trials."

From this general paradigm special cases can be derived. The simplest case is the one-group, before-after design, Design 16.2 (a), where one group of subjects was given an experimental treatment preceded by a pretest and followed by a posttest. Since the weaknesses of this design have already been mentioned, further discussion is not necessary. It should be noted, though, that this design, especially in its ex post facto form, closely approximates much common-sense observation and thinking. A person might observe educational practices today and decide that they are not too good. In order to make this judgment, he implicitly or explicitly compares today's educational practices with educational practices of the past. From a number of possible causes, depending on his particular bias, he will select one or more reasons for what he believes to be the sorry state of educational affairs: "progressive education," "educationists," "professors of education," "moral degeneration," "lack of firm religious principles," and so on.

Two-group, Experimental Group-Control Group Designs   This design has two forms, the better of which (repeated here) was described in Chap. 17 as Design 17.2:

$\boxed{M_r}$	X	Y	(Experimental)
	$(\sim X)$	Y	(Control)

In this design, subjects are first matched and then assigned to experimental and control groups at random. In the other form, subjects are matched but not assigned to experimental and control groups at random. The latter design can be indicated by simply dropping the subscript r from $\boxed{M_r}$ (described in Chap. 16 as Design 16.4, one of the inadequate designs).

The design-statistical paradigm of this warhorse of all designs is shown in Fig. 19.3. The insertion of the symbols for the means shows the two sources of systematic variance: *treatments* and *pairs, columns* and *rows.* This is in clear contrast to the randomized designs of Chap. 18, where the only systematic variance was *treatments* or *columns.*

Judging from published research, it seems that most uses of this classic structure fall into the Design 16.4, or nonrandomized, category. This is not surprising, since a general awareness of the importance and the logic of randomization is a relatively recent development.

Pairs	X_e	X_c	
1	Y_{1e}	Y_{1c}	M_1
2	Y_{2e}	Y_{2c}	M_2
3	Y_{3e}	Y_{3c}	M_3
.	.	.	.
.	.	.	.
.	.	.	.
n	Y_{ne}	Y_{nc}	M_n
	M_e	M_c	

FIG. **19.3**

The most common variant of the two-group, experimental group-control group design is the before-after, two-group design. (See Design 17.3 (b).) The design-statistical paradigm was shown in Fig. 17.3. The only alteration of the paradigm would be to insert a units (pairs) column on the left of the paradigm to indicate that subjects are matched. If D (difference) scores are used in the analysis, then the paradigm reduces to that of Fig. 19.3.

RESEARCH EXAMPLES OF TWO-GROUP DESIGNS

Hundreds of studies of the two-group, matched-subjects type have been published. This design has been especially popular in educational research. In many, probably most, studies using matched subjects, the subjects have not been assigned to experimental and control groups at random. It is often impossible to tell whether investigators have or have not used randomization, since research reports frequently fail to report how subjects are assigned to groups. The studies described below have been chosen not only because they illustrated correlated groups design, matching, and control problems, but also because they are historically, educationally, and psychologically important. Two of them are studies of rare scope.

Thorndike's Transfer of Training Study   In 1924, E. L. Thorndike published a remarkable study of the presumed effect on intelligence of certain school subjects.[3] (Since this study was summarized to some extent in Chap. 17, its discussion here is limited to Thorndike's use of matching.)

[3] E. Thorndike, "Mental Discipline in High School Studies," *Journal of Educational Psychology*, XV (1924), 1–22, 83–98.

Students were matched according to scores on Form A of the measure of the dependent variable, intelligence. This test also served as a pretest. The independent variable was One Year's Study of Subjects, such as history, mathematics, and Latin. A posttest, Form B of the intelligence test, was given at the end of the year. Thorndike used an ingenious device to separate the differential effect of each school subject by matching on Form A of the intelligence test those pupils who studied, for instance, English, history, geometry, and *Latin* with those pupils who studied English, history, geometry, and *shopwork*. Thus, for these two groups, he was comparing the differential effects of *Latin* and *shopwork*. Gains in final intelligence scores were considered a joint effect of growth plus the academic subjects studied.

Despite its weaknesses, this was a colossal study. Thorndike was aware of the lack of adequate controls, as revealed in the following passage on the effects of selection:

> The chief reason why good thinkers seem superficially to have been made such by having taken certain school studies, is that good thinkers have taken such studies . . . When the good thinkers studied Greek and Latin, these studies seemed to make good thinkers. Now that the good thinkers study Physics and Trigonometry, these seem to make good thinkers. If the abler pupils should all study Physical Education and Dramatic Art, these subjects would seem to make good thinkers.[4]

Thorndike pointed the way to controlled educational research, which has led to the decrease of metaphysical and dogmatic explanations in education. His work struck a blow against the razor strop theory of mental training, the theory that likened the mind to a razor that could be sharpened by stropping it on "hard" subjects.

It is not easy to evaluate a study such as this, the scope and ingenuity of which is impressive. One wonders, however, about the adequacy of the dependent variable, "intelligence" or "intellectual ability." Can school subjects studied for one year have much effect on intelligence? We now also believe that such large numbers of subjects are not necessary. Most important, though, Thorndike's experiment was not a "true" one. Strictly speaking, it was an ex post facto study in the sense in which this term has been defined in this text. No randomization, of course, was possible. Thorndike measured the intelligence of students and let the independent variables, School Subjects, operate. As mentioned above, he was aware of this control weakness in his experiment. Still, the matching and the ingenious "experimental" arrangements were the best that could be arranged in a natural situation. The study is still a classic that deserves respect and careful study despite its weaknesses in history (maturation was controlled) and selection.

[4] *Ibid.,* p. 98.

The Winnetka Experiment In 1932, Morphett and Washburne began an interesting experiment on an important educational problem.[5] A group of 25 children entering first grade was selected as the experimental group. Each child in this group was matched with three other children on home environment, mental age, and chronological age. The experimental group was given no systematic instruction in arithmetic, reading, and writing during the first one and a half years of their school life. The children did have opportunities to learn, however. The control-group children had a similar educational environment except that about one-third of the time was devoted to systematic study of reading, writing, and arithmetic. The children's progress was followed and they were tested periodically over a period of seven years. The number of experimental group subjects dwindled to 13. The control-group subjects dwindled similarly.

After the year and a half (middle of second grade), as might be expected, the experimental-group children were about a year behind the control-group children in achievement. But by the end of the third grade the two groups were approximately equal. At the end of the seven-year period, the experimental-group children exceeded the control-group children by about three-quarters of a grade. Both groups were approximately equal in intelligence at the end of the experiment, indicating, according to the authors, that survival selection of intelligence was not a factor.

The serious attempt of the Winnetka Experiment to obtain an empirical answer to the controversial question of when and how to begin formal instruction deserves commendation. Since it would take a great deal of space to analyze its weaknesses, this exercise is left to the reader. Despite the weaknesses, however, the results of this study, at the very least, cast doubt upon some of our traditional notions of early instruction and learning. As such, it was a very valuable experiment. It should have been followed by similar studies, because even today we have not found a clear answer to Morphett and Washburne's question.

The Eight-year Study Another ambitious attempt to answer an important educational question empirically was the Eight-Year Study,[6] which was designed to answer the question: How do "progressive" methods of education in high school compare with "traditional" methods in preparing youngsters for college? Thirty "progressive" high schools in different parts of the country were included in this study. Students in these schools studied under a core curriculum plan. After the students were in college, they were matched with students from "traditional" schools on sex, intel-

[5] M. Morphett and C. Washburne, "Postponing Formal Instruction: A Seven-Year Case Study," in *The Effect of Administrative Practices on the Character of the Education Program—Symposium.* Washington, D.C.: American Educational Research Association, 1940. Although three control children were matched to each experimental child, the basic design of this research remains the same.

[6] W. Aikin, *The Story of the Eight-Year Study.* New York: Harper & Row, 1942.

ligence, and other variables. The college performances of the two groups were compared. In general, the results indicated that the students of the progressive schools performed somewhat better than the students from traditional schools.

This large-scale study, like the Thorndike study, is ex post facto in nature with serious control weaknesses, probably the most important of which is self-selection. Despite the matching, there may have been other crucial variables that distinguished the progressive school students from the traditional school students *when the study started*. Do children, for example, who go to progressive high schools differ significantly in motivation from children who go to traditional high schools? Do the parents of the progressive school children engender better attitudes toward learning than do the parents of traditional school children? (Some of the schools were university laboratory schools.) Even though this study can be criticized, it remains an important attempt to get objective evidence on complex and difficult educational questions.[7]

Extensions of Two-group Designs   Since experimental and control groups, pretests, and posttests are used in the Solomon three- and four-group designs (Designs 17.5 and 17.6), these designs technically belong to the two-group designs just discussed. From the viewpoint of this chapter, they may be considered as extensions of two-group designs. Except for the factorial analysis of variance possible with Design 17.6, the four-group design, these designs, then, offer nothing essentially new in design and statistics.

An obvious extension of two-group, correlated-groups design is to add more experimental or control groups, which requires no change in principle or analysis. The only difficulties, as mentioned before, are practical.

MULTIGROUP, CORRELATED-GROUPS DESIGNS

Units Variance   While it is difficult to match three and four sets of subjects, and while it is ordinarily not feasible or desirable in behavioral research to use the same subjects in each of the groups, there are natural situations in which correlated groups exist. These situations are particularly important in educational research. Until recently, the variances due to differences between classes, schools, school systems, and other "natural" units have not been well controlled or even often used in the analysis of data. Perhaps the first indication of the importance of this kind of vari-

---

[7] The study also broke new ground in measurement. Realizing that progressive educators stress qualities not measured by the usual tests of intelligence and achievement, the investigators devised measurement instruments. The most important of these were tests to measure the ability to think. See E. Smith, *et al., Appraising and Recording Student Progress*. New York: Harper & Row, 1942.

ance was given in Lindquist's fine book on statistical analysis in educational research.[8] In this book, Lindquist placed considerable emphasis on *schools variance*. Schools, classes, and other educational units tend to differ significantly in achievement, intelligence, aptitudes, and other variables. The educational investigator has to be alert to these *unit differences*, as well as to individual differences.

Consider an obvious example. Suppose an investigator chooses a sample of five schools for their variety and heterogeneity. He is of course seeking external validity: representativeness. He conducts an investigation using pupils from all five schools and combines the measures from the five schools to test the mean differences in some dependent variable. In so doing, he is ignoring the differences among the schools' variance. It is understandable that the means do not differ significantly; the schools' variance is mixed in with the error variance.

Gross errors can follow from ignoring schools variance. One such error is to select a number of schools and to designate certain schools as experimental schools and others as control schools. Here the between-schools variance gets entangled with the variance of the experimental variable variance. Similarly, classes, school districts, and other educational units differ and thus engender variance. The variances must be identified and controlled, whether it be by experimental or statistical control, or both.[9]

A Hypothetical Example of Schools Variance   In running an experiment in several schools, the best procedure is to seek to reproduce the experiment in *each* of the schools. The procedure is somewhat as follows. First, randomly select m schools from the N schools of some well-defined schools population (district or county elementary schools). Run the experiment in *each* of the schools. Avoid setting up an experimental school here and a control school there, because the between-schools variance is confounded by doing this. Analyze the between-schools variance. A design-statistical paradigm would resemble Fig. 19.1, except that one might have means instead of individual scores in the cells. (One might also have several class means or the individual scores in the cells.)

Since school situations vary, it may not be possible to perform all the

---

[8] E. Lindquist, *Statistical Analysis in Educational Research*. Boston: Houghton Mifflin, 1940.

[9] To be prepared to do research in school situations, the student needs more study of the design and statistical problems involved than the scope of this text permits. For example, the differences between the situations where students can be assigned to experimental treatments at random and where intact classes must be used should be understood. Perhaps the three best references for such study are: E. Lindquist, *op. cit.*, chaps. IV and V, especially pp. 104–132, 145–163; E. Lindquist, *Design and Analysis of Experiments in Psychology and Education*, Boston: Houghton Mifflin, 1953, chaps. 7 and 8; A. Edwards, *Experimental Design in Psychological Research*, rev. ed., New York: Holt, Rinehart and Winston, Inc., 1960, chap. 11. The type of design considered above is also called *randomized blocks design* or *random replications design*.

experimental treatments in each school. It is possible in such cases, though much less desirable, to sample schools at random and to assign them to experimental treatments at random.[10] Even if the schools cannot be selected at random, a useful experiment can be performed.

FACTORIAL CORRELATED-GROUPS DESIGNS

Future educational research will very likely use the basic type of schools design discussed above. There is little doubt, too, that factorial models will be combined with the schools or units notion to yield a valuable design: *factorial correlated-groups design.* The more complex designs become, of course, the more difficult the statistical and interpretative problems. These problems should not block the use of such designs, however. To show how useful they can be, simply add sex or intelligence levels, or any other pertinent variable, to the design of Fig. 19.1. Conceptually there is nothing difficult about this—Fig. 19.4 shows what such a design might look like. Some individuals may find it easier to conceive the design if it

		Schools	A_1	A_2	A_3
			Methods (Treatments)		
		1			
		2			
	B_1	3			
		4			
Levels		5	*Y* MEANS		
(Devices,			OR		
Types,					
etc.)		1	MEASURES		
		2			
	B_2	3			
		4			
		5			

FIG. **19.4**

is set up a bit differently, as in Fig. 19.5. The advantage of this setup is that it preserves the form of the simpler design by showing the *schools* rows clearly.

10 See Lindquist, *Design and Analysis of Experiments in Psychology and Education,* chap. 7. On pp. 187 and 188, Lindquist gives a good research example.

	Methods					
	A_1		A_2		A_3	
Levels	B_1	B_2	B_1	B_2	B_1	B_2
1						
2						
Schools 3			Y MEANS OR MEASURES			
4						
5						

FIG. **19.5**

The strengths and weaknesses of the factorial correlated-groups design are similar to those of the more complex factorial designs. The main strengths are the ability to isolate and measure variances and to test interactions. Note that the two main sources of variance, *methods (A)* and *levels (B)*, and the *schools* variance can be evaluated, that is, the differences between the *A, B,* and *schools* means can be tested for significance. In addition, three interactions can be tested for significance: *methods* by *levels, methods* by *schools,* and *levels* by *schools.* If individual scores are used in the cells instead of means, the triple interaction, too, can be tested. Note how important such interaction can be, both theoretically and practically. For example, questions like the following can be answered: Do methods work differently in different schools? Do certain methods work differently at different intelligence levels or with different sexes or with children of different socioeconomic levels? Do levels of intelligence interact with schools?

ANALYSIS OF COVARIANCE

The invention of the analysis of covariance by Ronald Fisher has extraordinary potential importance in educational and psychological research. It is frequently necessary to study groups as they are; subjects cannot be matched or assigned at random. Analysis of covariance comes to the investigator's assistance. Here is a splendid example of the creative use of the variance principles common to correlation theory and to analysis of variance to solve a long-standing analytical problem. In essence, Fisher extended his basic notion of analyzing the total variance (sum of squares) of a set of measures into systematic and error variances (sums of squares) to the analysis of covariance.

Analysis of covariance is a form of analysis of variance that tests the significance of the differences between means of final experimental data by taking into account and adjusting initial differences in the data.

That is, the analysis of covariance analyzes the differences between experimental groups on Y after taking into account either initial differences in the Y measures or differences in some pertinent independent variable.

Consider the case of a school psychologist who plans a reading experiment. Knowing that intelligence is an important variable in any study of reading, he wishes to match the subjects of three experimental groups on intelligence. But administrative and other difficulties make this impossible. Since every child in his school has an intelligence test score on file, he uses these scores, together with reading scores, in an analysis of covariance. The analysis of covariance statistically matches the pupils for him, which is remarkable—he gets the advantages of random assignment as in simple one-way analysis and the benefits of matching, without the difficulties of arranging the matching. In addition, the analysis of covariance can easily give him three coefficients of correlation between the intelligence and reading scores, one of which is the best estimate of the "true" correlation between the measures.

Even if the school psychologist had no intelligence measures, he could use reading pretest measures in the same way. The analysis of covariance would be used to analyze the final measures for significant differences, but this analysis would be adjusted for pretest differences between the groups. If the assumptions behind the analysis of covariance are not violated, this method can be used in many educational research situations, because the scores on important educational variables are often available in school, college, and university files.

A PROCEDURAL DESCRIPTION OF ANALYSIS OF COVARIANCE

Covariance[11] was defined in Chap. 7 as the average of the cross products of the deviation scores of two variables, X and Y. (A deviation score is defined by $x = X - M_x$, or $y = Y - M_y$.) If a number of individuals have X scores and Y scores, intelligence test scores, and reading scores, we then have a set of ordered pairs, with X scores first in all pairs. Reducing these scores to deviation scores, x and y, we have another set of ordered pairs, (x, y). If the x's and y's are multiplied, and these cross products are summed, we have a measure analogous to the sum of squares of the analysis of variance. It is called the *sum of cross products* and is written Σxy. Just as the analysis of variance works with sums of squares and variances,

---

[11] A complete statistical description of the analysis of covariance is not apropos in this text. The objective is to acquaint the student with the general method and to show its relation to other forms of design and statistical analysis. A good brief discussion of the rationale of analysis of covariance can be found in M. Tate, *Statistics in Education.* New York: Macmillan, 1955, pp. 515–522. For computational purposes, Edwards' older book is good: A. Edwards, *Experimental Design in Psychological Research.* New York: Holt, Rinehart and Winston, Inc., 1950, chap. 17.

the analysis of covariance works with the sums of cross products and covariances, as well as with the sums of squares.

The net outcome of the procedure is an analysis of covariance table that tests the significance of the differences of the Y means of the experimental groups after adjustment of the Y sums of squares. This adjustment in effect removes from the Y sums of squares that part due to the relation between X and Y. The higher the correlation between X and Y, the more effective the analysis of covariance. (If the correlation is zero or quite low, analysis of covariance is a waste of time.) What emerges for a final analysis of covariance table are the adjusted total, between-groups, and within-groups sums of squares.[12] Variances (mean squares) and the F ratio are computed from these adjusted measures.

The paradigm of an analysis of covariance is the same as that of a before-after design. The general design is either Design 17.3 (a) or 17.3 (b). The data paradigm is similar to that of Fig. 17.3.

A data paradigm of Koenker's kindergarten study, as it might have been run, is shown in Table 19.1.[13] Koenker matched his subjects on intelligence and also administered a pretest. He analyzed the difference scores (posttest minus pretest scores), using a t test. He could also have used the analysis of covariance method in two or three different ways. Instead of matching on intelligence, he could have used intelligence test scores as the X scores of an analysis of covariance. Another way would have been to use the pretest scores as X scores, ignoring the intelligence scores, as shown in Table 19.1. A third way, called multiple analysis of covariance, would have been to use both intelligence test and pretest scores as two sets of X scores.

In Table 19.1 the Y means are the main concern. They were significantly different by t test. It is doubtful, in this case, that the analysis of covariance would have added anything of particular value to the analysis.

---

[12] It is well to note the three r's that were mentioned earlier. Since one formula for r is $r = \Sigma xy / \sqrt{\Sigma x^2 \Sigma y^2}$, and since analysis of covariance yields all these terms for total, between groups and within groups, obviously three r's can be computed. The r for total is the usual r computed between two sets of measures, and r for between groups is the correlation between the pairs of means. The key contribution of analysis of covariance is to yield the *within-groups* r. Since the sums of squares and cross products are computed *within* each group separately, main differences between groups do not influence the computed r. Thus, the within r is the "purest" and "best" estimate of the "true" r between X and Y. It is not often realized that many computed r's may be spuriously inflated or deflated by between-groups variance. Assume that an r is computed between intelligence and school achievement, and the scores of girls and boys are included in the computations. If there is a significant difference in achievement between girls and boys, and if most of the girls are in one group and most of the boys in another group, this between-groups difference may inflate the computed r. An analysis of covariance of the same data would yield a within-groups r that would probably be lower than the original total r.

[13] R. Koenker, "Arithmetic Readiness at the Kindergarten Level," *Journal of Educational Research*, XLII (1948), 218–223.

Yet in many other cases it might be very valuable, especially so in experiments using intact groups.

TABLE **19.1**   EXPERIMENTAL GROUP-CONTROL GROUP ANALYSIS OF COVARIANCE
PARADIGM; BASED ON KOENKER STUDY

Experimental		Control	
X (Pretest)	Y (Posttest)	X (Pretest)	Y (Posttest)
M_{xe}	M_{ye}	M_{xc}	M_{yc}

One of the major difficulties of educational and sociological research is our inability to set up experimental groups at will. Administrators and teachers, for example, are understandably reluctant to break up classes. The investigator often must use classes intact. Through the analysis of covariance it is often possible to control class or other group differences statistically. For example, three methods of teaching spelling, A_1, A_2, and A_3 are to be tested. The random assignment of subjects is not possible, but it *is* possible to use intact classes. It is known that intelligence is significantly related to spelling and that the classes will probably differ significantly in intelligence. The methods can be assigned to the intact classes at random, and intelligence test scores can be used as X measures in an analysis of covariance. The paradigm would look like that in Fig. 19.6, where X = intelligence test scores and Y = spelling scores. (The X measures might also be spelling pretest scores.)

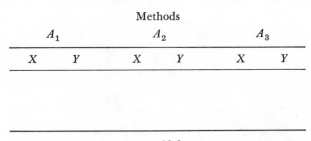

Methods

A_1		A_2		A_3	
X	Y	X	Y	X	Y

FIG. **19.6**

This type of experiment has certain decided advantages: one is that measures of intelligence and achievement usually exist before the experiment starts. Thus they can be used without the sensitization dangers of pretests; an experiment can also be run without the students' knowing that they are being tested. Closely allied to this is the advantage of experiments done in natural settings, a matter we take up in Part V. Still another advantage is the precision of the analysis and the information it can yield.

RESEARCH DESIGN AND ANALYSIS: CONCLUDING REMARKS

Four major objectives have dominated the organization and preparation of Part IV. The first was to acquaint the student of behavioral research with a knowledge of the principal designs of research. By so doing, it was hoped that narrowly circumscribed notions of doing research with, say, only one experimental group and one control group, or with matched subjects, or with one group, before and after, may be widened.

The second objective was to convey a sense of the balanced structure of good research designs. It is desirable to develop a sensitive feeling for the architecture of design, design that is formally as well as functionally fitted to the research problems we are seeking to solve.

The third objective was to help the reader understand the logic of experimental inquiry and the logic of the various designs. Research designs are alternative routes to the same destination: reliable and valid statements of the relations between variables. Some designs, if feasible, yield stronger relational statements than other designs.

In a certain sense, the fourth objective of Part IV has been the most difficult to achieve: to help the student understand the relation between research design and statistics. Statistics is, in one sense, the technical discipline of handling variance. And, as we have seen, one of the basic purposes of design is to provide control of systematic and error variances. This is the reason for treating statistics in such detail in Part III before considering design in Part IV. Fisher expresses this idea succinctly when he says, "Statistical procedure and experimental design are only two different aspects of the same whole, and that whole comprises all the logical requirements of the complete process of adding to natural knowledge by experimentation." [14]

A well-conceived design is no guarantee of the validity of research findings. Elegant designs nicely tailored to research problems can still result in wrong or distorted conclusions. Nevertheless, the chances of arriving at accurate and valid conclusions are better with sound designs than with unsound ones. This is relatively sure: if design is faulty, one can come to no clear conclusions. If, for instance, one uses a two-group, matched-subjects design when the research problem logically demands a factorial design, or if one uses a factorial design when the nature of the research situation calls for a correlated-groups design, no amount of interpretative or statistical manipulation can increase confidence in the conclusions of such research.

[14] R. Fisher, *The Design of Experiments,* 6th ed. New York: Hafner, 1951, p. 3.

It is fitting that Fisher should have the last word on this subject. In the first chapter of his book, *Design of Experiments,* he said:

> . . . If the design of an experiment is faulty, any method of interpretation which makes it out to be decisive must be faulty too. It is true that there are a great many experimental procedures which are well designed in that they *may* lead to decisive conclusions, but on other occasions may fail to do so; in such cases, if decisive conclusions are in fact drawn when they are unjustified, we may say that the fault is wholly in the interpretation, not in the design. But the fault of interpretation . . . lies in overlooking the characteristic features of the design which lead to the result being sometimes inconclusive, or conclusive on some questions but not on all. To understand correctly the one aspect of the problem is to understand the other.[15]

STUDY SUGGESTIONS

1. Read two or three research studies in which matching of subjects has been used. The Gates and Taylor, Koenker, and Dawe studies, cited later in these study suggestions, are good examples. Here are four more studies:

   Hilgard, J., "Learning and Maturation in Preschool Children," *Journal of Genetic Psychology,* XLI (1932), 36–56.

   Lehman, H., and L. Cole, "The Effectiveness of Drill in Handwriting to Remove Specific Illegibilities." *School and Society,* XXVII (1928), 546–548.

   Sears, P., "Levels of Aspiration in Academically Successful and Unsuccessful Children," *Journal of Abnormal and Social Psychology,* XXXV (1940), 498–536.

   Capehart, B., A. Hodges, and R. Roth, "Evaluating the Core Curriculum: A Further Look." *School Review,* LX (1953), 406–412.

   Consider these studies critically. If a study is faulty, ask yourself: Could the investigator have done a better job under the circumstances? In each case, ask yourself whether the conclusions can be trusted. Look especially at the Capehart, Hodges, and Roth study in reference to this question. Matching was not used in the Lehman and Cole study, which was included in the above list only because two intact classes were used, one an experimental group and the other a control group. Might the investigators have used the analysis of covariance? What is your opinion of the conclusions?

2. One useful means of control by matching is to use pairs of identical twins. Why is this method a useful means of control? If you were setting up an experiment to test the effect of environment on measured intelligence and you had 20 pairs of identical twins and complete experimental freedom, how would you set up the experiment?

[15] *Ibid.,* pp. 2, 3.

3. A number of years ago, Dawe planned a small but educationally important study.[16] She was interested in the possible effect of an enriched educational program on the intelligence and language ability, among other characteristics, of children living in an orphanage. Eleven pairs of children, who were matched on sex, age, intelligence, vocabulary, and school group, were divided into an experimental group and a control group. (The exact procedural details were not reported in the account of the study.) The experimental group was given an intensive educational program emphasing some of the factors known to be related to superior language development. At the end of the training period, the experimental group had made greater gains than the control group in measured intelligence and vocabulary. The initial and final means of the experimental-group and control-group intelligence test scores were:

	Experimental	Control
Initial	80.6	81.5
Final	94.8	79.5

(Standard deviations were not reported, but ranges were. Dawe reported that this difference was significant at the .01 level.)

   (a) What are the weaknesses of this research? Despite the weaknesses, do you believe the results are valid? If so, why?

   (b) Draw up a better design to answer the research question. Why do you think your design is better than Dawe's?

4. In their study of the transfer of training summarized in an earlier chapter, Gates and Taylor matched experimental and control group subjects on 12 variables: sex, age, mental age (on the Stanford-Binet tests), intelligence quotient, scholastic maturity (judged by teachers), and several forms of memory.[17] Aside from the obvious duplications of matching criteria (mental age *and* IQ), discuss Gates and Taylor's matching procedure critically. What were its good and bad points?

   The following question was asked: Does practice in a mental function (memory for digits) improve future learning of the mental function? Set up two different research designs, each of which is capable of giving a reasonably valid answer to this question. Discuss the relative merits of the two designs and compare them to the Gates and Taylor design.

16 H. Dawe, "A Study of the Effect of an Educational Program upon Language Development and Related Mental Functions in Young Children," *Journal of Experimental Education*, XI (1942), 200–209.

17 A Gates and G. Taylor, "An Experimental Study of the Nature of Improvement Resulting from Practice in a Mental Function," *Journal of Educational Psychology*, XVI (1925), 583–592.

5. Ability grouping is a subject on which there has been much discussion but little research. You are planning a study of ability grouping in one school, and the principal and the teachers are quite willing to cooperate. The measures of the dependent variable are scores on a mathematics test. Design three experiments to test ability grouping at the eighth-grade level as follows:

  (a) Match subjects on intelligence and assign subjects to experimental groups at random. Disregard any other variables.

  (b) Assign subjects at random and use a mathematics pretest and posttest. (What types of analysis are possible?)

  (c) Assume that you must use intact classes, that there are six eighth-grade classes, and that you know the classes differ in mathematics ability.

  Evaluate the three experimental designs.[18]

6. An unusual use of television instruction is reported by Hartman who asked whether educational television courses (ETV) could be used to help make up deficiencies in the science background of college freshmen.[19] An entire freshman class, about 180 students, was randomly divided into two groups, ETV and no-ETV. A pretest in physics was administered. One group was shown a television film on electricity and magnetism, the other group a television film on mechanics. Each group served as a control on the other group in this dual experiment. Hartman used the analysis of covariance to analyze his data. The X measures were scores on the physics pretest. The results on one of the subexperiments were as follows: the electricity and magnetism group had a mean of 13.26; the control group's mean was 11.85. The F ratio was 7.75, significant at the .01 level.

  (a) Sketch Hartman's design.

  (b) Comment on the strengths and weaknesses of ths study. Could Hartman have done any better than he did? If so, how?

  (c) Why did Hartman use the analysis of covariance? Could he have used another method of analysis? For example, could he have analyzed difference scores (posttest minus pretest scores)? Could he have matched subjects? Contrast the three methods.

7. In Footnote 12, it was said that three r's could be computed using the

[18] For a competent and complex experiment of ability grouping in which a factorial analysis of variance and covariance was used, see N. Wallen and R. Vowles, "The Effect of Intraclass Ability Grouping on Arithmetic Achievement in the Sixth Grade," *Journal of Educational Psychology*, LI (1960), 159–163. Another quite different study of ability grouping was recently made in Sweden. See T. Husen and N. Svensson, "Pedagogic Milieu and Development of Intellectual Skills," *School Review*, LXVIII (1960), 36–51.

[19] F. Hartman, "Filmed Physics Lectures as Supplementary and Refresher College Physics Instruction." In W. Schramm, ed., *The Impact of Educational Television.* Urbana, Ill.: University of Illinois Press, 1960, pp. 117–124.

terms yielded in the analysis of covariance. Here are some simple figures to illustrate what was meant:

A_1		A_2	
X	Y	X	Y
1	5	3	7
2	2	4	4
3	4	5	6
4	6	6	8
5	3	7	5

Assume that an experiment has been done with two methods. The X measures are intelligence test scores; the Y measures are achievement test scores. Unknown to the experimenter, all the subjects of Group A_1 are boys and all the subjects of Group A_2 are girls. There is a difference between the Y means and between the X means. (In fact, if 2 is subtracted from each of the scores of the A_2 group, the result is the A_1 scores.)

The r between all ten X and Y scores is .33. But if r is computed between X and Y of the A_1 group alone, it is 0, and also for the A_2 X and Y scores. The average within groups r, then, is 0, but the total r is .33. This difference is due to the between-groups variance.

Compute the r's and verify the above figures. Is the r of .33 "spurious"? If the r of 0 is the "true" r, why? Discuss this problem. Can this situation be expressed algebraically?

PART FIVE

TYPES OF RESEARCH

20 *EX POST FACTO RESEARCH*

Among the dangerous fallacies used by man, one of the most dangerous to science is that known as *post hoc, ergo propter hoc,* after this, therefore caused by this. We may joke, with a tinge of seriousness, "If I take an umbrella, it won't rain." We may even seriously say that delinquents are delinquent because of a lack of discipline in the schools or that religious education makes children more virtuous. It is very easy to assume that one thing causes another simply because it occurs before the other, and because one has such a wide choice of possible "causes." Then, too, many explanations often seem plausible. It is easy to believe, for instance, that the learning of children improves because we institute a new educational practice or teach in a certain way. We assume that the improvement in their learning was due to the new spelling method, to the institution of group processes into the classroom situation, to stern discipline and more homework (or little discipline and less homework). We rarely stop to realize that children will usually learn something if they are given the opportunity to learn.

The social scientist and the educational scientist constantly face the problem of the post hoc fallacy. The sociologist who seeks the causes of delinquency knows that he must exercise extreme care in studying this problem. Slum conditions, broken homes, lack of love—each, or all, of these conditions can be possible causes of delinquency. The psychologist seeking the roots of adult personality faces an even subtler problem: hereditary traits, child-rearing practices, educational influences, parental personality, and environmental circumstances are all plausible explanations. The educational scientist, with the goal of understanding the basis of successful school achievement, also faces a large number of reasonable possibilities: intelligence, aptitude, motivation, home environment, teacher personality, pupil personality, and teaching methods.

The danger of the post hoc assumption is that it can, and often does, lead to erroneous and misleading interpretations of research data, the effect being particularly serious when the scientist has little or no control over time and independent variables. When he is seeking to explain a phenomenon that has already occurred he is confronted with the unpleasant fact that he does not have real control of the possible causes. Hence he must pursue a course of research action different in execution and interpretation from that of the scientist who experiments.

Definition   Ex post facto research[1] may be defined as *that research in which the independent variable or variables have already occurred and in which the researcher starts with the observation of a dependent variable or variables. He then studies the independent variables in retrospect for their possible relations to, and effects on, the dependent variable or variables.*

Assume that an investigator is interested in the relation between sex and creativity in children. He measures the creativity of a sample of boys and girls and tests the significance of the difference between the means of the two sexes. The mean of boys is significantly higher than the mean of girls. He concludes that boys are more creative than girls. This may or may not be a valid conclusion. The relation exists, true. With only this evidence, however, the conclusion is doubtful. The question is: Is the demonstrated relation really between sex and creativity? Since many other variables are correlated with sex, it might have been one or more of these variables that produced the difference between the creativity scores of the two sexes.

BASIC DIFFERENCE BETWEEN EXPERIMENTAL RESEARCH AND EX POST FACTO RESEARCH

The basis of the structure in which the experimental scientist operates is simple. He hypothesizes: If x, then y; if frustration, then aggression. Depending on circumstances and his personal predilections in research design, he uses some method to manipulate or measure x. He then observes y to see if concomitant variation, the variation expected or predicted from the variation in x, occurs. If it does, this is evidence for the validity of the proposition, $x \rightarrow y$, $x \rightarrow y$ meaning "If x, then y." Note that the scientist here predicts from a controlled x to y. To help him achieve control, he can use the principle of randomization and active manipulation of x and can assume, other things equal, that y is varying as a result of the manipulation of x.

In ex post facto research, on the other hand, y is observed. Then a retrospective search for x ensues. An x is found that is plausible and agrees

---

[1] The complete definition of ex post facto research used in this book is somewhat different from that often accepted. The term was originally used by Chapin and Greenwood to mean a quasi-experiment in which an attempt is made to control independent variables by matching and symbolic means. Since this meaning is not broad enough for our purposes, "ex post facto" is here expanded to include all research that has the characteristics discussed in the text.

with the hypothesis. Due to lack of control of x and other possible x's, the "truth" of the hypothesized relation between x and y cannot be asserted with the confidence of the experimental situation. Basically, then, ex post facto research has, so to speak, a built-in weakness: lack of control of independent variables.

CONTROL AND EX POST FACTO RESEARCH

The most important difference between experimental research and ex post facto research, then, is *control*. In the experimental case, the investigator at least has manipulative control: he has at least one active variable. If an experiment is a "true" experiment, as defined in Part IV, he can also exercise control by randomization. He can assign subjects to groups at random. Or, at the very least, he can assign treatments to groups at random.

In the ex post facto research situation, this control of the independent variables is not possible, and what is perhaps more important, neither is randomization. The ex post facto investigator must take things as they are and try to disentangle them.

Take a well-known case. When an experimenter paints the skins of rats with carcinogenic substances (x), adequately controls other variables, and the rats ultimately develop carcinoma (y), the argument is valid because x (and other possible x's, theoretically) is controlled and y is predicted. But when an investigator finds cases of lung cancer (y) and then goes back among the possible multiplicity of causes $(x_1, x_2, \cdots, x_n)$ and picks cigarette-smoking (say x_3) as the culprit, he is in the midst of a difficulty similar to that of the fallacy of the affirmation of the consequent. Both cases are of course probabilistic. In the first case the investigator can be *more* sure, considerably more sure if he has made "other things equal," that $x \rightarrow y$. In the ex post facto case, however, the investigator is always on shakier ground because he cannot say, with nearly as much assurance, "other things equal." He cannot control the independent variables by manipulation or by randomization. In short, the probability that x is "really" related to y is greater in the experimental situation than it is in the ex post facto situation, because the control of x is greater.

SELF-SELECTION AND EX POST FACTO RESEARCH

In an ideal social scientific research world, the possibility of finding random samples of subjects, and randomly assigning subjects to groups and treatments to groups would always be possible. In the real world, however, one, two, or even all three of these possibilities do not exist. It is possible to draw subjects at random in both experimental and in ex post facto research. But it is not possible, in ex post facto research, to assign subjects to groups at random or to assign treatments to groups at random. Thus subjects can "assign themselves" to groups, can "select themselves" into the groups on the basis of characteristics other than those in which the investigator may be interested. The subjects and the treatments come, as it were, already assigned to the groups.

Self-selection, then, is the research case in which the members of the groups being studied are in the groups, in part, because they differentially possess traits or characteristics extraneous to the research problem, characteristics that possibly influence or are otherwise related to the variables of the research problem. Two examples of self-selection, which will aid understanding, follow.

In the well-known cigarette-smoking–cancer research, the smoking habits of a large number of people were studied. This large group was divided into those who had lung cancer—or who had died of it—and those who did not have it. The dependent variable was thus the presence or absence of cancer. The investigator probed the subjects' backgrounds to determine whether they smoked cigarettes, and if so, how many. Cigarette-smoking was the independent variable. The investigator found that the incidence of lung cancer rose with the number of cigarettes smoked daily. He also found that the incidence was lower in the cases of light smokers and nonsmokers. He came to the conclusion that cigarette-smoking caused lung cancer.[2] This conclusion may or may not be true. But the investigator cannot come to this conclusion, although he *can* say that there is a statistically significant relation between the variables.

The reason he cannot state a causal connection is because there are a number of other variables, any one of which, or any combination of which, may have caused lung cancer. And he has not controlled other possible independent variables. He *cannot* control them, except by testing alternative hypothesis, a procedure to be explained later. Even when he also studies a "control group" of people who have no cancer, self-selection may be operating. Maybe tense, anxious men are doomed to have lung cancer if they marry blonde women, for instance. It may just happen that this type of man also smokes cigarettes heavily. The cigarette-smoking is not what kills him—he kills himself by being born tense and anxious—and possibly by marrying a blonde. Such men are selected into the sample by investigators only because they smoke cigarettes. But such men select themselves into the sample because they commonly possess a temperament that happens to have cigarette-smoking as a concomitant.

---

[2] Careful scientific investigators will usually not say "cause." They may simply say "is related to," which is proper. The word "cause" is used here to make the point more emphatic and because authoritative sources here so use it: see *The New York Times,* Dec. 6, 1959, p. E–11, where the Surgeon General of the United States Public Health Service is directly quoted as saying: "the weight of evidence at present implicates smoking as the principal etiological (causative) factor in the increased incidence of lung cancer."

Self-selection can be a subtle business. There are two kinds of self-selection: self-selection into *samples* and self-selection into *comparison groups*. Self-selection into comparison groups occurs when subjects are selected because they are in one group or another: cancer and no cancer, college and no college, underachievement and no underachievement. That is, they are selected *because* they possess the dependent variable. Self-selection into samples occurs when subjects are selected in a nonrandom fashion into a sample.

The crux of the matter is that when *assignment* is not random, there is always a loophole for other variables to crawl through. When we put subjects into groups, in the above case and in similar cases, or they "put themselves" into groups, on the basis of one variable, it is possible that another variable (or variables) correlated with this variable is the "real" basis of the relation. The usual ex post facto study uses groups that exhibit differences in the dependent variable. In some longitudinal-type studies the groups are differentiated first on the basis of the independent variable. But the two cases are basically the same, since group membership *on the basis of a variable* always brings selection into the picture.

For example, we might select college freshmen at random and then follow them to determine the relation between intelligence and success in college. The students selected themselves into college, so to speak. One or more of the characteristics they bring with them to college, other than intelligence—socioeconomic level, motivation, family background —may be the principal determinants of college success. That we start with the independent variable, in this case intelligence, does not change the self-selective nature of the research situation. In the sampling sense, the students selected themselves into college, which would be an important factor if we were studying college students and noncollege students. But if we were interested only in the success and nonsuccess *of college students,* self-selection into college would be irrelevant, whereas self-selection into success and nonsuccess groups is crucial. That we may have measured the intelligence of the students when they entered college and followed them through to success and nonsuccess does not change either the selection problem or the ex post facto character of the research. In sum, the students selected themselves into college and selected themselves to succeed or not to succeed in college.

LARGE-SCALE EX POST FACTO RESEARCH

The further study of examples is necessary to achieve a perspective for evaluating the contribution of ex post facto research to social scientific and educational research. Several examples of this kind of research have already been given, for example, the research on cigarette-smoking and cancer and the studies of teacher characteristics. Kinsey's studies of sexual behavior are ex post facto; so are many studies of the relations between political and religious affiliation and attitudes, although the body of experimental attitude research is growing. Studies of the relations between school achievement and such variables as social class, race, sex, aptitude, and intelligence are ex post facto in nature. Indeed, it is probably no exaggeration to say that a large proportion of educational and sociological research is ex post facto. It is harder to make a statement about psychological research, because psychological researchers freely use active and assigned variables, but it is probably safe to say that a large proportion of psychological studies are ex post facto, perhaps half or more than half. The following summarized studies have been chosen for their variety and importance.

The Authoritarian Personality Study[3]   The Authoritarian Personality Study was actually a series of studies which together constitute an important and influential contribution to social scientific, particularly psychological, research. The general hypothesis of the study was that political, economic, and social beliefs are related to deep-seated personality characteristics. Another hypothesis was that adult personality is derived from early childhood experiences. In short, attitudes and beliefs were related to underlying personality trends. The investigators, among other traits, studied anti-Semitism as part of a general characteristic called *ethnocentrism*. Later, the investigators exended their thought and work to a still larger construct, *authoritarianism,* which they conceived to be a broad personality syndrome that determines in part ethnocentrism, social attitudes, and certain other behaviors. The authoritarian personality was conceived to be conventional, cynical, destructive, aggressive, power-centered, and ethnocentric.

While this is an inadequate summary of the basic problems of a very complex study, it is sufficient for the present purpose. By definition of the problem, the study had to be ex post facto—although there have been later experimental studies in which high authoritarianism and low authoritarianism, for instance, are independent assigned variables. The variables of *The Authoritarian Personality* were assigned variables. One of the major results of the study was information on the relation between authoritarianism and prejudice. It is obvious that when one studies such variables one is studying already existing sets of personality characteristics and attitudes. The subjects are ready-made authoritarians or nonauthoritarians (with gradations between) and more or less ready-made conserva-

---

[3] T. Adorno, *et al., The Authoritarian Personality.* New York: Harper & Row, 1950. An extensive critique of this book has been published: R. Christie and M. Jahoda, eds., *Studies in the Scope and Method of "The Authoritarian Personality."* New York: Free Press, 1954. Study of the latter volume is rewarding for the intermediate or advanced student of social scientific research. See, especially, the chapter by H. Hyman and P. Sheatsley, "The Authoritarian Personality—A Methodological Critique," pp. 50–122.

tives and liberals. One can conceive, somehow, of manipulating such variables, but such manipulation, as indicated previously, changes the nature of the variables. At any rate, whenever one studies the relations between variables that "already exist" in the individuals studied, or whenever one studies the determinants of such variables, one is deeply imbedded in ex post facto study and its problems.

Social Class Influences on Learning Studies[4]   An extensive set of investigations into social-class influences on learning, the details of which do not concern us here, has greatly affected modern educators. These studies are ex post facto studies and, as such, are laden with interpretative difficulties. One of the principal aims of research in such studies is to attempt to explain differences in school achievement between middle-class and lower-class children. An investigator notes that there are striking differences in school achievement. Can these differences be attributed in part to social class membership? He examines the collective achievement scores of middle-class and lower-class children and consistently notes significant differences: middle-class children do better in school than lower-class children. He may then come to the conclusion that social class is a determinant of school achievement.

The ex post facto character of such research is clear. The investigator starts with the dependent variable, school achievement (or "learning"), and among the many possible influential independent variables, he selects social class. Naturally, he may pick other independent variables as well, variables such as intelligence and motivation, both of which are also related to school achievement and to social class. This makes no difference. It is not a matter of complexity· it is a matter of control. The social class researcher has no power to manipulate social class, nor has he the power of randomization. In this case, the relation between social class and school achievement seems well-established.

Even the relation between social class and measured intelligence seems to be well-established. Yet these "established" relations may be spurious, and they are more likely to be spurious in ex post facto than in experimental research, other things being equal. The major determinants of the difference between the two groups in school achievement may be intelligence and motivation. Middle-class children may tend to have higher *measured* intelligence and higher motivation for school work than lower-class children. It may be these two variables that are the major determinants of school achievement—not social class. Social class mem-

4 There are a large number of studies of social class and its relation to a number of variables, including such educational variables as curriculum choice, testing, grades, and educational motivation. Two of the most pertinent references are A. Davis, *Social-Class Influences upon Learning,* Cambridge: Harvard University Press, 1948; and W. Warner, R. Havighurst, and M. Loeb, *Who Shall Be Educated?* New York: Harper & Row, 1944.

bership happens to be a correlate of these two variables. It is, so to speak, part of the correlational baggage of intelligence, motivation, and school achievement rather than a determinant of school achievement in its own right. (This argument has more force when we discuss the relation between race and school achievement, because race is substantially correlated with social class. If a relation between race and school achievement is found, the common variance may more likely be social class and school achievement than race and school achievement.)

A Two-century Achievement Study[5]   The debate on whether the old days in education were better than those of the present rages today as it did last year, a decade ago, and in the last century. A study that attempted to compare the results of twentieth-century education with nineteenth-century education is so purely ex post facto in nature that, like the cigarette-smoking–cancer research, it is almost a classic. Caldwell and Courtis compared the achievements of Boston high school children in history, geography, arithmetic, grammar, and so on in 1845 and of high school children all over the United States in 1919. Actually, the "selected best" of the 1845 pupils were compared to the unselected lower 40 percent of the 1919 pupils. The same tests that were given to the 1845 pupils were given to the 1919 pupils.

It was found, among other things, that the 1919 pupils tended to make lower scores on memory and abstract-skill questions and higher scores on thought questions. The results were consistent throughout the United States. The authors said that the pupils today were much like those of 1845: they tended to achieve the same successes and make the same errors.[6]

The lack of control in this ex post facto study is of course obvious. For its purpose the study is a good one, although it probably has little scientific value. From a practical point of view, however, it provides evidence that some common-sense generalizations about pupil achievement are meaningless.

Sears, Maccoby, and Levin's Study of Child-Rearing Practices[7]   One of the landmark studies of this century, Sears, Maccoby, and Levin's study of child-rearing practices is one of the largest and best empirical attempts to study the effects of child-rearing practices on children. The investigators interviewed mothers of kindergarten children to determine what methods the mothers used in raising their children. (The sample was not random.) Child-rearing methods were carefully categorized into major dimensions: disciplinary techniques, permissiveness, severity, the mother's

5 O. Caldwell and S. Courtis, *Then and Now in Education*. New York: Harcourt, 1925.

6 *Ibid.*, p. 97.

7 R. Sears, E. Maccoby, and H. Levin, *Patterns of Child Rearing*. New York: Harper & Row, 1957.

temperamental qualities, and the encouragement of mature behavior.[8] The mothers were also asked about their feelings and attitudes toward self, husband, pregnancy, and child-rearing practices. In addition, mothers were asked about their children's behavior. In an analytical tour de force, the relations between the mothers' feelings about and attitudes toward self, husband, pregnancy, and so forth, and their attitudes toward their children and child-rearing practices were studied, as well as the relations between both of these sets of feelings and attitudes and the children's behavior.

Although the results of this study are much too complex and numerous to summarize here, one or two of them may give some indication of the scope of the study. Coldness on the part of the mother was associated with persistent bed-wetting, feeding problems, aggression, emotional upset during toilet training, and a slow development of conscience.[9] Another important result that seems to be confirmed by psychological thought is: punishment is inversely related to success in child-rearing.[10]

SMALL-SCALE EX POST FACTO RESEARCH

Pettigrew Study of Regional Differences in Prejudice[11] In a well-executed study of a social problem that is difficult to probe experimentally, Pettigrew asked the question: Is anti-Negro prejudice more closely related to social factors and less so to personality factors in the South than in the North? In effect, this amounts to contrasting sociological and psychological explanations of prejudice. To test hypotheses derived from this question, Pettigrew administered authoritarianism, anti-Semitism, and anti-Negro scales to random samples of white adults in four northern and four southern towns.

One hypothesis predicted a simple difference between northern and southern anti-Negro prejudice, with the result that the southern sample had a significantly higher mean score than the northern sample. There was no significant mean difference on the authoritarianism measure, which was used as a control test. Pettigrew reasoned that, since the authoritarianism scale is presumed to measure "externalizing personality potential," and since the two regions did not differ on this scale but *did* differ on the anti-Negro scale, the hypothesis that externalizing personality factors are of equal importance in the North and the South, and that social-cultural factors are more important in the South than in the North, was supported.

[8] *Ibid.*, pp. 15, 16.
[9] *Ibid.*, pp. 482, 483.
[10] *Ibid.*, p. 484.
[11] T. Pettigrew, "Regional Differences in Anti-Negro Prejudice," *Journal of Abnormal and Social Psychology*, LIX (1959), 28–36.

A Cross-Cultural Study of School Children's Anxiety[12]   In good ex post facto educational research existing differences in environment are often deliberately selected to test theoretical and practical hypotheses. An example of this kind of research is a cross-cultural study of school children's anxiety by Sarnoff, *et al.* Sarnoff and his colleagues used the English eleven-plus examination system, in which the outcome of a group of tests determines the direction of the child's educational future. The investigators reasoned that, since the eleven-plus examinations were so crucial to the British children, they would probably produce *test anxiety*. They further reasoned that American children would probably not have as high test anxiety, because of the difference in our educational system. The basic hypothesis, therefore, was that a difference would be found between English and American children in the degree of test anxiety and that there would be no difference between the groups in *general anxiety* if comparable English and American groups were studied.

This study skillfully utilized an existing independent variable, test examinations, to test a hypothesis on *presumed* existing differences between national groups. Because the researchers seemingly predicted from *x* to *y,* and because they matched their samples so carefully, some students of research might say that this is not an ex post facto study, but actually the study is probably a good example simply because it is not experimental. Experimental manipulation and randomization were lacking, so that the basic approach was the same as that of the cigarette-smoking–cancer studies and the Pettigrew North-South, anti-Negro attitude study. It is particularly noteworthy that Sarnoff and his colleagues tested a "control hypothesis"—the difference between the two groups on general anxiety. (This alternative hypothesis idea was also used by Pettigrew when he tested North-South differences on authoritarianism.)

A Study of Children's Reactions to Finger Painting[13]   A study that is particularly interesting, because it combines experimental and ex post facto approaches, is the Alper, Blane, and Adams Study of the reactions of children of different social classes to finger-painting experience. Experimental manipulation was certainly involved, but the independent variable was not manipulated. Indeed, one might almost say that the dependent variable was manipulated! The general question the authors asked was: Do social-class differences in child-training practices result in class differences in personality? More specifically: Are there differences in approaches to finger painting between middle- and lower-class children?

[12] I. Sarnoff, *et al.*, "A Cross-Cultural Study of Anxiety among American and English School Children," *Journal of Educational Psychology,* XLIX (1958), 129–136.

[13] T. Alper, H. Blane, and B. Adams, "Reactions of Middle and Lower Class Children to Finger Paints as a Function of Class Differences in Child-Training Practices," *Journal of Abnormal and Social Psychology,* LI (1955), 439–448.

Two groups of nursery school children, 18 middle-class children and 18 lower-class children, were introduced in Experiment I to two different finger-painting tasks. The children's behavior was measured on 16 variables: time began painting, acceptance of task, requests for help, washing, and so on. The two groups differed greatly in their reactions, and the differences were significant on most of the measures.

In a second experiment, a "control experiment," the same procedure was followed using crayons rather than finger paints. The only differences were procedural changes necessitated by the use of two different media (some of the subjects were different also). The two groups did not differ significantly in any of the 11 variables measured, a rather surprising contrast to the results of Experiment I.

To call the Alper, Blane, and Adams study ex post facto may be questionable, because a control experiment was included. It is possible, however, to suppose that the two groups varied in the finger-painting tasks, not because of different child-rearing practices between the social classes, but perhaps because of some other variable. The study is classified as ex post facto research because it was not possible to manipulate the independent variable and because the subjects came to the study with their reactions ready-made, as it were.

Another noteworthy point is the ingenuity of the control experiment. The running of this second experiment is analogous to Pettigrew's testing of authoritarianism and the testing of general anxiety by Sarnoff, *et al.* Imagine the researchers' consternation if the differences between the two groups had been significant on the crayon tasks! Obviously their theoretical thinking would have to have been reviewed with a very critical eye.

TESTING ALTERNATIVE OR "CONTROL" HYPOTHESES

Most empirical investigations begin with hypotheses; the implications of these hypotheses are deduced and then tested empirically. Although we "confirm" hypotheses in the manner indicated in earlier chapters, we can also "disconfirm" hypotheses by trying to show that alternative plausible hypotheses are not correct. Let us consider first alternative independent variables as antecedents of a dependent variable. The reasoning is the same. If we say "alternative independent variables," for example, we are also stating alternative hypotheses or alternative explanations for the occurrence or variation of a dependent variable.

In ex post facto studies, although one cannot have the confidence in the "truth" of the statement, If x, then y, that one has in the experimental situation, it *is* possible to set up and test alternative or "control" hypotheses. (Of course, alternative hypotheses can and should be tested in experimental studies, too.)

Let x_1, x_2, and x_3 be three alternative independent variables, and let y be the dependent variable, the phenomenon to be "explained" with a statement of the form: If x, then y. Assume that x_1, x_2, and x_3 exhaust the possibilities. This assumption cannot actually be made—in scientific research it is practically impossible to exhaust all the causal possibilities. This difficulty is especially aggravating to researchers in the social sciences and education. Still, it is assumed here for pedagogical reasons.

An investigator having reason to believe that x_1 is the causative factor, holds x_2 and x_3 constant. He is assuming that one of the three factors is *the* factor, that either x_1 or x_2 or x_3 is *the* "true" independent variable. (Again, note the assumption. It may be none of them or some combination of all three.) Suppose that the investigator succeeds in eliminating x_2, that is, he shows that x_2 is not related to y. If he also succeeds in eliminating x_3, he can then conclude that x_1 is the influential independent variable. Since the alternative or "control" hypotheses have not been substantiated, the original hypothesis is strengthened.

Similarly, we can test alternative *dependent* variables, which imply alternative hypotheses, of course. We merely shift the alternatives to the dependent variable, as Alper, Blane, and Adams did when they set up the crayon experiment in juxtaposition to the finger-paint experiment. Pettigrew used the same method to test the relation between geographical region and authoritarianism and prejudices. In both of these studies alternative hypotheses were tested—and found wanting.

Now consider the Sarnoff, *et al.* study where it was predicted that American and English children would differ significantly in test anxiety but not in general anxiety. The hypothesis was carefully and specifically delineated: If eleven-plus examinations are taken, then test anxiety results. Since it was possible that there might be other independent variables causing the difference between the English and American children on test anxiety, the investigators evidently wished to rule out at least some of the major contenders. This they accomplished by carefully matching the samples: they probably reasoned that the difference in test anxiety might be due to a difference in general anxiety, since the measure of test anxiety obviously must reflect some general anxiety. If this were found to be so, the major hypothesis would not be supported. Therefore Sarnoff and his colleagues, in addition to testing the relation between examination and test anxiety, also tested the relation between examination and general anxiety.

In this kind of ex post facto control, instead of having alternative independent variables, say x_1 and x_2, we have alternative dependent variables, y_1 and y_2. We again assume that the alternatives exhaust the possibilities. If this is so, then x is either associated with y_1 (test anxiety), or with y_2 (general anxiety), or with both. To paraphrase the Sarnoff argument: Either the examination influences test anxiety or it influences general anxiety, or both; the examination influences test anxiety and it does not influence general anxiety. Therefore the examination influences test anxiety.

The method of testing alternative hypotheses, though important in all research, is particularly important in ex post facto studies, because it is one of the only ways to "control" the independent variables of such research. Lacking the possibility of randomization and manipulation, ex post facto researchers, perhaps more so than experimentalists, must be very sensitive to alternative hypothesis-testing possibilities.

EVALUATION OF EX POST FACTO RESEARCH

The reader may have concluded from the preceding discussion that ex post facto research is inferior to experimental research, but this conclusion would be unwarranted. It is easy to *say* that experimental research is "better" than ex post facto research, or that experimental research tends to be "trivial," or that ex post facto research is "merely correlational." Such statements, in and of themselves, are oversimplifications. What the student of research needs is a balanced understanding of the strengths and weaknesses of both kinds of research. To be committed unequivocally to experimentation or to ex post facto research may be poor policy.[14]

The Limitations of Ex Post Facto Interpretation Ex post facto research has three major weaknesses, two of which have already been discussed in detail: (1) the inability to manipulate independent variables, (2) the lack of power to randomize, and (3) the risk of improper interpretation. In other words, compared to experimental research, other things being equal, ex post facto research lacks control; this lack is the basis of the third weakness: the risk of improper interpretation.

The danger of improper and erroneous interpretations in ex post facto research stems in part from the plausibility of many explanations of complex events. It is easy for us to accept the first and most obvious interpretation of an established relation, especially if we work without hypotheses to guide the investigation, or proceed from the dependent variable to the independent variable. These two circumstances are closely related because research unguided by hypotheses, research "to find out things," is most often ex post facto research. Experimental research is more likely to be based on carefully defined hypotheses.

[14] The reader will find stimulating discussion of approaches to educational research in the following references: R. Travers, *An Introduction to Educational Research.* New York: Macmillan, 1958, chap. 13; J. Stanley, "Studying Status vs. Manipulating Variables." In R. Collier and S. Elam, eds., *Research Design and Analysis.* Bloomington, Ind.: Phi Delta Kappa, 1961, chap. 6; J. Stanley, "Controlled Experimentation in the Classroom," *Journal of Experimental Education,* XXV (1957), 195–201; J. Carroll, "Neglected Areas in Educational Research," *Phi Delta Kappan,* XLII (1961), 339–343.

Hypotheses are if-then predictions. In a research experiment the prediction is from a well-controlled x to a y. If the prediction holds true, we are relatively safe in stating the conditional, If x, then y. In an ex post facto study under the same conditions, however, we are considerably less safe in stating the conditional, for reasons discussed earlier. Careful safeguards are more essential in the latter case, especially in the selection and testing of alternative hypotheses, such as the predicted lack of relation between the eleven-plus examination and general anxiety in the Sarnoff study. A predicted (or unpredicted) relation in ex post facto research may be quite spurious, but its plausibility and conformity to preconception may make it easy to accept. This is a danger in experimental research, but it is *less* of a danger than it is in ex post facto research because an experimental situation is so much easier to control.

Ex post facto research that is conducted without hypotheses, without predictions, research in which data are just collected and then interpreted, is even more dangerous in its power to mislead. Significant differences or correlations are located if possible and then interpreted. Assume that an educator decides to study the factors leading to underachievement. He selects a group of underachievers and a group of normal achievers and administers a battery of tests to both groups. He then computes the means of the two groups on the tests and analyzes the differences with t tests. Among, say, twelve such differences, three are significant. The investigator concludes, then, that underachievers and normal achievers differ on the variables measured by these three tests. Upon analysis of the three tests, he thinks he understands what characterizes underachievers. Since all three of the tests seem to measure insecurity, therefore the cause of underachievement is insecurity.

Although the simplicity of this example is a bit exaggerated, studies very similar to this hypothetical one are often undertaken. When guided by hypotheses the results of such studies are more valid, but the results are still weak because they capitalize on chance relations, and above all, the explanation of the results seems so plausible—once a plausible explanation has been found. According to Merton, *post factum* explanations do not lend themselves to nullifiability, because they are so flexible. Whatever the observations, he says, new interpretations can be found to "fit the facts." [15]

The Value of Ex Post Facto Research   Despite its weaknesses, much ex post facto research must be done in psychology, sociology, and education simply because many research problems in the social sciences and education do not lend themselves to experimental inquiry. A little reflection on some of the important variables in educational research—intelligence,

[15] R. Merton, *Social Theory and Social Structure.* New York: Free Press, 1949, pp. 90, 91.

aptitude, home background, parental upbringing, teacher personality, school atmosphere—will show that they are not manipulable. Controlled inquiry is possible, of course, but true experimentation is not. Sociological problems of education, such as extreme deviation in group behavior and its effect on educational achievement, and board of education decisions and their effects on teacher and administrator performance and morale, are mostly ex post facto in nature. Even if we would avoid ex post facto research, we cannot.

It can even be said that ex post facto research is more important than experimental research. This is, of course, not a methodological observation. It means, rather, that the most important social scientific and educational research problems do not lend themselves to experimentation, although many of them do lend themselves to controlled inquiry of the ex post facto kind. Consider the study of the effect of the English eleven-plus examination on English children, current studies of children's creativity, Piaget's studies of children's thinking, Gross's studies of boards of education and superintendents, and the authoritarianism studies of Adorno, *et al.* If a tally of sound and important studies in psychology, sociology, and education were made, it is likely that ex post facto studies would outnumber and outrank experimental studies.

CONCLUSIONS

Some students of research believe that much behavioral research, but particularly educational research, suffers from a serious lack of a rigorous experimental approach and that it will lag as long as this situation exists. The author believes that good experimental research is badly needed in all fields, and that large doses of poor ex post facto research should be avoided. Improvements in *educational* ex post facto research are badly needed. Perhaps a good rule to follow would be to ignore the results of any ex post facto study that does not test hypotheses. Exceptions to this stricture should be few and far between. Perhaps another good rule would be to be highly skeptical of any ex post facto study that tests only one hypothesis; that is, alternative "negative" hypotheses should be routinely tested. Researchers should predict significant relations *and* nonsignificant relations whenever possible.

A final piece of advice is this: always treat the results and interpretations of the data of ex post facto investigations with great care and caution. Where one must be careful with experimental results and interpretations, one must be doubly careful with ex post facto results and interpretations.

1. A social psychologist plans to investigate factors behind anti-Semitism. He believes that people who have had authoritarian parents and authoritarian upbringing tend to be anti-Semitic. Would a research project designed to test this hypothesis be experimental or ex post facto? Why?

2. An educational psychologist decides to test the hypothesis that intelligence and motivation are the principal determinants of success in school. Would his research be experimental or ex post facto? Why?

3. An investigator is interested in the relation between role perception and attitudes toward education.
   (a) Which is the independent variable? The dependent variable?
   (b) Whatever judgment you have made, could you justifiably reverse the variables?
   (c) Do you think a research project designed to investigate this problem would be basically experimental or ex post facto?
   (d) Could the investigator do two researches, one experimental and one ex post facto, both designed to test the same hypothesis?
   (e) If your answer to (d) was Yes, would the variables of the two problems be the same? Assuming that the relations in both researches were significant, would the conclusions be substantially the same?

4. A researcher is interested in teacher success. He selects two groups of teachers: one that has been highly successful and one that has not been too successful. He finds that successful teachers tend to be more outgoing, somewhat more dependent, and more interested in people than less successful teachers. Assuming that everything has been methodologically well-done, discuss the possible strengths and weaknesses of this research. Can the researcher plan an experiment to test these relations?

5. Suppose that you want to study the effects of the decisions of boards of education on various aspects of education, such as teacher morale, pupil achievement, relations between teachers and administrators, teacher clique formation. Would your research be experimental or ex post facto? Why?

6. In the study suggestions of Chap. 2, a number of problems and hypotheses were given. Take each of these problems and hypotheses and decide whether research designed to explore the problems and test the hypotheses would be basically experimental or ex post facto. Can any of the problems and hypotheses be tackled in both ways?

LABORATORY EXPERIMENTS, FIELD EXPERIMENTS, AND FIELD STUDIES

Social scientific research can be divided into four major categories: laboratory experiments, field experiments, field studies, and survey research.[1] This breakdown stems from two sources, the distinction between experimental and nonexperimental research and that between laboratory and "field" research. With the background of Chap. 20, with its emphasis on the differences between experimental and ex post facto research, it is now possible to concentrate on other important aspects of experiments.

A LABORATORY EXPERIMENT: SHERIF'S STUDIES OF GROUP INFLUENCE ON NORMS

In the 1930's, a remarkably original set of research studies of importance to social science was done by Sherif.[2] Sherif asked whether individuals, when placed in an objectively unstable situation with external frames of reference removed, would establish consistent frames of reference of their own.[3] He also asked whether these subjectively established frames

[1] This chapter owes much to the competent treatments of laboratory experiments, field experiments, and field studies in L. Festinger and D. Katz, *Research Methods in the Behavioral Sciences.* New York: Holt, Rinehart and Winston, Inc., 1953, chaps. 2, 3, and 4.

[2] M. Sherif, "Group Influences upon the Formation of Norms and Attitudes." In E. Maccoby, T. Newcomb, and E. Hartley, eds., *Readings in Social Psychology,* 3rd ed. New York: Holt, Rinehart and Winston, Inc., 1958, pp. 219–232. (This is a good combination of two of Sherif's reports.)

[3] To understand Sherif's study and other studies in this chapter, certain social psychological terms must be defined. A *frame of reference* is a perceptual context that may influence judgments, attitudes, and behavior. It is a standard for evaluating people, objects, and events. "It depends on how you look at it" expresses the idea. A businessman, for example, may view education from an efficiency frame of reference, whereas a teacher may view it from a learning frame of reference. A *norm,* or *social norm,* is a rule governing the behavior of group members, a set of expectations or standards of behavior in certain situations. "Students should study," "Teachers should be kind but firm," and "Behave like a good girl" express social norms. An *attitude* is a predisposition to behave toward persons or objects in one's environment, or a predisposition to perceive, feel, think, and behave toward something. Important social attitudes are attitudes toward

of reference would carry over to group situations. A third question centered on whether a group in the same objectively unstable situation would form a group frame of reference, a group norm, that would influence the individual in subsequent similar situations.

Sherif imaginatively seized on the autokinetic phenomenon as a stimulus situation. When an individual is put into a completely dark room and a stationary point of light is shown briefly, the individual will see the light move, this way, that way, this much distance, that much distance. Sherif showed a point of light to individual subjects in a dark room after telling them that the light would move. The subjects were to tell how much the light had "moved" (in inches) in a series of 100 tests. Each subject's *subjective* judgments stabilized to a norm (in this case an average) and a range; different subjects had different norms. Sherif found that, put into other similar situations, a subject would carry his norm with him.

A similar procedure was used with eight groups of two subjects each and eight groups of three subjects each. Half the individuals of these groups started with the individual situation, as described above, and then functioned as groups. Half of them started with a group situation in which judgments of the "movement" of the light were made with the other group members present, and then their judgments were studied individually.

The results were interesting. When an individual, after establishing a "norm," was put into an individual situation again, he brought the established norm with him, as indicated above. But when he was put into a group situation with others whose norms were different from his own, the different norms tended to converge on a new "group norm." When individuals new to the situation were put into it in groups they tended rather quickly to establish a group norm that was peculiar to the group. Sherif, in a second series of experiments with two-subject groups, used a confederate, who had been assigned to display certain predetermined ranges and norms. The aim of the experiment was to see if the naïve subject would "conform" to the confederate's "norm." When tested alone later, the new subjects, who had "conformed" to the confederate's "norm," continued to use it in judging the supposed movement of the light. Sherif concluded that an experimentally manipulated norm can influence perception of an indefinite stimulus.

---

racial or religious groups, education, etc. These concepts are interrelated. For further discussion, see T. Newcomb, *Social Psychology*. New York: Holt, Rinehart and Winston, Inc., 1950; M. Sherif and C. Sherif, *An Outline of Social Psychology*, rev. ed. New York: Harper & Row, 1956; D. Krech, R. Crutchfield, and E. Ballachey, *Individual in Society*. New York: McGraw-Hill, 1962.

A FIELD EXPERIMENT: VERPLANCK'S STUDY
OF THE REINFORCEMENT OF OPINION STATEMENTS

Verplanck, in a highly original experiment,[4] tested part of the theory of reinforcement in a realistic setting. People say such things as: "Ignore him; he'll go away," and "People like to talk to people who are interested in what they are saying." They are assuming the validity of reinforcement theory, which holds that if responses are reinforced they will be repeated and if they are not reinforced they will tend to die away. Most of the research on this theory has been done using animals as subjects. In the Verplanck experiment human beings who did not know that they were being used as subjects were studied.

Verplanck used 24 subjects, 20 men and 4 women, and 17 "experimenters." Each experimenter (E) engaged a subject (S) in conversation on a variety of topics for at least a half hour. The half hour was divided into three ten-minute periods. During the first ten-minute period, E determined S's rate of opinion output. A comparison baseline of S's opinion utterance rate was thus established. (Of course, individuals differ in the rates at which they express opinions.) In the second ten-minute period, E reinforced S's opinion statements. Each time S uttered an opinion, E would say something affirmative, "Yes, you're right," "That's so," and the like, or would paraphrase S's remarks. This was *positive reinforcement*. In the third ten-minute period, E tried to extinguish opinion statements either by withdrawing *all* reinforcement, by saying nothing when S uttered an opinion, or by disagreeing with S's opinion. This was *no reinforcement* or *negative reinforcement*. E recorded S's opinion statements by coding certain marks in the form of doodling. Each time an opinion was expressed, a certain mark was made.

In summary, Ss' opinion statements were *reinforced* by *agreement* or by *paraphrase* and then *extinguished* by *no response* or by *disagreement*. The independent variable was *reinforcement;* the dependent variable was *rate of opinion utterance*. Relative frequencies of expressed opinions were the measures of the dependent variable.

The results were rather dramatic. All 24 Ss showed an increase in relative frequency of opinion statement during the second, or reinforcement, period; 21 of the 24 Ss showed reduced relative frequencies of expressed opinion during the third, or extinction, period. *Agreement* was found to be slightly more effective than *paraphrase,* though both were effective. There seemed to be little difference between *disagreement* and *no reinforcement*. Verplanck, in a footnote at the end of the report, says that after describing the experiment to someone else he had the interesting

4 W. Verplanck, "The Control of the Content of Conversation: Reinforcement of Statements of Opinion," *Journal of Abnormal and Social Psychology,* LI (1955), 668–676.

and perhaps disconcerting experience of finding himself being used as a subject by the person to whom he was talking. He says that he showed the expected effect and was quite unaware that he had been a subject!

A FIELD STUDY:
NEWCOMB'S BENNINGTON COLLEGE STUDY

In one of the most important studies yet done of the influence on students of a college environment, Newcomb[5] studied the entire student body of Bennington College, about 600 young women, from 1935 to 1939. An unusual facet of the study was Newcomb's attempt to explain both social and personality factors in influencing attitude changes in the students.

Although other hypotheses were tested, the principal hypothesis of the Bennington Study was that new students would converge on the norms of the college group, and that the more the students assimilated to the college community, the greater would be the change in their social attitudes.

Newcomb used a number of paper-and-pencil attitude scales, written reports on students, and individual interviews. The study was longitudinal and ex post facto. The independent variable, while not easy to categorize, might be said to be the social norms of Bennington College. The dependent variables were social attitudes and certain behaviors of the students.

Newcomb found significant, mean-score changes in attitudes between freshmen, on the one hand, and juniors and seniors, on the other. The changes were toward less conservatism on a variety of social issues. For example, the political preferences of juniors and seniors in the 1936 presidential election, when Roosevelt and Landon were candidates, were much less conservative than those of freshmen and sophomores. Of 52 juniors and seniors, 15 percent preferred Landon (Republican), whereas of 52 freshmen, 62 percent preferred Landon. The percentages of preferences for Roosevelt (Democrat) were 54 percent and 29 percent. The mean scores of all students for four years on a scale designed to measure political and economic conservatism were: freshmen, 74.2; sophomores, 69.4; juniors, 65.9, and seniors, 62.4. Evidently the college had affected the students' attitudes.

Newcomb asked a further question: Would these attitudes have changed in other colleges? To answer this question, Newcomb administered his conservatism measures to students of Williams College and Skid-

[5] T. Newcomb, *Personality and Social Change.* New York: Holt, Rinehart and Winston, Inc., 1943. A shorter account, called "Some Patterned Consequences of Membership in a College Community," can be found in T. Newcomb and E. Hartley, eds., *Readings in Social Psychology.* New York: Holt, Rinehart and Winston, Inc., 1947, pp. 345–357.

more College. The comparable mean scores of Skidmore students, freshmen through seniors, were: 79.9, 78.1, 77.0, and 74.1. Although Newcomb does not report a significance test, it seems that Skidmore (and Williams) students did not change as much and as consistently over time as did the Bennington students.

CHARACTERISTICS AND CRITERIA
OF LABORATORY EXPERIMENTS,
FIELD EXPERIMENTS, AND FIELD STUDIES

A *laboratory experiment* is a research study in which the variance of all or nearly all of the possible influential independent variables not pertinent to the immediate problem of the investigation is kept at a minimum. This is done by isolating the research in a physical situation apart from the routine of ordinary living and by manipulating one or more independent variables under rigorously specified, operationalized, and controlled conditions.

Strengths and Weaknesses of Laboratory Experiments The laboratory experiment has the inherent virtue of the possibility of relatively complete control. The laboratory experimenter can, and often does, isolate the research situation from the life around the laboratory by eliminating the many extraneous influences that may affect the dependent variable.

In addition to situation control, laboratory experimenters can ordinarily use random assignment and can manipulate one or more independent variables at will. There are other aspects to laboratory control: the experimenter in most cases can achieve a high degree of specificity in the operational definitions of his variables. The relatively crude operational definitions of field situations, such as many of those associated with the measurement of values, attitudes, aptitudes, and personality traits, do not plague the experimentalist, though the definitional problem is never simple. (The Sherif experiment is a good example. The operational definition of "social norm" is relatively straightforward and clear.)

Closely allied to operational strength is the precision and replicability of laboratory experiments. *Precise* means accurate, definite, unambiguous. Precise measurements are made with precision instruments. In variance terms, the more precise an experimental procedure is, the less the error variance. The more accurate or precise a measuring instrument is, the more certain we can be that the measures obtained do not vary very much from their "true" values. This is the problem of reliability, which will be discussed in a later chapter (Chap. 24).

Precise laboratory results are achieved mainly by controlled manipulation. By specifying exactly the conditions of the experiment, we reduce the risk that subjects may respond equivocally and thus introduce random variance into the experimental situation.

The greatest weakness of the laboratory experiment is probably the lack of strength of independent variables. Since laboratory situations are, after all, situations that are created for special purposes, it can be said that the effects of experimental manipulations are usually weak. The inducing of convergence on the norm by the announced estimates of light movement by Sherif's confederates, while striking, was only a matter of inches and fractions of inches. Compare this to the relatively massive effect of a large group majority on an individual group member in a real-life situation. The board of education member, who knows that an action he wants carried goes against the wishes of the majority of his colleagues and perhaps the majority of the community, is under heavy and massive pressure to converge on the norm. The teenager who loves to study may find it difficult to withstand the social pressure of other teenagers who do not want to study.

One reason for the preoccupation with laboratory precision and refined statistics is the weakness of laboratory effects. To detect a significant difference in the laboratory requires (1) situations and measures with a minimum of random noise, and (2) accurate and sensitive statistical tests that will show relations and significant differences when they exist.

Another weakness is a product of the first: the artificiality of the experimental research situation. Actually, it is difficult to know if artificiality is a weakness or simply a neutral characteristic of laboratory experimental situations. When a research situation is deliberately contrived to exclude the many distractions of the environment, it is perhaps illogical to label the situation with a term that expresses in part the result being sought. The criticism of artificiality does not come from experimenters, who know that experimental situations are artificial; it comes from individuals lacking an understanding of the purposes of laboratory experiments.

The temptation to interpret the results of laboratory experiments incorrectly is great. While Sherif's results are highly significant, in the opinion of many social scientists, they can only tentatively be extrapolated beyond the laboratory. In fact, only with great care can they be generalized beyond the laboratory. Similar results may be obtained in real-life situations, and there is some evidence (Sherif has provided some) that they do. But this is not necessarily the case. The relations must always be tested anew under nonlaboratory conditions.

Although laboratory experiments have internal validity, then, they suffer from a lack of external validity. In Chap. 17 we asked the question: Did X, the experimental manipulation, really make a significant difference? The stronger our confidence in the "truth" of the relations discovered in a research study, the greater the internal validity of the study. When a relation is discovered in a well-executed laboratory experiment, we generally can have considerable confidence in it, since we have exercised the maximum possible control of the independent variable and other possible extraneous independent variables. When Sherif uncovered the relation between the group situation and the phenomenon of convergence on the norm, he could be relatively assured of the "truth" of this relation—in the laboratory. He had achieved a fairly high degree of internal validity. This does not mean, however, that he had necessarily achieved external validity.

One can say: If I study this problem using field experiments, *maybe* I will find the same relation. This is an empirical, not a speculative, matter; we must put the relation to test in the situation to which we want to generalize. Does the convergence on the norm phenomenon work in community groups, faculties, legislative bodies? This lack of external validity is the basis of the objections of many educators to animal studies of learning theory. Their objections are only valid if an experimenter generalizes from the behavior and learning of laboratory animals to the behavior and learning of children. Capable experimentalists, however, rarely blunder in this fashion—they know that the laboratory is a contrived environment.

Purposes of the Laboratory Experiment Laboratory experiments have three related purposes. First, they attempt to discover relations under "pure" and uncontaminated conditions. The experimenter asks: Is x related to y? How is it related to y? How strong is the relation? He seeks to reduce a discovered relation to functional form. He would like to write an equation of the form $y = f(x)$, make predictions on the basis of the function, and perform further laboratory, and perhaps even field tests, to see if the empirical values of the dependent variable y agree with or depart from the predicted values.

A second purpose should be mentioned in conjunction with the first purpose: the testing of predictions derived from theory, primarily, and other research, secondarily. For instance, on the basis of Sherif's norm-convergence finding, one might predict to a number of other laboratory and field experimental situations, as Sherif did in his later studies of boys in camp situations.[6] (See also the work of Asch.[7]) Asch, though, argued that Sherif's stimulus, the light, was ambiguous in the sense that different people would "interpret" it differently, that is, they would see

6 Sherif and Sherif, *op. cit.*, pp. 191ff.

7 S. Asch, "Studies of Independence and Conformity: I. A Minority of One against a Unanimous Majority," *Psychological Monographs*, LXX (1956), Whole No. 416; S. Asch, *Social Psychology*. Englewood Cliffs, N. J.: Prentice-Hall, 1952, chap. 16.

the light move different distances. He wondered whether the convergence phenomenon would work with clear stimuli in a more realistic setting. A series of experiments showed that it did.

A third purpose of laboratory experiments is to refine theories and hypotheses, to formulate hypotheses related to other experimentally or nonexperimentally tested hypotheses, and, perhaps most important, to help build theoretical systems. This was one of Sherif's major purposes in his work, and also of Hull in his many laboratory experiments of reinforcement and learning phenomena. Although some laboratory experiments are conducted without this purpose, of course, most laboratory experiments are strongly theory-oriented.

The aim of laboratory experiments, then, is to test hypotheses derived from theory, to study the precise interrelations of variables and their operation, and to control variance under research conditions that are uncontaminated by the operation of extraneous variables. As such, the laboratory experiment is one of man's greatest achievements. Although weaknesses exist, they are weaknesses only in a sense that is really irrelevant. Conceding the lack of representativeness (external validity) the laboratory experiment still has the fundamental prerequisite of any research: internal validity.

THE FIELD EXPERIMENT

A field experiment is a research study in a realistic situation in which one or more independent variables are manipulated by the experimenter under as carefully controlled conditions as the situation will permit. The contrast between the laboratory experiment and the field experiment is not sharp: the differences are mostly matters of degree. Sometimes it is hard to label a particular study "laboratory experiment" or "field experiment." Where the laboratory experiment has a maximum of control, most field studies must operate with less control, a factor that is often a severe handicap to the experiment.

Strengths and Weaknesses of Field Experiments   Field experiments have values that especially recommend them to educational investigators. (Their weaknesses are for the most part of a practical nature.) The manipulation of independent variables and the possibility of randomization are the most important characteristics of the field experiment. Theoretically, the criterion of control can be satisfied, and if this criterion is satisfied, the problem of establishing causal relations is that much closer to solution. The causal problem of ex post facto research is much less problematic in experimental field research.

The control of the experimental field situation, however, is rarely as tight as the control of the laboratory experimental situation. We have here both a strength and a weakness. The investigator in a field study, though he has the power of manipulation, is always faced with the unpleasant possibility that his independent variables are contaminated by uncontrolled environmental variables. We stress this point because the necessity of controlling extraneous independent variables is particularly urgent in field experiments (see Part IV where most of the research design discussion applied to field experiments). The laboratory experiment is conducted in a tightly controlled situation, whereas the field experiment takes place in a natural, often loose, situation. One of the main preoccupations of the field experimenter, then, is to try to make the research situation more closely approximate the conditions of the laboratory experiment. Of course this is often a difficult goal to reach, but if the research situation can be kept tight, the field experiment is very powerful because statements of causal relations of the if-then type can then be made.

As compensation for the blessing of control's being mixed, the field experiment has two or three unique virtues. The variables in a field experiment usually have a stronger effect than those of laboratory experiments. The reinforcement of the Verplanck study was strong enough to penetrate the distractions of the situations in which the experimental conversations took place. The principle is: The more realistic the research situation, the stronger the variables. This is one advantage of doing research in educational settings. For the most part, research in school settings is similar to routine educational activities, and thus need not be necessarily viewed as something special and apart from school life. Despite the pleas of many educators for more realistic educational research, there is no special virtue in realism, as realism. Realism simply increases the strength of the variables. It also contributes to external validity, since the more realistic the situation, the more valid are generalizations to other situations likely to be.

Another virtue of field experiments is their appropriateness for studying complex social influences, processes, and changes in lifelike settings. The dynamics and interactions of small groups have been fruitfully studied in field experiments. Verplanck, in the study summarized earlier, studied the social process of communication in a natural situation. Coch and French manipulated participation in planning and studied its effect on various dependent variables—production, resignations, and aggression.[8] The broad hypothesis tested was that resistance to change can be overcome by increased participation in decisions or processes that may lead to change. Factory workers were divided into three groups. The

8 L. Coch and J. French, "Overcoming Resistance to Change," *Human Relations*, I (1948), 512–532.

members of the control group did not participate in any of the discussions or decisions about changes in the factory. Two experimental groups did participate in discussion and decision in different degrees: total participation and participation by representation. The results supported the hypothesis.

The study of social processes and social change could be of great importance to education, but there are few educational field experiments in which they are the main focus of the experiment. Most field experiments in educational research have practical purposes, like seeking answers to problems of teaching and classroom management. Educational studies that are theoretical in nature tend to be ex post facto. As the outlook, methods, and content of social psychology, which is a relatively new discipline, influence educators, we can expect to see a pronounced increase in the number of field experiments on social process and social change in educational settings.

Field experiments are well-suited both to the testing of theory and to the solution of practical problems. While the Verplanck experiment was geared basically to the realistic testing of hypotheses derived from reinforcement theory, it also had practical results. Methods experiments in education are usually practical in purpose and seek to determine which methods get the best learning results. Koenker's arithmetic readiness study, studies of college teaching by Marr and McKeachie, studies of homogeneous and heterogeneous grouping, experiments on underachievers, studies of systematic versus nonsystematic early instruction, and many others are oriented to practical outcomes. Although some educators strongly believe that most educational research should be applied research, in recent years other educators have urged increased theoretical research.[9]

Another characteristic of field experiments is that they are suited to testing broad hypotheses. A good example is the cohesiveness-attraction hypothesis of group dynamics: The greater the cohesiveness of a group, the greater its power to influence its members.[10] This is a broad generalization, but one that is not difficult to operationalize and test in field experiments. An educational example, positive reinforcement produces better learning, is a broad hypothesis perhaps more difficult to test adequately in the field situation than is the cohesiveness hypothesis. An important hypothesis adaptable to field experimentation is that principles

9 For a good discussion of the issues involved, see R. Travers, *An Introduction to Educational Research.* New York: Macmillan, 1958, chap. 3ff. See also F. Kerlinger, "The Mythology of Educational Research: The Methods Approach," *School and Society,* LXXXVIII (1960), 149–151.

10 L. Festinger, S. Schachter, and K. Back, *Social Pressures in Informal Groups.* New York: Harper & Row, 1950, chap. 5; S. Schachter, *et al.,* "An Experimental Study of Cohesiveness and Productivity," *Human Relations,* IV (1951), 229–238.

learned through induction from concrete cases are transferred more to new situations than are principles taught as principles.[11]

Flexibility and applicability to a wide variety of problems are important characteristics of field experiments, the only two limitations being whether one or more independent variables can be manipulated and whether the practical exigencies of the research situation are such that a field experiment can be done on the particular problem under study. Surmounting these two limitations is not easy. When it *can* be done, a wide range of theoretical and practical problems is open to experimentation.

As indicated earlier, the main weaknesses of field experiments are practical. Although the manipulation of an independent variable may be conceivable, it may not be possible or practical to do so. Many variables, of course, cannot be manipulated, at least in our society and in our schools.

Another practical difficulty, especially in school situations, is the problem of randomization. There is no theoretical reason why randomization cannot be used in field experiments. The obstacles to its use are practical problems like the unwillingness to break up class groups or to allow children to be assigned to experimental groups at random. Even if the random assignment is permitted, the independent variable may be seriously blurred, because the effects of the treatment cannot be isolated. Teachers and children, for example, may discuss what is happening during the course of the experiment. To prevent such muddying of the variables, the experimenter should explain to administrators and teachers the necessity for random assignment and careful control. Lacking the ability to randomize, the experimenter must abandon the research, modify it to suit the situation, or seek another situation where randomization is feasible and permissible.

An experimental field characteristic of a different nature is to some experimenters a weakness and to others a strength. A field investigator has to be, to some extent at least, a socially skilled operator. He should be able to work with people, talk to them, and convince them of the importance and necessity of his research. He should be prepared to spend many hours, even days and weeks, of patient discussion with people responsible for the institutional or community situation in which he is to work. For instance, if he is to work in a rural school system, he should have a knowledge of rural as well as general educational problems, and of the particular rural system he wishes to study. Some researchers become impatient with these preliminaries, because they are anxious to get

[11] This is an altered form of the hypothesis of G. Haslerud and S. Meyers, "The Transfer Value of Given and Individually Derived Principles," *Journal of Educational Psychology*, XLIX (1958), 293–298.

the research job done. They find it difficult to spend the time and effort necessary in most practical situations. Others enjoy the inevitable socializing that accompanies field research.[12]

An important obstacle to good design, an obstacle that seems ordinarily to be overlooked, is the attitude of the researcher. For example, the planning of educational research often seems to be characterized by a negative attitude epitomized by such statements as, "That can't be done in schools," "The administrators and teachers won't allow that," and "Experiments can't be done on this problem in that situation." Starting with attitudes like this compromises any good research design before the research even begins. If, for example, a research design calls for the random assignment of teachers to classes, and if the lack of such assignment seriously jeopardizes the internal validity of the proposed study, every effort should be made to assign teachers at random. Educators planning research seem to assume that the administrators or the teachers will not permit random assignment. This assumption is not necessarily valid, however.

The consent and cooperation of teachers and administrators can often be obtained if a proper approach, with adequate and accurate orientation, is used, and if explanations of the reasons for the use of specific experimental methods are given. The points being emphasized are these: Design research to obtain valid answers to the research questions. Then, if it is necessary to make the experiment possible, and only then, modify the "ideal" design. With imagination, patience, and courtesy, many of the practical problems of implementation of research design can be satisfactorily solved.

One other weakness inherent in field experimental situations is lack of precision. In the laboratory experiment it is possible to achieve a high degree of precision or accuracy, so that laboratory measurement and control problems are usually simpler than those in field experiments. In realistic situations, there is always a great deal of systematic and random noise. In order to measure the effect of an independent variable on a dependent variable in the field experiment, it is not only necessary to maximize the variance of the manipulated variable and any assigned variables, but also to measure the dependent variable as precisely as possible. But in realistic situations, such as in schools and community groups, extraneous independent variables abound. And measures of dependent variables, unfortunately, are sometimes not sensitive enough to pick up the messages of our independent variable. In other words, the dependent variable measures are often so crude that they cannot pick up all the variance that has been engendered by the independent variable.

[12] Good advice on handling this aspect of field situations is given by J. French, "Experiments in Field Settings," in Festinger and Katz, op. cit., pp. 118–129, and D. Katz, "Field Studies," ibid., pp. 87–89.

FIELD STUDIES

Field studies are ex post facto scientific inquiries aimed at discovering the relations and interactions among sociological, psychological, and educational variables in real social structures. Many large studies, such as those discussed earlier—the Sears, Maccoby, and Levin study of child-rearing practices and the Sarason anxiety studies, for example—are field studies. In this book, *any* scientific studies, large or small, that systematically pursue relations and test hypotheses, that are ex post facto, that are made in life situations like communities, schools, factories, organizations, and institutions will be considered field studies.

The investigator in a field study first looks at a social or institutional situation and then studies the relations among the attitudes, values, perceptions, and behaviors of individuals and groups in the situation. He ordinarily manipulates no independent variables. Before discussing and appraising the various types of field studies, it will be helpful to consider three or four examples. (See Chap. 20 for discussions of two large-scale studies by Newcomb, and Sears, Maccoby, and Levin.)

Examples of smaller field studies are numerous. An excellent example is Getzels and Guba's study of role conflict and role-taking effectiveness.[13] Getzels and Guba studied Air Force officers who were also instructors at an Air Force school. The amount of conflict between the role of an officer as officer and his role as instructor was related to his rated effectiveness. It was found that the more acute this conflict became, the more ineffective the officer tended to be. Getzels and Guba thus used a ready-made educational situation to test hypotheses derived from role theory. This is a case where manipulation of the independent variable is rather unlikely.

Cook and Greenhoe in a large educational field study of different groups—school board members, teachers, citizens, and students—were asked to rate a number of applicants for "social fitness" for teaching positions.[14] Among the applicants presented were individuals of different religions and beliefs. In general, board of education members were found to be the least liberal, then citizens, then teachers; students were found to be the most liberal.

Marquis, Guetzkow, and Heyns, in a unique and significant field investigation, studied 72 actual decision-making conferences.[15] Through direct observation and questionnaires, the satisfaction of group members

13 J. Getzels and E. Guba, "Role, Role Conflict, and Effectiveness," *American Sociological Review*, XIX (1954), 164–175. This study is particularly distinguished by its strong theoretical orientation.
14 L. Cook and F. Greenhoe, "Community Contacts of 9122 Teachers," *Social Forces*, XIX (1940), 63–72.
15 D. Marquis, H. Guetzkow, and R. Heyns, "A Social Psychological Study of The Decision-Making Conference." In H. Guetzkow, ed., *Groups, Leadership, and Men*. Pittsburgh, Pa.: Carnegie Press, 1951, pp. 55–67.

with the conferences and their outcomes, and the productivity of the conferences, were determined. It was found that group-member satisfaction increased with procedural structuring of the meetings, with cohesiveness of the groups, and with *opportunity* to talk (but not actual participation of group members). Cohesive groups were found to be no more productive than noncohesive groups.

Types of Field Studies   Katz has divided field studies into two broad types: *exploratory* and *hypothesis-testing*.[16] The exploratory type, says Katz, *seeks what is* rather than *predict relations* to be found. The Cook and Greenhoe and the Marquis, Guetzkow, and Heyns studies more or less exemplify this type of study, though so categorizing them might be criticized. Exploratory studies have three purposes: to discover significant variables in the field situation, to discover relations among variables,[17] and to lay a groundwork for later, more systematic and rigorous testing of hypotheses.

Throughout this book up to this point, the use and testing of hypotheses has been emphasized. It is well to recognize, though, that there are activities preliminary to hypothesis-testing in scientific research. In order to achieve the desirable aim of hypothesis-testing, preliminary methodological and measurement investigation must often be done. Some of the finest work of the twentieth century has been in this area. An example of this work is that done by the factor analyst, who is preoccupied with the discovery, isolation, specification, and measurement of underlying dimensions of achievement, intelligence, aptitudes, attitudes, situations, and personality traits.

The second subtype of exploratory field studies, research aimed at discovering or uncovering relations, is indispensable to scientific advance in the social sciences. It is necessary to know, for instance, the correlates of the variables of our science. Indeed, the scientific meaning of a construct springs from the relations it has with other constructs.

Assume that we have no scientific knowledge of the construct "intelligence": we know nothing of its causes or concomitants. For example, suppose that we know nothing whatsoever about the relation of intelligence to achievement. It is conceivable that we might do a field study in school situations. We might carefully observe a number of boys and girls who are said to be intelligent or nonintelligent by teachers (though right here we introduce contamination, because teachers must obviously judge intelligence, in part at least, by achievement). We may notice that a larger number of "more intelligent" children come from homes of higher socioeconomic levels; they solve problems in class more quickly than other children; they have a wider vocabulary, and so on. We now have some

16 Katz, *op. cit.*, pp. 75–83.
17 *Ibid.*, p. 75.

clues to the nature of intelligence, so that we can attempt to construct a simple measure of intelligence. Note that our "definition" of intelligence springs from what presumably intelligent and nonintelligent children *do*. A similar procedure could be followed with the variable "achievement."

Strengths and Weaknesses of Field Studies Field studies are strong in realism, significance, strength of variables, theory orientation, and heuristic quality. The variance of many variables in actual field settings is large, especially when compared to the variance of the variables of laboratory experiments. Consider the contrast between the impact of social norms in a laboratory experiment like Sherif's and the impact of these norms in a community where, say, certain actions of teachers are frowned upon and others approved. Consider also the difference between studying cohesiveness in the laboratory where subjects are asked, for example, whether they would like to remain in a group (measure of cohesiveness) and studying the cohesiveness of a school faculty where staying in the group is an essential part of one's professional future. Compare the group atmosphere in the Bennington College Study and that in a field experiment where different atmospheres are planned by college instructors playing different roles. Variables such as social class, prejudiced attitudes, conservatism, liberalism, economic frustration, and mass communication can have a massive effect in these studies.

The strength of variables is not an unalloyed blessing. In a field situation there is usually so much noise in the communication channel that even though the effects may be strong and the variance great, it is not easy for the experimenter to separate the variables.

The realism of field studies is obvious. Of all types of studies, they are closest to real life. There can be no complaint of artificiality here. (The remarks about realism in field experiments apply, *a fortiori,* to the realism of field studies.)

The application of scientific method to such human problems as delinquency, morale, prejudice, social and educational attitudes, value conflicts, child-rearing practices, and authoritarianism was started in this century. Much has been learned by scientists seeking to understand the origin and the correlates of religious and other prejudice, or the relation between child-rearing practices and adult social behavior, or the relation between the values of society in general and the educational practices of schools. These are problems that are closer to practical men and women than are many other scientific problems.

Social significance, however, does not always mean scientific significance. Practical field studies designed only for the ultimate solution of practical problems will always be desirable. If they exclude theoretical scientific problems, however, they defeat the purpose of scientific research. The researcher can get so involved in the fascinating business of examining complex human attributes and activities that he may find it difficult to focus his mind on the theory he is trying to develop and to test. For instance, he may ask the question, Is there a relation between religious preference or political preference and authoritarian attitudes? But a more important scientific question lies behind this surface question: *Why* are religious and political preferences related to authoritarian attitudes? The answer to this theoretical problem would solve not just this one question but many other related, though perhaps not so obvious, questions. In other words, the social significance of field studies is definitely a strength, but without scientific vigilance social scientific and educational research can be weakened.

Field studies are highly heuristic. Any researcher knows that one of the research difficulties of a field study is to keep himself contained within the limits of his problem. Hypotheses frequently fling themselves at one. The field is rich in discovery potentiality. For example, he may decide to test the hypothesis that the social attitudes of board of education members is a determinant of board of education policy decisions. After starting to gather data, however, he stumbles upon many interesting notions that can deflect the course of his investigation: the relation between the attitudes of board of education members and their election to the boards, the relation between the scope of men's business and professional interests and their seeking board of education membership, and the different conceptions of the curriculum problems of board members, administrators, teachers, and parents.

Despite these strengths, the field study is a scientific weak cousin of laboratory and field experiments. Its most serious weakness, of course, is its ex post facto character. Thus statements of causal relations are much weaker than they are in experimental research. To complicate matters further, the field situation almost always has a plethora of variables and variance. Think of the many possible independent variables that we might choose as determinants of school achievement. In an experimental study, these variables can be controlled to a large extent, but in a field study, they must be related somehow to achieve whatever degree of control we can get by more indirect and less satisfactory means.

Another methodological weakness is the lack of precision in the measurement of field variables. In field *studies,* the problem of precision is more acute, naturally, than in field *experiments.* The problems of measurement encountered by Sears, Maccoby, and Levin is good evidence of the lack of precision of field studies. In measuring such variables as dependence and aggression, these traits had to be very indirectly inferred —through interviews with the children's mothers.

Other weaknesses of field studies are practical problems: feasibility, cost, sampling, and time. These difficulties are really *potential* weaknesses —none of them need be a real weakness. The most obvious questions that can be asked are: Can the study be done with the facilities at the investigator's disposal? Can the variables be measured? Will it cost too much? Will it take too much time and effort? Will the subjects be cooperative? Is random sampling possible? Anyone contemplating a field study has to ask and answer such questions. In designing research it is important not to underestimate the large amounts of time, energy, and skill necessary for the successful completion of most field studies. The field researcher needs to be salesman, administrator, and entrepreneur, as well as investigator.[18]

[18] For details, see Katz, *op. cit.,* especially pp. 65ff.

22 *SURVEY RESEARCH*

This chapter will be devoted to the use of survey research in social scientific and educational research.[1] The dictionary defines a *survey* as a "critical inspection, often official, to provide exact information; often, a study of an area with respect to a certain condition, or its prevalence; as, a *survey* of the schools."[2] A survey in education generally means gathering facts about schools, such as their facilities and personnel, the average salaries of teachers, pupil-teacher ratios, the availability of facilities and equipment, and so on. The purpose of a school survey is usually to assay conditions in a school, or schools, generally for some practical purpose. The largest surveys, called *status surveys,* are those done by the United States Bureau of the Census on such topics as school enrollment and school districts. The National Education Association has for years surveyed teachers' salaries throughout the country. Individual states survey the tax rates, school districts, bonded indebtedness, the average expenditure per pupil, and the curricula of local school districts. The aim of such studies is to learn the status quo rather than to study the relations among variables.

This type of study, so firmly entrenched in the educational mind, is not scientific. Except for sophisticated sampling designs, and the methods of the Census Bureau and of certain survey research agencies, it is more analogous to skilled clerical work. To ferret out pupil-teacher ratios, bonded indebtedness, curricular practices, and the like is basically routine fact-gathering and has little resemblance to scientific behavioral research. The practice of surveying strictly for fact-gathering will not be discussed in this book. The reader who learns the basic elements of scientific research will find status surveys, such as those described above, more

---

[1] Although important, the work of public opinion pollsters, such as Gallup, Crossley, and Roper, will not be considered here. For a good account of the polls and other surveys, see M. Parten, *Surveys, Polls, and Samples.* New York: Harper & Row, 1950, chap. 1.

[2] *Webster's New Collegiate Dictionary,* 2d ed. Springfield, Mass.: Merriam, 1949, p. 855.

or less routine.[3] The exceptions to this statement are sampling, questionnaire construction, and interviewing, topics we shall examine later.

A DEFINITION OF SURVEY RESEARCH

Survey research is that branch of social scientific investigation that
studies large and small populations (or universes) by selecting and
studying samples chosen from the populations to discover the relative
incidence, distribution, and interrelations of sociological and psychological variables. Surveys covered by this definition are often called *sample surveys,* probably because survey research developed as a separate
research activity, along with the development and improvement of sampling procedures. Surveys, as such, are not new. Social welfare studies were
done in England as long ago as the eighteenth century.[4] Survey research
in the social scientific sense, however, is quite new—it is a development
of the twentieth century.

As noted in the above definition, survey research is considered to be
a branch of social scientific research, which immediately distinguishes
survey research from the status survey. The procedures and methods of
survey research have been developed mostly by psychologists, sociologists,
anthropologists, economists, political scientists, and statisticians.[5] These
men have put a rigorous scientific stamp on survey research and, in the
process, have profoundly influenced the social sciences.

The definition also links populations and samples. The survey researcher is interested in the accurate assessment of the characteristics of
whole populations of people. He wants to know, for instance, how many
persons in the United States are going to vote for the Republican candidate. He wants to know the relation between a purchaser's economic
status and the kind of automobile he purchases, to give another example.
He wants to know the relation between the attitudes toward education
and the public support of a school bond issue of the population of a
school district. In short, the survey researcher wants to know something
about *U,* the universe.

Only rarely, however, do survey researchers study whole populations: they study *samples* drawn from populations. From these samples
they infer the characteristics of the defined population or universe. The
study of samples from which inferences about populations can be drawn

[3] There is no intention of derogating status surveys. They are important and
indispensable. The intention is to separate, clearly and unambiguously, status surveys
and scientific survey research.

[4] Parten, *op. cit.,* p. 5.

[5] A. Campbell and G. Katona, "The Sample Survey: A Technique for Social-
Science Research." In L. Festinger and D. Katz, *Research Methods in the Behavioral
Sciences.* New York: Holt, Rinehart and Winston, Inc., 1953, chap. 1.

are needed because of the difficulties of attempting to study whole populations. Random samples can often furnish the same information as a census (an enumeration and study of an entire population) at much less cost, with greater efficiency, and sometimes with greater accuracy.

Sample surveys attempt to determine the incidence, distribution, and interrelations among sociological and psychological variables. Although the approach and the techniques of survey research can be used on any set of objects that can be well-defined, survey research focuses on people, the vital facts of people, and their beliefs, opinions, attitudes, motivations, and behavior.

The social scientific nature of survey research is revealed by the nature of its variables, which can be classified as sociological *facts* and *opinions* and *attitudes. Sociological facts* are attributes of individuals that spring from their membership in social groups or sets: sex, income, political and religious affiliation, socioeconomic status, education, age, living expenses, occupation, race, and so on.[6]

The second type of variable is psychological and includes opinions and attitudes, on the one hand, and behavior, on the other. The survey researcher is not interested primarily in the sociological variables, as such: he is primarily interested in what people think and what they do. The sociological variables are then related in some manner to the psychological variables. An example will show this quite well. Table 22.1 gives some of the data from Gross's study of the members of boards of education and superintendents of schools in Massachusetts.[7] The board members and superintendents were asked whether they thought there should be specific academic standards for promotion in the first six grades. The table shows the pertinent percentages. Evidently there *is* a relation between role (the sociological and independent variable) and belief about promotion standards (the psychological and dependent variable). School board members seem to believe more in academic standards for promotion than do school superintendents.

TABLE 22.1   RELATION BETWEEN ROLE AND BELIEFS ABOUT PROMOTION
POLICIES—GROSS STUDY

| | *Belief about Academic Standards for Promotion* | | | |
	Desirable	No Opinion	Undesirable	*N*
School Board Members	84%	1%	15%	508
Superintendents	51%	0%	49%	105

6 For a complete description of such social and personal facts, see Parten, *op. cit.,* pp. 169–174.

7 N. Gross, *Who Runs Our Schools?* New York: Wiley, 1958, p. 115.

Survey researchers, of course, also study the relations among psychological variables. For example, Gross also reports the relation between the educational progressivism of board members and the number of hours spent on board activities.[8]

TYPES OF SURVEYS

Surveys can be conveniently classified by the following methods of obtaining information: personal interview, mail questionnaire, panel, telephone, and controlled observation. Of these, the personal interview far overshadows the others as perhaps the most powerful and useful tool of social scientific survey research. These survey types will be briefly described here; in a later chapter, when studying methods of data collection, we shall return to two of them: the personal interview and controlled observation.

Interviews and Schedules   The best examples of survey research use the personal interview as the principal method of gathering information. This is accomplished in part by the careful and laborious construction of a schedule or questionnaire.[9] Schedule information includes factual information, opinions and attitudes, and reasons for behavior, opinions, and attitudes. Interview schedules are difficult to construct; they are time-consuming, and relatively costly; but there is no other method that yields the information they do.

The *factual information* gathered in surveys includes the so-called sociological data mentioned previously: sex, marital status, education, income, political preference, religious preference, and the like. Such information is indispensable, since it is used in studying the relations among variables and in checking the adequacy of samples. These data, which are entered on a "face sheet," are called "face sheet information." Face sheet information, at least part of it, is ordinarily obtained at the beginning of the interview. Much of it is neutral in character and serves to help the interviewer establish rapport with the respondent. Questions of a more personal nature, such as those about income and personal habits, and questions that are more difficult to answer such as the extent of the knowledge or ability of the respondent, can be reserved for later questioning, perhaps at the end of the schedule.[10] The timing must necessarily be a matter of judgment and experience.

Other kinds of factual information include what respondents know

---

[8] *Ibid.,* p. 180.

[9] The term "schedule" will be used. It has a clear meaning: the instrument used to gather survey information through personal interview. "Questionnaire" has been used to label personal interview instruments and attitudinal or personality instruments. The latter are called "scales" in this book.

[10] Parten, *op. cit.,* p. 215.

about the subject under investigation, what respondents did in the past, what they are doing now, and what they intend to do in the future. After all, unless we observe behavior directly, all data about respondents' behavior must come from them or from other people. In this special sense, past, present, and future behavior can all be classified under the "fact" of behavior, even if the behavior is only an intention. A major point of such factual questions is that the respondent presumably knows a good deal about his own actions and behavior. If he says he voted for a school bond issue, we can believe him—unless there is compelling evidence to the contrary. Similarly, we can believe him, perhaps with more reservation (since the event has not happened yet), if he says he is going to vote for a school bond issue.

Just as important, maybe even more important from a social scientific standpoint, are the beliefs, opinions, attitudes, and feelings that respondents have about cognitive objects.[11] Many of the cognitive objects of survey research may not be of interest to the researcher: investments, certain commercial products, political candidates, and the like. Other cognitive objects are more interesting: the United Nations, UNESCO, integration. Among cognitive objects of probable interest to educational scientists are: teachers, students, boards of education, educational administrators, educational practices, Federal aid to education, integrated schools, school reorganization, bond issues, and education itself.

The personal interview can be very helpful in learning a respondent's own estimate of his *reasons* for doing or believing something. When asked his reasons for his actions, intentions, or attitudes, a person may say he has done something, intends to do something, or feels a certain way about something. He may specify that a group affiliation or loyalty or an event may have influenced him. Or he may have heard about the issue under investigation via public media of communication. For example, a respondent may say that, while he was formerly opposed to Federal aid to education because he and his political party have always opposed government interference, he now supports Federal aid because he has read a great deal about the problem in newspapers and magazines and has come to the conclusion that Federal aid would benefit American education.

A respondent's desires, values, and needs may influence his attitudes and actions. When saying why he favors Federal aid to education the respondent may indicate that his own educational aspirations were thwarted and that he has always yearned for more education. Or he may indicate that his religious group has, as a part of its value structure, a deep com-

---

11 *Cognitive object* is an expression used to indicate the object of an attitude. Almost anything can be the object of an attitude, but the term is ordinarily reserved for important social "objects," for example, groups (religious, racial, educational) and institutions (education, marriage, political parties, banks).

mitment to the education of children. If the individual under study has accurately sounded his own desires, values, and needs—and can express them verbally—the personal interview can be very valuable.

Other Types of Survey Research The next-important type of survey research is the *panel* technique.[12] A sample of respondents is selected and interviewed, and then reinterviewed and studied at later times. The panel technique enables the researcher to study changes in behaviors and attitudes.

Telephone surveys have little to recommend them beyond speed and low cost. Especially when the interviewer is unknown to the respondent they are limited by possible nonresponse, uncooperativeness, and by reluctance to answer more than simple, superficial questions. Yet telephoning can sometimes be useful in obtaining information essential to a study. Its principal defect, obviously, is the inability to obtain detailed information.

The *mail questionnaire,* another type of survey, is in popular use in education, although it has serious drawbacks unless it is used in conjunction with other techniques. Two of these defects are possible lack of response and the inability to check the responses given. These defects, especially the first, are serious enough to make the mail questionnaire worse than useless, except in highly sophisticated hands. Responses to mail questionnaires are generally poor. Returns of less than 40 or 50 percent are common. Higher percentages are rare. At best, the researcher must content himself with returns as low as 50 or 60 percent.

As a result of low returns in mail questionnaires, valid generalizations cannot be made.[13] Although there are means of securing larger returns and reducing deficiencies—follow-up questionnaires, enclosing money, interviewing a random sample of nonrespondents and analyzing nonrespondent data—these methods are costly, time-consuming, and often ineffective. As Parten says, "Most mail questionnaires bring so few returns, and these from such a highly selected population, that the findings of such surveys are almost invariably open to question." [14] The best advice would seem to be not to use mail questionnaires if a better method can possibly be used. If mail questionnaires are used, every effort should be made to obtain returns of at least 80 to 90 percent or more, and lacking such returns, to learn something of the characteristics of the nonrespondents.

[12] See P. Lazarsfeld, "The Use of Panels in Social Research," in B. Berelson and M. Janowitz, *Supplement to Reader in Public Opinion and Communication.* New York: Free Press, 1953, pp. 511–519.

[13] See Parten, *op. cit.,* pp. 391–402, for a discussion of the inadequacies of mail questionnaires and remedies for remediable deficiencies. For further discussion of mail questionnaires, see W. Goode and P. Hatt, *Methods in Social Research.* New York: McGraw-Hill, 1952, chap. 12.

[14] Parten, *op. cit.,* p. 400.

THE METHODOLOGY OF SURVEY RESEARCH

Survey research has contributed much to the methodology of the social sciences. Its most important contributions, perhaps, have been to rigorous sampling procedures, to the over-all design and the implementation of the design of studies, to the unambiguous definition and specification of the research problem, and to the analysis of data.

In the limited space of a section of one chapter, it is obviously impossible to discuss adequately the methodology of survey research. Only those parts of the methodology germane to the purposes of this book, therefore, will be outlined in this chapter: the survey or study design, the so-called flow plan or chart of survey researchers, and the check of the reliability and validity of the sample and the data-gathering methods. (Sampling was discussed in Part I; analysis will be discussed in Part VIII.)

Survey researchers use a "flow plan" or chart to outline the design and subsequent implementation of a survey.[15] The flow plan starts with the objectives of the survey, lists each step to be taken in the survey, and ends with the final report. First, the general and specific problems that are to be solved are as carefully and as completely stated as possible. Since, in principle, there is nothing very different here from the discussion of problems and hypotheses of Chap. 2, we can omit detailed discussion and give one simple hypothetical example. An educational investigator has been commissioned by a board of education to study the attitudes of community members toward the school system. On discussing the general problem with the board of education and the administrators of the school system, the investigator notes a number of more specific problems, such as: Is the attitude of the members of the community affected by their having children in school? Are their attitudes affected by their educational level?

One of the investigator's most important jobs is to specify and clarify the problem. To do this well, he should not expect just to ask people what they think of the schools, although this may be a good way to begin if one does not know much about the subject. He should have specific questions to ask that are aimed at various facets of the problem. Each of these questions should be built into the interviewing schedule and other instruments that may be used in the survey. Some survey researchers even design tables for the analysis of data at this point in order to clarify the research problem and to guide the construction of interview questions. Since this procedure is recommended, let us design a couple of tables in a simple manner to show how they can be used to specify survey objectives and questions.

Take the question: Is attitude related to educational level? The question requires that "attitude" and "educational level" be operationally defined. Positive and negative attitudes will be inferred from re-

15 Campbell and Katona, *op. cit.*, pp. 39–41.

sponses to schedule questions and items: If, in response to a broad question like, "In general, what do you think of the school system here?" a respondent says, "It is one of the best in this area," it can be inferred that he has a positive attitude toward the schools. Naturally, one question will not be enough. Related questions should be used, too. A definition of "educational level" is quite easy to obtain. It is decided to use three levels: (1) Some College, (2) High School Graduate, and (3) Non-High School Graduate. The analysis paradigm might look like Fig. 22.1.

	Positive Attitude	Negative Attitude
Some College		
High School Graduate		
Non-High School Graduate		

FIG. 22.1

The virtue of paradigms like this one is that the researcher can immediately tell whether he has stated a specific problem clearly and whether the specific problem is related to the general problem. It also gives him some notion as to how many respondents he will need to fill the table cells adequately, as well as providing him with guidelines for coding and analysis. In addition, as Katz says, "By actually going through the mechanics of setting out such tables, the investigators are bound to discover complexities of a variable that need more detailed measurement and qualifications of hypotheses in relation to special conditions." [16]

The next step in the flow plan is the sample and the sampling plan. Because sampling is much too complex to be discussed here,[17] we shall outline only the main ideas. First, the universe to be sampled and studied

[16] D. Katz, "Field Studies," in Festinger and Katz, op. cit., pp. 80, 81.
[17] For a good general discussion of sampling in relation to the present chapter, see Goode and Hatt, op. cit., chap. 14. A more technical discussion is: L. Kish, "Selection of the Sample," in Festinger and Katz, op. cit., chap. 5. Parten's chapters on the subject are detailed and useful: Parten, op. cit., chaps. 4, 7, 8, and 9. A good brief reference on so-called area sampling is: M. Hansen and P. Hauser, "Area Sampling—Some Principles of Sample Design," in Berelson and Janowitz, op. cit., pp. 546–554. Area sampling is the type of sampling most used in survey research. First, defined large areas are sampled at random. This amounts to partitioning of the universe and random sampling the cells of the partition. The partition cells may be areas delineated by grids on maps or aerial photographs of counties, school districts, or city blocks. Then further subarea samples may be drawn at random from the large areas already drawn. Finally, all individuals or families or random samples of individuals and families may be drawn.

must be defined. Are all citizens living in the community included: Community leaders? Those citizens paying school taxes? Those with children of school age? Those with children in school? Once the universe is defined, a decision is made as to how the sample is to be drawn and how many cases will be drawn. In the best survey research, random samples are used. Because of their high cost and greater difficulty of execution random samples are often bypassed for *quota samples*. In a quota (or quota control) sample, "representativeness" is presumably achieved by assigning quotas to interviewers—so many men and women, so many whites and Negroes, and so on. Quota sampling should be avoided in behavioral survey research: while it *may* achieve representativeness, it is impossible to *assume* representativeness because the procedure is nonrandom.

The next large step in a survey is the construction of the interview schedule and other measuring instruments to be used. This is a laborious and difficult business bearing virtually no resemblance to the questionnaires often hastily put together for research in education. The main task is to translate the research questions into an interview instrument and into any other instruments constructed for the survey. One of the problems of the study, for instance, may be: How are permissive and restrictive attitudes toward the discipline of children related to perceptions of the local school system? Among the questions to be written to assess permissive and restrictive attitudes, one might be: How do you feel children should be disciplined? After drafts of the interview schedule and other instruments are completed, they are pretested on a small representative sample of the universe. They are then revised and put in final form.

The steps outlined above constitute the first large part of any survey. Data collection is the second large part. Interviewers are oriented, trained, and sent out with complete instructions as to whom to interview and how the interview is to be handled. In the best surveys, interviewers are allowed no latitude as to whom to interview. They must interview those individuals and only those individuals designated, generally by random devices. Some latitude may be allowed in the actual interviewing and use of the schedule, but not much. The work of interviewers is also systematically checked in some manner. For example, every tenth interview may be checked by sending another interviewer to the same respondent. Interview schedules are also studied for signs of spurious answering and reporting.

The third large part of the flow plan is analytical. The responses to questions are coded and tabulated. *Coding* is the term used to describe the translation of question responses and respondent information to specific categories for purposes of analyses.[18] Take the example of Fig. 22.1. All

18 A discussion of simple coding is given by Goode and Hatt, *op. cit.*, pp. 315–325. For detailed discussions of coding and coding problems, mimeographed instructional

respondents must be assigned to one of the three educational-level categories and a number (or another symbol) assigned to each level. Then each person must also be assigned to a "positive attitude" or "negative attitude" category. To aid in the coding, content analysis may be used. Content analysis is an objective and quantitative method for assigning types of verbal and other data to categories. Coding can mean the analysis of factual response data and then the assignment of individuals to classes or categories, or the assigning of categories to individuals, especially if one is preparing machine cards for machine analysis. Such cards consist of a large number of columns with a number of cells in each column. The fifth column may be assigned, say, to sex, and the first two cells of the column, or the numbers 0 and 1, used to designate female and male.

Tabulation is simply the recording of the numbers of types of responses in the appropriate categories, after which statistical analysis follows: the computation of percentages, averages, relational indices, and appropriate tests of significance. If an attitude scale or other scales have been used, different types of analysis are of course necessary.

The analyses of the data are studied, collated, assimilated, and interpreted. Finally, the results of this interpretative process are reported.

Checking Survey Data The data of survey research can very often be checked. Some of the respondents can be reinterviewed and the results of both interviews checked against each other. It has been found that the reliability of personal factual items, like age and income, is high.[19] The reliability of attitude responses is harder to determine, because a change in response may signify a real change of attitude. The reliability of average responses is higher than the reliability of individual responses. It is fortunate that the researcher is usually more interested in averages, or group measures, than in individual measures.

Survey research has a unique advantage among social scientific methods: it is sometimes possible to check the validity of survey data without too much difficulty. In checking the validity of a measuring instrument, it is necessary to use an outside criterion. One compares one's results to some outside, presumably valid, criterion. For instance, a respondent tells us he voted in the last election of school board members. We can check whether he did or not by checking the registration and voting records. Ordinarily individual behavior is not checked because information about individuals is hard to secure, but group information is often available. This information can be used to check to some extent the validity of the survey sample and the responses of the respondents.

---

materials are available at small cost from the Survey Research Center, University of Michigan, Ann Arbor, Michigan.

[19] Parten, *op. cit.*, pp. 496–498.

Probably the best example of an outside check on survey data is to use the information provided by the last census. This is particularly useful in large-scale surveys, but may also be an aid in smaller surveys. In studying the attitudes toward education of the people of a school district, for example, we draw a sample of citizens and wish to check its adequacy. We can check the proportions of men and women, races, educational level, ages, and so on. National sample information has been found to be remarkably close to census information. Stouffer made such comparisons in a national study of civil liberties. Table 22.2 reports some of the comparisons, made by Stouffer in a large-scale study of civil liberties.[20]

TABLE 22.2   COMPARISON OF SAMPLE WITH CENSUS DATA, STOUFFER STUDY

Characteristic	Census	Survey
Urban	64.0%	66.0%
Male	47.7	46.6
Negro	9.2	8.9
College	15.4	17.1
High School	43.5	45.4
Grade School (or none)	41.1	37.5

With one exception, grade school education, no estimate is off by more than 2 percent, which is reassuring evidence of the adequacy of the sample. (It is also some evidence of the validity of the responses of individuals interviewed.) To be sure, Stouffer was dealing with a very large sample, but smaller samples have also been found to be quite accurate. In one of the Detroit-area studies of the University of Michigan, the sample was approximately 735. The check of the sample against the 1950 Census showed survey percentages on a number of items to be very close to census percentages. The percentages of religious affiliations of the Detroit people, as estimated by the sample and as reported by the Detroit Council of Churches were: Catholic: 37 percent (survey), 38 percent (Council); Protestant: 56 percent and 57 percent; Other: 5 percent and 2 percent; No preference: 2 percent and 3 percent.[21]

The same method or similar methods can and should be used in educational surveys. Certain routine factual questions should be put into all survey schedules for these checking purposes. School systems and colleges and universities usually have records of varied kinds that can be used to check survey information.

20 From S. Stouffer, *Communism, Conformity, and Civil Liberties.* Garden City, N.Y.: Doubleday, 1955, pp. 237, 238. Copyright © 1955 by Samuel A. Stouffer. Reprinted by permission of Doubleday & Company, Inc.

21 Detroit Area Study, University of Michigan, *A Social Profile of Detroit.* Ann Arbor: University of Michigan, 1952, p. 36.

A number of other checks, both internal and external, are useful in determining the reliability and validity of census data. The student is referred to Parten and other sources for detailed discussions of these kinds of checking methods.[22]

TWO STUDIES

Many surveys have been made, both good and bad. Most of them would probably not interest the student because they are only refined attempts to obtain simple information—certain studies of presidential voting, of industrial plants, and so forth. There are, however, other surveys of considerable, even great, interest and significance to behavioral scientists. Kornhauser's study of Detroit includes attitudes toward education and toward minority-group members.[23] Campbell and Metzner's survey of the use of the library is a straightforward, factual study of two important phenomena, the public library and American reading habits.[24]

Two important surveys will be summarized and discussed below. One is the Stouffer study already mentioned. Its content and methodology are so unusual, even imaginative, and yet representative of the best of survey research, that its inclusion in this chapter is well justified. The other is a study of the role relationships of board of education members and superintendents.[25] Its methodology, while following the lines of good survey research, goes beyond most surveys in certain respects. More important, it is strongly grounded in social scientific theory.

Stouffer's large and thorough study was anchored in the reactions of Americans to the danger of Communism inside and outside the United States and to danger from those individuals who, while trying to thwart the conspiracy, might sacrifice some of the liberties of Americans. A number of questions were asked and answered: How do the attitudes of community leaders compare to the attitudes of the rank and file within the community? Do attitudes vary from one region of the country to another, with education, with religion?

The study is quite unique in one methodological respect: two large and independent area random samples of the people of the United States were interviewed by two separate and independent agencies using the same schedule. Each sample included more than 2400 cases, a total of almost 5000 cases! By using two separate samples, not only could external

---

[22] Parten, *op. cit.,* chap. 16: Campbell and Katona, *op. cit.,* pp. 41–48. H. Hyman, *Survey Design and Analysis.* New York: Free Press, 1955, pp. 151–172.

[23] A. Kornhauser, *Detroit as the People See It.* Detroit: Wayne University Press, 1952.

[24] A. Campbell and C. Metzner, *Public Use of the Library.* Ann Arbor: Institute for Social Research, University of Michigan, 1950.

[25] N. Gross, W. Mason, and A. McEachern, *Explorations in Role Analysis.* New York: Wiley, 1958.

and internal checks of survey data be made; the results of one survey could be checked against the other. There has probably never been such a large-scale and thorough check on the adequacy of random sampling procedures (except, perhaps for certain Federal government studies and methods). In addition, about 1500 community leaders were selected and interviewed independently of the larger samples. These leaders were not selected at random, but by role: mayors, chambers of commerce presidents, American Legion commanders, and so on.

Stouffer exhaustively analyzed the data. The reader who follows the analyses, the numerical data, and the evaluative discussions of the analyses will find them rewarding. To summarize the data and findings here would be impractical. Instead, one very interesting example is reported in Table 22.3.[26] The question was asked of the leaders and the larger group in the sample: "If a person wanted to make a speech in your community against churches and religions, should he be allowed to speak or not?"

TABLE 22.3   TABULATION OF RESPONSES TO QUESTION ON TOLERANCE OF RELIGIOUS NONCONFORMITY, STOUFFER STUDY [a] (IN PERCENT)

| | | Response | | |
		No	No Opinion	Yes
Community	AIPO	33	1	66
Leaders	NORC	35	2	63
National	AIPO	60	3	37
Cross Section	NORC	61	2	37

[a] "No Opinion" percentages filled in by subtraction. AIPO: American Institute of Public Opinion (one of the survey agencies); NORC: National Opinion Research Center (the other survey agency).

The data of Table 22.3 indicate: one, there is a relation between position in the community and tolerance: community leaders seem to be more tolerant than the average citizen. Two, the sampling (area random method) was quite effective. Note the closeness of the percentages of the national cross sections. This is a remarkable demonstration of the power of random sampling.

The Gross, Mason, and McEachern study, using the role of the school superintendent as the main cognitive object, tested theoretically derived hypotheses about expectations and behaviors of superintendents and board of education members. One of these was that incumbents of a role position would assign more responsibility to the position than would incumbents of subordinate or superordinate positions.[27] Another

26 Figures taken from Stouffer, op. cit., pp. 32, 33.
27 Gross, Mason, and McEachern, op. cit., p. 123.

was that the longer the members of a social system interact, the greater the consensus of their expectations of the behavior of incumbents of positions in that social system.[28]

Of the universe of 217 superintendents in Massachusetts, 105 were randomly selected and interviewed. The board of education members associated with these 105 superintendents were also studied. There were 517 such members of whom 98 percent, or 508, were interviewed. The lengthy interview schedule was designed to test the hypotheses mentioned above, as well as to obtain other factual information. As in the Stouffer study, scales were also used, including scales to measure authoritarianism, ethnocentrism, political-economic conservatism, career satisfaction, level of aspiration, educational progressivism, and other variables.

TABLE 22.4 RELATION OF RELIGION TO CIVIC MOTIVATION, GROSS, MASON, AND MC EACHERN STUDY (IN PERCENT)

	Motivated by Civic Duty	
	Yes	No
Catholic	49.4	50.6
Non-Catholic	73.1	26.9

In the course of the study, superintendents were asked about the civic motivation of board members. The investigators then related civic motivation to religion, among other variables. According to the results (given in Table 22.4),[29] Catholics seem to be less motivated by civic duty than non-Catholics. Another interesting finding was the relation between board of education members having children and "goodness" of motivation to become board members. Of the board members with no children, 27 percent had "good" motivation (as reported by superintendents), whereas of those with children, 48 percent had "good" motivation.[30]

APPLICATIONS OF SURVEY RESEARCH TO EDUCATION

Despite its evident potential value in helping to solve theoretical and applied educational problems, scientific survey research has not been used to any great extent by educators. Its distinctive educational usefulness, moreover, seems not to have been realized. Therefore this section and the remainder of the chapter are for the most part devoted to applications of survey research to education and educational problems. First let us look at some of the possibilities.

28 *Ibid.*, p. 177.
29 *Ibid.*, p. 199.
30 Gross, *Who Runs Our Schools?*, p. 165.

Obviously, survey research is a useful tool for educational fact-finding. An administrator, a board of education, or a staff of teachers can learn a great deal about a school system or a community without contacting every child, every teacher, and every citizen. In short, the sampling methods developed in survey research can be very useful. It is unsatisfactory to depend upon relatively hit-or-miss, so-called representative samples based on "expert" judgments. Nor is it necessary to gather data on whole populations. Frequently, samples are sufficient for many educational purposes.

Most research in education is done with relatively small nonrandom samples. If hypotheses are supported, they can later be tested with random samples of populations, and if again supported, the results can be generalized to populations of schools, children, and laymen. In other words, survey research can be used to test hypotheses already tested in more limited situations, with the result that external validity is increased.

School district reorganization is taking place all over the United States. Little reliable and valid information is available on the attitudes of citizens toward this reorganization. It might be profitable to draw random samples of citizens in communities that are entering reorganization discussions. Then, by using the panel method, changes in attitude can be studied as reorganization progresses and the information or misinformation of citizens accurately weighed. Practical information helpful to administrators and boards of education may thus be obtained, not to mention rich possibilities for testing theoretical hypotheses on the subject of change in attitude and information due to public information programs.

Another important problem that survey research might enlighten is morale. The morale of teachers and administrators can be studied by the panel method. What changes in morale occur as a result of changes in employment or administrative policies or as a result of salary-schedule changes?

Survey research seems ideally suited to the study of integration and its impact on communities and their schools. Again, the panel method can be helpful. Or interviews of random samples of citizens and teachers of school districts just starting integration might provide valuable practical information on the fears and anxieties of the citizenry, so that appropriate measures to lessen these fears can be taken in other districts. The effect of these measures can also be studied similarly.

Survey research is probably best adapted to obtaining personal and social facts, beliefs, and attitudes. It is significant that, although hundreds of thousands of words are spoken and written about education and about what people presumably think about education, there is little dependable information on the subject. We simply do not know what people's attitudes toward education are. We have to depend on feature writers and so-called experts for this information. Boards of education frequently depend on administrators and local leaders to tell them what the people think. Will they support a bond issue? What would they think about a merger of two or three adjoining districts? How would they react to redistricting in neighborhood school areas to counteract segregation? Survey research can help answer these and many other similar educational questions.

ADVANTAGES AND DISADVANTAGES
OF SURVEY RESEARCH

Survey research has the advantage of wide scope: a great deal of information can be obtained from a large population. A large population or a large school system can be tested with much less expense than that incurred by taking a census. While surveys tend to be more expensive than laboratory and field experiments and field studies, for the amount and quality of information they yield they are economical. Furthermore, existing educational facilities and personnel can be used to reduce the costs of the research.

Survey research information is accurate—within sampling error ranges, of course. The accuracy of properly drawn samples is frequently surprising, even to experts in the field. A sample of 600 to 700 individuals or families can give a remarkably accurate portrait of a community—its values, attitudes, and beliefs.

With these advantages go inevitable disadvantages. First, survey information ordinarily does not penetrate very deeply below the surface. The scope of the information sought is usually emphasized at the expense of depth. This seems to be a weakness, however, that is not necessarily inherent in the method. The Gross, Mason, and McEachern, and other studies, show that it is possible to go considerably below surface opinions. Yet the survey seems best adapted to extensive rather than intensive research. Other types of research are perhaps better adapted to deeper exploration of relations.

A second weakness is a practical one. Survey research is demanding of time and money. In a large survey, it may be months before a single hypothesis can be tested. Sampling and the development of good schedules are major operations. Interviews require skill, time, and money. Surveys on a smaller scale can avoid these problems to some extent, even though it is generally true that survey research demands large investments of time, energy, and money. (When compared to the census, however, surveys are relatively inexpensive, as indicated earlier.)

Any research that uses sampling is naturally subject to sampling error. While it is true that survey information has been found to be relatively accurate, there is always the one chance in twenty or a hundred that an error more serious than might be caused by minor fluctuations of chance may occur. The probability of such an error can be diminished by building safety checks into a study—by comparing census data or other outside information and by sampling the same population independently.

A potential rather than an actual weakness of this method is that the survey interview can temporarily lift the respondent out of his own social context, which may make the results of the survey invalid. The interview is a special event in the ordinary life of the respondent. This apartness may affect the respondent so that he talks to, and interacts with, the interviewer in an unnatural manner. He is not himself, so to speak. For example, a mother, when queried about her child-rearing practices, may give answers that reveal methods she would like to use rather than those she *does* use. It is possible for interviewers to limit the effects of lifting respondents out of social context by skilled handling, especially by one's manner and by careful phrasing and asking of questions.[31]

Survey research also requires a good deal of research knowledge and sophistication. The competent survey investigator must know sampling, question and schedule construction, interviewing, the analysis of data, and other technical aspects of the survey. Such knowledge is hard to come by. Few investigators get this kind and amount of experience. Some sociology and psychology departments now train their graduate students adequately. It is doubtful, however, that more than one or two schools of education in the country systematically and adequately train their students in the necessary skills. Until students of education are exposed to this kind of training, lack of research knowledge will remain a major impediment to good survey research in education.

[31] E. Maccoby and N. Maccoby, "The Interview: A Tool of Social Science," in G. Lindzey, ed., *Handbook of Social Psychology*, vol. I. Cambridge, Mass.: Addison-Wesley, 1954, pp. 449–481. See, especially, pp. 462–464.

PART SIX

MEASUREMENT

23 *FOUNDATIONS OF MEASUREMENT*

"In its broadest sense, measurement is the assignment of numerals to objects or events according to rules." [1] This definition of measurement succinctly and accurately expresses the basic nature of measurement. To understand the definition, however, requires the definition and explanation of each important term —a task to which much of this chapter will be devoted.

Suppose that we ask a male judge to stand seven feet away from an attractive young woman. The judge is asked to look at the young woman and then to estimate the degree to which she possesses five attributes: niceness, strength of character, personality, musical ability, and intelligence. The estimate is to be given numerically. In the number system a scale of numbers from 1 through 5 is used, 1 indicating a very small amount of the characteristic in question and 5 indicating a great deal of the characteristic. In other words, the judge, just by looking at the young woman, is to assess how "nice" she is, how "strong" her character is, and so on, using the numbers 1, 2, 3, 4, and 5 to indicate the amount of each characteristic she possesses.

After the judge is finished, another male judge is asked to repeat the process with the same young woman. The numbers of the second judge are checked against those of the first judge. Then both judges similarly judge a number of other young women.

This example may seem to be a little ridiculous. Most of us, however, go through very much the same procedure all our lives. We often judge how "nice," how "strong," how "intelligent" people are simply by looking at them and talking to them. It only seems silly when it is given as a serious example of measurement. Silly or serious, it *is* an example of measurement, since it satisfies the definition. The judges assigned numerals to objects according to rules. The objects, the numerals, and the

[1] S. Stevens, "Mathematics, Measurement, and Psychophysics," in S. Stevens, ed., *Handbook of Experimental Psychology*. New York: Wiley, 1951, p. 1. Campbell first proposed a definition of this nature. One of his definitions is ". . . the assignment of numbers to represent properties." N. Campbell, *What is Science?* New York: Dover, 1952 (1921), p. 110.

rules for the assignment of the numerals to the objects were all specified. The numerals were 1, 2, 3, 4, and 5; the objects were the young women; the rules for the assignment of the numerals to the objects were contained in the instructions to the judges. Then the end-product of their work, the numerals, might be used to compute measures of relation, analyses of variance, and the like.

The definition of measurement includes no statement about the quality of the measurement procedure. It simply says that, somehow, numerals are assigned to objects or to events. The "somehow," naturally, is important—but not to the definition. Measurement is a game we play with objects and numerals. Games have rules. It is of course important for other reasons that the rules be "good" rules, but whether the rules are "good" or "bad," the procedure is still measurement.

Why this emphasis on the definition of measurement and on its "rule" quality? There are three reasons. First, measurement, especially psychological and educational measurement, is badly misunderstood. It is not hard to understand certain measurements used in the natural sciences—length, weight, and volume, for example. Even measures more removed from common sense can be understood without wrenching elementary intuitive notions too much. But to understand and accept the fact that the measurement of such characteristics of individuals and groups as intelligence, aggressiveness, cohesiveness, and anxiety involves *basically and essentially* the same thinking and general procedure is much harder to do. Indeed, many say that it cannot be done. Knowing and understanding that measurement is the assignment of numerals to objects or events by rule, then, helps to erase erroneous and misleading conceptions of psychological and educational measurement.

Second, the definition tells us that, if rules can be set up on some rational or empirical basis, measurement of anything is *theoretically* possible. This greatly widens the scientist's measurement horizons. He will not, in short, reject the possibility of measuring some property because the property is, say, a complex and elusive one. He understands that measurement is a game that he may or may not be able to play with this or that property at this time. But he never rejects the possibility of playing the game, though he may realistically understand its difficulties.

Third, the definition alerts us to the essential neutral core of measurement and measurement procedures and to the necessity for setting up "good" rules, rules whose virtue can be empirically tested. No measurement procedure is any better than its rules. The rules given in the example above were poor. The procedure was a measurement procedure; the definition was satisfied. But it was a poor procedure for reasons that should become apparent later.

DEFINITION OF MEASUREMENT

To repeat our definition, "measurement is the assignment of numerals to objects or events according to rules." [2] A *numeral* is a symbol of the form: 1, 2, 3, · · · , or I, II, III, · · · . A numeral has no quantitative meaning unless we give it such a meaning; it is simply a symbol of a special kind. It can be used to label objects, such as baseball players, billiard balls, or individuals drawn in a sample from a universe. We could just as well use the word "symbol" in the definition. It is quite possible, even necessary, to assign symbols to objects or sets of objects according to rules. "Numeral" is used because measurement ordinarily uses numerals which, after being assigned quantitative meaning, become *numbers*. A *number*, then, is a numeral that has been assigned quantitative meaning.

The term "assigned" in the definition means *mapping*. You may recall that earlier we talked about mapping the objects of one set on to the objects of another set. A function, *f*, is a rule, a *rule of correspondence*. It is a rule that assigns to each member of one set some one member of another set. The members of the two sets can be any objects at all. In mathematics, the members are generally numbers and algebraic symbols. In research, the members of one set can be individuals, or symbols standing for individuals, and the members of the other set can be numerals or numbers. In most psychological and educational measurement, numerals and numbers are mapped on to, or assigned to, individuals.[3]

The most interesting—and difficult—work of measurement is *the rule*. A *rule* is a guide, a method, a command that tells us what to do. A mathematical rule is *f*, a function; *f* is a rule for assigning the objects of one set to the objects of another set. In measurement a rule might say: "Assign the numerals 1 through 5 to individuals according to how nice they are. If an individual is very, very nice, let the number 5 be assigned to him. If an individual is not at all nice, let the number 1 be assigned. Assign to individuals between these limits numbers between the limits." Another rule is one we have already met a number of times: "If an individual is male, assign him a 1. If an individual is female, assign her a 0." Of course, we would have to have a prior rule or set of rules defining male and female.

Diagram this proposition as in Chap. 6. Assume that we have a set, *A*, of five persons, three men and two women: a_1, a_3, and a_4 are men; a_2

---

[2] *Ibid.*

[3] Usually, in a mapping, the members of the domain are said to be mapped on to members of the range. In order to preserve consistency with the definition of measurement given above and to be able always to conceive of the measurement procedure as a function, the mapping has been turned around. This conception of mapping, furthermore, is consistent with the earlier definition of a function as a rule that assigns to each member of the domain of a set some one member of the range. The rule tells *how* the pairs are to be ordered.

and a_5 are women. We wish to "measure" sex. Assuming we have a prior rule that allows us unambiguously to determine sex, we use the rule given in the preceding paragraph: "If a person is male, assign 1; if female, assign 0." Let 0 and 1 be a set. Call it B. Then $B = \{0, 1\}$. The measurement diagram is shown in Fig. 23.1.

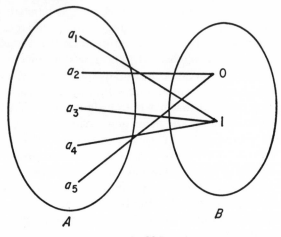

FIG. **23.1**

This procedure is the same as the one we used in Chap. 6 when discussing relations and functions. Evidently measurement is a relation. Since, to each member of A, the domain, one and only one object of B, the range, is assigned, the relation is a function. Are all measurement procedures functions, then? They are, provided the objects being measured are considered the domain and the numerals being assigned to, or mapped onto them, are considered the range.

Here is another way to bring set, relation-function, and measurement ideas together. Recall that a relation is a set of ordered pairs. So is a function. Any measurement procedure, then, sets up a set of ordered pairs, the first member of each pair being the object measured, and the second member the numeral assigned to the object according to the measurement rule, whatever it is. We can thus write a general equation for any measurement procedure:

$$f = \{(x, y); x = \text{any object, and } y = \text{a numeral}\}$$

This is read: "The function, f, or the rule of correspondence, is equal to the set of ordered pairs (x, y) such that x is an object and each corresponding y is a numeral." This is a general rule and will fit any case of measurement.

Let us cite another example to make this discussion more concrete. The events to be measured, the x's, are five children. The numerals, the *y*'s, are the ranks 1, 2, 3, 4, and 5. Assume that *f* is a rule that instructs a teacher as follows: "Give the rank 1 to the child who has the greatest motivation to do schoolwork. Give the rank 2 to the child who has the next greatest motivation to do schoolwork, and so on to the rank 5 which you should give to the child with the least motivation to do schoolwork." The measurement or the function is shown in Fig. 23.2.

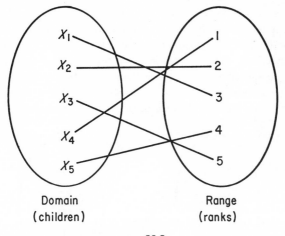

Domain
(children)

Range
(ranks)

FIG. 23.2

Note that *f*, the rule of correspondence, might have been: "If a child has high motivation for schoolwork, give him a 1, but if a child has low motivation for schoolwork, give him a 0." Then the range becomes $\{0, 1\}$. This simply means that the set of five children has been partitioned into two subsets, to each of which will be assigned, by means of *f*, the numerals 0 and 1. A diagram of this would look like Fig. 23.1 with the set *A* being the domain and the set *B* the range.

To return to *rules*. Here is where evaluation comes into the picture. Rules may be "good" or "bad." With "good" rules we have "good," or sound, measurement, other things being equal. With "bad" rules we have "bad," or poor, measurement. Many things are easy to measure, because the rules are easy to draw up and follow. To measure sex is easy, for example, since several simple and fairly clear criteria can be used to determine sex and to tell the investigator when to assign 1 and when to assign 0. It is also easy to measure certain other human characteristics: hair color, eye color, height, weight. Unfortunately, most human characteristics are much more difficult to measure, mainly because it is difficult to devise clear rules that are "good." Nonetheless, we must always have rules of some kind in order to measure anything.

MEASUREMENT AND "REALITY" ISOMORPHISM

Measurement can be a meaningless business, as we have seen. How can this be avoided? The definition of sets of objects being measured, the definition of the numerical sets from which we assign numerals to the objects being measured, and the rules of assignment or correspondence have to be tied to "reality." When the hardness of objects is measured, there is little difficulty. If a substance a can scratch b (and not vice versa), then a is harder than b. Similarly, if a can scratch b, and b can scratch c, then (probably) a can scratch c. These are empirical matters that are easily tested, so that we can find a rank order of hardness. A set of objects can be measured for its hardness by a few scratch tests, and numerals can be assigned to indicate degrees of hardness. It is said that the measurement procedure and the number system are *isomorphic* to reality.

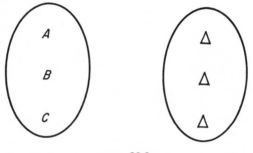

FIG. **23.3**

Isomorphism means identity or similarity of form. The question is asked: Is this set of objects isomorphic to that set of objects? Are the two sets the same or similar in some formal aspect? For example, the two sets of Fig. 23.3 are isomorphic as to cardinal number: they both have *three* members. They both have "threeness." In measurement, the question must be asked: Is the measurement game we are playing tied to "reality"? Do the measurement procedures being used have some rational and empirical correspondence with "reality"?

To show the nature of this question of isomorphism, we can again use the idea of the correspondence of sets of objects. We may wish to measure the *persistence* of seven individuals. Suppose, also, that I am an omniscient being. I know the exact amount of persistence each individual possesses, that is, I know the "true" persistence values of each individual. (Assume that *persistence* has been adequately defined.) But *you*, the measurer, do not know these "true" values. It is necessary for you to assess the persistence of the individuals in some fallible way and you think you have found such a way. For instance, you might assess persistence by giving the individuals tasks to perform and noting the total time an individual requires to complete a task, or you might note the total number of times he tries to do a task before he turns to some other activity.[4] You use your method and measure the persistence of the individuals. You come out with, say, the seven values 6, 6, 4, 3, 3, 2, 1. Now I know the "true" values. They are: 8, 5, 2, 4, 3, 3, 1. This set of values is "reality." The correspondence of this set is shown in Fig. 23.4.

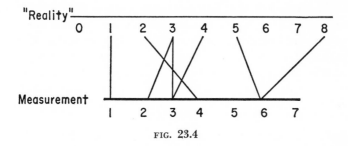

FIG. 23.4

In two cases, you have assessed the "true" values exactly. You have "missed" all the others. Only one of these "misses," however, is serious, and there is a fair correspondence between the two rank orders of values. Note, too, that in my omniscience I knew that the "true" values of persistence run from 0 through 8, whereas your measurement system only encompasses 1 through 6.

While this example is a bit fanciful, it does show in a crude way the nature of the isomorphism problem. The ultimate question to be asked of any measurement procedure is: Is the measurement procedure isomorphic to reality? You were not too far off in measuring persistence. The only trouble is that we rarely discover as simply as this the degree of correspondence to "reality" of our measurements. In fact, we often do not even know whether we are measuring what we are trying to measure! Despite this difficulty, the scientist must *test*, in some manner, the isomorphism of the measurement numbers game he is playing with "reality."

PROPERTIES, CONSTRUCTS, AND INDICANTS OF OBJECTS

We say we measure objects, but this is not quite true. We measure the properties, or the characteristics, of these objects. Even this qualification is not quite true, however. We actually measure *indicants* of the properties of objects, so that when we say we measure objects we are really saying that we measure indicants of the properties of objects. This is generally true of all science, though the properties of some natural objects are much closer to direct observation than others. For instance, the property of sex associated with animal objects is closely tied to direct ob-

[4] N. Feather, "The Study of Persistence," *Psychological Bulletin*, LIX (1962), 94.

servation. As soon as relatively simple physical properties are left behind for more complex and elusive properties—which are of much greater interest to social scientists and educators—direct observation of properties is impossible. Hostility cannot be directly observed, nor can morale, anxiety, intelligence, creativeness, and talent. We must always *infer* these properties or characteristics from observation of presumed indicants of the properties.

Indicant is merely a convenient word used to mean something that points to something else. If a boy continually strikes other boys, we *may* say his behavior is an indicant of his underlying hostility. If someone's hands sweat excessively, we *may* say that he is anxious. A child plays a Schubert impromptu beautifully; we say she has "talent." If a child marks a certain number of objective-type items in an achievement test correctly, we say he has a certain level of achievement. In each of these cases, some identifiable behavior is an indicant of an underlying property. Obviously we are on much shakier ground when making such inferences from observed behavior than when directly observing properties like skin color, size, and sex. To measure a child's cooperativenes, dependency, and imaginativeness is very different from measuring his height, weight, or wristbone development. The fundamental process of measurement is the same, but the rules are much more difficult to prescribe. Also, the observations of the psychological properties are much further removed from the actual properties than are those of the physical properties. This is perhaps the single greatest difficulty of psychological and educational measurement.

The indicants from which properties are inferred are specified by operational definitions, definitions that specify the activities or "operations" necessary to measure variables or constructs. A *construct* is an invented name for a property. Many constructs have been used in previous chapters: authoritarianism, achievement, social class, intelligence, persistence, and so on. Constructs, commonly and somewhat inaccurately called variables, are defined in two general ways in science: by other constructs and by experimental and measurement procedures. These were earlier called constitutive and operational definitions. An operational definition is necessary in order to measure a property or a construct. This is done by specifying the observations of the behavioral indicants of the properties.

Numerals are assigned to the behavioral indicants of the properties. Then, after making observations of the indicants, the numbers (numerals) are substituted for the indicants and analyzed statistically. As an example, consider an investigator who is working on the relation between intelligence and honesty. He operationally defines *intelligence* as scores obtained on the Lorge-Thorndike Intelligence Test. *Honesty* is operationally defined as observations in a contrived situation permitting pupils to cheat or not to cheat. The intelligence numerals assigned to pupils can be the total number of items correct in the test, IQ's, or some other form of score.

The honesty numerals assigned to pupils are the number of times they did not cheat when they could have cheated. The two sets of numbers may be correlated or otherwise analyzed. The coefficient of correlation, say, is .55, significant at the .01 level. All this is fairly straightforward and quite familiar. What is not so straightforward and familiar is this: if the investigator draws the conclusion that there is a significant positive relation between intelligence and honesty, he is making a very large inferential leap from behavior indicants in the form of marks on paper and observations of "cheating" behavior to psychological properties. That he may be seriously mistaken should be quite obvious.

LEVELS OF MEASUREMENT AND SCALING

Classification and Enumeration The first and most elementary step in any measurement procedure is to define the objects of the universe of discourse. Suppose U, the universal set, is defined as all tenth grade pupils in a certain high school. Next, the properties of the objects of U must be defined. All measurement requires that U be broken down into at least two subsets. The most elementary form of measurement would be to classify or categorize all the objects as possessing or not possessing some characteristic. Say this characteristic is maleness. We break U down into males and nonmales, or males and females. These are of course two *subsets* of U, or a *partitioning* of U. (Recall that partitioning a set consists of breaking it down into subsets that are *mutually exclusive* and *exhaustive*. That is, each set object must be assigned to one subset and one subset only, and all set objects in U must be so assigned.)

What we have done is to classify the objects of interest to us. We have put them into pigeonholes: we have partitioned them. The obvious simplicity of this procedure seems to cause difficulty for students. People spend much of their lives categorizing things, events, and people. Life could not go on without such categorizing, yet to associate the process with measurement seems difficult.

After a method of classification has been found, we have in effect a rule for telling which objects of U go into which classes or subsets or partitions. This rule is used and the set objects are put into the subsets. Here are the boys; here are the girls. Easy. Here are the middle-class children; here are the working-class children. Not as easy, but not too hard. Here are the delinquents; here are the nondelinquents. Harder. Here are the bright ones; here are the average ones; here are the dull ones. Much harder. Here are the creative ones; here are the noncreative ones. Very much harder.

After the objects of the universe have been classified into designated subsets, the members of the sets can be counted. In the dichotomous case, the rule for counting was given in Chap. 5: If a member of U has the characteristic in question, say *maleness,* then assign a 1. If the member does not have the characteristic, then assign a 0. (See Fig. 23.1.) When set members are counted in this fashion, all objects of a subset are considered to be equal to each other and unequal to the members of other subsets.

Measurement Postulates   There are four general levels of measurement: nominal, ordinal, interval, and ratio. These four levels lead to four kinds of scales. Some writers on the subject admit only ordinal, interval, and ratio measurement, while others say that all four belong to the measurement family. We need not be too fussy about this as long as we understand the characteristics of the different scales and levels.

Before discussing the levels themselves, it will be wise to discuss three of the postulates basic to measurement. A *postulate* is an assumption that is an essential prerequisite to carrying out some operation or line of thinking. In this case, it is an assumption about the relations between the objects being measured. Although postulates are usually assumed to be true, in measurement it is necessary to test the postulates whenever possible. More than three postulates are really necessary in order to make it possible to equate objects, to rank order them, and to add them.[5]

The three postulates can be written:

1. Either $(a = b)$ or $(a \neq b)$, but not both

2. If $[(a = b)$ and $(b = c)]$, then $(a = c)$

3. If $[(a > b)$ and $(b > c)]$, then $(a > c)$

The first postulate says: "*a* is either equal to *b* or not equal to *b*, but not both." This postulate is necessary for classification. We must be able to assert either that one object is the same in a characteristic as another or that it is not the same. In measurement "the same" does not necessarily mean complete identity. It can mean "sufficiently the same to be classed as members of the same set." Two boys are the "same" in maleness, though it is conceivable that one boy may actually be more masculine than another. And the two boys certainly differ in many other characteristics. This is a criterion matter. To be able to say "the two are the same," we must have a criterion or a set of criteria. If we wish to assign boys to social class categories, we might use the criterion of father's occupation and/or residence. The criterion must be sufficiently unambiguous to make classification possible, that is, to satisfy the condition the postulate states.

The second postulate says "If *a* equals *b,* and *b* equals *c,* then *a*

[5] See J. Guilford, *Psychometric Methods,* 2nd ed. New York: McGraw-Hill, 1954, pp. 11, 12. Some of the discussion that follows is based in part on Guilford and on the Stevens reference cited earlier. Another important source of guidance is W. Torgerson, *Theory and Methods of Scaling.* New York: Wiley, 1958, chaps. 1 and 2.

equals *c*." If one member of a universe is the same as another member, and this second member is the same as a third member, then the first member is the same as the third member. This postulate enables a researcher to establish the equality of set members on a characteristic by comparing objects. More important, if the postulate is satisfied, objects not ordinarily amenable to observation may be assigned to subsets of a universe. For example, suppose we wish to assign individuals to two categories, "prejudiced" and "unprejudiced." Consider one such individual. We know that all or most members of the association he belongs to are prejudiced. We may therefore feel safe in assigning him and others like him to the category "prejudiced." Or we may be able to assign him to the category "prejudiced" on the basis of his response to another measuring instrument which is highly correlated with a prejudice measuring instrument.

The third postulate is of more immediate and practical importance for our purposes. It says, "If *a* is greater than *b*, and *b* is greater than *c*, then *a* is greater than *c*." This is the *transitivity* postulate. (So is 2 a transitivity postulate.) Other symbols or words can be substituted for "greater than" ("$>$"), "less than" ("$<$"), "is at a greater distance than," "is stronger than," "precedes," "dominates," and so on. Most measurement in psychology and education depends on this postulate. It must be possible to assert ordinal- or rank-order statements like "*a* has more of a property than *b*; *b* has more of the property than *c*; therefore *a* has more of the property than *c*."

The preceding statements may seem obvious. It is easy and even justifiable to make many such statements, but not always. We cannot always take it for granted that the postulate is satisfied. In fact Coombs says that it is remarkably difficult to find examples of simple orders among social psychological variables.[6] In physical measurements the postulate is often satisfied: if stick *a* is longer than stick *b*, and stick *b* is longer than stick *c*, then stick *a* must be longer than stick *c*. If student *a* has more items right on a test than student *b*, and student *b* has more right than student *c*, student *a* must have more right than student *c*. But take the relation *dominance*: *a* may dominate *b* and *b* may dominate *c*, but it is possible that *a* does not dominate *c*. A wife may dominate her husband, and the husband may dominate the child, but the child may dominate his mother (the wife). If an investigator is studying dominance relations among children, he cannot simply assume that the postulate is correct. He must demonstrate that it is correct. This is then an empirical matter. Further, to disabuse oneself of the notion that transitivity is obvious, think about the relations "loves," "likes," "is a friend of," or "accepts."

[6] C. Coombs, "Theory and Methods of Social Measurement." In L. Festinger and D. Katz, *Research Methods in the Behavioral Sciences*. New York: Holt, Rinehart and Winston, Inc., 1953, p. 477.

Nominal Measurement   The rules used to assign numerals to objects are the criteria that define the kind of scale and the level of measurement. The lowest level of measurement is *nominal* measurement (see earlier discussion of categorization). The numbers assigned to objects are numerical without having a number meaning; they cannot be ordered or added. They are *labels* much like the letters used to label sets. If individuals or groups are assigned 1, 2, 3, · · · , these numerals are merely names. For example, baseball and football players may be assigned such numbers. (These numbers may then have a qualitative meaning, but not a quantitative meaning.) Telephones may also be assigned such numbers. Groups may be given the labels I, II, and III or A_1, A_2, and A_3. We use nominal measurement in our everyday thinking and living. We identify others as "men," "women," "Protestants," "Australians," and so on. At any rate, the symbols assigned to the objects, or rather, to the sets of objects, constitute nominal scales. Some experts think this is not measurement, as indicated previously. Such exclusion of nominal measurement would prevent much social scientific research procedure from being called measurement. Since the definition of measurement is satisfied, and since the members of labeled sets can be counted and compared, it would seem that nominal procedures *are* measurement.

The requirements of nominal measurement are simple. All the members of a set are assigned the same numeral and no two sets are assigned the same numeral.[7] Postulates 1 and 2 have to be satisfied. We must know when objects are or are not equal. In psychological, sociological, and educational measurement, however, the "equal" should be enclosed in quotation marks. This relation means *"approximately* equal," because of the complexity of human behavior, the fallibility of human judgment and response, and the usual errors of measurement.

Nominal measurement—at least in one simple form—was expressed in Fig. 23.1, where the objects of the range, $\{0, 1\}$, were mapped onto the a's, the objects of U, the five people, by the rule: If x is male, assign 1; if x is female, assign 0. This is how nominal measurement is quantified when only a dichotomy is involved. When the partition contains more than two categories, some other method must be used. Basically, nominal measurement quantification amounts to counting the objects in the cells of the subsets or partitions.

Ordinal Measurement   *Ordinal measurement* requires, as we saw earlier, that the objects of a set can be rank-ordered on an operationally defined characteristic or property. If the ordinal transitivity postulate is justified, then ordinal measurement is possible. That is, if we have three objects, a, b, and c, and a is greater than b, and b is greater than c; and if we can

[7] Guilford, *op. cit.*, p. 12.

justifiably say, also, that *a* is greater than *c*, then the main condition for ordinal measurement is satisfied.

The procedure can be generalized in three ways. One, any number of objects of any kind can be measured ordinally simply by extension to *a, b, c,* · · · , *n.* (Even though two objects may sometimes be equal, ordinal measurement is still possible.) We simply need to be able to say $a > b > c > \cdots > n$ on some property.

The second extension consists of using combined properties or combined criteria. Instead of using only one property, we can use two or more. For example, instead of ranking a group of college students on academic achievement by grade-point averages, we may wish to rank them on the combined criteria of grade-point average and test scores. (Grade-point averages, too, are composite scores.)

The third extension is accomplished by using criteria other than "greater than." "Less than" occurs to us immediately. "Precedes," "is above," and "is superior to" may be useful criteria. In fact, we might substitute a symbol other than ">" or "<." One such symbol is "∘." It can be used to mean any operation, such as those just named, in which the transitivity postulate is satisfied: $a \circ b$ might mean *"a precedes b,"* or *"a is subordinate to b,"* and $a \circ b \circ c$ might mean *"a is superior to b, b is superior to c, and a is superior to c."*

The numerals assigned to ranked objects are called *rank values.* Let *R* equal the set of *ranked objects:* $R = \{a > b > \cdots > n\}$. Let R^* equal the set of *rank values:* $R^* = \{1, 2, \cdots, n\}$. We assign the objects of R^* to the objects of *R* as follows: the largest object is assigned 1, the next in size 2, and so on to the smallest object which is assigned the last numeral in the particular series. If this procedure is used, the rank values assigned are in the reverse order. If, for instance, there are five objects, with *a* the largest, *b* the next, through *e,* the smallest, then:

Objects	*R*	R^*
a	1	5
b	2	4
c	3	3
d	4	2
e	5	1

Of course, one step can be skipped by assigning R^* directly: by assigning 5 to *a,* 4 to *b,* through 1 to *e.*

Ordinal numbers indicate rank order and nothing more. The numbers do not indicate absolute quantities, nor do they indicate that the intervals between the numbers are equal. For instance, it cannot be assumed that because the *numerals* are equally spaced the underlying properties they represent are equally spaced. If two subjects have the ranks 8 and 5 and two other subjects the ranks 6 and 3, we cannot say that the differences between the first and second pairs are equal. There is also no way to know that any individual has *none* of the property being measured. Rank-order scales are not equal-interval scales, nor do they have absolute zero points.

Interval Measurement (**Scales**)   *Interval* or *equal-interval* scales possess the characteristics of nominal and ordinal scales, especially the rank-order characteristic. In addition, numerically equal distances on interval scales represent equal distances in the property being measured. Thus, suppose that we had measured four objects on an interval scale and gotten the values 8, 6, 5, and 3. Then we can legitimately say that the difference between the first and third objects in the property measured, $8 - 5 = 3$, is equal to the difference between the second and fourth objects, $6 - 3 = 3$. Another way to express the equal-interval idea is to say that the *intervals* can be added and subtracted. An interval scale is assumed as follows:

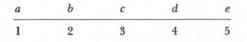

a	b	c	d	e
1	2	3	4	5

The interval from a to c is $3 - 1 = 2$. The interval from c to d is $4 - 3 = 1$. We can add these two intervals $(3 - 1) + (4 - 3) = 2 + 1 = 3$. Now note that the interval from a to d is $4 - 1 = 3$. Expressed in an equation: $(d - a) = (c - a) + (d - c)$. If these intervals were five pupils measured on an interval scale of achievement, then the differences in achievement between pupils a and c and between b and d would be equal. We could not say, however, that the achievement of d was twice as great as that of pupil b. (Such a statement would require one higher level of measurement.) Note that it is not *quantities* or *amounts* that are added and subtracted. It is *intervals* or *distances*.

Ratio Measurement (**Scales**)   The highest level of measurement is *ratio measurement,* and the measurement ideal of the scientist is the ratio scale. A ratio scale, in addition to possessing the characteristics of nominal, ordinal, and interval scales, has an absolute or natural zero that has empirical meaning. If a measurement is zero on a ratio scale, then there is a basis for saying that some measured object has none of the property being measured. Since there is an absolute or natural zero, all arithmetic operations are possible, including multiplication and division. Numbers on the scale indicate the actual amounts of the property being measured. If a ratio scale of achievement existed, then it would be possible to say that a pupil with a scale score of 8 has an achievement twice as great as a pupil with a scale score of 4.

COMPARISONS OF SCALES: PRACTICAL
CONSIDERATIONS AND STATISTICS

The basic characteristics of the four types of measurement and their accompanying scales have been discussed. What kinds of scales are used in behavioral and educational research? Mostly nominal and ordinal are used, though the probability is good that many scales and tests used in psychological and educational measurement approximate interval measurement well enough for practical purposes, as we shall see.

First, consider a great deal of measurement that is only nominal. Whenever real attributes (earlier defined as characteristics of an all-or-none nature, such as sex, yes-no answers to questions, married-single, children-no children, etc.) are involved, measurement is nominal. Or, whenever variates are converted to attributes, as when objects are arbitrarily divided into two groups such as high-low and old-young, on variables that are at least capable of being ordered, we have nominal measurement.

It is instructive to study the numerical operations and statistics that are, in a strict sense, legitimate and permissible with each type of measurement. With nominal measurement the counting of numbers of cases in each category and subcategory is, of course, permissible. Frequency statistics like x^2, percentages, and certain coefficients of correlation (contingency coefficients) can be used. This sounds thin. Actually, it is a good deal. A good principle to remember is this: If one cannot use any other method, one can almost always partition or cross-partition subjects. If we are studying the relation between two variables and do not have any way to measure them adequately in an ordinal or interval fashion, some way can probably be found to divide the objects of study into at least two groups. For example, in studying the relation between the motivation of board of education members to become board members and their religion, as Gross and his colleagues did, we may be able to have knowledgeable judges divide the sample of board members into those with "good" motivation and those with "poor" motivation. Then we can cross-partition religion with the motivation dichotomy and thus study the relation.

Intelligence, aptitude, and personality test scores are, *basically and strictly speaking,* ordinal. They indicate with more or less accuracy not the *amounts* of intelligence, aptitude, and personality traits of individuals, but rather the *rank-order positions* of the individuals. To see this, we must realize that ordinal scales do not possess the desirable characteristics of equal intervals or absolute zeroes. Intelligence-test scores are examples. It is not possible to say that an individual has zero intelligence. If he is alive, he must have some score above zero. But there is no absolute zero on an intelligence test scale. The zero is arbitrary, and without an absolute zero, addition of *amounts* of intelligence has little meaning, for arbitrary zero points can lead to different sums. On a scale with an arbitrary zero point the following addition is performed: $2 + 3 = 5$. Then the sum is 5 scale units above zero. But if the arbitrary zero point is inaccurate and the "real" zero point is at the scale position 4 scale points lower than the arbitrary zero position, then the former 2 and 3 should really be 6 and 7, and $6 + 7 = 13!$

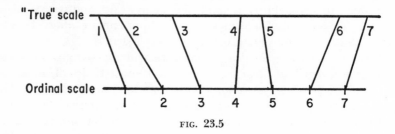

FIG. 23.5

The lack of a real zero in ordinal scales is not as serious as the lack of equal intervals. Even without a real zero, *distances* within a scale can be added, provided that these distances are equal (empirically). The situation might be somewhat as indicated in Fig. 23.5. The scale on the top ("true" scale) indicates the "true" values of a variable. The bottom scale (ordinal scale) indicates the rank-order scale used by an investigator. In other words, an investigator has rank-ordered seven persons quite well, but his ordinal numerals, which *look* equal in interval, are not "true," although they may be fairly accurate representations of the empirical facts.

Strictly speaking, the statistics that can be used with ordinal scales include rank-order measures such as the rank-order coefficient of correlation, ρ, Kendall's W, and the rank-order analysis of variance, medians, and percentiles. If only these statistics (and others like them) are legitimate, how can statistics like r, t, and F be used with what are in effect ordinal measures? And they are so used, without a qualm by most researchers.

Although this is a moot point, the situation is not as difficult as it seems. As Torgerson points out, some types of natural origin have been devised for certain types of measurement.[8] In measuring preferences and attitudes, for example, the neutral points (on either side of which are degrees of positive and negative favoring, approving, liking, and preferring) can be considered natural origins. Besides, ratio scales, while desirable, are not absolutely necessary because most of what we need to do in psychological measurement can be done with equal-interval scales.

The lack of equal intervals is more serious since distances *within* a scale theoretically cannot be added without interval equality. Yet, though most psychological scales are basically ordinal, we can with considerable assurance often assume an equality of interval. The argument is eviden-

8 Torgerson, *op. cit.*, p. 30.

tial. If we have, say, two or three measures of the same variable, and these measures are all substantially and linearly related, then equal intervals can be assumed. This assumption is valid because the more nearly a relation approaches linearity, the more nearly equal are the intervals of the scales. This also applies, at least to some extent, to certain psychological measures like intelligence, achievement, and attitude tests and scales.

A related argument is that many of the methods of analysis we use work quite well with most psychological scales. That is, the results we get from using scales and assuming equal intervals are quite satisfactory.

The point of view adopted in this book is, then, a pragmatic one, that the assumption of interval equality works. Still, we are faced with a dilemma: if we use ordinal measures as though they were interval or ratio measures, we *can* err seriously in interpreting data and the relations inferred from data, though the danger is probably not as grave as it has been made out to be. There is no trouble with the numbers, as numbers. *They* do not know the difference between ρ and r or between parametric and nonparametric statistics, nor do they know the assumptions behind their use. But *we* do, or should, know the differences and the consequences of ignoring the differences. On the other hand, if we abide strictly by the rules, we cut off powerful modes of measurement and analyses and are left with tools inadequate to cope with the problems we want to solve.

What is the answer, the resolution of the conflict? Part of the answer was given above: it is probable that most psychological and educational scales approximate interval equality fairly well. In those situations in which there is serious doubt as to interval equality, there are technical means for coping with some of the problems. The competent research worker should know something of scaling methods, especially methods of achieving approximate equality of intervals and certain transformations that change ordinal scales into interval scales.[9]

It is a goal of scientific measurement to construct and use interval and ratio scales. Once that goal is obtained, there is congruence between the properties being measured and the number system. In the state of measurement at present, however, we cannot be sure that our measurement instruments have equal intervals. Therefore, it becomes important to ask the question: How serious are the distortions and errors introduced by treating ordinal measurements as though they were interval measurements? With care in the construction of measuring instruments, and especially with care in the interpretation of the results, the consequences are evidently not serious.

The best procedure would seem to be to treat ordinal measurements as though they were interval measurements, but to be constantly alert to the possibility of *gross* inequality of intervals. As much as possible about

---

[9] M. Bartlett, "The Use of Transformations," *Biometrics*, III (1947), 39–52. (See, especially, pp. 49, 50.) Guilford, *op. cit.*, chaps. 8 and 9.

the characteristics of the measuring tools should be learned. Above all, we need to be particularly careful with the interpretation of ordinal data to which statistical analysis suitable for interval measurement has been applied. Much useful information has been obtained by this approach, with resulting scientific advances in psychology and education. In short, it is unlikely that the educational researcher will be seriously led astray by heeding this advice, if he is knowledgeable and careful in applying it.

Guilford has expressed the matter aptly. He says that psychologists have rarely hesitated to apply the statistics that assume interval-scale measurement to ordinal-scale data. He even says that there is little awareness of the interval-scale assumption. Then, comfortingly, he adds:

> . . . experimental data often approach the condition of equal units sufficiently well that there is tolerable error in applying the various statistics that call for them. This is one of those occasions for making use of approximations, even gross ones, in order that one may extract the most information from his data. This is often justified on the basis of evidence of the internal consistency of the findings and the validity of the outcomes. This does not excuse the investigator, however, from being on the alert for intolerable approximations and for results and conclusions that are essentially a function of his faulty application of statistics.[10]

[10] Guilford, *op. cit.*, pp. 15, 16. For related references, see C. Boneau, "A Note on Measurement Scales and Statistical Tests," *American Psychologist*, XVI (1961), 260, 261; N. Anderson, "Scales and Statistics: Parametric and Nonparametric," *Psychological Bulletin*, LVIII (1961), 305–316; F. Lord, "Further Comments on 'Football Numbers,'" *American Psychologist*, IX (1954), 264, 265.

24 *RELIABILITY*

After assigning numerals to objects or events according to rules, an investigator must face the two major problems of reliability and validity. He has devised his measurement game and has administered the measuring instrument to a group of subjects. He has a set of numbers, the end product of the measurement game. He must now ask and answer the questions: What is the reliability of the measuring instrument? What is its validity?

If one does not know the reliability and validity of one's data little faith can be put in the results obtained and the conclusions drawn from the results. The data of the social sciences and education, derived from human behavior and human products, are, as we saw in the last chapter, several steps removed from the properties of scientific interest. Thus they may constitute a major threat to validity. Concern for reliability comes from the necessity for dependability in measurement. The data of all psychological and educational measurement instruments contain errors of measurement. To the extent that they do so, to that extent the data they yield will not be dependable. And if data are not dependable, any conclusions drawn from them will not, of course, be dependable.

DEFINITIONS OF RELIABILITY

Synonyms for reliability are: dependability, stability, consistency, predictability, accuracy. A reliable man, for instance, is a man whose behavior is consistent, dependable, and predictable—what he will do tomorrow and next week will be consistent with what he does today and what he has done last week. We say he is stable. An unreliable man, on the other hand, is one whose behavior is much more variable. More important, he is unpredictably variable. Sometimes he does this, sometimes that. He lacks stability. We say he is inconsistent.

So it is with psychological and educational measurements: they are more or less variable from occasion to occasion. They are stable and relatively predictable or they are unstable and relatively unpredictable; they are consistent or not consistent. If they are reliable, we can depend upon them. If they are unreliable, we cannot depend upon them.

It is possible to approach the definition of reliability in three ways. One approach is epitomized by the question: If we measure the same set of objects again and again with the same or comparable measuring instrument, will we get the same or similar results? This question implies a definition of reliability in *stability, dependability, predictability* terms. It is the definition most often given in elementary discussions of the subject.

A second approach is epitomized by the question: Are the measures obtained from a measuring instrument the "true" measures of the property measured? This is an *accuracy* definition, which really asks whether measurements are accurate. Compared to the first definition, it is further removed from common sense and intuition, but it is also more fundamental. These two approaches or definitions can be summarized in the words *stability* and *accuracy*. As we will see later, however, the accuracy definition implies the stability definition.

There is a third approach to the definition of reliability, an approach that not only helps us better define and solve both theoretical and practical problems but also implies other approaches and definitions. We can inquire how much *error of measurement* there is in a measuring instrument. Recall that there are two general types of variance: systematic and random. *Systematic variance* leans in one direction: scores tend to be all positive or all negative or all high or all low. Error in this case is constant or biased. *Random* or *error variance* is self-compensating: scores tend now to lean this way, now that way. Errors of measurement are random errors. They are the sum or product of a number of causes: the ordinary random or chance elements present in all measures due to unknown causes, temporary or momentary fatigue, fortuitous conditions at a particular time that temporarily affect the object measured or the measuring instrument, fluctuations of memory or mood, and other factors that are temporary and shifting. To the extent that errors of measurement are present in a measuring instrument, to this extent the instrument is unreliable. In other words, reliability can be defined as the relative absence of errors of measurement in a measuring instrument. *Reliability is associated, then, with random or chance error.*

Reliability is the *accuracy* or *precision* of a measuring instrument. A homely example can easily show what is meant. Suppose a sportsman wishes to compare the accuracy of two guns. One is an old piece made a century ago but which is still in good condition. The other is a modern weapon made by an expert gunsmith. Both pieces are solidly fixed in granite bases and aimed and zeroed in by a sharpshooter. Equal numbers of rounds are fired with each gun. In Fig. 24.1, the hypothetical pattern of shots on a target for each gun is shown. The target on the left represents the pattern of shots produced by the older gun. Observe that the shots are considerably scattered. Now observe that the pattern of shots on the target on the right is more closely packed. The shots are closely clustered around the bull's-eye.

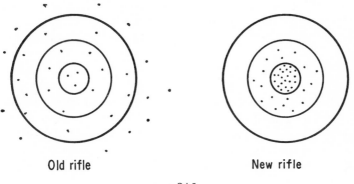

Old rifle   New rifle

FIG. 24.1

Let us assume that numbers have been assigned to the circles of the targets: 3 to the bull's-eye, 2 to the next circle, 1 to the outside circle, and 0 to any shot oustide the target. It is obvious that if we computed measures of variability, say a standard deviation, from the two shot patterns, the old rifle would have a much larger measure of variability than the newer rifle. These measures can be considered reliability indices. The smaller variability measure of the new rifle indicates much less error, and thus much greater accuracy. The new rifle is reliable; the old rifle is unreliable.

Similarly, psychological and educational measurements have greater and lesser reliabilities. A measuring instrument, say an arithmetic achievement test, is given to a group of children—usually only once. Our goal, of course, is a multiple one: we seek to hit the "true" score of each child. To the extent that we miss the "true" scores, to this extent our measuring instrument, our test, is unreliable. The "true," the "real," arithmetic scores of five children, say, are 35, 31, 29, 22, 14. Another experimenter does not know these "true" scores. His results are: 37, 30, 26, 24, 15. While he has not in a single case hit the "true" score, he has achieved the same rank order. His reliability and accuracy are surprisingly high.

Suppose that his five scores had been: 24, 37, 26, 15, 30. These are the same five scores, but they have a very different rank order. In this case, the test would be unreliable, because of its inaccuracy. To show all this more compactly, the three sets of scores, with their rank orders, have been set beside each other in Table 24.1. The rank orders of the first and second columns covary exactly. The rank-order coefficient of correlation

TABLE 24.1   "TRUE," RELIABLE, AND UNRELIABLE OBTAINED TEST SCORES
AND RANK ORDERS OF FIVE CHILDREN

1 "True" Scores	(Rank)	2 Scores from Reliable Test	(Rank)	3 Scores from Unreliable Test	(Rank)
35	(1)	37	(1)	24	(4)
31	(2)	30	(2)	37	(1)
29	(3)	26	(3)	26	(3)
22	(4)	24	(4)	15	(5)
14	(5)	15	(5)	30	(2)

is 1.00. Even though the test scores of the second column are not the exact scores, they *are* in the exact rank order. On this basis, using a rank-order coefficient of correlation, the test is reliable. The rank-order coefficient of correlation between the ranks of the first and third columns, however, is zero, so that the test is completely unreliable.

THEORY OF RELIABILITY

The example given in Table 24.1 epitomizes what we need to know about reliability.[1] It is necessary, now, to formalize the intuitive notions and to outline a theory of reliability. This theory is not only conceptually elegant; it is also practically powerful. It helps to unify measurement ideas and supplies a foundation for understanding various analytic techniques. The theory also ties in nicely with the variance approach emphasized earlier in this book.

Any set of measures has a total variance, that is, after administering an instrument to a set of objects and obtaining a set of numbers (scores), we can compute a mean, a standard deviation, and a variance. Let us be concerned here only with the variance. The variance, as seen earlier, is a *total obtained variance,* since it includes variances due to several causes. In general, any total obtained variance (or sum of squares) includes systematic and error variances.

Each person has an obtained score, X_t. (The "t" stands for "total.") This score has two components: a "true" component and an error component. We assume that each person has a "true" score, X_∞. (The "∞"

---

[1] The treatment of reliability in this chapter is based on traditional error theory. See J. Guilford, *Psychometric Methods,* 2d ed. New York: McGraw-Hill, 1954, chaps. 13 and 14. While this theory has been shown to have unnecessary assumptions, it is admirably suited to conveying to the beginning student the basic nature of reliability. For a brilliant criticism of the theory, see R. Tryon, "Reliability and Behavior Domain Validity: Reformulation and Historical Critique," *Psychological Bulletin,* LIV (1957), 229–249. In practice, the two approaches arrive at much the same formulas for computing reliability.

is the infinity sign, and is used to signify "true.") This score would be known only to an omniscient being.[2] In addition to this "true" score, each person has an error score, X_e. The error score is some increment or decrement resulting from several of the factors responsible for errors of measurement.

This reasoning leads to a simple equation basic to the theory:

$$X_t = X_\infty + X_e \qquad (24.1)$$

which says, succinctly, that any obtained score is made of two components, a "true" component and an error component. The only part of this definition that gives any real trouble is X_∞, which can be conceived to be the score an individual would obtain if all internal and external conditions were "perfect" and the measuring instrument were "perfect." A bit more realistically, it can be considered to be the mean of a large number of administrations of the test to the same person. Symbolically, $X_\infty = (X_1 + X_2 + \cdots + X_n)/n$.

With a little simple algebra, Eq. 24.1 can be extended to yield a more useful equation in variance terms:

$$V_t = V_\infty + V_e \qquad (24.2)$$

Equation 24.2 shows that the total obtained variance of a test is made up of two variance components, a "true" component and an "error" component. If, for example, it were possible to administer the same instrument to the same group 4,367,929 times, and then to compute the means of each person's 4,367,929 scores, we would have a set of "nearly true" measures of the group. In other words, these means are the X_∞'s of the group. We could then compute the variance of the X_∞'s yielding V_∞. This value must always be less than V_t, the variance computed from the obtained set of original scores, the X_t's, because the original scores contain error, whereas the "true," or "nearly true," scores have no error, the error having been washed out by the averaging process. (Errors of measurement are self-compensating.) Put differently, if there were no errors of measurement in the X_t's, then $V_t = V_\infty$. But, there are always errors of measurement, and we assume that if we knew the error scores and subtracted them from the obtained scores we would obtain the "true" scores.

We never know the "true" scores nor do we really ever know the error scores. Nevertheless, it is possible to estimate the error variance. By so doing, we can, in effect, substitute in Eq. 24.2 and solve the equation. This is the essence of the idea, even though certain assumptions and steps have been omitted from the discussion. A diagram or two may show the

---

[2] This does not mean that X_∞ may not include properties other than the property being measured. All *systematic* variance is included in X_∞. The problem of measuring *the* property is a validity problem.

ideas more clearly. Let the total variances of two tests be represented by two bars. One test is highly reliable; the other test only moderately so, as shown in Fig. 24.2. Tests A and B have the same total variance, but 90 percent of Test A is "true" variance and 10 percent is error variance. Only 60 percent of Test B is "true" variance and 40 percent is error variance. Test A is thus much more reliable than Test B.

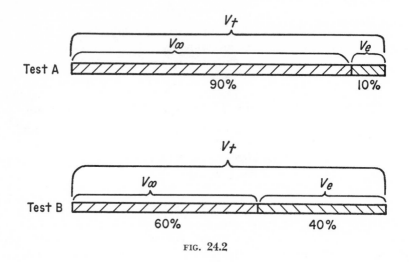

FIG. 24.2

Reliability is defined, so to speak, through error: the more error, the greater the unreliability; the less error, the greater the reliability. Practically speaking, this means that if we can estimate the error variance in any measure we can also estimate the measure's reliability. This brings us to two equivalent definitions of reliability:

1. Reliability is the proportion of the "true" variance to the total obtained variance of the data yielded by a measuring instrument.
2. Reliability is the proportion of error variance to the total obtained variance of the data yielded by a measuring instrument subtracted from 1.00, the index 1.00 indicating perfect reliability.

It is easier to write these definitions in equation form:

$$r_{tt} = \frac{V_\infty}{V_t} \tag{24.3}$$

$$r_{tt} = 1 - \frac{V_e}{V_t} \tag{24.4}$$

where r_{tt} is the reliability coefficient and the other symbols are as defined before. Equation 24.3 is theoretical and cannot be used for computation. Equation 24.4 is both theoretical and practical. It can be used both to conceptualize the idea of reliability and to estimate the reliability of an instrument. An alternate equation to (24.4) is

$$r_{tt} = \frac{V_t - V_e}{V_t} \qquad (24.5)$$

This alternative definition of reliability will be useful in helping us to understand what reliability is.

Two Computational Examples   To show the nature of reliability, two examples are given in Table 24.2. One of them, labeled I in Table 24.2, is an example of high reliability; the other, labeled II, is an example of low reliability. Note carefully that exactly the same numbers are used in both cases. The only difference is that they are arranged differently. The situation in both cases is this: five individuals have been administered a test of four items. (This is unrealistic, of course, but it will do to illustrate several points.) The data of the five individuals are given in the rows; the sums of the individuals are given to the right of the rows (Σ_t). The sums of the items are given at the bottom of each table (Σ_{it}). In addition, the sums of the individuals on the odd items (Σ_o) and the sums of the individuals on the even items (Σ_e) are given on the extreme right of each subtable. The calculations necessary for two-way analyses of variance are given below the data tables.

TABLE 24.2   DEMONSTRATION OF RELIABILITY AND COMPUTATION OF RELIABILITY COEFFICIENTS. HYPOTHETICAL EXAMPLES

| | I: $r_{tt} = .92$ | | | | | | | | II: $r_{tt} = .45$ | | | | | | |
| Indi-viduals | Items | | | | | | | Indi-viduals | Items | | | | | | |
	a	b	c	d	Σ_t	Σ_o	Σ_e		a	b	c	d	Σ_t	Σ_o	Σ_e
1	6	6	5	4	21	11	10	1	6	4	5	1	16	11	5
2	4	6	5	3	18	9	9	2	4	1	5	4	14	9	5
3	4	4	4	2	14	8	6	3	4	6	4	2	16	8	8
4	3	1	4	2	10	7	3	4	3	6	4	3	16	7	9
5	1	2	1	1	5	2	3	5	1	2	1	2	6	2	4
Σ_{it}	18	19	19	12	$\Sigma X_t = 68$			Σ_{it}	18	19	19	12	$\Sigma X_t = 68$		
					$(\Sigma X_t)^2 = 4624$								$(\Sigma X_t)^2 = 4624$		
					$\Sigma X_t^2 = 288$								$\Sigma X_t^2 = 288$		

$$C = \frac{(68)^2}{20} = 231.20 \qquad\qquad C = 231.20$$

$$\text{Total} = 288 - 231.20 = 56.80 \qquad\qquad \text{Total} = 56.80$$

$$\text{Between Items} = \frac{1190}{5} - 231.20 = 6.80 \qquad\qquad \text{Between Items} = 6.80$$

$$\text{Between Individuals} = \frac{1086}{4} - 231.20 \qquad\qquad \text{Between Individuals} = \frac{1000}{4} - 231.20$$

$$= 40.30 \qquad\qquad\qquad\qquad\qquad = 18.80$$

Source	df	s.s.	m.s.	F	Source	df	s.s.	m.s.	F
Items	3	6.80	2.27	2.80 (n.s.)	Items	3	6.80	2.27	1 (n.s.)
Individuals	4	40.30	(10.08)	12.44 (.001)	Individuals	4	18.80	(4.70)	1.81 (n.s.)
Residual:					Residual:				
I × Ind	12	9.70	(.81)		I × Ind	12	31.20	(2.60)	
Total	19	56.80			Total	19	56.80		

By Eq. 24.4:

$$r_{tt} = 1 - \frac{V_e}{V_{\text{ind}}} = 1 - \frac{.81}{10.08}$$

$$= .92$$

$$r_{tt} = 1 - \frac{2.60}{4.70}$$

$$= .45$$

By Eq. 24.5:

$$r_{tt} = \frac{V_{\text{ind}} - V_e}{V_{\text{ind}}} = \frac{10.08 - .81}{10.08}$$

$$= .92$$

$$r_{tt} = \frac{4.70 - 2.60}{4.70}$$

$$= .45$$

Odd-Even:

$$r_{oe} = .91$$

$$r_{oe} = .32$$

To make the examples more realistic, imagine that the data are scores on a six-point scale, say attitudes toward school. A high score means a high favorable attitude, a low score a low favorable (or unfavorable) attitude. (It makes no difference, however, what the scores are. They can even be 1's and 0's resulting from marking items of an achievement test right, 1, and wrong, 0.) In I, Individual 1 has a high favorable attitude toward school, whereas Individual 5 has a low favorable attitude toward school. These are readily indicated by the sums of the individuals (or the means): 21 and 5. These sums (Σ_t) are the usual scores yielded by tests. For instance, if we wanted to know the mean of the group, we would compute it as $(21 + 18 + 14 + 10 + 5)/5 = 13.60$.

The variance of these sums provides one of the terms of Eqs. 24.4 and 24.5, but not the other: V_t, but not V_e. By using the analysis of variance it is possible to compute both V_t and V_e. The analyses of variance of I and II show how this is done. These calculations need not detain us long, since they are subsidiary to the main issue.

The analysis of variance yields the variances: Between items, Between individuals, and Residual or Error. The F ratios for Items are not significant in I or II. (Note that both mean squares are 2.27. Obviously they must be equal, since they are calculated from the same sums at the bottoms of the two subtables.) Actually, we are not interested in these variances—we only want to remove the variance due to items from the total variance. Our interest lies in the Individual variances and in the Error variances, which are circled in the subtables. The total variance of Eq. 24.3, 24.4, and 24.5 is interesting because it is an index of differences between individuals. It is a measure of individual differences. Instead of writing V_t, then, let us write V_{ind}, meaning the variance resulting from individual differences. By using either (24.4) or (24.5), we obtain reliability coefficients of .92 for the data of I and .45 for the data of II. The hypothetical data of I are reliable; those of II are not reliable.

Perhaps the best way to understand this is to go back to Eq. 24.3. Now we write $r_{tt} = V_\infty / V_{ind}$. If we had a direct way to calculate V_∞, we could quickly calculate r_{tt}, but as we saw before, we do not have a direct way. There *is* a way to estimate it, however. If we can find a way to estimate V_e, the error variance, the problem is solved because V_e can be subtracted from V_{ind} to yield an estimate of V_∞. Obviously we can ignore V_∞ and subtract the proportion V_e / V_{ind} from 1 and get r_{tt}. This is a perfectly acceptable way to compute r_{tt} and to conceptualize reliability. Reasoning from $V_{ind} - V_e$ is perhaps more fruitful and ties in nicely with our earlier discussion of components of variance.

It was said in Chap. 11 that each statistical problem has a total amount of variance and each variance source contributes to this total variance. We translate the reasoning of Chap. 11 to the present problem. In random samples of the same population, V_b and V_w should be statistically equal. But, if V_b, the between-groups variance, is significantly greater than V_w, the within-groups (error) variance, then there is something in V_b over and above chance. That is, V_b includes the variance of V_w and, in addition, some systematic variance.

Similarly, we can say that if V_{ind} is significantly greater than V_e, then there is something in V_{ind} over and above error variance. This excess of variance would seem to be due to individual differences in whatever is being measured. Measurement aims at the "true" scores of individuals. The only way that we can know that this aim is accomplished is by learning the "true" *differences* between individuals. When we say that reliability is the accuracy of a measuring instrument, we mean that a reliable instrument more or less measures the "true" scores of individuals according to the reliability of the instrument. That "true" scores are measured can be inferred only from the "true" *differences* between individuals, although neither of these can be directly measured, of course. What we do is to infer the "true" differences from the fallible, empirical, measured differences, which are always to some extent corrupted by errors of measurement.

Now, if there is some way to remove from V_{ind} the effect of errors of measurement, some way to free V_{ind} of error, we can solve the problem easily. We simply subtract V_e from V_{ind} to get an estimate of V_∞. Then the proportion of the "pure" variance to all the variance, "pure" and "impure," is the estimate of the reliability of the measuring instrument. To summarize symbolically:

$$r_{tt} = \frac{V_\infty}{V_{ind}} = \frac{V_{ind} - V_e}{V_{ind}} = 1 - \frac{V_e}{V_{ind}}$$

The actual calculations are given at the bottom of Table 24.2.

Returning to the data of Table 24.2, let us see if we can "see" the reliability of I and the unreliability of II. Look first at the columns where the totals of the individuals are recorded (Σ_t). Notice that the sums of I have a wider spread, a greater range, than those of II: $21 - 5 = 16$ and $16 - 6 = 10$. Given the same individuals, the more reliable a measure the greater the range of the sums of the individuals. Think of the extreme: a completely unreliable instrument would yield sums that are like the sums yielded by random numbers, and, of course, the reliability of random numbers is zero. (The nonsignificant F ratio for Individuals, 1.81, in II indicates that $r_{tt} = .45$ is not significant.)

Now examine the rank orders of the values under the items, a, b, c, and d. In I, all four rank orders are about the same. Each item of the attitude scale, apparently, is measuring the same thing. To the extent that the individual items yield the same rank orders of individuals, to this extent the test is reliable. The items hang together, so to speak. They are internally consistent. Also, notice that the rank orders of the items of I are about the same as the rank order of the sums.

The rank order of the values under the items in II is a different case. The rank orders of a and c agree very well; they are the same as those of I. The rank orders of a and b, a and d, b and d, and c and d, however, do not agree very well. Either the items are measuring different things, or they are not measuring very consistently. This lack of congruence of rank orders is reflected in the totals of the individuals. Although the rank order of these totals is similar to the rank order of the totals of I, the range or variance is considerably less, and there is lack of spread between the sums (for example, the three 16's).

We conclude our consideration of these two examples by considering certain figures in Table 24.2 not considered before. On the right-hand side of both I and II the sums of the odd items (Σ_o) and the sums of the even items (Σ_e) are given. Simply add the values of odd items across the rows: $a + c : 6 + 5 = 11$, $4 + 5 = 9$, $4 + 4 = 8$, and so forth, in I. Then add the values of the even items: $b + d : 6 + 4 = 10$, $6 + 3 = 9$, and so forth, in I also. If there were more items, for example, a, b, c, d, e, f, g, then we would add: $a + c + e + g$ for the odd sums, and $b + d + f$ for the even sums. To calculate the reliability coefficient, calculate the product-moment correlation between the odd sums and the even sums, and then correct the resulting coefficient with the Spearman-Brown formula.[3] The odd-even r_{tt}'s for I and II are .91 and .32, respectively, fairly close to the analysis of variance results of .92 and .45. (With more subjects and more items, the estimates will ordinarily be close.)

[3] See any measurement text, for example, Guilford, *op. cit.*, p. 354. The sums of the odd and the sums of the even items are, of course, the sums of only half the items in a test. They are therefore less reliable than the sums of all the items. The Spearman-Brown formula corrects the odd-even coefficient (and other part coefficients) for the lesser number of items used in calculating the coefficient.

This simple operation may seem mystifying. To see that this is a variation of the same variance and rank-order theme, let us note, first, the rank order of the sums of the two examples. The rank orders of Σ_o and Σ_e are almost the same in I, but quite different in II. The reasoning is the same as before. Evidently the items are measuring the same thing in I, but in II the two sets of items are not consistent. To reconstruct the variance argument, simply remember that by adding the sum of the odd items to the sum of the even items for each person the total sum, or $\Sigma_o + \Sigma_e = \Sigma_t$, can be obtained.

THE INTERPRETATION
OF THE RELIABILITY COEFFICIENT

The reader may recall that if r, the coefficient of correlation, is squared, it becomes a coefficient of determination, that is, it gives us the proportion or percentage of the variance shared by two variables. If $r = .90$, then the two variables share $(.90)^2 = 81$ percent of the total variance of the two variables in common. The reliability coefficient is also a coefficient of determination. Theoretically, it tells how much variance of the total variance of a measured variable is "true" variance. If we had the "true" individual differences scores, and could correlate them with the scores of the measured variable and square the resulting coefficient of correlation, we would obtain the reliability coefficient.

Symbolic representation may make this clear. Let $r_{t\infty}$ be the coefficient of correlation between the obtained scores and the "true" scores, X_∞. The reliability coefficient is defined:

$$r_{tt} = r_{t\infty}^2 \qquad (24.6)$$

Although it is not possible to compute $r_{t\infty}$ directly, it is helpful to understand the rationale of the reliability coefficient in these theoretical terms.

Another theoretical interpretation is to conceive that each X_∞ can be the mean of a large number of X_t's derived from the test's being administered to an individual a large number of times, other things being equal.[4] The idea behind this notion has been explained before. The first administration of the test yields, say, a certain rank order of individuals. If the second, third, and further measurings all tend to yield approximately the same rank order, then the test is reliable. This is a stability or *test-retest* interpretation of reliability.

Another interpretation is that reliability is the *internal consistency* of a test. This means that the test items are homogeneous. This interpretation in effect boils down to the same idea as other interpretations: accuracy. Take any random sample of items from the test, and any other

4 *Ibid.*, p. 349.

random and different sample of items from the test. Treat each sample as a separate subtest. Each individual will then have two scores: one X_t for one subsample and another X_t for the other subsample. Correlate the two sets, continuing the process indefinitely. The average intercorrelation of the subsamples (corrected by the Spearman-Brown formula) shows the test's internal consistency.[5] But this means, really, that each subsample, if the test is reliable, succeeds in producing approximately the same rank order of individuals. If it does not, the test is not reliable.

THE STANDARD ERROR OF THE MEAN AND THE STANDARD ERROR OF MEASUREMENT

Two important aspects of reliability that have not been discussed yet are the reliability of means and the reliability of individual measures. These are tied to the standard error of the mean and the standard error of measurement. In research studies, ordinarily, the standard error of the mean—and related statistics like the standard error of the differences between means and the standard error of a correlation coefficient—is the more important of these. Since the standard error of the mean was discussed in considerable detail in an earlier chapter, it is only necessary to say here that the reliability of specific statistics is another aspect of the general problem of reliability. The standard error of measurement, or its square, the standard variance of measurement, needs to be defined and identified, if only briefly. This will be done through use of a simple example.

TABLE **24.3**   HYPOTHETICAL RELIABILITY AND STANDARD ERROR
OF MEASUREMENT EXAMPLE

	X_t	X_∞	X_e
	2	1	1
	1	2	-1
	3	3	0
	3	4	-1
	6	5	1
Σ:	15	15	0
M:	3	3	0
V:	2.80	2.00	.80

[5] See L. Cronbach, "Coefficient Alpha and the Internal Structure of Tests," *Psychometrika*, XVI (1951), 297–334; Tryon, *op. cit.* The formulas given by Cronbach and Tryon look different from Eqs. 24.3 and 24.4. They yield the same results, however. The originator of the use of the analysis of variance to estimate reliability seems to have been Hoyt. See C. Hoyt, "Test Reliability Obtained by Analysis of Variance," *Psychometrika*, VI (1941), 153–160.

$$r_{tt} = 1 - \frac{V_e}{V_t} = 1 - \frac{.80}{2.80} = .71 \qquad r_{t\infty} = .845$$

$$r_{tt} = \frac{V_\infty}{V_t} = \frac{2.00}{2.80} = .71 \qquad\qquad r_{tt} = r^2_{t\infty} = (.845)^2 = .71$$

$$SV_{\text{meas}} = V_t(1 - r_{tt}) = 2.80(1 - .71) = .81$$

$$SE_{\text{meas}} = SD_t \sqrt{1 - r_{tt}} = \sqrt{SV_{\text{meas}}} = \sqrt{.81} = .90$$

An investigator measures the attitudes of five individuals and obtains the scores given under the column labeled X_t in Table 24.3. Assume, further, that the "true" scores of the five individuals in the attitude are those given under the column labeled X_∞. (Remember, however, that we can never know these scores.) It can be seen that the instrument is reliable. While only one of the five obtained scores is exactly the same as its companion "true" score, the differences between those obtained scores that are not the same and the "true" scores are all small. These differences are shown under the column labeled "X_e"; They are "error scores." The instrument is evidently fairly accurate. The calculation of r_{tt} confirms this impression: .71.

A rather direct measure of the reliability of the instrument can be obtained by calculating the variance or the standard deviation of the error scores (X_e). The variance of the error scores and the variances of the X_t and X_∞ scores have been calculated and entered in Table 24.3. The variance of the error scores we now label, justifiably, *the standard variance of measurement,* which might more accurately be called "the standard variance of errors of measurement." The square root of this statistic is called the *standard error of measurement.* The standard variance of measurement is defined:

$$SV_{\text{meas}} = V_t(1 - r_{tt}) \tag{24.7}$$

This statistic can only be calculated, obviously, if we know the reliability coefficient. Note that if there is some way to estimate SV_{meas}, then it is possible to calculate the reliability coefficient. This bears further investigation.

We start with the definition of reliability given earlier: $r_{tt} = V_\infty/V_t = 1 - V_e/V_t$. A little algebraic manipulation yields the standard variance of measurement:

$$r_{tt} = 1 - \frac{V_e}{V_t}$$

$$r_{tt}V_t = V_t - V_e$$

$$V_e = V_t - r_{tt}V_t$$

$$V_e = V_t(1 - r_{tt})$$

The right side of the equation is the same as the right side of Eq. 24.7. Therefore $V_e = SV_{meas}$, or the error variance used earlier in the analysis of variance, *is* the standard variance of measurement. The standard variance of measurement and the standard error of measurement of the example have been calculated in Table 24.3. They are .81 and .90, respectively. As textbooks of measurement show, they can be used to interpret individual test scores. Such interpretation will not be discussed here; these statistics have been included only to show the connection between the original theory and ways of determining reliability.

One more calculation in Table 24.3 needs explanation. If we correlate the X_t and the X_∞ scores, we obtain a coefficient of correlation of .845, which was mentioned earlier. Now we obtain this coefficient, $r_{t\infty}$, directly, and square it to obtain the reliability coefficient. (See Eq. 24.6.) The latter, of course, is the same as before: .71.[6]

THE IMPROVEMENT OF RELIABILITY

The principle behind the improvement of reliability is the one previously called the *maxmincon principle*—in a slightly different form: "Maximize the variance of the individual differences and minimize the error variance." Equation 24.4 clearly indicates the principle. The general procedure follows.

First, write the items of psychological and educational measuring instruments unambiguously. An ambiguous event can be interpreted in more than one way. An ambiguous item permits error variance to creep in because individuals can interpret the item differently. Such interpretations tend to be random, and hence they increase error variance and decrease reliability.

Second, if an instrument is not reliable enough, add more items of equal kind and quality. This will usually, though not necessarily, increase reliability by a predictable amount. Adding more items increases the probability that any individual's X_t is close to his X_∞. This is a matter of the sampling of the property or the item space. With few items, a chance error, an essentially random response, looms large. With more items, it looms less large. The probability of its being balanced by another random error the other way is greater when there are more items. Summarily, more items increase the probability of accurate measurement. (Remember that each X_t is the sum of the item values for an individual.)

Third, clear and standard instructions tend to reduce errors of meas-

---

[6] It would be useful for the student to plot the X_t and X_∞ values of the little example of Table 24.3. On each side of an "average" line (regression line) drawn through the center of the points draw one standard error of measurement. Use the same unit of measurement that is used on the two axes. Note that all the points lie within, or not far outside, these lines. The space enclosed by the two outside lines might be called a "reliability space."

urement. Great care must always be taken, in writing the instructions, to state them clearly. Ambiguous instructions increase the error variance. Further, measuring instruments should always be administered under standard, well-controlled, and similar conditions. If the situations of administration differ, error variance can again intrude.

THE VALUE OF RELIABILITY

To be interpretable, a test must be reliable. Unless one can depend upon the results of the measurement of one's variables, one cannot, with any confidence, determine the relations between the variables. One goal of science, again, is to discover the relations among variables. Since unreliable measurement is measurement overloaded with error, the discovery of these relations becomes a difficult and tenuous business. Is an obtained coefficient of correlation between two variables low because one or both measures are unreliable? Is an analysis of variance F ratio not significant because the hypothesized relation does not exist or because the measure of the dependent variables is too crude, too unreliable?

Reliability, while not the most important facet of measurement, is still extremely important. In a way, this is like the money problem: the lack of it is the real problem. High reliability is no guarantee of good scientific results, but there can be no good scientific results without reliability. In brief, reliability is a necessary but not sufficient condition of the value of research results and their interpretation.

25 *VALIDITY*

The subject of validity is complex, controversial, and peculiarly important in psychological and educational research. Here perhaps more than anywhere else, the nature of reality is questioned. It is possible to study reliability without inquiring into the meaning of the variables whose reliable measurement is studied. It is not possible to study validity, however, without sooner or later inquiring into the nature and meaning of one's variables.

When measuring certain physical properties and relatively simple attributes of persons, validity is no great problem. There is often rather direct and close congruence between the nature of the object measured and the measuring instrument. The length of an object, for example, can be measured by laying off sticks, containing a standard number system in feet or meters, on the object. Weight is more indirect, but nevertheless not difficult: an object placed in a container displaces the container downward. The downward movement of the container is registered on a calibrated index, which reads "pounds" or "ounces." With some physical attributes, then, there is little doubt of what is being measured.

On the other hand, suppose an educational scientist wishes to study the relation between intelligence and school achievement or the relation between authoritarianism and teaching style. Now there are no rulers to use, no scales with which to weigh the degree of authoritarianism, no clear-cut physical or behavioral attributes that point unmistakably to teaching style. It is necessary in such cases to invent indirect means to measure psychological and educational properties. These means are often so indirect that the validity of the measurement and its products is doubtful.

TYPES OF VALIDITY

The commonest definition of validity is epitomized by the question: Are we measuring what we think we are measuring? The emphasis in this question is on *what* is being measured. For example, a teacher has constructed a test to measure *understanding* of scientific procedures and has included in the test only *factual* items about scientific procedures. The test is not valid, because while it may reliably measure the pupils' *factual knowledge* of scientific procedures, it does not measure their *understanding* of such procedures. In other words, it may measure what it measures quite well, but it does not measure what the teacher intended it to measure.

Although the commonest definition of validity was given above, it must immediately be emphasized that there is no one validity. A test or scale is valid for the scientific or practical purpose of its user. An educator may be interested in the *nature* of high school pupils' achievement in mathematics. He would then be interested in *what* a mathematics achievement or aptitude test measures. He might, for instance, want to know the factors that enter into mathematics test performance and their relative weights in this performance. On the other hand, he may be primarily interested in knowing the pupils who will probably be successful and those who will probably be unsuccessful in high school mathematics. He may have little interest in *what* a mathematics aptitude test measures. He is interested mainly in successful *prediction*. Implied by these two uses of tests are different kinds of validity. We now examine an extremely important development in test theory: the analysis and study of different kinds of validity.

The most important classification of types of validity is that prepared by a joint committee of the American Psychological Association, the American Educational Research Association, and the National Council on Measurements Used in Education.[1] Four types of validity are discussed: *predictive, concurrent, content,* and *construct.* Each of these will be examined briefly, though we put the greatest emphasis on construct validity, since it is probably the most important form of validity from the scientific research point of view.

Content Validity and Content Validation   A university psychology professor has given a course to seniors in which he has emphasized the understanding of principles of human development. He prepares an objective-type test. Wanting to know something of its validity, he critically examines each of the test's items for their relevance to understanding principles of human development. He also asks two colleagues to evaluate the content of the test. Naturally, he tells the colleagues what it is he is trying to measure. He has investigated the *content validity* of the test.

Content validity is the *representativeness* or *sampling adequacy* of the content—the substance, the matter, the topics—of a measuring instru-

[1] *Technical Recommendations for Psychological Tests and Diagnostic Techniques, Psychological Bulletin,* LI (1954), Supplement, 201–238. An important article that explains in detail the system and thinking of the committee is L. Cronbach and P. Meehl, "Construct Validity of Psychological Tests," *Psychological Bulletin,* LII (1955), 281–302.

ment.[2] *Content validation* is guided by the question: Is the substance or content of this measure representative of the content or the universe of content of the property being measured? Any psychological or educational property has a theoretical universe of content consisting of all the things that can possibly be said or observed about the property. The members of this universe, U, can be called items. The property might be "arithmetic achievement," to take a relatively easy example. U has an infinite number of members: all possible items using numbers, arithmetic operations, and concepts. A test high in content validity would theoretically be a random sample or subset of U. If it were possible to draw items from U at random in sufficient numbers, then any such sample of items would form a test high in content validity. If U consists of subsets A, B, and C, which are arithmetic operations, arithmetic concepts, and number manipulation, respectively; then any sufficiently large random sample of U would represent A, B, and C approximately equally. The test's content validity would be satisfactory.

Ordinarily, and unfortunately, it is not possible to draw random samples of items from a universe of content. Such universes of content exist only theoretically. True, it is possible and desirable to assemble large collections of items, especially in the achievement area, and to draw random samples from such collections for testing purposes. But the content validity of such collections, no matter how large and how "good" the items, is always in question.

If it is not possible to satisfy the definition of content validity, how can a reasonable degree of content validity be achieved? Content validation consists essentially in *judgment*. Alone or with others, one judges the representativeness of the items. One may ask: Does this item measure Property M? To express it more fully one might ask: Is this item representative of the universe of content of M? If U has subsets, such as those indicated above, then one has to ask additional questions; for example: Is this item a member of the subset M_1 or the subset M_2?

Some universes of content are more obvious and much easier to judge than others; the content of many achievement tests, for instance, would seem to be obvious. The content validity of these tests, it is said, can be assumed. While this statement seems reasonable, and while the content of most achievement tests is "self-validated" in the sense that the individual writing the test to a degree defines the property being measured (for example, a teacher writing a classroom test of spelling or arith-

[2] *Technical Recommendations, op. cit.*, p. 13. Two other definitions of content validity can be found in R. Ebel, "Obtaining and Reporting Evidence on Content Validity," *Educational and Psychological Measurement*, XVI (1956), 269–282; R. Lennon, "Assumptions Underlying the Use of Content Validity," *ibid.*, pp. 294–304. The first of these articles stresses the ultimate goals of instruction; the second, like the definition in the text above, is more pertinent to research, because it stresses the representativeness of the sampling of *subjects' responses* to a measurement instrument.

metic), it is dangerous to assume the adequacy of content validity without systematic efforts to check the assumption. For example, an educational investigator, testing hypotheses about the relations between social studies achievement and other variables, may assume the content validity of his social studies test. The theory from which the investigator derived his hypotheses, however, may require an *understanding* and *application* of social studies ideas, whereas the test he used may be almost purely factual in content. His test lacks content validity for his purpose. In fact, he is not really testing the hypotheses he thinks he is testing.

Content validation, then, is basically judgmental. The items of a test must be studied, each item being weighed for its presumed representativeness of the universe. This means that each item must be judged for its presumed relevance to the property being measured, which is no easy task. In many cases, other "competent" judges must also judge the content of the items. The universe of content must, if possible, be clearly defined; that is, the judges must be furnished with specific directions for making judgments, as well as with specification of what they are judging. Then, some method for pooling independent judgments must be used.[3]

Predictive and Concurrent Validity and Validation Predictive validity and concurrent validity are much alike. With few exceptions, they can be considered the same, because they differ only in the time dimension. It is perhaps unfortunate that the word *prediction* is associated so strongly with the future. In science, prediction does not necessarily mean *forecast*. Margenau points out that "pre-" implies "prior to completed knowledge" and does not contrast with "post-." [4] One "predicts" from an independent variable to a dependent variable. One "predicts" the existence or non-existence of a relation; one even "predicts" something that happened in the past! This broad scientific meaning of prediction is the meaning intended when discussing predictive validity. If this is so, then predictive validity and concurrent validity are virtually the same.

Whatever the difficulties of words, predictive or concurrent validity is characterized by prediction to an *outside criterion* and by checking a measuring instrument, either now or in the future, against some outcome. A test predicts a certain kind of outcome, or it predicts some present or future state of affairs. In a sense, then, all tests are predictive. Aptitude tests predict future achievement; achievement tests predict present and future achievement; and intelligence tests predict the present and future ability to learn and to solve problems.

[3] An excellent guide to the content validity of achievement tests has been prepared: B. Bloom, *et al.*, *Taxonomy of Educational Objectives*. New York: Longmans, 1956. This is a comprehensive attempt to outline and discuss educational goals in relation to measurement.

[4] H. Margenau, *The Nature of Physical Reality*. New York: McGraw-Hill, 1950, p. 105, footnote.

Predictive validity is ordinarily associated with practical problems and outcomes. Interest is not so much in what is behind test performance as it is in helping to solve practical problems. Tests are used by the hundreds for the predictive purposes of screening and selecting potentially successful candidates in education, in business, and in other occupations. Tests are also concurrently used as substitutes for perhaps less convenient, more difficult, or otherwise cumbersome modes of measurement and evaluation.

The single greatest difficulty of predictive validation is the criterion. Often criteria do not even exist or their validity is doubtful. Obtaining possible criteria may even be difficult. What criterion can be used to validate a measure of teacher effectveness? Who is to judge teacher effectiveness? Is getting the Ph.D. degree an adequate criterion of success in research? Is being a businessman a good index of interest in business? What criterion can be used to test the predictive validity of a musical aptitude test?

Construct Validity and Construct Validation   Scientifically speaking, construct validity is one of the most significant advances of modern measurement theory and practice. It is a significant advance because it unites psychometric notions with scientific theoretical notions.

The measurement expert, when he inquires into the construct validity of a test, usually wants to know what psychological property or properties can "explain" the variance of the test. He wishes to know the "meaning" of the test. If the test is an intelligence test, he may want to know what factors lie behind test performance. He asks: What factors or constructs account for variance in test performance? [5] He may specifically ask: Does this test measure verbal ability and abstract reasoning ability? Does it also "measure" social class membership? He is asking what proportion of the total test variance is accounted for by the constructs: verbal ability, abstract reasoning ability, and social class membership. In short, he seeks to *explain* individual differences in the test scores of a measuring instrument. His interest is more in the property being measured than in the test itself.

A researcher generally starts with the constructs or variables entering into the relations. He has discovered, say, a positive correlation between two measures, one a measure of educational traditionalism and the other a measure of the perception of the characteristics associated with the "good" teacher. Individuals high on the traditionalism measure see the "good" teacher as efficient, moral, thorough, industrious, conscientious, and reliable. Individuals low on the traditionalism measure may see the "good" teacher in a different way. The researcher now wants to know *why* this relation exists, what is behind it. To learn why, he must

[5] Cronbach and Meehl, *op. cit.*, p. 282.

know the meaning of the constructs entering the relation, "perception of the 'good' teacher" and "traditionalism." *How* he can study these meanings is a construct validity problem.

One can see that construct validation and empirical scientific inquiry are closely allied. It is not simply a question of validating a test. One must try to validate the theory behind the test. Cronbach says that there are three parts to construct validation: suggesting what constructs possibly account for test performance, deriving hypotheses from the theory involving the construct, and testing the hypotheses empirically.[6] This formulation is but a reduced précis of the general scientific approach discussed in Part I.

The significant point about construct validity, that which sets it apart from other types of validity, is its preoccupation with theory, theoretical constructs, and scientific empirical inquiry involving the testing of hypothesized relations. Construct validation in measurement contrasts sharply with empiric approaches that define the validity of a measure purely by its success in predicting a criterion. For example, a purely empiric tester might say that a test is valid if it efficiently distinguishes individuals high and low in a trait. *Why* the test succeeds in separating the subsets of a group is of no great concern. It is enough that it does.

A Hypothetical Example of Construct Validation Let us assume that an investigator is interested in the determinants of creativity and the relation of creativity to school achievement. He notices that the most sociable persons, who exhibit affection for others, also seem to be less creative than those who are less sociable and affectionate. He wants to test the implied relation in a controlled fashion. One of his first tasks is to obtain or construct a measure of the sociable-affectionate characteristic. The investigator, surmising that this combination of traits may be a reflection of a deeper concern or love for others, calls it Amorism. He assumes that there are individual differences in Amorism, that some people have a great deal of it, others a moderate amount, and still others very little.

He must first construct an instrument to measure Amorism. The literature gives him little help, since scientific psychologists have rarely investigated the fundamental nature of love. Sociability, however, has been measured. The investigator must construct a *new* instrument, basing its content on his intuitive and reasoned notions of what Amorism is. The reliability of the test, tried out with large groups, runs between .75 and .85.

The question now is whether or not the test is valid. The investigator correlates the instrument, calling it the *A* scale, with independent

[6] L. Cronbach, *Essentials of Psychological Testing*, 2d ed. New York: Harper & Row, 1960, p. 121.

measures of sociability. The correlations are moderately substantial, but he needs evidence that the test has construct validity. He deduces certain relations that should and should not exist between Amorism and other variables. He reasons that if Amorism is a general tendency to love others, then it should correlate with characteristics like cooperativeness and friendliness. Persons high in Amorism, he also believes, will approach problems in an ego-oriented manner as contrasted to persons low in Amorism, who will approach problems in a task-oriented manner.

Acting on this reasoning, the investigator administers the A scale and a scale to measure subjectivity to a number of sixth-grade students. To measure cooperativeness he observes the classroom and playground behavior of the same group of students. The correlations between the three measures are positive and significant.[7]

Knowing the pitfalls of psychological measurement, the investigator is not satisfied. These positive correlations may be due to a factor common to all three tests, but irrelevant to Amorism; for example, the tendency to give the "right" answers. (This would probably be ruled out, however, because the observation measure of Cooperativeness correlates positively with Amorism and Subjectivity.) So, taking a new group of subjects, he administers the Amorism and Subjectivity scales, has the subjects' behavior rated for Cooperativeness, and in addition, administers a creativity test that has been found in other research to be reliable (correlated with psychologists' ratings of the creativity of written compositions).

The investigator states the relation between Amorism and Creativity in hypothesis form: The relation between the A scale and the creativity measure will be negative and significant. The correlations between Amorism and Cooperativeness and between Amorism and Subjectivity will be positive and significant. "Check" hypotheses are also formulated: The correlation between Cooperativeness and Creativity will not be significant; it will be near zero, but the correlation between Subjectivity and Creativity will be positive and significant. This last relation is predicted on the basis of previous research findings. The six correlation coefficients are given in the correlation matrix of Table 25.1. The four measures are labeled as follows: A, Amorism; B, Cooperativeness; C, Subjectivity; and D, Creativity.

The evidence for the construct validity of the A scale is good. All the r's are as predicted; especially important are the r's between D (Creativity) and the other variables. Note that there are three different kinds of prediction: positive, negative, and zero. All three kinds are as predicted. This illustrates what might be called *differential prediction* or *differential validity*. It is not enough to predict, for instance, that the

[7] Note that we would not expect high correlations between the measures. If the correlations were too high, we would then suspect the validity of the A scale. It would be measuring, perhaps, Subjectivity or Cooperativeness, but not Amorism.

measure presumably reflecting the target property be positively correlated with one theoretically relevant variable. One should, through deduction from the theory, predict more than one such positive relation. In addition, one should predict zero relations between the principal variable and variables "irrelevant" to the theory.

TABLE 25.1 INTERCORRELATIONS OF FOUR HYPOTHETICAL MEASURES [a]

	B	C	D
A	.50	.60	−.30
B		.40	.05
C			.50

[a] A = amorism; B = cooperativeness; C = subjectivity; D = creativity. Correlation coefficients .25 or greater are significant at the .01 level. $N = 90$.

In the example above, although Cooperativeness was expected to correlate with Amorism, there was no theoretical reason to expect it to correlate at all with Creativity. Another example of a different kind is when an investigator deliberately introduces a measure that would, if it correlates with the variable whose validity is under study, invalidate other positive relations. One bugaboo of personality and attitude scales is the social desirability phenomenon, mentioned earlier. The correlation between the target variable and a theoretically related variable may be due to the fact that the instruments measuring both variables may be substantially tapping social desirability rather than the variables they were designed to tap. One can check whether this is so by including a measure of social desirability along with the other measures.

Despite all the evidence leading the investigator to believe that the A scale has construct validity, he may still be doubtful. He now sets up an experiment (of an ex post facto kind) in which he has pupils high and low in Amorism solve problems. He predicts that pupils *low* in Amorism will solve problems more successfully than those *high* in Amorism. If the data support the prediction, this is further evidence of the construct validity of his measure of Amorism. It is of course a significant finding in and of itself. Such an experimental procedure, however, is probably more appropriate with achievement and attitude measures. One can manipulate communications, for example, in order to change attitudes. If attitude scores change according to theoretical prediction, this would be evidence of the construct validity of the attitude measure, since the scores would probably not change according to prediction if the measure were not measuring the construct.

Research Examples of Construct Validation In one sense, any type of validation is construct validation.[8] Whenever hypotheses are tested, when-

8 J. Loevinger, "Objective Tests as Instruments of Psychological Theory," *Psychological Reports,* III (1957), 635–694, Monograph Supplement 9. Loevinger argues that

ever relations are empirically studied, construct validity is involved. Let us examine some actual examples of construct validation. In so doing, we note that aspects of predictive, concurrent, and content validities are also present.

SARASON'S TEST ANXIETY SCALE FOR CHILDREN   Sarason, *et al.*, in studying the validity of their Test Anxiety Scale for Children (TASC), used Cronbach and Meehl's notion of embedding the TASC and the anxiety construct in a "nomological network," an interrelated system of relations that constitute a theory.[9] One of the empirical tests was to correlate the TASC with teacher ratings of children's anxiety. The TASC was administered to over 2200 second- through fifth-grade pupils. The pupils were also rated by their teachers on a 17-item anxiety rating scale. Though the correlations between the TASC and the ratings were low, they were for the most part statistically significant, thus yielding evidence of the validity of the TASC.

Sarason and his colleagues also tested the relations between the TASC and intelligence and achievement. The *r*'s were low and negative, as predicted. The important relation between general anxiety and test anxiety was also studied. It, too, supported Sarason's expectations. Earlier we reviewed these investigators' study of the differences between American and English school children in test anxiety. The results also supported stated hypotheses, thus adding further weight to the researchers' confidence in the construct validity of the TASC.

ROKEACH'S DOGMATISM SCALE   An interesting and psychologically significant example of construct validation is Rokeach's work on the Dogmatism (*D*) scale and other related measures.[10] To some extent, disputing the validity of the well-known *F* scale as a measure of authoritarianism, Rokeach, on the basis of rather involved theoretical reasoning, constructed the *D* scale. This instrument consists of a number of items that he believed would tap closed-mindedness, a way of thinking presumably associated with any ideology regardless of content. Central to Rokeach's formulation is the notion that the ideological orientations of individuals are related to their personalities, thought processes, and behaviors. Two examples among many that can be given are his predictions that dogmatism is related to intolerance and to opinionation.

Rokeach undertook an extensive series of investigations aimed at testing his theory and the construct validity of his scales.[11] In one study

---

construct validity, from a scientific point of view, is the whole of validity. At the other extreme, Bechtoldt argues that construct validity has no place in psychology. H. Bechtoldt, "Construct Validity: A Critique," *American Psychologist*, XIV (1959), 619–629.

[9] S. Sarason, *et al.*, *Anxiety in Elementary School Children*. New York: Wiley, 1960, pp. 125–128.

[10] M. Rokeach, *The Open and Closed Mind*. New York: Basic Books, 1960.

[11] Rokeach specifically says that he was mainly preoccupied with construct valid-

he used what has been called the *known-groups method*. In this method groups of people with "known" characteristics are administered an instrument and the direction of differences is predicted. For example, if we were validating an attitude scale designed to measure conservatism, we might select groups "known" to be very conservative and groups "known" not to be conservative. Rokeach had college professors and graduate psychology students select graduate students and friends they considered to be open- and closed-minded. The *D* scale clearly differentiated the two groups.[12]

Perhaps a more cogent demonstration of the validity of the *D* scale using the known-groups method is Rokeach's testing of different religious groups.[13] He found that Catholic students in Michigan, as predicted, obtained significantly higher *D* scores than Protestant students. These results did not hold up in New York, however. With English subjects, Rokeach found that Communists scored significantly higher on *D* than did liberals, an interesting finding indeed, especially when the same Communists scored significantly lower on the *F* (Authoritarianism) scale.

In more direct tests of the *D* scale's validity in measuring individuals' total belief systems, Rokeach studied the relation between problem-solving in situations quite different from any encountered in everyday life,[14] the relations between belief-system closedness and perceptual analysis,[15] and even the relation between closedness and acceptance of new and unconventional music.[16] While the results of these studies were not clear-cut, they furnished evidence of the validity of Rokeach's theoretical derivations and the validity of the *D* measure.

Other Methods of Construct Validation   In addition to the examples just discussed, there are other methods that illustrate construct validity and construct validation. Any tester is familiar with the technique of correlating items with total scores. In using this technique, the total test score of any individual is assumed to be valid. To the extent that any item measures the same thing the total scores does, to that extent the item is valid.[17]

A much less frequently used method of studying measure validity is factor analysis. Factor analysis will be discussed more fully in Chap. 36, but its relevance to this chapter warrants brief comment.

Factor analysis is a method for reducing a large number of measures to a smaller number of measures (factors) by discovering which measures

---

ity. Though he was concerned with predictive, concurrent, and content validities, these were subordinate to construct validity. *Ibid.*, p. 99, footnote.

12 *Ibid.*, chap. 5.
13 *Ibid.*, chap. 6.
14 *Ibid.*, chaps. 8, 9, and 12.
15 *Ibid.*, chap. 14.
16 *Ibid.*, chap. 15.
17 For a thorough discussion of item analysis, see Guilford, *op. cit.*, pp. 417ff.

"go together" (which measures measure the same thing) and the relations between these clusters of measures that go together. For example, we may give a group of individuals twenty tests each presumed to measure something different. We may find, however, that the twenty tests are really only five measures or factors. This is discovered through correlational methods.

In order to study the construct validity of any measure, it is always helpful to correlate the measure with other measures. The Amorism example discussed earlier illustrated the method and the ideas behind it. But, would it not be more valuable to correlate a measure with a large number of other measures? How better to learn about a construct than to know its correlates? Factor analysis is a refined method of doing this. It tells us, in effect, what measures measure the same thing and to what extent they measure what they measure. In fact, factor analysis may almost be called the most important of construct validity tools.

One example from the author's research will illustrate what is meant by factor analysis. By means of Q methodology (a method to be described later; see Chap. 33) a number of items have been found to measure what appeared to be two relatively independent (uncorrelated) dimensions of educational attitudes, A (progressivism) and B (traditionalism). To test the hypotheses that these two dimensions (factors) constituted most of the variance of educational attitudes, that they were independent measures of the two factors, and that the items were valid measures of educational attitudes, the items were built into an attitude scale and administered to three groups presumed to be different in educational attitudes: graduate students of education, undergraduate students of education, and persons outside the university.[18] This is the known-groups method, of course.

A factor analysis of the intercorrelations of the items confirmed the factor or dimension hypotheses. The analysis of variance of the differences between the means of the three groups on A and B confirmed the group-differences hypothesis. Two dimensions or factors emerged from the factor analysis, the factors were relatively independent, and the differences between the means were significant. The means were also in the predicted direction. These results seemed to indicate that the scale was valid and that the "theory" behind its construction was also valid.

[18] F. Kerlinger and E. Kaya, "The Construction and Factor Analytic Validation of Scales to Measure Attitudes toward Education," *Educational and Psychological Measurement,* XIX (1959), 13–29; F. Kerlinger and E. Kaya, "The Predictive Validity of Scales Constructed to Measure Attitudes toward Education," *Educational and Psychological Measurement,* XIX (1959), 305–317. The authors used the term "predictive validity" in the second of these reports; perhaps they should have used "construct validity." The difference is not serious, however. "Predictive validity" was used because group membership was predicted, or rather, scale scores were predicted from group membership.

A VARIANCE DEFINITION OF VALIDITY: THE VARIANCE RELATION OF RELIABILITY AND VALIDITY [19]

In the last chapter, reliability was defined as

$$r_{tt} = \frac{V_\infty}{V_t} \tag{25.1}$$

the proportion of "true" variance to total variance. It is theoretically and empirically useful to define validity similarly. Validity, therefore, is defined:

$$\text{Val} = \frac{V_{co}}{V_t} \tag{25.2}$$

where Val is the validity; V_{co} the common factor variance; and V_t the total variance of a measure. Validity is thus seen as the proportion of the total variance of a measure that is common factor variance.

Unfortunately, we are not in a position yet to present the full meaning of this definition. An understanding of so-called factor theory is required, but factor theory will not be discussed until later in the book. Despite this difficulty, we must attempt an explanation of validity in variance terms if we are to have a well-rounded view of the subject. Besides, expressing validity and reliability mathematically will unify and clarify both subjects. Indeed, reliability and validity will be seen to be parts of one unified whole.

Common factor variance is the variance of a measure that is shared with other measures. In other words, common factor variance is the variance that two or more tests have in common.

In contrast to the common factor variance of a measure is its *specific variance*, V_{sp}, the systematic variance of a measure that is not shared by any other measure. If a test measures skills that other tests measure, we have common factor variance; if it also measures a skill that no other test does, we have specific variance.

Figure 25.1 expresses these ideas and also adds the notion of error variance. The A and B circles represent the variances of Tests A and B. The intersection of A and B, $A \cap B$, is the relation of the two sets. Similarly, $V(A \cap B)$ is the common factor variance. The specific variances and the error variances of both tests are also indicated.

From this viewpoint, then, and following the variance reasoning outlined in the last chapter, any measure's total variance has several com-

---

[19] The variance treatment of validity presented here is an extension of the variance treatment of reliability presented in the last chapter. Both treatments follow Guilford, *op. cit.*, pp. 354–357.

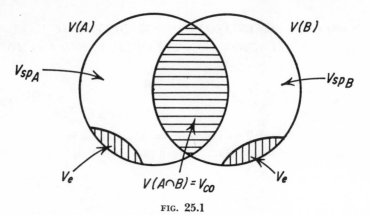

FIG. 25.1

ponents: *common factor variance, specific variance,* and *error variance.* This is expressed by the equation:

$$V_t = V_{co} + V_{sp} + V_e \tag{25.3}$$

To be able to talk of proportions of the total variance, we divide the terms of Eq. 25.3 by the total variance:

$$\frac{V_t}{V_t} = \frac{V_{co}}{V_t} + \frac{V_{sp}}{V_t} + \frac{V_a}{V_t} \tag{25.4}$$

How do Eqs. 25.1 and 25.2 fit into this picture? The first term on the right, V_{co} / V_t, is the right-hand member of (25.2). Therefore validity can be viewed as that part of the total variance of a measure that is not specific variance and not error variance. This is easily seen algebraically:

$$\frac{V_{co}}{V_t} = \frac{V_t}{V_t} - \frac{V_{sp}}{V_t} - \frac{V_e}{V_t} \tag{25.5}$$

By a definition of the previous chapter, reliability can be defined as

$$r_{tt} = 1 - \frac{V_e}{V_t} \tag{25.6}$$

This can be written:

$$r_{tt} = \frac{V_t}{V_t} - \frac{V_e}{V_t} \tag{25.7}$$

The right-hand side of the equation, however, is part of the right-hand side of (25.5). If we rewrite (25.5) slightly, we obtain

$$\frac{V_{co}}{V_t} = \frac{V_t}{V_t} - \frac{V_e}{V_t} - \frac{V_{sp}}{V_t} \tag{25.8}$$

This must mean, then, that validity and reliability are close variance relations. Reliability is equal to the first two right-hand members of (25.8). So, bringing in (25.1):

$$r_{tt} = \frac{V_t}{V_t} - \frac{V_e}{V_t} = \frac{V_\infty}{V_t} \tag{25.9}$$

If we substitute in (25.8), we get

$$\frac{V_{co}}{V_t} = \frac{V_\infty}{V_t} - \frac{V_{sp}}{V_t} \tag{25.10}$$

Thus we see that the proportion of the total variance of a measure is equal to the proportion of the total variance that is "true" variance minus the proportion that is specific variance. Or, the validity of a measure is that portion of the total variance of the measure that shares variance with other measures. Theoretically, valid variance includes no variance due to error, nor does it include variance that is specific to this measure and this measure only.

This can all be summed up in two ways. First, we sum it up in an equation or two. Let us assume that we have a method of determining the common factor variance (or variances) of a test. (Later we shall see that factor analysis is such a method.) For simplicity suppose that there are two sources of common factor variance in a test—and no others. Call these factors A and B. They might be verbal ability and arithmetic ability, or they might be liberal attitudes and conservative attitudes. If we add the variance of A to the variance of B, we obtain the common factor variance of the test, which is expressed by the equations,

$$V_{co} = V_A + V_B \tag{25.11}$$

$$\frac{V_{co}}{V_t} = \frac{V_A}{V_t} + \frac{V_B}{V_t} \tag{25.12}$$

Then, using (25.2) and substituting in (25.12), we obtain

$$\text{Val} = \frac{V_A}{V_t} + \frac{V_B}{V_t} \tag{25.13}$$

The total variance of a test, we said before, includes the common factor variance, the variance specific to the test and to no other test (at least as far as present information goes), and error variance. Equations 25.3 and 25.4 express this. Now, substituting in (25.4) the equality of (25.12), we obtain

$$\frac{V_t}{V_t} = \overbrace{\frac{V_A}{V_t} + \frac{V_B}{V_t}}^{h^2} + \underbrace{\frac{V_{sp}}{V_t} + \frac{V_e}{V_t}}_{r_{tt}} \tag{25.14}$$

The first two terms on the right-hand side of (25.14) are associated with the validity of the measure, and the first three terms on the right are associated with the reliability of the measure. These relations have been indicated. Common factor variance, or the validity component of the measure, is labeled h^2 (*communality*), a symbol customarily used to indicate the common factor variance of a test. Reliability, as usual, is labeled r_{tt}.

To discuss all the implications of this formulation of validity and reliability would take us too far astray at this time. All that is needed now is to try to clarify the formulation with a diagram and a brief discussion.

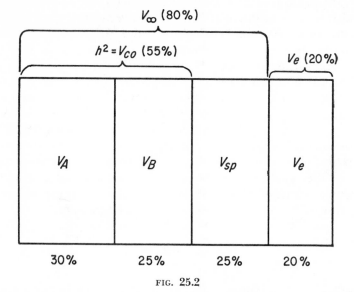

FIG. 25.2

Figure 25.2 is an attempt to express 25.14 diagrammatically. The figure represents the contributions of the different variances to the total variance (taken to be equal to 100 percent). Four variances, three systematic variances and one error variance, comprise the total variance in this theoretical model.[20] The contribution of each of the sources of variance is indicated. Of the total variance, 80 percent is reliable variance. Of the reliable variance, 30 percent is contributed by Factor A and 25 percent by Factor B, and 25 percent is specific to this test. The remaining 20 percent of the total variance is error variance.

The test may be interpreted as quite reliable (in most cases), since a sizable proportion of the total variance is reliable or "true" variance. The interpretation of validity is more difficult. If there were only one factor, say A, and it contributed 55 percent of the total variance, then we could say that a considerable proportion of the total variance was valid

[20] Naturally, practical outcomes never look this neat. It is remarkable, however, how well the model works. The variance thinking, too, is valuable in conceptualizing and discussing measurement outcomes.

variance. We would know that a good bit of the reliable measurement (about 70 percent) would be the measurement of the property known as *A*. This would be a construct validity statement. Practically speaking, individuals measured with the test would be rank-ordered on *A* with adequate reliability.

With the above hypothetical example, however, the situation is more complex. The test measures two factors, *A* and *B*. There could be three sets of rank orders, one resulting from *A*, one from *B*, and one from *specific*. While repeat reliability might be high, if we thought we were measuring only *A*, to the extent we thought so to this extent the test would not be valid. We might, however, have a score for each individual on *A* and one on *B*. In this case the test would be valid.[21] Indeed, modern developments in measurement indicate that such multiple scores are becoming more and more a part of accepted procedure.

THE VALIDITY AND RELIABILITY OF PSYCHOLOGICAL AND EDUCATIONAL MEASUREMENT INSTRUMENTS

Poor measurement can invalidate any scientific investigation. Most of the criticisms of psychological and educational measurement, by professionals and laymen alike, center on validity. This is as it should be. Achieving reliability is to a large extent a technical matter. Validity, however, is much more than technique. It bores into the essence of science itself. It also bores into philosophy. Construct validity, particularly, since it is concerned with the nature of "reality" and the nature of the properties being measured, is heavily philosophical.

Despite the difficulties of achieving reliable and valid psychological and educational measurements, great progress has been made in this century. There is growing understanding that *all* psychological and educational measuring instruments must be critically and empirically examined for their reliability and validity. The day of tolerance of inadequate measurement is ending. The demands imposed by professional psychologists and educators, the theoretical and statistical tools available and rapidly being developed, and the increasing sophistication of graduate students of psychology, sociology, and education have set new high standards that should be healthy stimulants both to the imaginations of research workers and to developers of scientific measurement.

---

[21] Note that even if we thought the test was measuring only *A*, predictions to a criterion might well be successful, especially if the criterion had a lot of both *A* and *B* in it. The test could have predictive validity even though its construct validity was questionable.

STUDY SUGGESTIONS

1. The following references are valuable guides to the study of measurement, although some of the theoretical and technical discussions are rather difficult. (The student can find elementary discussions of reliability and validity in most measurement and statistics texts.)

Bloom, B., *et al. Taxonomy of Educational Objectives. Handbook I: Cognitive Domain.* New York: Longmans, 1956. This unique book emphasizes the goals of education and their relation to measurement. It is invaluable for the researcher who has to measure educational variables.

Cronbach, L. *Essentials of Psychological Testing,* 2d ed. New York: Harper & Row, 1960, Chaps. 5 and 6. This book includes excellent elementary chapters on validity and reliability written by an outstanding expert. On p. 106, Cronbach gives a valuable table (Table 8) outlining types of validity and their characteristics and uses.

Cronbach, L., and P. Meehl. "Construct Validity in Psychological Tests." *Psychological Bulletin,* LII (1955), 281–302. This very important and influential article has stimulated much discussion and work. It stresses the relation of scientific theory and measurement.

Guilford, J. *Psychometric Methods,* 2d ed. New York: McGraw-Hill, 1954, Chaps. 1, 13, and 14. A basic source on measurement theory and practice, this text requires careful study, but is rewarding.

Harris, C., ed. *Encyclopedia of Educational Research,* 3d ed. New York: Macmillan, 1960. See articles on reliability, validity, and prediction.

Technical Recommendations for Psychological Tests and Diagnostic Techniques. Psychological Bulletin Supplement, Vol. LI, No. 2, Part 2, 1954. This small pioneering work is apparently having a great influence on psychological measurement. It defines and briefly discusses types of validity, among other things.

Thorndike, R. "Reliability." In E. Lindquist, ed. *Educational Measurement.* Washington, D.C.: American Council on Education, 1951, Chap. 15. A definitive discussion of reliability. Contains an exceptionally good table summarizing the possible sources of variance in measures: Table 8, p. 569.

Tryon, R. "Reliability and Behavior Doman Validity: A Reformulation and Historical Critique." *Psychological Bulletin,* LIV (1957), 229–249. This is an excellent and very important article on reliability. Some observers consider it to be a classic article that will significantly change thinking on reliability. It contains a good worked example.

2. Discuss and criticize the following statements:
    (a) "The reliability of my creativity test is .85. I can therefore be reasonably sure that I am measuring creativity."
    (b) "My creativity test really measures creativity, because I had an expert on creativity carefully screen all the items of the test."
    (c) "Since the reliability of the test of logical thinking is only .40, its validity is negligible."
3. Study the following assertions and decide in each case whether the assertion refers to reliability or validity, or both. Label the type of reliability and validity.
    (a) "The test was given twice to the same group. The coefficient of correlation between the scores of the two administrations was .90."
    (b) "Four teachers studied the items of the test for their relevance to the objectives of the curriculum."
    (c) "The items seem to be a good sample of the item universe."
    (d) "Between a test of academic aptitude and grade-point averages, $r = .55$."
    (e) "The mean difference between Republicans and Democrats on the conservatism instrument was highly significant."
4. An investigator wishes to study the relation between dogmatism and ethnocentrism. He uses a well-established measure of ethnocentrism and constructs an instrument to measure dogmatism. The correlation between dogmatism and ethnocentrism is .60. The investigator does not stop there, however, because it seems to him that the correlation may be due to factors other than those he is trying to measure. He is particularly dubious about the dogmatism measure. What should he do to obtain evidence that his dogmatism measure is really measuring dogmatism? (Pay particular attention to construct validity and construct validation.)
5. Imagine that you have given a test of six items to six persons. The scores of each person on each item are given below. Say that you have also given another test of six items to six persons. These scores are also given below. The scores of the first test, I, are given on the left; the scores of the second test, II, are given on the right.

	I Items							II Items					
Persons	*a*	*b*	*c*	*d*	*e*	*f*	Persons	*a*	*b*	*c*	*d*	*e*	*f*
1	6	6	7	5	6	5	1	6	4	5	6	6	3
2	6	4	5	5	4	5	2	6	2	7	4	4	4
3	5	4	7	6	4	3	3	5	6	5	3	4	2
4	3	2	5	3	4	4	4	3	4	4	5	4	5
5	2	3	4	4	3	2	5	2	1	7	1	3	5
6	2	1	3	1	0	2	6	2	3	3	5	0	2

The scores in II are the same as those in I, except that the orders of the scores of Items (*b*), (*c*), (*d*), and (*f*) have been changed.

(a) Do a two-way analysis of variance of each set of scores. Compare the *F* ratios and interpret them. Pay special attention to the *F* ratio for Persons (Individuals).

(b) Compute $r_{tt} = (V_{ind} - V_e)/V_{ind}$ for I and II. Interpret the two r_{tt}'s. Why are they so different?

(c) Add the odd items across the rows; add the even items. Compare the rank orders and the ranges of the odd totals, the even totals, and the totals of all six items. The coefficients of correlation between odd and even items, corrected, are .98 and .30. Explain why they are so different. What do they mean?

(d) Assume that there were 100 persons and 60 items. Would this have changed the procedures and the reasoning behind them? Would the effect of changing the orders of, say, five to ten items have affected the r_{tt}'s as much as in these examples? If not, why not?

(*Answers:* (a) I: $F_{items} = 3.78$ (.05); $F_{persons} = 20.35$ (.001); II: $F_{items} = 1.03$ (*n.s.*); $F_{persons} = 1.91$ (*n.s.*). (b) I: $r_{tt} = .95$. II: $r_{tt} = .48$.)

PART SEVEN

METHODS OF OBSERVATION AND DATA COLLECTION

INTRODUCTION

To implement general plans of research, methods of data collection must be used. There is always a mutual interplay of problem and method. Problems dictate methods to a considerable extent, but methods—their availability, feasibility, and relevance—also influence problems. Some problems cannot be satisfactorily studied, because methods do not at present exist to collect the data implied by the problems; or existing methods and even those that can be invented may not be capable of yielding the precise data needed. In such cases it may be necessary to alter the problem or perhaps even to abandon it temporarily. At any rate, the problem is the more fundamental consideration.

Methods of observation are systematic and standard procedures for obtaining data. They can be considered extensions of measurement theory and methods. The clue is furnished by the definition of measurement: the assignment of numerals to objects according to rules. In the last analysis, all methods have the technical purpose of enabling the researcher to so make observations that symbols or numerals can be assigned to the objects or to the sets of objects under study.

The approach to methods of observation used in this section is dictated by the conviction that such methods can only be learned through experience. It is possible to learn certain principles of schedule construction, but in order to construct an actual schedule, one requires considerable practice in writing and reviewing items and instructions. A book can explain how to interview, but in order to be able to interview, one must interview.

The following chapters, then, have three main purposes. The first is to acquaint the student with the most important observational methods that are available. Graduate students seem to concentrate on two or three methods, perhaps because of a lack of familiarity with available methods. This restriction to two or three methods unduly narrows the range of possible problems and inquiry. Thus one of the prime objectives of these chapters is to broaden the student's knowledge of available methods.

The second purpose is to help the student understand the main

465

characteristics and purposes of the methods. Methods differ considerably in what they can and cannot do. Users of methods must know these possibilities if they are to be able to choose methods suited to their problem s. Many a good problem has suffered from an inappropriate and inadequate method.

The third purpose is closely related to the second: to indicate, if incompletely, the strengths and weaknesses of the methods. One method may be well suited to a problem, but it may have grave weaknesses that disqualify it. The mail questionnaire, discussed earlier, is a case in point. A problem may require a wide geographical sampling of schools, which can be easily accomplished by the mail questionnaire. But its well-known weaknesses would perhaps disqualify it from consideration, unless it were the only possible way to obtain data.

26 INTERVIEWS AND INTERVIEW SCHEDULES

Data-collection methods can be categorized by the degree of their directness. If we wish to know something about someone, we can ask him about it directly. He may or may not give us an answer. On the other hand, we may not ask him a direct question. We may give him some ambiguous stimulus, like a blurred picture, a blot of ink, or a vague question; and then ask him for his impressions of the stimulus on the assumption that he will give the needed information without knowing he is giving it. This method would be highly indirect. Most of the data-collection methods used in psychological and sociological research are relatively direct or moderately indirect. Rarely are highly indirect means used.

Interviews and schedules (questionnaires) are ordinarily quite direct. This is both a strength and a weakness. It is a strength because a great deal of the information needed in social scientific research is fairly straightforward and can be gotten from respondents by direct questions. Though the questions may have to be carefully handled, respondents can, and usually will, give much information directly. There is much information, however, of a more difficult nature that respondents may be unwilling, reluctant, or unable to give readily and directly, for example, information on income, sexual relations, and attitudes toward religion and minority groups. In such cases, direct questions may yield data that are invalid. Yet, properly handled, even personal or controversial material can be successfully obtained with interviews and schedules.

The interview is probably man's oldest and most often used device for obtaining information. It has important qualities that objective tests and scales and behavioral observations do not possess. When used with a well-conceived schedule, an interview can obtain a great deal of information; it is flexible and adaptable to individual situations, and it can often be used when no other method is possible or adequate. These qualities make it especially suitable for research with children.[1] An interviewer

[1] L. Yarrow, "Interviewing Children," in P. Mussen, ed., *Handbook of Research Methods in Child Development.* New York: Wiley, 1960, chap. 14.

can know whether the respondent, especially a child, does not understand a question and can, within limits, repeat or rephrase the question. Questions about hopes, aspirations, and anxieties can be asked in such a way as to elicit accurate information. Most important, perhaps, the interview permits probing into the context of, and reasons for, answers to questions.

The major shortcoming of the interview and its accompanying schedule is practical. Interviews take a lot of time. Getting information from one individual may take as long as an hour or even two. This large time investment costs effort and money. So, whenever a more economical method answers the research purposes, interviews should not be used.

INTERVIEWS AND SCHEDULES AS TOOLS OF SCIENCE

For the most part, interviews and schedules have been used simply for gathering so-called facts. Little thought seems to have been given to their potentialities as instruments designed to measure the variables of research problems. The most important use of interviews should be to study relations and to test hypotheses. The interview, in other words, is a psychological measuring instrument. Perhaps more accurately, the products of interviews, respondents' answers to carefully contrived questions, can be translated into measures of psychological variables. Interviews and interview schedules are therefore subject to the same criteria of reliability, validity, and objectivity as any other measuring instruments.

An interview can be used for three main purposes. One, it can be used as an exploratory device to help identify variables and relations, to suggest hypotheses, and to guide other phases of the research. Two, it can be used as the main instrument of the research. In this case, questions designed to measure the variables of the research will be included in the interview schedule. These questions are then to be considered as items in a psychometric instrument, rather than as mere information-gathering devices. Three, the interview can be used to supplement other methods used in a research study: to follow up unexpected results, to validate other methods, and to go deeper into the motivations of respondents and their reasons for responding as they do.

In using interviews as tools of scientific research, we must ask the questions: Can data on the research problem be obtained in an easier or better way? To achieve reliability, for example, is not a small problem. Interviewers must be trained; questions must be pretested and revised to eliminate ambiguities and inadequate wording. Is it worth the effort? Validity, too, is no small problem. Special pains must be taken to eliminate interviewer bias; questions must be tested for unknown biases. The particular research problem and the nature of the information sought must, in the last analysis, dictate whether or not the interview will be used.[2]

The Interview   The *interview* is a face-to-face interpersonal role situation in which one person, the interviewer, asks a person being interviewed, the respondent, questions designed to obtain answers pertinent to the purposes of the research problem. There are two broad types of interview: *structured and unstructered* or *standardized and unstandardized*.[3] In the standardized interview, the questions, their sequence, and their wording are fixed. An interviewer may be allowed some liberty in asking questions, but very little. This liberty is specified in advance. Standardized interviews use interview schedules that have been carefully prepared in advance to obtain information pertinent to the research problem.

Unstandardized interviews are much more flexible and open. Although the research purposes govern the questions asked, their content, their sequence, and their wording are entirely in the hands of the interviewer. Ordinarily no schedule is used. In other words, the unstandardized, nonstructured interview is an open situation in contrast to the standardized, structured interview, which is a closed situation. This does not mean that an unstandardized interview is casual. It should be just as carefully planned as the standardized one. Our concern here is solely with the standardized interview. It is recognized, however, that many research problems may, and often do, require a compromise type of interview in which the interviewer is permitted leeway to use alternate questions that he judges fit particular respondents and particular questions in the interview.[4]

THE INTERVIEW SCHEDULE

Interviewing itself is an art, but the planning and writing of an interview schedule is even more of an art. It is unusual for a novice to produce a good schedule, at least without considerable prior study and practice. There are several reasons for this, the main ones probably being the multiple meaning and ambiguity of words, the lack of sharp and constant focus on the problems and hypotheses being studied, a lack of ap-

[2] The student will find detailed guidance in C. Cannell and R. Kahn, "The Collection of Data by Interviewing." In L. Festinger and D. Katz, eds., *Research Methods in the Behavioral Sciences*. New York: Holt, Rinehart and Winston, Inc., 1953, chap. 8.

[3] E. Maccoby and N. Maccoby, "The Interview: A Tool of Social Science," in G. Lindzey, ed., *Handbook of Social Psychology*, vol. I. Cambridge, Mass.: Addison-Wesley, 1954, pp. 449–487.

[4] The actual procedure of conducting an interview is not discussed in this book. The reader will find guidance in the excellent references given in the study suggestions at the end of the chapter.

preciation of the schedule as a psychometric instrument, and a lack of necessary background and experience.

Kinds of Schedule Information and Items   There are three kinds of schedule information that are included in most schedules: face sheet (identification) information, census-type (or sociological) information, and problem information.[5] Except for identification, these types of information were discussed in Chap. 22. The importance of identifying each schedule accurately and completely, however, needs to be mentioned. The careful researcher should learn to identify with letters, numbers, or other symbols, every schedule and every scale. In addition, identifying information for each individual must be systematically recorded.

Two types of schedule items are in common use: *fixed-alternative* (or closed) and *open-end* (or open). A third type of item, having fixed alternatives, is also used: *scale* items.

FIXED-ALTERNATIVE ITEMS   Fixed-alternative items, as the name indicates, offer the respondent a choice among two or more alternatives. These items are also called *closed* or *poll* questions. The commonest kind of fixed-alternative item is dichotomous, that is, it asks for Yes-No, Agree-Disagree, and other two-alternative answers. Often a third alternative, Don't Know or Undecided, is added.

Two examples of fixed-alternative items follow:[6]

> There are always some people whose ideas are considered bad or dangerous by other people, for instance, somebody who is against all churches and religion. If such a person wanted to make a speech in your city (town, community) against churches and religion, should he be allowed to speak, or not?
>
> Yes .... ☐
> No .... ☐
> Don't know .... ☐
>
> If the school board in your community were to say, some day, that there were no Communists teaching in your schools, would you feel pretty sure it was true, or not?
>
> Would feel it was true .... ☐
> Would not .... ☐
> Don't know .... ☐

Although fixed-alternative items have the decided advantages of achieving greater uniformity of measurement and thus greater reliability, of forcing the respondent to answer in a way that fits the response categories previously set up, and of being easily coded, they have certain

---

[5] M. Parten, *Surveys, Polls, and Samples.* New York: Harper & Row, 1950, pp. 162, 163. For a comprehensive description of information that can be gotten with interviews, see pp. 163–176.

[6] From *Communism, Conformity, and Civil Liberties* by Samuel A. Stouffer. Garden City, N.Y.: Doubleday, 1955, pp. 252 and 256. Copyright © 1955 by Samuel A. Stouffer. Reprinted by permission of Doubleday & Company, Inc.

disadvantages. The major disadvantage is their superficiality: Without probes they cannot get beneath the response surface. They may also irritate a respondent who finds none of the alternatives suitable. Worse, they can force responses. A respondent may choose an alternative to conceal ignorance. Or he may choose alternatives that do not accurately represent true facts or opinions. These difficulties do not mean that fixed alternative items are bad and useless. On the contrary, they can be used to good purpose if they are judiciously written, used with probes, and mixed with open items.[7]

OPEN-END ITEMS   Open or open-end items are an extremely important development in the technique of interviewing. *Open-end questions* are those that supply a frame of reference for respondents' answers, but put a minimum of restraint on the answers and their expression. While their content is dictated by the research problem, they impose no other restrictions on the content and manner of respondent answers. Examples will be given a little later.

Open-end questions have important advantages, but they have disadvantages, too. If properly written and used, however, these disadvantages can be minimized. Open-end questions are flexible; they have possibilities of depth; they enable the interviewer to clear up misunderstanding (through probing); they enable the interviewer to ascertain a respondent's lack of knowledge, to detect ambiguity, to encourage cooperation and achieve rapport, and to make better estimates of respondents' true intentions, beliefs, and attitudes. Their use also has another advantage: the responses to open-end questions can suggest possibilities of relations and hypotheses. Respondents will sometimes give unexpected answers that may indicate the existence of relations not originally anticipated.

A special type of open-end question is the *funnel*. Actually, this is a set of questions directed toward getting information on a single important topic or a single set of related topics. The funnel starts with a broad question and narrows down progressively to the important specific point. Cannell and Kahn say that the funnel has the purposes of preventing early questions in a sequence of questions from affecting those that come later and of determining something of the respondent's frame of reference.[8] Another form of funnel starts with an open general question and uses follow-up, specific closed questions.[9] The best way to get a feeling for good

---

[7] Parten gives good advice on the writing and use of fixed-alternative questions: Parten, *op. cit.*, pp. 184ff. See, also, Maccoby and Maccoby, *op. cit.*, pp. 457–459.

A *probe* is a device used to find out respondents' information on a subject, their frames of reference, or, more usually, to clarify and ascertain reasons for responses given. Probing increases the "response-getting" power of questions without changing their content. Examples of probes are: "Tell me more about that," "How is that?" "Could you please explain that." See Cannell and Kahn, *op. cit.*, p. 359.

[8] *Ibid.*, p. 349.

[9] Maccoby and Maccoby, *op. cit.*, p. 459.

open-end questions and funnels is to study examples, several of which follow.

To obtain information on child-rearing practices, Sears, Maccoby, and Levin used a number of good open-end and funnel questions. One of them, with the author's comments in brackets, is:

> All babies cry, of course. [*Note that the interviewer puts the parent at ease about her child's crying.*] Some mothers feel that if you pick up a baby every time it cries, you will spoil it. Others think you should never let a baby cry for very long. [*The frame of reference has been clearly given. The mother is also put at ease no matter how she handles her baby's crying.*] How do you feel about this?
> (a) What did you do about this with X?
> (b) How about in the middle of the night? [10]

This funnel question set not only reaches attitudes; it also probes specific practices.

Another good example from the same schedule is:

> We'd like to get some idea of the sort of rules you have for X in general —the sort of thing he is allowed to do and the sort of things he isn't allowed to do. What are some of the rules?
> (a) How about bedtime?
> (b) How about making noise in the house—how much of that do you allow? . . .
> (d) How far away is he allowed to go by himself? [11]

In a study of student attitudes toward the university done at the University of Michigan, two of the relations explored were (1) that between student contact with the faculty and the degree of satisfaction obtained, and (2) attitudes toward the university.[12] One of the funnel sets used was:

> Do you have any contacts with any members of the faculty outside of classes?
> (a) (If yes) How often is that?
> (b) What is the nature of your contacts (social, counseling, and so on)?
> Are you generally satisfied with the amount of personal contact you have with members of the faculty?
> (If no) What would you like to see done about it?

Simple and interesting questions were used by Campbell and Metzner in their survey of the public use of the library. One of the ways the

[10] R. Sears, E. Maccoby, and H. Levin, *Patterns of Child Rearing*. Evanston, Ill.: Row, Peterson, 1957, pp. 491–493.

[11] *Ibid.*, p. 494. Two specific questions are omitted.

[12] This selection is from an unpublished study done by a class in survey research at the University of Michigan, 1951.

authors found out whether people read books and used public libraries was to confront the respondents with situations and then to ask them questions about those situations. Two of their open-end questions were:

> If someone asked you how he could find out something about bringing up children, how would you tell him to go about it?
> (a) (if "from a book") Where would you get the book? (if library not mentioned in Q 1-4) I notice you didn't mention the public library. How does it happen you wouldn't go to a public library to find out things like this? [*This is of course a check on whether the respondent did go to a library and also a probe for reasons.*] 13

SCALE ITEMS   A third type of schedule item is the scale item. A *scale* is a set of verbal items to each of which an individual responds by expressing degrees of agreement or disagreement or some other mode of response. Scale items have fixed alternatives and place the responding individual at some point on the scale. (They will be discussed at greater length in Chap. 27.) The use of scale items in interview schedules is a new development of great promise, since the benefits of scales are combined with those of interviews. We can include, for example, a scale to measure attitudes toward education in an interview schedule on the same topic. Scale scores can be obtained in this way for each respondent and scale scores can be checked against open-end question data. Or one can measure the *tolerance of nonconformity,* as Stouffer did, by having a scale to measure this variable embedded in the interview schedule.14 It is of course possible to use one or more of a variety of scales: attitude scales, rating scales, rank-order scales, and others.

Criteria of Question-Writing   Criteria or precepts of question-writing have been developed through experience and research. Some of the most important of these are given below in the form of questions. Brief comments are appended to the questions. When confronted with the actual necessity of drafting a schedule, the student should consult more extended treatments, since the ensuing discussion, in keeping with the discussion of the rest of the chapter, is intended only as an introduction to the subject.15

1. *Is the question related to the research problem and the research objectives?* Except for factual and sociological information questions, all the items of a schedule should have some research problem function. This

---

13 A. Campbell and C. Metzner, *Public Use of the Library.* Ann Arbor: Institute for Social Research, University of Michigan, 1950, p. 69.

14 Stouffer, *op. cit.,* Appendix C.

15 Good practical guidance is given in A. Kornhauser and P. Sheatsley, "Questionnaire Construction and Interview Procedure." In C. Selltiz, *et al., Research Methods in Social Relations,* rev. ed. New York: Holt, Rinehart and Winston, Inc., 1959. Appendix C; Parten, *op. cit.,* chap. VI.

means that the purpose of each question is to elicit information that can be used to test the hypotheses of the research.

2. *Is the type of question the right and appropriate one?* Some information can best be obtained with the open-end question—reasons for behavior, intentions, and attitudes. Certain other information, on the other hand, can be more expeditiously obtained with closed questions. If all that is required of a respondent is his preferred choice of two or more alternatives, and these alternatives can be clearly specified, it would be wasteful to use an open-end question.

3. *Is the item clear and unambiguous?* A great deal of work has been done on item-writing. Certain precepts, if followed, help the item writer to avoid ambiguity. First, questions that contain more than one idea to which a respondent can react should be avoided. An item like, "Do you believe that the educational aims of the modern high school and the teaching methods used to attain these aims are educationally sound?," is an ambiguous question, because the respondent is asked about both educational aims and teaching methods in the same question. Second, avoid ambiguous words and expressions. A respondent might be asked the question, "Do you think the teachers of your school get fair treatment?" This is an ambiguous item because "fair treatment" might refer to several different areas of treatment. The word "fair," too, can mean "just," "equitable," "not too good," "impartial," and "objective." The question needs a clear context, an explicit frame of reference. (Sometimes, however, ambiguous questions are deliberately used to elicit different frames of reference.)

Long questions tend to be ambiguous, because the respondent may get lost in the verbiage. His comprehension may be stymied by a nonessential part of the question. The entire item, however, may be long, because it may be necessary to supply adequate informational context. (The first Sears, Maccoby, and Levin question given in the last section is such a question.) The actual question, though, should be focused on one idea.

4. *Is the question a leading question?* Leading questions suggest answers. As such, they threaten validity. If you ask a person, "Have you read about the local school situation?," you may get a disproportionately large number of "yes" responses, because the question may imply that it is bad not to have read about the local school situation.

5. *Does the question demand knowledge and information that the respondent does not have?* To counter the invalidity of response due to lack of information, it is wise to use information filter questions. Before asking a person what he thinks of UNESCO, first find out whether he knows what UNESCO is and means. Another approach is possible. You can explain UNESCO briefly and then ask the respondent what he thinks of it.

6. *Does the question demand personal or delicate material that the respondent may resist?* Special techniques are needed to obtain information of a personal, delicate, or controversial nature. Ask income and other personal matters late in the interview after rapport has been built up. When asking about something that is socially disapproved, show that some people believe one way and others believe another way. Don't make the respondent in effect disapprove himself. Use "soft" rather than "hard" expressions. Don't say "punishment" to a teacher. Softer words might be "correction" and "negative reinforcement." Maccoby and Maccoby's discussion of this subject outlines more precepts that are useful to keep in mind.[16]

7. *Is the question loaded with social desirability?* People tend to give responses that are socially desirable, responses that indicate or imply approval of actions or things that are generally considered to be good. We may ask a person about his feelings toward children. Everybody is supposed to love children. Unless we are very careful, we will get a stereotyped response about children and love. Also, when we ask a person if he votes, we must be careful since everyone is supposed to vote. If we ask respondents their reactions to minority groups, we again run the risk of getting invalid responses. Most educated people, no matter what their "true" attitudes, are aware that prejudice is disapproved. A good question, then, is one in which respondents are not led to express merely socially desirable sentiments. At the same time, as Cannell and Kahn point out, one should not question a respondent so that he is faced with the necessity of giving a socially undesirable response.[17]

THE VALUE OF INTERVIEWS AND INTERVIEW SCHEDULES

The interview, when coupled with an adequate schedule of pre-tested worth, is a potent and indispensable research tool, yielding data that no other research tool can yield. It is adaptable, capable of being used with all kinds of respondents in many kinds of research, and uniquely suited to exploration in depth. But do its strengths balance its weaknesses? And what is its value in behavioral research when compared to other methods of data collection?

The most natural tool with which to compare the interview is the so-called questionnaire. As noted earlier, "questionnaire" is a term used for almost any kind of instrument that has questions or items to which individuals respond. Although the term is used interchangeably with "schedule," it seems to be associated more with self-administered instruments that have items of the closed- or fixed-alternative type.

[16] Maccoby and Maccoby, *op. cit.*, p. 457.
[17] Cannell and Kahn, *op. cit.*, p. 346.

The self-administered instrument has certain advantages. With most or all of its items of the closed type, greater uniformity of stimulus and thus greater reliability can be achieved. In this respect, it has the advantages of objective-type, written tests and scales, if they are adequately constructed and pretested. A second advantage is that, if anonymous, honesty and frankness may be encouraged. This kind of test can also be administered to large numbers relatively easily. A somewhat dubious advantage is that it can be mailed to respondents. Further, it is economical. Its cost is ordinarily a fraction of that of interviews.

The disadvantages of the self-administered instrument seem to outweigh its advantages. The principal disadvantage of the self-administered instrument is low percentage of returns. A second disadvantage is that it may not be as uniform as it seems. Experience has shown that the same question frequently has different meanings for different people. As we saw, this can be handled in the interview. But we are powerless to do anything about it when the instrument is self-administered. Third, if only closed items are used, the instrument displays the same weaknesses of closed items discussed earlier in this chapter. On the other hand, if open items are used, the respondent may object to writing the answers, which reduces the sample of adequate responses. Many people cannot express themselves adequately in writing, and many who can express themselves dislike doing so.

Because of these disadvantages, the interview is probably superior to the self-administered questionnaire. (This statement does not include carefully constructed personality and attitude scales.) The best instrument available for sounding people's behavior, future intentions, feelings, attitudes, and reason for behavior would seem to be the structured interview coupled with an interview schedule that includes open-end, closed, and scale items. Of course, the structured interview must be carefully constructed and pretested and be used only by skilled interviewers. The cost in time, energy, and money, and the very high degree of skill necessary for its construction, are its main drawbacks. Once these disadvantages are surmounted, the structured interview is a powerful tool of behavioral research.

The self-administered questionnaire has been used too much, especially in educational research, and the structured interview too little. The success of the interview in sociology and psychology should encourage educational researchers to master its intricacies and to use it where it is clearly appropriate. At the very least, whenever a questionnaire is contemplated, the question should be asked: Would it be better to use an interview? If the answer is yes, then every effort should be made to do so.

STUDY SUGGESTIONS

1. There are many valuable references on the interview and the interview schedule, some of which are listed below. Those marked with an asterisk will probably be of most help to the reader whose knowledge of the field is limited.

> Cannell, C., and R. Kahn. "The Collection of Data by Interviewing." In L. Festinger and D. Katz, eds. *Research Methods in the Behaviorial Sciences.* New York: Holt, Rinehart and Winston, Inc., 1953, Chap. 8.

> * Goode, W., and P. Hatt. *Methods in Social Research.* New York: McGraw-Hill, 1952, Chaps. 11, 12, and 13.

> * Kornhauser, A., and P. Sheatsley. "Questionnaire Construction and Interview Procedure." In C. Selltiz, *et al. Research Methods in Social Relations,* rev. ed. New York: Holt, Rinehart and Winston, Inc., 1959, Appendix C.

> Maccoby, E., and N. Maccoby. "The Interview: A Tool of Social Science." In G. Lindzey, ed. *Handbook of Social Psychology,* Vol. I. Cambridge, Mass.: Addison-Wesley, 1954, Chap. 12.

> * Parten, M. *Surveys, Polls, and Samples.* New York: Harper & Row, 1950, Chaps. VI, X, and XI.

2. Interviews and interview schedules have been used in a number of excellent research studies. The reader should carefully study two or three well-constructed schedules. Here are five studies of particular value and interest. The specific references, when given, are to the interview schedules used.

> Campbell, A., and C. Metzner. *Public Use of the Library.* Ann Arbor: Institute of Social Research, University of Michigan, 1950, Appendix C. This is a simple, straightforward, excellent schedule.

> Detroit Area Study, University of Michigan. *A Social Profile of Detroit.* Ann Arbor: University of Michigan, 1953, Appendix B. This is a status study of the relations between social characteristics of the inhabitants of a large city: religion, occupation, participation.

> Miller, D., and G. Swanson. *The Changing American Parent.* New York: Wiley, 1958, Appendix 3. An involved schedule that required careful planning and work, this study contains several good funnel questions.

> Sears, R., E. Maccoby, and H. Levin. *Patterns of Child Rearing.* New York: Harper & Row, 1957, Appendix A. This is a long and detailed interview schedule.

> Stouffer, S. *Communism, Conformity, and Civil Liberties.* Garden

City, N.Y.: Doubleday, 1955, Appendix B. This schedule is unusual in that it contains many fixed-alternative items and scales especially designed to measure tolerance and perception of Communist threat. See Appendix C for the scales.

27 *OBJECTIVE TESTS AND SCALES*

Objective methods of observation are those in which anyone following the prescribed rules will assign the same numerals to objects and sets of objects as anyone else. An objective procedure is one in which agreement among observers is at a maximum. In variance terms, observer variance is at a minimum. This means that judgmental variance, the variance due to differences in judges' assignment of numerals to objects, is zero.

All methods of observation are inferential: inferences about properties of the members of sets are made on the basis of the numerals assigned to the set members with interviews, tests, scales, and direct observations of behavior. The methods differ in their directness or indirectness, in the degree to which inferences are made from the raw observations. The inferences made by using objective methods of observation are usually lengthy, despite their seeming directness. Most such methods permit a high degree of inter-observer agreement because subjects make marks on paper, the marks being restricted to two or more choices among alternatives supplied by the observer. From these marks on paper the observer infers the characteristics of the individuals and sets of individuals making the marks. In one class of objective methods, the marks on paper are made by the observer (or judge) who looks at the object or objects of measurement and chooses between given alternatives. In this case, too, inferences about the properties of the observed object or objects are made from the marks on paper. The main difference lies in who makes the marks.

It should be recognized that all methods of observation have *some* objectivity. There is not a sharp dichotomy, in other words, between so-called objective methods and other methods of observation. There is, rather, a difference in the degree of objectivity. Again, think of degrees of objectivity as degrees of extent of agreement among observers—the ambiguity and confusion often associated with the problem disappear. Another important point is that it is possible to objectify the subjective.

If, in fact, it were not possible to do so, it would not be possible to have scientific psychological procedures.

We will agree, then, that what are here called objective methods of observation and measurement have no monopoly on objectivity or on inference, but that they are more objective and no less inferential than any other methods of observation and measurement. The methods to be discussed in this chapter will by no means exhaust possible methods, since the subject is very large and varied. They are considered only *measures of variables,* to be viewed and assessed the same as all other measures of variables.

TESTS AND SCALES: DEFINITIONS

A *test* is a systematic procedure in which the individual tested is presented with a set of constructed stimuli to which he responds, the responses enabling the tester to assign the testee a numeral or set of numerals from which inferences can be made about the testee's possession of whatever the test is supposed to measure. This definition says little more than that a test is a measurement instrument.

A *scale* is a set of symbols or numerals so constructed that the symbols or numerals can be assigned by rule to the individuals (or their behaviors) to whom the scale is applied, the assignment being indicated by the individual's possession of whatever the scale is supposed to measure. Like a test, a scale is a measuring instrument. Indeed, except for the excess meaning associated with *test,* we can see that *test* and *scale* are similarly defined. Strictly speaking, however, *scale* is used in two ways: to indicate a measuring instrument and to indicate the systematized numerals of the measuring instrument. We use it in both senses without worrying too much about fine distinctions. Remember this, however: tests are scales, but scales are not tests. This can be said because scales do not ordinarily have the meanings of competition and success or failure that tests do. Significantly, we say "achievement testing," not "achievement scaling"; "intelligence testing" and not "intelligence scaling."

TYPES OF OBJECTIVE MEASURES

Hundreds, perhaps thousands, of objective inferential tests and scales have been constructed and used. Watson estimates that at least 500 personality inventories have appeared commercially.[1] There are probably as many ability, aptitude, intelligence, and achievement tests. How is the student to thread his way through this bewildering mass of

1 R. Watson, "Historical Review of Objective Personality Testing: The Search for Objectivity." In B. Bass and I. Berg, eds., *Objective Approaches to Personality Assessment.* Princeton, N.J.: Van Nostrand, 1959, chap I, p. 10.

measures? It is not easy. The best we can hope to do is to structure the subject so that the student can approach it intelligently.

Most tests and scales can be divided into the following classes: intelligence and aptitude tests, achievement tests, personality measures, attitude and value scales, and miscellaneous objective measures. We will discuss each of these types of measure from the point of view of behavioral research.

Intelligence and Aptitude Tests   While the nature and definition of intelligence are far from being fully determined, there are a number of good individual and group intelligence tests that the research worker can use when he needs a measure of intelligence. To control the intelligence variable, many researchers use short, so-called omnibus measures. (An omnibus measure is one that includes items of different kinds—verbal, numerical, spatial, and others—in one instrument.) These measures are ordinarily highly verbal and correlate substantially with school achievement. Buros' handbook is useful as a guide to such tests.[2]

Aptitude is potential ability for achievement. Although there are good aptitude tests available, they are used mainly for guidance and counseling. Still, general aptitude measures may sometimes be useful to the educational investigator, particularly as possible control variables. In studies in which school achievement is the dependent variable, pupils' aptitudes—verbal, numerical, and abstract reasoning aptitudes, for example—may need to be identified and controlled.

Achievement Tests   Achievement tests measure the present proficiency, mastery, and understanding of general and specific areas of knowledge. For the most part, they are measures of the effectiveness of instruction and learning. They are, of course, enormously important in education and educational research. Indeed, in research involving instructional methods, achievement, as we have seen, is often the dependent variable.

Achievement tests can be classified in several ways. For our purposes, we break them down into, first, standardized and specially constructed tests. Standardized tests are published group tests that are based on general educational content common to a large number of educational systems. They are the products of a high degree of professional competence and skill in test-writing and, as such, are usually quite reliable and generally valid. They are also provided with elaborate tables of norms (averages) that can be used for comparative purposes. Specially constructed tests are ordinarily teacher-made tests devised by teachers to measure more limited and specific achievements. They may also, of course, be constructed by educational researchers for measuring limited areas of achievement or proficiency.

[2] O. Buros, ed., *The Fifth Mental Measurements Yearbook*. Highland Park, N.J.: Gryphon Press, 1959.

Standardized achievement tests can also be classified into general and special tests. General tests are typically batteries of tests that measure the most important areas of school achievement: language usage, vocabulary, reading, arithmetic, and social studies. Special achievement tests, as the name indicates, are tests in individual subjects, such as history, science, and English.

Of the many achievement tests available, the researcher usually will have no choice, because the school system has probably already selected its tests. If the researcher can choose, however, he should carefully assess what kind of achievement his research problem requires. If his research variable is simply achievement in a particular area like social studies, then obviously the tests the school system uses are sufficient. But suppose the research variable is achievement in understanding concepts. Then, many tests used in schools will not be adequate. In such cases, the researcher can choose a test specifically designed to measure the understanding of concepts, or he can devise such a test himself. In the former case, he should consult a standard measurement text and actual tests and test manuals. The latter case is more difficult. The construction of any achievement test is a formidable job, the details of which cannot be discussed here. The student is referred to specialized texts, especially those given in Study Suggestion 3 at the end of this chapter.

Personality Measures   The measurement of personality is the most complex of the fields of psychological measurement—and the most challenging. In addition to the many personality inventories commercially available, hundreds of different measures have been used in published and unpublished research studies.

The major problem of personality measures is validity. While reliability, as mentioned in an earlier chapter, is a technical matter that can be handled without too great trouble, validity is not so tractable. To answer the validity question, "Are we measuring what we think we are measuring?," is a complex and difficult task.

There are two general approaches to the construction and validation of personality measures. One can be called the a priori method, after Ferguson, the other the construct or theoretical method. In the a priori method, items are constructed to reflect the personality dimension to be measured. Since the introvert is frequently a retiring person, we might write items about his preferring to be alone—shunning parties, for instance—in order to measure introverson. Since the anxious person will probably be nervous and disorganized under stress, we might write items suggesting these conditions in order to measure anxiety. In the a priori method, then, the scale writer collects or writes items that presumably measure the personality trait to be measured.

This approach is essentially that of early personality-test writers;

it is a content-validity method that is still used today. While there is nothing inherently wrong with the method—indeed, it will have to be used, especially in the early stages of test and scale construction—the results can be misleading. Items do not always measure what we think they measure. Sometimes, we even find that an item we thought would measure, say, social responsibility, actually measures a tendency to agree with socially desirable statements. For this reason, the a priori method, used alone, is insufficient.

The method of validation often used with a priori personality scales is the known-group method. To validate a scale of social responsibility, one might find a group of individuals known to be high in social responsibility, and another known to be low in social responsibility. If the scale differentiates the groups successfully, it is said to have validity.[3]

A priori personality measures will, of course, continue to be used in behavioral research. Their blind use, however, should be discouraged. At the very least, the predictive validities of such scales must be checked. Personality measures have been used too often, merely because the user *thinks* they are valid measures of whatever he is measuring. Before using any personality measure, the student should study recent critical discussions of personality and personality measures.

The construct or theoretical method of personality-measure construction emphasizes the relations of the variable being measured to other variables, the relations prompted by the theory underlying the research. (See Chap. 25.) While scale construction must always to some extent be a priori, the more personality measures are subjected to the tests of construct validity the more faith we can have in them. It is not enough simply to accept the validity of a personality scale, or even to accept its validity because it has successfully differentiated, say, artists from scientists, teachers from non-teachers, normal persons from neurotic persons. Ultimately, its construct validity, its successful use in a wide variety of theoretically predicted relations, must be established.

Attitude Scales   Attitudes, while treated separately here and in most textbook discussions, are really an integral part of personality. (Intelligence and aptitude, too, are considered parts of personality by modern theorists.) Personality measurement, however, is mostly of traits. A *trait* is an enduring characteristic of the individual to respond in a certain manner in all situations. If one is dominant, one exhibits dominant behavior in most situations. If one is anxious, anxious behavior permeates most of one's activities. An *attitude*, on the other hand, is a predisposition to think, feel, perceive, and behave toward a cognitive object. One has an attitude toward something "out there." A trait has subjective reference;

---

[3] See, however, Cronbach's analytic admonitions: L. Cronbach, *Essentials of Psychological Testing*, 2nd ed. New York: Harper & Row, 1960, p. 482.

an attitude has objective reference.[4] One who has a hostile attitude toward foreigners may be hostile only to foreigners, but one who has the trait *hostility* is hostile toward everyone (at least potentially).

There are three major types of attitude scales: *summated rating scales, equal-appearing interval scales,* and *cumulative (or Guttman) scales.* A summated rating scale (also called Likert-type scale) is a set of attitude items, all of which are considered of approximately equal "attitude value," and to each of which subjects respond with degrees of agreement or disagreement (intensity). The scores of the items of such a scale are summed, or summed and averaged, to yield an individual's attitude score. As in all attitude scales, the purpose of the summated rating scale is to place an individual somewhere on an agreement continuum of the attitude in question.

It is important to note two or three characteristics of summated rating scales, since many scales share these characteristics. First, U, the universe of items, is conceived to be a set of items of equal "attitude value," as indicated in the definition given above. This means that there is no scale of items, as such. One item is the same as any other item in attitude value. The *individuals* responding to items are "scaled"; this "scaling" comes about through the sums (or averages) of the individuals, responses. Any subset of U is theoretically the same as any other subset of U: a set of individuals would be rank-ordered the same using U_2 as U_1.

Second, summated rating scales allow for the *intensity* of attitude expression. Subjects can merely agree or they can agree strongly. There are advantages to this, as well as disadvantages. The main advantage is that greater variance results. When there are five or seven possible categories of response, it is obvious that the response variance should be greater than with only two or three categories (agree, disagree, no opinion, for example). The variance of summated rating scales, unfortunately, often seems to consist of response-set variance. Individuals have differential tendencies to use certain types of responses: extreme responses, neutral responses, agree responses, disagree responses. This response variance confounds the attitude (and personality trait) variance. The individual differences yielded by summated rating attitude scales (and similarly scored trait measures) has been shown to be due in part to response set and other similar extraneous sources of variance.[5]

Here are two summated rating items from a scale designed by the writer to measure attitudes toward the decision of the United States Supreme Court on the New York Regents' Prayer. Respondents are asked to indicate whether they *agree very strongly* (7), *agree strongly* (6), *agree*

[4] R. Stagner, *Psychology of Personality,* 2d ed. New York: McGraw-Hill, 1948, p. 202.

[5] The literature on response set is large and cannot be cited here. But see J. Guilford, *Psychometric Methods,* 2d ed. New York: McGraw-Hill, 1954, pp. 451–456, for a good summary discussion.

(5), *disagree* (3), *disagree strongly* (2), *disagree very strongly* (1). The values in parentheses are assigned to the responses indicated. (If there is no response to an item, 4 is given.) Thus, there is a seven-point scale of degree of agreement-disagreement.

1. The Supreme Court decision will aid American democracy by strengthening the principle of the separation of church and state.
2. The Supreme Court was right; the decision will help to protect religious freedom.

Thurstone *equal-appearing interval scales* are built on different principles. While the ultimate product, a set of attitude items, can be used for the same purpose of assigning individuals attitude scores or places along an agreement-disagreement continuum, equal-appearing interval scales also accomplish the important purpose of scaling the attitude items. *Each item* is assigned a scale value, and the scale value indicates the strength of attitude of an agreement response to the item. The universe of items is considered to be an ordered set; that is, items differ in scale value. The scaling procedure finds these scale values. In addition, the items of the final scale to be used are so selected that the intervals between them are equal, a most important and desirable psychometric feature.

The following equal-appearing interval items, with the scale values of the items, are from Thurstone and Chave's scale, Attitude toward the Church:[6]

> I believe the church is the greatest institution in America today. (Scale value: 0.2)
> I believe in religion, but I seldom go to church. (Scale value: 5.4)
> I think the church is a hindrance to religion for it still depends upon magic, superstition, and myth. (Scale value: 9.6)

In the Thurstone and Chave scale, the lower the scale value, the more positive the attitude toward the church. The first and third items were the lowest and highest in the scale. The second item, of course, had an intermediate value. The total scale contained 45 items with scale values ranging over the whole continuum. Usually, however, equal-appearing interval scales contain considerably fewer items.

The third type of scale, *the cumulative or Guttman scale,* consists of a relatively small set of homogeneous items that are unidimensional (or supposed to be). A *unidimensional* scale measures one variable, and one variable only. The scale gets its name from the cumulative relation between items and the total scores of individuals. For example, we ask

[6] L. Thurstone and E. Chave, *The Measurement of Attitude.* Chicago: University of Chicago Press, 1929, pp. 61–63, 78.

four children three arithmetic questions: (a) $28/7 = ?$, (b) $8 \times 4 = ?$, and (c) $12 + 9 = ?$ A child who gets (a) correct is very likely to get the other two correct. The child who misses (a), but gets (b) correct, is likely also to get (c) correct. A child who misses (c), on the other hand, is not likely to get (a) and (b) correct. The situation can be summarized as follows (the table includes the score of the fourth child, who gets none correct):

	(a)	*(b)*	*(c)*	*Total Score*
First Child	1	1	1	3
Second Child	0	1	1	2
Third Child	0	0	1	1
Fourth Child	0	0	0	0

(1 = Correct; 0 = Incorrect)

Note the relation between the *pattern* of item responses and total scores. If we know a child's total score, we can predict his pattern, if the scale is cumulative, just as knowledge of correct responses to the harder items are predictive of the responses to the easier items. Note, too, that both items and persons are scaled.

Similarly, people can be asked various questions about an attitudinal object. If upon analysis the patterns of responses arrange themselves in the manner indicated above (at least fairly closely), then the questions or items are said to be unidimensional. Therefore people can be ranked according to their scale responses. Here are three questions that were designed by Stouffer for his tolerance study:

> Now, I should like to ask you some questions about a man who admits he is a Communist.
> Suppose this admitted Communist wants to make a speech in your community. Should he be allowed to speak or not?
> If some people in your community suggested that a book he wrote favoring government ownership [of all the railroads and big industries] should be taken out of your public library, would you favor removing the book, or not?
> Suppose he is a clerk in a store. Should he be fired, or not? [7]

These items, part of Stouffer's total scale measuring tolerance, were scaled. A person who says "Yes" to the first item will tend to say "Yes" to the other two items. A person who says "Yes" to the second item will tend to say "Yes" to the third. A third person might say "Yes" to the third item and "No" to the first two, and a fourth person might "No" to all three. The scores and patterns of the four persons are the same as those given for the arithmetic questions: the first person (total score of 3) was

[7] From *Communism, Conformity, and Civil Liberties* by Samuel A. Stouffer. Garden City, N.Y.: Doubleday, 1955, pp. 263–265. Copyright © 1955 by Samuel A. Stouffer. Reprinted by permission of Doubleday & Company, Inc.

the most tolerant; the second person (total score of 2) the next most tolerant; and the fourth person (total score of 0) the least tolerant. Both persons and items are scaled for the degree of tolerance.

It is obvious that these three methods of constructing attitude scales are very different. Note that the same or similar methods can be used with other kinds of personality and other scales. The summated rating scale concentrates on the subjects and their places on the scale. The equal-appearing interval scale concentrates on the items and their places on the scale. Interestingly, both types of scales yield about the same results as far as reliability and the placing of individuals in attitudinal rank orders are concerned. Cumulative scales concentrate on the scalability of sets of items and on the scale positions of individuals.

Of the three types of scales, the summated rating scale seems to be the most useful in behavioral research. It is easier to develop, and as indicated above, yields about the same results as the more laboriously constructed, equal-appearing interval scale. Used with care and knowledge of its weaknesses, summated rating scales can be adapted to many needs of behavioral researchers. Cumulative scales would seem to be less useful and less generally applicable, though perhaps important and useful in certain areas of psychological measurement. If one clear-cut cognitive object is used, a short well-constructed cumulative scale may yield reliable measures of a number of psychological variables: tolerance, conformity, group identification, acceptance of authority, permissiveness, and so on. It should be noted, too, that the method can be improved and altered in various ways. Edwards gives detailed descriptions of such improvements and alterations.[8] It is possible that such scales, because of their relative simplicity and brevity, may be useful in research with children. There is no reason, either, why the method cannot be extended to observations. Teachers might be asked questions about children and about classes. Then both questions and children or classes can possibly be scaled.

Other methods of measuring and scaling attitude and personality variables have been developed. They include forced-choice, rank-order, rating, factor analytic, and other methods. Although they are important and point to better psychological and educational measurement, and consequently to better behavioral research, they cannot be discussed here. Some of them, however, will be considered later in this chapter and in subsequent chapters.

Value Scales   Scales to measure values are closely related to attitude scales. Unfortunately, the subject of values has not been the object of

[8] A. Edwards, *Techniques of Attitude Scale Construction*. New York: Appleton, 1957, chaps. 7 and 9.

much scientific investigation, to the detriment of the measurement of values. The only well-known commercially available values scale seems to be the Allport-Vernon-Lindzey Study of Values.[9] There can be little doubt, however, that social and educational values will become the focus of much more theoretical and empirical work in the next decade, since social scientists are becoming increasingly aware that values are important determinants of individual and group human behavior.[10]

A *value* is a culturally weighted preference for a thing or things, for people, for institutions, or for some kind of behavior.[11] Values have also been defined as very inclusive general attitudes. Simply put, values express the "good," the "bad," the "shoulds," the "oughts" of human behavior. Values put things and behaviors on an approval-disapproval continuum. The implications for measurement are obvious: we can write value scales very much as we write attitude scales. But we can go further, too. Values even more than attitudes imply choice. Alternatives of known scale values or weights can be presented to subjects with appropriate instructions for choosing among them according to some value criterion.

Miscellaneous Objective Measures   There are a number of objective inferential measures that do not conveniently fall into one of the above categories, although they are closely related to one or more of them. We shall consider several of these measures here to illustrate the variety of work already done and the possible nature of future objective inferential measurement.

Certain scales are important because of their theoretical value and the frequency of their use. The well-known *F* scale is one of these scales.[12] Designed to measure authoritarianism (*F* originally stood for fascism), it has been called both a personality and an attitude measure. Probably closer to being a personality measure, the *F* scale is a summated rating scale in which subjects are asked to respond to a number of general statements, usually 29 or 30. Here are three such items, agreement with which is supposed to indicate authoritarian trends in the respondent. These items were chosen for their variety and their possible interest to educators.

> Obedience and respect for authority are the most important virtues children should learn.

9 G. Allport, P. Vernon, and G. Lindzey, *Study of Values,* rev. ed. Boston: Houghton Mifflin, 1951.

10 See W. Dukes, "Psychological Studies of Values," *Psychological Bulletin,* LII (1955), 24–50. Also B. Friedman, *Foundations of the Measurement of Values.* New York: Teachers College, Columbia University, 1946.

11 C. Kluckhohn, *et al.,* "Values and Value-Orientations in the Theory of Action." In T. Parsons and E. Shils, eds., *Toward a General Theory of Action.* Cambridge, Mass.: Harvard University Press, 1952, pp. 388–433.

12 T. Adorno, *et al., The Authoritarian Personality.* New York: Harper & Row, 1950.

> What the youth needs most is strict discipline, rugged determination, and the will to work and fight for family and country.
>
> Science has its place, but there are many important things that can never possibly be understood by the human mind.[13]

That this is an attitude scale, in the strict sense, is doubtful, unless the definition of attitude can be broadened to include many of the important cognitive objects of life: family, love, discipline, man. There is little doubt, however, that the F scale taps broad general attitudes or cores of values, and personality traits or groups of traits. Many differences are found between high- and low-scoring persons and groups.[14] More important, however, are the sound theoretical reasoning behind the scale's construction, the empirical approach to an important social and psychological problem, and the stimulus to research in the measurement of complex variables. The F scale, though, has perhaps rightly fallen into disrepute under the critical onslaught of psychologists, because it does not hold up under the rigorous application of validity criteria.

A number of scales related to the F scale have been constructed by Adorno and his colleagues, and also by other behavioral scientists. One of the Adorno scales is the E (Ethnocentrism) scale, which attempts to measure prejudiced attitudes more directly.[15] (The F scale measures ethnocentrism indirectly.) Two more related scales that are exceptionally important, but that defy categorization, are Rokeach's Dogmatism (D) and Opinionation (O) scales.[16] Like the F and E scales, these are summated rating scales that presumably measure, in the case of the D scale, the openness and closedness of individuals' belief systems and general intolerance and authoritarianism, and in the case of the O scale, general intolerance. Rokeach built his scales deductively, that is, he studied characteristics of open and closed human belief systems and constructed items to tap these characteristics. Here is a sample of Rokeach's D scale items:

> Man on his own is a helpless and miserable creature.
> There are two kinds of people in the world: those who are for the truth and those who are against the truth.
> In the long run the best way to live is to pick friends and associates whose tastes and beliefs are the same as one's own.[17]

The first item was designed to measure helplessness, the second intolerance, and the third the avoidance of contact with persons whose

---

[13] *Ibid.,* pp. 255–257.

[14] R. Christie, "Authoritarianism Re-examined." In R. Christie and M. Jahoda, *Studies in the Scope and Method of "The Authoritarian Personality."* New York: Free Press, 1957, pp. 123–196; H. Titus and E. Hollander, "The California F Scale in Psychological Research: 1950–1955," *Psychological Bulletin,* LIV (1954), 47–64.

[15] Adorno, *et al., op. cit.,* p. 142.

[16] M. Rokeach, *The Open and Closed Mind.* New York: Basic Books, 1960, pp. 73–84.

[17] *Ibid.,* pp. 75, 78, and 79.

beliefs differ from one's own. It is interesting to note that Rokeach believes that the *D* scale measures authoritarianism better than the *F* scale and presents evidence to back his belief. One outstanding feature of Rokeach's work is his measurement of dogmatism of the right and the left and opinionation of the right and the left. The *F* scale measures only authoritarianism of the right. Rokeach's work is another serious and ambitious attempt to measure important and complex variables—with, it is believed, considerable success.

The measurement of *interests* is relatively easy. The most important measures are the Strong and Kuder tests.[18] In the Strong test, the subject responds to activities presumably related to different vocations: musician, artist, athletic director, physician, and so on. His responses are then compared to the responses of members of the various vocations. Kuder's inventory identifies clusters of occupational interest: scientific, musical, mechanical, and so on. It, too, uses activities presumably related to the different interest areas. An individual's responses identify his broad interests. The reliabilities of both measures are high and the validities are respectable. The Kuder inventory is probably more useful to educational researchers than the Strong inventory, since Kuder measures are more closely related to educational and psychological variables than are the Strong measures. For the researcher who wants a quick measure of occupational interests, the Thurstone Interest Schedule takes only ten minutes to administer.[19]

Occasionally, researchers may need a measure of self-perception. Wylie gives short descriptions of many of them.[20] One of particular interest to researchers working with school children is Coopersmith's Self-Esteem Inventory.[21]

In research studies on group processes, a measure of group cohesiveness, attraction to a group, or the extent to which members wish to stay in a group, is sometimes needed. A simple, easily administered and scored cohesiveness measure has been constructed by Libo.[22] Libo developed an interesting picture-projective measure of cohesiveness, but he found that the much simpler pencil-and-paper measure yielded better results.

[18] Good discussions of these scales can be found in J. Guilford, *Personality*. New York: McGraw-Hill, 1959, pp. 206–220.

[19] L. Thurstone, *Thurstone Interest Schedule*. New York: Psychological Corp., 1947.

[20] R. Wylie, *The Self Concept*. Lincoln: University of Nebraska Press, 1961, pp 86ff.

[21] S. Coopersmith, "A Method for Determining Types of Self Esteem," *Journal of Abnormal and Social Psychology*, LIX (1959), 87–94. The inventory itself has to be obtained from the American Documentation Institute. See *ibid.*, p. 88, footnote 2.

[22] L. Libo, *Measuring Group Cohesiveness*. Ann Arbor: Institute for Social Research, University of Michigan, 1953, pp. 24, 25.

A promising newer development is the measurement of *needs*. The most interesting, highly objective instrument that measures a variety of needs and that should be useful in behavioral research is Edwards' Personal Preference Schedule (PPS).[23] The PPS is theoretically oriented, being based on Murray's needs theory. It measures needs for achievement, dependence, succorance, deference, affiliation, and so on. The construction and rationale of this scale are psychometrically satisfying. In addition to basing the inventory on needs theory, for example, Edwards attempted to control the social desirability of items by pairing items approximately equal in social desirabilty.

CHOICE AND CONSTRUCTION OF OBJECTIVE MEASURES

One of the most difficult tasks of the behavioral researcher faced with the necessity of measuring variables is to find his way through a mass of already existing measures. If a good measure of a particular variable exists, there seems to be little point in constructing a new measure. The question is, however: Does a good measure exist? To answer this question may require much search and study. The student should first know what kind of variable he is trying to measure. Some guidance has been attempted with the structure just provided. One must know clearly whether the variable is an aptitude, achievement, personality, attitude, or some other kind of variable. The second step is to consult one or two texts that discuss psychological tests and measures.[24] Next, the periodical literature may need to be searched. Many worthwhile measures have never been published commercially. The *F* and *D* scales are examples; they are not commercially available, but anyone can use them for research purposes. One may prefer not to use a commercial test. While there is at least one good commercial measure of rigidity, for instance, there are others tucked away in research articles.

The *Psychological Bulletin* often features reviews of the literature in a field. So does the *Review of Educational Research*. There have been excellent reviews of the use of the *F* scale and related measures, of values and value measures, of rigidity, and other variables. One can track down measures, too, by checking the *Psychological Abstracts*, which includes sections on new tests and measures. Another source, particularly of educational measures, are pertinent articles in the *Encyclopedia of Educational Research*. Finally, when one has narrowed down the field and found a measure that seems suitable, one can try to find reviews of it in the Buros' yearbook.[25]

---

[23] A. Edwards, *Personal Preference Schedule, Manual*. New York: Psychological Corp., 1953.

[24] See the study suggestions at the end of the chapter.

[25] Buros, *op. cit.*

An investigator may find that no measure exists for measuring what he wants to measure. Or, if a measure exists, he may deem it unsatisfactory for his purpose. Therefore he must construct his own measure—or abandon the variable. The construction of objective tests and scales is a long and arduous task. There are no shortcuts. A poorly constructed instrument may do more harm than good, because it may lead the investigator to erroneous conclusions. The investigator who must construct a new instrument, then, has to follow certain well-recognized procedures and be governed by accepted psychometric criteria.

Three preliminary steps are recommended for any beginning behavioral scientist who plans to construct a test or scale. First, a course in psychometrics and test or scale construction would be very helpful. Unfortunately, such courses are not given in many schools, and especially not at an advanced level. Students are therefore often thrown on their own resources without adequate direction. Second, consult two or three good references on the subject, study them carefully, and then start the construction job. Third, consult a psychometrics expert, if possible, for assistance in working out complex problems.

TYPES OF OBJECTIVE SCALES AND ITEMS

Two broad types of items in general use are those in which responses are independent and those in which responses are not independent. Independence here means that a person's response to an item has no influence on his response to another item. True-false, yes-no, agree-disagree, and Likert items belong to the independent type. The subject responds to each item freely with a range of two or more possible responses from which he can choose one. Nonindependent items, on the other hand, force the respondent to choose one item or alternative that precludes the choice of other items or alternatives. These forms of scales and items are called forced-choice scales and items. The subject is faced with two or more items or sub-items and is asked to choose one or more of them according to some criterion, or even criteria.

Two simple examples will show the difference between independent and nonindependent items. First, a set of instructions that allows independence of response might be given to the respondent:

> Indicate beside each of the following statements how much you approve them, using a scale from 1 through 5, 1 meaning "Do not approve at all" and 5 meaning "Approve very much."

A contrasting set of instructions, with more limited choices (nonindependent) might be:

Forty pairs of statements are given below. From each pair, choose the one you *approve more*. Mark it with a check.

This distinction is the basis of much of the discussion that follows. Both kinds of items and scales have advantages and disadvantages, of course. An advantage of the type of item that allows independence is its economy. Also, when each item is responded to, a maximum of information is obtained, each item contributing to the variance. Less time is taken to administer such scales, too, but they suffer, sometimes severely, from response-set biases. An individual can give the same response to every item: he can endorse them all enthusiastically or all indifferently depending on his particular response bias. Response-bias variance, then, confounds the variable property variance with such items.

The forced-choice type of scale, on the other hand, avoids, at least to some extent, response bias. At the same time, though, it suffers from a lack of independence, a lack of economy, and overcomplexity. Forced-choice scales can also strain the subject's endurance and patience, resulting in less cooperation. Still, many experts believe that forced-choice instruments hold great promise for psychological and educational measurement. Other experts are skeptical.

Types of scales and items, then, can be divided into three types: *agreement-disagreement* (or *approve-disapprove,* or *true-false,* and the like), *rank order,* and *forced choice.* We discuss each of these briefly. Lengthier discussion can be found in the literature.[26]

Agreement-Disagreement Items   There are three general forms of *agreement-disagreement* items:
1. Those permitting one of two possible responses
2. Those permitting one of three or more possible responses
3. Those permitting more than one choice of three or more possible responses

The first two of these forms supply alternatives like "agree-disagree"; "yes-no"; "yes-?-no"; "approve-no opinion-disapprove"; "approve strongly-approve-disapprove-disapprove strongly"; "*1, 2, 3, 4, 5.*" The subject chooses one of the supplied responses to report his reaction to each item. In so doing he gives a report of himself or indicates his reaction to the item. Most personality and attitude scales use such items.

The third type of scale in this group presents a number of items; the subject is instructed to indicate those items that describe himself, items with which he agrees, or simply items that he chooses. The adjective check list is a good example. The subject is presented with a list of adjectives, some indicating desirable traits, like *thoughtful, generous,* and

---

[26] See, especially, Guilford, *Psychometric Methods, op. cit.*

considerate; and others indicating undesirable traits, like *cruel, selfish,* and *mean.* He is asked to check those adjectives that characterize himself. (Of course this type of instrument can be used to characterize other persons, also.) A better form, perhaps, would be a list with all positive adjectives of known scale values from which the subject is asked to select a specified number of his own personal characteristics. By using only positive items, response bias can be weakened. The equal-appearing interval scale and its response system of checking those attitude items with which one agrees is, of course, the same idea. The idea is a useful one, especially with the development of factor scales, scaling methods, and the increasing use of choice methods.

To illustrate the not inconsiderable possibilities, we can examine a scale constructed by the writer to measure perceptions or judgments of desirable characteristics of teachers. The subjects were presented with 18 descriptions of teachers. All elements of the descriptions were balanced in three groups of six items each, except for adjectival descriptions. These adjectival descriptions fell into three groups: *A, B,* and *N* (neutral). (*A* and *B* were dimensions derived from empirical studies using the method of factor analysis.) Subjects were asked to play the role of a superintendent of schools and to choose the six teachers he would hire from among the 18 teachers. Here are two of the items, the first a *B* item, the second an *A* item.

1. Davida Lester. Age 27. Single. B.S., University of Buffalo; M.A., City College. Has seven years teaching experience, all of it satisfactory. Her recommendations are good. She has been described by reliable sources as industrious, firm, efficient, moral, dependable, and self-controlled.

2. Ruth Simpson. Age 24. Single. B.S., Potsdam State Teachers College; M.A., New York University. Has five years teaching experience, all of it satisfactory. Her recommendations are good. Reliable evidence indicates that she is insightful, flexible, purposeful, enthusiastic, fair, and sympathetic.

Scoring methods for these types of items are usually simple. Numerals are assigned to the various choices. For instance, "agree-disagree" could be 1 and 0; and "yes-?-no" could be 1, 0, −1, or avoiding minus signs: 2, 1, 0. The responses of the Likert-type items described earlier were simply assigned 1 through 5 or 1 through 7. Various weighted scoring systems have been devised, but the evidence indicates that weighted and unweighted scores give much the same results.

Students seem to find it hard to believe this, especially when it comes to the weighting of items. (Note that we are now talking of the weighting of *responses* to items.) Although the matter is not completely settled, the evidence is strong that, in tests and measures of sufficient numbers of items—say 20 or more—weighting items differentially does not make much difference in final outcomes. Nor does the different weighting of responses make much difference.[27] This means that although you can have four responses weighted 4, 3, 2, 1, you can reduce them to 1 and 0 by letting 4 and 3 equal 1, and 2 and 1 equal 0. The reader is not advised to follow this practice indiscriminately, however, since in some cases it may make a noticeable difference. It makes no difference at all, in variance terms, if you transform scoring weights linearly. You may have subjects use a system, $+1$, 0, -1, and of course, these scores can be used in analysis. But you can add a constant of 1 to each score, yielding 2, 1, 0. The transformed scores are much easier to work with since they have no minus signs.

Rank-Order Items and Scales The second group of scale and item types is *ordinal* or *rank order,* which is a simple and most useful form of scale or item. A whole scale can be rank-ordered, that is, subjects can be asked to rank all of the items according to some specified criterion. We might wish to compare the educational values of administrators, teachers, and parents, for instance. A number of items presumed to measure educational values can be presented to the members of each group with instructions to rank-order them according to their preferences. We may be studying the different perceptions of professional educators and teachers. Administrators and teachers can be presented with descriptive adjectives and instructed to rank-order them, the number 1 rank indicating their notion of the most important characteristic a teacher should have, the number 2 rank indicating the next most important characteristic, and so on to the least important characteristic. Here is a sample of a short scale that might be used for this purpose:

sensitive	self-controlled
warm	flexible
efficient	sympathetic
imaginative	kind
dependable	firm
industrious	purposeful

Rank-order scales have three convenient analytic advantages. One, the scales of individuals can easily be intercorrelated and analyzed. Composite rank orders of groups of individuals can also easily be correlated. Two, scale values of a set of stimuli can be calculated using one of the

27 See *ibid.,* pp. 447ff. See, also, J. Guilford, C. Lovell, and R. Williams, "Completely Weighted versus Unweighted Scoring in an Achievement Examination," *Educational and Psychological Measurement,* II (1942), 15–21; and A. Phillips, "Further Evidence Regarding Weighted versus Unweighted Scoring of Examinations," *Educational and Psychological Measurement,* III (1943), 151–155.

rank-order methods of scaling.[28] Three, they partially escape response set and the tendency to agree with socially desirable items.

A useful, but relatively untried, method of constructing scales has been suggested by Stephenson in another context.[29] The writer some years ago followed Stephenson's suggestion and constructed sets of four items, each set of which was to be rank-ordered by the respondents. Here is one of the sets of items. (Try responding to it. Assign 1 to the item approved most highly, 2 to the item approved next and 3 to the next, and 4 to the item least approved.)

> It is unrealistic to expect education to be like real life; it is more a preparation for life.
> Pupils should be encouraged to evaluate their teachers, since they must learn to evaluate other people all their lives.
> The backbone of the school curriculum is subject matter; activities are useful mainly to facilitate the learning of subject matter.
> No subject is more important than the personalities of the pupils.

Items and scales like these are useful with very sophisticated individuals. But they have defects, one of which is the lack of independence of the items. Note that, in the set of items above, we have four choices at the start. After choosing the first item three are left. After three items have been chosen and ranked, only one item and one rank remain. This introduces spurious negative correlation between items, correlation that is a result of the measurement procedure. The reader is encouraged, nevertheless, to explore rank-order items and scales. They can be quite effective as well as economical.

Forced-Choice Items and Scales   The third group of items and scales consists of the so-called *forced-choice* methods. Forced-choice methods can further be divided into pair comparisons and triads, tetrads, pentads, and so forth. The essence of a forced-choice method is that the subject must choose among alternatives. By this means the investigator may be able to escape to some extent the response set and social desirability difficulties of objective methods of measurement. There are a number of possibilities of item construction, but two or three of them seem generally most useful.

The forced-choice technique is not new: Vernon and Allport used it in the first Study of Values.[30] One of the types of item they used was very much like the rank-order, educational attitudes item given above.

---

[28] Guilford, *op. cit.*, chap. 8.

[29] W. Stephenson, *The Study of Behavior.* Chicago: University of Chicago, 1953, pp. 205, 206.

[30] P. Vernon and G. Allport, "A Test for Personal Values," *Journal of Abnormal and Social Psychology*, XXVI (1931), 231–248.

But Vernon and Allport's scale, though theoretically oriented, lacked an important feature of the technique that has become associated with forced choice: the determination of discrimination and preference values of the individual items used in the subsets of items, which in effect ensures item validity and controls "item desirability." [31] ("Item desirability" means that one item might be chosen over another simply because it expresses a more desirable idea. For example, if a person is asked whether he is careless or efficient, he is likely to say he is efficient, even though he *is* careless.)

The method of *paired comparisons* (or *pair comparisons*) has a long and respectable psychometric past. It has, however, been used mostly for purposes of determining scale values.[32] Here we look at paired comparisons as a method of measurement. The essence of the method is that sets of pairs of stimuli, or items of different values on a single continuum or on two different continua or factors, are presented to the subject with instructions to choose one member of each pair on the basis of some stated criterion. The criterion might be: which one better characterizes the subject, or which does the subject prefer. The items of the pairs can be single words, phrases, sentences, or even paragraphs. For example, Dunkel, in studying the life goals of students, paired items like the following:

> Making a place for myself in the world; getting ahead.
> Living the pleasure of the moment.[33]

One use of paired comparisons is the pairing of statements in Edwards' Personal Preference Schedule (PPS). One item measuring the need for autonomy, for instance, is paired with another item measuring the need for change. The subject is asked to choose one of these items. It is assumed that he will choose the one item that fits his own needs. A unique feature of the scale is that the social desirability values of the paired members were determined empirically and the pairs matched accordingly. The instrument yields profiles of need scores for each individual.

In some ways, the two types of paired-comparisons technique, (1) the determining of scale values of stimuli, and (2) the direct measurement of variables, are the most satisfying of psychometric methods. They are simple and economical, because there are only two alternatives. Further, a good deal of information can be obtained with a limited amount of material. If, for example, an investigator has only 10 items, say 5 of Variable *A* and 5 of Variable *B,* he can construct a scale of 5 × 5 or 25 items, since each *A* item can be systematically paired with each *B* item. If

---

[31] Guilford, *op. cit.,* pp. 274ff.

[32] *Ibid.,* chap. 7.

[33] H. Dunkel, "An Inventory of Students' General Goals in Life," *Educational and Psychological Measurement,* IV (1944), 87–95.

he has 10 *A* items and 10 *B* items, he can construct a scale of 100 items. (The scoring is simple: assign a "1" to *A* or *B* in each item, depending on which alternative the subject chooses.) Most important, paired-comparison items force the subjects to choose. Although this may irk some subjects, especially if they believe that neither item represents what they would choose (that is, choosing between *coward* and *weakling* to categorize oneself), it is really a customary human activity. We must make choices every day of our lives. It can even be argued that agreement-disagreement items are artificial and that choice items are "natural."

Forced-choice items of more than two parts can assume a number of forms with three, four, or five parts, the parts being homogeneous or heterogeneous in favorableness or unfavorableness. We discuss and illustrate only one of these types to demonstrate the principles behind such items. By factor analysis, a procedure known as the critical incidents technique, or some other method, items are gathered and selected. It is usually found that some items discriminate between criterion groups and others do not. Both kinds of items—call them *discriminators* and *irrelevants*—are included in each item set. In addition, *preference values* are determined for each item.

A typical forced-choice item is a tetrad. One useful form of tetrad consists of two pairs of items, one pair high in preference value, the other pair low in preference value, one member of each pair being a discriminator (or valid), and the other member being an irrelevant (or not valid). A scheme of such a forced-choice item is

(a) high preference—discriminator
(b) high preference—irrelevant
(c) low preference—discriminator
(d) low preference—irrelevant

A subject is directed to choose the item of the tetrad that he most prefers, or that describes him (or someone else) best, and so on. He is also directed to select the item that is least preferred or least descriptive of himself.

The basic idea behind this rather complex type of item is, as indicated earlier, that response set and social desirability are controlled. The subject cannot tell, theoretically at least, which are the discriminator items and which the irrelevant items; nor can he pick items on the basis of preference values. Thus the tendencies to evaluate oneself (or others) too high or too low is counteracted, and validity is therefore presumably increased.[34]

Here is a forced-choice item of a somewhat different type, constructed by the author for illustrative purposes using items from actual research.

[34] For further discussion, see Guilford, *op. cit.*, pp. 274ff.

conscientious
agreeable
responsive
sensitive

One of the items (*sensitive*) is an *A* item, and one (*conscientious*) a *B* item. (*A* and *B* refer to the factors mentioned earlier.) The other two items are presumably irrelevant. Subjects can be asked to choose the one or two items that are most important for a teacher to have.

It is still too soon to evaluate forced-choice methods. They seem to have great promise. Yet there are technical and psychological difficulties, among which the most important seem to be the lack of independence of items, the perhaps too complex nature of some items (see the earlier attitudes-toward-education tetrad), and the resistance of subjects to difficult choices. The reader is referred to Guilford's discussion of the subject: it is brief, informed, and objective.[35]

EVALUATION OF OBJECTIVE TESTS AND SCALES

Tremendous progress has been made in the objective measurement of intelligence, aptitudes, achievement, personality, and attitudes. Opinion is divided, often sharply, on the value of objective measurement, however. The most impressive gain has been made in the objective measurement of intelligence, aptitudes, and achievement. Gains in personality and attitude measurement have not been as impressive. The problem, of course, is validity, especially the validity of personality measures.

Two or three recent developments are most encouraging. One is the increasing realization of the complexity of measuring any personality and attitude variables. A second is the technical advances made in doing so. Another closely allied development is the use of factor analysis to help identify variables and to guide the construction of measures. A third development (discussed in Chap. 25) is the increasing knowledge, understanding, and mastery of the validity problem itself, and especially the realization that validity and psychological theory are intertwined.

STUDY SUGGESTIONS

1. Among the large number of useful references on the objective measurement of psychological and educational variables, a few particularly useful ones are listed below. In addition, the student will find useful information on standardized tests in elementary textbooks.

   Buros, O., ed. *The Fifth Mental Measurements Yearbook.* Highland

   [35] *Ibid.*

Park, N.J.: Gryphon Press, 1959. Descriptions and reviews of published tests and measures of all kinds can be found in this book.

Edwards, A. *Techniques of Attitude Scale Construction*. New York: Appleton-Century-Crofts, 1957. This is an elementary how-to-do-it book on scaling.

Edwards, A. *The Social Desirability Variable in Personality Assessment and Research*. New York: Holt, Rinehart and Winston, Inc., 1958. Here is a good monograph by the principal investigator of this troublesome phenomenon.

Ellis, A. "The Validity of Personality Questionnaires," *Psychological Bulletin*, XLIII (1946), 385–440. This is a sobering review of earlier personality measures.

Ferguson, L. *Personality Measurement*. New York: McGraw-Hill, 1952. Good descriptions of measures are included in this book, along with many scales and items.

Guilford, J. *Personality*. New York: McGraw-Hill, 1959. Good discussions of many personality measures and other measures may be found in this book.

Guilford, J. *Psychometric Methods*, 2d ed. New York: McGraw-Hill, 1954. This textbook is thorough, competent, and difficult, but useful. The student needs statistical background—and competent guidance—to work with this valuable book.

Torgerson, W. *Theory and Methods of Scaling*. New York: Wiley, 1958. This is an authoritative, definitive, and well-written book on scaling.

2. To gain insight into the rationale and construction of psychological measuring instruments, it is helpful to study complete or relatively complete accounts of their development. It is also helpful to study and become familiar with good items in a variety of fields. The references given below contain both accounts of the development of interesting and important measurement instruments and items.

Allport, G., P. Vernon, and G. Lindzey. *Study of Values,* rev. ed. *Manual of Directions*. Boston: Houghton Mifflin, 1951.

Casteneda, A., B. McCandless, and D. Palermo. "The Children's Form of the Manifest Anxiety Scale." *Child Development*, XXVII (1956), 317–326. This account of scale construction is incomplete, but contains all the scale items.

Cattell, R., D. Saunders, and G. Stice. *Handbook for the Sixteen Personality Factor Questionnaire*. Champaign, Ill.: Institute for Personality and Ability Testing, 1957. A very important scale, based on factor analysis, this is perhaps the most promising of the personality measures.

Edwards, A. *Personal Preference Schedule, Manual*. New York: Psychological Corp., 1953.

Gordon, L. *Gordon Personal Profile, Manual.* Yonkers-on-Hudson, N.Y.: World Book, 1953. These are competently constructed, forced-choice personality scales.

Gough, H., H. McClosky, and P. Meehl. "A Personality Scale for Social Responsibility." *Journal of Abnormal and Social Psychology,* XLVII (1952), 73–80. This article describes a good example of an almost completely empirical approach to scale construction.

Likert, R. "A Technique for the Measurement of Attitudes." *Archives of Psychology,* No. 140, 1932. This is Likert's original monograph describing his technique, an important landmark in attitude measurement.

Morris, C., and L. Jones. "Value Scales and Dimensions." *Journal of Abnormal and Social Psychology,* LI (1955), 523–535. An unusual objective measure of values is given here. Although the measurement could be greatly improved, this is a fascinating study.

Rokeach, M. "Political and Religious Dogmatism: An Alternative to the Authoritarian Personality." *Psychological Monographs,* Vol. LXX, No. 18 (Whole No. 425), 1956. This is an account of the development of the Dogmatism and Opinionation scales.

Stern, G. "Preliminary Manual: Activities Index; College Characteristics Index." Syracuse: Syracuse University Research Institute, 1958. (Hectographed.) Designed to measure needs (cf. Edwards' PPS measure) and theoretically oriented, this index has 300 items developed from an original item pool of over 1000 items.

Stern, G., *et al.* "Two Scales for the Assessment Motivations for Teaching." *Educational and Psychological Measurement,* XX (1960), 9–29. This is an example of exceptionally thorough background work to develop a measuring instrument. It measures motivations for teaching. The scales and instructions can be obtained from the authors.

Thurstone, L., and E. Chave. *The Measurement of Attitude.* Chicago: University of Chicago Press, 1929. This excellent monograph describes the construction of the equal-appearing intervals scale to measure attitudes toward the church.

3. Here are five useful references on the construction of achievement tests:

Bloom, B., ed. *Taxonomy of Educational Objectives: The Classification of Educational Goals: Handbook I, Cognitive Domain.* New York: Longmans, Green,' 1956. This basic and unusual book at-attempts to lay a foundation for cognitive measurement by classifying educational objectives and by giving numerous precepts and examples. Pages 201–207, which outline the book, are extremely useful to test constructors and educational researchers.

Gerberich, J., *Specimen Objective Test Items.* New York: Longmans,

Green, 1956. Numerous examples of test items of all kinds may be found in this book.

Lindquist, E., ed. *Educational Measurement,* Part 2. Washington, D.C.: American Council on Education, 1951. This book contains authoritative chapters on the construction of achievement tests.

Travers, R., *How to Make Achievement Tests.* New York: Odyssey Press, 1950. Good practical guidance may be found here.

Wood, D., *Test Construction.* Columbus, Ohio: Merrill Books, 1960. This book offers succinct and clear guidance on writing achievement tests by an outstanding expert. See especially Chaps. 5, 6, and 7.

28 OBSERVATIONS OF BEHAVIOR

A university research institute, collaborating with several public school systems, studied teacher behavior and pupil work outcomes. One hypothesis explored was that flexible and alert teachers would stimulate pupils to more original and independent work. The research group elected to use Ryans' Classroom Observation Record to measure the behavior of teachers and students.[1]

The Classroom Observation Record is an 18-item objective observation instrument, each item being a bipolar pair of descriptive adjectives, such as partial-fair, harsh-kind, inflexible-adaptable, dull-stimulating. The Record was developed in two ways: by the study of research reports and opinions that named qualities thought to be desirable in teachers and essential to good teaching, and by the use of the critical-incidents technique. The first approach yielded 46 characteristics that seemed relevant. In the *critical-incidents technique,* a large number of experienced teachers were asked what specific behaviors in which specific situations would be used by effective and ineffective teachers.[2] Over 500 critical incidents were obtained, which were reduced to a list of 25 bipolar generalized kinds of behavior.[3] This list was further reduced to a working form of 18 behaviors.

Experienced teachers were used as observers and were carefully trained in the observation technique and use of the Record. In addition, they were retrained at appropriate intervals. Each observer used a glossary containing descriptions or behavioral summaries of the adjective pairs. For example, "inflexible-adaptable" was described as "rigid in conforming to routine" ("inflexible") and "flexible in adapting explanations" ("adaptable"); "impatient with interruptions and digressions" ("inflexible") and "met an unusual classroom situation competently" ("adaptable").[4]

---

[1] D. Ryans, *Characteristics of Teachers.* Washington, D.C.: American Council on Education, 1960, p. 86.

[2] See *ibid.,* pp. 79–83. For a long and competent general discussion, see J. Flanagan, "The Critical Incident Technique," *Psychological Bulletin,* LI (1954), 327–358.

[3] Ryans, *op. cit.,* p. 82.

[4] *Ibid.,* p. 91.

The observers observed a large number of teachers. Each teacher was observed twice by different observers. The unit of observation time was one class period. If there were discrepancies between the two observers in describing a teacher, a third observer was used. Observers made notes during the class hour. Each item of the Record was assessed on a seven-point scale, as in the following pair:

Dull   1   2   3   4   5   6   7   N   *Stimulating*

(N means "neutral.") The Record was filled out after each observation period, one class hour.

Averages of two (or three) Record assessments were calculated. Each teacher, then, had scores on the 18 descriptive pairs. The researchers did a number of analyses, using item scores, scores of groups of items, and total scores. These analyses do not concern us here, except to note that the objective observations of the behavior of the teachers yielded measures of the independent variable.

Everyone observes the actions of others. We look at other persons and listen to them talk. We infer what others mean when they say something, and we infer the characteristics, motivations, feelings, and intentions of others on the basis of these observations. We say, "He is a shrewd judge of people," meaning that his observations of behavior are keen and that we think his inferences of what lies behind the behavior are valid.

This day-by-day kind of observation of most people, however, is unsatisfactory for science. The social scientist must also observe human behavior, but he must be dissatisfied with the inadequacy of uncontrolled observations. He seeks reliable and objective observations from which he can draw valid inferences. He treats the observation of behavior as part of a measurement procedure: he assigns numerals to objects, in this case human behavioral acts or sequences of acts, according to rules.

PROBLEMS OF OBSERVATION OF BEHAVIOR

Basically, there are only two modes of observation: we can watch people do and say things and we can ask people about their own actions and the behavior of others. The principal ways of getting information are by either experiencing something directly, or by having someone tell us what happened. In this chapter we are concerned mainly with seeing and hearing events and observing behavior, and solving the scientific problems that spring from such observation. We approach the problem in two ways: (1) we examine the main problems of observation of behavior and formulate certain precepts or guides, and (2) we examine four or five working examples of sound observational systems.

The Observer The major problem of behavioral observation is the observer himself. One of the difficulties with the interview, recall, was the interviewer, because he was part of the measuring instrument. This problem was almost nonexistent in objective tests and scales. In behavioral observation the observer is both a crucial strength and a crucial weakness. Why? The observer must digest the information derived from his observations and then make inferences about constructs. He observes a certain behavior, say a child striking another child. Somehow he must process this observation and make an inference that the behavior is a manifestation of the construct "aggression" or "aggressive behavior," or even "hostility." The strength and the weakness of the procedure is the observer's powers of inference. If it were not for inference, a machine observer would be better than a man observer. (Sometimes it *may* be.) The strength is that the observer can relate the observed behavior to the constructs or variables of a study: he brings behavior and construct together. One of the recurring difficulties of measurement is to bridge the gap between behavior and construct. Competent observers and well-made observations help bridge this gap.

The basic weakness of the observer is that he can make quite incorrect inferences from observations, due to human fallibility. This is a formidable problem. Take two extreme cases. Suppose, on the one hand, that an observer who is strongly hostile to parochial school education observes parochial school classes. It is clear that his bias may well invalidate the observational measuring instrument. Referring again to the Ryans Classroom Observation Record, he can easily rate an adaptable teacher as somewhat inflexible because he perceives parochial school teaching as inflexible. Or he may judge the actually stimulating behavior of a parochial school teacher to be dull.

On the other hand, assume that an observer could be completely objective and that he knew nothing whatever about public or parochial education. In a sense any observations he makes would not be biased, but they would be inadequate. Observation of human behavior requires competent knowledge of that behavior, and even of the meaning of the behavior.

The observer-inference problem is the main difficulty. There is, however, another problem: the observer can affect the objects of observation simply by being part of the observational situation. Actually and fortunately, this is not a severe problem. Indeed, it is more of a problem to the uninitiated who seem to believe that people will act differently, even artificially, when observed. The classic educational case of this is the belief that a teacher under observation, especially by superiors, will put her best foot forward. She will act in an exemplary way not necessarily customary with her, it is thought. This may be true. A significant point is missed, however. It is not realized that a teacher cannot do what she cannot do. She cannot act in a way she has not learned to act. She cannot be "adaptable," to use one of Ryans' adjectives, if she has not learned to be adaptable.

Observers seem to have little effect on the situations they observe.[5] Individuals and groups seem to adapt rather quickly to an observer's presence and to act as they would usually act. This does not mean that the observer cannot have an effect. It means that if the observer takes care to be unobtrusive and not to give the people observed the feeling that judgments are being made, then the observer as an influential stimulus is mostly nullified.

Validity and Reliability   On the surface, nothing seems more natural, when observing *harsh-kind* behavior or *partial-fair* behavior, than to believe that we are measuring what we say we are measuring. And when Ryans gives the observer in the glossary of the Record fairly detailed (but not too detailed) definitions of *harsh-kind* or *partial-fair,* then there is good correspondence, presumably, between what is measured and what was intended to be measured. The main point, perhaps, is that, given his definitions, observers can and *do* apply the terms similarly to the same or similar types of behavior. For instance, part of his glossary for *partial-fair* is: "Gave most attention to one or a few pupils" (*partial*) and "Distributed attention to many pupils" (*fair*).[6]

When a greater interpretative burden is put upon the observer, however, validity may suffer (as well as reliability). Fouriezos, Hutt, and Guetzkow's measurement of self-oriented needs in conference behavior is an example.[7] Observers are given a simple ten-point rating scale, ranging from "No expression of self-oriented need" to "All behavior of the self-oriented type," on which they indicate integrated appraisals of group members' self-oriented needs. They are guided by five categories of need expression on which they make notes during conferences. While the system seems to have worked well, there would seem to be a rather large gap between the observed behaviors and the inferred needs. The more the burden of interpretation put upon the observer, then, the greater the validity problem. (This does not mean, however, that no burden of interpretation should be put upon the observer.)

A simple aspect of the validity of observation measures is their predictive power. Do they predict any relevant criteria dependably? The trouble, as usual, is in the criteria. As Heyns and Lippitt point out, inde-

[5] R. Heyns and R. Lippitt, "Systematic Observational Techniques," in G. Lindzey, ed., *Handbook of Social Psychology*, vol. I. Cambridge, Mass.: Addison-Wesley, 1954, chap. 10, p. 399.

[6] Ryans, *op. cit.,* p. 87.

[7] N. Fouriezos, M. Hutt, and H. Guetzkow, "Self-Oriented Needs in Discussion Groups." In D. Cartwright and A. Zander, eds., *Group Dynamics.* New York: Harper & Row, 1953, pp. 354–360.

pendent measures of the same variables are rare.[8] Can we say that an observational measure of teacher behavior is valid because it correlates positively with superiors' ratings? We might have an independent measure of self-oriented needs, but would this measure be an adequate criterion for observations of such needs? [9]

The important clue to the study of the validity of behavioral observation measures would seem to be construct validity. If the variables being measured by the observational procedures are imbedded in a theoretical framework, then certain relations should exist. Do they indeed exist? If we are working with a theoretical framework based on needs, for instance, we may deduce from the theory that teachers strong in succorance needs will score high (in Ryans' observation system) on *excitable* and *uncertain*, and low on *understanding*. If these relations hold up, then this is evidence for the construct validity of the observation system.

The reliability of behavioral observation measures is a simpler matter, though by no means an easy one. Reliability is usually defined as the agreement among observers. The reader will recall that this amounts to the definition of objectivity given earlier. While it is satisfactory so to conceive of reliability, at least for practical purposes, the broader conception of reliability developed earlier should be applied to observations as it is applied to all other measures.

Practically speaking, then, the reliability of observations can be estimated by correlating the observations of two or more observers. When assessing the reliability of the assignment of behaviors to categories, percentage of agreement between judges is often used. But, as with all kinds of measurement, there are other ways to estimate reliability, for example, repeat reliability and reliability estimated through analysis of variance.

CHARACTERISTICS OF OBSERVATIONS

The first and most important consideration in any observation system is to know clearly what is being observed. This seems so obvious as to be trite. Let us see that it is not so obvious. Suppose we are studying the relation between *independence* and *problem-solving*. We hypothesize that the more independent a child the better he will be able to solve problems, other things equal. We wish to observe *independence*, or more accurately, *independent behavior*. Now, what *is* independent behavior? If a child persistently works by himself is this independent behavior? If a child initiates projects and games with other children, is this independent

8 Heyns and Lippitt, *op. cit.*, p. 398.
9 For an excellent discussion of the criterion problem and validity in relation to teaching behaviors, see Ryans, *op. cit.*, chap. 2.

behavior? Take a much more difficult problem: What is democratic behavior in a teacher? If a teacher is nice to children, is this democratic?
If she organizes children into groups, is she being democratic? Just what
do we mean when we say "democratic behavior"? It should be obvious
that clear knowledge of what is being observed is not so obvious.

It is necessary, then, to define fairly precisely and unambiguously
what is to be observed. If we are measuring *curiosity*, we must tell the
observer what curious behavior is. If *cooperativeness* is being measured,
we must somehow tell the observer how cooperative behavior is distinguished from any other kind of behavior. This means that we must
provide the observer with some form of operational definition of the
variable being measured; we must define the variable behaviorally.

Categories   The fundamental practical job of the observer is to assign
behaviors to categories. The categories of the Ryans' Record are defined
by the adjective pairs. In another comprehensive system for observing
classroom behaviors, eight broad behavioral categories or dimensions are
used.[10] Two of these, for instance, are *Differentiation* and *Climate-
Teacher*. *Differentiation* includes behaviors aimed at providing or not
providing for individual differences of pupils. *Climate-Teacher* includes
teacher behaviors that set or influence the emotional and social atmosphere of the class. These broad categories are further broken down into
subcategories that indicate where along the dimension measured a particular behavior is to be placed. *Differentiation*, for instance, is broken
into 10 subcategories from "identical work—no teacher assistance" to
"differentiated work-ability and interest basis—individual-teacher assistance." [11] The observer may note, during an observation period, that
the teacher makes no attempt at all to help any individuals and that all
pupils are doing the same work. He would assign this set of behavioral
acts to the first subcategory.

From earlier work on partitioning, recall that categories must be
exhaustive and mutually exclusive. In order to satisfy the exhaustiveness
condition, one must first define *U*, the universe of behaviors to be observed. In some observation systems, this is not hard to do. In others it is
very difficult to do. In the Cornell, Lindvall, and Saupe system *U* was
the behavior of all the teachers and pupils in a classroom. But this is
much too large and vague an order. So, these investigators broke *U* down
into subsets: *A: Differentiation; B: Social Organization; C: Pupil Initiative; D: Content; E: Variety; F: Competency; G: Climate-Teacher; H:
Climate-Pupil*.[12] Careful study of this partitioning will show that most

10 F. Cornell, C. Lindvall, and J. Saupe, *An Exploratory Measurement of Indi-
vidualities of Schools and Classrooms.* Urbana, Ill.: Bureau of Educational Research,
University of Illinois, 1952.
    11 *Ibid.*, p. 53.
    12 *Ibid.*, pp. 53, 54.

classroom behaviors can be subsumed under one of these rubrics. Cornell, Lindvall, and Saupe further partitioned the above eight subsets of U into further subsets of the subsets. One of these breakdowns was described earlier.

It might sound as though *all* possible behaviors must be defined and observed. Not so. In many cases, an investigator may be interested only in the variable *social climate* (of a classroom or a group). In such a case the behavior subsumed under *Climate-Teachers* and *Climate-Pupils*, two of Cornell, Lindvall, and Saupe's subsets, would comprise U. (These include items like: "Respected pupil opinion," "Tried to see a pupil point of view," "Corrected or criticized excessively." [13]) In other words, U can be large, medium, or small, depending upon the research problem and objectives. One can range from an extremely broad variable like *teacher effectiveness*, including all Ryans' categories to a comparatively narrow variable like *aggressiveness* that may require only two or three subcategories, like *physical and verbal injury to another child* and *taking objects from another child*.

Units of Behavior What units to use in measuring human behavior is still an unsettled problem. Here one is often faced with a clash between reliability and validity demands. Theoretically, one can attain a high degree of reliability by using small and easily observed and recorded units. One can attempt to define behavior quite operationally by listing a large number of behavioral acts, and can thus ordinarily attain a high degree of precision and reliability. Yet in so doing one may also have so reduced the behavior that it no longer bears much resemblance to the behavior one intended to observe. Thus validity has been lost.

On the other hand, one can use broad "natural" definitions and perhaps achieve a high degree of validity. One might instruct observers to observe *cooperation* and define *cooperative behavior* as "accepting other persons' approaches, suggestions, and ideas; working harmoniously with others toward goals," or some such rather broad definition. If observers have had group experience and understand group processes, then it might be expected that they could validly assess behavior as cooperative and uncooperative by using this definition. Such a broad, even vague, definition enables the observer to capture, if he can, the full flavor of cooperative behavior. But it also allows considerable ambiguity of interpretation to creep into observers' perceptions, thus lowering reliability.

Some researchers who are strongly operational in their approach insist upon highly specific definitions of the variables observed. They might list a number of specific behaviors for the observer to observe. No others would be observed and recorded. Extreme approaches like this may produce high reliability, but they may also miss part of the essential

[13] *Ibid.,* p. 54.

core of the variables observed. Suppose ten specific types of behavior are listed for *cooperativeness*. Suppose, too, that the universe of possible behaviors consists of 40 or 50 types. Clearly, important aspects of *cooperativeness* will be neglected. While what is measured may be reliably measured, it may be quite trivial or at least partly irrelevant to the variable *cooperativeness*.

This is the molar-molecular problem of any measurement procedure in the social sciences. The *molar approach* takes larger behavioral wholes as units of observation. Complete interaction units may be specified as observational targets. Verbal behavior may be broken down into complete interchanges between two or more individuals, or into whole paragraphs or sentences. The *molecular approach*, by contrast, takes smaller segments of behavior as units of observation. Each interchange or partial interchange may be recorded. Units of verbal behavior may be words or short phrases. The molar observer will start with a general broadly defined variable, as given earlier, and consider and record a variety of behaviors under the one rubric. He depends on his experience and interpretation of the meaning of the actions he is observing. The molecular observer, on the other hand, seeks to push his own experience and interpretation out of the observational picture. He records what he sees—and no more.

Degree of Observer Inference   Observation systems differ on another important dimension: the *amount of inference* required of the observer. Molecular systems require relatively little inference. The observer simply notes that an individual does or says something. For example, a system may require the observer to note each interaction unit, which may be defined as any verbal interchange between two individuals. If an interchange occurs, it is noted; if it does not occur, it is not noted. Or a category may be "Strikes another child." Every time one child strikes another it is noted. No inferences are made in such systems—if, of course, it is ever possible to escape inferences (for example, "strikes"). Pure behavior is recorded as nearly as possible.

Observation systems with such low degrees of observer inference are rare. Most systems require some degree of inference. An investigator may be doing research on board of education behavior and may decide that a low inference analysis is suited to his problem. He may use observation items like "Suggests a course of action," "Interrupts another board member," "Disputes a point," "Asks a question," "Gives an order to superintendent," "Makes a motion," and the like. Since such items are comparatively unambiguous, the reliability of the observation system should be substantial.

Systems with higher degrees of inference required of the observer are more common and probably more useful in most research, especially in most educational research. The high inference observation system gives the observer labeled categories that require greater or lesser interpretation of the observed behavior. The observation system of Fouriezos, Hutt, and Guetzkow, mentioned earlier, is rather high in observer inference demands. Though five need areas are supplied and defined, the observer must infer that any particular behavior is self need-oriented. For instance, *dominance* is one of the five needs. It is defined as any individual's attempts to exhibit intellectual superiority over other individuals. The authors say, "Dominance in social situations includes attempts to control and direct in the social situation. . . . The leader here controls with little concern for the needs of the group . . ." [14] Then they say that dominance is shown when an individual refuses to hear arguments against his own ideas and tries to force the group to follow his plans. They stress, however, the necessity for the observer to distinguish between dominance based on ego needs and dominance based on situational demands. It is clear that this system is highly inferential. Lest the reader believe that this necessarily impairs reliability, note that test-retest coefficients of reliability ranged from .67 to .96. To attain such satisfactory reliability, the authors stress the necessity of training observers.

It is not possible to make flat generalizations on the relative virtues of systems with different degrees of inference.[15] Probably the best advice to the neophyte is to aim at a medium degree of inference. Too vague categories with too little specification of what to observe put an excessive burden on the observer. Different observers can too easily put different interpretations on the same behavior. Too specific categories, while they cut down ambiguity and uncertainty, may tend to be too rigid and inflexible, even trivial. Better than anything else, the student should study various successful systems, paying special attention to the behavior categories and the definitions (instructions) attached to the categories for the guidance of the observer.

Generality or Applicability Observation systems differ considerably in their *generality,* or degree of *applicability* to research situations other than those for which they were originally designed. Some systems are quite general: they are designed for use with many different research problems. The well-known Bales group interaction analysis is one such general system.[16] This is a low inference system in which all verbal and nonverbal behavior, presumably in any group, can be categorized into one of twelve categories: "shows solidarity," "agrees," "asks for opinion," and so on. The twelve categories are grouped in three larger sets: social-

---

14 Fouriezos, Hutt, and Guetzkow, *op. cit.,* p. 684.
15 Heyns and Lippitt discuss the dimension of inference in observations in each of several, rather completely described social psychological observation systems. Heyns and Lippitt, *op. cit.*
16 R. Bales, *Interaction Process Analysis.* Cambridge, Mass.: Addison-Wesley, 1951.

emotional-positive; social-emotional-negative; task-neutral. The Ryans system was obviously intended for general use in any classroom. The Cornell, Lindvall, and Saupe system, too, is general.

Some systems, however, were constructed for use in particular research problems and may or may not be generally applicable to other situations. Such, evidently, is the Fouriezos, Hutt, and Guetzkow system. Yet it can be applied to situations other than decision-making conferences. With some adaptation, it could probably be used in educational research—board of education meetings, perhaps. Children's groups and clubs might be observed with it. Most systems devised for specific research problems, with suitable revision and adaptation, can probably be applied to other research problems.

Sampling of Behavior   The last characteristic of observations, *sampling*, is, strictly speaking, not a characteristic. It is a way of obtaining observations. Before using an observation system in actual research, when and how the system will be applied must be decided. If classroom behaviors of teachers are to be observed, how will the behaviors be sampled? Will all the specified behaviors in one class period be observed? This is what Ryans does. Or will specified samples of specified behaviors be sampled systematically or randomly? In other words, a sampling plan of some kind must be devised and used.

There are two aspects of behavior sampling: *event sampling* and *time sampling*.[17] Event sampling was actually touched upon earlier when units of observation were discussed. An additional meaning attached to the term, however, needs brief explanation. *Event sampling* is the selection for observation of integral behavioral occurrences or events of a given class.[18] Examples of integral events are temper tantrums, fights and quarrels, games, emotional episodes, verbal interchanges on specific topics, problem-solving situations, classroom interactions between teachers and pupils, and so on. The investigator who is pursuing events must either know when the events are going to occur and be present when they occur, as with classroom events, or wait until they occur, as with quarrels.

Event sampling has three virtues: One, the events are natural lifelike situations and thus possess an inherent validity not ordinarily possessed by time samples. Two, an integral event possesses a continuity of behavior that the more piecemeal behavioral acts of time samples do not possess. If one observes a problem-solving situation from beginning to end, one is witnessing a natural and complete unit of individual and

---

[17] See H. Wright, "Observational Child Study," in P. Mussen, ed., *Handbook of Research Methods in Child Development.* New York: Wiley, 1960, chap. 3. For a complete review of time sampling, see R. Arrington, "Time Sampling in Studies of Social Behavior: A Critical Review of Techniques and Results with Research Suggestions," *Psychological Bulletin,* XL (1943), 81–124.

[18] Wright, *op. cit.,* p. 104.

group behavior. By so doing, one achieves a whole and realistic larger unit of individual or social behavior. As we saw in an earlier chapter when field experiments and field studies were discussed, naturalistic situations have an impact and a closeness to psychological and social reality that experiments do not usually have.

A third virtue of event sampling inheres in an important characteristic of many behavioral events: they are sometimes infrequent and rare. For example, one may be interested in decisions made in administrative or legislative meetings. Or one may be interested in the ultimate step in problem-solving. Teachers' disciplinary methods may be a variable. Such events and many others are relatively infrequent. As such, they can easily be missed by time sampling; they therefore require event sampling.

Time sampling is the selection of behavioral units for observation at different points in time. Observation units can be chosen in systematic or in random ways so as to be representative of a defined universe of behavior. A good example is teacher behavior. Suppose the relations between certain variables like *teacher alertness, fairness,* and *initiative,* on the one hand, and *pupil initiative* and *cooperativeness,* on the other hand, are studied. We may select random samples of teachers and then take time samples of their behavioral acts. These time samples can be systematic: three five-minute observations at specified times during each of, say, five class hours, the class hours being the first, third, and fifth periods one day and the second and fourth periods the next day. Or the time samples can be random: five five-minute observation periods selected at random from a specified universe of five-minute periods. Obviously, there are many ways that time samples can be set up and selected. As usual, the way such samples are chosen, their length, and their number must be influenced by the research problem.[19]

Time samples have the important advantage of assuring the investigator of obtaining representative samples of behavior. This is true, however, only of behaviors that occur fairly frequently. Behaviors that occur infrequently have a high probability of escaping the sampling net, unless huge samples are drawn. Creative behavior, sympathetic behavior, and hostile behavior, for example, may be quite infrequent. Still, time sampling is an outstanding contribution to the scientific study of human behavior.

Time samples, as implied earlier, suffer from lack of continuity, lack of adequate context, and perhaps naturalness. This is particularly true when small units of time and behavior are used. Still, there is no

[19] In a fascinating study of leadership and the power of group influence with small children, Merei points out that time sampling would show only leaders giving orders and the group obeying, whereas prolonged observations would show the inner workings of ordering and obeying. F. Merei, "Group Leadership and Institutionalization," *Human Relations,* II (1949), 23–39.

reason why event sampling and time sampling cannot sometimes be combined. If one were studying classroom recitations, one could draw a random sample of the class periods of one teacher at different times and observe all recitations during the sampled periods, being careful to observe each recitation in its entirety.

RATING SCALES [20]

To this point, we have been talking only about the observation of *actual behavior*. The observer looks at and listens to the objects of regard directly. He sits in the classroom and observes teacher pupil and pupil-pupil interactions. Or he may watch and listen to a group of children solving a problem behind a one-way screen. There is another class of behavioral observation, however, that needs to be mentioned. This type of observation will be called *remembered behavior* or *perceived behavior*. It is conveniently considered under the topic of rating scales.

In measuring remembered or perceived behavior, we ordinarily present the observer with an observation system in the form of a scale of some kind and ask him to assess an object on one or more characteristics, the object not being present. In order to do this, he must make his assessments on the basis of past observations or on the basis of his perceptions of what the observed object is like and how it will behave. A convenient way to measure both actual behavior and perceived or remembered behavior is with rating scales.

A *rating scale* is a pyschological measuring instrument that requires the rater or observer to assign the rated object to categories or continua that have numerals assigned to them. Rating scales are perhaps the most ubiquitous of psychological measuring instruments probably because they are seemingly easy to construct and, more important, easy and quick to use. Unfortunately, the apparent ease of construction is deceptive and the ease of use carries a heavy price: lack of validity due to a number of sources of bias that enter into rating measures. Still, with knowledge, skill, and care, ratings can be extremely valuable.

[20] For an excellent discussion of rating scales, see J. Guilford, *Psychometric Methods*, 2d ed. New York: McGraw-Hill, 1954, chap. 11. Eysenck ably summarized the most important substantive work, particularly factor analytic and related work, on ratings: H. Eysenck, *The Structure of Human Personality*. New York: Wiley, 1953, chap. II.

Although rating scales were mentioned earlier in this book, they were not systematically discussed. In reading what follows, the student should bear in mind that rating scales are really objective scales. As such, they might have been included in Chap. 27. Their discussion was reserved for this chapter because the discussion of Chap. 27 focused mainly on measures responded to by the subject being measured. Rating scales, on the other hand, are measures of individuals and their reactions, characteristics, and behaviors by observers. The contrast, then, is between the subject as he sees himself and the subject as others see him. It is important to note, too, that rating scales are used to measure psychological objects, products, and stimuli, such as handwriting, concepts, essays, interview protocols, and projective test materials.

Types of Rating Scales   There are four or five types of rating scales. Two of these types were discussed in the last chapter: check lists and forced-choice instruments. We consider now only three types and their characteristics. These are the *category rating scale,* the *numerical rating scale* and the *graphic rating scale.* They are quite similar, differing mainly in details.

The category rating scale presents the observer or judge with several categories from which he picks the one that best characterizes the behavior or characteristic of the object being rated. Suppose a teacher's classroom behavior is being rated. One of the characteristics rated, say, is *alertness.* A category item might be:

How alert is she? (Check one.)
Very alert
Alert
Not alert
Not at all alert

A slightly different category item might be:

How imaginative is she? (Check one.)
Extremely imaginative
Very imaginative
Imaginative
Unimaginative
Very unimaginative
Extremely unimaginative

A still different form uses condensed descriptions. Such an item might look like this:

Is she resourceful? (Check one.)
Always resourceful; never lacking in ideas
Resources are good
Sometimes flounders for ideas
Very unresourceful; rarely has ideas

Numerical rating scales are perhaps the easiest to construct and use. They also yield numbers that can be directly used in statistical analysis. In addition, because the numbers may represent equal intervals in the mind of the observer, they may approach interval measurement.[21] Any of the above category scales can be quickly and easily converted to numerical rating scales simply by affixing numbers before each of the categories. The numbers 3, 2, 1, 0, or 4, 3, 2, 1, can be affixed to the *alertness*

21 Guilford, *op. cit.,* p. 264.

item above. The *imaginative* item could have 5, 4, 3, 2, 1, 0 before the choices. A convenient method of numerical rating is to use the same numerical system, say 4, 3, 2, 1, 0, with each item. This is of course the system used in summated-rating attitude scales. In rating scales, it is probably better, however, to give both the verbal description and the numerals.

In graphic rating scales lines or bars are combined with descriptive phrases. The alertness item, just discussed, could look like this in graphic form:

| |_____| |_____| |_____| |
Very   Alert   Not   Not at all
alert   alert   alert

Such scales have many varieties: vertical segmented lines, continuous lines, unmarked lines, lines broken into marked equal intervals (as above), and others. These are probably the best of the usual forms of rating scales. They fix a continuum in the mind of the observer. They suggest equal intervals. They are clear and easy to understand and use. Guilford over-praises them a bit when he says, "The virtues of graphic rating scales are many; their faults are few," but his point is well-taken.[22]

Weaknesses of Rating Scales   Ratings have two serious weaknesses, one of them extrinsic, the other intrinsic. The extrinsic defect is that they are seemingly so easy to construct and use that they are used indiscriminately, frequently without any knowledge of their intrinsic defects. We will not pause to mention the many errors that can creep into the unskillful construction and use of rating scales. Rather, we warn the reader against seizing them for any and all measurement needs. One should first ask the question: Is there a better way to measure my variables? If so, use it. If not, then study the characteristics of good rating scales, work with painstaking care, and subject rating results to empirical test and adequate statistical analysis.[23]

The intrinsic defect of rating scales is their proneness to constant or biased error. This is not new to us, of course. We met this problem in the last chapter when considering response set. With ratings, however, it is particularly threatening to validity. Constant rating error takes several forms, the most pervasive of which is the famous *halo effect*. This is the tendency to rate an object in the constant direction of a general impression of the object. Everyday cases of halo are: believing a person to be intelligent because he agrees with us; believing a man to be virtuous because we like him; giving high praise to Republican presidents and damning Democratic ones.

[22] *Ibid.*, p. 268.
[23] Guilford's advice is invaluable: *ibid.*, pp. 264–268 and 293–296.

Halo manifests itself frequently in measurement, especially with ratings. The professor assesses the quality of essay test questions higher than they should be because he likes the testee. Or he may rate the second, third, and fourth questions higher (or lower) than they should be because the first question was well answered (or poorly answered). Teacher evaluation of children's achievement that is influenced by the children's docility or lack of docility is another case of halo. In rating individuals on rating scales, there is a tendency for the rating of one characteristic to influence the ratings of other characteristics.

Halo is extremely difficult to avoid. It seems to be particularly strong in traits that are not clearly defined, not easily observable, and that are morally important.[24]

Two important sources of constant error are the error of severity and the error of leniency. The *error of severity* is a general tendency to rate all individuals too low on all characteristics. This is the tough marker, the man who says, "Nobody gets an *A* in my classes." The *error of leniency* is the opposite general tendency to rate too high. This is the good fellow who loves everybody—and the love is reflected in the ratings.

An exasperating source of invalidity in ratings is the *error of central tendency,* the general tendency to avoid all extreme judgments and rate right down the middle of a rating scale. It manifests itself particularly when raters are unfamiliar with the objects being rated.

There are other less important types of error that will not be considered. More important is how to cope with the types listed above. This is a complex matter that cannot be discussed here. The reader is referred to Guilford's chapter in *Psychometric Methods* where many devices for coping with error are discussed in detail.[25]

Rating scales can and should be used in behavioral research. Their unwarranted, expedient, and unsophisticated use has been rightly condemned. But this should not mean general condemnation. They have virtues that make them valuable tools of scientific research. These have been summarized by Guilford: they require less time than other methods; they are generally interesting and easy for observers to use; they have a very wide range of application; they can be used with a large number of

---

[24] *Ibid.*, p. 279.

[25] Systematic errors can be dealt with to some extent by statistical means. Guilford has worked out an ingenious method using analysis of variance. The basic idea is that variances due to *subjects, judges,* and *characteristics* are extracted from the total variance of ratings. The ratings are then corrected. An easier method when rating individuals on only one characteristic is two-way (correlated-groups) analysis of variance. Reliability can also be easily calculated. The use of analysis of variance to estimate reliability, as we learned earlier, was Hoyt's contribution. Ebel applied analysis of variance to reliability of ratings. See Guilford, *op. cit.*, pp. 280–288, 383, 395–397; R. Ebel, "Estimation on the Reliability of Ratings," *Psychometrika*, XVI (1951), 407–424.

characteristics.[26] It might be added that they can be used as adjuncts to other methods. That is, they can be used as instruments to aid behavioral observations, and they can be used in conjunction with other objective instruments, with interviews, and even with projective measures (to be discussed in the next chapter).

EXAMPLES OF OBSERVATION SYSTEMS

Three or four observation systems were mentioned earlier. Several other behavioral observation systems are summarized below to help the student get a feeling for the variety of systems that are possible and the ways in which such systems are constructed and used. In addition, the student may gain further understanding of when behavioral observation is appropriate, when, in other words, a research problem requires direct measurement of behavior. Remembered behavior systems and rating scales are also summarized.

Merrill's Measurement of Mother-Child Interaction[27]   Wishing to measure the variables *Contact between Mothers and Children, Specificity of Control of the Child's Behavior,* and *Facilitation and Inhibition of the Child's Behavior,* Merrill set up an interesting and useful observation system. Mother and child were observed in an experimental room equipped with children's toys and a one-way screen. The mothers were told to imagine that they were at home with their children, unoccupied for half an hour. They had no idea that *they* were being observed, since they had been told that the research was on the child's play behavior.

A mother's behavior was recorded every five seconds, using a fairly complex notational system based on categories derived from the variables mentioned above. For example, *s* means M (Mother) *structurizes,* that is, she uses indirect means to stimulate or influence the child; *t* means M *teaches,* or gives information to increase the child's knowledge; *i* means the mother *interferes* with the child's activity in order to stop it. Each category is accompanied by clear definitions and examples. The category system is comprehensive: it embraces all possible behavior incidents that could occur in a play session. The average reliability for five sessions was .88.

Merrill performed a neat, effective, yet simple experiment using the observation system. Separating the mothers into experimental and control groups, she told the experimental group mothers, in a second half-hour session, that their children's play potential had not been realized, thus inducing motivation to stimulate the child to do "better." The

---

[26] Guilford, *op. cit.,* p. 297.
[27] B. Merrill, "A Measurement of Mother-Child Interaction," *Journal of Abnormal and Social Psychology,* XLI (1946), 37–49.

control group mothers were told the procedure would be the same as before. If the observation procedure were sensitive enough, it should show the result of the induced motivation. It did.

Student Rating of Instructors: Two Studies Student rating of instructors belongs to the category "observation of remembered behavior," which was discussed earlier. Many instruments have been constructed for this purpose. Until lately, however, instructors who have used such scales have had little idea of what they were actually measuring. Coffman attempted to find out what one such scale was measuring.[28] He used a five-point graphic rating scale consisting of 18 traits and behaviors. Each subscale used five descriptive phrases. Two of the 18 traits and the accompanying descriptions are:

> *Preparation for Class Meetings.* Class meetings very carefully planned. Usually well prepared. Preparation often inadequate. Little preparation. No preparation.
> *Organization of Course.* Every lesson well organized. Most lessons well organized. Some organization but not always clear. Very little organization. No organization.[29]

Coffman, through a factor analysis of the ratings on 55 instructors, found four factors which he called *empathy, organization, punctual-neat-normal,* and *verbal fluency.*

A similar but more complex study of teacher performance used a descriptive check list in order to compute scale values and preference and discrimination indices of 150 descriptive phrases.[30] Ten sets of four phrases each were constructed using the results of the previous analyses. Raters then rank-ordered the phrases in each set. That is, when rating an instructor, a student would choose the item in each tetrad that applied most to the instructor and put a "1" in front of it. He would then choose the next most applicable item and put a "2" in front of it. The least applicable item, of course, had a "4" placed before it. This is a forced-choice system like that encountered in the last chapter. Here is one of the tetrads:

Set *i*
_____ Always had class material ready. (3)
_____ Covered subject well. (1)
_____ Encouraged students to think out answers. (4)
_____ Rules and regulations fair. (2)[31]

[28] W. Coffman, "Determining Students' Concepts of Effective Teaching from Their Ratings of Instructors," *Journal of Educational Psychology,* XLV (1954), 277–286.
[29] *Ibid.,* p. 278. These were two of the best items as shown by a factor analysis.
[30] D. Cosgrove, "Diagnostic Rating of Teacher Performance," *Journal of Educational Psychology,* L (1959), 200–204.
[31] *Ibid.,* p. 202.

(The numbers in parentheses refer to the four factors built into each tetrad: 1) *Knowledge and Organization of Subject Matter;* 2) *Adequacy of Relations with Students in Class;* 3) *Adequacy of Plans and Procedures in Class;* and 4) *Enthusiasm in Working with Students.*)

Measurement of Educational Leadership   An instrument of considerable potential usefulness in the study of educational administration is the Leader Behavior Description Questionnaire (LBDQ), adapted by Halpin for educational use with school superintendents.[32] The LBDQ is a Likert-type instrument of 80 behavioral items responded to by observers on a five-point scale. The observer is instructed to describe, as he knows it, a superintendent's behavior by responding to each of the 80 items: "He *always (often, occasionally, seldom, never)* acts this way." The major dimensions of the instrument are *Initiating Structure* and *Consideration.* Two items of the former category are:

> He criticizes poor work.
> He lets staff members know what is expected of them.

Two of the *Consideration* items are:

> He finds time to listen to staff members.
> He gets staff approval on important matters before going ahead.

A unique feature of Halpin's research is the dual use of the LBDQ. First, it was used to learn about the *actual* behavior of superintendents: how superintendents *do* behave. This is LBDQ-Real. Second, it was used to learn how superintendents *should* behave. This is LBDQ-Ideal. Each group—superintendents, staff members, and board of education members—responded to the instrument in both ways. Thus, different perceptions of *actual* and *ideal* superintendent roles were studied.

Assessment of Parent Behavior   One of the most ambitious attempts to measure parent behavior in natural settings is the research of Baldwin, Kalhorn, and Breese.[33] Observers visit homes and, among other things, rate the behavior of parents on an observation rating scale of 30 items. The items consist of bipolar adjective pairs, such as *disapproving-approving, rejecting-devoted, nonchalant-anxious, dictatorial-democratic,* and so

---

[32] A. Halpin, *The Leadership Behavior of School Superintendents.* Chicago: Midwest Administration Center, University of Chicago, 1956. The LBDQ is given on pp. 91–95. See, also, A. Halpin, "The Leadership Behavior and Combat Performance of Airplane Commanders," *Journal of Abnormal and Social Psychology,* XLIX (1954), 19–22.

[33] A. Baldwin, J. Kalhorn, and F. Breese, "Patterns of Parent Behavior," *Psychological Monographs,* LVIII (1945), No. 3; "The Appraisal of Parent Behavior," *Psychological Monographs,* LXIII (1949), No. 4.

on. The behavior of a mother is observed in the home and rated on the 30 items. Each of the items has careful observer directions on what to observe and rate. Despite the directions, a good bit of inference is required of the observer. The researchers have found that the 30 items group themselves into a smaller number of factors, among which the most important are *warmth, democracy,* and *indulgence.* The *warmth* factor, for example, consists of the following items: *child-subordinating-child-centered, disapproval-approval, rejection-acceptance, hostile-affectionate, isolation-close rapport.*

Time Sampling of Children's Behavior In an important study of the personality structure of four- and five-year-old children as inferred from the children's actual behavior, Cattell and Peterson very appropriately used time sampling of behavioral acts.[34] Observers used a list of 76 items which they visually "swept" every five minutes to remind them of possible behavioral acts to observe and record. The observers mingled with other adults in a large garden and playground and inconspicuously made their observations. They concentrated wholly on one child for two half-hour play periods (plus five minutes at either end of the play periods).

The items are of considerable interest since they include items from other similar researches, 40 verbally defined traits previously found to measure children's personalities, and other items of possible relevance. Some of them are:

> Asks adult for help.
> Plays alone.
> Shows serious or anxious expression.
> Shows curiosity.
> Helps another child.

It should be noted that most of the 76 items are of the low inference type, though there are items requiring inference ("Expresses suspicion," "Shows fear of surroundings").

The elaborate analysis of the data (factor analysis) cannot be discussed. It is sufficient to comment on the method. The item sample covered a very wide range of possible behaviors and was clearly behavioral in character. The items form an excellent pool from which educational researchers can extract items for research on specific research problems. Furthermore, Cattell and Peterson's analysis supplies at least tentative identifications of what the items are measuring.

Point-Time Sampling of Classroom Activities Kowatrakul, in studying the relation between student behavior and classroom activities in various

---

34 R. Cattell and D. Peterson, "Personality Structure in 4-5 Year Olds, by Factoring Observed, Time-Sampled Behavior," *Estratto della Rassegna di Psicologia Generale e Clinica,* III (1958), 3–21.

subjects, developed a promising method of observation of classroom behavior to be used in conjunction with what he calls point-time sampling.[35] Six categories of behavior were used: *Intent on Ongoing Work*
(task-oriented), *Social Work-Oriented* (social remarks that are work-
oriented), *Social-Friendly* (any social remarks), *Momentary Withdrawal,
Intent on Work in Another Academic Area,* and *Intent on Work in Non-
academic Area.* Three kinds of classroom activity were also observed:
Independent Seat Work, Watching and Listening, and *Discussion.* The
two systems were used in conjunction with each other.

The unusual feature of Kowatrakul's system was the point-time
sampling. The observer observes a subject long enough to record one
behavior. He then immediately passes on to the next subject. The behavior of the next subject must be independent of that of the first subject.
(The author does not say how this is to be achieved, unfortunately.) This
procedure is used until one "behavior point" of each subject in the group
has been recorded. Then a new round of observations begins. Kowatrakul
reports that each round takes between three to five minutes in each class.

The reliabilities reported are extremely high, most of them being
greater than .90, some being as high as .98. (These were odd-even reliabilities.) In a special study of 1689 time samples done by two observers,
there was 94 percent agreement. Evidently this is a highly reliable method.

Students of educational research might well pay particular attention
to this system, since it seems well-suited to classroom observations of the
indicated variables. Its point-time sampling feature certainly deserves
further research and use. Few systems yield such high reliabilities. Further, validity, in this case, seems no great problem because of the almost
self-evident nature of the categories and the activities subsumed under
them.

ASSESSMENT OF BEHAVIORAL OBSERVATION

There is no doubt whatever that objective observation of human
behavior has advanced beyond the rudimentary stage. The advances, like
other methodological and measurement advances made in the last ten
to twenty years, have been striking. The growth of psychometric and
statistical mastery and sophistication has been felt in the observation and
assessment of actual and remembered behavior. Social scientific research
can and should profit from these advances. Many educational research
problems, for example, strongly demand behavior observations: children
in classrooms interacting with each other and with teachers, administrators and teachers discussing school problems in staff meetings, boards of

[35] S. Kowatrakul, "Some Behaviors of Elementary School Children Related to
Classroom Activities and Subject Areas," *Journal of Educational Psychology,* L (1959),
121–128.

education working toward policy decisions. Behavior observations can be used in natural situations and experimentally contrived situations, as we have seen. Here is one methodological approach that is essentially the same in both kinds of situations.

To sum up, researchers should pay more attention to the possibility of measuring some of their variables by the direct observation of behavior. Such observations can be used when other methods are inappropriate or impossible to use. They must be used when variables of research studies are interactive and interpersonal in nature. They must be used, in short, when the research variables are clearly behavioral. When administrator behavior, teacher behavior, pupil behavior, and parent behavior are independent or dependent variables, clearly it would seem more appropriate to observe and measure the kinds of behavior directly than simply to ask people about them, important as the asking may be. Finally, it must always be remembered that data and the analysis of data are no better than the original observations from which they come.

STUDY SUGGESTIONS

The student should study two or three behavior-observation systems. It is suggested that among the systems mentioned in this chapter, the Ryans and the Cornell, Lindvall, and Saupe monographs will yield the highest returns. These two systems are limited to classroom observation, however. Many students will profit from wider browsing and study. Here are some other good behavior-observation systems.

Anderson, H., "Domination and Socially Integrative Behavior." In R. Barker, J. Kounin, and H. Wright, eds., *Child Behavior and Development*. New York: McGraw-Hill, 1943, Chap. XXVII. This summary chapter of Anderson's well-known observational work includes a rather elaborate, well worked-out system for studying the effects of two types of teacher behavior on pupil behavior.

Barker, R., T. Dembo, and K. Lewin, "Frustration and Regression." *Ibid.*, Chap. XXVI. This is another well-known and competent study in which the *constructiveness* of children's behavior was observed under conditions of frustration. Interesting attempts at validation by correlating *constructiveness* with mental age and chronological age are discussed.

Bales, R., "Some Uniformities of Behavior in Small Social Systems." In G. Swanson, T. Newcomb, and E. Hartley, eds., *Readings in Social Psychology*, rev. ed. New York: Holt, Rinehart and Winston, Inc. 1952, pp. 146–159. A good and brief description of Bales' system is given here.

Gage, N., G. Leavitt, and G. Stone, "Teachers' Understanding of Their Pupils and Pupils' Ratings of Their Teachers." *Psychological Mono-*

graphs, LXIX (1955), Whole No. 406. This is a complex study using ratings. See, especially, the 12-item scale, "Our Teacher" (p. 14), to measure pupils' perceptions of teachers. The authors also used a paired-comparisons form of the same scale.

Olson, W., "The Measurement of Nervous Habits." In W. Dennis, *Readings in Child Psychology.* Englewood Cliffs, N.J.: Prentice-Hall, 1951, pp. 439–445. This is an excerpt from Olson's monograph on the subject, one of the pioneer studies using time sampling.

Parten, M., and S. Newhall, "Social Behavior of Preschool Children." In Barker, Kounin, and Wright, *op. cit.,* Chap. XXIX. This is a good example of behavioral observations and time sampling using children as subjects. The variables observed were *social participation* and *leadership.* The results were validated against teacher ratings.

29 *PROJECTIVE METHODS*

Men project some part of themselves into everything they do. Watch a man walk. Watch him drive a car. Listen to a woman talk to her husband. Examine an artist's paintings. Study a professor's lecture style. Observe a child play with other children or with toys and dolls. In all these ways human beings express their needs, their drives, their styles of life. If we want to know a person, then we can study *what* he does and the *way* he does it.

In its original psychoanalytic usage, *projection* means to eject unconscious, unacceptable impulses of one's own from oneself and to perceive them as belonging to others. An individual with unconscious hostile impulses, for example, may see other people as hostile. The offensive impulse is ejected, or "projected." One's own impulses are unconsciously projected upon the external world.

The notion of projection, however, has been broadened to include more than just unacceptable impulses. Values, attitudes, needs, wishes, as well as impulses and motives, are projected upon objects and behavior outside the individual. A hungry individual may invest inedible objects with food properties. A jealous individual sees other men as threats to his marriage. An individual with conservative social attitudes may see federal taxes as confiscatory. The teacher with progressive educational values will see children and curricula quite differently from the teacher with traditional educational values. Each person, then, views the world through his own projective glasses.

If these notions are correct, then it should be possible to study men's motives, emotions, values, attitudes, and needs by somehow getting them to project these internal states on to external objects. This potent idea is behind projective devices of all kinds.

When we present a child with objective items to measure the extent of his knowledge of subject matter, we allow him little room to project himself. If, on the other hand, we ask him to write about himself, we give him the opportunity to "express himself," to project his personality into the written product. As Getzels and Jackson have shown, creative and noncreative children write very different kinds of autobiography.[1] Two excerpts from the autobiographies of two children, the first written by a creative child, the second by a noncreative (but highly intelligent) child follow. Even these short excerpts show striking differences:

> In 1943 I was born. I have been living without interruption ever since. My parents are my mother and father—an arrangement I have found increasingly convenient over the years.[2]
>
> My autobiography is neither interesting or exciting and I see very little reason for writing it. However I shall attempt to write a certain amount of material which would be constructive.[3]

A basic principle of projective methods is that the more unstructured and ambiguous a stimulus, the more a subject can and will project his emotions, needs, motivations, attitudes, and values. The *structure* of a stimulus, at least from one important point of view, is the degree of choice available to the subject. A highly structured stimulus leaves very little choice: the subject has unambiguous choice among clear alternatives, as in an objective-type achievement test question. A stimulus of low structure has a wide range of alternative choices. It is ambiguous: the subject can "choose" his own interpretation. Projective devices range widely in degree of structure, but they are much less structured than the methods already considered.

Another important characteristic of projective methods is their lack of objectivity. Projectives lack objectivity in the sense that it is much easier for different observers to come to different conclusions about the responses of the same persons. Recall that one of the powerful advantages of objective methods was that different observers must agree on the scoring of responses. Projectives, on the other hand, lack this very desirable characteristic: different observers can score the same data quite differently. This is a serious weakness.

Suppose judges are reading autobiographies written by children in order to rate them on creativity. Take the first of the two passages quoted from Getzels and Jackson's book, above. One judge might rate the passage high in creativity because of its bright unusual approach. Yet another judge might discount the bright unusual approach. He may consider the approach to be merely flip, and he may rate the passage low in creativity. Similarly, two judges observing a child play with dolls may rate the child quite differently in aggressiveness. One may conclude, because the child throws a doll across the room, that this is a manifestation of aggressiveness. Another judge, however, may conclude that throwing

[1] Reprinted with permission from J. Getzels and P. Jackson, *Creativity and Intelligence.* New York: Wiley, 1962, pp. 99–103.

[2] *Ibid.,* p. 100.

[3] *Ibid.,* p. 101.

the doll was simply a sort of punctuation mark at the end of a play activity. All tests and measures involve inference, as we have seen. Projective tests and measures require very large inferential leaps indeed, larger than those of any other method. Thus the reliability and validity of projective devices are difficult problems.

A final point to remember about projection and projective methods is that almost anything at all can be used as a stimulus. Because there are well-known projective tests, like the Rorschach, the TAT (Thematic Apperception Test), and the Draw-a-Person Test, this does not mean that projectives are limited to standard published tests. There is actually a very large number of ways that the principle of projection can be used. Here are only a few of the possibilities: drawing pictures, using finger paint and clay, writing essays, playing with toys and dolls, role playing, handwriting, telling stories in response to vague stimuli, describing blots, clouds, or ambiguous pictures, associating words to other words, writing autobiographies, reacting to colors or sounds or both, interpreting music.

There is little doubt that projective devices are among the most imaginative and significant creations of psychology. There is also little doubt of their power, flexibility, and catholicity. But—and the "but" is a large one—the price paid is high: projective tests and measures are always on shaky reliability and validity grounds.

A CLASSIFICATION OF PROJECTIVE MEASURES

On the basis of previous efforts to classify projective measures, Lindzey proposed a sensible five-way classification that will serve very well to structure our discussion. Lindzey proposes that the classification of projective measures be based on types of response. There are, he says, five types: association, construction, completion, choice or ordering, and expression.[4] This taxonomy is particularly useful because it puts emphasis on the respondent and, by implication, on the variables measured. It brings us closer, in other words, to the operational thinking of earlier chapters, whereas preoccupation with projective tests as tests might lead us astray from our basic task: the collection of data for scientific purposes.

Association Techniques   *Association techniques* require the subject to respond, at the presentation of a stimulus, with the first thing that comes

[4] G. Lindzey, "On the Classification of Projective Techniques," *Psychological Bulletin*, LVI (1959), 158–168. Discussion of choice or ordering techniques is omitted in this text, since they are not true projective techniques. Essentially, they provide multiple-choice responses to projective stimuli. For example, there is a multiple-choice form of the Rorschach test. Perhaps it would be better to say that the technique is a mechanics of objectifying projective devices. An early general review of projectives is: H. Sargent, "Projective Methods: Their Origins, Theory, and Application in Personality Research," *Psychological Bullein*, XLII (1945), 257–293.

to mind. Although the association idea is old, its modern projective use seems to stem from Freud's invention of the free association technique, Jung's later studies in word association, and Rorschach's work with inkblots. The most famous and important projective device of this kind is the Rorschach test. The individual is asked by a highly skilled examiner to respond to ten inkblots of varying shapes and colors. The test is relatively unstructured and allows full play of the subject's responses. From the responses and associations produced to the inkblots the examiner infers the personality characteristics of the respondent. While there is little doubt of the Rorschach test's unique importance in modern psychology, particularly clinical psychology, it is doubtful that it has much use in educational and sociological research. It requires a high degree of skill acquired after long training and experience and much time to administer and score. In addition, its reliability and validity are, to say the least, doubtful and controversial.

Perhaps more immediately promising for social scientific and educational research are *word association* methods. Ordinarily, emotionally tinged words are included with neutral words, and subjects are asked to respond with the first word that comes to mind. The words produced presumably can indicate a subject's feelings, motives, and attitudes, especially toward other persons. If one were studying, say, the "adjustment" of adolescents, one might present them with a list of words with presumably significant associations for them. Here is a possible list: father, school, girls (boys), home, church, mother, sex, study, me, date, hate, friend.

More pertinent to the measurement of research variables, consider Getzels and Jackson's use of word association in their study of creativity.[5] The word association technique was used to measure a presumed aspect of creativity: the ability to shift frames of reference. Among the 25 words used were *arm, bolt, fair, leaf, policy.* Instead of asking for an immediate response of one word, however, Getzels and Jackson asked subjects to give as many meanings as they could. Score was the total number of meanings given *and* the number of different categories into which the definitions could be put.[6] For example, a subject might respond to *fair* with beautiful, light, just, equitable, unbiased, legible, average. The score of words produced is 7; category score might be 4 or 5, depending on the system used.

Construction Techniques   Projective techniques of the *constructive* type focus upon the *product* of the subject. The subject is required to produce, to construct, something at direction, usually a picture or a story. These

---

[5] Getzels and Jackson, *op. cit.,* pp. 199, 200, 224, 225.
[6] *Ibid.,* p. 17. While this usage departs somewhat from the traditional use of projectives, it is obvious that the idea of projection is behind the test.

are complex techniques that often demand a good deal from subjects. The stimulus can be very simple, like asking children to tell a story about their homes or what happened to them yesterday, or very complex, like the well-known Thematic Apperception Test. Generally some form of standardized stimulus is used.

The TAT, or parts or variants of it, has been used a good deal in research. It consists of a set of vague pictures of relatively low structure that tap a wide variety of feelings and needs of subjects. In its original form, it probably finds little use in educational research for much the same reasons given for the Rorschach. But the idea behind it has considerable research potential. One, two, or three vague pictures, for instance, can be shown to children with instructions to write brief stories. The protocols (a *protocol*, in research, is a record of what was said, written, or done by individuals or groups) are read and scored, then, on such variables as need for achievement, originality, divergent thinking, and so on.

One of the most interesting of recent developments of the projective construction type is the measurement of motivation through short stories written by subjects in responses to pictures shown them.[7] Veroff's method of measuring power motivation (PM) illustrates the idea very well.[8] In addition, it represents an unusual amount of effort spent to demonstrate the validity of the method; for this reason it is presented here in some detail.

Veroff presented five pictures in booklets to his subjects. Each picture represented a situation in which power, or control of other persons, was potential. Subjects were required to write brief stories about each picture. The stories were then analyzed for evidence of PM. A story was first identified as related or not related to PM. If it was not related to PM, no further scoring was done. If it was related to PM, it was scored according to three criteria: affect, control activity, and superior-subordinate role relations. That is, if a story contained a statement about one person demanding something from another person, this was scored under control activity. Similarly, it was scored under the third criterion if a statement was about a boss-worker activity and relationship.

Taking advantage of a student election, Veroff used students who were running for office, a natural power situation. These he called *aroused* students. Undergraduates not running for office were the *nonaroused* students. Both groups responded to the PM measure. Numbers of students in the *aroused* and *nonaroused* groups above and below the median on PM are given in Table 29.1.[9] This result is highly significant.

[7] D. McClelland, *et al.*, *The Achievement Motive*. New York: Appleton, 1953.
[8] D. Veroff, "Development and Validation of a Projective Measure of Power Motivation," *Journal of Abnormal and Social Psychology*, LIV (1957), 1–8.
[9] *Ibid.*, p. 4.

Evidently the PM measure has validity. Reliability, too, was found to be satisfactory.[10]

TABLE 29.1   TEST OF VALIDITY OF MEASURE OF POWER MOTIVATION, VEROFF STUDY

	Power Score	
	Above Median	Below Median
Aroused Group	22	12
Nonaroused Group	9	25

Completion Techniques   Getzels and Jackson, in the study of creativity and intelligence mentioned earlier, used two measures that illustrate completion techniques.[11] One of these was a disguised test of adjustment. Subjects were required to complete sentences at high speed. The items were scored for positive and negative affect. One of the items was:

Working with others all the time makes me————————.

The subject might respond: mad, nervous, tired, sick (negative affect), or content, feel good, happy (positive affect).

The other, somewhat more interesting measure was called the Fables Test, a measure of creativity. Four fables with the last line missing were presented to subjects, with instructions to supply three types of endings: moralistic, humorous, sad. The endings were scored for *appropriateness* and *relatedness*. Each individual's score was the sum of these two scores. Reliability was a substantial .87. Here is one of the fables:

The Mischievous Dog

A rascally dog used to run quietly to the heels of every passerby and bite them without warning. So his master was obliged to tie a bell around the cur's neck that he might give notice wherever he went. This the dog thought very fine indeed, and he went about tinkling it in pride all over town.

But an old hound said:

---

[10] A number of other tests of validity were made. For example, the stories were scored for achievement motivation to check the possibility that the difference might have been due to differences between the two groups in achievement motivation. There were no significant differences between the groups. This study is an excellent example of the sophisticated construction and validation of a complex measure.

[11] Getzels and Jackson, *op. cit.*, pp. 214–216, 248–253, 202–205, 227–229.

Moralistic: ....
Humorous: ....
Sad: ....[12]

Here are some examples of responses gotten by this test. They are labeled as *appropriate* or *not appropriate:*

Appropriate	Not Appropriate
You are only ringing out your guilt. (Moralistic)	You can't both bite and be quiet. (Moralistic)
This is your plight, you dogs that bite. (Humorous)	Now you should learn to sing. (Humorous) [13]

Completion projective measures, then, supply the subject with a stimulus that is incomplete, the subject being required to complete it as he wishes, as with the first of the cited Getzels and Jackson measures. Or the stimulus may be loosely structured, as with the second measure (the Fables Test). It is obvious that responses of completion techniques are simpler than those of association and construction measures, thus simplifying the tasks of scoring and interpretation. The famous sentence-completion method is the best-known of such techniques, but other types of completion measures, such as story completion, discussion completion, and others, are being developed.

Expressive Techniques Expressive projective techniques are similar to constructive techniques: the subject is required to form some sort of product out of raw material. But the emphasis is on the *manner* in which he does this— the end product is not so important. With the constructive methods, the content, and perhaps the style, of the story or other product are analyzed. With, say, finger painting or play therapy, it is the process of the activity and not the end product that is important. The subject *expresses* his needs, desires, emotions, and motives through working with, manipulating, and interacting with materials, including other people, in a manner or style that uniquely expresses his personality.

The principal expressive methods are play, drawing, painting, finger painting, and role playing. There are, however, other possibilities: working with clay, handwriting, games, and so on. The discussion that follows is limited to play techniques, finger painting, and role playing. These will be sufficient to illustrate expressive methods.

In the research use of play techniques, a child is brought into the presence of a variety of toys, very often dolls of some kind. He may be told that a set of dolls is a family and that he should play with them and tell a story about them. Or he may be given a set of toys representing a

[12] *Ibid.,* pp. 227, 228.
[13] *Ibid.,* pp. 203, 204.

miniature life situation. Or he may be put into a planned situation with one or two other children and told to play with them. Axline, for example, in studying racial conflicts in children, rotated children in four-child play groups in order to study white and Negro children's adjustability to each other.[14] Axline's verbatim reports vividly show how play techniques can tap the aggressiveness and racial attitudes of young children. Although the specific technique does not matter too much, some forms of play technique seem better suited to the expressive purpose than others.

Doll play seems well suited to research with young children, probably because it seems so easy and natural for children to project themselves into the dolls. Many variables can be measured, but the main ones have been aggression, stereotypy, and prejudice.[15] In their study of the effect of the presence of mothers on the aggressiveness of children, Levin and Turgeon used doll play to measure aggression.[16] Aggression was defined as acts that hurt, irritate, injure, punish, frustrate, or destroy the dolls or equipment. Two scores of aggression were used: total number of aggressive units per session and percent aggression (number of aggressive units divided by total number of units). Experimental-group children's doll play was observed by the experimenter and mothers. The control-group children's play was observed by the experimenter and a stranger. The children observed by their mothers were more aggressive than those not observed by their mothers.

Although it has evidently not been used much in educational research, doll play is a promising method for research with children in the nursery school, the kindergarten, and the early grades. The necessary equipment is simple, varied, and inexpensive. Certain common variables can readily be measured by combining doll play with a good behavioral observation method. Perhaps most important, experimental situations of considerable naturalness can be set up with no great trouble. In short, doll play can be used to measure the effects of manipulated independent variables, or it can be used to manipulate the independent variable or variables.

Finger painting is a particularly rich expressive method. Although used mostly with children, there is no really good reason why it cannot be used with adults. The subject is given pots of a special type of paint and told to draw what he likes with the paints, using his fingers and hands. Variables can be measured by counting numbers of certain kinds of manipulative and approach behavior or by rating subjects on the vari-

14 V. Axline, "Play Therapy and Race Conflict in Children," *Journal of Abnormal and Social Psychology,* XLIII (1948), 300–310.

15 H. Levin and E. Wardwell, "The Research Uses of Doll Play," *Psychological Bulletin,* LIX (1962), 27–56.

16 H. Levin and V. Turgeon, "The Influence of the Mother's Presence on Children's Doll Play Aggression," *Journal of Abnormal and Social Psychology,* LV (1957), 304–308.

ables using predetermined criteria. The best way to show how effective finger painting can be in ingenious hands is to study a good piece of research in which it has been used.

Considerably earlier we briefly considered a remarkable study in which finger paints were used to measure dependent variables.[17] Combining psychoanalytic and sociological theory, Alper, Blane, and Adams asked the question: Do social class differences in child training result in class differences in personality? Specifically they asked: Are there social class differences in the approach to, and the use of, finger painting? Lower- and middle-class children were given finger paints with instructions (1) to paint anything you want, and (2) to paint a picture of your family. (A control experiment in which crayons were used was also run. The assumption was that crayons do not have the expressive power of finger paints. Evidently they do not.)

Sixteen aspects of finger painting were measured in the experiment; among them: time to begin painting, use of whole hand vs. finger-tip approach, use of both hands, use of whole vs. partial use of sheet, and washing-up behavior. Significant differences were found in the behavior of the children in most of the tasks, for example, middle-class children more often tried to avoid the finger painting task and less often used both hands and the whole sheet. This is a fortunate use of a simple projective device to measure variables relevant to the theory underlying the research.

Role Playing Although role playing perhaps rightfully belongs among the expressive techniques, there are good reasons for treating it separately. First, it involves other persons. Second, and more important, it holds great promise as an experimental method and as an observation-measurement tool of behavioral research, though its research use has been quite limited.[18] Up to now, the use of role playing has been dominated by practical considerations, a characteristic it has in common with other projective devices. Yet its use in research in social psychology and education seems quite promising. It combines the advantages of controlled behavioral observations with the power of projective methods.

Role playing is the acting-out of an assigned personal or social situation for a brief period of time by two or more individuals who have been assigned specific roles. The investigator uses an observation system to measure his variables. Or role playing can be used as an experimental manipulation without observation. The research possibilities are many. Group processes and interpersonal interaction, especially, can be con-

[17] T. Alper, H. Blane, and B. Adams, "Reactions of Middle and Lower Class Children to Finger Paints as a Function of Class Differences in Child-Training Practices," *Journal of Abnormal and Social Psychology*, LI (1955), 439–448.

[18] J. Mann, "Experimental Evaluations of Role Playing," *Psychological Bulletin*, LIII (1956), 227–234.

veniently studied.[19] A wide range of variables can be measured: hostility, authoritarianism, prejudice, dominance-submission, and so on. It has been the experience of role players that they say things they would rarely say under ordinary circumstances. They "come out" with things that surprise even themselves. The method, in other words, tends to bring out motives, needs, and attitudes that are below the social surface.

Suppose, for instance, we are studying the relation between authoritarian trends and leadership behavior. We might measure authoritarianism with a pencil-and-paper test, set up two- or three-person groups, and instruct the groups to role-play a committee charged with planning a school function. While the groups were interacting, we could measure leadership behavior. We might even measure authoritarianism through role playing in the same or similar manner. The difficult part, of course, is to decide what authoritarian behavior is, and then to validate the decision.

In studying teaching effectiveness, we might have teacher trainees play various kinds of teacher roles. Or we can ask a teacher or teacher trainee to play the part of a child while another individual plays the part of a teacher. This might be a potent way to measure teacher empathy, or the ability of a teacher to identify with the thoughts and feelings of children. We could ask experienced teachers and teacher trainees to play the role of a teacher discussing a problem of poor work with a student, one of the individuals playing the part of the student. It might not be easy to set up an observation system geared to measure empathy, but it is far from impossible.

It is fairly easy to set up role-playing situations for practical purposes. There seems to be little knowledge on how to set up such situations for research purposes. The interested student will have to try out various approaches and techniques. Here are some ideas that may help.

In using role playing in research, it is necessary to remember that it is not being used for therapeutic or educational purposes. It is a projective device to aid in observing behavior and measuring variables that are conveniently observed and measured in no other ways. The role-playing situation should be structured so that the probability of eliciting behavior pertinent to the variable or variables being measured is high. Suppose it is necessary to measure the attitudes toward authority of small children. The children can be asked to take the roles of teachers, doctors, and parents. Some specific situation should be assigned. For instance, three children can be assigned the roles of mother, teacher, and child in a situation where the mother has been asked by the teacher to come to the school because the child has misbehaved. If it is found, as it well

[19] See W. Lambert, "Interpersonal Behavior," in P. Mussen, ed., *Handbook of Research Methods in Child Development.* New York: Wiley, 1960, chap. 20.

might be, that such a situation does not adequately elicit the appropriate behavior and attitudes, the situation may be simplified, say, to include only the teacher and the child. Other authority-figure roles can of course be used.

Subjects must be able to structure their roles and play their parts consistently. To do this, they need instructions that are just the right mixture of generality and specificity. If the instructions are too general, the actors may wander and consequently may not yield behavior relevant to the variables being measured. Rather than say "Play a teacher and a child," it would be better to say something like, "You be a teacher, and you be a child who has misbehaved in class. You (the latter child) have hit other children several times. The teacher has asked you to stay after school to talk to her. You have both just sat down and started to talk. Go ahead." Note that these instructions outline a general situation that could occur in any class anywhere, but they have a fairly clear structure: the actors know what to talk about. If, on the other hand, the instructions are too specific, the actors may be too bound up in the specificities of the situation. This is a matter of experience.

Closely related to the point just made is the keynote of role playing: spontaneity. Role-playing situations must be so planned that the actors can play their parts spontaneously. Remember that role-playing situations and instructions are not experimental situations and instructions where all details are carefully spelled out. They are projective situations. A good deal of leeway, even looseness, must be allowed so that the actors can project themselves into the roles they are playing.

Time limits should be carefully planned. Role-playing situations are generally brief, anywhere from 3 to 15 or 20 minutes. Most situations are best ended after about 10 minutes. This is usually sufficient time for the variables to be measured and not so long that the actors might lag.

A last point is that the researcher himself or a confederate can always play one of the roles and so be able to control and structure the situation to some extent. This may be especially necessary in the research use of role playing. Role players sometimes wander off the assigned subjects and roles. Confederates are often useful because they can keep the acting of the group concentrated on the assigned situation. More important, maybe, is the possibility of their deliberately saying and doing things to stimulate the actors' behavior relevant to the variable of interest. For example, if attitudes toward authority are measured, he might, in playing the role of a child, say something about hating teachers and other adults.

The possibilities are limited only by the ingenuity and energy of the researcher. One or two examples of the use of role playing in research may now be helpful. Borgatta, in a significant study mentioned earlier, explored the relation between verbal behavior about an action and actual behavior.[20] He conducted 166 three-man group, role-playing sessions in which he measured the Bales' variables mentioned earlier. First, the groups interacted in 4 six-minute periods to "get acquainted" and to plan the role-playing sessions. This was called *actual participation*. Its purpose was to obtain measures under actual conditions of discussion and planning. Two 12-minute *role-playing* sessions were held for the subjects to enact the situations they had planned. The Bales' variables were measured in both sessions. The measures of the *actual* and *role-playing* sessions were correlated. The *r*'s ranged from .04 to .74 and averaged about .50. Factor analysis showed that, for the most part, the same variables were measured in both situations. This is good evidence of the validity of the role-playing situations.

Steiner and Field, in a study of the effects of role taking on attitudes, measured the attitudes of students toward the desegregation of schools.[21] Those whose attitudes were for desegregation were put into 34 three-man groups. Two members of each group had similar attitude scores; the third member was an accomplice of the experimenters. The groups were instructed to discuss the desirability of desegregating public schools and to attempt to reach agreement during the 15-minute experimental period. They were urged to take account of the views of a typical Southern segregationist, a typical Northern minister, priest, or rabbi, and a typical member of the National Association for the Advancement of Colored People. Roles were assigned to each group member in half the groups. The experimental subjects in these groups were assigned the Northern clergyman and NAACP roles. The accomplice was always assigned the Southern segregationist role. The treatment for the other 17 groups was the same except that group members were not assigned roles. The results indicated that the role assignment affected group members' perceptions of each other. When specific roles were *not* assigned, for example, subjects yielded more to the segregationist arguments of the accomplice and indicated greater preference for one another (rather than for the accomplice).

PROJECTIVE TECHNIQUES AND BEHAVIORAL RESEARCH: AN ASSESSMENT

The same difficulties that face researchers in other fields using projective methods of course face the behavioral researcher. As Sargent said, in 1945:

---

[20] E. Borgatta, "Analysis of Social Interaction: Actual, Role Playing, and Projective," *Journal of Abnormal and Social Psychology*, LI (1955), 394–405. Though this is a methodological study, its original, ingenious, and creative use of role playing deserves special mention. In passing, it may be said that it is not easy to find research studies that have used role playing—especially educational research studies.

[21] I. Steiner and W. Field, "Role Assignment and Interpersonal Influence," *Journal of Abnormal and Social Psychology*, LXI (1960), 239–245.

The variety and richness of material which the projective methods provide is at once the delight of the clinician and the despair of the experimentalist. The research worker who attempts to use any of these methods is immediately impressed both with their infinite possibilities for interpretation and insight, and the seemingly insurmountable difficulties in the way of scientific treatment of the data.[22]

Projective measures are probably the most controversial of psychological measurement instruments. They have been extravagantly praised and extravagantly blamed.[23] In evaluating them, we must not confuse noble sentiments and mythology with reliable and valid methods of observation. The position taken in this book is that all methods of observation and measurement must satisfy the same scientific criteria. To argue that a method is valid because it encompasses the whole personality or plunges into the unconscious mind evades the issue. The fact of the projective matter seems to be that the scientific canons of reliability, validity, and objectivity have not been adequately satisfied. Worse, too few attempts have been made to put projective techniques to hard empirical test. Before marrying any method or set of methods, the student should keep these thoughts in mind. This is not the place, however, to labor the projective argument. The purpose here is to guide the student to rational and balanced perspective and use of all methods. What might a balanced view on projective methods be?

First, projective methods must be considered as methods of observation and measurement, just as any other methods are. As such, their purpose is to assign numerals to objects or events according to rules. This can clearly be seen in the examples given above. The Getzels and Jackson and the Borgatta measures, as different as they appear to be, for instance, from summated-rating scales or interviews, are methods of observing behavior and measuring variables. The same is true of any projective method. The questions to be asked, as always, are: Can the numerals be assigned to the objects reliably? How valid are the procedures?

Second, then, projective methods must be subjected to the same type of reliability testing and empirical validation as any other psychometric procedures. This is not too easy to do. Still, it must be done—and done well. Such empirical testing is almost more important with projectives than with other kinds of instruments because of the very long inferential leaps involved.

Third, attempts can and must be made to "objectify the subjective." Projective devices, as we saw earlier, have a large element of subjectivity of interpretation. Objectivity is defined as agreement among observers. This means, to repeat an earlier dictum, that independent and compe-

22 Sargent, *op. cit.*, p. 275.
23 For a severe criticism, see H. Eysenck, *Sense and Nonsense in Psychology.* Baltimore: Penguin, 1957, pp. 218–230.

tent judges must agree on the scoring and interpretation of the data yielded by an observation method. How can this be done with projective methods?

To illustrate the notion of objectifying the subjective—which is really not new to us—take a simple example of the measurement of a complex variable. Suppose an investigator is trying to measure creativity. He shows children a picture and asks them to write a story about it. After the stories are written, he can ask judges, whom he has already trained, to read the stories. In addition, he constructs a graphic seven-point rating scale (or a numerical rating scale) of five items. Each item is a criterion of creativity as he defines it. Say that two of them are *originality* and *unusual approach*. He now asks his judges to rate the stories of all the children using the rating scale. He can then correlate the ratings of the judges, or he can utilize analysis of variance. To the extent that the ratings correlate highly, to this extent he has achieved objectivity. Other objective procedures can similarly be applied to the products of projective tests.

To sum up, projective methods of observation, when considered as psychometric instruments and subjected to the same canons and criteria of scientific measurement as other instruments, and when used with circumspection and care, can be useful tools of psychological and educational research. A projective instrument should not be used, however, if you have a more objective instrument that adequately measures the same variable. There is no sense in taking the risk if you do not have to. Moreover, it is best to avoid complex projective techniques, like the Rorschach test and the TAT, that require highly specialized training and a great deal of perhaps questionable interpretation.

30 AVAILABLE MATERIALS AND CONTENT ANALYSIS

There is a vast store of materials produced by institutions, organizations, and individuals that is available for research purposes. Some of the more important possibilities of these resources are suggested in the first half of this chapter. The possibility of using the method of content analysis to study available and produced materials will be explored in the second half of the chapter.

USES OF AVAILABLE MATERIALS

Whether a researcher's interest is basically theoretical or basically practical, he has to steep himself in his materials. If he is going to study boards of education and their functioning, he must not only know a great deal about education and boards of education generally; he must be quite familiar with the particular boards of education he is going to study. Almost all board of education documents are public records and are thus available for research purposes. To become familiar with a sample of boards of education he can read the documents produced by the boards and their agents and the official and unofficial documents of the boards' policies, activities, and decisions. Thus the first purpose of the use of available materials is to *explore* the nature of the data and the subjects, to get an insight into the total situation.

A second purpose of available materials is to *suggest hypotheses*. While an investigator may have one or two hypotheses which he has deduced, say, from sociological or psychological theory, the study of available materials, like the minutes of board meetings, may suggest further hypotheses. In reading minutes, for example, an investigator may notice that certain boards seem always to reach unanimous decisions, whereas certain other boards rarely reach unanimous decisions. He may also notice that the boards that reach unanimous decisions also seem to have a higher level of education among their members. This suggests an interesting and perhaps theoretically important hypothesis.

A third use of available materials is to *test hypotheses*. For example,

Beale, in his great study of freedom—or rather, lack of freedom—in public schools and teachers' colleges, tested implicit hypotheses on the relation between lack of freedom and other variables.[1] Much of Beale's source data came from available materials: newspapers, periodicals, books, public documents, court decisions, and so on. Lewin, comparing the Hitler Youth and the Boy Scouts of America, was implicitly testing the hypothesis that similarly organized but ideologically different groups would stress quite different themes in their literature.[2] To test his implicit hypotheses, he analyzed and compared member and leader literature published by the Boy Scouts and by the Hitler Youth.

Although beset with certain methodological difficulties, there is no reason why available materials cannot deliberately be used to test hypotheses. Using the minutes of boards of education, one can test the hypothesis that motivations of board members to become board members is related to the decisions of the boards. Of course, one would have to measure the members' motivations in one of the ways previously discussed. The decisions of the boards and the votes of individual members, of course, are recorded in the minutes. Another hypothesis similarly testable is that the pressure group affiliation of board members is related to decisions. One might predict that boards of education with members who represent pressure groups tend to have split decisions on matters of import to the pressure groups.

A quite different type of hypothesis that can be tested with available materials is on the relations between different kinds of test scores with different kinds of pupils. One might predict, for instance, that the correlations between certain variables will be higher with girls than with boys. Or one might take available test scores from school files and compare the relations between certain sets of test scores of middle-class and lower-class children.

Available materials can be used to *check the results of data obtained by one or more other methods.* This is, of course, a validation use. Such validation can take two forms: validation of relations obtained through the use of other methods and validation of measuring instruments. It may have been found, through interviewing, that the attitudes of board of education members toward curriculum innovations and teacher participation in curriculum planning was largely positive. But a check of board records may show that boards rarely support policies that would make these improvements possible. Likewise, an analysis of newspaper editorials may show that the newspapers enthusiastically support "educational progress" and "better education for all our children." Yet a further analysis of editorials and news stories may show that the

---

[1] H. Beale, *Are American Teachers Free?* New York: Scribner, 1936.
[2] H. Lewin, "Hitler Youth and the Boy Scouts of America," *Human Relations,* I (1947), 206–227.

newspapers take a dim view of new educational policies that require the expenditure of money.[3]

Another use of available materials to check on research findings was mentioned earlier when survey research was discussed: the use of census data to *check sample data*. If one has drawn a random sample of dwellings in a community in order to interview individuals on their knowledge of, and attitudes toward, the local board of education and its policies, the accuracy of one's sample should be checked by comparing sociological data of the sample, like income, race, and education, with the same data of the most recent census or with available data in local government offices.

Census and other official data—voting lists, housing registration, license registration, school censuses, and so on—are also used to help *draw samples*. Researchers too often use hit-and-miss samples. To draw a random sample of a large geographical area is, as we saw earlier, an expensive and difficult job. But it is not too difficult to draw random samples of single, smaller communities. Some school systems, for example, maintain relatively complete and accurate lists of taxpayers or families with school children. For some educational research purposes, these lists may be helpful in drawing random samples. The point is that there are a number of available sources that can be used for drawing samples. Though none of these sources is perfect, since records are kept for different purposes, with different degrees of accuracy, by people of different levels of competence, they are much better sources of samples than the informed hunches of investigators.

Important Types of Available Materials Five or six kinds of available materials seem to be most important for research. Each of these will be mentioned and considered briefly. Though the emphasis in the following discussion will be upon educational research, the materials would of course be useful in psychological and sociological research.

Since they have already been discussed, we need not delay long over *census data* and *registration data*. If an investigator needs census data, perhaps the best thing to do is to write the United States Government Printing Office, Washington, D.C., for information. Pertinent catalogues will be sent on request. Specialized requests for information and help can be sent to the United States Census Bureau. In some cases, the Bureau may even prepare tabulations of data for researchers (at nominal cost).

For information on local registration data, write or visit the nearest county office (the County Clerk). For school data, of course, write or visit the chief administrative officer of the school district or districts in which you are interested. School census and registration data, especially for schools and school districts covering a wide geographic area within a state,

---

[3] See C. Foster, *Editorial Treatment of Education in the American Press.* Cambridge, Mass.: Harvard University Press, 1938, p. 39.

can be obtained from state education departments. Interstate school data and information can be obtained from the Office of Education, United States Department of Health, Education, and Welfare, Washington, D.C.

Data of various kinds on foreign countries can ordinarily be obtained from the consulates and embassies of the countries. (Write the appropriate embassy, Washington, D.C., for information.) A good deal of useful, foreign, educational information can also be obtained from UNESCO. (Write UNESCO, United Nations, New York.) The Institute for International Education is an excellent source of material on foreign education. (Information and Resources Division, New York.)

Newspapers and periodicals, especially the former, have two possible uses in educational research. One, they influence education and educational policy decisions and often reflect the values and attitudes of many citizens. As such, they can be studied and analyzed for their educational content. An educational researcher might wish to know how much accurate information about local education is available in the local press. This is a rich untapped source of data. There seem to be no studies of the undoubtedly important role newspapers play in influencing boards of education and local administrative officers. For example, it would be interesting to know how much accurate and inaccurate reporting of educational matters appears in newspapers. It would be interesting to know the relations between editorial policies and educational decisions. It is highly probable that teachers salaries, bond issues, curriculum policies, and other important educational matters have been profoundly influenced by newspapers and their reporting and editorial policies.

Two, newspapers maintain files that are useful sources of data. Reporters, editors, and publishers themselves are rich repositories of information about educational conditions and issues in their areas. Some newspaper people tend to view things from a larger viewpoint than do other people in a community. Moreover, even when biased, they tend to be more aware of their biases. Thus they can be of considerable assistance to an investigator studying school systems and their problems.

A third largely untapped source of materials of possible use to research are the records and the knowledge of the officers and members of *voluntary associations.* Although there has not been too much research on voluntary associations, there is little doubt of their impact on the thinking of millions of Americans. The most important of these associations are probably the fraternal associations (Masons, Oddfellows), church-affiliated associations (Knights of Columbus, Women's Society for Christian Service), and veterans' associations (Veterans of Foreign Wars, American Legion). Many of these organizations take an active interest in education. Indeed, some of them are active pressure groups. In addition to being interesting and important objects of study in their own right, these groups and their officers often know a great deal about local communities and their educational problems.

From an educational research viewpoint, *school records* are the most important available materials. Pupil records and test scores are useful in their own right, since much can be learned about a school system from a simple statistical compilation and analysis of the quantitative data available. It would seem important, for example, to know the average achievement, intelligence, and aptitude levels of the schools in a district in which one is doing research. It would also seem important to know whether the usual relations exist between the various measures of achievement and ability. If one is working in a school that deviates a good deal in one way or another from other schools, one should at least be aware of it.

School records and data have other uses, however. Sampling was mentioned earlier. When drawing samples of schools, classes, and pupils, the first stop should be the school administrative offices. A well-kept school filing system is an invaluable asset to the educational researcher—if he can gain direct or indirect access to it.[4] If a card for each child exists, it is an easy and routine matter to set the cards up to draw random samples. Class lists are useful for sampling purposes: one can number each class and draw random samples of classes.

A cautionary word is necessary. The records of many schools and school districts are not well kept. And in most cases no thought has been given to the research use of the records. Scores will be missing or inaccurately recorded. (The tests themselves may have been improperly administered and improperly scored. When using test scores from school records, some discreet attempt should be made to determine the quality of the administration and scoring of the tests.) The researcher who wants to use an analysis of variance or to compute a coefficient of correlation will most often find that raw scores or standard scores have not been recorded. Grade-point averages and percentiles are common. In such cases, the researcher must make an effort to obtain the raw scores. The day may come when school records are adequately kept. Meanwhile, investigators must be constantly alert to the possibilities of inaccuracies and to the

---

[4] The whole subject of research-school staff relations is too large a subject to discuss in this book. Besides, there are few set rules. Some advice may be helpful, however. The first person for the investigator to see is the chief administrative officer. If he is understanding and cooperative, half the problem is solved. But many administrators are not cooperative and understanding. In such cases, better abandon the school system—unless you have board of education influence. Next, it is good policy to get board of education approval for the research. The chief administrator can usually get such approval, if he wishes to. Still, it is wise for the investigator to discuss the research directly with the board. Obviously, principals and teachers have to be consulted, too. Planned discussion sessions of representative board members, administrators, and teachers should be arranged if it is possible to do so. In short, the educational investigator, or at least one or more of his colleagues, has to be skilled in social relations. Neglect of this side of research can have unfortunate consequences. On the other hand, successful social relations can yield not only interest and cooperation; they can help the investigator learn a great deal about the school system and the community. See D. Katz, "Field Studies," in L. Festinger and D. Katz, eds., *Research Methods in the Behavioral Sciences*. New York: Holt, Rinehart and Winston, Inc., 1953, pp. 85–89.

fact that school record scores are often not in adequate form for statistical treatment.

The last important type of available data is the *personal document*. Allport, in his study of personal documents, stresses their use to study the needs, motives, and values of individuals.[5] This is similar to the case study. With the aid of content analysis personal documents can also be used to test hypotheses. They are thus considered the same as any other available materials, subject to the same laws and rules. The difficulty with this use of personal documents—or expressive documents, as they have been called—is their relative scarcity. This severely limits sampling possibilities. Adequate samples of expressive materials, however, can be obtained by asking subjects to produce letters, autobiographies, essays, and diaries. But the scientific use of expressive documents, generally speaking, is to help the investigator develop hypotheses and insights.

CONTENT ANALYSIS

Content analysis[6] is a method of studying and analyzing communications in a systematic, objective, and quantitative manner for the purpose of measuring variables.[7] Most content analysis has not been done to measure variables, as such. Rather, it has been used to determine the relative emphasis or frequency of various communication phenomena: propaganda, trends, styles, changes in content, readability. In this chapter content analysis is brought into line as a method of observation and measurement.

It may seem a bit strange that a method of *analysis* is included in Part VII rather than in Part VIII of this book. The reason is that content analysis, while certainly a method of analysis, is more than that. It is, as indicated above, a method of observation. Instead of observing people's behavior directly, or asking them to respond to scales, or interviewing them, the investigator takes the communications that people have produced and asks questions of the communications. There is a logic and economy about so viewing content analysis. In effect, we take it out of the purely methodological or analytic class and put it into the same class as interviews, scales, and other methods of observation. Thus we realize that we are doing nothing essentially different from previous observational activities: we are observing and measuring variables.

5 G. Allport, *The Use of Personal Documents in Psychological Science*. New York: Social Science Research Council, 1942, p. xii.

6 The following discussion leans heavily on Berelson's excellent treatment of the subject: B. Berelson, "Content Analysis." In G. Lindzey, ed., *Handbook of Social Psychology*, vol. I. Cambridge, Mass.: Addison-Wesley, 1954, chap. 13. This is a condensed version of Berelson's book: B. Berelson, *Content Analysis in Communication Research*. New York: Free Press, 1952.

7 Berelson, "Content Analysis," *op. cit.*, p. 489. Although influenced by Berelson, this definition departs considerably from his.

RESEARCH EXAMPLES OF CONTENT ANALYSIS

Most content analyses are simpler than those summarized here (except for the first). But it is very likely that the future use of content analysis will be more complex than it has been, since it will probably be used more and more often to test theories and hypotheses.

Study of Radio Serials   In the simplest forms of content analysis, manifest content categories are set up, and the occurrences of category units are counted. This is well-illustrated by Arnheim's study of the daytime radio serial.[8] Arnheim wanted answers to general questions about soap operas: Do they offer healthy or unhealthy mental food? What sort of social life do they depict? What attitudes do they convey? Studies such as this are basically descriptive: they describe the nature and status of some phenomenon, rather than test relations among variables. Arnheim chose 43 serials at random from those scheduled between 8 A.M. and 6 P.M. during a three-week period. Observers listened to one serial each during the three-week period. The analysis consisted of counting the numbers of serials and settings belonging to categories such as locale of serials, social status of the main characters, kinds of problems (marriage, professional, crime, illness, for instance), moral evaluations, and so on. From the relative frequencies Arnheim drew conclusions, such as, radio serials have a firm grip on American women because they satisfy their psychological needs.

Content analysis is here a simple though laborious affair. The main problem is to set up a workable category system. Then trained coders assign persons and actions to the categories. The results are reported in frequencies or percentages. Little or no attempt is made to relate one variable to another. Propaganda analysis follows this simple formula. The messages of the propagandist—foreign country, the press, radio, television—are categorized and counted according to purpose, appeal, effect, devices, and so on.

Kounin and Gump Study   One of the few educational studies to use content analysis is Kounin and Gump's[9] interesting and important study of the effect of punitive and nonpunitive teachers on children's perceptions of misconduct. Three pairs of punitive and nonpunitive teachers were selected from three schools by agreement among raters. Other differences were controlled. Punitiveness-Nonpunitiveness was the independent variable. Individual interviews were held with the 174 first-grade children of these six teachers. The interviews and the content coding were structured

---

[8] R. Arnheim, "The World of the Daytime Serial." In P. Lazarsfeld and F. Stanton, eds., *Radio Research 1942–43*. New York: Duell, Sloan & Pearce, 1944, pp. 34–85.

[9] J. Kounin and P. Gump, "The Comparative Influence of Punitive and Nonpunitive Teachers upon Children's Concepts of School Misconduct," *Journal of Educational Psychology*, LII (1961), 44–49.

around the question, "What is the worst thing a child can do at school?" After a child replied, he was asked, "Why is that so bad?"

The content of the replies to the questions were analyzed by means of a rather complex code consisting of five major categories with subcategories in all but one of them. Table 30.1 is an abbreviated version of Kounin and Gump's summary table of results.[10] It shows three of the major categories with five of the subcategories. The particular items selected illustrate both the category system and the results. The relations between *punitiveness of teacher* and *perception of misconduct* are clearly demonstrated.

TABLE **30.1**   SOME RESULTS OF KOUNIN AND GUMP STUDY [a]

Misconducts and Explanations	Percent *Pu*	Percent *NPu*
I. Content and quality of misconducts		
A. Physical assaults on others	38	17
D. Abstract misconducts	27	52
II. Content and quality of explanations		
C. Serious harm to others	45	18
D. Reality-centered retributions	21	48
V. Concern with school-unique objectives		
A. Learning and achievement losses	20	43

[a] *Pu:* children who have punitive teachers; *NPu:* children who have nonpunitive teachers. $N = 174$. All differences are significant at the .05 level or beyond.

This study is a good example of the use of content analysis to test research hypotheses. The first of four hypotheses, for example, said that the school misconduct preoccupations of children with punitive teachers would contain more aggression than the misconduct preoccupations of children with nonpunitive teachers. Inspection of Table 30.1 shows that this hypothesis was confirmed. The study is also a good example of choosing methods to fit research purposes. Kounin and Gump reasoned that children would not give the same answers to interview questions that they would to forced-choice questions. And they had to know the misconducts with which the children were preoccupied. The interviews and content analysis naturally followed from this reasoning.

A Content Analysis of Children's Textbooks[11]   Children's books have often been studied and analyzed in the past hundred years. But only recently has content analysis been applied to the task. Earlier types of analysis were qualitative and relatively nonobjective. Some years ago, the writer

---

[10] *Ibid.,* p. 47.

[11] I. Child, E. Potter, and E. Levine, "Children's Textbooks and Personality Development: An Exploration in the Social Psychology of Education," *Psychological Monographs,* LX (1960), No. 3.

collected a large number of Japanese morals (*Shūshin*) textbooks and "analyzed" them.[12] The analysis consisted of the careful reading of selections thought to be particularly moralistic (in the Japanese sense). Conclusions were drawn from this somewhat impressionistic and certainly subjective approach. We now examine a more objective approach to children's textbooks.

Child and his colleagues analyzed third-grade textbooks for content that presumably influenced children's personalities. This was a descriptive study. Hypothesized relations were not tested, though hypothesis testing was implied. Our concern here is solely with the method.

First, all third-grade readers published since 1930 were obtained. There were 30 of them. Second, stories were selected on the basis of their containing characters in action. More than three-quarters of the contents of the 30 books, a total of 914 stories, were analyzed. Third, the unit chosen for analysis was the *thema*. A *thema* is a sequence of events that consists of a situation confronting a person, the response behavior, and the consequences of the behavior as perceived by the person himself. There were 3409 thema, an average of about 4 per story.

Fourth, a category system was set up. The general schema included *characters, behavior, circumstances, consequences,* and *type of story.* These general categories were broken down in a complex manner into subcategories. *Behavior,* for example, was broken down into a large number of needs. *Consequences of behavior* was broken down into *reward, punishment,* and *no consequence.*

Finally, each story was read and, if suitable, all the thema in the story fitting the analysis system were identified, counted, and entered under appropriate categories and subcategories. The results were then interpreted.

This study, while at a lower scientific level than the Kounin and Gump study, points the way to significant scientific study of material previously accessible only to relatively subjective critical study. The methodology is probably too complex to be as useful as it might be (it was overloaded by the needs system used). But the application of a highly objective and simple quantitative system applied to the extremely important field of children's educational materials certainly opens up wide and significant areas of research.

SOME ASPECTS OF METHOD IN CONTENT ANALYSIS

Content analysis, it is clear, can be applied to available materials and to materials especially produced for the particular research purpose.

[12] F. Kerlinger, "The Modern Origin of Morals Instruction in Japan," *History of Education Journal,* II (1951), 119–126.

One can content-analyze letters, diaries, ethnographic materials, newspaper articles, minutes of meetings, and so on. One can also ask children to write autobiographies, stories, or short essays. These products can then be content-analyzed. The possibilities are many. But how is content analysis done? A brief introduction to the subject is given below. The student who intends to use content analysis in actual research, however, should consult Berelson's book, which was cited earlier.

Definition and Categorization of Universe　The first step, as usual, is to define U, the universe of content that is to be analyzed. Kounin and Gump's U was all replies to the question on misconduct, or simply breaches of good behavior as perceived by the children. Then U was partitioned into five major categories and a number of subcategories. (See Table 30.1.)

In the study of children's textbooks summarized earlier, U was all the thema in a specified subset of third-grade textbooks. The categories were *character, behavior, circumstances, consequences,* and *type of story.* A large number of subcategories were also specified.

Categorization, or the partitioning of U, is perhaps the most important part of content analysis. It is most important because it is a direct reflection of the theory and the problem of any study. It spells out, in effect, the variables of the hypotheses. One of Kounin and Gump's main hypotheses was that *teacher punitiveness* is related to children's *perceptions of misconduct.* The dependent variable, children's *perceptions of misconduct,* was U. To test the basic hypothesis, however, U had to be partitioned into *kinds* of misconduct so that *teacher punitiveness* could be related to it. Study Table 30.1 and note some of the categories of U (verbal part of table) and how the categories are juxtaposed against the punitive and nonpunitive categories. For instance, the subcategories "Serious harm to others" and "Reality-centered retributions" are juxtaposed against "Percent Pu" and "Percent NPu." (We study such juxtaposition, or crossbreaks, in a later chapter.) A great deal of thought, work, and care must go into this first step.

Units of Analysis　Berelson lists five major units of analysis: words, themes, characters, items, and space-and-time measures.[13] The *word* is the smallest unit. Although not likely to be used too much, it may be useful in some educational research studies. An investigator might be studying value words in the writings of high school students. For some reason, he might wish to know the relation between sex or political preference of parents, or their religion, on the one hand, and the use of value words, on the other hand. The word unit may also be useful in studies of reading, because it is an easy unit to work with. U can ordinarily be clearly defined and categorized, for example, value words and nonvalue words; diffi-

---

[13] Berelson, *op. cit.*, pp. 508, 509.

cult, medium, and easy words. Then words can simply be counted—tedious, but easy.

The *theme* is a very useful though much more difficult unit. A *theme* is often a sentence, a proposition about something. Themes are combined into sets of themes. The letters of adolescents or college students may be studied for statements of *self-reference*. This would be the larger theme. The themes making this up might be defined as any sentences that use "I," "me," and other words indicating reference to the writer's self. *Discipline* is an interesting larger theme. *Child training* or *control* is another. Many observers take field notes in a thematic manner. Here is an example from the field notes of an observer in a small village in Japan:

> *Food-Training:* . . . Use cajolery in this family—but it varies. Parents will leave something disliked (if child should be obstreperous about it) out of child's diet.[14]
>
> Informant's first child was fed whenever he cried, and the second child was started out that way; but after one month, informant fed second child on schedule . . .[15]

It should be emphasized, as Berelson does, that if the themes are complex, content analysis using the theme as the unit of analysis is difficult and perhaps unreliable.[16] Yet it is an important and useful unit because it is ordinarily realistic and close to the original content.

Character and *space-and-time* measures are probably not too useful in educational research. The first is simply an individual in a literary production. We might use it in analyzing children's stories. The second is the actual physical measurement of content: number of inches of space, number of pages, number of paragraphs, number of minutes of discussion, and so on.

Like the theme, the *item* unit is important. The *item* is a whole production: an essay, a news story, a radio talk, a television program, a class recitation or discussion. In the last chapter, we examined Getzels and Jackson's use of autobiographies to measure creativity. The unit was the item, the whole autobiography. Each autobiography was judged either "creative" or "noncreative." Children can be asked to write projective stories in response to a picture. The whole story of each child can be the unit of analysis. Judges can be trained to use a rating scale to assess the creativity of the stories. Or judges can be trained to assign each story to a creative or noncreative category.

It is likely that the item as a unit of analysis will be particularly use-

---

[14] Center for Japanese Studies, University of Michigan, Okayama Field Station, *863, Niiike,* August 25, 1950 (GB). ("*863*" is the Yale field number; "*Niiike*" is the Japanese village; "GB" is the observer.)

[15] CFJS, UM, OFS, *853, Takashima,* Dec. 18, 1950 (MFN).

[16] Berelson, *op. cit.,* p. 508.

ful in behavioral research. As long as pertinent criteria for categorizing a variable can be defined, and as long as judges can agree substantially in their ratings, rankings, or assignments, then the item unit is profitable to use. But careful checks on reliability and validity must be made. Judges can wander from the criteria, and they can lose themselves in the masses of reading they must do. Yet it is surprising how much agreement can be reached, even for rather complex material. The writer and a student assistant have content-analyzed student essays to measure attitudes toward education. The *items,* that is, the whole essays, were the units. The agreement coefficients (r's) were about .60. Though not high, these coefficients are promising. In judging the creativity of student essays, teacher judges in the Hartsdale, New York, public school system achieved agreement coefficients of .70 to .80. Here, again, the whole essays were the units.

Quantification   All materials are potentially quantifiable. We can even rank the sonnets of Shakespeare or the last five piano sonatas of Beethoven in the order of our personal preferences, if nothing else. It is true that some materials are not as amenable to quantification as certain other materials. After all, it is much easier to assign numbers to children corresponding to their knowledge of spelling than it is to assign numbers to the original thinking or creativity of the same children. This does not mean, however, that no numbers can be legitimately assigned to children's products on the variables originality and creativity. It is not easy, but it can be done. How well it can be done is of course another matter.

There are three or more ways to assign numbers to the objects of the content analysis *U*. The first and most common of these corresponds to nominal measurement: count the number of objects in each category after assigning each object to its proper category. If we are reading reports of field observers, and we come to a passage, ". . . babies are breast fed until two years of age, then gradually weaned to rice and gruel." [17] This theme might be assigned to the category "Permissive" or the category "Late Weaning." Then, in going through the observer's notes, we assign similar passages to these categories. The quantification would simply be the counting of the number of themes in each of the categories.

A second form of quantification is *ranking,* or ordinal measurement. If one is working with not too many objects to be ranked—say not more than 30—judges can be asked to rank them according to a specified criterion. Assume that the relations between religiosity and other variables are being studied, and subjects are asked to write on the subject "What I Believe." Judges might be asked to rank the essays on the degree of religious belief. If a large number of essays are involved, they can still be ranked, but a more manageable system than total ranking can be used, for example, 10 or 11 ranks can be made available, and judges can assign the essays to the ranks in the Thurstone scale manner.

[17] CFJS, UM, OFS, *853, Niiike,* Aug. 25, 1950.

A third form of quantification is *rating*. Children's compositions, for example, can be rated as wholes for degrees of creativity, originality, inner-direction and other-direction, achievement orientation, interests, values, and other variables. Rating scales were discussed in Chap. 28. Their application to content analysis needs no new discussion.

Certain conditions have to be met before quantification is justified or worthwhile. Berelson has spelled out these conditions.[18] Two of his seven conditions should be noted: (1) to count carefully (or otherwise quantify) when the materials to be analyzed are representative, and (2) to count carefully when the category items appear in the materials in sufficient numbers to justify counting (or otherwise quantifying). The reason for both conditions is obvious: if the materials are not representative or if the category items are relatively infrequent, generalization from statistics computed from them is unwarranted.

The answer to these two and other conditions, then, is to so select materials or to so have materials produced that quantification is possible and necessary. If materials cannot meet the criteria, they can be used only for heuristic and suggestive purposes and not for the scientific purpose of relating variables to each other.

USE OF CONTENT ANALYSIS AND AVAILABLE MATERIALS IN PSYCHOLOGICAL AND EDUCATIONAL RESEARCH

In a new approach to an old subject, it is particularly appropriate that examples instead of explanations be used. Instead of an abstract discussion, then, uses of content analysis and available materials will be suggested. The suggestions apply mostly to content analysis, though available materials are not ignored.

A large number and variety of psychological variables can be measured through content analysis: needs, values, attitudes, stereotypes, authoritarianism, ethnocentrism, creativity, and so on. Content analysis is appropriate, however, only when other methods of measuring the same variables are inappropriate or impossible. If one were studying ethnocentrism, for instance, in veterans' associations, an attitude scale might be resisted. But association members would probably not object to being interviewed. Further, interview protocols can be content-analyzed. (Appropriate projective-type questions designed to elicit ethnocentric responses can be included in the interview schedule.)

Education has suffered from a lack of analysis of the educational information people absorb from the press and other media of public communication. Educational news articles, editorials, and special features might well be content-analyzed. (This use was mentioned earlier.)

The study of values with ordinary methods of measurement is difficult in part because social desirability and social acquiescence play so

[18] Berelson, *op. cit.*, pp. 512–514.

large a part in the measurement. But subjects, especially children, can be asked to produce verbal materials on specified topics, and the materials can be content-analyzed for expressed values.[19] This is a singularly neglected area of research. The reason, presumably, is that values, by their very nature, are taken for granted. At any rate, here is a large unplumbed area of possible research in which content analysis can play an important part.

In some educational experiments it may be possible to use content analysis to assess the effects of experimental treatments on dependent variables. For example, is it possible to stimulate the creativity of school children? How much does writing practice help students to write essays? Content analysis can help obtain answers to such questions.

Content analysis can be used to validate other methods of observation and measurement. A scale to measure, say, attitudes toward Jews is hard to validate because there are few external criteria against which to check it. Most people, moreover, know they should not be anti-Semitic. They thus give responses that may not be indices of their true attitudes. But projective-type questions can be asked of subjects, and the responses content-analyzed for their attitudes toward Jews. It is not easy to conceal anti-Semitism if one has to write a short essay on Jews.

Available materials and materials manufactured by request have an extremely valuable use that is often overlooked: as sources of items for objective tests and scales and interview schedules. If one is constructing a scale to measure educational values, for instance, there are vast resources for item construction available: newspaper editorials on education, magazine articles, organizational and institutional propaganda (for example, church and voluntary association literature on education and literature of educational pressure groups), books on education (especially on philosophy of education), speeches of public figures. One of the main difficulties for the investigator is to cut his way through the morass of pious sentiments to the hard core of the value matter. Though

---

[19] For a values content analysis suggestion, see R. White, *Value-Analysis: The Nature and Use of the Method,* Society for the Psychological Study of Social Issues, 1951. Some features of White's method are excellent; others are not too desirable. While he has touched upon most of the values of man, his system is fundamentally a priori. Furthermore, it is very complicated, though he does suggest that it can be cut down for specific purposes (p. 69). A great deal of research clearly needs to be done on values, their measurement, and their interrelations. As far as the role of content analysis in values research is concerned, the reader can profit from deCharms and Moeller's provocative study of the values and motives expressed in 150 years of children's readers: R. deCharms and G. Moeller, "Values Expressed in American Children's Readers: 1800–1950," *Journal of Abnormal and Social Psychology,* LXIV (1962), 136–142. These authors tested, among other things, the engaging hypothesis that *achievement motivation* is related to *inventiveness* as expressed by the number of patents issued. The coefficients of correlation between these variables was .79 in one sample of readers and .68 in a check sample. The authors also drew two entirely independent and different samples from their materials. The results are a remarkable demonstration of the power of sampling.

it seems not to have been so used, content analysis can be put to work to analyze such materials.

Other uses suggest themselves, of course. For instance, irrational and illogical thinking on educational matters and matters related to education—financing schools by bond issues at substantial rates of interest, religious manifestations in public schools, transportation for school children, school budgets, teachers salaries, curriculum changes—can all be content-analyzed. In fact, content analysis would seem to be the only method of analyzing materials on such subjects.

Content analysis and available materials, however, should not be used indiscriminately. Content analysis is laborious, time-consuming, and expensive. It should be used when the nature of a research problem is such as to require it. It should not be used when an easier method is available and appropriate. Although it can be used to measure achievement motivation, it cannot be used to measure achievement (except, perhaps, written composition). While it can be used to measure attitudes, there are usually better and easier ways to do so. Similarly for available materials. If one can deliberately select, sample, or produce one's own materials, so much the better. Frequently, however, one cannot. So available materials must be used.

In conclusion, then, judgment, circumspection, and careful thought are needed to decide whether the research problem requires or can profit from available materials and content analysis. As Berelson says, at the end of his fine presentation of content analysis:

> Unless there is a sensible, or clever, or sound, or revealing, or unusual, or important notion underlying the analysis, it is not worth going through the rigor of the procedure, especially when it is so arduous and so costly of effort.[20]

[20] Berelson, *op. cit.,* p. 518.

31 *SOCIOMETRY*

SOCIOMETRY: A DEFINITION

Sociometry is a broad term indicating a number of methods of gathering and analyzing data on the choice, communication, and interaction patterns of people in groups. One might say that sociometry is the study and measurement of social choice. It has also been called a means of studying the attractions and repulsions of members of groups.

Sociometric methods are based on *choice*. One person is asked to choose one or more other persons according to one or more criteria supplied by the researcher. The group member is asked: With whom would you like to work? With whom would you like to play? Whom would you like to work with you on this project? He then makes one, two, three, or more choices among the members of his own (usually) or of other groups. What could be simpler and more natural? People choose each other all their lives. Now the researcher simply asks them to make choices for specific research purposes. The method works equally well for kindergartners and for atomic scientists.

Types of Sociometric Choice As indicated above, the most essential ingredient of sociometric methods is choice. But choice should be rather broadly understood: it not only means "choice of people"; it may mean "choice of lines of communication," or "choice of lines of influence," or "choice of minority groups." The choices made depend upon the instructions and questions given to individuals. Here is a list of sociometric questions and instructions:

1. With whom would you like to work (play, sit next to, and so on)?
2. Who are your three best friends?
3. Which two members of this group (age group, class, school, club, for instance) do you like the most (like the least)?
4. Choose a partner with whom to work on this problem.
5. Who are the three best (worst) pupils in your class?
6. What two students would you pick to room with you?

7. Who should lead the group in this project?
8. Whom would you choose to represent you on a committee to improve faculty welfare?
9. What four individuals have the greatest prestige in your school (class, company, team)?
10. What two groups of people are the most acceptable (least acceptable) to you as neighbors (friends, business associates, professional associates)?

There are obviously many possibilities of choice questions.[1] In addition, these can all be multiplied simply by asking: Whom do you think would choose you to . . . ? and Whom do you think the group will choose to . . . ? Subjects can be asked to rank others on the criteria, providing there are not too many others to rank. Or rating scales can be used. We might ask the pupils of a class to rate each other class member using one or more types of choice. For example, we could phrase the sociometric instructions something like this: "Here is a list of the members of your class. Rate each of them according to whether you would like to work with them on homework. Use the numbers 3, 2, 1, 0, −1, −2,−3. The number 3 means you want to work with an individual *very much*. The number −3 means you would *dislike very much* working with him. The number 0 means that you do not care one way or the other. The other numbers, of course, express intermediate degrees of liking and disliking."

METHODS OF SOCIOMETRIC ANALYSIS

It is characteristic of most newer methods that their data-gathering and analytic aspects are intimately related. That is, one cannot properly understand the methods unless one also understands the methods used to analyze the data. Sociometry is probably the simplest method there is for gathering data. It also yields very simple scores—basically 1's and 0's. Yet sociometry has attracted mathematical (and some statistical) analysis of a high level of sophistication.

There are three forms of sociometric analysis: *sociometric matrices, sociograms,* and *sociometric indices.* Of all methods of sociometric analysis, *sociometric matrices,* to be defined presently, perhaps contain the most

[1] For further discussion, see N. Gronlund, *Sociometry in the Classroom.* New York: Harper & Row, 1959, chap. 2. This is an elementary reference. A reference for the researcher is: G. Lindzey and E. Borgatta, "Sociometric Measurement." In G. Lindzey, ed., *Handbook of Social Psychology,* vol. I. Cambridge, Mass.: Addison-Wesley, 1954, chap. 11. A useful technical reference is: C. Proctor and C. Loomis, "Analysis of Sociometric Data." In M. Jahoda, M. Deutsch, and S. Cook, *Research Methods in Social Relations,* part two. New York: Holt, Rinehart and Winston, Inc., 1951, chap. 17. Important technical articles can also be found in: J. Moreno, *et al., The Sociometry Reader.* New York: Free Press, 1960.

important possibilities and implications for the behavioral researcher. *Sociograms* are diagrams or charts of the choices made in groups. We shall discuss sociograms very little, since they are used more frequently for practical than for research purposes.[2] *Sociometric indices* are single numbers calculated from two or more numbers yielded by sociometric data. They indicate sociometric characteristics of individuals and groups. As such they are very useful in research.

Sociometric Matrices   We learned some time ago that a *matrix* was a rectangular array of numbers or other symbols. In sociometry we are concerned only with square, or $n \times n$ matrices, n being equal to the number of persons in a group. Rows of the matrix are labeled i; columns are labeled j; i and j, of course, can stand for any number and any person in the group. If we write a_{ij}, this means the entry in the ith row and jth column of the matrix, or, more simply, any entry in the matrix. It is convenient to write *sociometric matrices*. These are matrices of numbers expressing all the choices of group members in any group.

Suppose a group of five members has responded to the sociometric question, "With whom would you like to work on such-and-such a project during the next two months? Choose two individuals." The responses to the sociometric question are, of course, *choices*. If a group member chooses another group member, the choice is represented by 1. If a group member does not choose another, the lack of choice is represented by 0. (If rejection had been called for, -1 could have been used.) The sociometric matrix of choices, C, of this hypothetical group situation is given in Table 31.1.

TABLE 31.1   SOCIOMETRIC CHOICE MATRIX: FIVE-MEMBER GROUP, TWO-CHOICE QUESTION [a]

		j				
		a	b	c	d	e
	a	0	1	0	0	1
	b	1	0	0	0	1
i	c	0	0	0	1	1
	d	0	1	0	0	1
	e	1	1	0	0	0
	Σ:	2	3	0	1	4

C

[a] Individual i *chooses* individual j. That is, the table can be read by rows: b chooses a and e. It can also be read by columns: b *is chosen* by a, d, and e. The sums at the bottom indicate the number of choices each individual receives.

2 See W. Smith, *Manual of Sociometry for Teachers*. Ann Arbor: Child Development Laboratories, University of Michigan, 1951. Also M. Northway, *A Primer of Sociometry*. Toronto: University of Toronto Press, 1952; Gronlund, *op. cit.*, pp. 68–78.

It is possible to analyze C in a number of ways. But first let us be sure we know how to read the matrix. It is probably easier to read from left to right, from i to j. Member i chooses (or does not choose) member j. For example, a chooses b and e; c chooses d and e. Sometimes it is convenient to speak passively, "b was chosen by a, d, and e," or "c was chosen by no one."

The analysis of a matrix usually begins by studying it to see who chose whom. With a simple matrix like C this is easy. There are three kinds of choice: *simple* or one-way, *mutual* or two-way, and *no choice*. We look first at simple choices. (This was discussed in the preceding paragraph.) A *simple* one-way choice is where i chooses j, but j does not choose i. In Table 31.1, c chose d, but d did not choose c. We write: $i \rightarrow j$, or $c \rightarrow d$. A *mutual* choice is where i chooses j and j also chooses i. In the table, a chose b and b chose a. We write: $i \leftrightarrow j$, or $a \leftrightarrow b$. We might count mutual choices in Table 31.1: $a \leftrightarrow b$, $a \leftrightarrow e$, $b \leftrightarrow e$. Mutual choices are important because they can give us information about group relations and group structure.

The extent to which any member is chosen is easily seen by adding the columns of the matrix. Obviously, e is "popular": he was chosen by all the other group members; a and b received 2 and 3 choices, respectively. Evidently c is not at all popular: no one chose him; d is not popular either: he received only 1 choice. If individuals are allowed unlimited choices, that is, if they are instructed to choose any number of other individuals, then the row sums take on meaning.[3] We might call these sums indices of, say, *gregariousness*.

There are other methods of matrix analysis that are potentially useful to researchers. For example, by relatively simple matrix operations one can determine cliques and chains of influence in small and large groups. These matters, however, are beyond the scope of this book.[4]

Sociograms or Directed Graphs The simplest analyses are like those just discussed. But with a matrix larger than C it is almost impossible to digest the complexities of the choice relations. Here *sociograms* are helpful, provided the group is not too large. We now change the name "sociogram" to "directed graph." This is a more general mathematical term that can be applied to any situation in which i and j are in some relation R. Instead of saying "i chooses j," it is quite possible to say "i influences j," or "i communicates to j," or "i is a friend of j," or "i dominates j." In symbolic shorthand, we can write, generally: iRj. Specifically, we can write for

[3] Subjects can be told to choose one, two, three, or more other persons. Three seems to be a common number of choices to allow. The number allowed should be dictated by the research purposes. See Gronlund, *op. cit.*, pp. 48, 49; Lindzey and Borgatta, *op. cit.*, p. 408.

[4] See *ibid.*, pp. 416–419, and the references cited. A good explanation of elementary matrix operations and sociometric matrices can be found in: J. Kemeny, J. Snell, and G. Thompson, *Introduction to Finite Mathematics*. Englewood Cliffs, N.J.: Prentice-Hall, 1956, pp. 198–201, 307–320.

the examples just given: *iCj* (*i* chooses *j*), *iIj* (*i* influences *j*), *iCj* (*i* communicates to *j*), *iFj* (*i* is a friend of *j*), *iDj* (*i* dominates *j*). Any of these interpretations can be depicted by a matrix such as *C* and by a directed graph. A directed graph of *C* is given in Fig. 31.1.

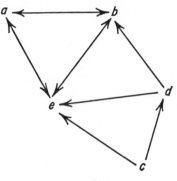

FIG. 31.1

We see at a glance that *e* is the center of choice. We might call him a leader. Or we might call him either a likable or a competent person. More important, notice that *a, b,* and *e* choose each other. This is a *clique*. Following Festinger, Schachter, and Back, we define a *clique* as three or more individuals who mutually choose each other.[5] Looking for more double-headed arrows, we find none. Now we might look for individuals with no arrowheads pointing at them: *c* is one such individual. We might say that *c* is not chosen or neglected.

Note that directed graphs and matrices say the same thing. We look at the number of choices *a* receives by adding the 1's in the *a* column of the matrix. We get the same information by adding the number of arrowheads pointing at *a* in the graph. For small and medium-size groups and for descriptive purposes, graphs are excellent means of summarizing group relations. For larger groups (larger than 20 members?) and more analytic purposes, they are not as suitable. They become difficult to construct and difficult to interpret. Moreover, different individuals can draw different graphs with the same data. Matrices are general, and, if handled properly, not too difficult to interpret. Different individuals must, with the same data, write exactly the same matrices.

Sociometric Indices[6] In sociometry, a large number of indices are possible. Three or four are given below. The student will find others in the literature.

5 L. Festinger, S. Schachter, and K. Back, *Social Pressures in Informal Groups.* New York: Harper & Row, 1950, p. 144.
6 The discussion that follows is for the most part based on Proctor and Loomis, *op. cit.* Some of the symbols are the author's.

A simple but useful index is

$$CS_j = \frac{\Sigma c_j}{n-1} \tag{31.1}$$

where $CS_j =$ the choice status of Person j; $\Sigma c_j =$ the sum of choices in Column j; and $n =$ the number of individuals in the group ($n - 1$ is used because one cannot count the individual himself). For C of Table 31.1, $CS_e = 4/4 = 1.00$ and $CS_a = 2/4 = .50$. How well or how poorly chosen an individual is is revealed by CS. It is, in short, his *choice status*. It is of course possible to have a choice rejection index. Simply put the number of 0's in any column in the numerator of Eq. 31.1.

Group sociometric measures are perhaps more interesting. If group members are free to choose as many other persons as they wish, then a measure of *group expansiveness, E*, as Proctor and Loomis call it, is

$$E = \frac{\Sigma c_{ij}}{n} \tag{31.2}$$

where $E =$ Expansiveness and $\Sigma c_{ij} =$ the sum of all the choices made by all group members. Here E is not applicable to C, since individuals were permitted only two choices.

A measure of the cohesiveness of a group is

$$Co = \frac{\Sigma(i \leftrightarrow j)}{\frac{n(n-1)}{2}} \tag{31.3}$$

Group cohesiveness is represented by Co and $\Sigma(i \leftrightarrow j) =$ sum of mutual choices (or mutual pairs).

This index is the proportion of mutual choices to the total number of possible pairs. In a five-member group, the total number of possible pairs is 5 things taken 2 at a time:

$$\binom{5}{2} = \frac{5(5-1)}{2} = 10$$

If, in an unlimited choice situation, there were 2 mutual choices, then $Co = 2/10 = .20$, a rather low degree of cohesiveness. In the case of limited choice, the formula is

$$Co = \frac{\Sigma(i \leftrightarrow j)}{dn/2} \tag{31.4}$$

where $d =$ the number of choices each individual is permitted. For C of Table 31.1, $Co = 3/(2 \times 5/2) = 3/5 = .60$, a substantial degree of cohesiveness.

There are other interesting and useful indices, some with mathematical and statistical justification, and some with none. One of the former, by Katz and Powell, is an index of conformity.[7] Though not hard to compute, its explanation is too lengthy to present here.

SOME RESEARCH APPLICATIONS OF SOCIOMETRY

Because the data of sociometry seem so different from other kinds of data, students find it difficult to think of sociometric measurement as measurement. There is no doubt that sociometric data are different. But they are the result of observation, *and they are measures.*[8] They are useful, for example, in classifying individuals and groups. In the Bennington College Study, summarized in Chap. 21, Newcomb measured individual prestige by asking students to name five students they would choose as most worthy to represent Bennington College at an important gathering of students from all types of American colleges.[9] He then grouped students by frequency of choice and related this measure of *sociometric prestige* to *political and economic progressivism.*

In another study, Newcomb ingeniously measured *general liking* (of one group member by another), or *attraction,* by having his subjects rank-order, according to degree of liking, 17 cards, on each of which was another subject's name. He also used a rating scale to accomplish much the same purpose with the same subjects a year later.[10] Liking, or attraction, was then related to other variables.

Gronlund studied the relation between the sociometric status of pupils and their teachers' preferences for having them in class.[11] A unique feature of this study was the sociometric nature of both independent and dependent variables. Gronlund asked the pupils of 40 sixth-grade classes to choose 5 classmates on the basis of work, play, and seating criteria. The responses were classified into High Average, Low Average, and Isolates and Neglectees. Teachers were asked to choose the three boys and the three girls they most preferred as pupils in class and the three boys and three girls they least preferred as pupils in class. To show in part how Gronlund analyzed the responses, part of his data on boys is given in Table 31.2 (The table should be read as follows: 56 percent of the pupils

7 L. Katz and J. Powell, "A Proposed Index of the Conformity of One Sociometric Measurement to Another." In Moreno, *op. cit.,* pp. 298–306. (Katz has been a creative pioneer in the application of mathematics to sociometry.)

8 For a discussion of the reliability and validity of sociometric measures, see Lindzey and Borgatta, *op. cit.,* pp. 420–424. See, also, Gronlund, *op. cit.,* chaps. 5 and 6.

9 T. Newcomb, *Personality and Social Change.* New York: Holt, Rinehart and Winston, Inc., 1943, pp. 54, 55.

10 T. Newcomb, *The Acquaintance Process.* New York: Holt, Rinehart and Winston, Inc., 1961, pp. 32, 33. Newcomb also had his subjects assign themselves to groups. These assignments were tabulated in a matrix, and an index of attraction of one person for another was then calculated. See pp. 34, 35.

11 N. Gronlund, "Relationship between the Sociometric Status of Pupils and Teachers' Preferences For or Against Having Them in Class," *Sociometry,* XVI (1953), 142–150.

who were not chosen by other pupils were nominated by teachers as least preferred, and so on.)

TABLE **31.2** GRONLUND DATA ON RELATION BETWEEN PUPIL AND
TEACHER SOCIOMETRIC CHOICES. (IN PERCENT)

		Pupil Choice		
		High Average	Low Average	Isolates-Neglectees
Teacher Choice	Most Preferred	23	19	11
	Least Preferred	13	28	56

Most sociometric studies have been ex post facto in nature. Some few have been experimental. One of these is Flanders and Havumaki's competent study of the effects of praise on sociometric choices.[12] Here a sociometric choice was used to measure the dependent variable. The authors' hypothesis was that praise of a student by a prestige figure would increase the student's "choice value." Tenth-grade pupils were divided into 33 groups of 10 subjects each. In 17 of the groups certain individuals were praised for their contributions to discussions about quiz program participation. In the other 16 groups, the subjects were not praised individually; the groups were handled as groups. After the experimental manipulation, the group members were asked to list five members of their groups who would be good quiz program participants. These choices constituted a measure of the dependent variable.

SOCIOMETRIC MEASUREMENT IN SOCIAL SCIENTIFIC AND EDUCATIONAL RESEARCH

Sociometry is a simple, economical, and naturalistic method of observation and data collection. Whenever such human actions as choosing, influencing, dominating, and communicating in group situations are involved, sociometric methods can usually be used. Sociometry also has the virtue of considerable flexibility. If it is defined broadly, it can be adapted to a wide variety of research. Its quantification possibilities, too, are rewarding. The simple assignment of 1's and 0's is probably used most often. Such assignment is particularly fortunate because powerful mathematical tools can be applied to the data, matrix methods being the outstanding example. But rank-order and rating methods can also be used to yield quantified sociometric data.

12 N. Flanders and S. Havumaki, "The Effect of Teacher-Pupil Contacts Involving Praise on the Sociometric Choices of Students," *Journal of Educational Psychology*, LI (1960), 65–68.

The research weaknesses of sociometry lie in the individuals who have used sociometry. As Lindzey and Borgatta point out, there is a scarcity of systematic theoretical investigation. They also point out the inadequate attention paid to sociometric criteria and the inadequate treatment of sociometric data.[13] The greatest weakness, however, is a weakness we have encountered before, particularly with projective methods. Many users of sociometric measures have relied upon them too much, have accepted rather than tested their reliability and validity, and have endowed sociometry with almost mystical qualities. This has been particularly true of practical applications of the method, but some of it has spilled over into its research use.

Sociometry, then, has considerable potential usefulness as one important approach to the observation and measurement of variables. The student who contemplates using the method, however, should study its rationale, its statistical limitations, and its possibilities of mathematical analysis. Some sources for such study are given in the study suggestions that follow. The student should also be aware that he can use criteria other than those of simple choice based on liking to work with, liking to play with, friendship, and so on. To repeat, whenever a conceptual arrow from one person to another person, or to a symbolic representation of another person, can be drawn—the arrow indicating "communicates with," "interacts with," "influences," "dominates," "leads," "accepts," "likes," "is friendly to," "perceives as good," "is like me," and so on— sociometric methods can be used and often should be used.

STUDY SUGGESTIONS

1. Four useful elementary references on sociometry have already been cited: Gronlund's book, Lindzey and Borgatta's chapter, and the Smith and Northway manuals. The more advanced student will find the following references stimulating:

> Bush, R., R. Abelson, and R. Hyman. *Mathematics for Psychologists: Examples and Problems.* New York: Social Science Research Council, 1956. This book contains a fine collection of examples of the applications of mathematics to psychological research problems, including a number of sociometric examples. (See pp. 27, 28, 29, 40, 42, 43.) Some background is required.

> Glanzer, M., and R. Glaser. "Techniques for the Study of Group Structure and Behavior: I. Analysis of Structure." *Psychological Bulletin,* LVI (1959), 317–332. An invaluable reference for readers with prior knowledge of the subject, this article reviews many sociometric indices, matrix operations, and so on.

13 Lindzey and Borgatta, *op. cit.,* pp. 442–444.

2. Let C mean "communicates with." In a four-man group, aCc, bCa, cCa, and dCb.
   (a) Write the matrix expressing these relations.
   (b) Draw a directed graph of the situation. Who would be likely to receive most communications?
   (c) Are there mutual choices? What are they?
   (d) A relation was earlier defined as a set of ordered pairs. Can the present situation be called a relation?

3. An investigator, studying the influence patterns of boards of education, obtained the following matrix from one board of education. (Note that this is like an unlimited choice situation because each individual can influence all or none of the members of the group.) Read the matrix: i influences j.

		j				
		a	b	c	d	e
	a	0	0	1	1	0
	b	0	0	0	0	1
i	c	1	0	0	1	0
	d	1	0	1	0	0
	e	0	1	0	0	0

   (a) What conclusions can you reach from study of this matrix? Is the board divided? Is there likely to be conflict?
   (b) Draw a graph of the influence situation. Interpret the graph.
   (c) Is there a clique on the board? (Define clique as given in the text.) If so, who are its members?
   (d) What members have the least number of influence channels? Are they, then, much less influential than the other members, other things being equal?
   (*Answers:* (c) Yes: a, c, d; (d) b and e.)

4. For the situation in Study Suggestion 3, calculate the cohesiveness of the group using Eq. 31.3.
   (*Answer:* $Co = .30$.)

32 *THE SEMANTIC DIFFERENTIAL*

The semantic differential (*SD*) is a method of observing and measuring the psychological meaning of things, usually concepts. Although everyone sees things a bit differently, sometimes very differently, there must be some common core of meaning in all concepts. Indeed the definition of *concept* makes this clear. People must to a great extent share behavioral and verbal definitions of things. We say, "I can't give you a definition of it, but I know what it means." We talk to one another only through shared meanings of words. The public-school parent and the parochial-school parent share the meaning of the word *school,* even though each has a different perception of the concept. Any concept, then, has a common cultural meaning. It also has other meanings, some of them shared by different groups of people, some of them more or less idiosyncratic.

Osgood invented the semantic differential, henceforth called *SD,* to measure the connotative meanings of concepts as points in what he has called "semantic space." [1] We illustrate the notion of semantic space with two- and three-dimensional examples.

A Spatial Example Imagine a three-dimensional space—the room you are sitting in, for instance. Assume that there are three sticks at right angles to each other, meeting in the center of the room and touching the walls, the floor, and the ceiling. Label these sticks *X, Y,* and *Z,* and call them axes or coordinates. Now imagine there are points scattered throughout the three-dimensional space with some of the points clustered near each other and near the *X* axis, others near the *Y* axis, and still others near the *Z* axis. Some points would be situated in the spaces between the axes. Label the points in any order with small letters, *a, b, · · · , n.* If the axes have been marked off in an equal-interval number system, then any point in the space can be unambiguously identified or "defined" by using the numbers on the three axes. (Let the center of the room,

[1] C. Osgood, G. Suci, and P. Tannenbaum, *The Measurement of Meaning.* Urbana, Ill.: University of Illinois Press, 1957.

where the three axes meet, be labeled 0 and the numbers on either side of 0 be plus or minus.)

Each point, then, has three numbers attached to it. For example, the point d might be $+6$ units on X, $+3$ units on Y, and -1 unit on Z. This could be written $d = \{6, 3, -1\}$. The point b might be $+4$ units on X, $+3$ units on Y, and 0 units on Z. Thus $b = \{4, 3, 0\}$.

If, through research, we had determined some general "meanings" for the axes X, Y, and Z, then the "meaning" of each point would be some combination of the meanings of X, Y, and Z. If $a = \{4, 0, 0\}$, for example, then a is pure "Xness"—4 units of it. If $c = \{1, 1, 6\}$, then c has a little of each of X and Y and a good deal of Z. We might say that a is an X-type and c a Z-type. Notice that if a point, say k, has coordinates $\{0, 0, 0\}$. then k has no meaning. In this circumstance, at least, k is meaningless.

While there is nothing difficult about such a conceptualization, our discussion up to now has been a bit abstract. Therefore let us take a hypothetical, two-dimensional, educational example and try to determine the "meaning" of certain key educational concepts. Suppose we have determined that there are two basic dimensions or factors of meaning. Our research has told us that most educational concepts, like SCHOOL, CURRICULUM, TEACHER, PRINCIPAL, and so on, can be related to two axes, X and Y, which, for good reasons, we have named *Evaluative* and *Potency*. Now, if we have some way to measure things on X, *Evaluative*, and Y, *Potency*, then we can describe these things in the same manner as we did before. Suppose we measured certain concepts in a particular school (by administering an appropriate instrument to teachers, say). SCHOOL may turn out to be $\{6, 1\}$, 6 units on X and 1 unit on Y, or, using seven-point scales, high on *Evaluative* and low on *Potency*. TEACHER may turn out to be $\{5, 2\}$, PUPIL $\{5, -1\}$, PARENT $\{2, 2\}$, PRINCIPAL $\{0, 5\}$, SUPERINTENDENT $\{1, 6\}$, TEACHING $\{6, 2\}$, STUDY $\{5, 1\}$, LEARNING $\{-2, 3\}$, and DISCIPLINE $\{1, 4\}$.

With this information we can "describe" this school (rather, the perception of this school) on the *Evaluative* and *Potency* dimensions. To see what the example just given looks like, we might plot the values of the concepts on the X and Y axes. This has been done in Fig. 32.1.

We now have a geometric, spatial, and quantitative description of the school on the two dimensions, X and Y. If X, *Evaluative*, is interpreted as "goodness," and Y, *Potency*, as "strength," and the measurements were obtained from the perceptions of teachers, we might say that the "atmosphere" of the school is such that concepts having to do with teaching—TEACHER, STUDY, SCHOOL, TEACHING, PUPIL—are "good" but not "strong," and that administrative concepts are "strong" but not "good." LEARNING, strange to say, is not "good" but somewhat "strong." PARENT is low on both "goodness" and "strength."

The "meaning" of this school has been specified. Other schools no doubt would have different "meanings." The main point is that concepts have been defined by reference to two known dimensions. If a concept has an ordered pair of numbers assigned to it, this ordered pair of numbers is its "meaning." In addition (and very important, as we shall see) the meaning of a concept comes from its relation not only to the two dimensions, X and Y, but also from its relations to other concepts. In Fig. 32.1, TEACHER, STUDY, TEACHING, and SCHOOL are evidently close in meaning. SUPERINTENDENT, PRINCIPAL, and DISCIPLINE, too, are close to each other in meaning, but removed from the first-named cluster. The meanings of PUPIL and LEARNING are somewhat apart from, though related to, the other meanings.

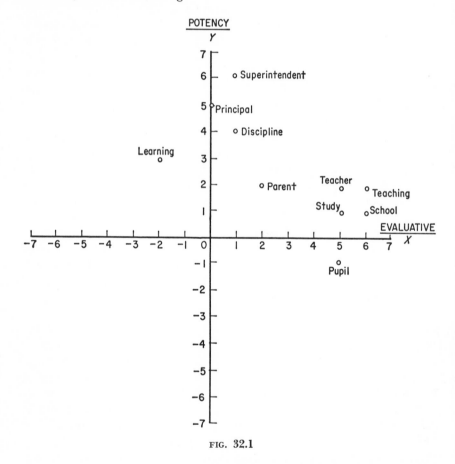

FIG. 32.1

THE CONSTRUCTION AND USE
OF THE SEMANTIC DIFFERENTIAL

An actual *SD* consists of a number of *scales*, each of which is a bipolar adjective pair, chosen from a large number of such scales for a particular research purpose, together with the *concepts* to be rated with the scales. The scales, or bipolar adjectives, are seven-point (usually) rating scales, the underlying nature of which has been determined empirically. That is, each scale measures one, sometimes two, of the basic dimensions or factors that Osgood and his colleagues have found to be behind the scales: *Evaluative, Potency, Activity*. These factors may be called clusters of adjectives.

Through research, Osgood has found that, when analyzed, adjective pairs like *good-bad, bitter-sweet, large-small,* and *clean-dirty* fall into clusters. The most important cluster seems to consist of adjectives that are *Evaluative*, such as *good-bad* and *pleasant-unpleasant*. A second cluster has adjectives that seem to share strength or *Potency* ideas. *Strong-weak* and *rugged-delicate* are examples. A third important factor is called *Activity* because its adjectives seem to express motion and action. *Fast-slow* and *hot-cold* are examples.

Here are nine of the bipolar adjectives.[2] They are each strongly identified with one of these dimensions or factors and are labeled *E, P, A,* accordingly. The nature of the dimensions or factors can be ascertained from study of these few scales.

(E)	good	: : : : : :	bad
(E)	beautiful	: : : : : :	ugly
(E)	clean	: : : : : :	dirty
(P)	large	: : : : : :	small
(P)	heavy	: : : : : :	light
(P)	strong	: : : : : :	weak
(A)	active	: : : : : :	passive
(A)	sharp	: : : : : :	dull
(A)	fast	: : : : : :	slow

These are only a few of the bipolar adjective pairs that are available for use and that have been empirically tested. Osgood gives a list of 50 scales with their factor identifications and the strength of the identifications.[3] Investigators can of course make up *SD* instruments using other adjective pairs.

Concepts   The first step in constructing or selecting an *SD* for research use is to choose the concepts or other stimuli one is going to rate with the bipolar adjectives. This is the most important part of the job. One

[2] From *ibid.*, p. 37.
[3] *Ibid.*

has to choose a number of concepts that are conceived to be relevant to the research problem. Osgood describes a study the main purpose of which was to determine the meanings of political concepts to three groups of subjects: Stevenson voters (*SV*), Eisenhower Republicans (*ER*), Taft Republicans (*TR*).[4] The investigators selected ten "Person" concepts and ten "Issue" concepts. Examples of the former are: ROBERT TAFT, ADLAI STEVENSON, GENERAL EISENHOWER. Examples of the latter are: FEDERAL SPENDING, SOCIALISM, UNITED NATIONS. The 20 concepts were then judged against a differential of 10 adjective pairs. The researchers assumed that the three different political biases would yield different "meaning spaces." Taft Republicans should rate EISENHOWER and FEDERAL SPENDING, for instance, similarly to each other and quite differently from Stevenson voters. In other words, the *SD* was used, in effect, to test the relation between political preference and the meanings assigned to concepts.

In a large and significant study of attitudes toward mental disorders, Nunnally had 250 representative subjects judge 12 concepts against a 17-scale differential.[5] To accomplish his purpose, Nunnally chose concepts related to mental disorders—NEUROTIC MAN, NEUROTIC WOMAN, INSANE MAN, INSANE WOMAN, PSYCHIATRIST—and concepts of ordinary life—AVERAGE MAN, AVERAGE WOMAN, OLD MAN, CHILD, ME, MOTHER, FATHER. With a sample of high school students, Nunnally used short expressions like METHODS FOR TREATING CANCER, METHODS FOR TREATING MENTAL ILLNESS, as well as single words like PSYCHOANALYSIS and DOCTOR.[6] His idea was that the meanings average people assign concepts suggestive of mental illness would be quite different from the meanings they assign concepts of ordinary life. The meaning of NEUROTIC MAN would be closer to the meaning of INSANE WOMAN, for instance, than it would be to AVERAGE MAN and ME.

A sample of concepts, then, must be judiciously chosen to represent some parts of the semantic space. If one were using the *SD* to measure social attitudes, one would carefully select concepts that would be likely to tap the attitudes and that would cover some parts of the semantic space. To choose concepts to tap the attitudes is not difficult. One can think of a number of concepts loaded with attitudinal meaning. These can include names of public figures like KENNEDY, EISENHOWER, NIXON, and TRUMAN. One assumes that the meanings associated with these names are intimately related to the people's social attitudes. A conservative's meaning space of these four names is probably very different from a liberal's. Perhaps more theoretically fruitful is the rich store of loaded words and expressions that trigger off expressions of attitude: GOVERNMENT AID

---

4 *Ibid.*, pp. 104–116.
5 J. Nunnally, *Popular Conceptions of Mental Health*. New York: Holt, Rinehart and Winston, Inc., 1961, chap. 4.
6 *Ibid.*, pp. 62–64.

TO EDUCATION, BIG BUSINESS, GOVERNMENT OWNERSHIP OF UTILITIES, SEX EDUCATION, PUBLIC HOUSING, SOCIALIZED MEDICINE, FOREIGN AID, WORLD PO- LITICAL ORGANIZATION, LABOR UNION, PROTECTIVE TARIFF, and so on. If the concepts used are not loaded with potential for different reactions by peo- ple holding different attitudes, they are useless for measurement purposes. In short, the concepts must be capable of eliciting varied responses and thus large variance.

The concepts must also cover, to some extent, the semantic space. If, in measuring social attitudes, one were to select concepts all of which were close in meaning, one could not adequately define the semantic space dimensions. In plain language, this means that one must not only use concepts like EISENHOWER, NIXON, and PROTECTIVE TARIFF; one must also include concepts like KENNEDY, GOVERNMENT AID TO EDUCATION, and SOCIALIZED MEDICINE. This is why Nunnally used everyday words like CHILD and AVERAGE WOMAN together with his mental illness concepts.

Scales The second step in the construction of the instrument, Osgood tells us, is to select appropriate *scales* or *adjective pairs*. Two main cri- teria determine the selection: factor representativeness and relevance to the concepts used. Perhaps in most cases investigators will want to use scales representative of the three main factors discussed earlier. It is possi- ble, however, that an investigator may wish to use scales of factors other than the three main ones. Nunnally, for instance, has found a factor he calls *Understandability*.[7] It would seem to be important for some research purposes. It consists of scales like *predictable-unpredictable, understand- able-mysterious, familiar-strange,* and *simple-complicated.*

On the other hand, the investigator may often need only the scales of one factor, most likely the *Evaluative* factor. This would be true in studies of attitudes and values. In some research cases, too, an investiga- tor may decide it is necessary to include scales whose factor identity is not known. After all, Osgood's original 50 scales by no means exhaust ad- jective possibilities. One might wish to use polarities like *progressive- traditional* and *permissive-restrictive* in a study of educational attitudes. These pairs do not appear in Osgood's original list. Generally, however, the original list will probably be adequate for most purposes.

Osgood and his colleagues use a small sample of factorially related scales: three scales to represent each factor, each scale highly "loaded" on one factor and not on the others. For example, nine scales may be used with three *Evaluative*, three *Potency*, and three *Activity* scales. The sums or averages of the three scales on each factor are ordinarily used as scores.

The second criterion of scale selection, *relevance* to the concepts used, is much more difficult to satisfy. In many cases, it is quite clear

---

7 *Ibid.,* pp. 43, 46, 54, *et* passim. Osgood's research indicates that there are cer- tainly other factors or dimensions, in fact no less than 7 or 8.

that an adjective pair is related to a concept. If one of the concepts being judged is FATHER, it is obvious that adjective pairs like *good-bad, large-small, young-old, loud-soft, pleasant-unpleasant,* and so on are suitable, since any of these pairs can be used to modify FATHER. But suppose, in a study of prejudice, one were using the concept BIGOT. While most of the cited adjective pairs are suitable, it may very well be necessary to include other adjectives not on Osgood's original list. *Flexible-rigid, intelligent-stupid,* and, perhaps, *democratic-autocratic* occur to one. If the concept TEACHER were used, one might wish to use adjective pairs presumably appropriate to teaching behavior, for example, *original-stereotyped, systematic-disorganized,* and *responsible-irresponsible.*[8] None of these is on Osgood's original list, though it is possible that one or more of them may have been used by Osgood or other researchers. Osgood says that scales of unknown factorial composition are often relevant to certain problems. When using such untried scales, however, one should attempt to determine the factorial identity of the scales. It is wise, too, to include scales of known factorial content.[9]

There is a subtle point here that is puzzling. Certain adjective pairs may seem irrelevant to the concepts judged. If one were judging musical compositions, adjective pairs like *loud-soft, pleasant-unpleasant,* and *beautiful-ugly* are clearly relevant. Other pairs like *honest-dishonest, rich-poor,* and *fair-unfair* would seem not to be relevant. But one cannot always be sure of relevance. Meanings are rich and complex, and an apparently irrelevant adjective pair may turn out to be relevant. If consistent systematic variance can be identified with an adjective pair, then one would have to conclude that the adjective pair is relevant to the concepts. (If an adjective pair is irrelevant to a set of concepts, there should be a large preponderance of midpoint ratings—4 on a seven-point scale—and relatively small variance.) In general, it is probably wise to select adjective pairs that are relevant to the concepts used and to use other adjective pairs sparingly. As Osgood, *et al.* put it, ". . . although there are, we believe, standard *factors* of judgment, the particular scales which may, in any given research problem, best represent these factors, are variable and must be carefully selected by the experimenter to suit his purpose." [10]

[8] D. Ryans, *Characteristics of Teachers.* Washington, D.C.: American Council on Education, 1960, pp. 86ff.

[9] Osgood, *et al., op. cit.,* p. 79. The words "factor," "factor structure," and "factorial content" may not be completely grasped at first. For the present think of a factor as a cluster of related things, or as more or less independent subsets of a larger set of things: tests, persons, concepts, and adjective pairs.

[10] *Ibid.,* p. 80.

FORMAT AND ADMINISTRATION
OF THE SEMANTIC DIFFERENTIAL

The format of *SD* instruments is simple. Although there are more complex forms possible, an effective form is illustrated below:

SCHOOL

(E)	1. pleasant	:	:	:	:	:	:	unpleasant
(A)	2. angular	:	:	:	:	:	:	rounded
(A)	*3. passive	:	:	:	:	:	:	active
(E)	*4. ugly	:	:	:	:	:	:	beautiful
(P)	*5. delicate	:	:	:	:	:	:	rugged
(A)	6. fast	:	:	:	:	:	:	slow
(E)	7. good	:	:	:	:	:	:	bad
(P)	*8. weak	:	:	:	:	:	:	strong
(A)	*9. dull	:	:	:	:	:	:	sharp
(P)	10. deep	:	:	:	:	:	:	shallow
(P)	11. heavy	:	:	:	:	:	:	light
(E)	*12. dark	:	:	:	:	:	:	bright

A concept, SCHOOL, has been inserted to show how a complete page of the instrument might look. The letters before each adjective pair indicate the three factors. The asterisks indicate that the polar adjectives have been reversed, that is, instead of *beautiful-ugly, ugly-beautiful* is used. Six of the 12 pairs were reversed at random. Reversals are used to counteract response bias tendencies. A subject cannot go down the list and check all scales at the same point. Notice that the scales are seven-point scales. Although three, five, or even nine-point scales can be used, Osgood has found the seven-point form to be effective. With children, a five-point scale would probably be more suitable.

Each concept appears on a separate sheet with the same set of scales. Subjects are instructed to judge the concepts according to the demands of the research. They might be asked to rate concepts like TEACHER, SCHOOL, ME, and so on, as they see them. This is the usual procedure. But subjects can also be asked to rate concepts "as boys see them," or "by what you think they mean to teachers." For detailed instructions, consult the book of Osgood, *et al.*

ANALYSIS OF SEMANTIC DIFFERENTIAL DATA

The *SD* yields a surprising amount of data, and with so many data, a number of analyses are possible. The scores are simply the numbers 1 through 7 assigned as follows:

good $\underline{7 \; : \; 6 \; : \; 5 \; : \; 4 \; : \; 3 \; : \; 2 \; : \; 1}$ bad

That is, if an individual checks the adjective pair *good-bad* between, say, the first and second sets of dots at the left, a 6 is assigned. Other checked points are assigned to the other numerals. It is possible to use the numerical system $+3, +2, +1, 0, -1, -2, -3$. This has the advantage of having a zero at the neutral point. But this advantage is more than offset by the disadvantage of having to work with negative quantities.

Viewed in variance and set terms, there are three main sources of variance or a three-way cross-partition of the total sample of scores. The sources of variance are: *concepts, scales,* and *subjects* (and, of course, *error*). That is, the scores can be analyzed for differences *between concepts, between scales, between subjects,* or any combination thereof. In most studies, however, there are ways of reducing the data to two categories, usually *concepts* and *scales,* or *concepts* and *factors.* The *SD* data, like *Q* data to be considered later, are unique in that the data of one individual can be analyzed, as well as the data of groups of individuals.

A small set of hypothetical data may be helpful. Suppose that the

TABLE 32.1 HYPOTHETICAL SEMANTIC DIFFERENTIAL DATA OF ONE SUBJECT: FIVE CONCEPTS, SIX SCALES

Scales	Concepts				
	A	*B*	*C*	*D*	*E*
1	6	2	6	5	3
2	5	2	5	5	2
3	6	1	4	6	2
4	7	1	5	6	3
5	5	3	5	7	1
6	6	2	7	7	2
M:	5.83	1.83	5.33	6.00	2.17

matrix of Table 32.1 contains the *SD* raw scores of one individual. This subject judged five concepts: TEACHING, DISCIPLINE, LEARNING, STUDY, CONTROL, against six scales selected from the scales of the *Evaluative* factor: *valuable-worthless, pleasant-unpleasant, bright-dark, good-bad, honest-dishonest, nice-awful.* (Notice that some of these scales seem relevant to all the concepts, whereas others do not.) We are interested in learning something about the individual's educational "meaning space." How does he "see," how does he evaluate key educational concepts? What relative values does he place on the different concepts? What concepts are close together in his meaning space? Which ones are far apart? What is the relation between his educational attitudes and his educational semantic space? We shall try to answer some of these questions from the data of Table 32.1. At the same time we can learn some of the main analytical possibilities of *SD* data, even though the hypothetical data are limited to only five concepts, judged by one subject using only one *SD* factor (*Evaluative*).

Means and Related Statistics The most obvious analysis of the data of Table 32.1 would be to compare the means of the concepts. There are two clusters of means: *A, C, D* and *B, E*. The subject puts high values on *A, C,* and *D*, and low values on *B* and *E*. That is, TEACHING, LEARNING, and STUDY are highly valued, but DISCIPLINE and CONTROL are not highly valued. With the data of a single individual, there is question of the legitimacy of the use of the usual statistical tests of significance. If the scores in Table 32.1 were averages—means or medians—of the scores of a group of individuals, it would be possible to use such tests. In this case, we might be interested in the significance of the differences between the five concept means and between the two clusters of means. Such analytic possibilities should be clear to the student. Instead of discussing them, we turn to the type of analysis stressed by Osgood.

Distance-Cluster Analysis If two concepts are close together in semantic space, they are alike in meaning for the individual or group making the judgments. Conversely, if they are separated in semantic space, they differ in meaning. What is needed is a measure of the distance between any two concepts. *Distance,* then, is the relation studied. The usual product-moment correlation coefficient is not considered suitable as a measure of the relation between two concepts, because it is a profile statistic; it does not take absolute distances into account. Osgood and his colleagues therefore use the so-called *D* statistic, a very simple measure which is defined:

$$D_{ij} = \sqrt{\Sigma d_{ij}^2} \qquad (32.1)$$

where *D* is the linear distance between any two concepts, *i* and *j*, and *d* is the algebraic difference between the coordinates of *i* and *j* on the same factor (*Evaluative, Potency,* or *Activity*).[11]

To compute *D* simply subtract the assigned values of one concept from the assigned values of another concept, square each of these differences, and sum the squared differences:

$$\Sigma d_{ij}^2 = \Sigma (X_i - X_j)^2 \qquad (32.2)$$

Then extract the square root of this sum, or

$$D_{ij} = \sqrt{\Sigma (X_i - X_j)^2} \qquad (32.3)$$

Take the values of concepts *A* and *B* of Table 32.1: $(6 - 2)^2 + (5 - 2)^2 +$

11 *Ibid.,* p. 91. Sometimes Σd_{ij}^2 is used instead of D_{ij}.

$(6 - 1)^2 + (7 - 1)^2 + (5 - 3)^2 + (6 - 2)^2 = 106$. Then $D = \sqrt{106} = 10.30$. The number of D's for any matrix is $n(n - 1)/2$, n being the number of concepts. For the data of Table 32.1, $(5)(4)/2 = 10$. The calculation of the 10 D's yields a symmetric matrix (a matrix that has the same values on both sides of the diagonal). The D matrix for the data of Table 32.1 is given in Table 32.2. It is labeled I. (Also given in Table 32.2 is a matrix of D's calculated from the ratings of a subject whose educational semantic space is very similar to that in I. It is labeled II. We consider it presently.)

TABLE 32.2 D MATRICES OF TWO SUBJECTS WITH SIMILAR SEMANTIC SPACES

			I						II		
	A	B	C	D	E		A	B	C	D	E
A		10.30	3.00	2.65	9.06	A		8.49	3.32	3.32	9.11
B	10.30		8.89	10.44	3.16	B	8.49		7.42	7.07	2.45
C	3.00	8.89		3.16	8.19	C	3.32	7.42		4.12	8.19
D	2.65	10.44	3.16		9.95	D	3.32	7.07	4.12		7.87
E	9.06	3.16	8.19	9.95		E	9.11	2.45	8.19	7.87	

One can analyze a D matrix in two or three ways. The basis of the different analyses, however, is the same: searching out concepts that cluster together. The *smaller* a D between two concepts, the closer the concepts are in meaning. Conversely, the *larger* a D the farther apart in meaning the two concepts are. With simple D matrices like those in Table 32.2, we can successively pair small D's to define clusters of concepts. Work row by row. For example, look at Row A of I. AC and AD are small: 3.00 and 2.65. Perhaps A, C, and D form a "close cluster." Check the C row. Is the D between C and D also small? It is 3.16. A, C, and D form a cluster because the distance between AC, AD, and CD are all small. Now take the next concept (row) that has not been considered, B. BE is 3.16, a small D value. Therefore B and E are close in meaning. All other D's are large. That is, $AB = 10.30$, $AE = 9.06$, $BC = 8.89$, and so on. There are, then, two clusters: A, C, D and B, E. Inspection of II will show the same clusters of concepts. We conclude, therefore, that the two subjects (or *groups* if the original scores from which the D's were computed were averages) have similar educational semantic spaces. They perceive the concepts alike.

TABLE 32.3 D MATRIX FOR A THIRD SUBJECT

	A	B	C	D	E
A		2.00	8.06	9.17	.3.46
B	2.00		7.94	9.17	2.83
C	8.06	7.94		2.65	6.86
D	9.17	9.17	2.65		7.75
E	3.46	2.83	6.86	7.75	

Suppose, now, that a third subject's *SD* data yielded the *D* matrix shown in Table 32.3. Analysis of this matrix shows that the concept clusters are *A, B, E* and *C, D*. The first two subjects perceived TEACHING, LEARNING, STUDY as close together but separate from DISCIPLINE, CONTROL, which were perceived as close together. The third subject's data, too, yielded two clusters: (1) TEACHING, DISCIPLINE, CONTROL and (2) LEARNING, STUDY. A little reflection should indicate that these two sets of perceptions are quite different. We might hypothesize that the basic educational value systems of the two sets of perceptions are also quite different. Such a hypothesis, of course, would have to be tested.

The above analysis contains the essence, if not all the substance, of *D* matrix analysis. It is somewhat descriptive and impressionistic. There are more objective methods which can only be briefly described.

If we wish to compare two or more matrices, we can compute coefficients of correlation between the *D*'s of each pair of matrices. The *D*'s of the same *ij* cells of two matrices form a set of ordered pairs. These pairs of *D*'s are correlated. (Only the values in the upper, or lower, half of the matrices are used.) For instance, take the data of Table 32.2. To find the similarity of the semantic structures of Matrices I and II, take the ordered pairs: (10.30, 8.49), (3.00, 3.32), $\cdot$ $\cdot$ $\cdot$, (9.95, 7.87), and compute r between the 10 pairs of *D*'s. In this case, $r = .93$, a very high degree of agreement. If we correlate the matrix of I, in Table 32.2, with the matrix of Table 32.3, $r = .06$. This is more objective evidence of the conclusions reached by the more impressionistic method.

Computing r's between matrices, however, we find out nothing about the clusters within the matrices. A *cluster* is a subset of a set of "objects"—persons, tests, concepts, and so on—the members of which are more similar or closer to each other than they are to members outside the cluster. The key question is how to define and identify clusters and their members. If we are working with correlation coefficients, the answer is easy and direct: we use factor analysis or some simpler form of cluster analysis. But with other statistics, such as *D*, the answer is not so simple. True, the three simple matrices of Tables 32.2 and 32.3 were easily handled. But the method was not objective. Suppose the *D*'s had not been so clearly divided? What if two of the concepts had had values in between 2 to 9? To what cluster do you assign two concepts whose *D* is 4 or 5?

Osgood, Suci, and Tannenbaum discuss this problem and outline methods of clustering concepts. They also outline a factor analytic method.[12] Cluster methods developed by other workers—McQuitty's *elementary linkage analysis,* for example—can be used.[13] The best sugges-

---

[12] *Ibid.,* pp. 102-104; 41, 42; 332-335.

[13] L. McQuitty, "Elementary Linkage Analysis for Isolating Orthogonal and Oblique Types and Typal Relevancies," *Educational and Psychological Measurement,* XVII (1957), 207–229. The author has tried this method with one or two *D* matrices and found it to work quite well, though not as well as a good factor analytic method.

tions, however, are perhaps Nunnally's.[14] He outlines and illustrates a method based on the sums of the cross-products of raw scores (ΣXY).

The Use of Factor Scores   Osgood customarily includes in his *SD* instruments equal numbers of *Evaluative, Potency,* and *Activity* scales. The scores of each of these are averaged separately to produce *E, P,* and *A* factor scores. Therefore, instead of the data of a subject or a group of subjects yielding one set of data, as above, three sets of data can be derived. Each of these sets can be analyzed and interpreted in the ways already described. For example, three *D* matrices can be produced and analyzed. (Osgood sometimes computes *D* matrices over all three factors; that is, factors are disregarded and *D*'s computed from the complete profiles of individual scores or group averages.) Or groups can be compared on one, two, or all three of the semantic factors.

SOME RESEARCH USES OF THE SEMANTIC DIFFERENTIAL

While psychologists have seized upon the semantic differential with enthusiasm, educators have shown much less ardor. Educational studies in which the *SD* is used are rare. The three researches now to be mentioned, therefore, are almost purely psychological. They are also highly original and significant.

Staats and Staats Attitude-Conditioning Study   Staats and Staats[15] asked whether attitudes elicited by significant words could be changed by conditioning. Further, could such attitudes be changed without the individuals involved being aware of the change? This is an important problem, because most attitudes are learned, conveyed, and reinforced with words. By attaching positive and negative affects to words, can we change attitudes? Staats and Staats tackled this problem, a problem slightly reminiscent of *Brave New World* and *1984.*

The experimenters used two groups of subjects to whom they presented, in one part of the experiment, six national names: GERMAN, SWEDISH, ITALIAN, FRENCH, DUTCH, and GREEK. Each time a name was presented on a screen, subjects heard the experimenter say another word. SWEDISH and DUTCH were always paired with evaluative words. For Group 1 DUTCH was paired with positive words, for example, *happy* and *sacred;* SWEDISH was paired with negative words: *ugly, bitter.* For Group 2 the

---

McQuitty has also developed other methods. See, for example, L. McQuitty, "Typal Analysis," *Educational and Psychological Measurement,* XXI (1961), 677–696; "Hierarchical Linkage Analysis," *Educational and Psychological Measurement,* XX (1960), 55–67.

[14] J. Nunnally, "The Analysis of Profile Data," *Psychological Bulletin,* LIX (1962), 311–319. A study of this valuable article is urged; its suggestions are applicable to all kinds of data.

[15] A. Staats and C. Staats, "Attitudes Established by Classical Conditioning," *Journal of Abnormal and Social Psychology,* LVII (1958), 37–40.

procedure was reversed. When this conditioning was completed, an *SD* was administered to the subjects. In a second experiment, male names were used instead of national names: HARRY, TOM, and so on. The same conditioning procedure was followed (with different subjects). After this second conditioning procedure, too, the *SD* was administered. The subjects were told that the experimenters had to find out the words they remembered and how they felt about them.

The data of each experiment were analyzed with a 2×2 analysis of variance. The seven-point *SD* scores of the two conditioned words were the dependent variable scores. It was found that the conditioning procedure was effective in attaching positive and negative evaluative effect to the conditioned words—a remarkable finding.

A Study of the Meaning of Human Values[16] The semantic differential was designed to be a general measurement instrument that could be used in a wide variety of research problems. This general quality was to follow, of course, from the generality of meaning. For instance, many different things can be labeled *good-bad, beautiful-ugly, fast-slow,* and so on. An unusual study of human values using the *SD* is a good example of its general nature and wide applicability.

Morris has postulated 13 broad "ways of life," values, or philosophic viewpoints.[17] Examples of these are: Sympathetic Concern for Others, Dignified Self-Control, Enjoyment of Simple Comforts, Preserve the Best in Society. For each "way to live," Morris has provided a fairly lengthy description, usually a paragraph. His whole instrument is called "Ways to Live."

Osgood, Ware, and Morris set themselves the task of bringing together two kinds of measurement, values and connotative meanings, in an unusual way: they measured the meaning of the value instrument, "Ways to Live," by having subjects judge the 13 ways on a form of *SD*. In other words, each of Morris' paragraph descriptions were judged by the subjects on a 26-scale *SD*.

In one analysis, inter-subject variance was ignored: all the subjects' judgments on each scale were averaged. Then the 13 ways were intercorrelated using these means as scores. For example, consider a 13×26 matrix of means: the 13 Ways and the 26 scales. Now we correlate Way 1 with Way 2, Way 1 with Way 3, and so on, over the 26 *SD* scales. This procedure yields a 13×13 matrix of *r*'s which can be factor-analyzed.

A Semantic Differential Study of Emotions It is striking that emotions, one of the two or three most important parts of man's life, have not been scientifically studied to any great extent. Some scientists would no doubt

16 C. Osgood, E. Ware, and C. Morris, "Analysis of the Connotative Meanings of a Variety of Human Values as Expressed by American College Students," *Journal of Abnormal and Social Psychology,* LXII (1961), 62–73.

17 C. Morris, *Varieties of Human Values.* Chicago: University of Chicago Press, 1955.

say that, since emotional experience is subjective and private, it is not amenable to scientific investigation. Block, in a highly significant and competent study,[18] has shown that it *is* possible to study emotions scientifically. In effect, he asked the questions: What are the factors behind emotions? Do the emotions of men and women differ in meaning? Do the emotions of different national groups differ in meaning?

To answer these questions, Block first had 40 male and 48 female American students judge 15 emotions, such as LOVE, ANGER, PRIDE, FEAR, and GRIEF, on a 20-item *SD*. The sums of all 40 men subjects on each of the 20 items (scales) for each emotion were assigned ranks. The same was done for women separately. That is, the adjective pairs sums for each emotion were rank-ordered. For the emotion FEAR, for example, the adjective pair *tense-relaxed* had a rank of 1, whereas the adjective pair *good-bad* had a rank of 17 (for the female students). This means that FEAR was seen as *tense* and *bad*. The rank-order correlations between men and women were all high, from .84 to .98, except that for GRIEF (.66).

The same procedure was used with 34 Norwegians (after appropriate translation of the instrument from English to Norwegian). Then the similarities and differences in meanings of the emotions to Americans and Norwegians were studied. The results seemed to indicate the appropriateness of the *SD* for cross-cultural study.

THE SEMANTIC DIFFERENTIAL
IN BEHAVIORAL RESEARCH

The semantic differential can be applied to a variety of research problems. It has been shown to be sufficiently reliable and valid for many research purposes.[19] It is also flexible and relatively easy to adapt to varying research demands, quick and economical to administer and to score. The main problems, as indicated earlier, are to select appropriate and relevant concepts or other cognitive objects to be judged, and appropriate and relevant analyses. In both cases the researcher is faced with a plethora of possibilities. Selection and choice, as usual, are determined by the nature of the problems explored and the hypotheses tested. Here are some suggested uses of the method.

The *SD* should be useful in exploring the meaning structures of children at different ages. Concepts are the foundation stones of the meaning structures of human beings; they are basic essentials in all human thinking. What concepts has the child of five, six, or nine learned? What are their connotative meanings? What does *teacher* mean to a child of six, a child of nine, a child of twelve? Is the semantic space in which

---

[18] J. Block, "Studies in the Phenomenology of Emotions," *Journal of Abnormal and Social Psychology*, LIV (1957), 358–363.

[19] See Osgood, *et al., op. cit.,* pp. 140–153, 192, 193, *et passim.*

teacher is imbedded one that will promote learning? Or will it impede learning? Questions such as these can be answered, in part at least, with the aid of the semantic differential.

Concepts are essential parts of the learning of attitudes. The relatively rigid and standardized perceptions of minority group members, called stereotypes, are important parts of prejudiced attitudes. Is it possible to change stereotypes? Attitude learning and change studies might well have a sensitive and helpful companion in the semantic differential. If the Staats and Staats study is any criterion, it is a fairly sensitive measure of attitude change. Indeed, Osgood believes that the *SD* can be used as a generalized attitude measurement technique, provided that *Evaluative* adjective pairs are used.[20]

One of the difficulties in communicating about education is the different interpretations put upon educational ideas. Take "progressive education," the "3 R's," "discipline," and so on. It is likely that different kinds of people have quite different connotative meaning structures of these words. It is likely, for example, that exponents of progressive education have sharply different semantic spaces surrounding these concepts than exponents of more traditional viewpoints. Investigating such structures and their correlates should enrich psychological theory pertinent to education. The *SD* might aid such research.

There has been little cross-cultural scientific educational research. Students of comparative education have done fine work in comparing the educational systems and philosophies of different countries. But little is known of the different meanings put upon educational concepts in different countries. What is the relation between such meanings and educational thinking and practice? Research into such problems is important not only for its own sake; it is also important because it could perhaps yield theoretical information valuable to social psychologists and educators and because it might throw light on American educational problems. The *SD* has already been shown to be a useful adjunct to such cross-cultural research.

If the *SD* can be conceived as a values and attitude measurement instrument, it may be possible to study children's values and attitudes by having teachers and other judges rate their compositions on an *Evaluative* form of the *SD*. A related possibility is the study of the attitudes and semantic spaces of teacher trainees. What effect does a teacher-training program have on the educational semantic space of teacher trainees? What effect does actual teaching experience have on the semantic space of teachers? And if changes take place, do concomitant changes in educational attitudes take place?

These are only a small sample of the possibilities. We have here a

20 *Ibid.,* p. 195.

useful and perhaps sensitive tool to help in the exploration of an extremely important area of psychological and educational concern: connotative meaning. The next decade should see many results of this exploration.

33 Q METHODOLOGY

Q methodology is a general name used by William Stephenson to express a group of pyschometric and statistical procedures he developed.[1] *Q technique* is a set of procedures used to implement *Q* methodology. It centers particularly in the sorting of decks of cards called *Q* sorts and in the correlations among the responses of different individuals to the *Q* sorts. We study *Q* methodology and *Q* technique in this chapter, though we will not be as concerned as Stephenson with distinguishing between the two.

Persons Correlations and Clusters   *Q* technique is mainly a sophisticated form of rank-ordering objects and then assigning numerals to subsets of the objects for statistical purposes. Take a set of six objects, say national figures: Eisenhower, Johnson, Rockefeller, Stevenson, Humphrey, Nixon. If we ask individuals to rank-order these men according to the criterion, "Whom would you most want to represent you to improve the welfare of the country?" we would expect different rank orders from different individuals. Two Republicans and two Democrats might give the rank orders shown in Table 33.1 (1 being first choice and 6 being last choice).

TABLE 33.1   HYPOTHETICAL RANK ORDERS GIVEN TO SIX POLITICAL FIGURES BY TWO REPUBLICANS AND TWO DEMOCRATS

	Rep–1	Rep–2	Dem–1	Dem–2
Eisenhower	1	1	5	4
Rockefeller	2	3	4	5
Nixon	3	2	6	6
Johnson	4	6	1	2
Stevenson	6	5	2	1
Humphrey	5	4	3	3

Inspection shows what might have been expected: the two Republicans have similar rank orders, as do the two Democrats. The rank orders

[1] W. Stephenson, *The Study of Behavior*. Chicago: University of Chicago Press, 1953.

of Republicans and Democrats, on the other hand, are unlike. To be more objective, we compute rank-order coefficients of correlation between all possible pairs of rankers. This yields a 4×4 correlation matrix, as shown in Table 33.2.

TABLE 33.2   CORRELATION MATRIX: CORRELATIONS BETWEEN REPUBLICANS
AND DEMOCRATS, TABLE 33.1 DATA

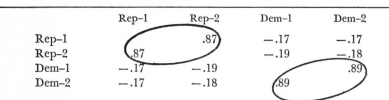

	Rep–1	Rep–2	Dem–1	Dem–2
Rep–1		.87	−.17	−.17
Rep–2	.87		−.19	−.18
Dem–1	−.17	−.19		.89
Dem–2	−.17	−.18	.89	

Note that the clusters, Rep-1, Rep-2 and Dem-1, Dem-2, stand out clearly. Rep-1 correlates highly with Rep-2 (.87), but very low with Dem-1 and Dem-2 (−.17 and −.17). Similarly, Dem-1 and Dem-2 correlate highly with each other (.89), but not with Rep-1 and Rep-2.

This oversimplified example illustrates two of the important basic ideas behind Q: *correlations between persons* and *persons clusters* or *factors.* The usual correlational procedure, loosely called R methodology, uses correlations between tests. The above example might have been four tests given to six persons, the tests measuring two variables. With Q, the four persons break down into two clusters.

Q Sorts and Q Sorting   The example given above used a straightforward rank-order procedure. Q technique uses a rank-order procedure of piles or groups of objects. A set of objects—verbal statements, single words, phrases, pictures, musical compositions—is given to an individual to sort into a set of piles according to some criterion. For example, the cards may have typed on them statements about educational practices. The subject may be asked to sort the cards according to whether he approves or disapproves the statements on them. With a large number of cards—Q sorts usually contain between 60 and 120 cards—it would be very difficult to rank order them. For statistical convenience, the sorter is instructed to put varying numbers of cards in several piles, the whole making up a normal or quasi-normal distribution.

Here is a Q sort distribution of 90 items:

Most Approve									*Least Approve*	
3	4	7	10	13	16	13	10	7	4	3
10	9	8	7	6	5	4	3	2	1	0

This is a rank-order continuum from "Most Approve" to "Least Approve" with varying degrees of approval and disapproval between the extremes.

The numbers 3, 4, 7, $\cdots$, 7, 4, 3 are the numbers of cards to be placed in each pile. The numbers below the line are the values assigned to the cards in each pile. That is, the 3 cards at the left, "Most Approve," are each assigned 10, the 4 cards in the next pile are assigned 9, and so on through the distribution to the 3 cards at the extreme right, which are assigned 0. The center pile is a neutral pile. The subject is told to put cards that are left over after he has made other choices, cards that seem ambiguous to him or about which he cannot make a decision, into the neutral pile. In brief, this Q distribution has 11 piles with varying numbers of cards in each pile, the cards in the piles being assigned values from 0 through 10. All statistical analyses are based on these latter values.

Sorting instructions and the objects sorted vary with the purposes of the research. Subjects can be asked to sort attitudinal statements on an approval-disapproval continuum. They can be asked to sort personality items on a "like me"-"not like me" continuum. Judges can sort behavioral statements to describe an individual or a group. Aesthetic objects, like pictures or abstract drawings, can be sorted according to strength of preference.

The number of cards in a Q distribution is determined by convenience and statistical demands. For statistical stability and reliability, the number should probably be not less than 60 (40 or 50 in some rare cases) nor more than 140, in most cases no more than 100. A good range is from 60 to 90 cards.[2]

In part, Q distributions are an arbitrary matter. It is possible to use rectangular distributions. That is, we could have the same number of cards in all the piles. Or we can even permit subjects to place the cards in a number of piles where they will. The normal or quasi-normal forced distribution has distinct advantages, mainly statistical, that make its use desirable. Here are some Q sort distributions.

$n = 80$

2	4	6	9	12	14	12	9	6	4	2
4	6	9	13	16	13	9	6	4
4	6	10	12	16	12	10	6	4

$n = 70$

| 2 | 3 | 5 | 8 | 11 | 12 | 11 | 8 | 5 | 3 | 2 |
| 2 | 3 | 4 | 8 | 11 | 14 | 11 | 8 | 4 | 3 | 2 |

$n = 60$

| 2 | 3 | 6 | 11 | 16 | 11 | 6 | 3 | 2 |
| 2 | 3 | 4 | 7 | 9 | 10 | 9 | 7 | 4 | 3 | 2 |

[2] The author has gotten good results with as few as 40 items. These 40 items were culled from a larger pool of items, all of which had been tested. It is rarely necessary or desirable to have more than 90 or 100 items.

A Miniature Q Sort   A semi-realistic example may help to clarify a number of technical points. Suppose we wish to explore attitudes toward education. We can assemble a large number of statements from which we randomly sample or systematically select a smaller number to put into a Q sort. We select 10 statements (naturally many more than 10 would actually be required). Subjects are asked to sort the 10 statements into the following distribution:

Most Approve				Least Approve
1	2	4	2	1
4	3	2	1	0

Again, the figures above the line are the numbers of cards in the piles; those below the line are the values assigned to each of the piles.

Suppose four subjects sort the cards as instructed and that the values below the line have been assigned to the cards in the piles. The four sets of values are given in Table 33.3. The numbers in the four columns under

TABLE 33.3 Q SORT VALUES OF FOUR PERSONS: MINIATURE Q SORT

Items	Persons			
	a	*b*	*c*	*d*
1	2	2	1	1
2	1	1	0	0
3	0	0	3	4
4	2	2	4	2
5	2	1	3	3
6	1	2	2	2
7	3	3	2	2
8	2	2	2	2
9	4	4	2	3
10	3	3	1	1

a, b, c, and *d* are the values assigned to the cards in the five piles after the four persons, *a, b, c* and *d,* have sorted the cards. By inspection we can see that the Q sorts of Persons *a* and *b* are very similar. The Q sorts of Persons *c* and *d* are also similar. (With these two pairs of persons, note that the high values and the low values tend to go together.) We can also see that there seems to be little relation between the Q sorts of *a* and *c, b* and *c,* and *b* and *d.* To be more precise, we need to compute coefficients of correlation.

The computation of coefficients of correlation with Q sorts is quite simple, because the formula for the *r*'s between pairs of subjects has quantities that never change. A convenient formula is

$$r = \frac{\Sigma xy}{\sqrt{\Sigma x^2 \, \Sigma y^2}} \qquad (33.1)$$

The denominator of this formula is always the same. The calculation of the denominator requires only the calculation of Σx^2, since $\Sigma x^2 = \Sigma y^2$. On the other hand, Σxy must be calculated for each pair of persons. Edwards gives simple and straightforward instructions for such calculations.[3]

The r's between the four sets of values of Table 33.3 are given in the correlation matrix of Table 33.4.

TABLE 33.4   CORRELATION MATRIX FROM THE Q SORT VALUES OF TABLE 33.3

	a	b	c	d
a		.92	−.08	−.08
b	.92		−.17	−.17
c	−.08	−.17		.75
d	−.08	−.17	.75	

The interpretation of these correlations presents no difficulties. Obviously Persons a and b sort the cards very similarly: $r = .92$. Persons c and d, too, are similar: $r = .75$. All the rest of the r's are near zero. Evidently there are two kinds or "types" of persons, insofar as attitudes toward education are concerned: "A-kind" and "B-kind."

To get an idea of what A and B are, we would have to go back to the Q sort and examine the items highly approved by A's and those highly approved by B's. Suppose the three highly approved A items were:

Learning is experimental; the child should be taught to test alternatives before accepting any of them.

No subject is more important than the personalities of the pupils.

Right from the very first grade, teachers must teach the child at his own level and not at the level of the grade he is in.

Suppose the three highly approved B items were:

Learning is essentially a process of increasing one's store of information about the various fields of knowledge.

The curriculum should contain an orderly arrangement of subjects that represent the best of our cultural heritage.

Schools of today are neglecting the three R's.[4]

3 A. Edwards, *Statistical Analysis*, rev. ed. New York: Holt, Rinehart and Winston, Inc., 1958, pp. 71–73. In computing ΣXY, a term the reader will find in this textbook, it is only necessary to multiply each pair of values and punch the products into an adding machine or desk calculator.

4 Items are from the author's Q sort of educational attitudes. See F. Kerlinger, "The Attitude Structure of the Individual: A Q-Study of the Educational Attitudes of Professors and Laymen," *Genetic Psychology Monographs*, LIII (1956), 283–329 (see pp. 323–327).

Obviously, these pairs of people are very different. One, the *A* pair, seems to favor "progressive" educational notions; the other, the *B* pair, seems to favor "traditional" educational notions. Perhaps these individuals are "progressives" and "traditionalists."

The miniature example just discussed contains the essential ingredients of much *Q* analysis. Obviously most *Q* studies have to have more subjects, even though it is theoretically possible. to have a *Q* study with one individual.[5] Also, the impressionistic kind of analysis used would in most cases not be satisfactory. A more objective method of ascertaining clusters of persons, or persons factors, would have to be used. The highly approved items of clusters of individuals also require a more objective method for their identification. Nevertheless, the example at least outlines the *Q* correlational method.

THEORY; STRUCTURED AND UNSTRUCTURED *Q* SORTS; ANALYSIS OF VARIANCE

Unstructured Q Sorts   Most published *Q* studies have used unstructured *Q* sorts. An *unstructured* *Q* sort is a set of items assembled without specific regard to the variables or factors underlying the items. Theoretically, any sample of homogeneous items can be used in an unstructured *Q* sort. Perhaps the most extensive use of unstructured *Q* sorts has been done by Rogers and his colleagues and students.[6] The idea is simple. A large number of statements are taken from various statement sources—personality inventories, what patients in therapy say to therapists, items specifically constructed by the researcher—and put together in a *Q* sort. The items of an unstructured *Q* sort are like the items of a personality or attitude scale: they are selected and used because they presumably measure one broad variable, like neuroticism, attitudes toward Negroes, or adjustment.

There is a theoretical infinite population of items, and the hope is that the set of items used by the investigator in his *Q* sort is a random, and thus representative, sample of this item population. One important population of items, used by Rogers and others, is focused on the perception of self and others. A large number of statements about the self is assembled or constructed: "I like people," "I am a failure," "I just can't seem to make up my mind on things," and so on.

Individuals are asked to sort the cards to describe themselves as they think they are, as other people see them, and the like. The cards are sorted into a *Q* distribution, the sorts intercorrelated, and the resulting

---

[5] An interesting example of this kind of study is: J. Nunnally, "An Investigation of Some Propositions of Self-Conception: The Case of Miss Sun," *Journal of Abnormal and Social Psychology*, L (1955), 87–92. Nunnally studied, via *Q* sorts, changes in the self-conception of a young woman during two years of therapy.

[6] C. Rogers and R. Dymond, eds., *Psychotherapy and Personality Change.* Chicago: University of Chicago Press, 1954.

R matrix factor analyzed. In Rogers' studies, inferences about personality and the results of therapy are then drawn from the correlations and the factor analysis. For example, subjects sort the cards before, during, and after therapy; the correlational and factor analytic results are compared. If a neurotic person has benefited from therapy, the reasoning goes, there should be a low *r* between his pretherapy and post-therapy *Q* sorts. The person who has not had therapy or who has not profited from therapy should have a high *r* between any two *Q* sorts, provided that the instructions were the same (and the sort reliable).

This is the approach that has more or less dominated *Q* studies.[7] One of Stephenson's most important contributions, the testing of "theory" and the principle of building "theory" into *Q* sorts by means of structured samples of items, has been neglected.[8]

Structured *Q* Sorts In a *structured Q sort,* the variables of a "theory," or of a hypothesis or set of hypotheses, are built into a set of items along Fisherian experimental and analysis of variance design principles. What does this mean? The theoretical principle behind the unstructured *Q* sort calls for a random sample of items from a population of such items. Now we make no pretense of randomness; we "structure" the *Q* sort.

In one sentence, the theory we seek to test is built into the *Q* sort. Instead of constructing instruments to measure the characteristics of individuals and individual differences, as such, instruments are constructed to embody or epitomize "theories." In the use of *Q* as Stephenson sees it, individuals as such are not tested; theoretical singular propositions are tested. Naturally, individuals must do the *Q* sorting. And *Q* sorts can of course be used to measure characteristics of individuals. But the basic rationale of *Q* as Stephenson sees it is that individuals sort the cards not so much to test the individuals as to test "theories" that have been built into the cards.[9]

One-Way Structured *Q* Sorts Building a theory into a measurement instrument, while not frequent, is not new. A well-known example is the Allport-Vernon-Lindzey Study of Values, a values instrument based on Spranger's theory of six "ideal" types of men: Theoretical, Economic, Aesthetic, Social, Political, and Religious.[10] The purpose of the instrument is not to test the theory but to measure the values of individuals. If a person is, say, basically a religious "type," he should select items of the Religious category over items of other categories.

---

[7] J. Wittenborn, "Contributions and Current Status of *Q* Methodology," *Psychological Bulletin,* LVIII (1961), 132–142.

[8] *Ibid.,* pp. 138, 139. See Stephenson, *op. cit.,* pp. 66–85.

[9] The word "theories" should here be taken to mean interrelated sets of hypotheses, variables, and propositions derived from larger generalizations.

[10] G. Allport, P. Vernon, and G. Lindzey, *Study of Values,* rev. ed. Boston: Houghton Mifflin, 1951.

The Stephenson approach to the same problem would be to test the Spranger theory. (Note that the Study of Values could be used to test the Spranger theory.) A Q sort would be constructed using the Spranger system as a guide. Items would be selected from various sources and specially written to represent the six Spranger values. There would be 10 to 15 Theoretical items, 10 to 15 Aesthetic items, and so forth, making a total of 60 to 90 items in the entire Q sort. Individuals would then be deliberately and systematically selected to "represent" the six values. For example, the investigator might select ministers and priests (Religious), businessmen (Economic), artists and musicians (Aesthetic), scientist and scholars (Theoretical), and so on.[11]

If the theory is "valid," and if the Q sort adequately expresses the theory, two rather big "if's," the statistical analyses of the sorts should show the theory's validity. That is, if any individual with "known" values—a minister or priest could be expected to have strong religious values, an artist strong aesthetic values—takes the sort with instructions to place favored or approved statements high and disapproved statements low, we would expect him to place the 10 or 15 statements congruent with his role and its associated values high. Statements associated with other roles and values we would expect him to place lower. If a scientist sorts the cards, we would expect him to place the cards in the Theoretical category high and cards of other categories relatively lower. Naturally, there will be few individuals whose sorts will be so clear-cut. Human beings and their attitudes and values are too complex. But we can expect some such results to occur beyond chance expectation if the theory is valid.

A Q sort suggested by the above considerations can be called a "one-way structured sort," because there is one basis of variable classification.[12] This is directly analogous to simple one-way analysis of variance. To make the matter clear, an example from a research study designed in part to test the Spranger theory in Q fashion can be given. A 90-item Q sort was used. Each item was a single word, each word having been previously categorized by judges in the six Spranger values. There were 15 Theoretical words—*science, knowledge, reason,* and so on; 15 Religious words—*God, church, sermon,* and so on; to a total of six categories and 90 words.

The cards were sorted by a number of persons chosen for their presumed possession of the six values. They were asked to sort the cards ac-

[11] In an interesting Q study of religious attitudes, Broen selected 24 clergymen to represent the full spectrum of religious beliefs and attitudes. There were four representatives of each of five major religious groupings. Broen says that the subjects were selected from churches and institutions known to have religious orientations in the directions of his hypothesized religious categories. W. Broen, "A Factor Analytic Study of Religious Attitudes," *Journal of Abnormal and Social Psychology,* LIV (1957), 176–179.

[12] Stephenson does not stress the possibility of Q sorts of the one-way type. His Q designs are almost all of the factorial two- and three-way type. There seems to be no reason why one-way designs cannot be used.

cording to the degree to which they favored or did not favor the words on the cards.

To illustrate the results, here are the mean values in rank order of the sort of one subject, a musician:

a	*s*	*t*	*p*	*e*	*r*
7.13	6.27	6.13	4.73	4.33	1.40

$F = 26.82$, significant at the .001 level. This means that the musician significantly differentiated the six values. What is the pattern of differentiation? The wider spaces indicate significant gaps.[13] Although it is the highest mean, there is no significant gap between Aesthetic and the next highest mean, Social (6.27). In fact, Aesthetic, Social, and Theoretical form a subset which is separated by a significant gap from all the other means. Political and Economic form another subset. Religious, the lowest mean (1.40), is significantly separated from all the other means. Evidently the musician highly favors Aesthetic, Social, and Theoretical words, and strongly disfavors Religious words. From this analysis we may perhaps draw inferences as to her value system, at least insofar as the measurement system allows. Independent knowledge of the subject confirmed this analysis.

If a set of stimuli can be categorized in this fashion, a one-way structured Q sort may be possible to construct and desirable to use. Small theories and hypotheses can be tested in this manner by having subjects of known values, attitudes, personality, roles, and so forth sort the cards. The student should realize that in addition to the analysis of variance structured sort approach, correlation analysis is always applicable. Simply correlate the Q sorts of different persons, and disregard the structure built into the sort.

Two-Way (Factorial) Structured Q Sorts   Many theories and hypotheses that can be structured along the lines of analysis of variance paradigms

---

[13] A simple way to do this test is to compute the standard error of the difference between means. The formula is

$$SE_{M_i - M_j} = \sqrt{V_w \left(\frac{1}{n_i} + \frac{1}{n_j} \right)}$$

where V_w = within-groups variance (from the analysis of variance). Multiply this value by 2:

$$2 \sqrt{2.34 \left(\frac{1}{15} + \frac{1}{15} \right)} = 2 \sqrt{2.34 \times .133} = 2 \times .558 = 1.12$$

Any difference equal to or greater than 1.12 is significant. Perhaps a more legitimate but more conservative test is Scheffé's. See A. Edwards, *Experimental Design in Psychological Research*, rev. ed. New York: Holt, Rinehart and Winston, Inc., 1960, pp. 154–156. Another good test is Tukey's. See A. Edwards, *Statistical Methods for the Behavioral Sciences*, New York: Holt, Rinehart and Winston, Inc., 1954, pp. 330–332.

have the potentiality of being tested with Q methods. The Spranger example just discussed is a case in point. Other one-way examples might be: introversion-extroversion; oral eroticism-anal eroticism; progressivism-traditionalism; liberalism-conservatism; open mindedness-closed mindedness; and so on. But how about more complex theories and hypotheses? Taking the next logical step, we add another dimension or variable to the Q paradigm. This makes a two-variable Q sort and a two-variable or factorial analysis of variance design. The Q sort is structured in two ways rather than one.

To illustrate two-way structured Q sorts, the paradigm of a 60-item sort constructed by the author to explore social attitudes is given in Table 33.5. The means of a known conservative individual have been inserted in the cells and on the margins.

TABLE 33.5   A TWO-WAY STRUCTURED Q SORT WITH THE MEANS OF A
CONSERVATIVE INDIVIDUAL

	Attitudes		
Areas	Conservative (1)	Liberal (2)	
Economic-Political (a)	5.13	3.07	4.10
General-Social (b)	5.27	4.53	4.90
	5.20	3.80	

First note the Q sort structure. The two main variables are *Attitudes* and *Areas*. *Attitudes* is partitioned into Conservative (1) and Liberal (2), *Areas* into Economic-Political (a) and General-Social (b). Any statement in the Q sort must fit into one of the four cells of the cross partition. Any attitude statement must be either Conservative or Liberal and at the same time either Economic-Political or General-Social. This structure was developed through study of the literature on social attitudes. It was found that almost any social attitudinal statement could be fitted into the structure. Whether the structure is valid is of course an empirical matter. At any rate, here are four statements representing each of the four cells. The labels correspond to those given above with the category names.

A first consideration in any society is the protection of property rights. (1a)

The gradual social ownership of industry needs to be encouraged if we are ever to cure some of the ills of our society. (2a)

If civilization is to survive, there must be a turning back to religion. (1b)

College and university professors should have complete freedom to teach whatever and however they choose. (2b)

The data of this individual's *Q* sort can be analyzed with analysis of variance, provided we use care and circumspection in the interpretation of the data. (The questionable nature of using analysis of variance with *Q* sorts will be discussed later.) The analysis to use, of course, is the factorial type. If we do so, we obtain *F* ratios between *Attitudes,* between *Areas,* and for the interaction of *Attitudes* and *Areas.* In this case only one pair of means, the Conservative and Liberal ones of 5.20 and 3.80, was found to be significantly different (at the .01 level). We conclude, therefore, that this individual is probably conservative in his attitudes. Since it was known that he was a conservative before he took the *Q* sort, this is some small confirmation of the validity of the reasoning that went into the sort.

Note that in this case we would not expect a significant *Areas F* ratio, but that a significant interaction *F* ratio would make good sense. It is quite possible that an individual can be an economic and political liberal and a social conservative. Many Catholics, for example, are political liberals and religious conservatives. In general, however, significant interactions are not expected; the principal interest in *Q* is ordinarily in the main effects.[14]

It should be mentioned that *Q* designs need not be limited to the simple 2 × 2 case shown above. Other combinations—3 × 2, 4 × 3, 2 × 4 —are possible. Three- and four-variable designs are also possible, if not too practicable. Another possibility is the application of the structure idea to objective tests and scales. The items of the social attitudes *Q* sort could be put into a summated rating scale form, for instance, and scored and analyzed accordingly.

FACTOR ANALYSIS AND FACTOR ARRAYS IN Q METHODOLOGY

The impossibility of doing justice to *Q* methodology without discussing factor analysis is nowhere more evident than in describing factor arrays, the final technical step of a *Q* study. One of the strong points of *Q* methodology is its analytic possibilities. Of these possibilities, factor arrays are very important. A *factor array* is a *Q* sort constructed from factor analytic results. Conceive factors as similar clusters of objects—in this case persons, or rather, the responses of persons. Those individuals who respond to a *Q* sort similarly will form clusters of persons. Oversimplified, conceive of summing the responses of the individuals of a cluster to any *Q* sort item. If we did this for every item in a *Q* sort, we would

---

[14] See Stephenson, *op. cit.,* pp. 103, 163, 164. See Stephenson, too, for other examples of structured *Q* sorts.

have sums (really weighted sums) for all items. These sums would of course vary a great deal. They can be rank ordered and then fitted into the original Q distribution.[15] This "new" synthetic Q sort is literally a description of the factor. It can be directly interpreted by the investigator. Usually, only the top and bottom two or three piles of the Q distribution are used for interpretative purposes. Factor arrays are calculated and prepared for each factor.

In a Q study of perceptions of desirable characteristics of teachers, the author asked judges to sort a Q deck of 90 cards on each of which was typed a single adjective. A factor analysis of the data yielded two main persons factors (clusters). The factor arrays of these two kinds of judges— call them A and B judges—showed two quite different perceptions of the characteristics a good teacher should possess. Here are the seven top adjectives of the A and the B arrays:

A	B
Intelligent	Conscientious
Imaginative	Moral
Insightful	Religious
Warm	Intelligent
Open-Minded	Efficient
Flexible	Just
Purposeful	Self-Controlled

Ordinarily, more positive items might be required to help identify and interpret the arrays. In addition, the negative end of the arrays would be used, since they might be helpful in the interpretation. For example, the three lowest items in the A array were Exacting, Strict, Religious, whereas the lowest B items were Inquisitive, Attractive, Sensitive. We do not attempt to interpret these arrays now. It is sufficient to show the nature of the Q factor array idea.

STRENGTHS AND WEAKNESSES OF Q METHODOLOGY

Like factor analysis which it uses liberally, Q methodology is controversial. It has been highly praised and harshly criticized. The truth of the critical matter is probably that the method is not as powerful and all-embracing as Stephenson has claimed it to be, nor is it as poor and defective as some critics have said it is. It is probably safe to say that Q is a flexible and useful tool in the armamentarium of the psychological and educational investigator. It also has defects, however, as we shall see.

The main strength of Q is its close affinity to theory. Structured Q

15 For details of computing factor arrays, see *ibid.*, pp. 176–179. A more detailed account is given in my manual: "Q Methodology and the Testing of Theory." New York: School of Education, New York University, 1958, pp. 45–48.

sorts, by definition, are theoretically oriented. In order to build a structured sort, one has perforce to enunciate some kind of theory. The theoretical emphasis becomes especially prominent in two- or three-way factorial sorts. In order to juxtapose two variables and to build them into an instrument, one must relate them to each other in some sensible fashion. While often rudimentary, this is the essence of theory: variables related in logical and empirical fashion.

Many individuals will no doubt believe that the possibilities of Q for the objective study of the individual in more than test score fashion are more important than the structured sort idea. With Q we have a methodology peculiarly suited to intensive study of the individual. One individual can be given two, three, or more related Q sorts. One individual can sort a Q sort many times. The data of such sortings can be analyzed quite objectively without entirely sacrificing the richness of the usual clinical, and much less objective, methods.

In addition, Q can be used to test the effects of independent variables on complex dependent variables. One difficulty in studying attitude change under the impact of communication, interaction, and other change agents is that the effects are not simple. Ordinarily the attitude mean of an experimental group is expected to increase or decrease under the impact of the independent variable or variables. With Q, we can rather sensitively assess such changes of single individuals by using analysis of variance and factor analysis of the data of structured Q sorts. Although they have hardly been used, such methods hold great promise for experimental social psychological and educational studies.

Another strength of Q is its usefulness in exploratory research. Suppose that one has little clear idea of the variables of a field of study but one has good hunches on some of the specific content of the variables. For example, Riesman talks a great deal about inner-direction and other-direction and the presumed characteristics and behaviors of inner- and other-directed individuals. But he has little to say about how his theoretical notions can be tested. An analysis of the things he says about inner-direction and other-direction seems to show certain themes or categories of statements around which one could structure a one-way Q sort. Such themes might be *achievement, privacy, abstract principle, conscience, group-interpersonal relations, niceness or emphasis on personality,* and *reality.* Or one might select, say, three or four of these themes and build a two-way structured sort somewhat like this:

	Individual-Group	Morality	Achievement
Inner-Direction			
Other-Direction			

While this paradigm might or might not be an adequate representation of the Riesman theory, it may at least give a good start to its empirical testing. Similarly, we may be able to lay out the operational structure of speculative and theoretical formulations in education, albeit rather crudely in the beginning. Then the reality of empirical data can help us refine the theory—or discard it, if need be.

Q methodology has other advantages. As indicated earlier, analysis of variance and correlation can be applied to Q data. Q sorting is interesting to subjects: most persons seem to enjoy sorting Q decks, perhaps because the method is realistic as well as challenging. Factor arrays are an important contribution to analysis and interpretation. The salient parts of factors are laid out for us to see and to interpret. One sees, so to speak, the verbal or other expression of the essence of whatever it is that is common to several individuals.

As usual, disadvantages accompany advantages. First, take the matter of sampling of persons. One can rarely work with sufficiently large samples in Q. It is not a method well-suited to cross-sectional or large sample purposes. One does not draw a random sample of persons for study with Q. While Stephenson argues the point vigorously, there is no escaping the inability of the investigator using Q to generalize to populations of individuals. Q therefore always requires cross-sectional supplementation. No matter how promising Q results may be, one cannot escape the necessity of testing theory on larger numbers of individuals.[16]

Q sorting has been adversely criticized, mostly on statistical grounds.[17] It will be remembered from a much earlier discussion that statistical operations and tests assume independence. This means that the response to one item should not be affected by responses to other items. In Q the placement of one card somewhere along the continuum should not affect the placement of other cards. If Q placements affect each other, then the independence assumption is violated. Unfortunately, this assumption is violated in all forced-choice procedures. And Q, of course, is a forced-choice procedure, since it is a rank-order method.

The real question is: How serious is the violation of the assumption? Is it serious enough to invalidate the use of correlational and analysis of variance procedures? There is no doubt that in an 80-item sort, there are not really 79 degrees of freedom. Thus, to some extent at least, the analysis of variance procedure is vitiated. It is doubtful, however, that too much is risked in Q statistical situations, if there is a fairly large number of items. One can perhaps fall back on Fisher's advice given long

---

[16] Stephenson argues vigorously against this point of view. See, for example, Stephenson, *op. cit.*, pp. 193, 194, 218.

[17] D. Sundland, "The Construction of Q Sorts: A Criticism," *Psychological Review*, LXIX (1962), 62–64; L. Cronbach and G. Gleser, "William Stephenson. *The Study of Behavior: Q-Technique and Its Methodology.* Chicago: University of Chicago Press, 1953," *Psychometrika*, XIX (1954), 327–330 (book review).

ago: raise the requirements for statistical significance. Instead of accepting the .05 level in Q sorts, require the .01 level of significance. In most cases of Q statistical significance encountered by the author, F ratios are so high they leave little doubt as to statistical significance.[18]

Another criticism of Q has focused on the forced-choice feature of Q sorting. It has been said that the forced procedure is unnatural, that it requires the subject to conform to an unreasonable requirement. Some subjects, too, complain about the forced-choice constraint of Q sorts. Furthermore, important information on elevation and scatter is said to be lost with the forced Q procedure. This means, for example, that two individuals could correlate highly because their profiles are alike. Yet these two individuals might be quite unlike: one might be high on a scale and the other low on the scale. (The computation of r takes no account of mean differences, or differences in level or elevation.) The Q procedure throws away levels differences between individuals.

On the constraint argument, all psychometric procedures are constraints on the individual. Because an individual feels constrained or pinched in sorting Q sorts, however, is no really good reason for declaring the procedure invalid. Most such inferences are probably made by critics who *think* forced procedures constrain the individual. In the experience of the author and his students, very few individuals complain about the procedure. Most of them, indeed, seem to enjoy it. Livson and Nichols say that the Q sorter is his own worst critic and that researchers should not be unduly alarmed by adverse sorter criticisms of the method.[19] They recommend use of the forced procedure after careful study of alternatives.

The evidence on the relative virtues of forced and unforced Q sorts is mixed. Block finds forced sorting equal or superior to unforced procedures.[20] Jones, on the other hand, finds the forced procedure wanting.[21] Definitive evidence one way or the other is lacking. So opinion must rule. It is the author's belief that *for its purpose* the forced sorting pro-

---

[18] It is well, however, to bear the independence stricture in mind. Instructions to subjects should not encourage lack of independence. That is, tell subjects that they can always move any card or cards from one pile to another right to the end of the sorting procedure.

[19] N. Livson and T. Nichols, "Discrimination and Reliability in Q-Sort Personality Descriptions," *Journal of Abnormal and Social Psychology*, LII (1956), 159–165. The author recalls an amusing and instructive incident. Colleagues had been asked to sort a 90-item unstructured Q sort the items of which were single words. One colleague, a philosopher, complained about the procedure. When he had finished, he said that the procedure was highly questionable, and that if he had to do it over again the results would certainly be quite different. He did the sort again *eleven months later*. The coefficient of correlation between the first and second sorts was .81!

[20] J. Block, "A Comparison of Forced and Unforced Q-Sorting Procedures," *Educational and Psychological Measurement*, XVI (1956), 481–493.

[21] A. Jones, "Distribution of Traits in Current Q-Sort Methodology," *Journal of Abnormal and Social Psychology*, LIII (1956), 90–95.

cedure is a useful device. Whether the distribution of cards is normal, rectangular, or otherwise is not so important, though the normal distribution works well and fits into statistical assumptions nicely. The important thing is to force individuals to make discriminations that they often will not make unless required to do so. The resulting measures are extremely useful in furthering the purposes outlined earlier in this chapter.

The criticism on the loss of information in Q sorting through lack of elevation and scatter is more serious.[22] The argument is too complex to discuss here. The reader should realize, however, that every time a coefficient of correlation is computed, the elevation (mean) and scatter (standard deviation) of the sets of scores are lost. Q is not unique here. Q is unique, however, in systematically using a procedure that sacrifices level and scatter. All individuals have the same *general* mean and the same *general* standard deviation. When sets of scores have these two characteristics they are called *ipsative* scores, in contrast to *normative* scores which are the usual scores derived from tests and scales.[23]

The practical answer is simple to state but not simple to implement: when elevation and scatter are important, do not use ipsative measures. If you are comparing the mean performances of two groups, for example, ipsative scores are of course inappropriate. If, on the other hand, mean differences are not important but the relations among variables *within* individuals or groups are important, then ipsative scores may well be appropriate. In the last analysis, the experience and judgment of the researcher are the final arbiters of whether Q sorting should be used.

Q METHODOLOGY IN SOCIAL SCIENTIFIC AND EDUCATIONAL RESEARCH

Although it is possible, and sometimes quite desirable, to use Q to assess the effects of experimental manipulations, simpler procedures are usually more appropriate. This stricture applies whenever a hypothesis is tested by comparing the central tendencies, variabilities, or relative frequencies of characteristics of groups of individuals. Q can profitably be used for comparing the characteristics of groups of individuals only when comparing the relations *within* the groups. For example, we might test a hypothesis that two specified groups of individuals, categorized on the basis of holding different values or attitudes, will also cluster together

---

22 See L. Cronbach and G. Gleser, "Assessing Similarity Between Profiles," *Psychological Bulletin*, L (1953), 456–473.

23 R. Cattell, "Psychological Measurement: Normative, Ipsative, Interactive," *Psychological Review*, LI (1944), 292–303. An easy way to see the normative-ipsative difference is to compare ratings, say on a scale of 1 through 7, and ranks. Rank scores are ipsative measures. No matter who ranks a set of k objects, the means and standard deviations must always be the same.

similarly on some other measure presumably related to the values or attitudes.

Suppose we believe that children of high creativity (assuming an adequate measure of creativity) will show similarity of aesthetic design preference. *Q* methodology might be useful in testing such a hypothesis. We locate a number of "high creatives" and an equal number of "noncreatives" on our measure and give them a structured sample of abstract designs. We predict that the "high creatives" will cluster together, say, but that the "noncreatives" will show much wider diversity. Now, it is true that the hypothesis could have been tested in the more usual way by counting numbers of similar preferences or by using ratings for both groups. But such tests might tell us nothing about the relations within the sets of aesthetic preferences. A technique like *Q* can do this by enabling us to interrelate and factor the responses of the individuals and to use analysis of variance procedures.

As indicated earlier, *Q* can be used to open up new areas, to test preliminary theories, to explore heuristic hunches. Examples were the suggested tentative structuring of the Riesman and Spranger theories. The problem of creativity has been tackled up to now almost entirely with large *N* cross-sectional methods. One might take a Guilford theory of convergent-divergent thinking or a Barron originality theory and explore them with *Q*.[24] Complex areas, especially psychological areas where intensive study of the individual is required, do not always yield too readily to large *N* approaches. *Q* methods, adequately used, should be useful in laying some of the research foundations in these areas.

Q is well adapted to studying certain aspects of intensive educational programs. Take attitude change in schools. Most research concentrates on the study of mean changes in attitudes under the impact of educational programs. But attitudes and attitude structures are complex. A group mean may not change much, but there may be pronounced changes in the structure of an attitude. Then, too, a group mean may change significantly, but we may have little or no idea of the nature of the change. Suppose a class is taught for a year with a new approach to social studies, an approach with several facets, say historical, economic, and social. Administration of an attitude scale before and after the program might show a significant change. But this can well leave out of account what aspects changed, the possible interactions of aspects of the general subject, and the changes in attitude factors. Again, *Q* might be a distinct aid in evaluating the program.

[24] J. Guilford, "Three Faces of Intellect," *American Psychologist*, XIV (1959), 469–479; F. Barron, "Complexity-Simplicity as a Personality Dimension," *Journal of Abnormal and Social Psychology*, XLVIII (1953), 163–172; "The Disposition toward Originality," *Journal of Abnormal and Social Psychology*, LI (1955), 478–485.

Although it cannot replace the methods discussed earlier in this book, Q methodology has a valuable contribution to make to social scientific and educational research. In competent and imaginative hands it has an important place, perhaps mainly in opening up new areas of research. It is not well-suited to testing hypotheses over large numbers of individuals, nor can it be used too well with large random samples. One can rarely generalize to populations from Q persons samples. Indeed, one usually does not wish to do so when using Q. Rather, one tests theories on small sets of individuals carefully chosen for their "known" or presumed possession of some significant characteristic or characteristics. One explores unknown and unfamiliar areas and variables for their identity, their interrelations, and their functioning. It may even be said that one uses Q for heuristic purposes. Used thus, Q is an important and unique approach to the study of psychological, sociological, and educational phenomena.

STUDY SUGGESTIONS

1. Unfortunately, there are no elementary references on Q methodology. The best advice that can be given the beginner is both positive and negative. First, the negative advice: do not try to use Q unless you have a pretty fair understanding of analysis of variance and factor analysis. It is hopeless to try to use Q mechanically via precept and formula.

   The positive advice is this: work with as many actual Q sorts as you can. Use the data examples in Stephenson's book. Do the analyses of variance.

   To get a feeling for the intercorrelation of Q sorts, type out, on 3×5 cards, the Jung Q sort that Stephenson gives on pp. 83–85, *The Study of Behavior*. Use the distribution Stephenson gives on p. 72. Ignore the categories. Sort the cards to describe yourself. Have six or seven friends do the same. Pick some introverted friends and some extroverted friends (according to your best judgment). Intercorrelate the sorts.[25] Try a simple cluster analysis by grouping persons with high r's together. After a while, you can acquire a knack for doing this.

   To learn something about the building of structured sorts, study Stephenson's Q testing of aesthetic preference in *The Study of Behavior*, pp. 128–141. Then try structuring some problem of interest

---

[25] It is useful, in recording an individual's Q sort data, to write the values of the pile placements on the backs of the cards with the individual's initials, being careful to record the initials and numbers of an individual in the same relative position on each card. With structured sorts, record the structure category symbols on the back of each card. Number the faces of the cards with random numbers 1 through n, n being the number of cards in the deck. There are more elaborate systems for sorting and recording data—for example, racks for sorting and scoring sheets for entering pile placement values—but these are not recommended.

to you. Write or select the items and try out the sort with friends.

2. Pick 12 prominent political names, six Republicans and six Democrats. Type the names on sheets in random order. Ask some individuals, whom you know to be Republicans and Democrats, to rank order the names according to their preference for the men. Intercorrelate the ranks using the rank-order coefficient of correlation. Enter the *rho*'s in a correlation matrix. Can you identify the individuals who have rank ordered the names by the intercorrelations? Do the political party preferences show in the correlations? Is this like *Q* methodology? (See Table 33.1 and accompanying discussion.)

3. Intercorrelate the data of Table 33.3. Do you get the correlation matrix of Table 33.4? Substitute other persons (and, of course, other variables) and interpret the matrix.

PART EIGHT

ANALYSIS AND INTERPRETATION

34 PRINCIPLES OF ANALYSIS AND INTERPRETATION

The research analyst breaks down data into constituent parts in order to obtain answers to research questions and to test research hypotheses. The analysis of research data, however, does not in and of itself provide the answers to research questions. Interpretation of the data is still necessary. To interpret is to explain, to find meaning. In most cases it is difficult or impossible to explain raw data: one must first analyze the data and then interpret the results of the analysis.

DEFINITIONS

Analysis is the ordering, the breaking down of data into constituent parts in order to obtain answers to research questions. A researcher hypothesizes a relation between methods of teaching and pupil achievement. He plans an experiment, executes it, and gathers data from his subjects. Then he must so order, break down, and manipulate the data that he can obtain an answer to the question: Do the methods affect pupil achievement? Actually, ordering and breaking down the data should be planned very early in the research. The researcher should lay out analysis paradigms when working on the problem and the hypotheses. Then, in the actual analysis phase of the research, only mechanical analytic manipulations are required.

Interpretation takes the results of analysis, makes inferences pertinent to the research relations studied, and draws conclusions about these relations. The researcher who interprets research results searches them for their meaning and implications. This is done in two ways. One, the relations *within* the research study and its data are interpreted. This is the narrower and more frequent use of the term interpretation. Here interpretation and analysis are closely intertwined. One almost automatically interprets as one analyzes. That is, when one computes, say, a coefficient of correlation, one almost immediately infers the existence of a relation and draws out its significance for the research problem as one orders, breaks down, and manipulates the data.

Two, the broader meaning of the research data is sought. This is done by comparing the results and the inferences drawn within the data to theory and to other research results. One seeks the meaning and implications *between* one's research results and conclusions either of one's own or of other researchers.[1] More important, one compares one's results with the demands and expectations of theory.

An example that may illustrate these ideas is the perception of teacher characteristics research described earlier. Reasoning from so-called directive-state and social perception theory,[2] we might predict that perceptions or judgments of desirable characteristics of effective teachers will in part be determined by the attitudes toward education of the individuals making the judgments. Suppose, now, that we have measures of attitudes toward education and measures of the perceptions or judgments of the characteristics of effective teachers. We correlate the two sets of measures: the correlation is substantial. This is the analysis. The data have been broken down into the two sets of measures, which are then compared by means of a statistical procedure.

The result of the analysis, a correlation coefficient, now has to be interpreted. What is its meaning? Specifically, what is its meaning within the study? What is its broader meaning in the light of previous related research findings and interpretations? And what is its meaning as confirmation or lack of confirmation of theoretical prediction? The first and last questions usually have to be considered together, since the meaning of a finding can ordinarily be interpreted only by relating the internal data to theoretical expectation. If the "internal" prediction holds up, one then relates the finding to other research findings which may or may not be consistent with one's present finding.

The correlation was substantial. Within the study, then, the correlation datum is consistent with theoretical expectation. Directive-state theory says that central states influence perceptions. Attitude is a central state; it must therefore influence perception. The specific deduction is that attitudes toward education influence perceptions of the effective teacher. We measure both variables and correlate the measures. From the

---

[1] This distinction is due to M. Jahoda, M. Deutsch, and S. Cook. See *Research Methods in Social Relations,* part 1. New York: Holt, Rinehart and Winston, Inc., 1951, pp. 252ff.

[2] *Directive-state theory* is a broad theory of perception that says in effect that our perceptions of cognitive objects are colored by our emotions, needs, wants, motives, attitudes, and values. These latter are, so to speak, directive-states within the individual influencing his perceptions and judgments. See J. Bruner, "Social Psychology and Perception." In E. Maccoby, T. Newcomb, and E. Hartley, eds., *Readings in Social Psychology,* rev. ed. New York: Holt, Rinehart and Winston, Inc., 1958, pp. 85–94. A more complete discussion can be found in: F. Allport, *Theories of Perception and the Concept of Structure.* New York: Wiley, 1955, chaps. 13, 14, and 15.

correlation coefficient we make an inferential leap to the hypothesis: since it is substantial, as predicted, the hypothesis is upheld. We then attempt to relate the finding to other research and other theory. In this case the finding is consistent with much of the research on directive-state and social perception theory, though it may be a far cry from laboratory experiments on perceptions of sizes of coins and perceptions of food objects to measurement of educational attitudes and perceptions of desirable teacher characteristics.

FREQUENCIES AND CONTINUOUS MEASURES

Quantitative data come in two general forms: frequencies and continuous measures. Although we have earlier seen that it is possible to view both types of measure in the same frame of reference by our definition of measurement, in practice it is necessary and useful to distinguish them.

Frequencies are simply the numbers of objects in sets and subsets. Let U be the universal set with N objects. Then N is the *number* of objects in U. Let U be partitioned into A_1, A_2, $\cdots$, A_k. Let n_1, n_2, $\cdots$, n_k be the numbers of objects in A_1, A_2, $\cdots$, A_k. Then n_1, n_2, $\cdots$, n_k are called frequencies.

It is helpful to look at this as a function. Let X be any set of objects with members $\{x_1, x_2, \cdots, x_n\}$. We wish to measure an attribute of the members of the set; call it M. Let $Y = \{0, 1\}$. Let the measurement be described as a function:

$$f = \{(x, y);\ x \text{ is a member of the set } X, \text{ and } y \text{ is either}$$
$$1 \text{ or } 0 \text{ depending on } x\text{'s possessing or not possessing } M\}$$

This is read: f, a function, or rule of correspondence, equals the set of ordered pairs (x, y) such that x is a member of X, y is 1 or 0, and so on. If x possesses M (determined in some empirical fashion), then assign a 1. If x does not possess M, assign a 0. Obviously this works very well with attributes like sex, religious preference, social class membership, and so on. It can also be adapted to variates (continuous measures) by definition and convention, as we learned earlier. To find the frequency of objects with characteristic A, count the number of objects that have been assigned 1.

With continuous measures or variates, the basic idea is the same. Only the rule of correspondence, f, and the numerals assigned to objects change. The rule of correspondence is more elaborate and the numerals are generally 0, 1, 2, $\cdots$ and fractions of these numerals. In other words, we write the measurement equation:

$$f = \{(x, y);\ x \text{ is an object, and } y = \text{any numeral}\}$$

which is the generalized form of the function. This digression or review is important, because it helps us to see the basic identity of frequency analysis and continuous measure analysis.

THE FIVE RULES OF CATEGORIZATION

The first step in any analysis is categorization. Categorization is merely another word for partitioning, that is, a *category* is a partition or a subpartition. If a set of objects is categorized in some way, it is simply partitioned according to some rule. The rule tells us, in effect, how to assign set objects to partitions and subpartitions. If this is so, then the rules of partitioning we studied earlier apply to problems of categorization. We need only explain the rules, relate them to the basic purposes of analysis, and put them to work in practical analytic situations.

Five rules of categorization are given below. Two of them, (2) and (3), are the exhaustiveness and disjointness rules discussed earlier in the book. Two others, (4) and (5), can actually be deduced from the fundamental rules, (2) and (3). Nevertheless, we list them as separate rules for practical reasons.

1. Categories are set up according to the research problem and purpose.
2. The categories are exhaustive.
3. The categories are mutually exclusive and independent.
4. Each category (variable) is derived from one classification principle.
5. Any categorization scheme must be on one level of discourse.

Rule 1 is the most important. If categorizations are not set up according to the demands of the research problem, then there can be no adequate answers to the research questions. We constantly ask: Does my analysis paradigm conform to the research problem? Does the analysis scheme enable me to test my hypotheses adequately? Suppose the hypothesis were: Religious education enhances the moral characteristics of children. Religious education has been defined as "parochial school education," moral characteristics as "honesty." The hypothesis is, therefore: Parochial children are more honest than public school children. (We ignore the great difficulty in designing an adequate test of this and related hypotheses.) Whatever data are gathered, whatever analysis is used, both data and analysis must bear directly on this hypothesis.

The simplest type of analysis is a frequency analysis. We randomly sample parochial and public schools, randomly sample n children from each school, and measure their honesty. Let us suppose that the best we can do is to label each child as *honest* or *not honest*. The paradigm for the frequency analysis would look like this:

	Honest	Not Honest
Parochial		
	FREQUENCIES	
Public		

If we had continuous measures for the *honesty* variable, then the paradigm would be different:

Parochial (1)	Public (2)
.	.
. Y Measures	.
.	.
.	.
M_{Y_1}	M_{Y_2}

It is obvious that both paradigms bear directly on the hypothesis: both enable the researcher to test the hypothesis, albeit in quite different ways. The point is that an analytical paradigm is, in effect, another way to state a problem, a hypothesis, a relation. That one paradigm uses frequencies while the other uses continuous measures in no way alters the relation tested. In other words, both modes of analysis are logically the same: they both test the proposition that the type of education affects honesty. They differ in the data they use, in statistical tests, and in sensitivity and power.

There are several things a researcher might do that would be irrelevant to the problem. If he included one, two, or three variables in the study with no theoretical or practical reason for doing so, then the analytic paradigm would be at least partly irrelevant to the problem. To take an extreme example, suppose a researcher collected achievement-test data from both types of schools and tested the achievement differences. This would probably have no bearing on the problem, since the researcher is interested in the moral differences and not the achievement differences between the two types of schools and, of course, between religious instruction and no religious instruction. He might bring other variables into the picture that have little or no bearing on the problem, for example, differences in teacher experience and training or teacher-pupil ratios. If, on the other hand, he thought that certain variables, like sex, family religious background, and perhaps personality variables, might interact with religious instruction to produce differences, then he might be justified in building such variables into the research problem and consequently into the analytic paradigm.

Rule 2, on exhaustiveness, is quite familiar to us. To repeat briefly, it simply means that all subjects, all objects of U, must be used up. All individuals in the universe must be capable of being assigned to the cells of the analytic paradigm. With the example just considered, each child either goes to parochial school or to public school. If, somehow, the sampling had included children who attend private schools, then the rule would be violated because there would be a number of children who could not be fitted into the 2×2 paradigm. If the research problem called for private-school pupils, then the 2×2 paradigm would have to be changed to a 3×2 paradigm, the rubric Private being added to Parochial and Public.

The exhaustiveness criterion is not always easy to satisfy. With true attributes, there is no problem. If sex is one of the variables, any individual has to be male or female. Suppose, however, that a variable under study were religious preference and we set up, in a paradigm, Protestant-Catholic-Jew. Now suppose some subjects were atheists or Buddhists. Clearly the categorization scheme violates the exhaustiveness rule: some subjects would have no cells to which to be assigned. Depending on numbers of cases and the research problem, we might add another rubric, Others, to which we assign any subjects who are not Protestants, Catholics, or Jews. Another solution, especially when the number of Others is small, is to drop these subjects from the study. Still another solution is to put these other subjects, if it is possible to do so, under an already existing rubric. Other variables where this problem is encountered are political preference, social class, types of education, types of teacher training, and so on.

Rule 3 is one that often causes research workers concern. To demand that the categories must be mutually exclusive means, as we learned earlier, that each object of U, each research subject (actually the measure assigned to each subject), must be assigned to one cell and one cell only of an analytic paradigm. This is a function of operational definition. Definitions of variables must be clear and unambiguous so that it is unlikely that any subject can be assigned to more than one cell. If religious preference is the variable being defined, then the definition of membership in the subsets Protestant, Catholic, and Jew must be clear and unambiguous. It might be "registered membership in a church." It might be "born in the church." It might simply be the subject's identification of himself as a Protestant, a Catholic, or a Jew. Whatever the definition, it must enable the investigator to assign any subject to one and only one of the three cells.

The independence part of Rule 3 is often difficult to satisfy, especially with continuous measures—and sometimes with frequencies. *In-*

dependence means, as we have seen before, that the assignment of one object to a cell in no way affects the assignment of any other object to that cell or to any other cell. Random assignment from an infinite or very large universe, of course, satisfies the rule. Without random assignment, however, we run into problems. When assigning objects to cells on the basis of the object's possession of certain characteristics, the assignment of an object now may affect the assignment of another object later.

Among the five rules, Rule 4, that each category (variable) must be derived from one classificatory principle, is sometimes violated by the neophyte. If one has a firm grasp of partitioning, this error is easily avoided. The rule means that, in setting up an analytic design, each variable has to be treated separately, because each variable is a separate dimension. One does not put two or more variables in one category or one dimension. If one were studying, for instance, the relations between social class, sex, and school achievement, one would not put social class and sex on one dimension. If one were studying the relations between methods of teaching, types of motivation, and school achievement, one would not lump together methods of teaching and types of motivation on one dimension. Such an error might look like one of the following designs:

(*a*)

	Method 1	Method 2	Type *a*	Type *b*
High School Achievement				
		FREQUENCIES		
Low School Achievement				

(*b*)

Method 1	Method 2	Type *a*	Type *b*
	ACHIEVEMENT SCORES		

It is clear that both paradigms violate the rule: they have one category derived from two classificatory principles. Correct paradigms might look like those of Fig. 34.1 (frequency analysis) or Fig. 34.2 (continuous measure analysis). If the student will use different letters for each variable, $A, B, C, \cdots$, with breakdowns $A_1, A_2, \cdots, B_1 B_2 \cdots$, he is not as likely to make this error.

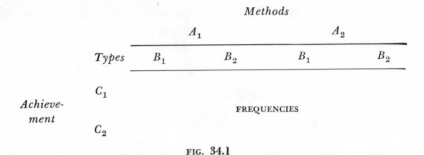

FIG. 34.1

Rule 5 is the hardest to explain because the term "level of discourse" is hard to define. It was defined in an earlier chapter as a set that contains all the objects that enter into a discussion. If we use the expression "universe of discourse," we tie the idea to set ideas. When talking about U_1, do not bring in U_2 without good reason and without making it clear that you are doing so.

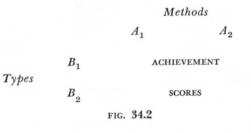

FIG. 34.2

In research analysis, it is usually the measures of the dependent variable that are analyzed. Take the problem of the relations among methods, intelligence, and achievement in an analysis of variance framework. Methods and intelligence are the independent variables; achievement is the dependent variable. The objects of analysis are the achievement measures. The independent variables and their categories are actually used to structure the dependent variable analysis. The universe of discourse, U, is the set of dependent variable measures. The independent variables can be conceived as the partitioning principles that are used to break down or partition the dependent variable measures. If, suddenly, we switch to another kind of dependent variable measure, then we may have switched levels or universes of discourse.

STATISTICAL PRESENTATION AND ANALYSIS

There are a number of types of statistical presentation. In this section, we merely glance at the main types in order to put them into perspective. We do not go into the presentation and analysis of statistical data, since these topics are well covered in almost any elementary statistics text.[3]

Frequency Distribution The simplest type of statistical presentation is the *frequency distribution,* which is, as the name indicates, the numbers of cases, or distribution of cases, falling into different categories. More specifically, a frequency distribution is a tabulation of quantitative data in classes. The classes can be the partitions of a variable or they can be frequency intervals.

There are two general types of frequency distribution: primary and secondary. *Primary presentation and analysis* is descriptive. One tells the reader how many cases of the sample or universe fall into each class. Here is a simple example. I tossed four coins 20 times. The frequency distribution of numbers of heads that turned up in each of the classes 4 Heads, 3 Heads, 2 Heads, 1 Head, 0 Heads is as follows:

Number of Heads	f
4	1
3	6
2	11
1	2
0	0
	20

More elaborate frequency distributions are mainly variations on this simple theme. Though the purpose of primary analysis is mainly descriptive, sometimes hypotheses can be tested with it. For example, we might be testing observed frequencies against frequencies expected by chance.

Secondary analysis consists of comparing frequencies and percentages. Analyzing the data of an $m \times n$ frequency or percentage table is secondary analysis. We have already seen examples. The basic idea is that variables—actually the categories of variables—are juxtaposed so that relations can be studied. Primary analysis is not concerned with relations; secondary analysis is. The simplest example of secondary analysis is the 2×2 crossbreak which is in essence the same as a double frequency distribution. If we had two columns of frequencies in the little distribution above, one for men and one for women, and proportions in the table, we might be able to say something about sex and coin-tossing behavior. Any crossbreak is in effect a frequency distribution, then, though we ordinarily do not use the two terms interchangeably.

---

[3] A good elementary text, especially for students of education, is M. Tate, *Statistics in Education.* New York: Macmillan, 1955. See, especially, chap. II.

Central Tendencies of Groups of Measures   It is possible that measures of central tendencies, statistical averages, are used more than any other measures. The reason is not hard to find. Groups of measures are too many and too complex for the eye and understanding to grasp. To compare groups of measures and to represent all the measures of a group with indices, and to interpret individual measures, measures of central tendency are used. They accomplish these purposes succinctly and efficiently.

The three principal measures of central tendency are the mean, the median, and the mode. They are averages by definition. The *mean* is the arithmetic average of a set of measures and is the most important and most-used central tendency average. The mean is the staple statistic of statistics, because of its reliability and its useful algebraic properties. There are three or four other kinds of means, but they will not be discussed here.[4]

The *median* is the midmost measure of any set of measures. It is a useful average when there are only a few very high or very low measures. The mean is unduly affected by such measures; the median is not. Compared to the mean, however, its usefulness is limited. It is a nonalgebraic measure that lacks the manipulative flexibility of the mean. Lately statisticians have been working out statistical tests that require the use of the median. Perhaps its most frequent use in social scientific and educational research is to help split a group into two equal parts, high intelligence and low intelligence, high anxiety and low anxiety, for instance.

The *mode* is the most frequently occurring measure of a set of measures. Modes are sometimes important in describing distributions. For example, it may be important for an educational investigator to know that a distribution of achievement scores is bimodal, a distribution with two points at which many similar scores cluster. In fact, such an occurrence may indicate that important factors, unknown to the investigator, are operating.

Variability of Sets of Measures   It is perhaps superfluous to mention here that the variability of any set of scores is one of its most important characteristics. In Chap. 7 and elsewhere, variability was discussed rather thoroughly; a few practical words will suffice here.

Research data reports should contain measures of variability. Generally speaking, a mean should not be reported unless a standard deviation (and the N) is also reported. The reader of a report should be able to interpret the data, always difficult or impossible without variability measures. In addition, some readers may wish to reanalyze the data of research reports. To do so they need variability measures.

[4] Types of means, as well as other measures of central tendency, are well discussed in Tate, *op. cit.*, chap. III.

The measures of variability in most use are the range, the standard deviation, the variance, and the semi-interquartile range.[5] In most behavioral research, the standard deviation and the variance are used. If the median is used as a measure of central tendency, as it must be with certain kinds of data, the semi-interquartile range, or more briefly, the quartile deviation, is used. One quartile deviation above and below the median includes 50 percent of the cases. This measure is independent of extreme values, unlike the range and the standard deviation, but, because of its nonalgebraic properties, it is useful mainly as a descriptive measure.

Until recent years the *range,* the difference between the highest and lowest measures of a set of measures, had little usefulness. Lately, however, it has come into research use, particularly in statistical tests with small samples (with N about 20 or 15, or less). For example, there are one-way and two-way analysis of variance methods that use the range as a measure of variability.[6] The range can also be used for quick estimates. Rough estimates of the standard deviation can be obtained by taking fractions of the range. If samples are small, say 30 or less, divide by 4; if larger, divide by 5 or 6. More useful, perhaps, a good estimate of the standard error of the mean can be calculated easily and quickly with the range. If the sample size is 15 or less, simply divide the number of cases (N) into the range; t tests are also possible with the range.[7]

Measures of Relations   There are many measures of relation in use. In this book we have already examined the product-moment coefficient of correlation (r), the rank-order coefficient of correlation (ρ), and the distance measure (D). All coefficients of relation, no matter how divergent in derivation, appearance, and use, do the same thing. They express the extent to which the members of the pairs of a set of ordered pairs vary concomitantly. It should also be pointed out that there is no essential and basic difference in purpose between a coefficient of correlation, a crossbreak frequency or percentage table, and an F or t test. They all have the same essential purpose: to tell the researcher whether a relation exists. Some of them, coefficients of correlation or association, tell the degree of the relation.

Coefficients of correlation usually vary in value from -1.00 through 0 to $+1.00$, or from 0 to $+1.00$, -1.00 and 1.00 indicating perfect negative and positive association, respectively, and 0 indicating no discernible relation. Whether the student is going to do research or read research re-

[5] See *ibid.,* chap. IV.

[6] See F. Mosteller and R. Bush, "Selected Quantitative Techniques." In G. Lindzey, ed., *Handbook of Social Psychology,* vol. I. Cambridge, Mass.: Addison-Wesley, 1954, pp. 304–307.

[7] *Ibid.,* pp. 323, 324.

ports, he will need a rather thorough knowledge of correlation and measures of correlation. Fortunately there are good references on the subject.[8]

Analysis of Differences   The analysis of differences, particularly the analysis of mean differences, was discussed in detail in Part III. We merely need to add that analysis of differences is by no means confined to measures of central tendency. The variances of different groups can be compared. An investigator might predict, for example, that a certain method of teaching social studies will make groups of pupils more heterogeneous than some other method. In such a case the variances or ranges of two or more groups can be compared and the differences tested for statistical significance. (An *F* test is appropriate.)

A very common form of the analysis of differences is the analysis of frequencies and percentages. The differences studied are those between obtained frequencies and percentages and those expected by chance. If these differences are found to be statistically significant, the existence of a relation between independent and dependent variables is inferred.

The differences between coefficients or correlation often have to be analyzed. One might predict on the basis of theory that a relation between *A* and *B* is stronger than between *C* and *D*. Say that $r_{AB} = .62$ and $r_{CD} = .51$. We compare the two: $.62 - .51 = .11$. Is this difference significant? A statistical test exists to answer this question.[9]

Profile Analysis   Recent developments have expanded the possibilities of analysis of profiles. A *profile* is a set of different measures of an individual or a group, each of which is expressed in the same unit of measure. An individual's scores on a group of different tests, if all scores have been converted to a common measure system (like percentiles, ranks, standard scores), constitute a profile. Although profiles are used mostly for diagnostic purposes, they are becoming increasingly important in psychological research. The scores yielded by the semantic differential and by *Q* sorts are profiles, for example. Factor analysis is partly concerned with profiles.

Important analytical problems are the assessment of the similarities of profiles and the related problem of how profiles cluster to form homogeneous groups of profiles. In Chap. 32, the cluster problem was considered in some detail. In Table 32.1, for instance, one subject's responses to five concepts on six semantic differential scales were given. The scores on the six concepts formed profiles. The cluster analysis of these profiles was given in Table 32.2, where *D* measures, measures of the similarity of the six profiles, were given. We might also have corre-

---

[8] See Tate, *op. cit.*, chap. VI. Most of the statistics and measurement texts cited in this book have good explanations of correlation and coefficients of correlation.

[9] A. Edwards, *Statistical Methods for the Behavioral Sciences*. New York: Holt, Rinehart and Winston, Inc., 1954, pp. 304–307; Tate, *op. cit.*, pp. 443, 444 and 467–468.

lated these data using r. Thus r can also be called a measure of profile similarity.

Another simple but instructive example of profile data was given in Table 33.3, where the scores of four persons on one Q sort were given. These profiles were intercorrelated with r.

There are a number of interesting possible applications of profile analysis to psychological and educational research problems. A child's meaning space, as well as the meaning spaces of groups of children, can be studied through profile analysis. We might ask: How do the meaning spaces of a child change over time? Is this child's meaning space similar to those of other children of his age and grade? Is the meaning space of the children of Group A similar to, or different from, the meaning space of the children of Group B?

We might be interested in the different perceptions of educational ideas and practices of educators and laymen, of teachers and administrators, of administrators and board of education members. Profile analysis can aid in the solution of these and many other research problems.

Profile analysis has special problems that require careful consideration. One of these problems is that similarity is not a general quality of persons. As Cronbach and Gleser point out, similarity is similarity only with respect to specified dimensions or complexes of characteristics.[10] Therefore it behooves the researcher to specify and define just what characteristics or complexes of characteristics are similar.

Another difficulty, or rather, set of difficulties, lies in what information one is willing to sacrifice in computing indices of profile similarity. Such decisions, of course, depend on the research problem. When one uses the product-moment coefficient of correlation (r), one loses level, that is, differences between means are sacrificed. This is loss of *elevation*. Product-moment r's take only *shape* into account. Further, *scatter,* differences in variability of profiles, is lost when computing, for instance, Q correlations. Obviously, much information is lost.[11] A measure that preserves these differences is the distance measure, D.[12]

---

[10] L. Cronbach and G. Gleser, "Assessing Similarity between Profiles," *Psychological Bulletin*, L (1953), 456–473 (p. 457).

[11] *Ibid.*, pp. 460, 461.

[12] See *ibid.* Cronbach and Gleser compare a number of profile similarity measures. They come to the general conclusion that D should in most cases be used. Until recently the analysis of D measures has been cumbersome and tricky. Nunnally, however, has published an excellent article that discusses the analysis of profile data. For the difficult factoring problem, he suggests factoring the cross-products of the raw scores. Nunnally also comes to different conclusions from Cronbach and Gleser about level, scatter, and shape. J. Nunnally, "Analysis of Profile Data," *Psychological Bulletin*, LIX (1962), 311–319.

INDICES

Index can be defined in two related ways. One, an index is an observable phenomenon that is substituted for a less observable phenomenon or for a phenomenon that cannot be directly observed. A thermometer, for example, gives readings of numbers that stand for degrees of temperature. The numerals on a speedometer dial indicate the speed of a vehicle. Test scores indicate achievement levels, verbal aptitudes, degrees of anxiety, and so on.

A definition perhaps more useful to the researcher is: An index is a number that is a composite of two or more other numbers. An investigator makes a series of observations, for example, and derives some single number from the measures of the observations to summarize the observations, to express them succinctly. By this definition, all sums and averages are indices: they all include in a single measure more than one measure. But the definition also includes the idea of indices as composites of different measures. Coefficients of correlation are such indices. So are F and t ratios. All of these combine different measures in single measures or indices.

IQ is an index: mental age divided by chronological age. (Mental age is itself an index since it is a composite of more than one measure.) There are indices of social-class status. For example, one can combine income, occupation, and place of residence to obtain a rather good index of social class. Sociometric indices were discussed in Chap. 31. They are based on the expression of choices by single numbers. An index of cohesiveness can be obtained by asking members of a group whether they would like to stay in the group. Their responses can be combined in a single number.

Indices are most important in scientific analysis. They simplify comparisons. Indeed, they enable research workers to make comparisons that otherwise could not be made or that could be made only with great difficulty. Raw data are usually much too complex to be grasped and used in mathematical and statistical manipulations. They must be reduced to manageable form. The percentage is a good example. Percentages transform raw numbers into comparable form.

Indices generally take the form of quotients: one number is divided by another number. The most useful such indices range between 0 and 1.00 or between -1.00 through 0 to $+1.00$. This makes them independent of numbers of cases and aids comparison from sample to sample and study to study. (They are generally expressed in decimal form.) There are two forms of quotients: ratios and proportions. A third form, the percentage, is a variation of the proportion.

A *ratio* is a composite of two numbers that relates one number to the other in fractional or decimal form. Any fraction, any quotient, is a ratio. Either or both the numerator and denominator of a ratio can themselves be ratios. The chief purpose and utility of a ratio is relational: it permits the comparison of otherwise noncomparable numbers. In order to do this, it is perhaps best to put the larger of the two numbers of the quotient in the denominator. This of course satisfies the condition mentioned above of having the ratio values range between 0 and 1.00, or between -1.00 through 0 to $+1.00$. This is by no means absolutely necessary, however. If, for example, we wished to compare the ratio of male to female high school graduates to the ratio of male and female graduates of junior high school graduates over several years, the ratio could sometimes be less than 1.00 and sometimes greater than 1.00, since it is possible that the preponderance of one sex over the other in one year might change in another year.

Sometimes ratios give more accurate information (in a sense) than the parts of which they are composed. If one were studying the relation between educational variables and tax rate, for instance, and if one were to use actual tax rates, an erroneous notion of the relation could be obtained. This is because tax rates on property are often misleading. Some communities with high *rates* actually have relatively low levels of taxation. The assessed valuation of property may be low. To avoid the discrepancies between one community and another, one can compute, for each community, the ratio of assessed valuation to true valuation. Then an adjusted tax rate, a "true" tax rate, can be computed by multiplying the tax rate in use by this fraction. This will yield a more accurate figure to use in calculations of relations between the tax rate and other variables.

Newcomb, in his study of the acquaintance process, invented an interesting ratio index.[13] As an index of agreement, Newcomb counted the issues among a large number of issues on which pairs of individuals agreed and disagreed. For each pair of subjects, the following ratio was computed:

$$\frac{\text{Number of agreeing responses to items of importance to both members}}{\text{Number of disagreeing responses to items of importance to both members}}$$

As an index of "reality-irreality" of the perceptions of group members of themselves and each other, one could use a sociometric index: the number of perceived choices by other members (on some appropriate criterion) divided by the number of actual choices. Such a ratio might be called an index of perceived acceptance or perceived rejection.

A *proportion* is a ratio, a fraction, but it is a special kind of ratio.

[13] T. Newcomb, *The Acquaintance Process*. New York: Holt, Rinehart, and Winston, Inc., 1961, pp. 281, 282.

It is a fraction with the numerator one of two or more observed frequencies and the denominator the sum of the observed frequencies. The probability definition given earlier, $p = s/(s + f)$, where s = number of successes and f = number of failures, is a proportion. Take any two numbers, say 20 and 60. The ratio of the two numbers is $20/60 = .33$. (It could also be $60/20 = 3$.) If these two numbers were the observed frequencies of the presence and lack of presence of an attribute in a total sample, where $N = 60 + 20 = 80$, then a proportion would be: $20/(60 + 20) = 20/80 = 1/4 = .25$. Another proportion, of course, is $60/80 = .75$.

A *percentage* is simply a proportion multiplied by 100. With the above example, $20/80 \times 100 = 1/4 \times 100 = 25$ percent. The main purpose of proportions and percentages is to reduce different sets of numbers to comparable sets of numbers with a common base. Any set of frequencies can be transformed to proportions or percentages in order to facilitate statistical manipulation and interpretation.[14]

A word of caution is in order. Because they are often a mixture of two fallible measures, indices can be dangerous. The IQ is a good example. The numerator of the fraction is itself an index since MA, mental age, is a composite of a number of measures. A better example is the so-called Achievement Quotient: $AQ = 100 \times EA/MA$, where EA = Educational Age, and MA = Mental Age. Here, both the numerator and the denominator of the fraction are complex indices. Both are mixtures of measures of varying reliability. To make matters worse, they are now thrown together. What is the meaning of the resulting index? How can we interpret it sensibly? It would be hard to say. In short, while indices are indispensable aids to scientific analysis, they must be used with circumspection and care.

THE INTERPRETATION OF RESEARCH DATA

Scientists, in evaluating research, can disagree on two broad fronts: data and the interpretation of data. Disagreements on data focus on such problems as the validity and reliability of measurement instruments, the adequacy and inadequacy of research design and methods of observation, and the adequacy and inadequacy of analysis. Assuming a certain degree of competence and adequacy, however, we find that major disagreements ordinarily focus upon the interpretation of data. Most psychologists, for example, will agree on the data of reinforcement experiments. Yet they disagree vigorously on the interpretation of the data of the experiments.

[14] Percentages should not be used with small numbers, though proportions may always be used. The reason for the percentage computation restriction is that the relatively larger percentages give a sense of accuracy not really present in the data. For example, suppose 6 and 4 are two observed frequencies. To transform these frequencies to 60 percent and 40 percent is a bit absurd.

Such disagreements are in part a function of theory. In a book like this we cannot labor interpretation from theoretical standpoints. We must be content with a more limited objective: the clarification of some common precepts of the interpretation of data *within* a particular research study or series of studies.

Adequacy of Research Design, Methodology, Measurement, and Analysis

One of the major themes of this book has been the appropriateness of methodology to the problem under investigation. The researcher usually has a choice of research designs, methods of observation, methods of measurement, and types of analysis. All of these elements must be congruent; they must all fit together. One does not plan, for example, a factorial design with nominal data, nor does one use an analysis appropriate to frequencies with, say, the continuous measures yielded by an attitude scale. Most important, the design, the methods of observation and measurement, and the statistical analysis must all be appropriate to the research problem.

An investigator obviously must carefully scrutinize what might be called the technical adequacy of the methods, the measurement, and the statistics. The adequacy of data interpretation crucially depends upon such scrutiny. A frequent source of interpretative inadequacy, for example, is randomness. Investigators frequently interpret ex post facto research data as though they were experimental data in which random assignment has been used.

Another frequent source of interpretative inadequacy is neglect of measurement problems. It is urgently necessary, in all social scientific and educational research, to pay particular attention to the reliability and validity of the measures of the variables. Simply to accept without question the reliability and validity of psychological measuring instruments is a gross error.

The researcher must be especially careful to question the validity of his measures, since the whole interpretative framework can collapse on this one point alone. If an educational investigator's problem includes the variable anxiety, and the statistical analysis shows a positive relation between anxiety and, say, achievement, the investigator must ask himself and the data whether the anxiety measured is the type of anxiety warranted by the problem. He might, for example, be measuring test anxiety when the problem calls for general anxiety. Similarly, he must ask himself whether his measure of achievement is valid for the research purpose. If the research problem demands application of principles but the measure of achievement is a standardized test that emphasizes factual knowledge, the interpretation of the data can be quite erroneous.

In other words, we face here the obvious, but too easily overlooked, fact that adequacy of interpretation is dependent on each link in the methodological chain, as well as on the appropriateness of each link to the research problem and the congruence of the links to each other. This is clearly seen when we are faced with negative or inconclusive results.

Negative or inconclusive results are much harder to interpret than positive results. When results are positive, when the data support the hypotheses, one interprets the data along the lines of the theory and the reasoning behind the hypotheses. Although one carefully asks critical questions, upheld predictions are evidence for the validity of the reasoning behind the problem statement. In addition, positive results are evidence that the methodology, the measurement, and the analysis are satisfactory.

This is one of the great virtues of scientific prediction. When we predict something and plan and execute a scheme for testing the prediction, and things turn out as we say they will, then the adequacy of our reasoning and our execution seems supported. We are never sure, of course. The outcome, though predicted, may be as it is for reasons quite other than those we fondly espouse. Still, the fact that the whole complex chain of theory—deduction from theory, design, methodology, measurement, and analysis—has led to a predicted outcome is cogent evidence for the adequacy of the whole structure. We make a complex bet with the odds against us, so to speak. We then throw the research dice or spin the research wheel. If our predicted number comes up, the reasoning and the execution leading to the successful prediction would seem to be adequate. If we can repeat the feat, then the evidence of adequacy is even more convincing.

But now take the negative case. Why were the results negative? Why did the results not come out as predicted? Note that any weak link in the research chain can cause negative results. If the design and the observation methods are not appropriate to the problem, clearly positive results can only be fortuitous or erroneous. If the measurement lacks reliability, inconclusive results will almost necessarily follow. If the statistical analysis is unsuited to the data, the results can easily be inconclusive. If, for example, a weak nonparametric test is used when a strong parametric one is needed, an actual relation can go undetected. But which of these possible causes of inconclusiveness, if any, is the true cause? Or are the theory and hypotheses at fault? It is an extremely difficult if not impossible task to answer these questions. Why?

Negative results can be due to any one, or several, or all of the following: incorrect theory and hypotheses, inappropriate or incorrect methodology, inadequate or poor measurement, and faulty analysis. All these factors must be carefully examined in turn. All must be scrutinized and the negative results laid at the door of one, several, or all of them. If we can be fairly sure that the methodology, the measurement, and the analysis are adequate, then negative results can be definite contributions to scientific advance, since then and only then can we have some confidence that our hypotheses are not correct.

The Interpretation of Unhypothesized Relations The testing of hypothesized relations has been strongly emphasized in this book. This does not mean, however, that other relations in the data are not sought and tested. Quite the contrary. The practicing researcher is always keen to seek out and study relations in his data. The unpredicted relation may be an important key to deeper understanding of theory. It may throw light on aspects of the problem not anticipated when the problem was formulated. Therefore researchers, while emphasizing hypothesized relations, should always be alert to unanticipated relations in their data.

Suppose we have hypothesized that the homogeneous grouping of pupils will be beneficial to bright pupils but not beneficial to pupils of lesser ability. The hypothesis is upheld, say. But we notice an apparent difference between suburban and rural areas: the relation seems stronger in the suburban areas; it is reversed in some rural areas! We cross-partition the data using the suburban-rural variable. We find that homogeneous grouping seems to have a marked influence on bright children in the suburbs, but that it has little or no influence in rural areas.[15] This would be an important finding indeed.

But such unpredicted findings must be treated with more suspicion than predicted findings. Before accepting them, they should be substantiated in independent research in which they are specifically predicted and tested. Only when a relation is deliberately and systematically tested with the necessary controls built into the design can we have much faith in it. The unanticipated finding may be fortuitous or spurious.

Proof, Probability, and Interpretation The interpretation of research data culminates in conditional probabilistic statements of the "If p, then q" kind. We enrich such statements by qualifying them in some such way as: If p, then q, under the conditions r, s, and t. Ordinarily we eschew causal statements, because we are aware that such statements cannot be made without grave risk of error.

Perhaps of greater practical importance to the researcher interpreting data is the problem of proof. Let us flatly assert that nothing can be "proved" scientifically. All one can do is to bring evidence to bear that such-and-such a proposition is true. Proof is a deductive matter, and experimental methods of inquiry are not methods of proof. They are controlled methods of bringing evidence to bear on the probable truth or falsity of relational propositions. No scientific investigation ever proves anything, in short. Thus the interpretation of the analysis of research data can never use the term proof in the logical sense of the word. Inter-

[15] I am indebted to Dr. Bernard Bryan, Superintendent, Second Supervisory District, New York State, for suggesting this hypothesis.

pretation, rather, must concern itself with the evidence for or against the validity of tested hypotheses.

Fortunately, for practical research purposes it is not necessary to worry excessively about causality and proof. Evidence at satisfactory levels of probability is sufficient for scientific progress. Causality and proof were discussed in this chapter to sensitize the reader to the danger of loose usage of the terms. The understanding of scientific reasoning, and practice and reasonable care in the interpretation of research data, while no guarantees of the validity of one's interpretations, are helpful guards against inadequate inference from data to conclusions.

STUDY SUGGESTIONS

1. Suppose you wish to study the relation between intelligence and school achievement. What are the two main possibilities for analyzing the data (omitting the possibility of computing a coefficient of correlation in the usual way)? Set up two analytic structures.
2. Assume that you want to add social class as a variable to the problem of Study Suggestion 1. Set up the two kinds of analytic paradigms.
3. An investigator has tested the differential effects of three methods of teaching reading on reading achievement. He had 30 subjects in each group and a reading achievement score for each subject. What does the analysis paradigm look like? What type of statistical analysis should he use?

    Set up a frequency analysis paradigm of the same data. What statistical test should be used? Which of the two methods, generally speaking, is better? Why?
4. In a study of the effects of group psychotherapy on the reading of retarded readers, Fisher reported the following scores and means for matched pairs of subjects:[16]

Pairs	Therapy	Nontherapy
A	16.0	9.0
B	8.5	9.0
C	18.5	16.5
D	6.0	13.5
E	7.5	2.0
F	12.5	— .5
M:	11.50	8.25

The therapy group received remedial reading instruction plus therapy. The nontherapy group received only remedial reading instruction.

[16] S. Fisher, "Group Therapy of Retarded Readers," *Journal of Educational Psychology,* XLIV (1953), 354–360.

The author says that the final results show that the group that had therapy showed the greater improvement in reading. He bases this conclusion on the fact that the nontherapy group's range of improvement scores was −.5 to 16.5 (months) with a mean gain of 8.25 (months), whereas the therapy group's range was 6.0 to 18.5 with a mean gain of 11.5. He says that the therapy group gained 3.25 months or 39.4 percent more than the nontherapy group.

Analyze these data. (*Hint:* Use two-way analysis of variance.) What conclusion do you come to? Discuss Fisher's results and his conclusions.

5. Fahey and Ball, in an evelution of a core curriculum program in general education at the college level, used volunteer teachers and, in effect, volunteer students.[17] Students for the core classes were invited to participate and were given tuition remission if they did so. Tests were given "to all students who would take them." That is, the students were notified of the tests and were urged to take them (but not required to do so). After a number of statistical analyses, the authors report their results and the interpretation of the results.

Comment on the interpretation of the results of this study. How much faith can we have in any conclusions of the authors? (The student is urged to read the original report. There is enough material here, however, for critical comment.)

6. Do simple one-way analysis of variance paradigms represent partitioning of variables? How about factorial analysis of variance paradigms? If your answer to both questions is yes, *why* do you say so? Why is partitioning important in setting up research designs and in analyzing data? Do partitioning and partitioning rules have any effect on the interpretation of data? If so, what effects might they have? Why?

[17] G. Fahey and J. Ball, "Objective Evaluation of a Program in General Education," *Journal of Educational Psychology*, LI (1960), 144–151.

35 *THE ANALYSIS OF CROSSBREAKS*

In a study of the personality differences between violators and nonviolators of moral prohibitions, MacKinnon reported interesting data on the relation between guilt feelings and actual moral transgression.[1] Of 24 violators and 24 nonviolators of prohibitions—violation consisted of looking at available solutions to problems being solved after instructions not to do so—7 violators said they often felt guilty about things they had done or had not done, while 14 violators said they had never experienced guilt. Eighteen nonviolators reported often feeling guilty, whereas 5 nonviolators said they rarely felt guilty. This information can be conveniently condensed into a 2×2 table (Table 35.1).

TABLE 35.1   RELATION BETWEEN VIOLATION OF PROHIBITION AND GUILT, MACKINNON STUDY

	Violators	Nonviolators
Feel Guilty	7	18
Do Not Feel Guilty	14	5

There seems to be a relation between the two variables. Among violators there are more subjects who report that they do not feel guilty about their actions than subjects who report that they feel guilty, whereas among nonviolators there are more subjects who report that they feel guilty about their actions than subjects who report that they do not feel guilty.

Teacher mortality has plagued the education profession. Why do teachers leave teaching and go into other occupations? Some indirect light was thrown on the subject by Rosenberg who, in a study of students' values, asked students, in 1950 and again in 1952, whether they would

[1] D. MacKinnon, "Violation of Prohibition." In H. Murray, *Explorations in Personality.* New York: Oxford, 1938, pp. 491–501.

like to become teachers.[2] He also determined whether the students held values that were "people-oriented" (work with people rather than things; be helpful to others) or "non-people-oriented." One of the relations he reported is given in Table 35.2.[3]

TABLE 35.2 PEOPLE-ORIENTED VALUES AND CHANGE OF OCCUPATIONAL CHOICE, ROSENBERG STUDY. (IN PERCENT)

	Remained Teachers, 1952	Left Teaching, 1952
People-Oriented	57	43
Non-People-Oriented	19	81

The data in the table seem to say that, among students who choose teaching as a profession, those who are not oriented toward people are more likely to leave teaching than those who are oriented toward people.

CROSSBREAKS: DEFINITIONS AND PURPOSE

The examples of Tables 35.1 and 35.2 are called crossbreaks. A *crossbreak* is a numerical tabular presentation of data, usually in frequency or percentage form, in which variables are juxtaposed in order to study the relations between them.[4] In the MacKinnon example the variables were Guilt and Violation of Prohibition. The variables of the Rosenberg example were People Orientation and Change of Occupational Choice. The term "crossbreak" is most appropriately used in frequency and percentage analysis, though it is possible to call a table of means a crossbreak. In this book the term is limited to tables of frequencies and percentages.

The crossbreak is a common and useful form of analysis that can be used with almost any kind of data. Its principal use, however, is with nominal data, especially of a dichotomous nature. Apart from its actual research use, the crossbreak is a valuable pedagogical device. Its clarity

2 M. Rosenberg, "Factors Influencing Change in Occupational Choice." In P. Lazarsfeld and M. Rosenberg, eds., *The Language of Social Research*. New York: Free Press, 1955, pp. 250–259.

3 *Ibid.*, p. 251. Rosenberg's table has been changed slightly by reversing the variables.

4 Crossbreaks are also used in descriptive ways. The investigator may not be interested in relations as such: he may want only to describe a situation that exists. For instance, take the case where a table breaks social-class membership against possession of TV sets, refrigerators, and so on. This is a descriptive comparison rather than a variable crossbreak, even though we might conceivably call possession of a TV, for instance, by some variable name. Our concern is exclusively with the analysis of data gathered to test or explore relations.

and simplicity, plus its usefulness in structuring variables, make the cross-break an effectve tool for learning how to structure research problems and how to analyze data.

Crossbreaks are cross partitions. Consequently we already know a good deal about them. Most important, we know the rules governing their construction and their tie to sets and subsets. Therefore the partitioning rules and the set notions already learned can easily be applied to cross-break analysis.

The major purpose of crossbreaks is simply stated: to facilitate the study and analysis of relations. Crossbreaks, by conveniently juxtaposing research variables, enable the researcher to determine the nature of the relations between the variables. But crossbreaks have other side purposes. They can be used to organize data in convenient form for statistical analysis. A χ^2 test, for example, is easily applied to any crossbreak table. Indices of association, too, are readily computed.

Another purpose of crossbreaks is to control variables. As we shall see later, crossbreaks enable us to study and test a relation between two variables while controlling a third variable. In this way "spurious" relations can be unmasked and the relations between variables can be "specified," that is, differences in degree of relationship at different levels of a control variable can be determined.

A fourth purpose of crossbreaks was alluded to above: the pedagogical benefit. The study and use of crossbreaks, and familiarity with crossbreak paradigms, sensitize the student and practicing researcher to the design and structure of research problems. There is something very salutary about reducing a research problem to a crossbreak. In fact, it can probably be said that if you cannot write a diagrammatic paradigm of your research problem in either analysis of variance or frequency crossbreak form, then the problem is not clear in your mind, there is an error in your conceptualization, or maybe you do not really have a research problem.

SIMPLE CROSSBREAKS AND RULES
FOR CROSSBREAK CONSTRUCTION

The simplest form a crossbreak can take is the 2×2 table. Both variables are dichotomized (if they are not already natural dichotomies) and stacked up against each other. Two examples of 2×2 crossbreaks, one in frequency form and one in percentage form, have already been given. Another example of a 2×2 crossbreak is given in Table 35.3. The data in the table are from an unpublished study by the author.[5]

---

[5] A study on the relations among Authoritarianism, Intelligence, and Political and Religious Preferences. Hi *F* and Lo *F* indicate high and low scores (above and below the mean of the original group of subjects) on the *F* scale, a presumed measure of authoritarianism.

TABLE 35.3 TWO-BY-TWO CROSSBREAK: POLITICAL PREFERENCE AND AUTHORITARIANISM, KERLINGER DATA

	Hi F	Lo F	
Democrat	13	31	44
Republican	63	35	98
	76	66	(142)

Before discussing how to interpret this table, we should know how it was set up. There seem to be no generally accepted rules on the setup of crossbreaks. We know, however, that they are cross partitions and thus must follow the rules of partitioning or categorization discussed earlier: the categories are set up according to the research hypotheses; they are independent and mutually exclusive; they are exhaustive; each category is derived from one and only one classification principle; all categories are on one level of discourse.

In addition to the rules of categorization, we need two other rules. One, in constructing any frequency or percentage table, *juxtapose the variables orthogonally. Orthogonal,* recall, means right-angled or rectangular. With two variables this is simple. The familiar 2×2 table looks like Fig. 35.1.

	B_1	B_2
A_1	A_1B_1	A_1B_2
A_2	A_2B_1	A_2B_2

FIG. 35.1

In Fig. 35.1 A_1 and A_2 are the partitions of the variable A; B_1 and B_2 are the partitions of the variable B; and A and B are said to be orthogonal to each other. The cells A_1B_1, $\cdots$, A_2B_2 are simply the intersections of the subsets of A and B: $A_1 \cap B_1$, $\cdots$, $A_2 \cap B_2$. Any object in U, the universe of objects, can be categorized as A_1B_1, A_1B_2, A_2B_1, or A_2B_2. If U is a sample of children, and A is sex and B is anxiety, then an A_1B_1 might be an anxious boy, whereas an A_2B_2 child might be a non-anxious girl. The 2×3, 2×4, 3×2, and similar tables are merely extensions of the idea.

The orthogonal rule is harder to follow in the three-dimensional case. Strictly speaking, a cube is necessary. Let there be three variables A, B, C, each dichotomized (for simplicity). The actual situation would look like Fig. 35.2. Each cell is a cube with a triple label. All visible cubes have been appropriately labeled. If the variables A, B, and C were sex, anxiety, and intelligence, then, for example, an $A_2B_2C_1$ cell number might be a nonanxious girl of high intelligence.

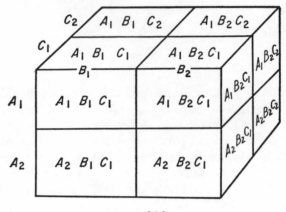

FIG. 35.2

Since handling cubes is cumbersome, we use a simpler system. The three-variable crossbreak table can look like that of Fig. 35.3. We return to three-dimensional crossbreaks later.

	B_1		B_2	
	C_1	C_2	C_1	C_2
A_1	$A_1B_1C_1$	$A_1B_1C_2$	$A_1B_2C_1$	$A_1B_2C_2$
A_2	$A_2B_1C_1$	$A_2B_1C_2$	$A_2B_2C_1$	$A_2B_2C_2$

FIG. 35.3

The second rule can be called the "percentage computation rule": *Compute percentages from the independent variable to the dependent variable.* In studies where it is not possible to label the variables as independent and dependent, the rule, of course, does not apply. But in most cases it does apply.[6]

Return to Table 35.3. Does the table indicate a relation between Political Preference and Authoritarianism? The first step in the analysis of any frequency table is to test statistical significance. That is, do the

[6] Zeisel states the rule differently: ". . . *percentages should be computed in the direction of the causal factor.*" H. Zeisel, *Say It With Figures*, rev. 4th ed. New York: Harper & Row, 1957, p. 24.

frequencies in the four cells of Table 35.3 depart significantly from the frequencies to be expected by chance? If they do, there is a relation between Political Preference and Authoritarianism. If we do a χ^2 test of the data, we find $\chi^2 = 14.74$, which is significant at the .001 level. There is, then, a statistically significant relation between Political Preference and F (Authoritarianism). But what is the nature of the relation? We can determine this by inspection of the table. It can be seen that proportionately more Republicans have high F scores than Democrats.

In many cases this much information would be sufficient for the research purpose. But it is possible to clarify the analysis by converting the tabled frequencies to percentages. It is reasonable to conceive, in this case, Political Preference as the independent variable and Authoritarianism as the dependent variable (though the opposite interpretation is not unreasonable). At any rate, we do so now (and in subsequent examples), and we compute the percentages from Political Preference to Authoritarianism, or from Democrat-Republican to Hi F and Lo F. To do this, treat each *row* separately. The frequencies of the Democrat row are 13 and 31, totaling 44. Computing $100 \times 13/44$ and $100 \times 31/44$, we obtain 30 percent and 70 percent. A similar calculation for the Republican row yields 64 percent and 36 percent. (Notice that each row must total 100 percent.) The percentage crossbreak is given in Table 35.4.

TABLE 35.4   PERCENTAGE CROSSBREAK OF TABLE 35.3 DATA

	Hi F	Lo F	
Democrat	30	70	100
Republican	64	36	100

The relation is now clearer than it was before: Republicans tend to have high, and Democrats low, F scores. There is a significant relation between Political Preference and Authoritarianism (as measured by the F scale). Note how the percentage crossbreak highlights the relation. The reason is that due to an unequal number of Democrats (44) and Republicans (98) in the sample, the relation is obscured in the frequency table. The percentage calculation transforms both rows to a common base and enhances the comparison.

It may have occurred to the reader that the percentages could have been calculated in two other ways: (1) over the whole table, and (2) down the columns. Crossbreaks resulting from these two methods are given in Table 35.5.

There is nothing fundamentally wrong with these crossbreaks. The one on the left of the table can be used for some research purposes. By adding the rows and the columns, for example, we learn the proportions

TABLE 35.5 PERCENTAGE CROSSBREAKS OF TABLE 35.3 DATA: (a) OVER
WHOLE TABLE; (b) DOWN COLUMNS

	Hi F	Lo F			Hi F	Lo F
Dem	9	22	31	Dem	17	47
Rep	44	25	69	Rep	83	53
	53	47	(100)		100	100
	(a)				(b)	

of Democrats and Republicans in the sample (rows) and the proportions
of high F's and low F's (columns). Certain measures of association can
be computed from such tables.[7] These tables do not essentially differ,
however, from the tables from which they were computed. They are simply transformations of the original data. As such, they may not be as
useful for interpretative purposes as the method mainly used in this
chapter, a method that clearly outlines the relations.

Subtable 35.5(b) is merely the case of conceiving Authoritarianism
as the independent variable and Political Preference as the dependent
variable. Notice that the interpretations of Table 35.4 and Table 35.5(b)
are different. The interpretations can be put in implication form. The
argument of Table 35.4, on the basis of the percentages, is: If Democrat,
then low F; if Republican, then high F. (Such statements are always quali-
fied by words like "tendency" and "probability." For simplicity we omit
such words here.) The argument of Table 35.5(b) is: If high F, then Republican; if low F, then either Democrat or Republican.

TYPES OF CROSSBREAKS AND TABLES

In general there are three types of tables: (1) one-dimensional, (2)
two-dimensional, and (3) k-dimensional. The number of dimensions of a
table is determined by the number of variables: a one-dimensional table
has one variable, a two-dimensional table has two variables, and so on.
It makes no difference how many categories any single variable has; the
dimensions of a table are always fixed by the number of variables. We
have already considered the two-dimensional table where two variables,
one independent and one dependent (usually), are set against each other.
In one sense, all analyses must come down to the two-dimensional break.
Indeed, most research analyses consisted, until a decade or two ago, of the
analysis of one variable against another. But it is often fruitful and nec-

---

[7] See L. Goodman and W. Kruskal, "Measures of Association for Cross Classifica-
tions," *Journal of the American Statistical Association*, XLIX (1954), 732–764; and
J. Cohen, "A Coefficient of Agreement for Nominal Scales," *Educational and Psychological Measurement*, XX (1960), 37–46.

essary to consider more than two variables simultaneously. Theoretically, there is no limit to the number of variables that can be considered at one time. The only limitations are practical ones: insufficient sample size and difficulty of comprehension of the relations contained in a multidimensional table.

One-Dimensional Tables There are two kinds of one-dimensional table. One is a "true" one-dimensional table; it is of little interest to us since it does not express a relation. Such tables occur commonly in newspapers, government publications, magazines, and so forth. In reporting the number or proportion of males and females in San Francisco, the number of cars of different makes produced in 1959, the number of children in each of the grades of X school system, we have "true" one-dimensional tables. One variable only is used in the table.

A type of table that is similar to the "true" one-dimensional table is one in which a relation is expressed, but the relation is of little or no scientific interest. We might call these "sociographic" tables. ("Sociographic" means to describe social facts.) They occur frequently in mass media of communication. When the incomes of different occupational groups are presented in a table, we have sociographic presentation. Obviously the relation expressed is between occupation and income, and equally obviously such tables are important in studying facts and trends of social, political, and economic life. Generally speaking, however, social scientists use such tables for special purposes, such as background and sampling. Occasionally a sociologist may use and analyze the data of such tables, but he does so usually for sociographic and not scientific purposes. They are, in short, tables whose purpose is essentially descriptive and practical.

Social scientists sometimes choose to report their data in tables that look one-dimensional but are really two-dimensional. Consider a table reported by Child, Potter, and Levine.[8] In this study the values expressed in third-grade children's textbooks were content-analyzed. Table 35.6 shows the percentages of instances in which rewards were given for various modes of acquisition. (In the original table, only the column of percentages on the left was given.) The table looks one-dimensional, but it really expresses a relation between two variables, Mode of Acquisition and Reward.

The key point is that tables of this kind are not really one-dimensional. In Table 35.6, one of the variables, Reward, is incompletely expressed. To make this clear, simply add another column of percentages beside those in the original table. (This has been done in Table 35.6.)

---

[8] I. Child, E. Potter, and E. Levine, "Children's Textbooks and Personality Development: An Exploration in the Social Psychology of Education," *Psychological Monographs*, LX (1946), No. 3.

TABLE 35.6   CHILD, POTTER, AND LEVINE DATA

Mode of Acquisition	% in which rewarded	(% in which not rewarded)
Effort	93	(7)
Buying, Selling, Trading	80	(20)
Asking, Wishing, Taking What is Offered	68	(32)
Dominance, Aggression, Stealing, Trickery	41	(59)

This column can be labeled "Not Rewarded." Now we have a complete two-dimensional table, and the relation becomes obvious. (Sometimes this cannot be done because data for "completing" the table are lacking.)

Two-Dimensional Tables   Two-dimensional tables or crossbreaks have two variables, each with two or more subclasses. The simplest form of a two-dimensional table, as we have seen, is called two-by-two, or simply 2×2. Two-dimensional tables are by no means limited to the 2×2 form. In fact, there is no logical limitation on the number of subclasses that each variable can have. Let us look at a few examples of $m \times n$ tables.

In their recent book, Miller and Swanson reported tests of a number of interesting hypotheses.[9] One hypothesis predicted a relation between the social-class membership of parents and the type of discipline they use, as shown in Table 35.7:[10]

TABLE 35.7   RELATION BETWEEN SOCIAL CLASS AND TYPE OF DISCIPLINE, MILLER AND SWANSON STUDY

	Discipline		
	Psychological	Mixed	Corporal
Middle Class	29 .76	5 .13	4 .11
Working Class	9 .12	28 .36	40 .52

χ^2 is 49.45, highly significant. This is, of course, a 2×3 table which the reader can easily interpret for himself. (The percentages, in proportion form, have been inserted in the cells to aid interpretation.)

---

9 D. Miller and G. Swanson, *Inner Conflict and Defense*. New York: Holt, Rinehart and Winston, Inc., 1960. Appendix D of this book contains a large number of crossbreaks.

10 *Ibid.*, p. 426. The textual discussion is on pp. 73ff. It would be profitable for the student to study the authors' theoretical reasoning and predictions in connection with the tables given in Appendix D. This book is a sophisticated theoretical-empirical study which, aside from its intrinsic interest, well replays study.

TABLE 35.8   RELATION BETWEEN SOCIAL CLASS AND TYPE OF REWARD,
MILLER AND SWANSON STUDY

	Type of Reward		
	Psychic	Neither	Concrete
Middle Class	25 .66	6 .16	7 .18
Working Class	12 .16	37 .48	28 .36

A similar table from the same book is given in Table 35.8.[11] Again, χ^2 is highly significant (29.52), and the interpretation is fairly simple. (The student should be sure he is able to interpret Tables 35.7 and 35.8, as well as earlier tables, before reading further.)

TABLE 35.9   RESPONSES OF SCHOOL BOARD MEMBERS AND SUPERINTENDENTS
TO SUBJECT MATTER-PUPIL INDIVIDUAL INTEREST QUESTION,
GROSS STUDY. (IN PERCENT)

	Desirable	No Opinion	Undesirable	N
School Board Members	33	1	66	508
Superintendents	13	2	85	105

A slightly different kind of 2×3 table is reported in Gross's excellent study of superintendents and school boards.[12] To the question "Should more emphasis be placed on teaching subject matter than on developing individual interests of the pupils?" school board members and superintendents responded as indicated in Table 35.9. Note three things: (1) the relation under study is between Role (school board members and superintendents), the independent variable, and Attitudes toward Subject Matter, the dependent variable; (2) the percentages are calculated from the independent variable to the dependent variable; (3) the table differs from those of Tables 35.7 and 35.8 in that one of the variables is what might be called a "response" variable. That is, Attitude toward Subject Matter (or Curriculum or Education) is inferred from the responses of Desirable and Undesirable to the question, whereas the sub-

[11] *Ibid.*
[12] N. Gross, *Who Runs Our Schools?* New York: Wiley, 1958. The study on which this book is based is one of the few large-scale, theoretically oriented researches in education. The more complete report is: N. Gross, W. Mason, and A. McEachern, *Explorations in Role Analysis: Studies of the School Superintendency Role.* New York: Wiley, 1958.

classes of the dependent variable, Discipline, of Table 35.7—Psychological, Mixed, and Corporal—and those of the dependent variable, type of reward, of Table 35.8—Psychic, Neither, and Concrete—directly reflect the variables. In other words, when the reader sees "Psychological-Mixed-Corporal" it is obvious to him that here is a variable (nominal), in this case a dependent variable. But when he sees "Desirable-Undesirable," it is usually not obvious that a variable is implied.[13]

Another example of a two-dimensional table that can help us make two or three important points, as well as give us interesting data to study, is from Stouffer's conformity-tolerance study.[14] Stouffer studied the relation between Tolerance, on the one hand, and several other sociological variables, on the other hand. One of the latter was Education. Stouffer was trying to get an answer to the question: What is the relation between the amount of education and degree of tolerance? The crossbreak given in Table 35.10 is instructive because (1) it is a 5 × 3 type and thus more complex than previous types; (2) it juxtaposes an ordinal variable, Education, against a classification of a presumably continuous variable, Tolerance; and (3) it illustrates a point that seems to confuse students, namely that the m and n numbers of an $m \times n$ crossbreak tell the number of subclasses or subcategories, and not the number of variables. Study of the table shows that a relation between the two variables exists: evidently the more education the more tolerance.[15]

Two-Dimensional Tables, "True" Dichotomies, and Continuous Measures
Many two-dimensional tables report "true" nominal data, data of variables that are truly dichotomous: sex, political preference, alive-dead, and

---

13 Note that all these cases involve nominal measurement.

14 S. Stouffer, *Communism, Conformity, and Civil Liberties.* New York: Doubleday, 1955. Copyright © 1955 by Samuel A. Stouffer. Reprinted by permission of Doubleday & Company, Inc. This book contains exhaustive crossbreak analyses. It can almost be considered a text and model of how to analyze relations via crossbreaks. Stouffer's untiring specifications of his data are especially valuable. For example, see chap. 4 where he juxtaposes age, education, tolerance, and other variables.

15 Note that it is possible to collapse the table into a simpler one, perhaps in order to show the relations more clearly. For example, if we ignore the In-Betweens and crossbreak College (Graduates plus Some College) against No-College, we would have:

	Less Tolerant	More Tolerant
College	45	372
No College	364	617

which becomes, in percentages:

	Less Tolerant	More Tolerant
College	11	89
No College	37	63

TABLE 35.10 RELATION BETWEEN EDUCATION AND TOLERANCE, STOUFFER STUDY

Education	Percentage of Distribution of Scores on Scale of Tolerance			
	Less Tolerant	In-Between	More Tolerant	N
College Graduates	5	29	66	308
Some College	9	38	53	319
High School Graduates	12	46	42	768
Some High School	17	54	29	576
Grade School	22	62	16	792

the like. Yet many such tables have one or both variables presumably continuous and artificially dichotomized or trichotomized. For example, the crossbreaks of Tables 35.3, 35.4, and 35.5 have as variables Political Preference and Authoritarianism. Political Preference is obviously nominal: Democrats and Republicans are discrete categories; an individual is usually one or the other and can be unambiguously assigned to one subcategory or the other. The *F* scale scores, on the other hand, are continuous. The categories Hi *F* and Lo *F* were artificially created by dividing the group approximately in half, and considering those scores above a certain point high and those scores below the point low.

An interesting example of a 2×2 table with one variable, Oral Explanation, a "natural" or "true" dichotomy, and the other variable, Oral Anxiety, a continuous variable artificially dichotomized at the median was used by Whiting and Child in their book, *Child Training and Personality*.[16] In studying their larger problem, the authors hypothesized that societies fostering oral anxiety in their socialization process would explain illness orally. Part of their evidence is given in Table 35.11. The data are statistically significant. The hypothesis is upheld.[17]

Three and k-Dimensional Tables It is theoretically possible to crossbreak any number of variables, but in practice the limit is three or four, more often three. The reasons for such limitation are obvious: very large

[16] J. Whiting and I. Child, *Child Training and Personality*. New Haven: Yale University Press, 1953, p. 156. The frequencies in the table are numbers of societies and not individuals. The total *N* was 75 (75 societies). This book, like others previously cited (Miller and Swanson; Sears, Maccoby, and Levin; Gross) is an excellent example of sophisticated theoretical reasoning and careful empirical testing of hypotheses. It is particularly instructive because of the ingenuity and flexibility shown in quantifying complex variables.

[17] Whiting and Child used a somewhat unusual method of testing statistical significance. See *ibid.*, pp. 163–166. Percentages are not given in Table 35.11 because the use of percentages with so few cases is questionable. Percentage computation with small numbers of cases is misleading. It is difficult, however, to define "small numbers of cases." A rule of thumb might be: do not compute percentages if a marginal frequency is less than 30. (Marginal frequencies are the totals of the rows and the columns.)

TABLE 35.11   RELATION BETWEEN ORAL ANXIETY AND ORAL EXPLANATIONS
OF ILLNESS, WHITING AND CHILD STUDY

	Societies with Oral Explanation	Societies without Oral Explanation
Societies above Median on Oral Anxiety	17	3
Societies below Median on Oral Anxiety	6	13

N's are required and, more important, the interpretation of data becomes considerably more difficult. Another point to bear in mind has been made previously: never use a complex analysis when a simpler analysis will accomplish the analytic job. Still, three and even four-dimensional tables can be useful and can supply indispensable information.

The analysis of three or more variables simultaneously has two main purposes. One is to study the relations among three or more variables. Take a three-dimensional example, and call the variables A, B, and C. We can study the following relations: between A and B, between A and C, between B and C, and between A, B, and C. The second purpose is to control one variable while studying the relation between the other two variables. For instance, we can study the relation between B and C while controlling A. An important use of this notion is to help us detect spurious relations. Another use is to help us "specify" a relation, to tell us when or under what conditions a relation is more or less pronounced.

Suppose that an investigator is interested in the hypothesis that level of aspiration is related to school achievement, and that he has relatively crude dichotomous measures of level of aspiration. He also has teacher grades which he dichotomizes. The variables and categories, then, are Hi LA (high Level of Aspiration), Lo LA, Hi SA (high School Achievement) and Lo SA. He randomly samples 400 children from a large city school system, divides them into two groups of 200 each on the basis of their grades (Hi and Lo), and then administers a level of aspiration instrument the measures of which, as indicated above, he dichotomizes.[18] Suppose, further, that he gets the results shown in Table 35.12.[19] A relation exists. ($\chi^2 = 100$, significant at the .001 level.)

18 Note that there is no logical reason why he could not use three, four, or even five categories for the Level of Aspiration and School Achievement variables. In fact, with adequate continuous measures there are more powerful methods of analysis than the one being discussed. For instance, a product-moment r might be computed.

19 The LA marginal totals have been made equal to simplify the analysis. Naturally, we will get equal marginals for the SA measures since we dichotomized them to begin with. But the LA marginals could take on a large range of values. (See Footnote 20.)

The investigator shows the results to a colleague, a rather sour individual, who says he thinks the results are nonsense, that it is obvious that if social class were brought into the picture the relation might be quite a different story. He reasons that social class and level of aspiration are strongly related, and that the original relation might hold for middle-

TABLE 35.12 RELATION BETWEEN LEVEL OF ASPIRATION AND SCHOOL
ACHIEVEMENT, HYPOTHETICAL DATA

	Hi *SA*	Lo *SA*	
Hi *LA*	150	50	200
Lo *LA*	50	150	200
	200	200	(400)

class youngsters but not for working-class youngsters. Disconcerted, the investigator goes back to his data, and, since he luckily has indices of social class on all children, he finds, when he works out the three-dimensional crossbreak, the results given in Table 35.13.[20]

TABLE 35.13 RELATIONS AMONG LEVEL OF ASPIRATION, SOCIAL CLASS,
AND SCHOOL ACHIEVEMENT, HYPOTHETICAL DATA

	MC		WC		
	Hi *SA*	Lo *SA*	Hi *SA*	Lo *SA*	
Hi *LA*	80	20	60	40	200
Lo *LA*	20	80	40	60	200
	100	100	100	100	(400)
	(200)		(200)		

The over-all χ^2 is 144, significant at the .001 level. The table frequencies depart very significantly from chance expectations. But what contributes to this result? Inspection of the table shows that the investigator's colleague was right: the relation between Level of Aspiration and School Achievement is considerably more pronounced with middle-class children than with working-class children.

The investigator can be more sure of this conclusion if he separates the middle-class and working-class data and does separate analyses. He sets up the tables and computes χ^2 and C, a coefficient of association to be

[20] The marginal totals are unrealistic. It is unlikely that the investigator would get equal frequencies of middle-class (*MC*) and working-class (*WC*) children—unless, of course, he sampled *MC* and *WC* populations equally.

explained later, for each table. (Simply compute χ^2's for the left and right halves of Table 35.13.) He obtains $\chi^2 = 72$, significant at .001, for the middle-class crossbreak (left four cells of Table 35.14). He obtains $\chi^2 = 8$, significant at .01, for the working-class crossbreak. The two C's are .51 and .20.[21] Evidently the relation between Level of Aspiration and School Achievement is considerably stronger with the middle-class children than it is with the working-class children.

Suppose, additionally, that the investigator wants to study the relation between Level of Aspiration and Social Class and between Social Class and School Achievement. By combining the appropriate frequencies of Table 35.13, he obtains the crossbreaks of Table 35.14. Obviously the relation is zero in both cases. (This is quite unlikely, of course.)

TABLE 35.14   RELATIONS BETWEEN SOCIAL CLASS AND LEVEL OF ASPIRATION (a)
AND BETWEEN SOCIAL CLASS AND SCHOOL ACHIEVEMENT (b)

	Hi *LA*	Lo *LA*		Hi *SA*	Lo *SA*
MC	100	100	*MC*	100	100
WC	100	100	*WC*	100	100
	(a)			(b)	

We have just been studying what might be called *specification*. "Specification . . . is the process of describing the conditions under which a particular relationship may exist or not exist, or may exist to a greater or lesser degree." [22] Specifying relations through crossbreaks is a very important part of analysis because, by means of it, one can possibly detect spurious relations and spell out conditions under which a relation exists or does not exist. The idea is better illustrated than expatiated. For the purpose we use a well-known example.

TABLE 35.15   RELATION BETWEEN EDUCATION AND MILITARY RANK,
THE AMERICAN SOLDIER DATA. (IN PERCENT)

	High School Graduate or Better	Less Than High School Graduate
Noncommissioned Officer	61	43
Private, Pfc.	39	57
Total Cases	3222	3152

21 For the time being, interpret C as an ordinary coefficient of correlation or association. $C = .51$, for example, indicates the degree of relation between *LA* and *SA* in the *MC* sample.

22 W. Goode and P. Hatt, *Methods in Social Research*. New York: McGraw-Hill, 1952, p. 356.

During World War II investigators studied the relation between Education and Military Rank and found the relation presented in Table 35.15 (in percentage form).[23] Kendall and Lazarsfeld "specified" the data of Table 35.15 by adding the variable Length of Service. The new $2 \times 2 \times 2$ crossbreak is given in Table 35.16. The new breakdown indicates that Length of Service seems to be an important independent variable, since the relation is relatively weaker when men whose service was less than two years are considered, whereas the relation is stronger when men whose service was more than two years are considered.

TABLE 35.16 DATA OF TABLE 35.15 "SPECIFIED" BY ADDITION OF VARIABLE LENGTH OF SERVICE. (IN PERCENT)

	Served Less Than 2 Years		Served More Than 2 Years	
	H. S. Grad. or Better	Less Than H. S. Grad.	H. S. Grad. or Better	Less Than H. S. Grad.
Noncomm. Officer	23	17	74	53
Private, Pfc.	77	83	26	47
Total Cases	842	823	2380	2329

The χ^2's for the three 2×2 tables are 206.82 (Table 35.15), 8.83 (left side of Table 35.16), and 224.39 (right side of Table 35.16). The first and third are highly significant (.001), the second very significant (.01). The relation exists significantly in the three crossbreaks. But how about the degree of relation? It is important to note that χ^2 is not a very useful measure of association, since it can increase without limit. In addition, it is not a measure of association, as such. Although C, the coefficient of contingency used earlier but not explained, has definite drawbacks, it is a useful measure of degree of association or relation:

$$C = \sqrt{\frac{\chi^2}{\chi^2 + N}} \qquad (35.1)$$

Computing C's for the three crossbreaks, we obtain .18 for Table 35.15, .07 for the left side of Table 35.16, and .21 for the right side of Table 35.16. Since the χ^2's were all significant, these C's are significant. They

[23] Actually, the data of Tables 35.15 and 35.16 were derived by Kendall and Lazarsfeld from the original data. See P. Kendall and P. Lazarsfeld, "Problems in Survey Analysis," in R. Merton and P. Lazarsfeld, eds., *Studies in the Scope and Method of "The American Soldier."* New York: Free Press, 1950. The original data can be found in S. Stouffer, *et al., The American Soldier.* Princeton, N. J.: Princeton University Press, 1949, vol. I, p. 249 (Table 7).

support analytic inspection of the tables: evidently the relation between Education and Military Rank is stronger with longer length of service than it is with shorter length of service.[24]

TABLE 35.17   RELATION BETWEEN LENGTH OF SERVICE AND MILITARY RANK, THE AMERICAN SOLDIER DATA. (IN PERCENT)

	Served More Than 2 Years	Served Less Than 2 Years
Noncomm. Officer	64	20
Private, Pfc.	36	80

Suppose we go a step further and determine the relation between Length of Service and Military Rank. This has been laid out in Table 35.17. Inspection of the data indicates that this relation is stronger than any of those yet studied.[25] Here $x^2 = 934.67$, and $C = .36$, which corroborates the inspection analysis. Apparently Length of Service is a more important variable than Education.

TABLE 35.18   RELATION BETWEEN LENGTH OF SERVICE AND MILITARY RANK, CONTROLLING EDUCATION

	High School Graduate or Better		Less Than High School Graduate	
	Served More Than 2 Years	Served Less Than 2 Years	Served More Than 2 Years	Served Less Than 2 Years
Noncomm. Officers	1761 .74	194 .23	1234 .53	140 .17
Private, Pfc.	619 .26	648 .77	1095 .47	683 .83

[24] Comparisons like these must be made with great care, especially by checking the original data, since C's are not directly comparable if computed from tables with different N's. There are other ways to handle situations like this, but they are beyond the scope of this book.

[25] If the student has difficulty following how the figures in the table were computed, start with Table 35.16 and compute the frequencies of each cell as follows: $.23 \times 842 = 194$; $.77 \times 842 = 648$; $.17 \times 823 = 140$; $\cdots$ $.47 \times 2329 = 1095$. (Note that the numbers have been rounded.) Then, to make up any 2×2 table, simply add the appropriate frequencies: $1761 + 1234 = 2995$; $194 + 140 = 334$; and $2995/4709 = .64$, and so on. Then compute percentages for the new table, for example, the percentages of Table 35.17 were derived from the following frequencies:

2995	334	3329
1714	1331	3045
4709	1665	(6374)

To verify this conclusion, let us now control Education. We lay out the $2 \times 2 \times 2$ table in Table 35.18. The percentages, computed from Length of Service to Military Rank, are inserted in the cells. For the left side of the table, High School Graduate or Better, $\chi^2 = 676.72$, and $C = .42$. For the right side, $\chi^2 = 320.04$, and $C = .30$.

Inspection of the two subtables of Table 35.18 and consideration of the C values indicate that (1) the relation between Length of Service and Military Rank is substantially present both with high school graduates and non-high school graduates, but (2) the relation is evidently stronger among the former than the latter.[26] Note that with the former group (left side of Table 35.18) the relation is straightforward: among those soldiers who graduated from high school, those who had served more than two years tended to become noncommissioned officers, whereas those who had served less than two years tended not to become noncommissioned officers. With the latter group (right side of Table 35.18), on the other hand, the relation is not two-sided: among those soldiers who did not graduate from high school, there was little difference if they had served more than two years (.53 and .47), but there was a marked difference if they had served less than two years (.17 and .83). That is, if a soldier had graduated from high school, and if he had served more than two years, there was a considerably greater chance of his becoming a noncommissioned officer than if he had served less than two years, but this was not true if he had less than high school education.

CROSSBREAKS, RELATIONS, ORDERED PAIRS, GRAPHING

The relations among crossbreaks, relations, and correlations are interesting and instructive. A relation is a set of ordered pairs. Two of the ways in which a set of ordered pairs can be expressed are (1) by listing the pairs and (2) by graphing the pairs. A coefficient of correlation is an index expressing the degree of relation. A crossbreak expresses the ordered pairs in a table.

To show how these notions are related, take the fictitious data of Table 35.19 where $U = 23$ pupils. The relation being studied is between Social Class (SC) and School Achievement (SA). We partition U into middle class (MC) and working class (WC). We also partition U into high school achievement (Hi SA) and low school achievement (Lo SA). We thus have a two-variable cross partition or crossbreak.

Suppose that of the 23 members of U we count 12 MC's and 11 WC's. We also count 13 Hi SA's and 10 Lo SA's. This gives us the marginal totals of a crossbreak. It does not tell us how many members there are in

---

[26] "Evidently" is used here because there is no way to test the significance of the differences between the C's. In this case, however, another coefficient, phi, can be computed. The phi's are .46 and .32. Since phi is a product-moment coefficient, we can compute the significance of the difference between two phi's. The difference, so tested, is highly significant.

TABLE 35.19   CROSSBREAK TABLE OF RELATION BETWEEN SOCIAL CLASS AND
SCHOOL ACHIEVEMENT, FICTITIOUS DATA

		B_1 Hi SA	B_2 Lo SA	
A_1	MC	10	2	12
A_2	LC	3	8	11
		13	10	

each cell. We must now count the number of *MC* pupils who are also
Hi *SA*, the number of *MC* pupils who are also Lo *SA*, the number of *WC*
pupils who are also Hi *SA*, and the number of *WC* pupils who are also
Lo *SA*. We find the numbers to be those of Table 35.19. These frequencies depart significantly from chance.[27] There is a significant relation between Social Class and School Achievement.

Look at this another way. Let $A_1 = MC$, $A_2 = LC$, $B_1 = $ Hi *SA*, and
$B_2 = $ Lo *SA*. How do we set up the ordered pairs of the crossbreak? We
do so by assigning each of the 23 subjects one of the combinations (1, 1),
(0, 1), (1, 0), and (0, 0). Assign 1's to A_1 and B_1 and 0's to A_2 and B_2. If a
subject is middle class (A_1) *and* a high school achiever (B_1), then he is an
A_1B_1; consequently the ordered pair assigned to him is (1, 1). The first 10
subjects in Table 35.20 belong to the A_1B_1 category and are thus assigned
(1, 1). Similarly, the remaining subjects are assigned ordered pairs of numbers according to their subset membership. The full list of 23 ordered pairs
is given in Table 35.20. The categories or crossbreak (set) intersections
have been indicated.

The relation is the set of ordered pairs of 1's and 0's. Table 35.20
is simply a different way of expressing the same relation shown by Table
35.19. We can compute a coefficient of correlation for both tables. If,
for example, we compute a product-moment *r* of the Table 35.20 data,
we obtain .56. (The product-moment *r* computed with 1's and 0's is
called a *phi* (ϕ) coefficient.[28])

Graph the relation. Let there be two axes, *A* and *B*, at right angles
to each other, and let *A* and *B* represent the two variables of Tables
35.19 and 35.20. We are interested in studying the relation between *A*
and *B*. Figure 35.4 shows the graphed ordered pairs. Where is the relation? We ask: Is there a set of ordered pairs that defines a significant relation between *A* and *B*? We have *paired* each individual's "score" on *A*

[27] As judged by Finney's tables. See S. Siegel, *Nonparametric Statistics*. New York:
McGraw-Hill, 1956, pp. 256–270. When the frequencies are relatively small, the Finney
tables give a more accurate test of significance than the χ^2 test.

[28] This is not a recommended procedure. It is used here to help clarify analytic
procedures and not to illustrate how ϕ is calculated. When both variables are true dichotomies, ϕ is used. This is not the case here.

TABLE 35.20   ORDERED PAIR ARRANGEMENT OF THE DATA OF TABLE 35.19

Ss	A	B	
1	1	1	
2	1	1	
3	1	1	
4	1	1	
5	1	1	
6	1	1	$A_1 B_1$
7	1	1	
8	1	1	
9	1	1	
10	1	1	
11	0	1	
12	0	1	$A_2 B_1$
13	0	1	
14	1	0	
15	1	0	$A_1 B_2$
16	0	0	
17	0	0	
18	0	0	
19	0	0	$A_2 B_2$
20	0	0	
21	0	0	
22	0	0	
23	0	0	

with his "score" on B and plotted the pairs on the A and B axes. Going back to the substance of the relation, we pair each individual's "score" on social-class membership with his achievement "score." In this manner we obtain a set of ordered pairs, and this subset *is* a relation. Our real question, then, is not: Is there a relation between A and B? but rather: *What* is the relation between A and B?

We can see from Fig. 35.4 that the relation between A and B is fairly strong. This is determined by the ordered pairs: the pairs are mostly (a_1, b_1) and (a_2, b_2). There are comparatively few (a_1, b_2) and (a_2, b_1). In words, middle-class scores pair with high achievement scores (1, 1), and working-class scores pair with low achievement scores (0, 0) with comparatively few exceptions (5 cases out of 23). We cannot name this relation succinctly, as we can relations such as "marriage," "brotherhood," and the like. We might, however, call it "social class-achievement," meaning that there is a relation in the ordered pair sense.

Two- and three-dimensional crossbreaks can be graphed in a fairly simple and convenient way to give pictures of the relations involved. In the case of two-dimensional breaks, compute percentages, set up two axes at right angles to each other, lay out percentages of the dependent variable on the ordinate (vertical axis), and the independent variable on the abscissa (horizontal axis).

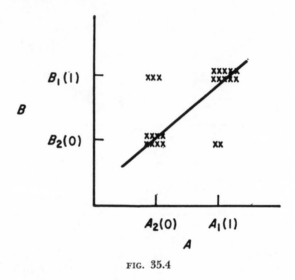

FIG. 35.4

　　The percentage crossbreak of Table 35.4 has been graphed in Fig. 35.5. On the ordinate lay out Hi F in percentages. On the abscissa mark off two points, Democrat and Republican. Make the distance from Democrat to Republican on the abscissa the same as the distance from 0 to 100 percent on the ordinate. The Democrat point is placed at the zero point on the abscissa; the Republican point is placed at a point the length of the total abscissa. Then plot on the ordinate the percentage of Democrats who had Hi F scores (30 percent) and the percentage of Republicans who had Hi F scores (64 percent) on a line erected at the Republican point and parallel to the ordinate. Draw a line connecting the two points. The angle between this line and the horizontal indicates the degree of relation. In Fig. 35.5 this angle is approximately 19 degrees. An angle of 90 degrees would be a correlation of .00; an angle of 45 degrees would be a correlation of 1.00. An angle of 19 degrees is a correlation of approximately .34. (Look up the tangent of the angle in a table of trigonometric functions.)

　　With three-dimensional tables, follow the same procedure, but draw two "relation" lines, one for each condition. For example, take the data of Table 35.16, the Army example. Lay out the axes and plot the points and "relation" lines as shown in Fig. 35.6. The reader can interpret this graph for himself. Note that "Private, Pfc." could just as well have been

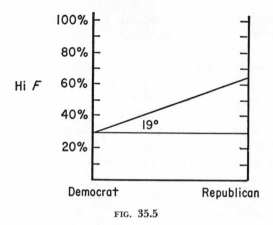

FIG. 35.5

used as "Noncommissioned Officers." (The angles of the two lines with the horizontal are 4 and 12 degrees. The tangents of these angles are .07 and .21.)

It should be clear that there are several ways to analyze the same data. The importance of understanding the different methods, their relations to the problems under investigation, and their relations to each other cannot be overemphasized. It is not so much technical competence as depth and flexibility of comprehension that one gets from using and understanding different methods. Too much analysis is done routinely and uncomprehendingly. While it is pointless to think when one does not need to—as Whitehead long ago pointed out—it is dangerous not to think and not to know what one is doing, both when planning research and the analysis of the data to be obtained in the research and when actually doing the analysis.

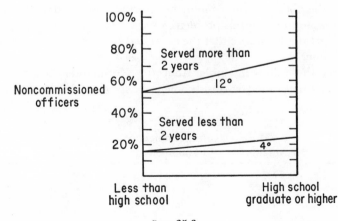

FIG. 35.6

No method of analysis is perfect. For a benefit obtained by one method, we often lose a benefit obtained by another method. Pick the method that seems best suited to the research problem and the research data. Study it, use it, and interpret results obtained by it with care. Understand the methods you use as best you can, and, as with statistics, do not allow yourself to worry excessively about assumptions and restrictions. They are important, of course, but significant research is more important. Few investigators can hope to understand thoroughly all statistics, all methods of observation, and all methods of analysis, especially in the early stages of study. Understanding in depth comes only with study and experience. Try the methods described above. You will probably find that as you do so you will begin to enjoy yourself. When this happens, real learning has begun.

STUDY SUGGESTIONS

1. Kornhauser, in his study of the attitudes of the people of Detroit toward a number of public issues,[29] obtained the following data on attitudes toward Negroes:

Educational Level	Percentage of Unfavorable Attitudes toward Negroes
College Graduates	27
Some College	42
High School Graduates	52
Below High School	64

  (a) Verbalize the relation expressed by this table. What is the problem implied by the table?
  (b) Can you think of any reasons or circumstances under which the above relation might be spurious? What are they? If you were studying this problem, what could you do to give yourself greater assurance that the expressed relation was not a spurious one?

2. Interpret the following table from the Kornhauser Detroit Study. Might the conclusion you could come to be spurious? Why?

Attitudes toward Negroes

Religious Preference	Favorable	Neutral, Ambiguous, and so on	Unfavorable	N
Protestant	17%	30%	53%	264
Catholic	12%	25%	63%	208
All Others	43%	25%	32%	53

[29] A. Kornhauser, *Detroit As The People See It*. Detroit: Wayne University Press, 1952, pp. 86, 87.

    (a) Reconstruct the original frequency table, and compute χ^2 and C. Interpret. (Be careful with this example. It is rather difficult. *Hint:* Think about which cells contribute most to χ^2.)

    (b) What additional information do you get from the frequency table (and perhaps one more percentage computation) that you cannot get from the above table?

    (*Answers:* $\chi^2 = 32.49$ (.001); $C = .24$.)

3. In a study of the relation between Political Preference, Religious Preference, Intelligence, and presumed Authoritarianism, using university music students as subjects, Kerlinger constructed several crossbreak tables, among which was the following:

	High Intelligence		Low Intelligence	
	Hi F	Lo F	Hi F	Lo F
Republican	30	22	33	13
Democrat	5	19	8	12

    Do a complete analysis of the data in the table. Study all 2×2 crossbreaks, compute χ^2's and C's. Compute χ^2 for the whole table. From the results, can you say there is a relation somewhere in the table? Where is it mostly? Interpret.

    (*Answers:* Whole table $\chi^2 = 15.00$ (.01); Political Preference by Intelligence $\chi^2 = .03$ (*n.s.*); F by Intelligence $\chi^2 = 3.67$ (*n.s.*); Political Preference by F $\chi^2 = 14.73$ (.001).)

4. In their study of defense mechanisms and social class, Miller and Swanson[30] published a large number of interesting tables, among which are the following. Interpret each of these tables, first computing percentages, χ^2's, and C's. (The variables are self-explanatory.)

(a) *Obedience Requests*

	Arbitrary	Explained
Middle Class	16	27
Working Class	28	10

(b) *Weaning*

	Early	Late
MC	33	22
WC	17	31

(c) *Type of Reward*

	Psychic	Mixed	Concrete
MC	25	6	7
WC	12	37	28

(d) *Discipline*

	Psychological	Mixed	Corporal
MC	29	5	4
WC	9	28	40

[30] Miller and Swanson, *op. cit.*, pp. 426ff.

Notice, particularly, in these four examples, that studying frequencies and χ^2's alone does not tell us very much about the relations. Interpret the tables.

(*Answers:* χ^2's: (a) 9.40; (b) 5.26; (c) 29.52; (d) 49.45. *C*'s: (a) 32; (b) .22; (c) .45; (d) .55. Note that these χ^2's were computed using the correction for continuity. Simply subtract .5 from $f_o - f_e$ before squaring.)

5. Search the literature and find two or three good examples of frequency and/or percentage crossbreaks. After analyzing the data yourself, read the authors' interpretations of the data and their conclusions. Criticize. Note inadequacies of analysis (reporting percentage tables without reporting N's; no statistical tests of significance; computing percentages with too small N's; and so on).

6. Shortly after President Kennedy took office, there was a battle in the Rules Committee of the House of Representatives. It will be recalled that Rayburn wanted to increase the members of the committee so that it would no longer be dominated by a conservative coalition. When the vote was taken in the House, the Rayburn forces won 217 to 212. It is interesting to ask: Is there a relation between political preference and voting on the issue? The data are:[31]

	For	Against
Democrats	195	64
Republicans	22	148

Compute χ^2 and *C*. Also compute the appropriate percentage table. Interpret. Is there another possible interpretation? That is, might there be an independent variable other than political preference operating? (Note that we have here two truly dichotomous variables.) (*Answers:* $\chi^2 = 159.61$ (.001); $C = .52$.)

7. Schachter reports the following data in his book, *The Psychology of Affiliation*:[32]

	High Anxiety		Low Anxiety	
	Together	Don't Care or Alone	Together	Don't Care or Alone
First-Born and Only Children	32	16	14	31
Later-Born Children	21	39	23	33

    [31] Organized from figures published in the *New York Times*, February 15, 1961, sec. 4, p. 1.

    [32] S. Schachter, *The Psychology of Affiliation*. Stanford: Stanford University Press, 1959, pp. 44 and 45 (Tables 11 and 12). Adapted with permission of the publisher.

These are experimental data. Schachter manipulated anxiety to study its differential effect on children with different ordinal positions in their families. "Together" means that subjects chose to spend time in the company of others after the experimental manipulation.

Interpret the data after doing appropriate analyses.

36 *FACTOR ANALYSIS*

Factor analysis is a method for determining the number and nature of the underlying variables among large numbers of measures. More succinctly, factor analysis is a method for determining k underlying variables (factors) from n sets of measures, k being less than n. It may also be called a method for extracting common factor variances from sets of measures.

Factor analysis serves the cause of scientific parsimony. Generally speaking, if two tests measure the same thing, the scores obtained from them can be added together. If, on the other hand, the two tests do not measure the same thing, their scores cannot be added together. Factor analysis tells us, in effect, what tests or measures can be added and studied together rather than separately. It thus limits the variables with which the scientist must cope. It also (hopefully) helps the scientist to locate and identify unities or fundamental properties underlying tests and measures.

A *factor* is a construct, a hypothetical entity that is assumed to underlie tests and test performance. A number of factors have been found to underlie intelligence, for example: verbal ability, numerical ability, abstract reasoning, spatial reasoning, and memory. Similarly, aptitude, attitude, and personality factors have been isolated and identified.

A HYPOTHETICAL EXAMPLE

Suppose we administer six tests to a large number of seventh-grade pupils. We suspect that the six tests are measuring not six but some smaller number of variables. The tests are: *vocabulary, reading, synonyms, numbers, arithmetic* (standardized test), *arithmetic* (teacher-made test). The names of these tests indicate their nature. We label them, respectively, *V, R, S, N, AS, AT*. (The last two tests, though both arithmetic, have different content and reliabilities. We assume a good reason for including both of them in our little test battery.) After the tests are administered and scored, coefficients of correlation are computed between each test and every other test. We lay out the r's in a correlation matrix (usually called R matrix). The matrix is given in Table 36.1.

TABLE 36.1 R MATRIX: COEFFICIENTS OF CORRELATION AMONG SIX TESTS

		V	R	S	N	AS	AT
Cluster I	V		.72	.63	.09	.09	.00
	R	.72		.57	.15	.16	.09
	S	.63	.57		.14	.15	.09
	N	.09	.15	.14		.57	.63
	AS	.09	.16	.15	.57		.72
	AT	.00	.09	.09	.63	.72	

Cluster II

Recall that a matrix is any rectangular array of numbers (or symbols). Correlation matrices are always square and symmetric. This is because the lower half of the matrix below the diagonal (from upper left to lower right) is the same as the upper half of the matrix. That is, the coefficients in the lower half are identical to those in the upper half, except for their arrangement. (Note that the top row is the same as the first column, the second row the same as the second column, and so on.)

The problem before us is expressed in two questions: How many underlying variables, or factors, are there? What are the factors? The factors are presumed to be underlying unities behind the test performances. They are reflected in the correlation coefficients. If two or more tests are substantially correlated, then the tests share variance. They have common factor variance. They are measuring something in common.

The first question in this case is easy to answer. There are two factors. This is indicated by the two clusters of r's, circled and labeled I and II in Table 36.1. Note that V correlates with R, .72; V with S, .63; and R with S, .57. V, R, and S appear to be measuring something in common. Similarly, N correlates with AS, .57, and with AT, .63; and AS correlates with AT, .72. N, AS, and AT are measuring something in common. It is important to note, however, that the tests in Cluster I, though themselves intercorrelated, are not to any great extent correlated with the tests in Cluster II. Likewise, N, AS, and AT, though themselves intercorrelated, are not substantially correlated with the tests V, R, and S. What is measured in common by the tests in Cluster I is evidently not the same as what is measured in common by the tests of Cluster II. There appear to be two clusters or factors in the matrix.[1]

[1] In this presentation, occasional oversimplifications and somewhat unrealistic examples are used. For example, the R matrix of Table 36.1 is unrealistic. All the tests

By inspecting the R matrix, we have determined that there are two factors underlying these tests. The second question (What are the factors?) is almost always more difficult. When we ask what the factors are, we seek to name them. We want *constructs* that explain the underlying unities or common factor variances of the factors. We ask what is common to the tests V, R, and S, on the one hand, and to the tests N, AS, and AT, on the other hand. V, R, and S are vocabulary, reading, and synonym tests. All three involve words, to a large extent. Perhaps the underlying factor is *verbal ability*. We name the factor *Verbal*, or V. N, AS, and AT all involve numerical or arithmetic operations. Suppose we named this factor *Arithmetic*. A friend points out to us that test N does not really involve arithmetic operations, since it consists mostly of manipulating numbers nonarithmetically. We overlooked this in our eagerness to name the underlying unity. Anyway, we now name the factor *Numerical*, or *Number*, or N. There is no inconsistency: all three tests involve numbers and numerical manipulation and operation.

Both questions have been answered: there are two factors, and they are named *Verbal, V*, and *Numerical, N*. It must be hastily and urgently pointed out, however, that neither question is ever finally answered in actual factor analytic research. This is especially true in early investigations of a field. The number of factors can change in subsequent investigations using the same tests. One of the V tests may also have some variance in common with another factor, say K. If a test measuring K is added to the matrix, a third factor would emerge. Perhaps more important, the name of a factor may be incorrect. Subsequent investigation using these V tests and other tests may show that V is not now common to all the tests. The investigator must then find another construct, another source of common factor variance. In short, factor names are tentative; they are hypotheses to be tested in further factor analytic and other kinds of research.

FACTOR MATRICES AND FACTOR LOADINGS

If a test measures one factor only it is said to be factorially "pure." To the extent that a test measures a factor, it is said to be *saturated* or *loaded* with the factor. Factor analysis is not really complete unless we know whether a test is factorially pure and how saturated it is with a factor. Of course, we would naturally want to know, if a measure is not factorially pure, what other factors it is saturated with. If a test is saturated with more than one factor it is said to be *factorially complex*.

Some tests and measures are factorially quite complex. The Stan-

---

would be positively correlated, though the two factors would probably emerge. In addition, clusters, while similar to factors, are not factors. For simplicity and pedagogical ends, however, we risk these discrepancies.

ford-Binet Intelligence Test, the Otis intelligence tests, and the *F* (Authoritarianism) scale are good examples. A desideratum of scientific investigation is to have pure measures of variables. If a measure of numerical ability is not factorially pure, how can we have confidence that a relation between numerical ability and school achievement, say, is really the relation we think it is? If the test measures both numerical ability and verbal reasoning, doubt is thrown upon relations discovered by using the test.

To help solve these and other problems, we need more than the inspection method used to analyze Table 36.1. The factorial facts are not usually as self-evident as in this oversimplified example. We need an objective method to determine (1) the number of factors, (2) the tests saturated or loaded on the various factors (the clusters), and (3) the magnitudes of the saturations or loadings. There are several factor analytic methods that accomplish these purposes. We shall discuss some of them later in the chapter.

TABLE **36.2** FACTOR MATRIX OF DATA OF TABLE 36.1, ROTATED SOLUTION

Tests	A	B	C	h^2
V	.86	.00	.03	.74
R	.83	.09	.11	.71
S	.75	.10	−.09	.57
N	.10	.75	−.09	.57
AS	.09	.83	.11	.71
AT	.00	.86	.03	.74

One of the final outcomes of a factor analysis is called a *factor matrix*, a table of coefficients that expresses the relations between the tests and the underlying factors. The factor matrix yielded by factor analyzing the data of Table 36.1 with the Thurstone Centroid Method, one of the several methods available, is given in Table 36.2.[2] The entries in the table are called *factor loadings*. They can be written a_{ij}, meaning the loading *a* of Test *i* on Factor *j*. In the second line, .83 is the factor loading of Test *R* on Factor *A*.[3] In the fourth line, .75 is the factor loading of Test *N* on Factor *B*. Test *AS* has the following loadings: .09 on Factor *A*, .83 on Factor *B*, and .11 on Factor *C*.

Factor loadings are not hard to interpret. They range between −1.00 through 0 to +1.00, like correlation coefficients. They are inter-

[2] L. Thurstone, *Multiple Factor Analysis*. Chicago: University of Chicago Press, 1947, chap. VIII. Actually, the centroid and most other factor analytic methods do not yield final solutions such as that in Table 36.2. They yield arbitrary solutions that require what is called "rotation of axes." Rotation will be briefly discussed later.

[3] Some factor analysts label final solution factors I, II, · · · , or I', II', · · · . In this chapter we label unrotated factors I, II, · · · and rotated (final solution) factors *A*, *B*, · · · .

preted similarly. In short, they express the correlations *between tests and factors*. For example, Test V has the following correlations with Factors A, B, and C, respectively: .86, .00, .03. Evidently Test V is highly loaded on A, but not at all on B and C.[4] Tests V, R, and S are loaded on A but not on other factors. Tests N, AS, and AT are loaded on B but not on other factors. All the tests are "pure."

The entries in the last column are called *communalities*, or h^2's. They are the sums of the squares of the factor loadings. For example, the communality of Test R is $(.83)^2 + (.09)^2 + (.11)^2 = .71$. The communality of a test or variable is its common factor variance. This will be explained later when factor theory is presented.

TABLE 36.3   ORIGINAL FACTOR MATRIX FROM WHICH THE R MATRIX
OF TABLE 36.1 WAS DERIVED

Tests	A	B	h^2
V	.90	.00	.81
R	.80	.10	.65
S	.70	.10	.50
N	.10	.70	.50
AS	.10	.80	.65
AT	.00	.90	.81

Before going further, it should again be noted that this example is unrealistic. Factor matrices rarely present such a clear-cut picture. Indeed, the factor matrix of Table 36.2 was "known." The author first wrote the matrix given in Table 36.3. If this matrix is multiplied by itself, the R matrix of Table 36.1 (with diagonal values) will be obtained. In this case, all that is necessary to obtain R is to multiply each row by every other row. For example, multiply row V by row R: $(.90)(.80) + (.00)(.10) = .72$; row V by row S: $(.90)(.70) + (.00)(.10) = .63$; row S by row AS: $(.70)(.10) + (.10)(.80) = .15$; and so on. The resulting R matrix was then factor-analyzed.[5]

It is instructive to compare Tables 36.2 and 36.3. Note the discrepancies. They are all small. That is, the fallible factor analytic method cannot perfectly reproduce the "true" factor matrix. It estimates it. In this case the fit is very close because of the deliberate simplicity of the

[4] Unfortunately, there is no generally accepted standard error of factor loadings. A crude rule is to use the standard error of r, or easier, to find the r that is significant for the N of the study. For example, with $N = 200$, an r of about .18 is significant at the .01 level. Some factor analysts in some studies do not bother with loadings less than .30, or even .40. Others do. The loadings considered "significant" in Table 36.2 are italicized.

[5] This matrix multiplication operation springs from what is called the basic equation of factor analysis: $R = FF'$ which says succinctly in matrix symbols what was said more laboriously above. A thorough understanding of factor analysis requires a good understanding of matrix algebra. Thurstone has written an excellent exposition. See *ibid.*, chap. II. Other somewhat easier discussions can be found in the references given in the study suggestions at the end of the chapter.

problem. Real data are not so obliging. Moreover, we never know the "true" factor matrix. If we did, there would be no need for factor analysis. We always estimate the factor matrix from the correlation matrix. The complexity and fallibility of research data frequently make this estimation a difficult business.

SOME FACTOR THEORY

In Chap. 29, we wrote an equation that expressed sources of variance in a measure (or test):

$$V_t = V_{co} + V_{sp} + V_e \tag{36.1}$$

where V_t = total variance of a measure; V_{co} = common factor variance, or the variance that two or more measures share in common; V_{sp} = specific variance, or the variance of the measure that is not shared with any other measure, that is, the variance of that measure and no other; V_e = error variance.

The common factor variance V_{co} was broken down into two sources of variance, A and B, two factors (see Eq. 25.11):

$$V_{co} = V_A + V_B \tag{36.2}$$

V_A might be verbal ability variance, and V_B might be numerical ability variance.

This is reasonable if we think of the sums of squares of factor loadings of any test:

$$h_i^2 = a_i^2 + b_i^2 + \cdots + k_i^2 \tag{36.3}$$

where a_i^2, b_i^2, . . . are the squares of the factor loadings of test i, and h_i^2 is the communality of test i. But $h_i^2 = V_{co}$. Therefore $V(A) = a^2$ and $V(B) = b^2$, and the theoretical equation (36.2) is tied to real factor analytic operations.

But there may of course be more than two factors. The generalized equation is

$$V_{co} = V_A + V_B + \cdots + V_K \tag{36.4}$$

Substituting in (Eq. 36.1), we obtain

$$V_t = V_A + V_B + \cdots + V_K + V_{sp} + V_e \tag{36.5}$$

Dividing through by V_t we find a proportional representation:

$$\frac{V_t}{V_t} = 1.00 = \underbrace{\overbrace{\frac{V_A}{V_t} + \frac{V_B}{V_t} + \cdots + \frac{V_K}{V_t}}^{h^2} + \frac{V_{sp}}{V_t}}_{r_{tt}} + \frac{V_e}{V_t} \tag{36.6}$$

The h^2 and r_{tt} parts of the equation have been labeled as they were in Chap. 25.

This equation has beauty. It ties tightly together measurement theory and factor theory.[6] h^2 is the proportion of the total variance that is common factor variance. r_{tt} is the proportion of the total variance that is reliable variance. V_e/V_t is the proportion of the total variance that is error variance. In Chap. 25 an equation like this enabled us to tie reliability and validity together. Now, it shows us the relation between factor theory and measurement theory. We see, in brief, that *the main problem of factor analysis is to determine the variance components of the total common factor variance.*

Take Test V in Table 36.2. A glance at Eq. 36.6 shows us, among other things, that the reliability of a measure is always greater than, or equal to, its communality. Test V's reliability, then, is at least .74. Suppose we say that $r_{tt} = .85$. Since $V_t/V_t = 1.00$, we can fill in all the terms:

$$\frac{V_t}{V_t} = 1.00 = \overbrace{(.86)^2 + (.00)^2; (.03)^2}^{h^2 = .74} + \overbrace{.11}^{V_{sp}} + \overbrace{.15}^{V_e}$$
$$\underbrace{\hphantom{(.86)^2 + (.00)^2; (.03)^2 + .11}}_{r_{tt} = .85}$$

Test V, then, has a high proportion of common factor variance and a low proportion of specific variance.

The proportions can be seen clearly in a circle diagram. Let the area of the circle equal the total variance, or 1.00 (100 percent of the area), in Fig. 36.1. The three variances have been indicated by blocking out areas of the circle. V_{co} or h^2, for example, is 74 percent, V_{sp} is 11 percent, and V_e is 15 percent of the total variance.

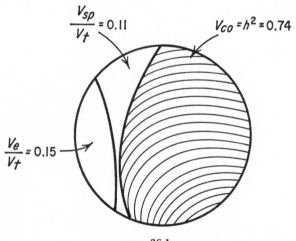

FIG. **36.1**

6 See Guilford, *op. cit.*, pp. 354–357, and Thurstone, *op. cit.*, chap. II.

A factor analytic investigation including Test V would tell us only about V_{co}, the common factor variance. It would tell us the proportion of the test's total variance that is common factor variance. It would also give us clues to the nature of the common factor variance by telling us what other tests share the same common factor variance and what other tests do not share it. Figure 25.1 in Chap. 25 shows the total variances of two tests represented by two circles. The common factor variance, V_{co}, is also indicated there by the set expression $V(A \cap B)$. The specific variances and the error variances, too, have been labeled.

GRAPHICAL REPRESENTATION OF FACTORS AND FACTOR LOADINGS

The student of factor analysis must learn to think spatially and geometrically if he is to grasp the essential nature of the factor approach. There are two or three good ways to do this. A table of correlations can be represented by the use of vectors and the angles between them.[7] We here use a more useful and common method. We treat the row entries of a factor matrix as coordinates and plot them in geometric space. In Fig. 36.2 the factor matrix entries of Table 36.2 have been plotted.

The two factors, A and B, are laid out at right angles to each other. These are called *reference axes*. Appropriate factor loading values are indicated on each of the axes. Then each test's loadings are treated as coordinates and plotted. For example, Test R's loadings are (.83, .09). Go out .83 on A and up .09 on B. This point has been indicated in Fig. 36.2 by a circled letter indicating the test. Plot the coordinates of the other five tests similarly.

The factor structure can now be clearly seen. Each test is highly loaded on one factor but not on the other factor. They are all relatively "pure" measures of their respective factors. A seventh point has been indicated in Fig. 36.2 by a circled cross in order to illustrate a presumed test that measures both factors. Its coordinates are (.60, .50). This means that the test is loaded on both factors, .60 on A and .50 on B. This test is not "pure." Factor structures of this simplicity and clarity, where the factors are orthogonal (the axes at right angles to each other), the test loadings substantial and "pure," no tests loaded on two or more factors, and only two factors, are not common.

Most published factor analytic studies report more than two factors. Four, five, even nine, ten, and more factors have been reported. Graphi-

---

[7] *Vectors* are directional arrows of given lengths. They are also ordered collections or sets of numbers. In two-dimensional space, for example, (.60, .20) and (.10, .70) are vectors. (.55, .20, .10) would be a vector in three-dimensional space. Since vectors have ordered numbers, they can be plotted in their respective spaces. (.60, .20), for example, can be plotted by going out .60 on an X axis and .20 up on a Y axis, the axes being orthogonal or at right angles to each other.

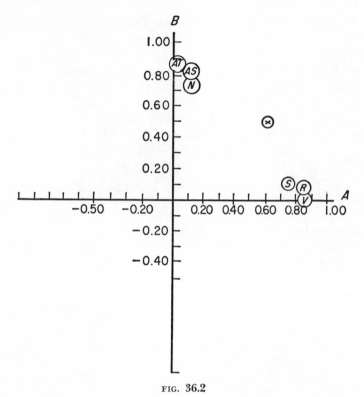

FIG. 36.2

cal representation of such factor structures in one graph is, of course, not possible. Factor analysts customarily plot factors two at a time, though it is possible to plot three at a time. It must be admitted, however, that it is difficult to visualize or keep in mind complex n-dimensional structures. One therefore visualizes two-dimensional structures and generalizes to n dimensions algebraically.

METHODS OF FACTOR ANALYSIS

Faced with the necessity of factor-analyzing a correlation matrix, the researcher has a number of methods available. The purpose of the present section is to familiarize the student with three or four of the principal methods in general use. To do so, two cluster methods and the principal factors and centroid methods will be briefly described. The centroid method will be illustrated with a simple example. Discussion of other methods of factor analysis—the diagonal method, group methods, statistical estimation methods, and so on—is beyond the scope of this book. The interested reader should consult one or two of the references given in Study Suggestion 1 at the end of the chapter.

It should be noted that factor analysis is going through an important transitional period. The increasing accessibility of high-speed computers and computing programs for factor analysis is making some of the methods obsolete. Thurstone's well-known centroid method, for example, will, in a few years, probably be little used. It is a computational compromise, as Thurstone said, to avoid the excessive computational labor of more satisfactory solutions.[8] It will no doubt be replaced in time by the principal factors and other mathematically and statistically more satisfying methods. Still, the centroid method occupies an honorable and worthy place among factor analytic methods. It will probably continue to be used for desk calculator solutions and for teaching purposes.

Cluster Methods The inspection method used earlier in this chapter can be called a cluster method. Cluster methods depend upon the identification of clusters and presumed factors by searching for interrelated groups of correlation coefficients or other measures of relation (for example, *D* measures). In Table 36.1, simple inspection identifies two clusters. In most *R* matrices, however, the clusters cannot be so easily identified. Take the *R* matrix given in Table 36.4. This table of correlation coefficients was reported by Rokeach and Fruchter in a factor analytic study of dogmatism and other variables.[9] Although one can fairly readily pick out a cluster of substantially related variables like {1, 2, 3}, one runs into difficulties with the other variables. A more objective method is needed.

TABLE **36.4** *R* MATRIX: ROKEACH AND FRUCHTER STUDY

	1	2	3	4	5	6	7	8	9	10
1		.65	.71	.33	.17	.14	.13	−.13	.22	−.05
2	.65		.52	.41	.30	.29	.20	−.08	.31	−.03
3	.71	.52		.30	.14	.07	.10	−.14	.11	−.02
4	.33	.41	.30		.64	.62	.52	.23	.12	.33
5	.17	.30	.14	.64		.69	.63	.43	−.08	.56
6	.14	.29	.07	.62	.69		.54	.35	.02	.40
7	.13	.20	.10	.52	.63	.54		.44	−.22	.62
8	−.13	−.08	−.14	.23	.43	.35	.44		−.39	.60
9	.22	.31	.11	.12	−.08	.02	−.22	−.39		−.51
10	−.05	−.03	−.02	.33	.56	.40	.62	.60	−.51	

One such objective cluster method has been recommended by McQuitty.[10] The method is quick, easy, and sometimes useful. It consists

---

[8] Thurstone, *op. cit.*, p. 178.

[9] M. Rokeach and B. Fruchter, "A Factorial Study of Dogmatism and Related Concepts," *Journal of Abnormal and Social Psychology*, LIII (1956), 356–360.

[10] L. McQuitty, "Elementary Linkage Analysis for Isolating Orthogonal and Oblique Types and Typal Relevancies," *Educational and Psychological Measurement*,

of identifying clusters or "types" by locating, through the size of *r*'s, the variables or tests most highly related, most closely clustered together. If this method is used, as is, with the *R* matrix of Table 36.4, it yields two clusters, I: $\{1, 2, 3\}$ and II: $\{4, 5, 6, 7, 8, 9\ (-), 10\}$.

The factor matrix reported by Rokeach and Fruchter, however, reports three factors. (See Table 36.5.) Note particularly that the non-quantitative cluster method does not show the third factor, though refinement of the method might conceivably turn up this factor. Another difficulty with the method is its lack of clarity in showing variables loaded on two or more factors. In other words, the method is sometimes not very precise, though McQuitty has provided more precise methods.[11]

TABLE 36.5   UNROTATED AND ROTATED FACTOR MATRICES, ROKEACH AND FRUCHTER STUDY [a]

| Variable | Unrotated Matrix | | | Rotated Matrix | | | |
	I	II	III	A	B	C	h^2
1. Anxiety	442	−708	173	77	−25	27	727
2. Paranoia	468	−600	134	72	−14	26	597
3. Self-Rejection	412	−656	313	69	−29	37	698
4. Dogmatism	708	−139	341	46	21	62	637
5. Authoritarianism (*F* scale)	784	185	297	27	48	66	737
6. Rigidity	680	123	421	23	32	71	652
7. Ethnocentrism (*E* scale)	728	273	099	21	59	47	614
8. Conservatism (*PEC* scale)	487	519	−129	−07	69	19	523
9. Left Opinionation	−169	−500	468	17	−63	26	498
10. Right Opinionation	642	549	−227	03	85	19	765

[a] Decimal points are omitted. The higher loadings in the rotated matrix have been italicized by the author to facilitate interpretation.

A useful quantitative method of cluster analysis has been advocated by Tryon.[12] One first lists the correlations in order of size. Then one builds up clusters of variables that "belong" together. The so-called *B* coefficient is used as a criterion of "belongingness." The method is fairly simple, dependable, and useful. But it does not yield a table of factor

XVII (1957), 207–229. This method seems to work best with clear-cut factor structure. Unmodified it is not always satisfactory. McQuitty, however, has worked out other methods. For example, see L. McQuitty, "Typal Analysis," *Educational and Psychological Measurement,* XXI (1961), 677–696.

[11] See, for example, McQuitty, "Elementary Linkage Analysis," *op. cit.,* pp. 222ff.

[12] A good exposition of the method can be found in B. Fruchter, *Introduction to Factor Analysis* Princeton, N. J.: Van Nostrand, 1954, chap. 2.

loadings. Like the McQuitty and other cluster methods, this method would seem most useful in preliminary or exploratory work.

The Principal Factors and Centroid Methods The principal factors method [13] is mathematically satisfying because it yields a mathematically unique solution of an R matrix. Perhaps its major solution feature is that it extracts a maximum amount of variance as each factor is calculated. In other words, the R matrix is expressed in the smallest number of factors by the method. Its principal shortcoming in the past has been its computational laboriousness. An R matrix of 20 variables, for example, required an inordinate amount of time to analyze. With the availability of modern high-speed electronic computers, however, laboriousness of computation is no longer an obstacle. Even fairly large R matrices can be solved in minutes. It is strongly recommended, therefore, that social scientific and educational researchers use the principal factors method.

To show the logic of the principal factors method without considerable mathematics is difficult. One can achieve a certain intuitive understanding of the method by approaching it geometrically. Conceive tests or variables as points in m-dimensional space. Variables that are highly and positively correlated should be near each other and away from variables with which they do not correlate. If this reasoning is correct, there should be swarms of points in space. Each of these points can be located in the space if suitable axes are inserted into the space, one axis for each dimension of the m dimensions. Then any point's location is its multiple identification obtained by reading its coordinates on the m axes. The factor problem is to shoot axes through neighboring swarms of points and to so locate these axes that they "account for" as much of the variances of the variables as possible.

Take the example we used in the chapter on the semantic differential (Chap. 32): imagine the room you are sitting in to have swarms of points in various parts of the three-dimensional space of the room. Imagine that some of the points cluster together in the upper right center of the room (from your vantage point). Now imagine another cluster of points at another point in the room, say in the lower right center. Part of the problem is to locate axes—three axes in this case, since the room is three-dimensional—so as to identify and appropriately label the swarms and the points in the swarms.

We can demonstrate these ideas by using a simple two-dimensional

[13] Thurstone, *op. cit.*, chaps. VIII and XX. An easy-to-follow exposition of the principal factors method is given in G. Thomson, *The Factorial Analysis of Human Ability*. Boston: Houghton Mifflin, 1951, chap. VII. A thorough mathematical exposition, with computational details and analytic discussion, is given in H. Harman, *Modern Factor Analysis*. Chicago: University of Chicago Press, 1960, chap. 9 and pp. 109–116. This method has usually been called the *principal axes* or *principal components* method. In this chapter, Harman's expression *principal factors* is used.

example. Since the basic ideas behind the principal factors method and the centroid method are similar, and since the centroid idea is a bit simpler, we lean on centroid notions, though we will not explain the centroid method in detail.

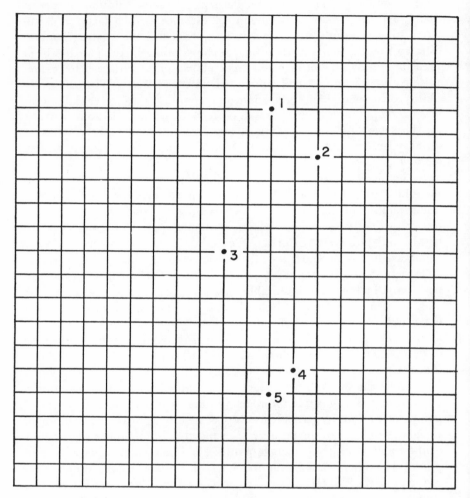

FIG. 36.3

Suppose we have five tests. These tests, let us say, are situated in two-dimensional space as indicated in Fig. 36.3. The closer two points are the more they are related. The problem is to determine: (1) how many factors there are; (2) what tests are loaded on what factors, and (3) the magnitudes of the test loadings.

The problem will now be solved in two different ways, each

interesting as well as instructive. First, we solve directly from the points themselves. Follow these directions. Draw a vertical line three units to the left of Point 3. Draw a horizontal line one unit below Point 3. Label these reference axes I and II. Now read off the coordinates of each point, for instance, Point 2 is (.70, .50), Point 4 is (.60, −.40). Write a "factor matrix" with these five pairs of values.

Rotate the axes orthogonally and clockwise so that axis I goes between Points 4 and 5. Axis II, of course, will go through Points 1 and 2. (The use of a protractor is recommended: the rotation should be approximately 40 degrees.) Label these "new" rotated axes A and B. Cut a strip of four-to-the-inch graph paper. (The points are plotted on this size graph paper.) Count the base of each square as .10 (.10 = 1/4 inch; ten units, of course, equal 1.00). Using the strip as a measure, measure the distances of the points on the new axes. For example, Point 2 should be close to (.22, .83), and Point 5 should be close to (.71, −.06). (It does not make too much difference if there are small discrepancies.) The original (I and II) and rotated (A and B) reference axes and the five points are shown in Fig. 36.4.

Now write both factor matrices, unrotated and rotated. They are given in Table 36.6.

TABLE **36.6** UNROTATED AND ROTATED FACTOR MATRICES, POINT-DISTANCE PROBLEM

Points	Unrotated I	II	Points	Rotated A	B
1	.50	.70	1	−.07	*.86*
2	.70	.50	2	.22	*.83*
3	.30	.10	3	.17	.27
4	.60	−.40	4	*.72*	.08
5	.50	−.50	5	*.71*	−.06

The problem is solved: There are two factors. Points (tests) 1 and 2 are high on Factor B, Points 4 and 5 are high on Factor A, and Point 3 has low loadings on both factors. The three questions originally asked have been answered.

This procedure is analogous to psychological factor problems. Tests are conceived as points in factor m-dimensional space. The factor loadings are the coordinates. The problem is to introduce appropriate reference frames or axes and then to "read off" the factor loadings. Unfortunately, in actual problems we do not know the number of factors (the dimensionality of the factor space and thus the number of axes) or the location of the points in space. These must be determined from data.

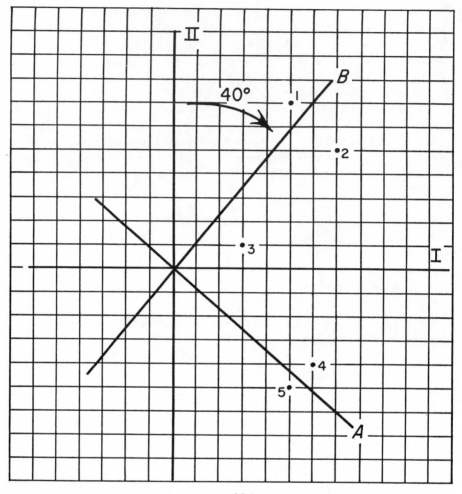

FIG. 36.4

The centroid method uses the data to "position" the reference axes. Instead of locating the axes visually, as we just did, the method in effect arithmetically locates the *centroid*, or average, of all the points in the factor space. An axis is "shot" through this centroid and the loadings of the points are "read off" this axis. This is done successively until all factors are accounted for. In this manner the number of factors and the loadings of the tests on the factors are determined. It must be emphasized, however, that this description is figurative. In using the method, for instance, one does not "read off" the loadings on the centroid axis. One calculates the loadings through an averaging process.

We may get a glimpse of the outlines of the procedure by generating numerical data from the points in space (Fig. 36.3) and then showing the matrix produced by a form of the method. Follow directions again. Go back to the original points in space (Fig. 36.3). Use the strip previously cut out: Measure the *distances* between each point and every other point. For instance, the distance from 1 to 2 is .29, that from 1 to 3 is .63, that from 2 to 4 is .90, and so on. If you do this you will obtain the distance matrix given in Table 36.7. (While the entries in the matrix are not *r*'s, recall that distance measures *are* measures of relation.)

TABLE **36.7**   MATRIX OF DISTANCES BETWEEN POINTS OF FIG. 36.3

	1	2	3	4	5
1		.29	.63	1.10	1.20
2	.29		.58	.90	1.02
3	.63	.58		.58	.62
4	1.10	.90	.58		.14
5	1.20	1.02	.62	.14	

It is possible to factor this matrix. If we do so, using an altered form of the centroid method (the alteration does not really matter now), we obtain the unrotated factor matrix given in Table 36.8.[14] The cen-

TABLE **36.8**   UNROTATED AND ROTATED FACTOR MATRICES OBTAINED
BY CENTROID METHOD

	Unrotated			Rotated	
Points	I	II	Points	A	B
1	.86	.76	1	.05	*1.15*
2	.74	.63	2	.06	*.97*
3	.64	−.16	3	*.56*	*.35*
4	.72	−.59	4	*.93*	.11
5	.79	−.70	5	*1.05*	.08

troid method yields this matrix, as indicated above, by a successive averaging process. The rotated matrix is also given in Table 36.8. (Note that the centroid and principal factors methods do not yield rotated matrices.) It was obtained by rotating the I and II axes 46 degrees clockwise and then reading off the "new" rotated values by means of the measuring strip, as shown in Fig. 36.5.

[14] If the student wishes to get more of the flavor of the centroid method, he can add the columns of the matrix of Table 36.7, add these column totals, take the square root of this sum, and then divide this square root into each of the column sums. This procedure will yield fair approximations of the first factor loadings. (The actual centroid method requires certain values in the diagonal, values that are missing in Table 36.7.) By a process too complicated to explain here, the variance due to the first factor is then substracted from the original *R* matrix (in this case, *D* matrix). Whatever is left after this substraction is then factored in a similar manner. The process is repeated until little or no variance is left.

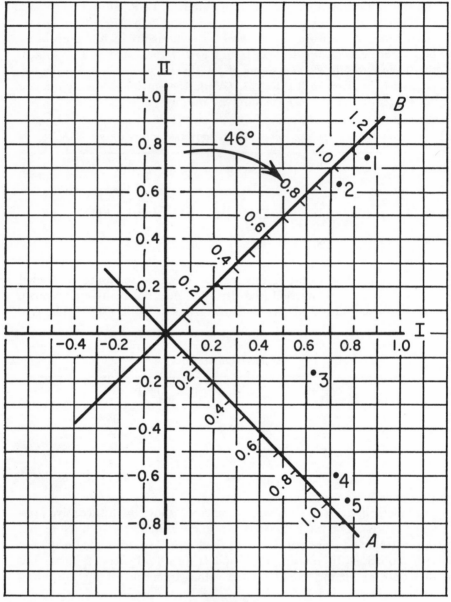

FIG. 36.5

Compare Figs. 36.4 and 36.5. They are, of course, very much alike: the factor structures are almost the same. The main differences are that (1) the loadings of Fig. 36.5, the centroid solution, are higher, and (2) the positions of the points are different. These differences are due mainly to the different methods used; they need not concern us here.

It is necessary to reemphasize a point made previously. With real problems we cannot use the simple direct method shown in Fig. 36.4. We do not know the positions of the points in space. We do not know how tests and variables cluster together. We do not know that there are two— or three, four, or more—factors. We do not know the loadings of the variables. The number of factors, the variable clusters, and the loadings must be estimated using methods like the centroid and principal factors methods.

Rotation and the Principle of Simple Structure Most factor analytic methods supply raw data in a form that is difficult or impossible to interpret. Thurstone argued that it was necessary to rotate factor matrices if one wanted to interpret them adequately.[15] He pointed out that original factor matrices are arbitrary in the sense that an infinite number of reference frames (axes) can be found to reproduce any given R matrix.[16] A principal factors matrix and its loadings account for the common factor variances of the test scores, but they do not in general provide scientifically meaningful structures. It is the configurations of tests or variables in factor space that are of fundamental concern. In order to discover these configurations adequately, the arbitrary reference axes must be rotated. In other words, we assume a psychological factor "reality" behind tests or variables. If this is so, there must be some unique and correct position for the axes, some unique and correct way to "view" the variables in n-dimensional space.

Among Thurstone's important contributions, his invention of the ideas of simple structure and factor axes rotation are perhaps the most important. With them he laid down relatively clear guidelines for achieving psychologically meaningful and interpretable factor analytic solutions.

Earlier we reported, in Table 36.2, a factor matrix obtained from the data of Table 36.1. This was the final *rotated* matrix and not the matrix originally produced by the centroid analysis. The matrix originally produced by centroid analysis is given in Table 36.9.

TABLE **36.9** UNROTATED FACTOR MATRIX, TABLE **36.1** R MATRIX

Tests	I	II	III a	h^2
V	.61	−.60	.03	.73
R	.65	−.52	.11	.70
S	.60	−.46	−.09	.57
N	.60	.46	−.09	.57
AS	.65	.52	.11	.70
AT	.61	.60	.03	.73

a The loadings of the third factor are given to show their relative insignificance and to provide a table congruent to the rotated matrix of Table 36.1.

15 Thurstone, *op. cit.*, pp. 508, 509.

16 *Ibid.*, p. 93. See also R. Cattell, *Factor Analysis*. New York: Harper & Row, 1952, p. 66.

If we try to interpret this table of loadings, we run into trouble. It might be said that all the tests are loaded on a general factor, I, and that the second factor, II, is bipolar. (A *bipolar factor* is one that has substantial positive and negative loadings.) This would amount to saying that all the tests measure the same thing (Factor I), but that the first three measure the negative aspect of whatever the second three measure (Factor II). But aside from the ambiguous nature of such an interpretation, we know that the reference axes, I and II, and consequently the factor loadings, are arbitrary. Look at the factor plot of Fig. 36.2. There are two clearly defined clusters of tests clinging closely to the axes *A* and *B*. There is no general factor here, nor is there a bipolar factor. The second major problem of factor analysis, therefore, is to discover a unique and compelling solution or position of the reference axes.

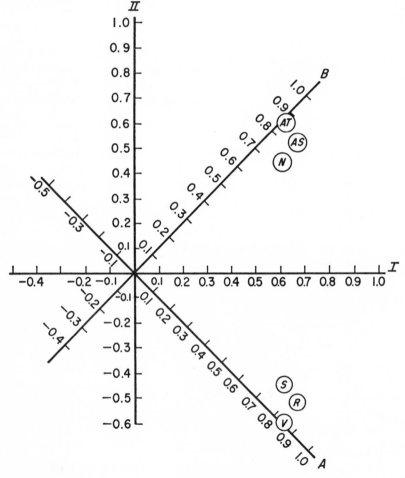

FIG. **36.6**

If we plot the loadings of I against II, we easily see what the story is. This has been done in Fig. 36.6. If we swing or rotate the I and II axes 45 degrees, we obtain essentially the structure of Fig. 36.2. That is, the new rotated positions of the axes and the positions of the six tests are the same as the positions of the axes and tests of Fig. 36.2. It simply leans to the right a bit. Turn the figure so that the *B* of the *B* axis points directly up and this becomes clear. It is now possible to read off the new rotated factor loadings on the rotated axes. (The reader can confirm this by reading off and writing down the loadings of the tests on the rotated axes of Fig. 36.6.)

This example, though unrealistic, may help the reader understand that the factor analyst searches for the unities that presumably underlie test performances. Spatially conceived, he searches out the relations among variables "out there" in multidimensional factor space. Through knowledge of the empirical relations among tests or other measures, he probes in factor space with reference axes until he finds the unities or relations among relations—if they exist.

To guide the factor analyst in his rotations, Thurstone laid down five principles or rules of simple structure.[17] The rules are applicable to both orthogonal and oblique rotations, though Thurstone emphasized the oblique case. (Oblique rotations are those in which the angles between axes are acute or obtuse.) The simple structure principles are as follows:

1. Each row of the factor matrix should have at least one loading close to zero.
2. For each column of the factor matrix there should be at least as many variables with zero or near-zero loadings as there are factors.
3. For every pair of factors (columns) there should be several variables with loadings in one factor (column) but not in the other.
4. When there four or more factors, a large proportion of the variables should have negligible (close to zero) loadings on any pair of factors.
5. For every pair of factors (columns) of the factor matrix there should be only a small number of variables with appreciable (nonzero) loadings in both columns.

In effect, these criteria call for as "pure" variables as possible, that is, each variable loaded on as few factors as possible, and *as many zeros as possible in the rotated factor matrix*. In this way the simplest possible interpretation of the factors can be achieved. In other words, rotation to achieve simple structure is a fairly objective way to achieve variable simplicity or to reduce variable complexity.

To understand this, imagine an ideal solution in which simple

[17] Thurstone, *op. cit.*, p. 335; Harman, *op. cit.*, p. 113; Fruchter, *op. cit.*, p. 110.

structure is "perfect." It might look like this, say, in a three-factor solution:

Tests	A	B	C
1	X	0	0
2	X	0	0
3	X	0	0
4	0	X	0
5	0	X	0
6	0	X	0
7	0	0	X
8	0	0	X
9	0	0	X

X's indicate substantial factor loadings, 0's near-zero loadings. Of course,
such "perfect" factor structures are rare. It is more likely that some of the
tests have loadings on more than one factor. Still, good approximations
to simple structure have been achieved, especially in well-planned and
executed factor analytic studies.

Before leaving the subject of factor rotations it must be pointed
out that there are a number of rotational methods. The two main types
of rotation are called "orthogonal" and "oblique." *Orthogonal* rotations
maintain the independence of factors, that is, the angles between the axes
are kept at 90 degrees. If we rotate factors I and II orthogonally, for
instance, we swing both axes together, maintaining the right angle between them. This means that the correlation between the factors is zero.
The rotation just performed in Fig. 36.6 was orthogonal. If we had four
factors, we would rotate I and II, I and III, I and IV, II and III, and so
on, maintaining right angles between each pair of axes. Some researchers
prefer to rotate orthogonally. Others insist that orthogonal rotation is
unrealistic, that actual factors are not usually uncorrelated, and that
rotations should conform to psychological "reality." [18]

Rotations in which the factor axes are allowed to form acute or
obtuse angles are called *oblique*. Obliqueness, of course, means that factors are correlated. There is no doubt that factor structures can be better
fitted with oblique axes and the simple structure criteria better satisfied.
Some researchers might object to oblique factors because of the possible
difficulty of comparing factor structures from one study to another. We
leave this controversial subject with two remarks. One, the type of rotation seems to be a matter of taste, as a statistical colleague of the author
has said. Two, the reader should understand both types of rotation to the
extent that he can interpret both kinds of factors. He should be particularly careful when confronted with the results of oblique solutions. They
contain peculiarities and subtleties not present in orthogonal solutions.

[18] See Thurstone, *op. cit.*, pp. 139, 140; Cattell, *op. cit.*, pp. 116–118, 122, 123, 210.

RESEARCH EXAMPLES

Six factor analytic studies are summarized below. Most factor analytic studies factor intelligence, aptitude, and personality tests and scales, the tests or scales themselves being intercorrelated and factored. Items of a single test can be factored, however. Persons, or the responses of persons, can also be factored. In other words, the variables entered into the correlation and factor matrices can be tests, scales, items, persons, concepts, or whatever can be intercorrelated in some way. The studies given below were selected, then, not to represent factor analytic investigations in general, but rather to familiarize the student with different uses of factor analysis.

Thurstone-Davis One-Factor Reading Study Thurstone,[19] suspecting that a study of reading tests made by Davis[20] had a simpler interpretation than the original one, factor-analyzed the intercorrelations of the nine tests used in the study. He found one factor! (There was very little variance left after one factor had been extracted.) The factor loadings and communalities (h^2's) are given in Table 36.10.

TABLE 36.10 THURSTONE FACTOR SOLUTION OF DAVIS DATA [a]

Tests	Loading	h^2
Word Meaning	.803	.645
Contextual Meaning	.810	.656
Organization	.469	.220
Thought	.409	.168
Specifics	.677	.458
Express Ideas	.895	.801
Inferences	.846	.716
Literary Devices	.658	.434
Determine Writer Purpose	.844	.713

[a] Test names were made up from the short descriptions given by Davis. Note that factor analysts sometimes report two, three, sometimes more, decimal places.

One might judge from these results that reading skills are unifactorial. Such an interpretation might be a serious mistake, however. As Thurstone points out, this is no evidence of the components of reading ability. The addition of other kinds of tests might well show other factors behind reading ability. Still, it is remarkable that the various abilities measured by the nine tests should be unifactorial. The usefulness of factor analysis is here nicely demonstrated.

19 L. Thurstone, "Note on a Reanalysis of Davis' Reading Tests," *Psychometrika,* XI (1946), 185–188.
20 F. Davis, "Fundamental Factors of Comprehension in Reading," *Psychometrika,* IX (1944), 185–197.

Thurstone Factorial Study of Intelligence   Thurstone and Thurstone, in their monumental work on intelligence factors and their measurement,[21] factor-analyzed 60 tests plus the three variables Chronological Age, Mental Age, and Sex. The analysis was based on the test responses of 710 eighth-grade pupils to the 60 tests. It revealed essentially the same set of so-called primary factors that had been found in previous factor analytic studies.

The Thurstones chose the three best tests for each of seven of the ten primary factors. Six of these tests seemed to have stability at different age levels sufficient for practical school use. They then revised and administered these tests to 437 eighth-grade school children. The main purpose of the study was to check the factor structure of the tests. In other words, they predicted that the same primary factors of intelligence put into the 21 tests would emerge from a new factor analysis on a new sample of children.

The rotated factor matrix (oblique rotation) is given in Table 36.11. This is a remarkable validation of the primary factors. The seven factors and their loadings are almost exactly as predicted.

Rokeach-Fruchter Study of Dogmatism and Other Variables   Rokeach and Fruchter administered a battery of ten scales to 207 college students in order to explore the factorial nature of dogmatism as measured by Rokeach's D scale.[22] *Dogmatism* is defined as a relatively closed cognitive organization of beliefs and disbeliefs, related to intolerance and organized around central beliefs about absolute authority.[23] Rokeach and Fruchter believed that dogmatism has its motivational basis in anxiety, that the D scale measures *general* authoritarianism and *general* intolerance, and that dogmatism refers to total systems of beliefs and not to single beliefs. They thus predicted the factor structure that should emerge from a factor analysis of dogmatism, authoritarianism, ethnocentrism (prejudice), anxiety, rigidity, and certain other measures. They factor analyzed the intercorrelations of the ten measures and obtained three factors which they rotated orthogonally to approximate simple structure.

The unrotated and rotated factor matrices were reported in Table 36.5 and the R matrix of this study in Table 36.4. Five of the variables reported in Table 36.5 were not mentioned above. Variables 2, 3, and 4 are subscales of the D scale. One purpose of the study was to determine whether paranoia and self-rejection, theoretically assumed to be parts of

21 L. Thurstone and T. Thurstone, *Factorial Studies of Intelligence*, Psychometric Monograph No. 2. Chicago: University of Chicago Press, 1941, chap. III. Copyright 1941 by The University of Chicago. The student interested in factor analysis and the testing of intelligence can profit greatly from study of this fine monograph.

22 Rokeach and Fruchter, *op. cit.*

23 M. Rokeach, "The Nature and Meaning of Dogmatism," *Psychological Review*, LXI (1954), 194–204.

TABLE **36.11** OBLIQUE ROTATED FACTOR MATRIX, THURSTONE AND THURSTONE STUDY [a]

Tests	P	N	W	V	S	M	R
Identification Numbers	42	40	05	−02	−07	−06	−06
Faces	45	17	−06	04	20	05	02
Mirror Reading	36	09	19	−02	05	−01	09
First Names	−02	09	02	00	−05	53	10
Figure Recognition	20	−10	02	−02	10	31	07
Word-Number	02	13	−03	00	01	58	−04
Sentences	00	01	−03	66	−08	−05	13
Vocabulary	−01	02	05	66	−04	02	02
Completion	−01	00	−01	67	15	00	−01
First Letters	12	−03	63	03	−02	00	−00
4–Letter Words	−02	−05	61	−01	08	−01	04
Suffixes	04	03	45	18	−03	03	−08
Flags	−04	05	03	−01	68	00	01
Figures	02	−06	01	−02	76	−02	−02
Cards	07	−03	−03	03	72	02	−03
Addition	01	64	−02	01	05	01	−02
Multiplication	01	67	01	−03	−05	02	02
3–Higher	−05	38	−01	06	20	−05	16
Letter Series	−03	03	03	02	00	02	53
Pedigrees	02	−05	−03	22	−03	05	44
Letter Group	06	06	13	−04	01	−06	42

[a] Decimal points are omitted. P = Perception; N = Number; W = Word Fluency; V = Verbal; S = Space; M = Memory; R = Reasoning.

the dogmatism complex, really belong to dogmatism. Variable 8 consisted of five items that measure political and economic conservatism. Variables 9 and 10 are scales devised by Rokeach to measure opinionation of the left and the right. Left Opinionation and Right Opinionation are supposed to be measures of general intolerance.[24] The authors believed that these three measures would emerge on a single factor of liberalism-conservatism.

Study of the R matrix (Table 36.4) shows a cluster of Variables 1, 2, and 3 and another of 4, 5, and 6. Variables 8 and 10 form another cluster. It should be obvious to the reader, however, that it is hard to disentangle the clusters, especially when there is overlapping.

The rotated factor matrix tells the story much more clearly and precisely. Recall that the authors hypothesized factors and factor loadings. Their hypotheses are: (1) Dogmatism (D) can be discriminated (factorially) from Authoritarianism (F), Ethnocentrism (E), Rigidity; (2) Para

[24] For a complete discussion of Rokeach's theory and the scales he has devised, see M. Rokeach, *The Open and Closed Mind*. New York: Basic Books, 1960. See, particularly, chap. 4.

noia, Self-Rejection, Dogmatism, and Anxiety will emerge on one factor; (3) Liberalism-Conservatism, Right-Opinionation, and Left-Opinionation will emerge on a separate factor.[25] Study of the rotated matrix confirms these hypotheses. It shows, in addition, certain cross-factor relations. It shows, for instance, that Dogmatism is factorially related both to Anxiety, Paranoia, and Self-Rejection, on the one hand, but more strongly related to Authoritarianism and Rigidity, on the other hand. The student can complete the interpretation of the matrix as an exercise.

This study is an excellent example of theoretical and factor analytic reasoning. It shows, further, that factor analysis is quite capable of testing hypotheses.

A Q Study of Perceptions of Effective Teacher Characteristics   In Chap. 33, it was said that the responses of individuals to a measurement instrument could be intercorrelated and factor-analyzed. Such analysis was called Q methodology in contrast to the intercorrelation and factor analysis of tests or variables which is called R methodology. (Q factor analysis is also called "inverse" or "obverse" factor analysis.)

No new factor analytic principles are involved. Instead of clusters or factors and factor loadings of tests, one has clusters or factors and factor loadings of persons, or rather, persons' responses. The six tests of Tables 36.1 and 36.2, for example, might have been six persons who all sorted the same Q sort. The correlation coefficients of Table 36.1 and the factor loadings of Table 36.2 might have been obtained by intercorrelating the Q sorts of the six persons, as outlined in Chap. 33, factor-analyzing the resulting R matrix (Table 36.1), and obtaining rotated factor loadings (Table 36.2). V, R, and S would be three persons who constitute one factor, and N, AS, and AT would be three persons who constitute another factor. In order to interpret the "persons" factors, one would search for something common to V, R, and S and something else common to N, AS, and AT. One would also compute factor arrays so that the substantive nature of the factors would be revealed.

On the basis of an earlier study and as part of a larger study of the relation between attitudes toward education and perceptions of the characteristics of effective teachers, the author constructed a Q sort, using 90 adjectives as items.[26] The set of Q adjective-items was sorted by 38 judges in response to instructions to sort the items to indicate their judgments as to the characteristics a "good" teacher should possess. The data of the 38 Q sorts were intercorrelated and the correlations factor-analyzed. Three factors were rotated to approximate simple structure. The rotated factor matrix (orthogonal) of 12 of the 38 judges is given in Table 36.12.

25 Rokeach and Fruchter, *op. cit.*, pp. 359, 360 and Footnote 7, p. 358.
26 Part of an unpublished study. For a discussion of the theoretical reasoning behind the study, see F. Kerlinger, "Educational Attitudes and Perceptions of Teachers: Suggestions for Teacher-Effectiveness Research," *School Review*, LXXI (1963), 1–11.

TABLE 36.12 ROTATED FACTOR MATRIX OF 12 JUDGES,
ATTITUDE-PERCEPTION STUDY [a]

Judges	A	B	C	h^2
1	*72*	06	17	55
2	*80*	02	15	66
3	*41*	39	−09	33
4	*65*	36	14	57
5	*67*	18	17	51
6	*65*	08	25	49
7	09	*62*	36	52
8	35	04	*61*	50
9	−11	24	*56*	38
10	15	15	*62*	43
11	−03	*72*	06	52
12	06	*65*	27	50

[a] Decimal points are omitted. Judges 1, 2, 3, and 4 are professors of education, 5 and 6 elementary teachers, 7 and 8 secondary teachers, 9 and 10 military officers teaching at a large Army school, and 11 and 12 nuns teaching in a parochial school. Significant loadings are italicized.

The judges were carefully selected to represent presumably different perceptions of the effective teacher. They included professors of education, elementary and secondary public school teachers, military instructors (officers), and parochial school teachers (nuns). The 12 judges of Table 36.12 represent all these groups. (See Footnote *a* to Table 36.12.) That is, the Table 36.12 data represent the data of the complete factor matrix.

It can be seen that a fairly good simple structure has been achieved. The professors of education and the elementary teachers are on one factor (Judges 1 through 6). One of the secondary teachers is on Factor *B*, and one is on Factor *C* (Numbers 7 and 8). The secondary teachers' loadings were more mixed than these two loadings indicate. The two military instructors (8 and 9) are on Factor *C*, and the two nuns (11 and 12) are on Factor *B*.

Evidently there are three different kinds of judges and thus three different kinds of judgments of the effective teacher.[27] These different judgments, or factors, seem also to be related to the judges' teaching roles. If we somehow average the values of the *Q* card placements of the judges on each factor separately, taking care to choose only those judges who are substantially loaded on one factor and not on the other two, we may be able to infer the nature of the factor, the underlying unity, or the source of the common factor variance. For example, we might use the

[27] The student should plot the factor loadings on graph paper (use 4-to-the-inch paper). Plot *A* and *B*, *A* and *C*, and *B* and *C*. In learning factor analysis and in interpreting factor analytic results, there is no substitute for plotting and careful study of plots.

data of Judges 1, 2, 5, and 6 for *A;* Judges 7, 11, and 12 for *B;* and Judges 8, 9, and 10 for *C*—though we would ordinarily want more judges for each factor.

"Calculating" the factor arrays as indicated above and in Chap. 33, but using more judges for each factor, the highly chosen or judged characteristics (important for teachers to have) are given in Table 36.13.

TABLE **36.13**   FACTOR ARRAYS OF *Q* DATA OF TEACHER CHARACTERISTICS PERCEPTION STUDY [a]

Factor *A*	Factor *B*	Factor *C*
Intelligent	Conscientious	Enthusiastic
Imaginative	Moral	Inquisitive
Insightful	Religious	Decisive
Warm	Intelligent	Purposeful
Open-Minded	Efficient	Sincere
Flexible	Just	Practical
Purposeful	Self-Controlled	Respectable
Enthusiastic	Trustworthy	Resourceful
Sympathetic	Refined	Imaginative
Sensitive	Firm	Just
Fair	Learned	Confident
Patient	Industrious	Definite
Sincere	Reliable	Persevering
Resourceful	Healthy	Forceful

[a] Adjectives are roughly in rank order. That is, the first three were assigned the highest values, the next four the next highest, and the next seven the next highest.

It is clear that there are three different perceptions of the "good" teacher, even though some adjectives occur on two of the arrays. Interpretation is left to the reader. In attempting to interpret these (or any other) factors, the student should ask: What is the underlying unity, the common factor running through these adjectives—or these tests, or persons, or test items? Whatever construct or constructs are chosen to epitomize the factor should express the communality running through the factor. For example, two psychologists judging the *B* factor array thought it expressed a "traditional" teacher outlook.

Ryans' Factor Analysis of Teacher Behavior   In his classical studies of the behaviors and characteristics of teachers, Ryans factor-analyzed actual observations of classroom behavior.[28] Judges observed large numbers of elementary and secondary teachers and rated them on a number of

28 D. Ryans, *Characteristics of Teachers.* Washington, D.C.: American Council on Education, 1960, chap. 4.

characteristics (see Table 36.14) using a seven-point rating scale. The ratings on each characteristic were correlated with the ratings on each of the other characteristics. This was done for elementary and secondary teachers separately. The resulting matrices of correlations among the characteristics were factor-analyzed and the resulting factor matrices rotated obliquely to simple structure. The rotated factor matrix of the secondary teacher characteristics (behaviors), as well as pupil characteristics, is given in Table 36.14.

TABLE 36.14 ROTATED FACTOR MATRIX OF TEACHER CHARACTERISTICS, RYANS STUDY [a]

Dimension	I	II	III	IV	V	VI
Pupil Behavior						
Apathetic-alert	07	01	*53*	21	05	−05
Obstructive-responsible	−02	03	*46*	04	−06	10
Uncertain-confident	17	02	*43*	−01	17	−03
Dependent-initiating	00	−05	*55*	04	21	−02
Teacher Behavior						
Partial-fair	*42*	26	−04	10	−11	05
Autocratic-democratic	*54*	−05	−02	01	*47*	−04
Aloof (Group)-responsive	*36*	−08	25	*34*	03	12
Aloof (Individual)-responsive	*54*	05	−02	*35*	06	03
Restricted-understanding	*44*	17	08	26	10	03
Harsh-kindly	*52*	07	−02	−05	12	15
Dull-stimulating	−08	06	*32*	14	28	17
Stereotyped-original	01	05	17	01	*40*	13
Apathetic-alert	04	08	12	*41*	−01	02
Unimpressive-attractive	02	00	01	−04	07	*39*
Monotonous-pleasant (voice)	05	−06	−01	05	−07	*46*
Inarticulate-articulate	−14	17	−04	08	−05	*35*
Evading-responsible	14	*52*	−08	20	03	−07
Erratic-steady	07	*43*	08	−25	08	17
Excitable-poised	04	20	06	−*39*	16	*36*
Uncertain-confident	−01	20	20	−11	12	27
Disorganized-systematic	−02	*50*	02	02	02	03
Inflexible-adaptable	*48*	09	00	09	*35*	00
Pessimistic-optimistic	*34*	−08	19	14	09	17
Immature-integrated	14	16	20	−06	09	*30*
Narrow-broad	05	*34*	−06	−03	*30*	03

[a] Decimal points are omitted. Loadings greater than .30 are italicized.

Ryans' able interpretations of the factors are here briefly summarized.[29]

[29] *Ibid.*, pp. 100, 101. The author has rephrased some of the descriptions slightly.

     I. Understanding-democratic vs. aloof, harsh, autocratic
    II. Businesslike, systematic, responsible vs. unorganized, slipshod
   III. (Teachers) Challenging, interesting, helpful;
       (Pupils) Pupil participation and controlled activity vs. apathy, dependence, lack of control
   IV. Alertness, enthusiasm, excitability
    V. Originality, adaptability, ability to stimulate vs. dullness, inflexibility, stereotypy
   VI. Pleasing voice, fluency, charm, dignity

Ryans, analyzing and interpreting the results of the elementary and secondary factor analyses, came to the conclusion (which he tested extensively) that there are three correlated factors, or sets of characteristics or behaviors, that stand out and that may be common to both elementary and secondary teachers:

X_o Understanding, friendliness, responsiveness vs. aloofness, egocentrism (Factor I)

Y_o Responsible, businesslike, systematic vs. evading, unplanned, slipshod (Factor II)

Z_o Stimulating, imaginative, original vs. dull, routine (Factor V)

A Factor Analytic Validation of Attitude Items[30]   In two Q studies, the author found two attitudes factors, one that seemed to be a reflection of progressive beliefs, the other a reflection of traditional beliefs. These factors were called A and B, respectively, and scales were constructed to measure them. The scales were administered to large numbers of school of education graduate and undergraduate students and individuals outside the university. It was predicted that, if the *items* of the instrument containing the two scales were intercorrelated, A items would correlate positively with other A items and B items would correlate positively with other B items. There should be near-zero correlations between A and B items.

    It was also predicted that a factor analysis of the item intercorrelations should produce two factors. The A items should be loaded positively and substantially on one factor and not on the other. The B items should be loaded positively and substantially on one factor and not on the other.

    The correlations conformed rather closely to the expectations outlined above. The A items intercorrelated positively: the r's ranged from .06 to .34, with a mean of .20. (Note: Item correlations are usually rather low.) The B items, too, intercorrelated positively: they ranged from .09 to .46, with a mean of .26. The correlations between the A and B items

    30 F. Kerlinger and E. Kaya, "The Construction and Factor Analytic Validation of Scales to Measure Attitudes Toward Education," *Educational and Psychological Measurement,* XIX (1959), 13–29.

were almost all negative and low. They had a range of from .00 to −.41, with a mean of −.11.

The rotated factor matrix and its loadings also conformed closely to expectations. This matrix is given in Table 36.15. (A third factor was found. It does not seem to have meaning.)

TABLE 36.15   ROTATED FACTOR MATRIX: *A* AND *B* ITEMS OF EDUCATIONAL ATTITUDES SCALE [a]

Items	*A*	*B*	*C*	h^2
(*A*)				
1	*.440*	.010	.167	.222
2	*.386*	−.136	.074	.173
5	*.416*	−.133	−.210	.235
7	*.356*	−.135	−.284	.226
8	*.450*	.011	−.273	.277
9	*.512*	−.046	−.134	.282
15	*.546*	−.026	−.185	.333
16	*.366*	−.089	.022	.142
17	*.577*	−.259	.117	.414
20	*.352*	−.032	−.277	.202
(*B*)				
3	*−.379*	*.349*	−.268	.337
4	−.096	*.379*	.185	.187
6	−.046	*.522*	−.161	.301
10	−.094	*.496*	.165	.282
11	−.019	*.581*	.097	.347
12	*−.305*	*.544*	−.158	.414
13	−.114	*.478*	.276	.318
14	−.013	*.411*	.221	.218
18	*−.330*	*.523*	−.156	.407
19	−.102	*.636*	.133	.433

[a] Significant loadings (≧ .30) are italicized.

The factor structure is almost perfect. All *A* items are loaded significantly on Factor *A*, and all *B* items are loaded significantly on Factor *B*. The only exceptions to the predictions are the three rather substantial negative loadings of *B* items 3, 12, and 18 on Factor *A*. This is cogent evidence, then, for the construct validity of the scale. If the reader will take the trouble to plot the factor loadings on graph paper, he will see the two clear, unmistakable, and independent clusters.

FACTOR ANALYSIS AND SCIENTIFIC PSYCHOLOGICAL
AND EDUCATIONAL RESEARCH

Factor analysis has two basic purposes: (1) to explore variable areas in order to identify the factors presumably underlying the variables as well as the variables, and, as in all scientific work, (2) to test hypotheses about the relations among variables. The first purpose is well known and fairly well accepted. The second purpose is not so well known nor so well accepted.

In conceptualizing the first purpose, the exploratory or reductive purpose, one should keep construct validity and constitutive definitions in mind. Factor analysis can be conceived as a construct validity tool. Recall that validity was defined in Chap. 25 as common factor variance. Since the main statistical preoccupation of factor analysis is common factor variance, by definition factor analysis is firmly tied to measurement theory. Indeed, this tie was expressed earlier in the section headed "Some Factor Theory," where equations were written to clarify factor analytic theory. (See, especially, Eq. 36.6.)

Recall, too, that construct validity seeks the "meaning" of a construct through the relations between the construct and other constructs. In Part I when types of definitions were discussed, we learned that constructs could be defined in two ways: by operational definitions and by constitutive definitions. Constitutive definitions are definitions that define constructs with other constructs. Essentially this is what factor analysis does. It may be called a constitutive meaning method since it enables the researcher to study the constitutive meanings of constructs— and thus their construct validity.

The measures of three variables, say, may share something in common. This something itself is a variable, presumably a more basic entity than the variables used to isolate and identify it. We give this new variable a name; in other words, we construct a hypothetical entity. Then, to inquire into the "reality" of the variable we may systematically devise a measure of it, testing its "reality" by correlating data obtained with the variable with data from other measures theoretically related to it. Factor analysis helps us check our theoretical expectations.

Part of the basic life-stuff of any science is its constructs. Old constructs continue to be used; new ones are constantly being invented. Note some of the general constructs directly pertinent to psychological and educational research: achievement, intelligence, learning, aptitude, attitude, problem-solving ability, needs, interests, creativity, conformity, teacher traits. Note some of the more specific variables important in psychological and educational research: test anxiety, verbal ability, traditionalism, convergent thinking, spatial perception, arithmetic reasoning, attitudes toward self, and social class. Clearly, a large portion of scientific psychological and educational research effort has to be devoted to what might be called construct investigation or construct validation. This requires factor analysis.

Although a good deal of psychological research pertinent to education and aimed at construct validation has been done, it is remarkable how ignorant we are. Take a very obvious example, school achievement, or simply achievement. After almost half a century of educational research we know little about achievement *as a construct*. We know something of the relations between achievement and other constructs, for example, intelligence, social class, anxiety, and sex. But we know strikingly little about the nature of achievement itself.[31] Thousands of tests are constructed and administered by teachers every year. But there is little research into what these tests measure. Beyond simple factual tests of circumscribed areas, it is evident that most teacher-made achievement tests—and most standardized achievement tests—are factorially complex. If this is so, it is equally evident that the construct validity of achievement tests is seriously in question. Almost any social studies, mathematics, science, or English test probably measures various aspects of achievement factors. The basic assumption behind most achievement testing is that the tests used to measure whatever achievement is being tested are themselves unitary measures of the achievement in question. And the assumption is quite probably false.

The assumption, moreover, is quite probably false with many other psychological-educational variables and measures. To talk about the relation between achievement and anxiety, for example, is easy. But it is not so easy to say that we are measuring unitary variables. Like achievement, anxiety is evidently multidimensional. Even types of tests and types of items may produce factors.

Many research areas, then, could well be preceded by factor analytic explorations of the variables of the area. This does not mean that a number of tests are thrown together and given to any samples that happen to be available. Factor analytic investigations, both exploratory and hypothesis-testing, have to be painstakingly planned. Variables that may be influential have to be controlled—sex, education, social class, intelligence, and so on.[32] Variables are not put into a factor analysis just to put them in. They should have legitimate purpose. If, for instance, one cannot control intelligence by sample selection, one might include a measure of intelligence (verbal, perhaps) in the battery of measures. By

[31] See E. Kaya, "Construct Validity in Achievement: An Inverse Factor Analytic Study of the Meaning of Achievement for Professors and Students of Psychology." Unpublished Ph.D. Thesis, New York University, 1959.

[32] J. Guilford, "Factorial Angles to Psychology," *Psychological Review*, LXVIII (1961), 1–20. This is an important article that any investigator who uses factor analysis should study. Another excellent statement is D. Wolfle, *Factor Analysis to 1940*, Psychometric Monographs No. 3. Chicago: University of Chicago Press, 1940.

identifying intelligence variance one has in a sense controlled intelligence.

One can also learn whether one's measures are contaminated by response biases by including response bias measures in factor analyses. For example, the writer had reason to suspect that the scales constructed to measure attitudes toward education mentioned previously might have been contaminated with intelligence and social desirability variance. An intelligence measure (verbal) and two social desirability measures were included with the educational attitudes scales in a factor analytic study. Evidently there was no contamination, since the scales were not loaded on the same factors as the intelligence and response bias measures.

The second major purpose of factor analysis is to test hypotheses. One aspect of hypothesis-testing has already been hinted: one can put tests or measures into factor analytic batteries deliberately to test the identification and nature of factors. The typical design of such studies has been well outlined by Thurstone, Cattell, Guilford, and others. First, factors are "discovered." Their nature is inferred from the tests that are loaded on them. This "nature" is set up as a hypothesis. New tests are constructed and given to new samples of subjects. The data are factor-analyzed. If the factors emerge *as predicted,* the hypothesis is to this extent confirmed, the factors would seem to have "reality." This would certainly not end the matter. One would have to test, among other things, the factors' relation to other factors. One would have to place the factors, as constructs, in a nomological network of constructs.

A less well-known use of factor analysis as a hypothesis-testing method is in testing experimental hypotheses. One might hypothesize that a certain method of teaching reading changes the ability patterns of pupils, so that verbal intelligence is not as potent an influence as it might be with other teaching methods. An experimental study could be planned in such a way as to test this hypothesis. The effects of the teaching methods could be assessed by factor analyses of a set of tests given before and after the different methods were used. Woodrow tested a similar hypothesis when he gave a set of tests before and after practice in seven tests: adding, subtracting, anagrams, and so on.[33] He found that factor loading patterns *did* change after practice.

In like manner, it might well be possible to assess the effects of important curriculum changes. A school system that radically changed its curriculum approach from, say, factual learning to a problem-oriented approach would have the possibility of assessing the effects of the change

---

[33] H. Woodrow, "The Relation between Abilities and Improvement with Practice," *Journal of Educational Psychology,* XXIX (1938), 215–230. For an important creative discussion of the possibilities of combining factor analysis and experimentation, see R. Cattell, *Factor Analysis, op. cit.,* chap. 20.

in part through factor analysis. Shifts in factor loading structures and magnitudes could be expected under the impact of so radical a curriculum change.

Factor analysis has many other uses in educational research. Schutz, for example, in a factor analysis of 18 social-cultural variables (college graduates in adult population, median grade of school in the population, professional workers, income, monthly rental, and so forth) and two test measures (a paragraph meaning test and an arithmetic reasoning test) found that, contrary to what might be expected, achievement was not related to the social-cultural variables.[34] The two achievement variables had high loadings on a factor independent of four other factors.

In considering the scientific value of factor analysis, the reader must be cautioned against attributing "reality" and uniqueness to factors that may not exist. The danger of reification is great. It is easy to name a factor and then to believe there is a reality behind the name. But giving a factor a name does not give it reality. Factor names are simply attempts to epitomize the essence of factors. They are always tentative, subject to later confirmation or disconfirmation. Then, too, as Wolfle and others have pointed out, factors can be produced by many things. Anything that introduces correlation between variables "creates" a factor.[35] Differences in sex, education, social and cultural background, and intelligence can cause factors to appear. Factors also differ—at least to some extent—with different samples. Response sets or test forms may cause factors to appear. Despite these cautions, it must be said that factors do repeatedly emerge with different tests, different samples, and different conditions. When this happens, we can have fair assurance that there is an underlying trait which we are successfully measuring.

There are serious criticisms of factor analysis. The major valid criticism centers around the statistical inadequacy of the method and the element of subjectivity that enters rotations. In an introductory chapter, these problems can only be mentioned. The reader is referred to the several discussions of Guilford, Cattell, and Harman. A criticism of a very different order seems to bother educators and some psychologists. This takes two or three forms, all of which seem to boil down to a profound distrust of the method due to its statistical complexity and, strangely enough, its objectivity.

The argument runs something like this. Factor analysts throw a lot of tests together into a statistical machine and get out factors that have little psychological or educational meaning. The factors are simply artifacts of the method. They are averages that correspond to no psycho-

[34] R. Schutz, "A Factor Analysis of Academic Achievement and Community Characteristics," *Educational and Psychological Measurement,* XX (1960), 513–518.

[35] Wolfle, *op. cit.,* p. 25.

logical reality, especially the psychological reality of the individual, other than that in the mind of the factor analyst.[36] Besides, you can't get any more out of a factor analysis than you put into it.

Actually, the argument is basically irrelevant. To say that factors have no psychological meaning and that they are averages is both true and untrue. If the argument were valid, no scientific constructs would have any meaning. They are all, in a sense, averages. They are all also inventions of the scientist. This is simply the lot of all science. The basic criterion of the "reality" of any construct, any factor, is its empirical, scientific "reality." If, after uncovering a factor, we can successfully predict relations from theoretical presuppositions and hypotheses, then the factor has "reality." There is no more reality to a factor than this, just as there is no more reality to an atom than its empirical manifestations.

The argument about only getting out what is put into a factor analysis is meaningless as well as irrelevant. No competent factor analytic investigator would ever claim more than this. But this does not mean that nothing is discovered in factor analysis. Quite the contrary. The answer is, of course, that we get nothing more out of a factor analysis than we put into it, but that we do not know *all* we put into it. Nor do we know what tests or measures share common factor variance. Nor do we know the relations between factors. Only factor analysis can tell us these things. We may write an attitude scale that we believe measures a single attitude. A factor analysis of the attitude items, naturally, cannot produce factors that are not in the items. But it can show us, for example, that there are two or three sources of common variance in a scale that we thought to be unidimensional. Similarly, a scale that we believe measures authoritarianism may be shown by factor analysis to measure intelligence, dogmatism, and other variables.

If we examine empirical evidence rather than opinion, it is impossible to escape the conclusion that factor analysis is one of the most powerful tools yet devised for the design and analysis of complex areas of scientific psychological and educational concern. It is also impossible to escape the conclusion that factor analysis has great potential importance in educational research.

It is fitting that this chapter—and the book—conclude with some words of a great psychological scientist, teacher, and factor analyst, Louis Leon Thurstone:

> As scientists, we have the faith that the abilities and personalities of people are not so complex as the total enumeration of attributes that can be listed. We believe that these traits are made up of a smaller number of primary factors or elements that combine in various ways to make a long

[36] See G. Allport, *Pattern and Growth in Personality*. New York: Holt, Rinehart and Winston, Inc., 1961, pp. 329, 330; G. Allport, *Personality*. New York: Holt, Rinehart and Winston, Inc., 1937 pp 242–248.

list of traits. It is our ambition to find some of these elementary abilities and traits . . .

All scientific work has this in common, that we try to comprehend nature in the most parsimonious manner. An explanation of a set of phenomena or of a set of experimental observations gains acceptance only in so far as it gives us intellectual control or comprehension of a relatively wide variety of phenomena in terms of a limited number of concepts. The principle of parsimony is intuitive for anyone who has even slight aptitude for science. The fundamental motivation of science is the craving for the simplest possible comprehension of nature, and it finds satisfaction in the discovery of the simplifying uniformities that we call scentific laws.[37]

STUDY SUGGESTIONS

1. There are several good references on factor analysis. The student should use one or two of these, working through the centroid method and perhaps the principal axes (factors) method.

   Cattell, R. *Factor Analysis*. New York: Harper & Row, 1952. An excellent text by a master of factor analysis, this book has an especially good discussion of controversial issues.

   Fruchter, B. *Introduction to Factor Analysis*. Princeton, N. J.: Van Nostrand, 1954. This is probably the simplest of the texts; it might well be used in conjunction with one of the more advanced works.

   Guilford, J. *Psychometric Methods,* 2d ed. New York: McGraw-Hill, 1954, Chap. 16. This excellent, brief presentation of the rationale of factor analysis is strongly recommended for the student who wants to learn the centroid method. See, also, pp. 354–357 for a presentation of factor and validity theory.

   Harman, H. *Modern Factor Analysis*. Chicago: University of Chicago Press, 1960. This text is very fine, but more difficult than other texts (except Thurstone's). It is at present the definitive work on factor analysis and thus indispensable for the student who wants breadth and depth.

   Thomson, G. *The Factorial Analysis of Human Ability*. Boston: Houghton Mifflin, 1939. This clear, well-written text has well-conceived and pointed explanations and examples. It is especially helpful in learning the principal axes method.

   Thurstone, L. *Multiple-Factor Analysis*. Chicago: University of Chicago Press, 1947. The classic of factor analysis, this work is highly recommended for the student who has studied more elementary expositions.

2. In addition to studying the logic and technique of factor analysis, the student should read factor analytic studies and discussions of factor

[37] L. Thurstone, *The Measurement of Values*. Chicago: University of Chicago Press, 1959, p. 8.

analysis topics. Here are several references that may be useful and interesting.

Eysenck, H. *The Structure of Human Personality*. New York: Wiley, 1953. This is a fine review of many factor analytic studies of physique, interests, attitudes, and traits.

French, J. *The Description of Aptitude and Achievement Tests in Terms of Rotated Factors*. Psychometric Monographs No. 5. Chicago: University of Chicago Press, 1951. This is an exhaustive review, with data, of many factor analytic studies of aptitude and achievement.

Stephenson, W. *The Study of Behavior*. Chicago: University of Chicago Press, 1953. A number of Stephenson's interesting factor analytic *Q* studies are contained in this book.

Thompson, J. "Meaningful and Unmeaningful Rotation of Factors." *Psychological Bulletin*, LIX (1962), 211–223. This is a competent and sensible article on the controversial rotation problem.

Wolfle, D. *Factor Analysis to 1940*. Chicago: University of Chicago Press, 1940. The author gives a brief and enlightening review of the field of factor analysis to 1940.

3. Here is a small fictitious correlation matrix, with the tests labeled.

	1	2	3	4	5	6
1. Vocabulary		.70	.22	.20	.15	.25
2. Analogies	.70		.15	.26	.12	.30
3. Addition	.22	.15		.81	.21	.10
4. Multiplication	.20	.26	.81		.31	.29
5. Recall First Names	.15	.12	.21	.31		.72
6. Recognize Figures	.25	.30	.40	.29	.72	

(a) Do an "armchair" factor analysis. That is, by inspection of the matrix determine how many factors there probably are and which tests are on what factors.

(b) Name the factors. How sure are you of your names? What would you do to be more sure of your conclusions?

4. Given below is the obliquely rotated factor matrix of the intercorrelations among 13 variables produced by the superiors of school principals when they rated the principals. The matrix is one among many such matrices in Hemphill, Griffiths, and Frederiksen's large study of educational administrator behavior.[38] (Note: All decimal points are omitted.)

(a) Name the factors, giving reasons for naming them as you do. (Use loadings .25 and higher to help in this naming.)

[38] J. Hemphill, D. Griffiths, and N. Frederiksen, *Administrative Performance and Personality*. New York: Teachers College, Columbia University, 1962, p. 232.

Rating Item	A	B	C	D	E
Interest in Work	06	15	41	−01	02
Sticking to a Job	03	−18	52	02	02
Getting Along with Teachers	69	07	−07	12	01
Getting Along with Parents	62	−02	04	08	04
Getting Along with Superiors	52	02	05	−17	31
Knowledge of Administration	−07	−11	30	02	26
Knowledge of Teaching	01	33	08	−09	31
Rapport with Children	56	32	−04	09	−12
Written Communication	−03	00	−06	07	45
Understanding	08	−04	05	07	39
Oral Communication (Formal)	−08	01	05	49	01
Oral Communication (Informal)	09	01	−05	48	07
Over-all Impression	25	09	15	01	26

(b) Check your names with the names reported in the study.

(c) This is an obliquely rotated matrix, which means that the factors are correlated. For example, the correlation between *A* and *C* is .47. What does this mean? How does this affect the interpretation of the data?

5. Interpret the rotated factor matrix given below. The data are taken from a larger table reported by Sears, Maccoby, and Levin.[39] (Note: All decimal points omitted.)

Scale	A	B	D
Permissiveness for Going without Clothes Indoors	66	−11	09
Masturbation Permissiveness	70	−04	05
Standards for Neatness and Orderliness	−35	−19	38
Extent of Use of Tangible Rewards	−04	−14	40
Extent of Use of Deprivation of Privileges	−16	−08	51
Parents' Agreement on Child-Rearing Policies	01	60	15
Husband's Reaction to Wife's Pregnancy	13	51	07
Mother's Child-Rearing Anxiety	−10	−56	−17

[39] R. Sears, E. Maccoby, and H. Levin, *Patterns of Child Rearing*. New York: Harper & Row, 1957, pp. 516–518. Only three factors of seven and eight measures of 44 are given. Some of the original signs (plus and minus) have been changed to facilitate interpretation.

APPENDIXES

A THE RESEARCH REPORT

This appendix has two purposes: to outline some of the main points of report writing and to cite appropriate references to guide the reader.

THE PURPOSE

The purpose of the research report is to tell readers the problem investigated, the methods used to solve the problem, the results of the investigation, and the conclusions inferred from the results. It is not the function of the investigator to *convince* the reader of the virtue of the research. Rather, it is to *report*, as expeditiously and clearly as possible, what was done, why it was done, the outcome of the doing, and the investigator's conclusions. The report should be so written that the reader himself can reach his own conclusions as to the adequacy of the research and the validity of the reported results and conclusions.

To achieve this purpose is not easy. The writer must strive for the right blend of detail and brevity, for objectivity, and for clarity in presentation. Perhaps the best criterion question is: Can another investigator replicate the research by following the research report? If he cannot, due to incomplete or inadequate reporting of methodology or to lack of clarity in presentation, then the report is inadequate.

THE STRUCTURE

The structure of the research report is simple. It is almost the same as the structure of the research itself: the problem, the methodology, the results. Here is a general outline:

I. Problem
1. Theory, hypotheses, definition
2. Previous research; the literature
II. Methodology-Data Collection
1. Sample and sampling method
2. How hypotheses were tested (methodology), experimental procedures, instrumentation

3. Measurement of variables
4. Methods of analysis, statistics
5. Pretesting and pilot studies
III. Results, Interpretation, and Conclusions

The Problem The problem section differs greatly in different reports. In theses and books, it is usually long and detailed. In published research reports, it is kept to a minimum. The basic precept to keep in mind, though seemingly obvious, is not easy to follow: Tell the reader what the research problem is. Tell it to him in question form. For example, What is the effect of set on problem solving behavior? What is the effect on learning of mutual similarity of items being learned?[1] Do school subjects have transfer value? Does past experience with materials have a negative effect on problem-solving involving the materials?[2] Do sex role and school location have a moderating effect on the cognitive and noncognitive performances of junior high school students?[3]

The statement of the general problem is usually not precise and operational. Rather, it sets the general stage for the reader. The subproblems, however, should be more precise. They should contain implications for testing. For example, Are principles derived by the learner solely from concrete instances more readily used in new situations than principles given to him?[4] Does practice in digit memorizing improve future memorizing of digits?[5] Can a person conversing with another person manipulate that person's conversation by agreeing or disagreeing with him, or by paraphrasing what he has said?[6]

Some report writers, rather than state the problems, state the general and specific hypotheses. A good practice would seem to be to state the broader general problem and then to state the hypotheses, both general and specific. The reader is referred to Chap. 2 for examples. Whatever way is used, bear in mind the main purpose of informing the reader of the main area of investigation and the specific propositions that were tested.

An important part of the statement of the problem is the definition of the variables. At some point in the problem discussion the variables should be defined. The subject of research definitions was handled in Chap. 3 and need not be repeated here, except for the admonition: Inform the reader not only of the variables but also what you mean by them. Define in general and operational terms giving justification for your definitions.

---

[1] E. Gibson, "Intra-List Generalization as a Factor in Verbal Learning," *Journal of Experimental Psychology*, XXX (1942), 185–200.

[2] H. Birch and H. Rabinowitz, "The Negative Effect of Previous Experience on Productive Thinking," *Journal of Experimental Psychology*, XLI (1951), 121–125.

[3] C. McGuire, "Sex Role and Community Variability in Test Performances," *Journal of Educational Psychology*, LII (1961), 61–73.

[4] G. Haslerud and S. Meyers, "The Transfer Value of Given and Individually Derived Principles," *Journal of Educational Psychology*, XLIX (1958), 293–298.

[5] A. Gates and G. Taylor, "An Experimental Study of the Nature of Improvement Resulting from Practice in a Mental Function," *Journal of Educational Psychology*, XVI (1925), 583–592.

[6] W. Verplanck, "The Control of the Content of Conversation: Reinforcement of Statements of Opinion," *Journal of Abnormal and Social Psychology*, LI (1955), 668–676.

There are two main reasons for discussing the general and research literature related to the research problem. The first of these is the more important: to explain and clarify the theoretical rationale of the problem. Suppose, like Haslerud and Meyers, one were interested in investigating the relative effectiveness for transfer of self-discovery of principles by learners and systematic enunciation of the principles to learners. Since the problem is in part a transfer of training problem, one would have to discuss transfer and some of the literature on transfer, but especially that part of the literature particularly pertinent to this problem.

In addition, one might well want to discuss to some extent philosophical and pedagogical writings on the theory of formal discipline, for instance. In this manner the investigator provides a general picture of the research topic and fits his problem into the general picture.

A second reason for discussing the literature is to tell the reader what research has and has not been done on the problem. Obviously, the investigator must show that his particular investigation has not been done before. The underlying purpose, of course, is to locate the present research in the existing body of research on the subject and to point out what it contributes to the subject.

Methodology-Data Collection   The function of the methodology-data collection section of the research report, of course, is to tell the reader what was done to solve the problem. Meticulous care must be exercised to so report that the criterion of replicability is satisfied. That is, it should be possible for another investigator to reproduce the research, to reanalyze the data, or to arrive at unambiguous conclusions as to the adequacy of the methods and data collection. In books and theses there can be little question of the applicability of the criterion. In research journal reports, unfortunately, the criterion is difficult, sometimes even impossible, to satisfy. Due to lack of journal space, investigators are forced to condense reports in such a way that it is sometimes difficult to reconstruct and evaluate what a researcher has done. Yet the criterion remains a good one and should be kept in mind when tackling the methodology section.

The first part of the methodology-data collection section should tell what sample or samples were used, how they were selected, and why they were so selected. If eighth-grade pupils were used, the reason for using them should be stated. If the samples were randomly selected, this should be said. The method of random sampling should also be specified. If pupils were assigned at random to experimental groups, this should be reported. If they were not, this, too, should be reported with reasons for the lack of such assignment.

The method of testing the hypotheses must be reported in detail. If the study has been experimental, the manner in which the independent variable(s) has been manipulated is described. This description includes instruments used—teaching machines, audio-visual aids, and so on—instructions to the subjects, control precautions, and the like. If the study has been ex post facto, the procedures used to gather data are outlined.

The report of any empirical study must include an account of the measurement of the variables of the study. This may be accomplished in a few sentences in some studies. For example, in an experiment with one independent variable and a dependent variable whose measurement is simple, all that may be necessary is a brief description of the measurement of the dependent variable. Such measurement may entail only the counting of responses. In other studies, the description of the measurement of the variables may take up most of the methodology section. A factor analytic study, for instance, may require lengthy descriptions of measurement instruments and how they were used. Such descriptions will of course include justification of the instruments used, as well as evidence of their reliability and validity.

An account of the data analysis methods used is sometimes put into the methodology section, sometimes in the analysis-interpretation section. It is probably better to include these methods in the methodology section, though space can sometimes be saved the other way. Whichever practice is followed, the analysis methods must be outlined and justified. Since most of the common methods of analysis are well known, it is ordinarily sufficient to say, for example, that a 2 x 3 x 3 factorial analysis of variance was done, or that χ^2 was used, or that principal factors factor analysis with orthogonal rotations was used. If an unusual method of analysis is used, or if a common method is used in an unusual way, the investigator should describe what was done in sufficient detail to enable a competent reader to understand it. If space is at a premium, as it usually is, sometimes a reference to a technical source of the analytic method is sufficient.

In many investigations, pilot studies and pretesting are used. (Indeed, they should be used in all or most studies.) If so, what was done and the outcome of what was done are reported. If the pilot study was solely for trying out the instruments or the variable manipulation method on a small scale, little need be said. If, however, the pilot study or the pretesting supplied actual research data, the reader is entitled to know methodological details.

Results, Interpretation, Conclusions   This part of the report, though logically a unit, is often broken down into two or three sections. We treat it here as one section, since the interpretation of results and the conclusions drawn from the results are so often reported together in journal research reports. In a thesis or book, however, it may be desirable to separate the data from their interpretation and from the conclusions.

The results or data of a research study are the raw materials for the solution of the research problem. The data and their analysis are the hypothesis-testing stuff of research. Methodology and data collection are tools used to obtain the raw material of hypothesis-testing, the data. The main question is this: Do the data support or not support the hypotheses? It cannot be emphasized enough that methodology, data collection, and analysis are selected and used for the purpose of testing the operational hypotheses deduced from the general research questions. Therefore the report writer must be exceptionally careful to report his results as accurately and completely as possible, informing the reader how the results bear on the hypotheses.

Before writing this part of the report, it is helpful to reduce the data and the results of the data analysis to condensed form, particularly tables. The researcher should thoroughly digest the data before writing. The question, "Do the data support the hypotheses?," must be clearly answered in his mind. Then, after outlining the results section, he should write.[7] While writing, the investigator should guard against wandering from the task at hand, the solution of the

[7] Goode and Hatt give good advice on writing up results: W. Goode and P. Hatt, *Methods in Social Research.* New York: McGraw-Hill, 1952, chap. 21.

research problem. Everything he writes must be geared to letting the data bear on the problem and the hypotheses.

Somewhere in the final section of the research report the limitations and weaknesses of the study should be discussed. This can be overdone, of course. All scientific work has weaknesses, and many pages can be written belaboring a study's weaknesses. Still, the major limitations, which, of course, may have been mentioned earlier when discussing the problem or the methodology, should be pointed out. This is done, not to show humility or one's technical competence, but rather to enable the reader to judge the validity of the conclusions drawn from the data and the general worth of the study.

Limitations of social scientific and educational research generally come from sampling and subject assignment inadequacies, methodological weaknesses, and statistical deficiencies. Lack of random sampling, as we have seen, limits the conclusions to the particular sample used. Lack of random assignment casts doubt on the adequacy of the control of independent variables and thus on the conclusions. Statistical deficiencies, similarly, can lead to incorrect conclusions. Deficiencies in measurement always affect conclusions, too. If a measurement instrument, perhaps through no fault of the writer, is only moderately reliable, a conclusive finding may have been made inconclusive. More important, the questionable validity of an instrument may seriously change a conclusion.

These matters have been discussed in the text and need no further elaboration here. It may be added, however, that the writing of the conclusions is naturally affected by the recognized and acknowledged limitations and weaknesses. Not only is the reader entitled to know these things; it is the professional responsibility of the writer to inform him of them.

THE WRITING

It is not easy to write simply and clearly. One has to work at it. One should realize that almost no writer can escape the necessity of constant revision by reorganizing and paring—deleting circumlocutions, redundancies, and other verbal fat. Suggestions for better research report writing follow.

Although research reports should be fairly detailed, there is no need to waste words. State the problem, the methodology, and the results as clearly, simply, and briefly as possible. Avoid hackneyed expressions like "in terms of," "with respect to," "with reference to," "give consideration to," and the like. Delete unnecessary words and expressions when revising. For example, sentences with expressions like "the fact of the matter is," "owing to the fact that," and "as to whether" can always be revised to remove such clumsy inelegancies. For good advice on simplicity and clarity, study Strunk and White's little classic, *The Elements of Style*. Fowler's and Nicholson's book are most helpful.[8]

Writing scholarly papers and research reports requires a certain amount of routine drudgery that few of us like. Bibliographies, footnotes, tables, figures, and other mechanical details, however, cannot be escaped. Yet a little systematic study can help solve most problems. That is, do not wait until you sit down to write and then find out how to handle footnotes and other mechanical details.

[8] See the references at the end of this appendix.

Get a good reference book or two and study and lay out footnote and biblio-graphical forms, tables, figures, and headings. Put three or four types of footnote entries on 3 by 5 cards. Similarly, learn two or three methods of laying out tables. Lay out skeleton tables. Then use these samples when writing. In short, put much of the drudgery and doubt behind you by mastering the elements of the methods, instead of impeding your writing by constant interruptions to check on how to do things.

Presentation of statistical results and analyses gives students considerable trouble. Hit the problem head-on. Perhaps the best way to do this is to study statistical presentation in two or three good journals, like the *Journal of Abnormal and Social Psychology,* the *Journal of Educational Psychology,* and the *American Sociological Review.* There are fairly standard ways to present tables of means and standard deviations, analysis of variance results, factor analytic results, and the like. In theses the problem of presenting data is not so acute, since space is not a major consideration. In journals, however, the space problem is acute. Tables must be condensed, even omitted. An excellent source of good statistical and tabular reporting help is the manual put out by the American Psychological Association. Turabian's manual is also good. The University of Chicago *Manual of Style* also contains excellent advice.

The purpose of statistical, tabular, and other condensed presentation should be kept in mind. A statistical table, for instance, should clearly tell the reader what the data essentially say. This does not mean, of course, that a statistical table can stand by itself. Its purpose is to illuminate and clarify the textual discussion. The text carries the story; the table helps make the text clear and gives the statistical evidence for assertions made in the text. The text may say, for example, "The three experimental groups differed significantly in achievement," and the tables will report the statistical data—means, standard deviations, F ratios, levels of significance—to support the assertion. There is often no need for a table. If a hypothesis has been tested by computing one, two, or three coefficients of correlation, these can simply be reported in the text without tabular presentation.

A fairly safe generalization to guide one in writing research reports is: first drafts are not adequate. In other words, almost any writing, as said earlier, improves upon revision. It is almost always possible to simplify first-draft language and to delete unnecessary words, phrases, and even sentences and paragraphs. A first rule, then, is to go over any report with a ruthless pencil toward the end of greater simplicity, clarity, and brevity. With experience this not only becomes possible; it becomes easier.

If an adequate outline has been used, there should be little problem with the organization of a research paper. Yet sometimes it is necessary to reorganize a report. One may find, for example, that one has discussed something at the end of the report that was not anticipated in the beginning. Reorganization is required. In any case, the possibility of improvement in communication through reorganization should always be kept in mind.

Anyone's research writing can be improved in two ways: (1) by letting something one has written sit for a few weeks; (2) by having someone else read and criticize one's work. It is remarkable what a little time will do for one's objectivity and critical capacity. One sees obvious blemishes that somehow one could not see before. Time helps salve the ego, too. Our precious inventions do not seem so precious after a few weeks or months. We can be much more objective about them.

The second problem is harder. It is hard to take criticism, but the researcher must learn to take it. Scientific research is probably the most complex activity of man. Writing research reports is not easy, and no one can be expected to be perfect. It should be accepted and routine procedure, therefore, to have colleagues read our reports. It should be accepted routine, too, to accept our readers' criticisms in the spirit in which we should have asked for them. There is of course no obligation to change a manuscript in line with criticism. But there is an obligation to give each criticism the serious, careful, and objective attention it deserves. Doctoral students have to consider seriously the criticisms of their sponsors—whether or not they like them or agree with them. All scholarly and scientific writers, however, should voluntarily learn the discipline of subjecting their work to their peers. They should learn that the complex business of communicating scholarly and scientific work is difficult and demanding, and that in the long run they can only profit from competent criticism and careful revision.

SOME USEFUL REFERENCES

A Manual of Style. Chicago: University of Chicago Press, 1949 (1906). A basic reference, this book should be consulted for moot points, for example, hyphenation, capitalization, tables, types, and so forth.

American Psychological Association. *Publication Manual of the American Psychological Association.* 1957 Revision. Washington, D.C.: American Psychological Association, 1957. This is the basic manual for writers of reports in psychological journals, especially APA journals. It is particularly good for mechanical details such as tables, typing, and the like. Note, however, that many journals, especially education journals, do not use the APA referencing system (all references at the end of the report).

Campbell, W. *Form and Style in Thesis Writing.* Boston: Houghton Mifflin, 1954. Here is a useful reference for thesis writers.

Fowler, H. *A Dictionary of Modern English Usage.* Oxford: Oxford University Press, 1926. A classic reference work, Fowler's book is enjoyable reading as well as a good guide.

Goode, W., and P. Hatt. *Methods in Social Research.* New York: McGraw-Hill, 1952, Chap. 21. The general discussion in this book makes many useful points for the report writer.

Nicholson, M. *A Dictionary of American-English Usage.* New York: Oxford University Press, 1957. Since this is a valuable American revision of Fowler's book, anyone who plans to write much, should get this book.

Parten, M. *Surveys, Polls, and Samples.* New York: Harper & Row, 1950, Chap. XVII. This detailed chapter is useful for educational researchers, though written originally for survey researchers.

Scott, W., and M. Wertheimer. *Introduction to Psychological Research.* New York: Wiley, 1962, Chap. 14. The presentation in this textbook is practical and readable. It contains a number of very useful suggestions, especially for psychological researchers. See, also, Chap. 2, which discusses, among other things, psychological periodicals and their characteristics.

Strunk, Jr., W., and E. White. *The Elements of Style.* New York: Macmillan, 1959. This little gem, which every writer should own, is dedicated to clarity, brevity, and simplicity.

Turabian, K. *A Manual for Writers of Term Papers, Theses, and Dissertations,* rev. ed. Chicago: University of Chicago Press, 1955. An excellent, invaluable reference, this manual might well be called the handbook of the doctoral student. It is based on the *Manual of Style.*

B HISTORICAL AND METHODOLOGICAL RESEARCH

Two important and very different types of research are not discussed in this book: *historical research* and what will be called *methodological research*. The limits of the book forbid an adequate discussion of both of these kinds of research. The purpose of this appendix is to acquaint the reader with the nature of historical and methodological research and to point out the part they play in social scientific and educational research.

HISTORICAL RESEARCH

Historical research is the critical investigation of events, developments, and experiences of the past, the careful weighing of evidence of the validity of sources of information on the past, and the interpretation of the weighed evidence. The historical investigator, like other investigators, then, collects data, evaluates the data for validity, and interprets the data. Actually, the historical method, or *historiography*, differs from other scholarly activity only in its rather elusive subject matter, the past, and the peculiarly difficult interpretative task imposed by the elusive nature of its subject matter.

Obviously, historical research is important in education. Outside of the intrinsic interest of history, it is necessary to know and understand educational accomplishments and developments of the past in order to gain a perspective of present and possibly future directions. To understand modern trends like progressivism, for instance, it is necessary to put it in a broader context than the present. One must search for its historical roots. One must know something of Froebel, Rousseau, Dewey, and even Freud. The current emphasis on "hardcore" learning is understood to be a recrudescence of a very old point of view, if one understands the historical roots of modern educational practices, values, and attitudes. It is in part the old razor strop theory of the mind revivified and dressed up in modern clothes.

If we look at one or two canons of historiography, we may be able to understand why historiographical discipline is valuable in and of itself and also valuable for the social scientist. One of the basic rules of research in history is: Always use primary sources. A *primary source* is the original repository of an historical datum, like an original record kept of an important occasion, an eye-witness description of an event, a photograph, minutes of organization meetings, and so on. A *secondary source* is an account or record of an historical event or circumstance one or more steps removed from an original repository. Instead of the minutes of an organization meeting, for example, one uses a newspaper account of the meeting. Instead of studying and citing the original report of a research, one studies and cites someone else's account and digest of it.

To use secondary sources when primary sources are available is a major historiographical error. And with good reason. Materials and data, especially those about human beings and their activities, become changed and often distorted in transmission. The reputable historian never completely trusts secondary sources, though he of course studies them and weighs them for their validity. (Often he is forced to use them for lack of primary sources.) The dangers of distortion and consequent erroneous interpretation are too great.

The precept of the primary source is a good one for behavioral investigators. While the sheer mass of published studies is so great that one has to depend upon secondary sources, such as competent digests and abtracts, one should always attempt to study primary sources, especially of important studies in one's own field. This suggestion applies to both the scientist and the practitioner. If the precept of the primary source were taken more seriously, fewer erroneous generalizations would be made. Generalizations like "Democratic group atmosphere produces better learning than autocratic or laissez-faire group atmosphere" would be examined more critically.

Two other canons of historiography are expressed by the terms *external criticism* and *internal criticism*.[1] The historian critically examines the sources of data for their genuineness, or, more accurately, for their validity. Is the document or source genuine? Did X really write this paper? If X wrote the paper, was he a competent and truthful witness? This is *external criticism*. *Internal criticism* is preoccupied with the *content* of the source or document and its meaning. Are the statements made accurate representations of the historical facts? A document may survive external criticism and still be suspect as evidence. There may be no doubt of the "true" author or recorder of events—and he may be competent. Wittingly or unwittingly, however, he may have distorted the truth. Internal criticism, in brief, seeks the "true" meaning and value of the content of sources of data.

Social scientific and educational investigators obviously use both external and internal criticism, but particularly internal criticism. If an author of a research report comes to an erroneous conclusion because of inadequate statistical analysis or interpretation, for example, it is clearly the task of other scientists to correct the error. There is a very well-known study on transfer of training whose authors seemed to have erred in the interpretation of their data.[2] The study was well done. Its conception and execution were imaginative and competent. But the conclusions and the interpretation of the data are questionable, because of inadequate statistical analysis and inadequate interpretation of the

[1] C. Good, A. Barr, and D. Scates, *The Methodology of Educational Research.* New York: Appleton, 1936, pp. 257–264.

[2] G. Hendrickson and W. Schroeder, "Transfer of Training in Learning to Hit a Submerged Target," *Journal of Educational Psychology*, XXXII (1941), 205–213.

statistical analysis that was done.[3] Any investigator can make, and does make, such errors. This is not the point. The point is that the study has been reproduced in anthologies and cited in texts as evidence of the effect of knowledge of principles on the transfer of learning. Perhaps the conclusion *is* correct. But this study did not yield adequate evidence of its correctness. Careful internal criticism of published and unpublished research studies is clearly needed.

The contributions to knowledge of the educational historian have been many and important. The history of education and historical research in education have suffered a serious decline, in part because of the impact of scientific research.[4] Prior to the 1920s, historical and related inquiry dominated educational attention. After the investigations of men like Thorndike, Terman, Hall, and others, however, historical inquiry was subordinated to the type of inquiry that became prevalent in education. Despite a contemporary recrudescence of historical inquiry among historians in schools of education, the history of education never recovered. This is most unfortunate. Without good history and good historians, a discipline can lose perspective, not to mention the serious consequences on the intellectual development of students of education of this neglect, even derogation, in education of the philosophy and history of education. Rigorous historiography is needed, just as good scientific research is needed.

The following excerpt from a report of a committee of historians on historiography summarizes the importance of historiography to the social sciences—and, by implication, to education:

> Historiography has a necessary relevance to all the social sciences, to the humanities, and to the formulation of public and private policies, because (1) all the data used in the social sciences, in the humanities, and in the formulation of public and private policies are drawn from records of, experience in, or writing about the past; because (2) all policies respecting human affairs, public or private, and all generalizations of a nonstatistical character in the social sciences and in the humanities involve interpretations of or assumptions about the past; and because (3) all workers in the social sciences and in the humanities are personalities of given times, places, and experience whose thinking is consequently in some measure conditioned and determined by the historical circumstances of their lives and experiences.[5]

METHODOLOGICAL RESEARCH

Methodological research is controlled investigation of the theoretical and applied aspects of measurement, mathematics and statistics, and ways of obtaining and analyzing data. Without methodological research, modern social scien-

---

[3] Analyses of variance of the data reported by Hendrickson and Schroeder in no case yielded significant F ratios. None of their results was significant, yet they say that theoretical information aided transfer from one situation to another.

[4] M. Borrowman, "History of Education." In C. Harris, ed., *Encyclopedia of Educational Research*, 3d ed. New York: Macmillan, 1960, pp. 661–668. (See especially pp. 663, 664.)

[5] Social Science Research Council, *Theory and Practice in Historical Study: A Report of the Committee on Historiography*. New York: Social Science Research Council, 1946, pp. 134, 135.

tific and educational research would still be in the research dark ages. Like historical research, it is an extremely important part of the body scientific. This strong statement is made to counteract the somewhat negative sentiments that many professionals in psychology, sociology, and education seem to hold about methodological research.

Methodology is called "mere" methodology. The methodologist is called a "mere" methodologist. This is a curious state of affairs. Among the most competent, imaginative, and creative men in modern psychology and educational psychology, "mere" methodologists hold high rank. Indeed, it is almost impossible to do outstanding research, though one can do acceptable research, without being something of a methodologist. It is needless to pursue the prejudice further. My point is that methodological research is a vital and absolutely indispensable part of social scientific and educational research. Let us look at what the methodological researcher does and see why these statements have been made.

Perhaps the largest and most rigorous area of psychological and educational methodological research is measurement. The methodologist—and it should be emphasized that good researchers in education have to be, to some extent, measurement methodologists—is preoccupied with theoretical and practical problems of identifying and measuring psychological variables. These problems have a number of aspects. Reliability and validity, in and of themselves, are large areas of preoccupation and investigation. Then there are the theoretical and practical problems of the construction of psychological and educational measuring instruments: scaling, item writing, item analysis, and so on. One man can easily spend a lifetime on any one of these aspects of measurement.

Statisticians long ago turned their talents to solving the problem of the objective evaluation of research data. Their contributions were considered at length in Part III and need not be repeated here. It is significant to add, however, that some of the most outstanding methodological contributions of statistics have come from applied researchers—Fisher, Thurstone, Cattell, to name only three.

The application of modern mathematics to social scientific research is really just beginning. A great deal of methodological as well as substantive work needs to be done. But already there is evidence of a lively stimulus to research. Applications of set theory and thinking were discussed earlier. We are also familiar with probability theory and its application to research. Matrix theory has been successfully applied to factor analysis and to sociometry. Its applications to other research problems are being developed; for example, power relations in groups are studied mathematically. Game theory is a new development that may have fruitful applications to behavioral research. A branch of mathematics known as linear programming has promise for the solution of certain complex educational problems. The prospects of the applications of modern mathematics and logic are exciting and important.

The third large area of methodological research, investigations of methods of data collection and analysis, has thrived for many years. This area includes interviews and the construction of interview schedules, content analysis, methods of sampling, systematic observational techniques, and other methods. An example or two may help the student appreciate the significance of such work.

Interviews can yield biased data. The study of the causes and prevention of biases in the schedule and in the interview situation, if successful, can help investigators increase the validity of their data. Which is the more reliable of two methods of direct observation of behavior: the observation and recording of small clearly defined acts of individuals or of larger molar units of behavior? What method of analysis of the content of written documents or of interview material yields the most reliable results? Such questions and many others are being successfully answered by methodologists.

REFERENCES ON HISTORICAL AND METHODOLOGICAL RESEARCH

Historical Research

Brickman, W. *Guide to Research in Educational History*. New York: New York University, 1949. This book is an excellent standard source for guidance in historical research.

Good, C., A. Barr, and D. Scates. *The Methodology of Educational Research*. New York: Appleton, 1936, Chap. VI. This is a good brief source.

Social Science Research Council. *Theory and Practice in Historical Study: A Report of the Committee on Historiography*. New York: Social Science Research Council, 1946. A good reference prepared by an outstanding committee of historians.

Methodological Research

There are no books, as such, on methodological research. The *Review of Educational Research,* however, is a basic source of review and bibliographical information. Every three years an issue called "Methodology of Educational Research" is published. It has articles summarizing or referring to publications in experimental design, measurement, statistics, and the like. The outstanding source of original publications on measurement and testing is the quarterly journal *Educational and Psychological Measurement.* The books listed below contain sections on social scientific methodology. Other, more specialized references were cited earlier in this book.

Bush, R., R. Abelson, and R. Hyman, *Mathematics for Psychologists: Examples and Problems*. New York: Social Science Research Council, 1956. This book is unique. It gives a large number of examples and exercises, culled from the literature, of applications of mathematics to psychological research problems. The discussion, however, is relatively condensed and requires mathematical background.

Lindquist, E., ed., *Educational Measurement*. Washington, D.C.: American Council on Education, 1951. This standard and excellent work covers a wide range of methodological research in measurement.

Lindzey, G., ed., *Handbook of Social Psychology*, Vol. I. Cambridge, Mass.: Addison-Wesley, 1954, Part 3, "Research Methods." This is the latest and perhaps the best compendium of social scientific research methods. Much of the discussion in the several chapters is methodological.

Mussen, P., ed., *Handbook of Research Methods in Child Development*. New York: Wiley, 1960. This book has several chapters that are primarily methodological; in general it is oriented toward research in child development.

C THE ELECTRONIC DIGITAL COMPUTER AND BEHAVIORAL RESEARCH[1]

The high-speed electronic digital computer is profoundly influencing behavioral research and behavioral scientists. The days of statistical and mathematical computational drudgery are over: the computer now does in minutes and seconds statistical and other operations that took days, weeks, and even months of clerical and desk calculator work. Research projects that would not have been attempted five years ago because of the sheer bulk of necessary calculations to analyze the data of the projects are now readily approachable with the computer and computer auxiliary equipment.

The intent of this appendix is to indicate the importance, even indispensability, of computers in behavioral research, and to try to stimulate the student to learn enough of computer technique to enable him to use the computer as a research tool. A subsidiary purpose is to acquaint the student with the basic characteristics of high-speed computers, with statistical computer programs that are generally available, and with a very remarkable achievement: the intermediary language with which the researcher communicates with the machine.

SOME IMPORTANT COMPUTER CHARACTERISTICS

The modern high-speed computer is an elaborate complex of electronic hardware whose chief characteristics are tremendous speed, easy ability to do thousands of repetitive operations with a high degree of accuracy, flexibility, and what will here be called "ductility." Everyone has heard that computers are fast. Few people know, however, how fast they are. They are faster than almost anything else man works with. Their operations approximate the speed of light. Most students are familiar with the calculation of correlation coefficients. With 100 cases of two sets of one-digit numbers, one correlation coefficient might

[1] I am deeply indebted to the Computing Center of the Courant Institute of Mathematical Sciences, New York University, for its generosity in allowing me to use the computer complex both to learn computer technique and to analyze research data. I owe the Center's Mr. Howard Walowitz a special debt for his patient and skillful instruction and guidance during my year of study and work at the Center and for a critical reading of this appendix. To Professor Nathan Jaspen, who needled my professional conscience until I overcame a curious resistance to learning programming, a note of thanks is also due.

take about 20 to 30 minutes to calculate. In contrast, here is an actual example of computer speed from the author's work. The responses of 164 individuals to two attitude scales totaling 50 items were analyzed on the IBM-7094. The means, standard deviations, and intercorrelations of the 50 items (1225 correlation coefficients) were calculated. In addition, a complete principal axes factor analysis with Varimax rotations of nine factors was done. The factor analysis and rotations, alone, would take weeks on a desk calculator. In fact, few researchers would be hardy enough to attempt them. The machine took about three minutes to do all the calculations from sums to rotated factor loadings!

This example also illustrates the second basic characteristic of computers: easy ability to do thousands of repetitive operations with a relatively high degree of accuracy. With 50 variables, there are 50 sums, 50 sums of squares, 50 means, 50 standard deviations, 1225 cross-products sums, and thousands, even millions, of other calculations. The machine handles these lengthy and laborious operations repetitively at great speed. For example, one common way to program the necessary statistics to calculate cross products, a very laborious business by hand, is to read in the data of one subject on all 50 variables, store the 50 values temporarily, and calculate and store the cross products for the one subject. In effect, a 50-element vector and a 50 x 50 matrix (actually less than 50 x 50, since the matrix is symmetric) for the one subject are stored. Then the scores of the next subject are read in, the scores added to the previously stored values, and the cross products of the subject's scores calculated and added to those already stored. The process is repeated until all the scores of all the subjects are read in and calculated. It should be mentioned in passing that by using special language these operations are quite simple to implement on a computer.

The ease with which such operations can be implemented, however, can be a hazard to the scientist. The computer calculates with a high but finite accuracy. This is because the computer's memory is limited to numbers of finite accuracy within a wide range of magnitude. In calculating sums of squares or cross products of large sets of numbers, for example, if the number of significant digits exceeds the machine's finite accuracy, the resulting sums will not be correct. In other words, computer output *can* be meaningless numbers, which the researcher may or may not recognize as meaningless.[2] It is therefore necessary for machine users to be constantly alert to the possibilities of inaccurate results.

The third characteristic of computers, flexibility, might better be called a characteristic of the use of the machine. What is meant is that there are several ways to make a computer do a particular job. Virtually identical results can be achieved with different sets of instructions to the machine. In other words, the way the machine operates permits flexibility of programming. It is in this sense that the machine is flexible. For example, with the 50-variable example just discussed, it is quite possible to read in all the scores before doing the calculations. Indeed, such a procedure is sometimes necessary, though a great deal more machine storage is required. The end results, of course, are the same.

Ductility, the last computer characteristic to be discussed, may be loosely

---

[2] Some computers have double-precision features, that is, computer accuracy is effectively doubled by means of a special increased storage feature. On the IBM-7094, for example, the usual accuracy is eight significant digits. With double precision arithmetic, the accuracy is increased to 16 significant digits.

translated as stupidity. The electronic computer is utterly stupid: it will do exactly what a programmer tells it to do. If a programmer solves a difficult problem brilliantly, the machine will perform "brilliantly." If the programmer programs a set of instructions incorrectly, the machine will faithfully and obediently make the errors its programmer has told it to make. This is a great strength, because it means that computers are highly reliable; they seldom make mistakes. Their logic is irrefragable. The researcher can therefore depend upon the machine's "logic" and accuracy, within the limitations mentioned previously.

HOW COMPUTER PROGRAMS WORK:
PROGRAMMING AND FORTRAN

A computer program is a set of instructions, in some sort of machine language, that tells the machine what operations to perform and how to perform them in order to analyze data and to calculate solutions of problems.

To understand to some extent how computers and computer programs work, let us look at some basic machine or program operations. Before anything else, however, we must be aware that an important problem for the researcher is to be able to communicate with the machine. He must be able to tell it what to do. One common and highly ingenious and useful communication medium is called Fortran (*For*mula *Trans*lation).[3] Fortran and similar languages constitute a major breakthrough in the research use of the computer. Fortran is an intermediary language that enables the researcher, as well as the machine expert, to communicate with the machine. Prior to its invention, the researcher had to communicate with the machine in highly detailed machine language or through a professional programmer. Since direct machine language is very complex, and since professional programmers are scarce and often do not understand research problems, the researcher was severely handicapped. The invention of Fortran and similar languages effectively solved this problem. The researcher writes his program in Fortran, and a computer program called a compiler translates the Fortran into an equivalent machine language program. If Fortran errors are made (that is, actual language and not logical errors), the compiler terminates the translation and prints out a so-called diagnostic, which informs the programmer of his errors and where they are in the Fortran program.[4]

Fortran, among other things, uses several basic statements like DO, GO TO, READ, WRITE, PUNCH, CALL, CONTINUE, and IF. These instructions mean what they say: they tell the machine to do this, do that, go to this instruction, read that instruction, and write the outcome. The power and flexibility of this seemingly simple language cannot be exaggerated. There is almost no numerical or logical operation that cannot be accomplished with it.

[3] Although Fortran is here used as an example, it must be remembered that there are other machine intermediary languages. It is quite possible, in fact, that Fortran may in the future be supplanted by other languages.

[4] This description may make programming sound easy. It is not easy, even though it is a great deal simpler than it used to be. To master Fortran and to program effectively takes considerable application, effort, concentrated thought, and actual machine work.

The reader who intends doing research is strongly urged to explore the possibilities of learning Fortran (or other intermediary language). To use the computer intelligently demands at least rudimentary knowledge and skill in programming. Many researchers believe that they can depend upon professional programmers and so-called "package" programs. Such dependence has pitfalls. Many professional programmers are not familiar enough with the purposes and details of the analytical tools of the scientist, particularly those of the social scientist, to be able to help solve many analytic problems adequately. If, in the analysis of an attitude scale, a researcher wants two factor analyses, one with total item scores and one without total scores, a "package" program supplied by a computing center is unlikely to have the total item scores in it. Or an analysis of variance package program may not have relational indices as part of its output. Moreover, while professional programmers are usually highly competent people, many of them would not know the reasons for such special requirements, nor would it be economical for them to adapt package programs or to write new programs for such special use.

One of the most difficult problems associated with computer work, then, is communication between researcher and programmer. It is probably unrealistic to expect researchers to be highly expert in programming. But it is even more unrealistic to expect professional programmers to understand the substance and methodology of behavioral science analysis. The best solution of the problem of communication between scientist and programmer is clear: the scientist must learn at least enough about programming to enable him to talk knowledgeably and intelligently to the programmer. The researcher can learn to do this in a matter of months, whereas it would take the programmer years to learn enough about behavioral science and behavioral science analysis to communicate with the researcher at the researcher's level.

AVAILABLE PROGRAMS

A fine example of the fruits of intelligent cooperation and open-minded dedication to science is the ready and open availability of many computer programs for scientific use.[5] Most of the following list of programs is available at many computing centers, especially those in universities. To authorized users of machines—and some universities now grant free computer time to unsupported faculty members and students—programs, facilities, and professional help are often available. The programs described below usually come, as indicated above, in ready-made packages. The user needs only familiarity with how to process the

---

[5] Computer personnel share their programs with each other. It is common to write another installation requesting a program that it has developed. There is even an organization known as SHARE (Society to Help Avoid Repetitive Effort), which maintains a readily available pool of computer programs. Note, too, that requests for program information to computer manufacturers are attentively answered. Like certain large university centers, the manufacturers maintain libraries and indexes of programs and their sources. They also supply programs. The most important sources of programs for social scientific use, however, are undoubtedly university computing centers. It is suggested that the potential user of the computer consult the individual in charge of the nearest computing center for information on university centers and the programs they have available.

programs and the data through the machine complex and, most important, how to interpret the machine output.

CORRELATION Correlation programs calculate and output means, standard deviations, and correlation matrices. They are probably the most ubiquitous of programs. With the larger machines, the program capacity is large, often well over a 100 x 100 matrix.

ANALYSIS OF VARIANCE Most analyses of variance can probably be done just as well on a desk calculator as on a computer. Certain analytic problems, however, are very laborious and call for computer help. For example, two-way analysis of variance (also called matched-groups or randomized blocks) with large numbers of blocks or subjects is time-consuming, laborious, and subject to error. Simple one-way analysis of variance with large numbers of measures and groups and with post hoc comparisons of means (via the Scheffé test, for instance), too, is often better done on a computer. Standard programs are widely available. The user should be careful, however, to be sure that the form of analysis of variance in a program is the form he needs to analyze his data. One does not need a complex factorial analysis of variance or covariance to do a simple one-way or two-way analysis of variance. And standard programs may not do post hoc comparisons of means or calculate relational indices.

ITEM ANALYSIS Item-total correlations, reliability, difficulty indices, and intercorrelations among items are best done on a computer because of the large number of calculations involved. Excellent programs have been written. The person in charge of the computing center one plans to use should be consulted.

FACTOR ANALYSIS Almost any university computing center will have one or two factor analysis programs available. The virtues of the high-speed computer are particularly evident with factor analysis. In earlier years, many factor analytic problems eluded solution because of the very large amount of calculation involved. This is now completely changed. Factor analysis has become almost commonplace.

But the use of factor analysis programs can be a good example of the danger of uncritical computer use, particularly the uncritical use of package programs. In order to interpret factor analytic results properly, one needs considerable understanding of, and experience with, factor theory, methodology, and practice. One must know the characteristics of different types of rotations; one must understand the principles of simple structure; one must be able to reach intelligent decisions as to the number of factors to be extracted and rotated. No one can supply this knowledge and understanding but the researcher himself. Factor analysis programs, however, can be rather fixed and rigid. The communality estimates, the type of rotation, and the number of factors extracted may not be suited to the problem being investigated. In other words, while factor analysis programs are readily available and a great boon to the researcher, great care must be exercised in their use.

OTHER PROGRAMS Many other programs have been written to accomplish a variety of analytical purposes. These include canonical correlations, discriminant analysis, multiple regression, and variable plots. The reader is referred to the Cooley and Lohnes and the Borko books, which are cited in the references at the end of this appendix.

CONCLUDING REMARKS

There is no doubt whatever of the importance and far-reaching implications and consequences of high-speed computers. Like everything else, of course, computers can be used wisely and not so wisely. One of the worst things one can do is to use a computer program without understanding the statistical and analytical principles behind the program. In addition to the danger of uncritically accepting incorrect results—something that occasionally happens, especially with new programs—one can err badly when using programs for more complex operations. In the preceding section, the example of factor analysis was used to point up the danger of the uncritical use of computer programs and the necessity for understanding and experience to interpret factor analytic solutions. We can here add to the previous remarks that, at the present stage of factor analysis theory and practice, judgments have to enter the analytic picture—at least to some extent. How many factors should be rotated? What kind of rotations should be used? Are the machine rotations adequate? The undiscriminating user of computer programs can blunder quite seriously here, as he can with many other kinds of problems.

Computers, then, are extremely useful, obedient, and reliable servants, though one must always remember that they are utterly stupid and that their facile output can never substitute for competent and imaginative theoretical, research-design, and statistical thinking. Despite the danger, the reader is urged to explore and learn about this enormously fascinating and powerful analytic tool. One thing is certain: the researcher who learns a little Fortran and who puts one or two programs through a machine complex successfully will never be the same again. He has participated in one of the most exciting adventures he will ever experience. The main problem will then be to maintain the balance and the discretion to keep the machine where it belongs: in the background and not in the foreground of research activity.

REFERENCES

Behavioral Science and *Educational and Psychological Measurement* These journals regularly feature descriptions and availability of computer programs for social scientific and educational use.

Bernstein, J., "The Analytical Engine," *New Yorker,* XXXIX (Oct. 19, 1963), 58–93; XXXIX (Oct. 26, 1963), 54–108. The author has outlined, in this long and interesting article, the history and characteristics of computers.

Borko, H., ed., *Computer Applications in the Behavioral Sciences.* Englewood Cliffs, N.J.: Prentice-Hall, 1962. This diverse and informative book describes, among other things, machines, programs, and techniques useful to psychologists, sociologists, and educators.

Cooley, W., and P. Lohnes, *Multivariate Procedures for the Behavioral Sciences.* New York: Wiley, 1962. This book is unique. It gives the complete Fortran listings (programs) of the most important statistical and mathematical routines, together with good discussions and examples of the methods behind the routines.

McCracken, D., *A Guide to Fortran Programming*. New York: Wiley, 1961. McCracken's manual attempts to teach Fortran to the beginner. While its emphasis is not on behavioral statistical methods, it supplies the student with a good foundation.

Wrigley, C., "Electronic Computers and Psychological Research," *American Psychologist*, XII (1957), 501–508. Though old by present-day standards, and thus technically obsolete, this article should be read by the social scientific user of the computer. It is an excellent introduction to some of the major problems associated with computer use.

Note: Technical and descriptive materials and manuals are available from the manufacturers of computers.

INDEXES

INDEX TO AUTHORS CITED

INDEX TO SUBJECT MATTER